EMOTIONAL TERRORS IN THE WORKPLACE: PROTECTING YOUR BUSINESS' BOTTOM LINE

Emotional Continuity Management in the Workplace

By Vali Hawkins Mitchell, Ph.D., LMHC

Philip Jan Rothstein, FBCI, Editor

ISBN 1-931332-27-4

BCI

Endorsed by The Business Continuity Institute

Rothstein Associates Inc.
Brookfield, Connecticut USA
www.rothstein.com

ISBN #1-931332-27-4

PUBLISHER:
Philip Jan Rothstein, FBCI
Rothstein Associates Inc.
The Rothstein Catalog On Service Level Management
4 Arapaho Rd.
Brookfield, Connecticut 06804-3104 U.S.A.
203.740.7444
203.740.7401 fax
www.rothstein.com
www.ServiceLevelBooks.com
info@rothstein.com

PREFACE
by James E. Lukaszewski

The failure to adequately address the victims and the emotional dimensions of corporate problems is what changes adverse events into crises and catastrophes. Buildings can be replaced; machines can be fixed; products can be re-engineered and re-marketed; but leaving the needs of victims unmet, denied, or trivialized, and failing to address the emotional impact of events and behaviors can cause permanent damage and often defines careers.

EMOTIONAL TERRORS IN THE WORKPLACE: PROTECTING YOUR BUSINESS' BOTTOM LINE is an interesting, comprehensive, and constructive approach to adding this key management ingredient to the manager's role. This book's goal is to arm the individual with enough information and structure to persuade the boss to take a shot at adding this skill and knowledge that will help managers and leaders preempt or at least begin to recognize the signs of corrosive emotional distress.

Two great weaknesses of today's business and management education are the intentional de-emphasis of the emotional component of work and working life, and only the flimsiest, most circumspect teaching of integrity and workplace ethics. These concepts are, in reality, connected. When a boss has difficultly managing or even acknowledging the emotional dimension of problems, the first response of observers is to question the ethics, humanity, or empathy of the manager faced with the problem. From the perspective of the victim of such behavior, the thoughtless, dollar-driven manager seems more like a perpetrator, rather than someone who is uncomfortable with the circumstances of the problem.

Management, as the author cites from time-to-time, hates this stuff. It's the fuzzy, mushy, sissy-type, right-brained stuff managers have been trained to ignore and, in fact, remove from their management skill set from the instant they begin their graduate school training. This aversion is powerful. Management remains unwilling to learn even though there are important and fairly frequent publicly embarrassing circumstances, which one might think would help business leaders "get it." I refer to this as the "General Patton Syndrome." During World War II, Major General George Patton slapped a soldier in a field hospital because the soldier ran from battle. Patton called the man a "coward," a "sissy," and a "sympathizer." His single act struck like thunderbolt throughout the military. General Patton was disciplined and made to publicly apologize. Did it change the views of military leaders and commanders about cowardice in battle? Probably not, but military leaders don't go around slapping solders anymore, at least not in public.

Today's business managers still approach emotional issues and questions more like General Patton — if you get emotional, you are disloyal, or malingering, or distracting yourself and others from important efforts, and even, heaven forbid, sabotaging management's best efforts.

One of the most powerful concepts explored by Vali Hawkins Mitchell in this book is the difference between arrogance and empathy. Today's managers are taught to be arrogant, that is, to make decisions based on criteria that are totally objective (read "non-emotional") and totally measurable and justifiable (read "fit a kind of dispassionate formula or structure"). This results in behaviors and attitudes that are cold, hard, and so seemingly callous as to be driven only by success measured in dollars, bonuses, and options.

What is management's excuse? Management has such difficulty answering this question that they conduct a reactive exercise I call "Death by Question." How can you measure emotion? How do you quantify empathy? How do you calculate the value of an apology? It's the old and false notion that management is science. In fact, management is far *more* than science.

Arrogance is making decisions for others without their participation or permission. *Empathy*, on the other hand, is frequently confused with *sympathy*, which is the verbalization of concern or recognition that someone else is about to or is suffering something that the sympathetic observer had no hand in and cannot help with. Empathy, in reality, is what is done to alleviate, replace, or be the substitute for someone else's pain, suffering, agony, or emotional distress. Saying we are sorry or that we recognize someone else's pain is meaningless and often comes across as superficial and insincere.

Empathy is all about doing something for that individual, relieving the pain, solving the problem, soothing the emotional distress, or even standing in the victim's place to suffer the potential for danger or threat. This book is about being an empathetic manager — a manager who acts with emotionally sensitive certainty then lets those actions speak for themselves. The reader will find a variety of quizzes and self-analyses sufficient to determine their management archetype: cold, arrogant, intrusive, abusive, reclusive; or, warm, effusive, helpful, or empathetic.

This book is an eye-opener. There are many case histories with frequent efforts to connect the type of manager and management behavior to forecast success or the need for more effort. There is an interesting methodology for calculating the cost of emotional distress and disturbance. There are lists and descriptions of all types of employees and managers, and how to recognize the destructive emotional dislocations that category can cause.

This book and your guidance can help your boss prepare for changes in their personal behavior and concept of management, fill a serious gap in their experience and training, and truly become an "empathetic manager."

James E. Lukaszewski, ABC, APR, Fellow PRSA
Snug Harbor, Danbury, Connecticut USA
September 2004

JAMES E. LUKASZEWSKI is Chairman and President, THE LUKASZEWSKI GROUP INC. (www.e911.com).

THE LUKASZEWSKI GROUP (White Plains, New York) provides strategic guidance to the managements of major U.S. and international businesses and organizations on the most sensitive reputation and ethical problems — the kind that can redefine the reputation of an organization, executive, company, or brand. They help organizations manage tough, touchy, sensitive communication problems. They focus on issues and situations with enormous organizational impact. Clients engage them to work across the spectrum of management communications and operational issues, reduce reputation risk, make things happen, move issues forward, provide second opinions, and resolve conflict and controversy.

THE BUSINESS CONTINUITY INSTITUTE

"Vali Hawkins Mitchell has produced an unusual and authoritative work. Packed with case study and "sound bytes," Vali will touch the corporate nerve and conscience. The words addressing what it was really like for the people touched by the aftermath of the events of 9/11 are particularly telling.

"The Preface sums up very well what is to follow: "... *Today's business managers still approach emotional issues and questions more like General Patton — if you get emotional, you are disloyal, or malingering, or distracting yourself and others from important efforts, and even, heaven forbid, sabotaging management's best efforts.*"

"Vali upholds many of the principles you will find promoted and supported by the BCI and encouraged as part of BCM good practice."

Julia Graham FBCI

Director of Risk Management, DLA LLC (United Kingdom)

Board of Directors, the Business Continuity Institute

The Mission of the Business Continuity Institute is to promote the art and science of business continuity management.

The Business Continuity Institute (BCI) was established in 1994 to provide opportunities to obtain guidance and support from fellow professionals. The Institute provides an internationally recognized status in relation to the individuals experience as a continuity practitioner. The BCI has over 1650 members in 45 countries.

The wider role of the BCI is to promote the highest standards of professional competence and commercial ethics in the provision and maintenance of business continuity planning and services.

THE AIMS AND OBJECTIVES OF THE BCI

- To define the professional competencies expected of business continuity professionals
- To provide an internationally recognized Certification scheme for the business continuity profession.
- To provide a program of Continuous Professional Development to enable members to maintain their professional competencies.
- To initiate, develop, evaluate and communicate BCM thinking, standards and good practices
- To influence policymakers, opinion-formers and other stakeholders worldwide in Business Continuity Management.

www.thebci.org

DEDICATION

Dedicated To All Noble Workplace Warriors Who Would,
At The End Of Their Long Day,
Rather Sing To Children
Than Scream At Them.

... And To My Granddaughters, Melanie Grace And Charity Faye, Who
Make Me Want To Sing... *And to Keep Working to Make More Money
So I Can Buy Them Cool Stuff!*

ACKNOWLEDGMENTS

Thank You to my Personal and Professional Continuity Team:
Robbie (*Kindness Drive-By And Introduction To Philip Rothstein*) Atabaigi
The American Red (*Yes, Vali Can Make A Sandwich And Be A Counselor*) Cross
Dan (*Knew I'd Really "Seen" Ground Zero And Not Just "Been There"*) Blasdel
Dr. B. Ed (*Suits Up And Shows Up Warrior*) Bohart
Mary (*FDNY Angel With Rose Petals*) Cole
Patti (*Caught My Heart After 9-11*) Courson
Janet (Somehow Always Finds Me) Davis
Sharon (*Boojum Tree*) Frizzell
Dr. Sheila (*Pair-A-Docs Conference*) Dunlop
Fire Department Of New (*Yes, Vali Does Know Where The Good Bagels Are*) York City
Victoria (*Integrity Matters*) Grayland
Floyd (*Get Some Red Bull And Keep Writing*) Ivy
Dr. Hal (*It's Only A Tornado!*) Lanse
Dr. Al (*36 Hours A Day*) Marcella
Ashley (*Karate And Research Expert*) Mitchell
The (*You People*) Mitchells And Cutters (*Especially Brad*)
Deb (*We Can Do This*) Ticknor
Dr. Joe (*Oklahoma City Mentor*) Westerheide
Kirsha (*Died On A Different September 11th But Still Teaching Me Daughter*) Melanie
Kyrin (*Sparkly-Artist-Heart Daughter*) And Parris (*Poet-Heart*) Pack
Donna (*Sisterfriend-I-Can't-Do- It-Without -Ya Firefighter*) Wendling
David (*Fearless Editor, Computer-Hero, 9/11 Heart-Partner, Spiffy Husband*) Mitchell

And to:
My (Anonymous) Noble Clients
My Brave (*On The Promise Of Total Confidentiality*) Colleagues
Business Continuity (*BCI*) Institute
Disaster Recovery Institute (*DRII*) International
Disaster Recovery (*DRJ*) Journal
Sheila (*It's Edgy*) Kwiatek
Jim (*Great Preface and Vision*) Lukaszewski

And my deepest appreciation to Philip Jan (*Every Writer's Dream Of A Publisher and Editor Who Actually Read What I Wrote, Even The Poetic*) Rothstein

Finally — to All Emotional (*You Know Who You Are*) Terrorists Who Inspire Me To Help The Good-Guys!

CONTENTS

12 READINESS: TOOLS FOR DEVELOPING AN EMOTIONAL MANAGEMENT CONTINUITY PLAN 227

13 READINESS: TOOLS FOR MANAGING INCIDENTS AND FOR DRILLING 253

THE LITTLE WARS
by Vali Hawkins Mitchell

It's not the nuclear holocausts that we worry about!
It's the Little Wars that wear us down,
The fights and feuds,
The conflicts and sorrows,
Today's and tomorrow's
Of never-ending non-resolves
That fatigue and tire,
Bog and mire
Us down in emotions
Too frequent to bear
That lead to despair.

Our battlefields are:
Work Sites
Bodies
Children
Relationships
Aging
Money
Marriage

And the Weapons of Mass Destruction are:
Despair
Loneliness
Isolation
Antagonism
Righteousness
Hopelessness
Grief
Fear
Errors
Anger
Longing
Yearning
Wanting
Giving up
Surrenders
Suspicions
Attacks
Terrors

Finding Peace is all we ask.
Making Peace is a daily task.

FIRST THOUGHTS

The universe is in motion, spinning, spinning. Atoms spin around atoms and galaxies spin around themselves in precise choreographies. Spinning is not unnatural. However, if a planet spins off its axis, it can be thrown light years from its original orbit. The consequences are extreme.

Humans are micro-representatives of the universal design of spinning atoms and organic galaxies, bioelectrical systems in motion. If a human being becomes unbalanced and emotionally tumbles away from its original pattern the consequences in terms of human dynamics can also be extreme. Any human that tries to maintain his or her orbit in the presence of a collapsing one is at risk.

The science of change within a system is understood through sound principles, laws of physics, and by considering the nature of Energy in Motion. These same principles make it possible to study and understand the underlying principles of Emotions in the Presence of Business Change.

The purpose of this book is to aid in the understanding of some of the dynamics of emotions in the presence of change that occur in the workplace. Although change and movement are known factors of life, movement can be either productive or counter-productive. Spinning out of orbit is generally counterproductive to life. Emotionally spinning out of orbit at the workplace is rarely fiscally productive if an employee spins out of the workplace gravity system.

How is the gravity at your company? Are the human emotions orbiting pleasantly about or wobbling into pre-collapse? What is your company doing with its human energy? Is the direction that managers and employees are spinning productive or destructive? Is the human energy of your company spinning positively within the framework of the galaxy of your industry? Or is it Stuck? Blocked? Running Amok? Exploding? Short-Circuited? Leaking? Or, Spinning Wildly Out of Control? What level of spin can your organization tolerate? A small wobble, or a single rotation? Or, can it withstand the daunting effects of a catastrophic, whirling spinout? And, do you want to be the one in your department who manages all that force? If so...how?

HOW TO READ THIS BOOK

Although it is beneficial to read an entire text on any topic some people don't like to read and prefer to skim and dip for goodies. Skimming and dipping is fine as long as you know what you are looking for and know when you have it. Reading, pondering, embracing and taking ownership of every word may not be your style or you are in a crisis and don't have time to meditate on the higher values of life. You need something helpful RIGHT NOW!

Taking in any information within a complete context will strengthen your knowledge base, language usage, comprehensions, advocacy stance, and consciousness as well as establish more depth and integration. Reading the width, breadth and depth of a topic is useful. Application of material without breadth and depth is less powerful.

Because this book discusses spinning and emotional tornadoes, approaching the topic of emotions at work would be best served by reading to seek a deep personal solid foundation that can't be blown away. But if you skim and dip, use this book as only one resource as you build a very complete awareness of the dynamics of human emotions at the workplace. If it is the first book on emotions you read, read it carefully. If it just another book for you, you should read even more carefully — there might be one more idea that you haven't read yet. Any book with one more good idea is worth your time. In a world that is spinning like a top on a daily basis an idea that offers safety in the workplace may indeed be worth your time.

Vali Hawkins Mitchell

October, 2004

xx

SECTION I

READINESS:
Rotations, Recognition And Risks

I hear stories. When I tell people I'm an Emotional Continuity Management consultant they say something like, "I could have used your help last month when we had an emotional meltdown at work. No one knew what to do. It was horrible but we figured it out eventually."

Eventually isn't cost effective. Eventually isn't compassionate for people who are either uncomfortable or at risk. Eventually is a luxury that competitive markets do not have. While every emotional incident is not necessarily a crisis, being prepared for managing workplace emotions is part of business continuity and appropriate risk assessment. Eventually people have emotional issues at the workplace.

How do you pay attention to emotions at work? How do you manage them? What emotions are appropriate and what emotions are counterproductive? When is enough venting at work enough? How are emotions useful when changes need to be made in the organization? How do you tell if someone is having normal emotions without getting an advanced degree in psychology? Why aren't emotional issues just a Human Resources (HR) thing? What if your HR person is emotionally unstable? What if your boss, supervisor, or manager is an emotional tornado? What if you are?

Most healthy people are influenced emotionally by the consequences of unexpected deaths, natural disasters, disgruntled employees, rumors, gossip, and threats of layoffs. Does your company have a policy and plan in place to manage the emotions of healthy employees? What about staff who are less than emotionally healthy to begin with?

Is it reasonable to worry about money, costs, and bottom-line issues when someone is hurting? Of course it is. It is quite simple to attend to the bottom-line issues with grace and compassion. Business and emotions are <u>not</u> mutually exclusive.

1

ROTATIONS:
WHAT IS SPINNING?

School Principal has been on secret administrative leave for one month. Officials will not say why. (Tri City Herald, April 22, 2004)

Internet company Terra Lycos reported that, for the first time since it started, searches for prisoner abuse images last week propelled the war in Iraq to the top of it's "top 10 Search Term" list. (Associated Press, May 15, 2004)

Thousands of laid-off workers will lose job-retraining opportunities because of a little-noticed change in the way the government pays for such programs. Thinly populated states like Iowa will be hardest hit, since many people there work at smaller companies. The new dictate is most likely to affect workers at companies with 150 or fewer employees. National emergency grants which have been used to help workers at shuttered manufacturing plants learn new skills will not be available to many. (Associated Press, May 15, 2004)

The first woman to be appointed Washington State fire marshal has resigned for unexplained reasons after six years in charge. (Daily Olympian, May, 2004)

Two Portland disc jockeys were fired from a local radio station after playing an audiotape of the beheading of American Nick Berg by Iraqi militants and then laughing over the sounds of the grisly death. (Associated Press, May 15, 2004)

Mad cow costs 150 jobs in Fort Morgan. Meatpacker Excel Corp. has laid off 150 employees at its Fort Morgan processing plant, a consequence of mad cow disease (Denver Post, January 11, 2004)

WHY YOU SHOULD READ THIS CHAPTER

If an event in your town or workplace spins out of control, will it disappear into thin air or turn into a global event? Will you and your company be ready to deal with the human emotional responses and business risks? How do you think your employees will react and respond to an unexpected change or event? Do you think emotions matter at the workplace? If you read this chapter you may begin to think how emotional responses are natural responses and to manage Emotional Continuity is as critical to your job as any other form of continuity practice.

BY THE END OF CHAPTER 1 YOU SHOULD BE ABLE TO

- Define and characterize issues associated with the challenges of managing human emotions at the work site to be able to explain the concept of workplace spinning to your employer or employees as you begin to develop buy-on procedures.

- Have detailed explanations of how emotions are to be expected and accepted while at the same time viewed as risk potential at the workplace.

- Create an index of what emotions are appropriate in your worksite during normal operations as well as during abnormal operations.

- Use the tornado analogy to prepare a rough draft document justifying a position on establishing an *Emotional Continuity Management Plan*.

- Using real examples from your experiences or current events, take a proactive stand to initiate a discussion about emotions. Make certain you move any discussion beyond the "touchy-feely" elements of emotions toward clear business-serve-the-bottom-line elements to specific fiscal risks of emotional spinning.

OVERVIEW

Reasonable variations of human emotions are expected at the workplace. People have feelings. Emotions that accumulate, collect force, expand in volume and begin to spin are another matter entirely. Spinning emotions can become as unmanageable as a tornado, and in the workplace they can cause just as much damage in terms of human distress and economic disruption.

All people have emotions. Normal people and abnormal people have emotions. Emotions happen at home and at work. So, understanding how individuals or groups respond emotionally in a business situation is important in order to have a complete perspective of human beings in a business function. Different people have different sets of emotions. Some people let emotions roll off their back like water off a duck. Other people swallow emotions and hold them in until they become toxic waste that needs a disposal site. Some have small simple feelings and others have large, complicated emotions. Stresses of life tickle our emotions or act as fuses in a time bomb. Stress triggers emotion. Extreme stress complicates the wide range of varying emotional responses. Work is a stressor. Sometimes work is an *extreme* stressor.

Since everyone has emotion, it is important to know what kinds of emotion are regular and what kinds are irregular, abnormal, or damaging within the business environment. To build a strong, well-grounded, value-added set of references for professional discussions and planning for Emotional Continuity Management a manager needs to know at least the basics about human emotion. Advanced knowledge is preferable.

Emotional Continuity Management planning for emotions that come from the stress caused by changes inside business, from small adjustments to catastrophic upheavals, requires knowing emotional and humanity-based needs and functions of people and not just technology and performance data. Emergency and Disaster Continuity planners sometimes posit the questions, *"What if during a disaster your computer is working, but no one shows up to use it? What if no one is working the computer because they are terrified to show up to a worksite devastated by an earthquake or bombing and they stay home to care for their children?"* The Emotional Continuity Manager asks, *"What if no one is coming or no one is producing even if they are at the site because they are grieving or anticipating the next wave of danger? What happens if employees are engaged in emotional combat with another employee through gossip, innuendo, or out-and-out verbal warfare? And what if the entire company is in turmoil because we have an Emotional Terrorist who is just driving everyone bonkers?"* The answer is that, in terms of bottom-line thinking, productivity is productivity — and if your employees are not available because their emotions are not calibrated to your industry standards, then fiscal risks must be considered. Human compassion needs are important. And so is money.

Employees today face the possibility of biological, nuclear, incendiary, chemical, explosive, or electronic catastrophe while potentially working in the same cubicle with someone ready to suicide over personal issues at home. They face rumors of downsizing and outsourcing while watching for anthrax amidst rumors that co-workers are having affairs. An employee coughs, someone jokes nervously about SARS, or teases a co-worker about their hamburger coming from a Mad Cow, someone laughs, someone worries, and productivity can falter as minds are not on tasks. Emotions run rampant in human lives and therefore at work sites. High-demand emotions demonstrated by complicated workplace relationships, time-consuming divorce proceedings, addiction behaviors, violence, illness, and death are common issues at work sites which people either manage well — or do *not* manage well. Low-demand emotions demonstrated by annoyances, petty bickering, competition, prejudice, bias, minor power struggles, health variables, politics and daily grind feelings take up mental space as well as emotional space.

It is reasonable to assume that dramatic effects from a terrorist attack, natural disaster, disgruntled employee shooting, or natural death at the work site would create emotional content. That content can be something that develops, evolves and resolves, or gathers speed and force like a tornado to become a spinning energy event with a life of its own. Even smaller events, such as a fully involved gossip chain or a computer upgrade can lead to the voluntary or involuntary exit of valuable employees. This can add energy to an emotional spin and translate into real risk features such as time loss, recruitment nightmares, disruptions in customer service, additional management hours, remediations and trainings, consultation fees, Employee Assistance Program (EAP) dollars spent, Human Resources (HR) time spent, administrative restructuring, and expensive and daunting litigations. Companies that prepare for the full range of emotions and therefore emotional risks, from annoyance to catastrophe, are better equipped to adjust to any emotionally charged event, small or large. It is never a question of if something will happen to disrupt the flow of productivity, it is only a question of when and how large.

Emotions that ebb and flow are functional in the workplace. A healthy system should be able to manage the ups and downs of emotions. Emotions directly affect the continuity of production and services, customer and vendor relations and essential infrastructure. Unstable emotional infrastructure in the workplace disrupts business through such measurable costs as medical and mental health care, employee retention and retraining costs, time loss, or legal fees. Emotional Continuity Management is reasonably simple for managers when they are provided the justifiable concepts, empirical evidence that the risks are real, a set of correct tools and instructions in their use. What has not been easy until recently has been convincing the "powers that be" that it is value-added work to deal directly and procedurally with emotions in the workplace. Businesses haven't seen emotions as part of the working technology and have done everything they can do to avoid the topic. Now, cutting-edge companies are turning the corner. Even technology continuity managers are talking about human resources benefits and scrambling to find ways to evaluate feelings and risks.

Yes, times are changing. Making a case for policy to manage emotions is now getting easier. For all the pain and horror associated with the terrorist attacks of September 11, 2001, employers are getting the message that no one is immune to crisis. In today's heightened security environments the demands of managing complex workplace emotions have increased beyond the normal training supplied by in-house Human Resources (HR) professionals and Employee Assistance Plans (EAPs). Many extremely well-meaning HR and EAP providers just do not have a necessary training to manage the complicated strata of extreme emotional responses. Emotions at work today go well beyond the former standards of HR and EAP training. HR and EAP providers now must have advanced trauma management training to be prepared to support employees. The days of easy emotional management are over. Life and work is much too complicated.

Significant emotions from small to extreme are no longer the sole domain of HR, EAP, or even emergency first responders and counselors. Emotions are spinning in the very midst of your team, project, cubicle, and company. Emotions are not just at the scene of a disaster. Emotions *are* present. And because they are not "controllable," human emotions are not subject to being mandated. *Emotions are going to happen.*

There are many times when emotions cannot be simply outsourced to an external provider of services. There are many times that a manager will face an extreme emotional reaction. Distressed people will require management regularly. That's your job! Your job today includes acquiring the skills necessary to know when you can manage emotions yourself, when you are way over your head, and when you need to call for backup. Emotional Continuity Management is a collection of ideas and skills supported by scientifically designed tools that help you manage, not control, human emotions.

Many twenty-first century organizations are beginning to agree that, to be comprehensive, Business Continuity Planning must include managing people's emotions. They are discovering that a system-wide approach to creating an emotionally spin-free workplace, means preparing themselves and all employees for potential emotional impact, thus lowering the risks of collective system-wide spinning. This planning also prepares everyone for rapid recovery no matter the size or conditions of the impact event. Organizations that develop Emotional Continuity policy, procedures, practice drills, multiple resources, and management tools are more ready to withstand whatever comes along with a healthy rapid-recovery mentality. Good days are good. Bad days are bad. But what happens if things go terribly, terribly, terribly bad? Then what?

MANAGEMENT IN THE MIDST OF EMOTIONAL CHAOS

When there is a local, regional, state or national disaster, some official has to "call" it a disaster. Governmental agencies are generally responsible for officially "declaring" when an event is of worthy merit to be defined within the rigorous guidelines and definitions to qualify an event or incident as a "declared" disaster. These official standards and markers control funding, emergency relief services, public assistance, debris clearance, repair, demolitions, replacements, housing, loans, grants, counseling, health care services, search and rescue, transportation, mass care, mutual aid, changing regulations, tax relief, restoration costs, corpse removals, some litigations and legal implications and exemptions, and immediate and long term financial support or relief. In other words, if it is a "REAL" disaster, it counts for something and procedures are put in place to aid recovery. Rapid recovery happens only after the official has decided it is officially official. Sometimes this happens with astonishing rapid speed and other times it can take what seems like a lifetime. In the meantime, people may be waiting and can be terribly upset and distressed. They know it was a disaster because they are sitting in the rubble that used to be their organized lives.

Case Example

The earthquake hit at 8:34 a.m. The epicenter was on the west side of Washington State which was declared an official disaster. FEMA (Federal Emergency Management Agency) was on the scene quickly to give support and manage media coverage. Teams evaluated damage and made dollar assessments. Across the state, on the east side of the mountains, the earthquake was recorded as minor and these counties were not within the official disaster area. They did not qualify for FEMA response.

The Skinners, who lived in a rural county, discovered that their driveway, the only entrance to their home and their home-based business, had buckled. The way the highway was set, their customer-based productivity depended on the turn-around in their driveway off the highway. Someone suggested the earthquake might have caused it. This idea had not occurred to them so they began making phone calls. No one had claimed any damage in the county. As channels began to shift, FEMA was suspicious but officially polite and came to their home to evaluate. After seeing the damage, the FEMA representative did a thorough investigation and discovered that their brick home had been split down the middle. The representative was clear that indeed this was earthquake damage and helped them file a report. Within 24 hours the county had received FEMA's report and was declared an official disaster area. Other people started calling with damage reports of disrupted hot water heaters, cracked fences, well damage, and various effects of the tremblor. The Skinners received a check from FEMA that helped pay for the repair of the driveway. FEMA paid $732.00 for the driveway. The damage from disrupted services was a loss of approximately $24,000 in revenue.

Learning Byte

The Skinners were happy with FEMA. Their representatives were courteous and professional and didn't treat the couple like they were trying to bilk the system. But they did wait a long time to get financial help. The neighbors, who had waited longer to report, became angry that FEMA had not come sooner and rallied together in angry meetings. Several home businesses and farms had delays, loss of productivity, and additional expenses incurred prior to the official declaration of disaster.

DO THIS: Learn how disasters are officially declared in your city, county, and state. New Homeland Security regulations may determine how disaster services work in your area.

DON'T: Make assumptions without good information, and don't wait too long to ask for help.

MANAGERS ARE SITE DISASTER OFFICIALS

As a manager, you are an important disaster "official" on the site. You are often the one who decides if an emotional incident is a disaster, or just a quick-fix problem. You determine if policy-level criteria have been met to implement procedures for intervention. You determine when an incident is a disaster — or just an annoyance. Managers are somewhat like FEMA on the job site. Despite the variety of incidents possible in a workplace, managers must make assessments that could help or disrupt employees. No matter what is happening, you may be the constant, common-denominator in a swirly system. Your employees will look to you to validate that they are in a disaster zone, real or perceived. Just like the Skinners and their neighbors, you will be standing in the midst of the after-effects of emotional damage and will have to make the tough calls. No matter if the event or incident is small or large in scope — the manager is the one that everyone turns to for help and guidance. It would be useful if you had a great windbreaker jacket with big yellow letters on it that stated you were the OFFICIAL and you had all the power to make things right. FEMA professionals get good jackets. But of course managers don't get cool jackets even thought they have similar job tasks with less power. In fact management not only do not get cool jackets, they are consistently blamed if things do not go well and people are not taken care of immediately. Employees can quickly become like the Skinners' distressed neighbors and group together to become a cranky mob. But, there you are, standing in the middle of the chaos as your company's first responder, and everyone is looking to you for leadership. You may be having feelings also, but your emotions must temporarily be put aside. Your feelings must be tucked away. The manager has to symbolically put on the FEMA jacket and walk into the midst of the chaos with a good plan. You have to have the mind set and the tools to walk into the spinning emotions of others and remain the stable influence. Are you ready? Because no matter the level of emotional energy in the workplace, *you* are the one who will be faced with managing it. You may be in the middle of a company crisis and experiencing your own emotional issues and will still be expected to keep the company on task. The smallest emotional issue such as annoyed IT workers who can't work because there is temporary technical downtime caused by a squirrel who inconsiderately fried itself in the electrical box will fall to your leadership. Big events, like the unexpected death of a beloved colleague who dies horribly in a freak car accident will require your strength of leadership presence. Likewise, a natural disaster like an earthquake or fire, or man-made catastrophe such as a terrorist attack, will fall on your skills to manage. And, not surprisingly, statistics indicate these events happen more than you would like to think. According to Albert Marcella, a specialist in the area of Information Technology (IT) Emergency Contingency Planning, there will be more problems in the future. His research shows that:

*   Computer downtime costs US businesses $4 billion a year
*   20% of all small to medium-size businesses suffer a major disaster every five years
*   Companies now have to think about the loss of life of key employees
*   Customers expect supplies and services to continue no matter what
*   Shareholders expect management control to remain operational through any crisis
*   Suppliers expect their revenue streams to continue .

In other words, the show must go on! Life continues. Work progresses. Sometimes it might seem like you are managing alone. In fact, you just *might be* managing alone. Small incidents come and go and you cannot run to administration with every emotional fluctuation. Bigger events will have a life of their own. Just like the official declarations of emergencies from agencies that control help and assistance may or may not arrive in a timely fashion, you may isolated in your management situation. The factors may include administrative ignorance, resistance or simple absence. You may have to make the call yourself. If there is a huge event, your isolation may be technical due to losses of power, technology or communications streams. You may not be able to call in your mentors or managers. You may be the whole game!

In fact, you may be without help or information for days, especially if there is no electrical power. No power could mean no communications. It could also mean no work. But it doesn't *ever* mean no human emotions! Managers are there in the field managing human emotions, as well as products and technology, while administrators are absent or desperately scrambling to keep the entire business alive. So if the emotional event is small you will be expected to manage it alone and not bother the higher-ups. If it is huge, you may also be alone for a variety of reasons. Sometimes during a large incident the administrators are the folks who are trying to drive the ambulance at top speed to get things back to function while you are alone, dear manager, in the back of the rig giving everyone on your staff CPR.

CAN YOU MANAGE MANAGING?

Managers are employees with emotions also. Not everyone is wired to be a manager. Even people with good intentions may not have the emotional grounding to stand in the middle of chaos. Some managers use the workplace to work out their own emotional issues. This isn't helpful and can lead to more emotional chaos. A manager must decide if they can handle the job and if they are willing to grow into the position. Management isn't about power; it is about leadership. Managers who do not have a good sense of their own emotions or leadership power may use the workplace to flex their autocratic muscles. Managers who are afraid are even worse.

Frightened managers clearly have no sense of themselves and their position as a manager. They may be overwhelmed and under-trained, or try to use force tactics to maintain authority because they have no other skills. Of course they may also just be mean people. But more than ever, when random emotions, chaos, or fears of terror and threat swirl around offices, the manager is under extreme pressure to be less afraid than his or her human counterparts or staff. This expectation is erroneous and dangerous. Managers are human also (well perhaps a few are not!) and are in a unique position to be either very helpful or very unhelpful to employees who are caught in an emotional spin. Most employees go to their jobs to work to survive their lives. After a hard day at work they may require additional support services to survive their jobs if they have a tyrannical manager who is attempting to maintain his or her own little kingdom of control. Employees need a certain level of leadership to feel safe and secure in their jobs, and that is what management is intended to supply. Managers who cannot manage are a risk.

Employees relate personally to perceived or real control issues at a work setting. From minor irritations to violent rages, employees react to their environment, and those who are held "hostage" by tyrannical managers at work are the least likely to maintain an emotional equilibrium under duress. Managers who are weak, indecisive, or frightened of making waves, do not add to the emotional stability of a company. Social scientists who have studied antisocial behavior in the workplace have found that dishonesty or unethical behaviors from management have influenced some employees to act counterproductively to the workplace. Emotionally frustrated employees apparently have a tendency to steal, manipulate records, slow pace, do poor work and essentially move from a high order of integrity and ethics to the lower status of the management. Managers set the emotional tone of a company.

Dysfunctional managers or supervisors come in a variety of styles:

- Hostile
- Violent
- Colluding
- Controlling
- Weak
- Manipulative
- Politically aggressive

- Wishy-washy
- Passive-aggressive
- Undertrained
- Emotional hostage takers
- Subtle Covert Emotional Terrorists
- Blatant, Overt Emotional Terrorists

Anyone who has ever been employed for any length of time has run into someone who manifests the qualities on this list. Clearly, managers are not the only employees who fall into these categories. But managers, who set the emotional tone in a company, can either stand in the midst of emotional content and add elements of competent and calm leadership, or toss emotional energy into the fray and add to the chaos. Managers, good, bad and neutral are in the midst of the action. A manager who does not have some sort of leadership presence in the turmoil is not managing. That leadership can come in the form of a physical presence, or a competent policy.

Managers stand in the middle of the small and large flows of human dynamic energy and have to deal with whatever comes their way. Good managers at their best are like midwives who stand at the apex of production to keep things moving. They don't necessarily have the baby or have the pain, but they are right there at the center of the action. Managers at their worst are people who create problems that stop the flow of production. They are afraid or ignorant of the birthing process and do not particularly like babies. Good managers and bad managers have the same work to do. How they do it is up to them. Managers have the same choices as everyone else. How these personal choices influence the work site emotional climate, production and eventually the bottom line, is usually up to what kind of choices these managers make. Managers are often seen as either wonderful mentors, inspirations, creative forces, and dynamic leaders or, at the other end of the emotional spectrum, as tyrannical and petty thieves who steal all the hope, life force, and warmth they can find to add to their own personal power addiction. Middle ground is not a common reaction to management.

Case Example

Misty was promoted to day shift Nurse Manager. She had never wanted to be a manager but appreciated the raise. She struggled for two years to make her best decisions about people and production. When the consultant arrived to help reorganize the company's administrative hierarchy, Misty had received a vote of "no-confidence" from former friends and colleagues. They complained she was a bad manager and that she spent some portion of every workday shut inside her office crying. Misty felt humiliated and made grand efforts to rise to the tasks required. She attended management trainings, read books, and talked with her family. She told the consultant that she regretted her decision daily when she saw the other nurses doing the nursing work that she missed. She had a passion for nursing but was now required to spend most hours in her office working on paperwork and mediating emotional issues between co-workers. Misty had come from a dysfunctional childhood home and hated conflict. She was relieved when the consultant encouraged her to return to the work she loved, as a floor nurse. Within two weeks the facility hired a Nurse Manager who had extensive managerial experience and was pursuing a career track toward administration. It was a better fit for all.

Learning Byte

This institution lost approximately 35 hours a week of productive time while the nurses were fussing and fuming about Misty's lack of managerial skills. Misty lost over 70 hours a week as she was becoming more and more consumed by her emotions and fears of failure. Misty had never been trained to deal with conflict and had entered nursing as a way to just help bodies get better, not feelings. The company policy now includes language that does not allow promotion from within based solely on seniority.

Management selection and hiring has a policy that includes such questions as "What experience or training do you have that will allow you to handle the extreme and minor emotions of employees?" It also has questions about willingness, competency, and training in conflict management and dispute resolution, and provides training dollars for non-industry-specific management training. In other words, a Nurse Manager needs management skills training in addition to medical seminars. This facility found that many independent companies provide management training and now support their managers attending non-medical courses. Nurse managers still must also maintain their industry-specific training requirements, such as continuing education units or CPR/First Aid status.

DO THIS: Evaluate your decision to be a manager on a regular basis. Look at how your company hires managers.

DON'T: Assume anyone can be a manager without advanced, ongoing training in management skills.

STARTING TO THINK ABOUT EMOTIONS

To start to think about emotions as a manager you will have to think about yours and your employees. Both are in the same location so both need attention. There is limited precedent for managers to start thinking about emotions, so this is where you can start raising your emotional management Grade Point Average. (GPA) You can start today to become fluent.

The word "emotions" can bring up an emotional reaction because traditionally emotions have seemed difficult to define. Most simply put, emotions are human feelings, sentiments, and sensations. The science of emotions studies physical, mental, and spiritual constructs to describe "feelings." Feelings are intangible although the results of emotions and feelings can be quite tangible. Emotion is the stuff of love and hate, peace and conflict, music and poetry, art and madness, politics and principles, philosophy and religion. Emotions are defined and redefined, scientifically analyzed, researched, dissected and sorted into bite-sized categories. Emotions are completely unfathomable and exquisitely human. Any attempt to define, much less comprehend the emotional nature of human beings, for the purpose of mandating or controlling human emotional response, is whimsy at best, and dangerous at its worst.

You can learn to expand your emotional vocabulary and explore the fascinating complications and ambiguities that are human emotions. Human emotions are more wonderfully complicated and dynamic than most people can imagine. Many people spend so much time avoiding and suppressing their feelings that they have actually come to believe they *are* controllable. Paul Ekman, in *Emotions Revealed*, explores just one aspect of emotions in cross-cultural research on facial expressions as windows to emotional states. He writes, "It is hard to overestimate the importance of emotions in our lives." Scientists, writers, philosophers, poets and mystics cannot agree on what an emotion is, but most would concur that the existence and importance of emotions, in life — as well as the workplace — must not be ignored. Avoidance and denial of emotions, especially at the workplace, is not only a behavior — it is also an emotion. Thinking about emotions is different than feeling emotions. Both are necessary to have a complete and comprehensive appreciation for human experience. And managers, in the midst of the chaos, need to be leaders of human experience to understand and feel emotions. Thinking about emotions is a precious journey that doesn't end in an adventure that never fails.

STARTING TO THINK ABOUT MANAGING EMOTIONS

Managers at the epicenter of employee emotional dynamics need to have their manager "game-on." Today's marketplace requires managers to be part of creating policies and procedures to manage many complicated functions, including emotions, at work. Today's management is not limited to the cubicle, so the range of creative management approaches must be comprehensive. Emotional Continuity Management plans that attend fully to the broad emotional strata of employees is very complex and can take years of top-end planning, discussions, research, drills, trainings, auditing, assessments, evaluations, and ethics determinations. Emotional Continuity Management is a cutting-edge activity and so must begin somewhere even if there is not a large volume of easily accessible information or support. And because of the emotional content of our times, Emotional Continuity Management planning must begin now, from where you are today. You cannot wait to be an expert to be *the* expert. The world is volatile and business economic securities are teetering on emotional whims of emotionally based issues. The issues of outsourcing, massive layoffs, wars in the Middle East, national security, rising fuel prices, endangered species, scandals, daily rumors of potential terrorists threats, and constant disruptions are defining countless new task and performance functions while creating emotional storms. Given the volatile nature of the world situation, a cutting-edge manager must begin first efforts to establish policies and procedures for managing emotions at the workplace. Policy and planning can begin by establishing basic criteria for Emotional Continuity Management.

Any plan, policy, or procedure of Emotional Continuity Management will be best served if it is:

- *Positive*: not fear based. Based in possibilities of recovery, and not horror.
- *Practical*: it should work across the board for all strata of employees
- *Technical*: empirical and repeatable, science-based, auditable, data producing
- *Non-technical*: include non-visible, intuitive, human "feelings" data
- *Auditable*: measurable outcomes
- *Assessable*: transparent and teachable in a variety of learning styles
- *Accessible*: available to all on not controlled by one domain
- *Repeatable*: created in a form that has continuing presentations and upgrades
- *Documentable*: lends itself to paper trails
- *Researchable*: provides data that can be evaluated and adjusted as trends change
- *Fiscally sound*: inexpensive to encourage regular use
- *Standard setting*: visible, transparent, higher-ground thinking
- *Ethical*: Moral, principled, fair, decent and just for all humans
- *Compassionate*: thoughtful, sympathetic, kind, benevolent, and humane
- *Economically rational*: supports the bottom line and is value-added.

WHAT IS EMOTIONAL SPINNING?

You have started thinking about emotions, yours and others, at the worksite, and understand that managers are in the midst of the complicated energy of human emotions. You have started to think that emotions may indeed be a professional management issue. You have made your professional decision to include Emotional Continuity Management in your work and at your workplace. You are ready. You are emotional-inspired. Then you are faced with an emotional incident that is beyond the scope of your regular management skills. You see the emotion and know it is your job to manage it, but you don't have any tools yet.

Then you see something that is bigger. You see a subset of emotions that seem to have another dimension. You see an emotional content that contains or represents something other than the regular daily grind feelings of people who have to work with people. You aren't just seeing the emotions; you are seeing something that seems to be attached to the feelings. This "something" seems to have a life of its own. What you may be seeing is *emotional spinning*.

Emotional spinning is what happens when an employee or a group of employees experience what could be seen as normal emotions that, for some reason, escalate and continue to develop an additional energy beyond the emotions of the original event. Emotional spinning occurs when one or more employees join forces with someone else to form a mutual or collective energy spin. The emotions are present, but the spin itself begins to take form and shape. A spin may start as a simple feeling state, then escalate to interfere with work functions.

Emotional spinning can center on one person or can consume entire systems and whole industries. Emotional spinning can feel like a mob mentality but is significantly subtler. Remember the old horror movies where someone in the village stirs up everyone to go kill the monster? Emotional spinning doesn't have to evolve into such dramatic scenes of angry villagers with torches in order to be disruptive. In fact, a subtle, scornful expression or undertone of disgust can initiate emotional havoc in a workplace quite effectively and surprisingly extensively. A well-placed rumor can create cascading turmoil and emotional spin-offs that lead to deep emotional distresses, leading to extraordinary fiscal carnage. A "soft" incident like a broken promise can turn into "hard" date of lost revenue. An angry facial expression can have more influence on feelings than words, as emotions fill in the gaps of meaning that lead people to make wild, emotional assumptions. Emotional spinning can take a regular workday and turn it into your worst management disaster nightmare!

As stated previously, creating anti-spinning policy or being the first one in your company to take a position of advocacy for Emotional Continuity Management is not yet an easy task. Business Continuity and Disaster Planners are making brave efforts to have "feelings" included in any body of contingency planning work. But even if your company is not ready to establish formalized policies and procedures, emotional management of human beings remains necessary for companies to survive. Perhaps your company is not ready to take good care of itself. Maybe your only interest in this information is that you want to provide yourself the best in professional self-care within a chaotic worksite. In either case, understanding the causes, attributes and variations of emotional spinning, as well as the prevention, recognition and management of human emotions in the workplace is time well spent. Brave managers are suiting up and showing up to inform and educate employees and bosses about the compassionate and fiscal issues of unmanaged spinning at the workplace. Some CEOs, business leaders, administrators, managers and owners are slowly but surely learning how emotions at the workplace is one discussion, and that spinning at the workplace is another discussion. Some emotions are well managed by HR and EAP representative. Spinning is a management issue.

DEFINITIONS:

Emotional: all human feelings, those defined as positive and negative

Spinning: normal emotions that, for some reason, escalate and continue to develop an additional energy beyond the emotions of the original event. Emotional spinning occurs when one or more person joins forces with someone else to form a mutual or collective energy spin. The increasing collective emotional dynamic created by rampant, unmanaged, or poorly managed feelings

Unintentional Spinning: Being unconsciously caught in someone else's strong emotional process and temporary emotional repercussions or consequences associated with the effects of an emotionally charged event

Intentional Spinning: The intentional use and action of displaying and using emotions of self or others to control a situation or to accumulate territory, either literal or figurative, using force through physical, mental, emotional or psychological mechanisms of fear, intimidation, implied threats, or outright control

Emotional Terrorism: The use of emotional mechanisms and behaviors to force or coerce an emotional agenda on someone else with the intention or action of controlling a situation, or accumulating territory; either real, perceived, or symbolic:

> a) When normal daily emotional levels of healthy/stable employees are used by someone or a group to escalate emotions to levels which interfere with production and/or well being;

> b) When dysfunctional, impaired or pathologically disturbed, non-healthy, unstable employees begin to influence healthy and stable workers to experience diminished feelings of work satisfaction levels, production, or general well-being;

> c) When covert (hidden) emotional agendas begin surfacing to overt (visible) levels causing small but perceivable effects in structure or infrastructure which result in tension, conflict, and/or other forms of disruption;

> d) When the primary, first signs of chaos which can lead to decay, destruction, damage, immobilization or death of an organism/system cause effect; and/or

> e) When severe levels of emotions based destruction or damage take place with terminal (end of operations) results

WHAT EMOTIONAL SPINNING IS *NOT*

Emotional spinning is *not* the regular day-to-day feelings that people experience and demonstrate. Emotional spinning is *not* the acute, short-lived moments of agitation or disturbance that are a reaction to normal challenges.

Emotional spinning is an effect, or process, which endures long enough to have consequences. Acute processes are like breezes; they come and go with a bit of a dramatic flair, but are non-consequential, unless the breeze is carrying a contagious disease. (The consequences of a toxic-laden breeze may be quite collectively impressive.) When people get together day after day at work, tension happens and conflicts happen. Tension and conflict are normal gusts and breezes associated with human beings that hang out with other human beings. No matter what else human beings produce throughout a day, they have emotions that produce feelings. People working together are going to find joy and annoyance as they associate with one another to create products and complete performance tasks. Human feelings happen and spin into all the nooks and crannies of human life, including the worksite like simple breezes blowing across the face of planet Earth. No part of the Earth is untouched by the wind. This is a *good* thing. Emotions are good. Emotions are breezes, dust devils and short windy gusts. Emotional spins are more like big winds, tempests, gales, storms, typhoons, hurricanes, cyclones and batten-down-the-hatch-and-head-for-the-cellar tornadoes!

Many human feelings are the kind that can be described as positive — like happy, enthusiastic, hopeful, ambitious, energized, loyal, and so forth. Some feelings are the kind that can be described as negative — like angry, fearful, gloomy, annoyed, tense, and so forth. Some feelings are comfy and some are uncomfortable. Both kinds of emotions, positive and negative, are normal, human, useful and to be expected. Emotions are okay, even at the work site. Most healthy adults can handle periods of joy and periods of discomfort without it interfering with their jobs. Most businesses can handle periods of joy and periods of discomfort without significant risk or losses. Businesses that employ human beings should expect and be willing and able to handle the full range of human emotional expression without coming apart at the seams.

HOW TO KNOW THE DIFFERENCE BETWEEN SPINNING AND ABUSE AND VIOLENCE

Emotional context is reasonable in life. Emotions are normal. Even big emotions can be useful and creative. But emotions that escalate to conflict must be stopped long before violence. Violence and abuse does happen and it happens at work and at home. Women abuse men. Men abuse women. Men abuse men. Women abuse women. There are some very scary human beings in the world and in our work sites. Battering spouses, child abusers, sex offenders, criminals, and even mass murders have jobs.

Emotional spinning is not necessarily abuse or violence. But no one is immune to the potential dangers of abuse and violence, not even at work. Abuse and violence are not culturally, ethnically, racially, politically, socioeconomically, or in any other way limited to one group or another. Workplace spinning is an equal-opportunity issue. So is abuse and violence. It is necessary for managers to learn how to recognize the difference between normal conflict that includes big emotions, and abuse or violence.

Some industries require their employees to be mandated reporters of abuse and violence. Health professionals, teachers, law enforcement and even day-care providers are usually required to take training on violence and abuse. You and your employees can opt to become mandated reporters of abuse violence toward other people and find a local or national educator to train your team. Abusers do not want you to have that information and will downplay the seriousness of their emotions and yours to create a deflection. The courts are becoming more and more concerned with domestic and child violence and it is becoming more important for businesses not to covertly support perpetrators, and take positions of anti-abuse advocacy in their companies.

If you suspect violence or abuse is happening at your work site, or someone on your team is either perpetrating or suffering from abuse, check your employee handbook and follow your company's policies. Then if needed go ahead and call Child or Adult Protective Services, a Mental Health Crisis Response Unit, or 911. If you are wrong it will certainly be embarrassing. If you are right it will certainly be upsetting. If you are wrong you might lose your job. If you are right you might lose your job. If you are right you may save a life. If you are right and don't make the call you may read your name or someone else' in the headlines tomorrow. Which headline would you rather read?

You May Be in an Abusive or Potentially Violent Situation if You:

- Are frightened of someone's temper
- Are feeling crazy because someone says you are the cause of the problems
- Feel controlled by someone's actions, silences, moods, looks, gestures, voice, threats
- Have the urge to rescue someone when he/she is in trouble
- Apologize for someone's bad behavior
- Make decisions about your activities, friends, ideas, according to what someone else wants or how they might react
- Were abused as a child or in another relationship
- Have been teased, pushed, ignored, slapped, chased, punched, tickled, thrown, hit, humiliated, or worse and that person has not responded to your needs for safety
- Are forced to have sex, commit a crime, do something unethical or against your will, or are humiliated for refusal
- Are forcibly isolated from others
- Are afraid to express your feelings for fear of someone's response, or told your feelings were invalid, or that you were to blame for any problems

You May Be Contributing to Abuse or Potential Violence if You:

- Lose your temper frequently or easily
- Drink alcohol or use drugs excessively
- Are very jealous, sulk silently when upset, use silence as a weapon, use explosive behavior as a weapon, have difficulty expressing your feelings
- Criticize and put down people
- Blame others for problems
- Monopolize the free time of others
- Have rigid ideas about roles and control
- Have broken things, hit, shoved, kicked, tickled, punched, pushed, slapped, chased, humiliated, teased, physically controlled or worse, and blamed others for these behaviors
- Frightened others with displays of anger or threats of danger to self, children, pets, property, or others
- Were physically or emotionally abused as a child
- Saw violence in your family home

WORKPLACE SPINS ARE LIKE EMOTIONAL TORNADOS

Just like a tornado of the weather variety, the outcome of an emotional tornado is often surprisingly destructive. The winds of these complicated forces can pick up you, beloved colleagues, friends, enemies, loved ones, communities, states, nations and in fact the entire world community and toss them about like a plastic cup. Reasonable, kind, hard-working individuals or entire systems can be relocated from a happy employment site right into an unemployment line with no references. A once vital person can be decimated and left languishing in a health care or mental health facility. Brilliant individuals can land in psychiatric or legal incarceration, alcohol and drug rehab, bankruptcy, divorce court, and even the grave. Emotional winds can swirl your co-worker into time-consuming child custody battles or a favorite boss into a fight for his or her personal or professional reputation. Emotional tornadoes can spin one person or entire systems. Just as the wind of nature isn't very picky about location, emotional tornadoes are not subject to specific places or industries.

Case Example

Prior to her faculty position at the college Paula had worked for a government educational team as a teacher and was well liked by students and faculty, administrators and parents. Paula was rather odd. She was well-traveled, dramatic, dressed non-traditionally, and loved telling a good story. The new president of the college did not like her. She did not fit his agenda or perception of success. He summarily created covert chaos in her department and overtly sabotaged her at staff meetings. Paula started feeling disconnected and began to isolate. When an accident in her office left her with a minor head injury she was denied sick leave by the president. He told her and others that he thought she was making up the symptoms and had possibly staged the accident to discredit him as the new president. This confused her because she had always had excellent credibility. Her complaints began to sound like paranoid fantasies even to herself. She had no witnesses on her behalf and no one stood up to defend her position. Her doctor put her on medications. Her complaints became less clear and her position weakened. Her frustration left her unable to coherently discuss what she experienced as some sort of covert agenda by the president to get her out of the college. She began crying at work. She resigned her tenure position at the college and within a week was committed to a local psychiatric, in-house treatment center. No one spoke up for her and the doctors were evaluating her for paranoia.

A new employee, Karla, had seen a similar emotional campaign in another college so took a professional risk and went to Paula's doctors to tell them that Paula wasn't crazy, the president really was out to get her. Karla risked her own job, as she did not have tenure. Because Karla was a counselor at the college, the doctors listened and responded well. They helped Paula quickly and successfully resolve the emotional impact of this episode. Karla quit quietly and moved on to another university. Both employees survived but suffered extreme financial difficulties.

Learning Byte

Sometimes, when everyone is out to get you, paranoia is just good thinking! This institution of higher education was spinning out of control and several employees were terminated without references by a powerful centrifugal force from an extremely tyrannical administrator. The college lost accreditation during this president's reign.

DO THIS: Pay attention to emotional tornadoes to protect yourself and your company

DON'T: Assume it will avoid you or your organization

An emotionally spinning boss or employee who works alone or in isolation and is not in a position to do much damage to anyone else can usually be managed successfully. However, if an emotionally spinning employee starts to take over territory, moves into another area, or joins another spinner, the velocity and risk of potential damage escalates exponentially. With each addition of an emotional spin the stability of an entire system is at risk and becomes weaker as it becomes compromised. An emotional tornado can threaten infrastructure just as a real tornado can do untoward damage.

One employee spinning is difficult enough to manage, but one in a key position is very challenging. When several employees gather forces, their collective energy is daunting. If the emotional tornado continues adding force, with or without intentionality, the consequences can reach "inconceivable" levels. An emotional spin that completely sabotages business productivity develops a life of it's own while the office grinds itself into an emotional spin frenzy. Anger and sadness, indignation and rage, fear and jealousy, sweeping through a system may leave a trail of emotional carnage, chaos and destruction with profound immediate long-term requirements for reconciliation and repair. An emotional tornado leaves a swath of emotional rubble. The effects of an emotional tornado can be managed or left to chance. Do you think your company is safe? Does it have the shelter of a policy to protect your people? Do you think it won't hit your company? Think again!

Case Example

A young employee was seduced by another employee and began an email love affair. Tamara got more and more involved and became careless with the "secret." Her email lover, Randy, manipulated her into a vulnerable position by threatening to tell her spouse. He emotionally and poetically claimed that he was her best friend and devoted lover who feared losing her. This seduction worked and she took more risks to keep the sexy communication going, thinking it was "love."

Eventually her husband, Brandon, suspected something was going on and discovered the relationship. She continued the email relationship that now spanned two departments of interconnected agencies. Randy began to email pornography. She tried to stop this, but failed. He persisted and encouraged her to join him for their special "love." Communications dwindled as she got disgusted and he threatened to move on to another woman because his "heart was broken."

Tamara was directed to an EAP provider when her supervisor saw her productivity drop and her moods become erratic. She told Randy to stop mailing her pornography. He refused. Now, even more involved with pornography, he threatened to use her old email to set in motion another emotional agenda to control her. Riddled with guilt and fear, Tamara bravely rebuked him again. Starting to lose control, Randy set up a revenge plan to make their email affair public. Tamara, ignorant of his entrenched sexual control agenda, emailed Randy to tell him she was reconciled with her spouse, in counseling, and wanted him to go away. Randy, knowing her seduction vulnerabilities, tried to pull her back in to the affair again. She was able, with much difficulty and professional support to rebuke these advances and he became very angry. Randy emailed Tamara some of her original responses to earlier love notes to remind her of their "love" and "accidentally" forwarded them to other staff in the office. He followed it with a very well written apology email to everyone claiming he had been the silent victim of her misplaced sexual aggressions for desperate months and that he has been so "embarrassed and humiliated beyond belief and would never want anyone to know about this." He performed well and then went to his manager complaining that Tamara was pursuing him. He cried. He used the word "stalking," and implied that there may be a sexual harassment lawsuit at stake, but he "didn't want to make waves." He explained sympathetically that he had heard that she was in counseling and must be mentally ill after all and he didn't want to hurt her. He eloquently punctuated his grievance with, "I hope she isn't dangerous."

Employees blamed Tamara because they saw him as non-emotional, calm, charming and sad while she appeared emotionally distracted, visibly upset, emotional, and unstable. The team became systemically agitated. Someone anonymous did some research and was "accidentally" able to find some very raunchy porno with her name attached to the document. Randy, with good IT skills, cleverly removed all evidence that would lead to him and claimed ongoing victimhood. Almost everyone rallied around him. There was one woman who didn't participate in discussions about any of this and quit unexpectedly. Management was too busy to pay any attention to this sudden exit because Randy escalated his spinning by using his ethnicity as a defense and attack against Tamara.

Tamara worked in a high security industry and the inappropriate use of email destroyed her security status. She was fired. Her dismissal threatened the security of Brandon's position in a closely related security industry, and under the extreme pressure applied from external sources, the young couple could not restore their marriage.

Learning Byte

There was no fast resolution to this event. Although Tamara's initial participation in the flirtation should not be minimized, it was Randy, an Emotional Terrorist, who was able to pull off the heist of this woman's career and life without apparent consequences. His success led him to getting better at Emotional Terror. Within a few weeks the corporation offered him significant perks including a raise. Management was held hostage with a threat of discrimination litigation.

Tamara and Brandon suffered extreme secondary financial damages associated with their losses of employment, social status, costs associated with a difficult and messy divorce and child custody battle. A teacher who didn't have time to "counsel kids of divorce" in a busy classroom advised that one of their young children be put on prescription drugs for stress at age six. Tamara and Brandon were torn apart by a sequence of cascading consequences which impoverished both these young parents and their children. This family was destroyed.

Within four months, two other female employees quit suddenly without reasonable explanations. Management began to see a pattern of female employees quitting without adequate explanation, and observed they were women who were within the same age group as Tamara, and worked in proximity to Randy. Eventually an older male manager, Ron, questioned Randy's ongoing "victimhood" behavior, and began slowly moving him away from key projects with sensitive security issues. Randy was not able to manipulate Ron and eventually transferred. Ron began a series of training for all employees on the topics of harassment, email usage, ethnicity and diversity issues, and how to recognize emotional manipulation. Randy used an Emotional Continuity Management plan that offered excellent information to his staff. It was too late for Tamara and Brandon. The potential estimated ongoing costs of spinning from Emotional Terrorism to this family and community, and ultimately to society, will continue for decades.

DO THIS: Avoid emotional entrapments before they spin into large events that hold you hostage.

DON'T: Try to manage large emotional spins alone. Some are too big to avoid and secrecy and isolation are dangerous.

EVALUATING WORKPLACE SPINNING AND EMOTIONAL TORNADOS

The effects of emotions in the workplace are significant and measurable. There is not a strong or long history of evaluating the effects of misplaced emotions in the workplace. Research is just beginning to ask the right questions. Feelings have been diminished in value to an extreme. Companies continue to spend millions of dollars evaluating tasks, performance productivity, IT security, competitive market strategies, ergonomic furniture, and customer service and still spend little or nothing on how people are feeling at work. Eventually research will catch up and prove its worth — but, in the meantime, managers have to convince themselves and others that emotions are a risk that employers need to consider.

Evaluating workplace emotions and more specifically, emotional spinning in its overt and covert expressions is no different than measuring other "intangibles" in the universe. The work begins subjectively and includes empirical data. Most scientific endeavors begin with a feeling, hunch, idea, hypothesis, belief, or partial observation that requires data to be complete. Only a few decades ago, scientists were unable to evaluate or measure many things we now take for granted. Evaluation starts when someone has a question and then gets an idea about how to measure it in order to answer the original question. Thus begins a rather tedious process of developing standards and practices, tests and measurements, assessments and evaluations. Although we are far from having an Emotion-o-Meter, (thank goodness!) science has come to standardize other important life-saving information through thorough and thoughtful evaluations, tests, tools, measuring devices, and is now able to make some generally consistent predictions.

Only a few decades of science and advocacy has produced the wonder of measuring and assessing such variables as: (1) fevers, with a thermometer; (2) elevated blood pressure, with a sphygmomanometer; (3) earthquakes, with a Seismograph; and, (4) blood glucose, with a glucometer. But some effects of nature do not so easily lend themselves to physical tools and measurements so they have needed other means of measurement. Science is constantly evolving ways to effectively assess such intangibles as intelligence, learning, personality, anxiety, trauma, and joy. Other methods used to evaluate and predict visible and invisible effects are comparative scales and graphs. One such tool is used extensively in tornado evaluations. It is called The Fujita Scale.

Ted Fujita and Allen Pearson were scientists who wanted to predict and evaluate the activities of tornadoes. Prior to 1971, weather experts used a variety of means to try to measure and describe tornadoes. Now experts use the Fujita Scale (also known as the Fujita-Pearson Scale) as a way of linking damage risks to wind speed. It is an easy, simple and accessible tool to use for describing and categorizing tornadoes. Fujita and Pearson organized the size of tornadoes into categories from F-0 to F-6, determined by the amount of their damage potential.

The following is a basic interpretation of the now well-accepted and used scale:

THE FUJITA-PEARSON SCALE
(adapted from www.disastercenter.com)

F-0 Gale tornado 40-72 m.p.h.	Damage to brick structures such as chimneys; breaks tree branches and limbs; pushes over shallow-rooted trees; damages billboards
F-1 Moderate tornado 73-112 m.p.h.	Peels surface off some roofs; mobile homes moved from foundations or overturned; blows moving autos off roads; may destroy attached garages and outbuildings
F-2 Significant tornado 113-157 m.p.h.	Tears roofs off frame houses; mobile homes and boxcars demolished; large trees snapped or uprooted; makes light objects act like missiles flying through the air
F-3 Severe tornado 158-206 m.p.h.	Roofs and walls are torn off well-constructed houses; trains can be blown off tracks or overturned; trees can be uprooted
F-4 Devastating tornado 207-260 m.p.h.	Can level well-constructed houses, structures with weak foundations can be blown some distance; cars can be thrown with other large objects that become flying missiles.
F-5 Incredible tornado 261-318 m.p.h.	Strong frame houses can be lifted off their foundations and carried considerable distances to disintegrate; automobile sized missiles can fly through the air in excess of 100 meters; trees become debarked; steel reinforced concrete structures are badly damaged.
F-6 Inconceivable tornado 319-379 m.p.h.	This force is unlikely. The small area of damage they might produce would probably not be recognizable along with the mess produced by F-4 and F-5 winds that would surround the F-6 winds. Missiles, such as cars and refrigerators would do serious secondary damage that could not be directly identified as F-6 damage. If this level is ever achieved, evidence for it might only be found in some manner of ground swirl pattern, for it may never be identifiable through engineering studies.

Even an F-0 tornado has structure, substance and merit. It causes damage. The tornado is a natural event. What it does to living things is simple: it destroys. A tornado has no conscience, nor does it necessarily have evil intent. The damage it does, however, can be significant and have long-term impact on the victims and survivors in its path.

What if an F-1 tornado ran smack dab into another F-1 tornado? Would an F-2 be created? If an F-2 joined another F-2 might an F-4 be a potential risk? Add more energy and force and, before long, you have a big, fat, nasty F-5 tornado with significant destruction potential and collateral damage risk. It makes sense to hit the basement cellar if tornadoes began to clump together and combine forces.

There is another, smaller tornadic process which is euphemistically called a *dust-devil* or *whirlwind*. These small gusts and breezes rarely cause significant damage and require little or no attention. They are not significant although they can blow your hairdo a bit, rearrange napkins during a picnic, or cause a few weepy eyes with their dust. They are worth mentioning in any discussion of wind. How many little dust-devil breezes does it take to make a gust? How many gusts make an F-1? What level of wind force creates damage?

Now, translate that wind into an analogy to discuss emotional energy. What is an emotional dust devil? Gust? Gale? Tornado? How much emotional wind at the work site will it take to create chaos? Carnage? What level emotional force can temporarily annoy productivity and what level can level it into rubble? What can your company manage?

THE ATTRIBUTES OF AN EMOTIONAL TORNADO

Fujita and Pearson have helped wind scientists. But what can managers use to describe emotional spin phenomena in the workplace? What language speaks of evaluating emotions? Since September 11, 2001, people are struggling to deal with the adjustments to new language, terms, and concepts like Homeland Security, Disaster Readiness, Critical Incident Stress Management (CISM), Trauma Counseling, Color-Coded Alert Levels, and Zero Tolerance. Before the Columbine school shootings, the word 'Columbine' was the name of a place. Now it is a noun and verb associated with disaster, death, trauma management, children, and national horror. Businesses are going to require a new language about emotions at the workplace that include the small, non-dramatic feelings of everyday human life and the catastrophic terms associated with death and destruction. If managers are going to talk about emotions, the language is going to need to be technical, business friendly, and less "mental health" stigmatized. Human emotions must be discussed at least as well and at the same level as a discussion about ergonomic furniture.

The good news is that tornadoes have attributes and emotions do also. Tornado experts use terms like volume, speed, force, area (crossing boundaries), location, point of origin, range, level, frequency and duration to discuss the attributes of wind. Using these same terms, managers can now begin to think in a new way about emotions in the workplace and consider how an emotional tornado could suddenly spin into a work site. Consider the following tornado attributes and begin to apply them to human feelings and emotional spinning.

Volume

Volume is about the accumulation of mass that takes up space.

A workplace spin usually involves more than one person or system and, if unmanaged, begins to increase in capacity.

Case Example

Florence was a hard worker with a long and noteworthy career. She worked independently and had excellent evaluations. Zella was a young go-getter who had a positive reputation. Their managers thought it would be a natural move to put them together for a new project. They respected one another and were eager to take on this exciting challenge.

In less than a week they were at one another's throats. Complaints and verbal accusations escalated. Managers were stunned and decided their reactions were due to normal and simple adjustments associated with any new project of this magnitude. Neither employee was able to emotionally adjust to the change. The project became secondary to the fight. Their arguments became loud and spilled into staff meetings and the cafeteria. Florence and Zella, who had been seen as icons and mentors to many staff, were now vicious to each other and anyone who supported the other. They had control battles and power struggles over their escalating fears that success meant job security. They were both convinced that the other one was sabotaging the project. They became enraged and paranoid.

Staff was just as shocked as the administration. Florence demonstrated extreme dependence and victimhood behaviors. The staff that sided with her was went to their managers frequently with odd complaints. Zella began drinking for the first time in her life and had public outbursts that included verbal attacks. The staff on her side began taking small liberties such as longer breaks and open gossiping. The managers called in the Human Resource professional who was unable to deal with the extreme nature of these powerful emotions and became impotent in the face of explosive emotions. Knowing her company hated "outsiders" she was desperate and called in an external consultant on her own. The staff now felt threatened, betrayed by HR, and terrorized that their departments were being exposed to external scrutiny. The collective paranoia was palpable.

The Consultant discovered both of these employees were appalled at this development and neither could explain it. They attempted to work through the difficulty, but were unable to avoid triggering each other into defensive outbursts. Zella and Florence, capable and expert professionals, when put in the same "container" developed a toxic emotional reaction that led to systemic emotional spinning.

Learning Byte

The emotional extremes demonstrated at this work site were new and first-time behaviors for Zella and Florence. A predisposition had been circumstantially triggered by what seemed to be a reasonable business decision. Both employees expressed to the Consultant that they were grieving the loss of their comfort zones in their old positions where they were successful and revered by others. The CEO at that time did not think that their emotional behaviors warranted much attention. But when they both had to be replaced, the costs for releasing and replacing these employees topped $200,000.00. One year later, Florence had found a new position, although her newfound aggressive behaviors from this experience had eroded many of her people skills and rapidly diminished her former reputation in the community. She was now considered a troublemaker. Zella was not able to find adequate work in the community and relocated. Whether Zella took the new alcohol and outburst behavior into a next workplace remains a question. Management now does much more extensive screening and interviewing before team placements. The CEO now insists that group projects begin with a brief training on grief management and tools for taking care of personal emotions under stress. The external consultant fees, at $150.00 per hour, are prohibitive to this small company. The HR department is overwhelmed.

DO THIS*: Take the creative risks to put people together for productivity. See how it goes. If it isn't working within a short period of time, rethink the combination.*

DON'T*: Hesitate to change your mind if the hostility volume goes up. Some things just don't work. Some people just don't work well together.*

Speed

Pace, rate, velocity, tempo. How fast is it going and is it getting faster because its own energy giving it more energy and momentum? Like a centrifuge or merry-go-round, the speed of a spin increases its own speed. Emotional spinning is *fast*. It can pick up added speed that is self-generative. Small beginnings quickly gain velocity.

Case Example

Dennis, a seasoned Emergency Medical Technician (EMT) began to complain more than usual, which stirred up his partner Tina. The manager, Tyke, who had worked with Dennis for a long time and had considered him a steady force, a solid cornerstone, a foundation on the squad, now found himself having a difficult time staying neutral. Their chief told the manager that he better "take care of it." Dennis' wife began calling Tyke thinking that her husband might be having an affair with Tina. Tina took Tyke aside and said that the partnership between her and Denis was decaying after years of working together and that Dennis was "losing it." Tyke felt out of control as the tensions rose.

Opinions began to create more opinions until everyone had voiced their position to everyone else. It evolved into a full-tilt emotional spin. Within a few weeks the entire community, which was small and prided itself on its "everyone-knows-everything" mentality, was divided by rumors and politics. The Chief, who based his prestige on election consequences in the community and depended on favorable perceptions for funding generosity, was extremely nervous. He began an affair. Dennis continued to complain while the troubled manager became more defensive at work and sullen at home

Learning Byte

Tyke was not neutral. As a friend he needed to be connected, as a manager he needed to see how the rumors were adding to more speed. Before it got out of control and entered into the community, Tyke needed to stop the speed at its source and find out what was happening with Dennis. This community lost confidence in services. The private EMT company lost primary funding sources.

DO THIS: Watch emotions to see if they are revving up faster than people can adjust. Find out what is going on.

DON'T: Add to the energy by rumors, gossip, or isolation.

Force

Emotional energy comes and goes. If the energy gathers strength and cohesion it becomes a force. A force can generate creativity or destruction. When strong influences combine with other powerful energies a strong dynamic occurs. Hitler was a force. He started as a voice, with an opinion, and that energy combined with other influences to become a larger force. Gandhi was a force. He started as a voice, with an opinion, and that energy combined with other influences to become a larger force.

Case Example

Keller was informed that his job was being outsourced. He felt confused and management didn't explain what this would mean. He took management's poor communication personally, began increasing his drinking and was verbally less supportive of his company. He started looking for another job. His loyalty shifted. A drinking buddy, Miles, met him at a local bar. Their usual complaints about work and marriage turned serious when Keller started fuming about loss of income, foreign workers taking his life away, the government being out to get him and his desire for "justice." The forces of alcohol plus anger escalated to revenge fantasies ripe with righteous indignation and patriotism. Miles "jokingly" suggested he hack into some of the proprietary information to take some of his "share" before he exited to "show them a thing or two." Keller had not thought of this before and saw an opportunity to maintain some control. The two buddies combined forces, planned, then committed a cyber crime which caused fiscal damage to the company as they destroyed historical and research databases.

Learning Byte

Management did not have an Emotional Continuity Plan, and so forgot to help Keller maintain his sense of self-esteem and personal empowerment by not keeping him in the loop of problem-solving his own situation. Outsourcing was not as much of a problem as was management just "dropping the emotionally charged bomb" and assuming Keller would adjust to the new situation. The losses to the company were not discovered for several months after Keller found a new job, and the increased savings from outsourcing were cancelled by the losses of data that had to be recreated.

DO THIS: Pay attention to the forces of change that are coming your way by becoming informed on your own. Education is a powerful force,

DON'T: Take the forces personally by trying to control forces with more force.

Area (Crossing Boundaries)

A boundary defines a limit to an area of domain. Putting up a boundary is a fence, real, perceived or symbolic, around an area. Putting up an emotional boundary, ideally, should be automatically honored and accepted by the recipient.

One way a person can make an emotional boundary is to say "no" to an action that is offensive. Another way is to create protection by policies that define areas of control or domain. Initially, individuals may feel some loss or disappointment from what may seem like a limitation, but most regular, healthy, well-boundaried people adjust quickly to disappointment and appreciate some level of clarity.

Spinning, like a tornado, does *not* like boundaries. Spinning does what it does, goes where it goes, and has its own agenda of spinning. Rules, policies, walls, boundaries, borders, guidelines, laws, limits or definitions are counter-forces that define areas. Creating a no-spin zone, for example, is creating a boundary where spinning is not appropriate.

Case Example

Caroline could not keep office supplies at her desk. She somehow always lost them. Every employee in the unit had seen her rummaging through their cubicle or desk seeking a pen or paper clip. It was not uncommon to find Caroline going through everyone's desk on a daily basis. No one complained of her stealing from them but her patterns and excuses became the topic of many lost work minutes, annoyances, and hallway gossip time. When confronted, Caroline always apologized and giggled that she was just an "airhead" while she actually leaned over other people in their workspace to "borrow" their equipment for "just a second." The company hired Jeann as a new manager. The first time Caroline was rifling her drawers for a paperclip, Jeann calmly told her not to do that again, because it was inappropriate. Caroline was shocked, and giggled about being an airhead. Jeann repeated the boundary and informed Caroline that is was not okay to rummage through her desk. Caroline had hurt feelings and complained to the staff. The staff immediately solidified into a "team" when they realized that they had never appreciated having their boundaries crossed. The team backed the new manager and learned to use better boundary-making language.

Learning Byte

Jeann was new and had not been part of the mythology that accepted and enabled Caroline's inappropriate workplace behavior without question. The collective expectation at the workplace was that it was more inappropriate to complain than to make a boundary. Jeann put new light on the issue and the staff was receptive and grateful for a way to establish boundaries. The staff genuinely liked Caroline so everyone was more than willing to encourage her to take care of her own property. They assisted her in redefining her boundaries, and encouraged her to stop calling herself an air-head. Caroline was encouraged to mature professionally through appropriate boundaries.

DO THIS: Be aware of boundaries, yours and others.

DON'T: Cross boundaries without permission.

Location

Location defines where something is happening. It can also refer to its point of origin. Since workplaces are now global, the location called "workplace" of where a spin may start might include:

- desks
- cubicles
- computers
- web sites
- cell phones
- telephones
- lounges
- transportation
- hotels
- business meetings
- restrooms
- hallways
- stairwells
- parking lots

Case Examples

- John travels more than he is in the main office. He talks to strangers about his work.
- Susanne and Melissa discuss their new project over lunch in a cafe.
- Warren works at home. His wife complains about the time.
- Louisa shares a cubicle with Edith and Frank. Edith hates Louisa.
- Charles and Ed cut the deal in the parking lot after the meeting.
- Fiona and Elizabeth are washing their hands in the ladies room and discuss the highpoints of a potential deal while they comb their hair
- Chrissy gossips with Deena in the hallway.

Learning Byte

All potential locations for employees need to be managed by managers. Where is management's domain? Do you need different skills for different locations like parking lots, bars, restrooms, or cafés? When Chrissy gossips with Deena, there are no boundaries in that location. Perhaps security is not an issue, but is privacy important? Managers need to redefine work locations and differentiate them from other more social locations. And Emotional Continuity Management now happens *everywhere* people are located. Chrissy set in motion a series of gossip spins that resulted in the unionization of the company. The costs of the unionization process cost hundreds of lost man-hours. Supporters of unionization were pleased with the outcome. Those opposed to unionization were unhappy. The location of this entire process began in a hallway.

DO THIS: Know that wherever you go, there you are, and you aren't alone.

DON'T: Manage only from behind your desk.

Point of Origin

Where did the spin originate? Did the spin start in the middle of the system, from the bottom up, or from the top down? Did it start internally from an employee? Did it start externally from a vendor, customer, client, or other outside force?

Case Example

The consultation team, after interviewing everyone in the a rural medical facility, at $120.00 an hour, found that the originating thought which triggered an expensive workplace drama came from a belief, nurtured by the C.E.O. He liked to be adored, and encouraged employees to think that they were "picked by the boss" to be special and receive special treatment. Each employee then believed that they had entitlement to the "special favor" of the C.E.O. The C.E.O. was playing both sides against the middle. This company had a "The-C.E.O.-Likes-Me-Best" game that was the point of origin for a violent organizational sibling rivalry. The conflict bordered on an almost religious belief of personal value with concurrent demands for territory and priority. Each person with "favored status" ran to the C.E.O. for protection and validation, and languished in the C.E.O.'s need to be needed. He enjoyed being the rescuing guru to whoever came to his office.

The C.E.O. hired the consultant and sabotaged the consultation with, "Well, I'll help everyone get back to their game. After all, they do turn to me. I'm their leader!" The division turned what were once reasonable humans into enemies fighting a Holy War for special favors. This subtle dynamic ultimately affected several hundred individuals in eight departments. After time-consuming investigations, interventions and remediations, it became evident that the C.E.O. generated this conflict because of a need to be perceived as All-Knowing. This C.E.O. did not appreciate that his leadership style created division between the ranks. A trickle down dysfunction turned into a full system emotional spin. The C.E.O. hired manager after manager, and consultant after consultant, providing himself a constant flow of new people to "mentor." He would give them special favors and then drop them on their heads as his favors shifted to someone else. point of origin dysfunction came from the top down and interventions were sabotaged at the top.

Learning Byte

The fourth consultant in a series of hires was paid $23,000.00 over a one-year period. During the consultation, the CEO brought in another consultant for a one-time consultation to consult on the consultation. That one meeting cost the company an additional $1,500.00. Individual meetings with the extra consultant resorted in the loss of approximately 23 additional work hours.

DO THIS: Look above you, below you, and beside you to find a point of origin for a spin.

DON'T: Be surprised if it is hard to locate the point of origin. Take your time, be patient, it will appear.

Size

Micro: Small, minute, barely discernible

Macro: Large, obvious, visible

Case Example

Jody is bulimic. She vomits routinely at work. Sometimes her ritualized vomiting schedule makes her late to meetings. When she enters meetings late her use of excessive perfume and loud gum chewing is temporarily disruptive and not appreciated by anyone.

Case Example

The earthquake leveled the building. Several employees were killed.

Learning Byte

It is easy to see the earthquake as a problem. Jody's bulimia is taking a toll on Jody and the staff in small micro-units. Size can be the difference between a slow leak and a deluge. Both companies lost money this year. One company can apply for insurance recovery benefits. One cannot.

DO THIS: Remember that a relatively small hole sank the Titanic

DON'T: Ignore the small stuff just because the big stuff is more dramatic.

Range

Emotional spins come in a fascinating assortment and array. The range includes:

• Annoying	to	Deadly
• Entry Level	to	Career Commitment
• Amateur	to	Professional
• Intermittent	to	Constant
• Subtle	to	Blatant
• Acute	to	Chronic

Case Example

While management focused on Gloria's constant tardiness, no one noticed an unusually shaped brown paper package sitting by the water cooler. When a manager finally saw the package and called 911 the company shut down for 8 hours while investigators searched the premises and removed the suspicious package.

Learning Byte

The risks are significant when a company either minimizes or overreacts to threats of security. This business lost $4,000.00 in eight hours of time loss. They were also losing money due to Gloria's behavior. Risk management needs to consider ranges of incidents and ranges of losses, from small to large, critical to non-critical.

DO THIS: Pay attention to the full range of possibilities, including the most extreme

DON'T: Downplay the need to think bigger and smaller than your normal range of experiences

Levels

Ranking incidents is very subjective, but they usually fall between small with a small impact to large with a large impact.

Case Example

Miss Roo was a new teacher who was devoted to making a good impression and consumed by the expectations of her new job. She started work on September 3 ʳᵈ, and was hoping she was making credibility points. She felt young and inexperienced, and hoped it didn't show. She hadn't felt too involved with the World Trade Center attacks because it was clear across the country. Certainly it was horrible, and she truly cared about the tragedy, but it didn't really touch her in a personal way. She wanted to focus on her students and her job performance. On a morning shortly after 9/11, Miss Roo was on recess duty when a small plane flew above the schoolyard. Her knees buckled under her and she threw herself to the ground in panic.

Learning Byte

Research has shown that anxiety, stress, trauma, depression and Post-Traumatic Stress symptoms do not depend entirely upon size or proximity to critical or catastrophic incidents. Even small events, perceived as life-threatening, can create significant emotions.

DO THIS: Pay attention to all levels of threat, from very small to large when making and Emotional Continuity Management plan.

DON'T: Minimize the risk potential of even a small threat level. One person's molehill is another persons avalanching mountain of death.

Frequency

Most people can usually keep their emotions in line while working. They don't fall apart, have tantrums, or dissolve into lengthy crying binges every shift. If emotions erupt on a frequent or regular basis, the frequency of the reaction can indicated that something beyond the regular levels of emotional response is present. Something may be seriously wrong.

Case Example

Sierra blew up at her manager on Tuesday. The following Monday, Sierra was found crying in the restroom. Two weeks later, Sierra stormed out of the work at the end of the day. At the end of the month, Sierra was late for work three days in a row. Sierra blew up at her manager again, this time during an all-staff meeting.

Learning Byte

Management did not see a pattern of frequency here. A good rule-of-thumb for attending to frequency might follow something like this:

1 episode = this may be acute, short, a random event, it may be a fluke, accident, or anomaly

2 episodes = pay attention because a pattern may be establishing itself

3 episodes = respond, because now a pattern has emerged

Some emotional events such as sexual harassment, violence, drug use, alcohol use, abusive language, racism, criminal behavior and other extremes may require immediate response after one episode. For some issues frequency means once.

DO THIS: Pay attention to patterns of frequency

DON'T: Wait too long to intervene. There is nothing more uncomfortable than saying, "I should have done something earlier" after something awful has happened.

Duration

Most emotional crises begin some sort of resolution process within two to five days. They may not resolve ever, or may take years to complete to closure, but even tragedies and catastrophic traumas look quite different after the initial first few days. Strong emotions begin to give way to either a softening or a strengthening of other emotions, but the original set of feelings does not last for long. If nothing has changed and the force and volume remain high, something else may be going on. Critical incidents that come and go quickly, such as an accident, tornado, or earthquake may have a different emotional impact on people than an incident that lasts longer, such as a hurricane, flooding, mass layoff, or long-term emotional chaos process.

Case Example

It had been three months since the fire destroyed the building. The new location was working well; Employees had restored operations and were making new customer contacts. As the days passed, there were fewer references made to the disaster. Except for Larry. Larry mentioned it every day. He asked people their opinions and solicited advice about his. He suggested there might be a lawsuit on its way, or that perhaps someone should look into the accountability of the management team. He kept newspaper clippings of the front-page story on his door and continued to ask people, "How are you doing?" A new employee was hired and Larry made a point to bring him into his office to discuss the incident.

Learning Byte

Something other than normal adjustment was going on with Larry. His manager just assumed that this was because Larry had an annoying personality. If it was his personality, then management needed to create some boundaries for this employee. But the manager did not consider that fact that Larry was a Vietnam veteran and was displaying symptoms of PTSD through his hyper-vigilance. By the time Larry entered counseling to manage his ongoing anxiety, he had lost all of his accrued sick leave. He used vacation leave and missed 30 hours of work to attend his counseling sessions.

DO THIS: Watch how emotions to begin to shift after an incident.

DON'T: Hurry anyone in their adjustment, but pay careful attention to someone who is not making some adjustments. If someone is still stirred up to the same level after 2-3 months post-incident, then it is an appropriate assumption that something else may be going on and they will need assistance.

Dr. Vali's Emotional Tornado Scale©

Range	Damage	Potential Behaviors and Examples
V-0	None	Normal general whining, non-specific complaints about life's annoyances and daily challenges. No demand for alignments. Share and vent.
		I hate Mondays when everything is a mess.
V-1	Noteworthy	Specific complaints focused on specific people and issues. Some expectation for alignment.
		Joe never cleans his desk. Don't you think he" a loser?
V-2	Significant	Specific complaints focused on specific people and issues. Elevated emotional charge, more expectation for alignment and support. Early generalized references to outcome.
		Joe's a loser, he is such a slob. Don't you just hate his desk? We should do something about him!
V-3	Critical	Specific complaints focused on specific people and issues. Increased emotional charge, elevated demands for alignment. More references to outcome and generalized plans for actions.
		I can't stand Joe. It's driving me crazy. Why don't we tell management and get him out of here. Let's ask Sue to join us.
V-4	Extreme	Specific complaints focused on specific people and issues. Increased charge, elevated demands for alignment and allegiance. Specific demands for outcomes, and specific plans and direct actions.
		It's got to be Joe or me. Even Louise hates his attitude. We're going to the union and getting him out of here. I heard he had an affair.
V-5	Catastrophic	Specific complaints focused on specific people and issues. Increased emotional charge, elevated demands for alignment, allegiances and loyalties, with threats of abandonment. Demands for outcomes at all cost. Actions being taken. Threats.
		Sue won't help us get Joe out of here. She must be having sex with him too. We can get rid of her easy, just go to HR and tell them she's not doing her work. I'll hide some of her project data and then she'll either join us or get out of here.

HOW TO RECOGNIZE A SPIN

Since people are going to be people, and emotions are not going away, how can you recognize when an emotion is just something of the moment or a sign that something else should be managed? To begin any discussion about people and their feelings it must be said that there are individuals who thrive on the emotions associated with light and hope, growth and creativity. There are others who thrive on the emotions of despair and darkness, death and destruction. There are people who thrive on working within the flow of growth with strong or weak positive energies and others who thrive on working against the flow of growth with equally strong or weak energy. There are people who are aggressively or passively seeking growth and others, equally aggressive or passive, which are pulled toward destruction. The reasons for this and the ranges of behaviors and practices are as varied as are the people involved. Psychologists and social scientists have many theories, but suffice it to say that both kinds of people work in all areas of commerce and service and can be found in all cities and walks of life. Some people jump at life and others aggressively dig their heels into life and refuse to move forward with it. Some people leap toward death and dig their heels into it and hope that someone will keep them company and join their misery. There are people who like to Rain on everyone's Parade, and there are people who like Parading on everyone's Rain. Some people seek transformation and others refuse to change. People are people.

Extreme behaviors can be a first recognition sign of an impending workplace spin event. Extreme positions do not lend themselves to the necessary flexibility of workplace demands. An unwillingness or inability to adjust to necessary changes within a reasonable adjustment time frame is not conducive to workplace productivity. In truth, there is *no* correct timeframe for someone to adjust to change. Time is an artificial arrangement loosely agreed upon by socialized people and is not cross-cultural. Time demands in a competitive workforce suggest that people need to adjust rather quickly. Resistance can be a sign that a spin is starting. Recognizing the attributes of spinning takes some practice. Workplaces are not intended to be counseling offices, confessionals, churches, temples, cathedrals, mystical retreat centers or Aunt Sophie's kitchen table. Attending to *every* emotional problem is not Emotional Continuity Management. Work is where work is meant to happen. Emotional Continuity Management is intended to increase rapid recovery as a necessary practice to keep things moving. Recognition of emotions and spinning is a management task.

SIGNS, CLUES AND HUNCHES

There are obvious and less than obvious signs of spinning. Many times management begins to recognize spinning through a series of observations and hunches. Resistances and extreme positions should lead you to a hunch that something in the movement of the energy in your system is not moving correctly or flowing smoothly. That is a clue. There is a scene in a movie about tornado chasers where the hero of the story, a former tornado specialist and scientist, suspects a twister is imminent. He doesn't confer with technology, like his counterpart the anti-hero who is presented as an unfeeling, human techno-robot bad guy. The hero has a hunch and smells the air. He notes the color of the sky. He picks up a handful of dirt and lets it fall between his fingers and watches how it falls to the earth. He closes his eyes. He hunches down and becomes quiet and still. He listens, smells, sees, touches, and attends to the signs, visible and invisible. He recognizes the early signs of a potential spin. He has a hunch first because he has seen spins very close up.

Case Example

The consultant had presented the seminar 28 times. The meetings were in the conference room and limited to 5 employees at a time. The timed sessions were exactly two hours to allow for shift work, coverage, and lunch breaks. Everyone was mandated to attend. Employees were instructed to be on time and to set up procedures for coverage within their departments. Word was out that the consultant was interesting, active, entertaining and that the information was useful.

Group 29 came late. The first employee to come was five minutes late and the last entry was 23 minutes late and entered without apology or explanation. The consultant had a powerful hunch that the resistance demonstrated indicated that he had found the troublemakers in the institution.

Learning Byte

Hunches are a good place to begin paying attention. A hunch is a feeling that can generate research data. All good science begins with a hunch.

DO THIS: Pay attention to your hunches

DON'T: Use hunches as complete data. Hunches include bias and opinions. They are important as a starting point only when backed by data.

Some Early, Recognizable Signs Of A Spin Risk

Incongruent Giggling	Avoidance
Malicious Compliance	Non-Compliance
Blame Statements	Eye Contact
Body Language	No Eye Contact
Littering	Procrastination
Gossiping	Self Projection
Unsolicited Opinions	Avoidance Of Tasks
Not Returning Phone Calls	Humiliation
Excessive Perfumes	Inappropriate Humor
Unsolicited Religious Evangelism	Trashing Shared Space
Invalidation	Anger
Seductions	Minimizing
Leaving Tasks 1/4 Undone	Innuendo
Whisperings	Raised Eyebrows
Nagging	Dismissing
Ignoring	Interrupting
Discrediting	Partial Truth
Partial Lie	Arrogance
Intimidation	Distance
Disgust	Corrections
Jealousy	Inattention
Boredom	Incongruence
Denial	Unwillingness
Criticism	Questions
Intimacy	Manipulations
Poor Grooming	Compliments
Negation	Poor Boundaries
Poor Hygiene	Untreated Health Issues
Outbursts	Drug/Alcohol Abuse
Excessive Perfume	Offensive T-Shirts/Clothes
Illegal Activities	Sexual Innuendo
Incongruent Perkiness	Demanding Praise
Non-Completion of Agreements	Gestures
Negative Facial Expressions	Mind Games
Rebelling Against Dress Code	Power Plays
Loud Stereos in Quiet Spaces	Manipulative Silences
Teasing	Harassment
Jokes	Eating Loudly During Meetings
Illicit Love Affairs	Spreading Rumors
Starting Rumors	False Charm
Guilt Language	Shame Language
Cursing	Exclusions/Racism

HOW TO PAY ATTENTION TO EARLY WARNING SIGNS

Managers, like most people, generally do not see emotions until they leap out into the open. This is because most employees are busy working and normal emotions will stay hidden, protected, private or underground. Emotions can remain covert for quite a while picking up speed and volume.

Managers don't want to spend their days in hyper-vigilance watching for signs of covert emotions. What fun is that? Good managers just want to do their jobs and not focus on the negative. Unfortunately while others are allowed the luxury of ignorance, today's cutting-edge managers have no choice. Neither do administrators, owner, directors, and CEOs who want to increase the bottom line have the luxury of turning away from watching for changes in the wind..

Learning how to keep an eye out for signs of emotional spinning means raising your awareness levels and creating a fine-tuned set of recognition skills. Managing emotions does *not* mean becoming a psychologist or a spy, although there are skills in these areas you must learn. Emotional Continuity Management is *risk management*. When everyone in your company becomes aware of the risk of emotional mismanagement. your company will have the upper hand in predicting, managing and avoiding unnecessary emotional spin events.

Managers are concerned if they spend time trying to recognize emotional spinning they are wasting company time looking for trouble. They complain that they are not showing faith in people. Regular people don't want to appear paranoid. The hard fact is that emotional spinning does not care about your opinions or resistance to learning how to manage, because emotional spinning has a life of its own. And intentional spinners, like Emotional Terrorists, are counting on your resistance so they can take more emotional or physical territory. Emotional Terrorists are expansionists seeking new collections of people, places and things to increase their empires. Ask yourself if you really think it a waste of company time and money, not showing good faith, or demonstrating paranoia to purchase a fire extinguisher? Then go have that discussion with a fire. Then go ask an arsonist. If you are still worried about good stewardship over the corporate dollar, call five attorneys and ask them to give you their hourly fees for court appearances. Pay attention.

A set up for an intentional emotional spin can look like this:

*   Andrew starts a rumor about layoffs
*   Bryan tells Nora that his marriage is ending and asks whether she would be willing to listen to him later after work because he needs a special friend right now, someone who would understand and appreciate him like she does. He tells Nora she is special.
*   Lonni cozies up to Desmond and tells him that she thinks it is a crime that Frank was given the assignment he wanted and now she thinks that Frank might be having an affair with the supervisor. She tells him she is on his side if he wants to fight it
*   Gena repeats Jeanne's rumor, but adds her beliefs that it might have something to do with Bruce getting an attorney
*   Carl calls all his team members after work encouraging them not to go to the meeting with the new consultant, because he heard that he might be taping the meeting, and then would share that with the bosses
*   Krissy blows off the new training meeting and tells her co-workers that if they go they are just "kiss-asses" and that if they want to keep their jobs they should just let the manager know how absurd it is to keep on getting all this training when it doesn't help
*   Hanna tells the manager what Gene said with the additional information that "everyone is now upset" and that Jared, the assistant manager, mentioned he might quit over this
*   Karen has been trying to stir people up for years to keep her power and control base. She is in a union. The rest of the business is not union. She brings in union reps that start promoting their cause. She uses this information to terrorize people who are under-represented.

•   Jorge is an anti-union manager who uses threats of lay-offs and bankruptcy to terrorize people against joining a union

WHAT CAUSES EMOTIONAL SPINNING?

Spins are the emotional responses to changes in the wind. A group can spin into excitement over a potentially lucrative merger. A group can spin into rage over the unjust termination of a favored colleague. Emotional spinning results from a combination and cumulative effect of other emotions. Spinning is multicausal. Factors that cause spinning are not only psychological. Spinning, like other group responses can be generated from agendas that are personal, moral, political, physical, symbolic, religious, sociological, economic, or totally without meaning as a response to itself. Personal causes of spinning can be generated from different perceptions, ideologies, belief systems, opinions, status, stress, traditions, environment, causes, desires, preferences, demands, hopes, fantasies, and perceived injustices.

When things are running smoothly businesses generally hum along nicely. The challenge is that life rarely runs along smoothly for very long. Life happens. And along with life happening comes a variety of emotions, weak and strong, pleasant and unpleasant, managed and uncontrollable. Life consists of change. Change is the only unchanging constant. Change demands adjustment. Some people adjust emotional well to change; others do not. Some people are in themselves agents of change. Consciously or unconsciously, intentionally or unintentionally, people interacting with people create change. Change causes spinning. It stirs up the breeze.

Planning for the full range of human responses to change is what Emotional Continuity Management planning is about. It may be less important to have a deep comprehension of the causes of spinning than to appreciate that change creates reaction. A reaction is what a spin is at its onset. A research scientist, terrorism expert, psychologist, psychiatrist, security specialist, or someone writing a book on emotional spinning, should have a comprehensive appreciation of the dynamics of change. The manager should know that spinning doesn't just happen for "no-good-reason." Spinning is *always* a reaction to something else.

The wonderful thing about human beings is their resiliency. One great feature of resiliency is dramatically evidenced as people recover rapidly to massive changes, even under duress. Stories of the emotional flexibility and adjustments of human beings in overwhelming circumstances are legendary. Most people rise to the occasion. Changes do not spin everyone emotionally. Some people are challenged by change and ascend to greatness and experience deeper calms and transcendent peace. There are countless wonderful stories of significant and traumatic life events that lead people to becoming devoted to a spiritual path, or entering into a life devoted to stillness and serenity, and becoming peaceful change leaders.

There are people who have been in catastrophic situations who have gone beyond their own needs and moved beyond amazing circumstances to act in heroic ways. However, people who have had heroic personalities in one situation can also radically transform into less than heroic stances. Previously strong leaders can just as easily become completely incapable of functioning during crisis and the changes associated with a catastrophe. One small event can be the last straw in an already crumbling psyche. Kind and gentle folks can suddenly become monsters and fiends while just as unexpectedly a former fiend becomes a saint. Changes at all levels, from annoying adaptations to catastrophic upheavals, tend to bring out the best and the worst reactions and responses in people. A positive emotional spin of support, care, compassion, love, peace and hope can easily be cancelled by a negative spin of abandonment, retribution, anger, rage, and revenge.

Case Example

Sergeant Miller was the perfect embodiment of command and respected by his troops who readily turned to the officer for strength and direction. When an air crash happened near the base, the unit was deployed and assigned the grisly task of body recovery. The young troops stood ready for their orders. No one expected that Sgt. Miller would be huddled down in the corner of the office weeping uncontrollably. The sergeant was hospitalized and replaced by a new officer. The young troops felt confused, abandoned, and betrayed by Sgt. Miller. They were overwhelmed by the assigned duty of body retrieval and the loss of leadership. Twenty years later this incident continued to be an unresolved issue for one of the soldiers, Troy, who entered counseling because he kept losing relationships and jobs due to his antagonism toward collaborative partnership and authority figures. At 45, this former soldier had experienced being terminated from 11 jobs, had 4 marriages and 3 divorces.

Learning Byte

Troy was never debriefed after the traumatic events of that awful day of the airline accident and carried his emotions around unconsciously, seeking a safe place to vent his rage. He was emotionally unstable by being forced into a large-change event that was not under his control. He felt even more chaotic because of his shame that he seemed to be the only one of his buddies that was still upset over this old incident. Any manager he worked with became a symbolic Sgt. Miller and Troy acted out his unresolved pain. Troy had an internal spin that he needed to externalize and ventilate. He created emotional spins wherever he went in his distorted effort to release his anguish.

Case Example

Andrea feared horses. Tuesday she was at a neighborhood horse ranch to visit her friend Lanny who taught riding to supplement his income. A large horse spooked and tried to jump a fence. The stallion's leg caught a metal edge of fencing and ripped open an artery. Lanny, busy with his business hurried to take care of students while Andrea stood in horror seeing the pool of blood get bigger. Lanny began to panic and scream at the students. Andrea knew this was a prized horse, the center of Lanny's financial security, and at risk. She grabbed gauze, knelt into the pool of blood, and put pressure on the wound to stop the bleeding. The horse was saved. The cost of the vet bill was less than the loss that the death of this horse would have brought to Lanny's new business

Learning Byte

Emotional spinning comes from a reaction to something internal or external. Troy reacted emotionally to old information. Lanny reacted to new information. Andrea rose to the occasion in an unpredictable manner.

DO THIS: Anticipate that emotional spinning may happen in unexpected circumstances and create unexpected reactions.

DON'T: Try to predict the unpredictable. Just be prepared for it for it to happen.

Why People Make Decisions to Spin

Trying To Avoid Something or Someone
Trying to Control Something or Someone
Fear
Pressure
Retaliation
Inattention
Ambition
Doing Something For The Company Against Best Interests
Doing What's Rewarded
Misguided Loyalties
Path Of Least Resistance

Politics
Anxiety
Empathy
Accountability
Fatigue
Uncertainty
Ignorance
Dysfunction
Pathology
Emotional Terrorism

A TECHNICAL WAY TO VIEW SPINNING

If you were to put the concept of emotional spinning into a mathematical equation, it might look something like this:

$$\text{CHANGE EVENT} + X = \text{HUMAN EMOTIONAL RESPONSE}$$

CHANGE EVENT

Life is change. And all businesses have changes if they are going to keep up with world markets. All changes create some loss. Even with gain there is loss through a change event. All loss leads to grief. With either small losses or large losses, the human emotion that goes with loss is grief. When a human loses a pen or loses a pet, a loved one or a job, they experience grief. Even people who do not recognize the behaviors or feelings associated with grief, experience grief.

Elisabeth Kübler-Ross (Scribner, 1997) was the first to provide a good template to discuss the grief process. And although she focused on the extreme emotions of grief associated with death, she described a set of grieving stages, which can apply to all loss that comes from change, even small loss from small change. What most people who are not in the emotions industry do not realize is that these stages are not limited to physical death. It doesn't take a death to grieve. It only takes a change. The stages are:

Denial, Bargaining, Anger, Depression, and Acceptance.

Case Example

Denial

The new manager instructed Annie not to use the company car until it was serviced, and to sign a new waiver before driving. Annie went ahead and used the car because she always had used it without having to ask permission. The manager reprimanded Annie. Her response was, "But this is how it's always been done."

Bargaining

When the manager repeated the policy, Annie said, "Well I'll just do it this way today, okay? And I'll pay for the gas myself."

Anger

The manager was consistent and courteously repeated the new rules. Annie reacted with, "Well this is pointless and annoying. I've always had free use of the company vehicle, and now you're telling me I have to ask 'mother-may-I' every time I have a client call me and I need to use the car?"

Depression

The manager explained the rationale for the new policy, which Annie agreed made sense. She stated, "Yeah, I can see that is a better policy for the organization, but it sure is difficult for me now that I have to re-think this entire logistics process for my project team. It was so easy before to just pop out on a client run without a bunch of paperwork and hassle."

Acceptance

The manager supported Annie by calmly listening to her as she went through the stages dealing with this change. When Annie seemed to be more in acceptance, the new manager complemented her on her history of teamwork, and suggested she review the policy and paperwork as soon as she had time, and offered to answer any questions that might come up. Annie responded with, "Yup, we're all in this new merger together I guess. I'll figure it out. Thanks."

Learning Byte

Because the manager was aware of the stages of normal grief cycle, she didn't take Annie's resistance personally and was able to remain calm, focused, and supportive while Annie moved through the stages. The manager also tracked her own stages as she bumped into the resistance of Annie that was a change from her fantasy that everyone would just be easily willing to comply to her new authority. The manager noted her own emotional content, and put it on hold for the moment. She did not resist the resistance and did not counter it with more resistance and escalating emotional power plays. The resistance went away. The manager knew Annie to be a solid employee, and with the tool of understanding grief stages, actually facilitated Annie's adjustment to a rather small change. The entire transition took only a few minutes and did not evolve into an emotional spin.

DO THIS: Learn the stages of grieving and apply them to any change.

DON'T: Make the error of thinking that it takes a death to experience the stages of grieving.

All change brings some degree of loss and some degree of gain. For example, you choose the pudding over the chocolate cake; you gain pudding but lose cake. You may gain a pound and lose your diet. If you stand up and move across the room to look out the window, you have lost your chair, warmed pillow, your original posture and perspective. You may have gained a view of the river and a more comfortable back. Loss and gain are consequences of all change. The ratio or value of loss to gain is defined by the perception of the one who is changing, the value or meaning of the change, and the level of real or perceived control of outcome. Managers help people manage feelings when they see they are losing control. The closer a change gets to threatening control over comfort, security or mortality, the more serious it is perceived and the more loaded with spin potential.

In business, most people would agree that their paycheck determines a significant portion of their security. Few people work just for the sport of it. For some the paycheck is literally the difference between life and death. Some people are totally dependent on a paycheck or some of the benefits, such as retirement or health insurance. People take mortality risk levels of their jobs very seriously and any change, no matter how much gain is potential, triggers fear of losses, real or perceived. Because all loss leads to grieving to some degree, managers who are familiar with the stages of grieving and see those stages as natural will be more compassionately efficient during change events.

The stages of grieving are tools for Emotional Continuity Management. It is amazing to discover how much more receptive and non-spinning a person can be, and how quickly they adjust, turn to teamwork, increase loyalty and respond with open communication when change responses are seen as grief responses and not as emotional spins.

Case Example

Management needed a consultation because the front desk receptionists in financing were becoming agitated and abrupt when the clients came for their paychecks. The clients often complained to the receptionists angrily about errors in their checks. The receptionists had no authority and were bombarded by these outbursts. The consultant helped the receptionists understand that the clients were merely grieving, and in denial, bargaining, anger, or depression. The receptionists didn't know that they were the first line of Emotional Continuity Management.

Learning Byte

The receptionists softened their approaches to clients who were angry or trying to bargain through potential losses of control. They stopped taking the client outbursts personally and regained composure, increased compassionate language, and were able to support one another as a team. They found some humor and were able to be more pleasant to clients and each other.

DO THIS: See how grief plays into your relationships with clients or co-workers.

DON'T: Assume that angry people are obnoxious when they just might be frightened.

Case Example

Leona didn't like her husband Hal and she hated her job. She had recently fallen in love with a wonderful man who made her life seem worth living. She was offered a new job in his company the same week her husband was diagnosed with a life-threatening health condition. The diagnosis would mean many years of ongoing medical intervention. Hal had to quit his job. Leona was now stuck in her job because it had excellent health insurance. She realized that if she divorced her husband, the consequences could truly be terminal for him. She talked with her counselor and discovered she didn't hate Hal enough to be homicidal, and that at this point she would need support to keep her job and her hope. She decided to discuss this openly with her husband. The two of them found a way to keep the marriage and the health insurance while moving on with their adult lives. They had to re-think their marriage vows and both agreed that they would help each other have the best life they could under the circumstances. They decided to stay married, but Leona continued the relationship with her new man. Hal moved in with another family member. Leona grieved the loss of the new job opportunity each day as she entered her old job worksite. Her co-workers never knew any of the details of her personal choices, but some of them became distant and blamed her for being less friendly. She was thus never chosen for the promotions that might have helped her be more financially independent.

Learning Byte

This was a difficult and unusual situation. Management may not know the emotional factors of the private lives of their employees from day to day. And there is generally no reason they should, unless work is impaired. Leona's work did not suffer, but her spirits declined. An observant and compassionate manager might have offered her some creative problem solving, a special assignment, or personal encouragements.

Do This: Watch for signs of despair that may indicate that an employee is struggling with a personal challenge.

Don't: Invade the privacy of someone who is coping, but encourage them toward hopeful solutions.

Human beings grieve everything from pens to pets, jobs to hairlines, cars to lovers, parking spots to waistlines. Because grieving is a natural part of our everyday lives, managers, employers and employees need to understand how it translates into the workplace. Grieving is somewhat of a multi-dimensional emotional state that moves feelings from one stage to another. A person can be in one stage of grieving about one issue, while in another stage about a completely different loss. Twelve people experiencing the same loss will go through the stages at different speeds and with different perceptions and responses. Some will resolve the loss quickly; some will take time and need additional support from co-workers, management, or from resources outside the workplace. Some people stay stuck in one stage or another and act from that emotional location for a long time. These individuals perceive their other experiences from a perception of loss that can be managed by understanding that their choices may continue to be predisposed to bargaining, anger, or depression. Moving between stages until resolution of one stage can seem to create endless spins of discomfort. Being stuck in one stage feels permanent. Being in a different stage than someone in the same situation can feel odd and is occasionally perceived as betrayal to the value of the loss.

The speed of recovery from a stage of grief is a variable. Rapid recovery through a change cannot be forced or mandated, but also depends on a willingness and ability to move through the grief work adequately. Avoiding the task does not help the process; it only delays it and leads it to becoming distorted into some other set of feelings. Most adults have experienced losses in their lives but that doesn't mean they are efficient at moving through their grief in a healthy and efficient manner. Grieving can accomplish character building, or be the source of an emotional spin that can turn a person, situation, or business into emotional turmoil for the wrong reasons. Grieving is serious business, and business should take it seriously.

Grief doesn't just happen when there is a high-drama event, terrorist incident, natural disaster, death, or traumatic episode. There is no need for body bags and carnage to trigger significant and elaborate grieving states. Grief happens hundreds of times a day. Managers need to know that although most people adjust to grief, some do not. Some people get stuck in one stage for a very long time. Have you ever known someone who was stuck in anger for a long time? Have you known someone who was stuck in depression for a long time? Have you ever bargained to try to maintain control of some difficult situation? Do you have any employees in your company who are emotionally stuck in one stage of grief work? Emotional Continuity Management means being an expert on grief work.

Case Example

Denial

John went to work at the mall on Christmas Eve. It was freezing and he hoped for his usually close-up parking place near the entrance.

Bargaining

John cruised the lot for open spots close to the entrance for 15 minutes.

He saw a spot up close and zoomed toward it. There was a motorcycle in the spot.

Anger

John cursed the motorcyclist under his breath and moved on.

Depression

John decided to park in the outer lot and walk farther.

Acceptance

John parked far away and trudged to his job in the mall.

Learning Byte

John didn't get stuck. If he had gotten stuck in anger he may have gone to work in a sour mood and stayed upset all evening. If he had been stuck in depression he may have questioned working at the mall or turned it into some other self-depreciating thought. If he had stayed stuck in bargaining he may have driven around for much longer looking for that easy parking spot. Grief happens. John wasn't devastated emotionally by this change and his adjustment.

DO THIS: Become and efficient griever.

DON'T: Make changes without expecting grief to be a part of the process.

Business losses from change are emotionally loaded because work is so intimately associated with safety and survival. Work is associated with key perceptions about the self, ego, status, worth, value, money and character. Business changes link many areas of human behavior. Work represents internal perceptions that are key to the foundational infrastructure of the personality and stability of the self. Changes in work can fragment the very foundations of self worth. What this means emotionally is that change can unhinge people from the inside out causing temporary or permanent unbalancing, which can lead to emotional spins. Something as simple as someone taking a parking spot that an employee has "territorialized" can lead to emotional grief and spinning behaviors.

Even removing an outdated vending machine can become a symbol for survival. If a vending machine becomes symbolic to survival, the vending machine is now emotionally charge and the change attached to the loss of it by its removal can become a grief event loaded with bargaining, anger and depression.

Case Example

The cafeteria at the hospital closed at 7:00pm. The only food available for graveyard shift came from home or the one vending machine in the lounge. Without evaluating the effect, administration removed the vending machine, claiming it wasn't necessary or financially viable. The uproar was extreme. Graveyard shift workers took it personally blaming everything from favoritism to outright loss of civil liberties. After many loud and angry meetings where administrators explained the fiscal rationale behind the economic losses associated with the machine, three employees resigned. The cost to the hospital topped $95,000.00

Learning Byte

No one asked what emotional needs were met with a vending machine available for middle-of-the-night emergency services personnel. To them it was "lifeline" and symbolized comfort and security. Many Emotional Continuity Management defusings were accomplished over group "let's-go-get-something-out-of-the-vending-machine" pilgrimages. For example, during one short-staffed night shift, the community experienced a particularly grisly multiple car accident that included many fatalities. The small hospital was crawling with grieving relatives, press, medical examiners, emergency personnel, and other previously admitted or emergency patients. The staff was running at full speed for hours on end. The vending machine became the "safe harbor" to run to for a "quick candy bar" to get through the next hours of work. Someone would say, "I'm getting a candy bar" and take the 3 minutes to breathe, recompose themselves, and emotionally regroup to go back into the fray.

The loss of this whimsical old vending machine, the night staff's symbolic safe harbor and nurturing mother with a cookie in the middle of a hard night, became personal. A previously tense, but covert low-level rivalry between day shift perk of ready-to-eat-food and the self-defined "food-less heroes of the night" became overt warfare of words and disgruntled employees. The battle that had been underground for years was now spinning wildly into the open. Administrations didn't see it coming and it created an unfixable rift between administration and night medical staff, days-only employees and nights-only employees and the three employees that quit. The Emotional Continuity Management consultant immediately asked what the vending machine meant to people and was told. The staff was collectively appalled that no one in administration or management had even had the courtesy, much less the wisdom, to ask if the vending machine was useful to anyone. It became very personal.

DO THIS: Assume that everything matters to someone.

DON'T: Forget to do your research! Don't neglect to ask everyone before a change. You don't want someone you missed asking to show up disgruntled because you didn't anticipate that a simple loss might be catastrophic to someone.

Business changes range between very small and very large. Changes can be for the good, such as a multi-billion-dollar dream contract. Business changes can also be negative, such as an unthinkable, unpredictable publicly humiliating scandal and bankruptcy. Change can range between relocating the vending machine to catastrophic destruction of an entire facility such as the destruction of the two towers at the World Trade Center. Between these extremes lies a universe with small and large changes including business and personal changes that influence emotions. There are simple as well as wildly complicated changes. There are changes that are short and instantaneous and some that take tedious decades to accomplish. Change isn't bad. Change is just life.

To assume that all changes, simple or complex, affect people in the same way is limited and potentially very dangerous. Since business changes can range from small to huge, emotional reactions to change can have the same range. Oddly enough, it is often the apparently smaller changes that trigger huge irrational spinnings that lead to time consuming terrors. People fill in the blanks of emotional events with their own emotional assumptions. A small incident can become catastrophic quickly if unattended. Events that lead to expensive consultations or litigation always begin with something small that escalates into something big. A small emotion that if managed well could just resolve politely becomes an F-5 tornado of emotions with carnage. Companies that don't see the need for Emotional Continuity Management have not understood how moving a small vending machine could begin the undoing of an entire system. Mental Health Counselors see this all the time. Wars have begun by one simple misunderstanding.

Business is about change, because business is about life. Life is change - easy change and difficult change. Current Business Continuity Planning focuses on the idea that change must always look big. It is reasonable that the focus of planning is on big events like the Terrorists Attacks of September 11, the Oklahoma City Bombing, high profile downsizings, corporate corruption trials, massive industry-wide layoffs, cybercrime, natural disasters, crime, vandalism, the outsourcing of America, trade agreements, and disgruntled employee homicides. Certainly some large terminal changes can destroy a business with a mortal blow. What is under-recognized are the little micro-changes, more like paper cuts, which can bleed a business to death without anyone noticing until it is too late. Disasters come in all sizes, from catastrophic to micro-incidents, or smaller changes that are perceived as disastrous. Change can come externally, from outside the system, or internally, from within it. Change can be hidden (covert), or very obvious (overt).

Examples Of Business Change

Changes, small and large	Moving the Pens
Remodeling/Painting	Changing Letterhead/Logos
Outsourcing/Downsizing	Re-Sizing/Layoffs
Awards/Loss of Awards	Losses
Personal Tragedies	Catastrophic Trauma
Organizational Change	Project Groupings
Furniture Arrangements	Access to People/Information
Redefinitions of Tasks	New Administration
Illness of a Co-worker	Death of Co-worker
Suicide/Murder of Co-worker	Rumors of Changes
Marriages/Divorces/Affairs	Computer Upgrades
Natural Disasters	Economic Changes
Hirings and Firings	Policy Shifts
Local/National/International News Events	A New Custodian
A New Water Cooler	Resizing

SOCIAL AND STYLE BUSINESS CHANGES

Sociology, anthropology, biology, psychology, medicine and most sciences are based on the study of change, change in the past, change in process or the study of future change. Change scientists do research in order to understand history, gather current data, or predict and control outcomes. In the last few decades, change has become more than a natural force in the universe, it has become an icon for progress. People tend to think that change represents what is right and what is wrong with the world. Those who value the status quo are in the fight of their life as progress moves and marches forward at an alarming pace. Shakers and movers can't get enough change fast enough.

From 1940 to 1944, over six million women joined the workforce in America. As men returned from the war overseas, many women left the factories, but the social and economic roles for women in the country had been altered permanently. Social changes are always reflected in the workplace. Overseas outsourcing, the introduction of man-made synthetic pharmaceuticals, wars in the Middle East taking young men out of the job pool, escalating divorce statistics increasing the number of single parents with complicated emotional issues, the increase of grandparents who are raising their grandchildren, are examples of the sociology of business change.

People are trying to survive in a world that is in the process of constantly reinventing itself. Businesses are on the move. Employees are on the move. Some employees are moving toward corporate agencies for the protective systems of safety and security. Others are moving away from corporate systems for the same reasons. Massive layoffs and economic instability leave employees seeking changes to survive. When employees move from the private sector to a hierarchical employment setting, or vice versa, the change can create a number of challenges. Expectations are different. Styles of communication and levels of aggression that have worked in one form may not match new settings. The employee who has been a private entrepreneur for many years may struggle with the adjustments necessary to attend staff meetings and report to authorities. And the "company man" who wants to be a consultant on his own may struggle with the details of setting up a business without an existing infrastructure and someone to report to on a regular basis.

Case Example

Viola spent between 30-50% of her management time on one staff member, Ron, for over 6 months. Ron had owned a business for many years and did not easily adjust to bureaucratic authority structure. Ron had a spouse who was important in another department of the company so was hired for special projects. Ron was always bucking authority and procedures. It became unmanageable when he decided that Viola being the manager wasn't convenient so went to a different manager, and upset the chain of authority. Ron was informed this wasn't going to work, but refused to change behaviors. The company had procedures for removing people, but they were tedious and expensive. Viola documented for six months and then took it before a committee to review it. She presented her findings. At that point the Human Resources director, Louisa, decided to redirect the goals and established an entirely new agenda. Louisa was non-effective, mild, non-assertive and hated to make recommendations that upset anyone, so she suggested that everyone go back to square one to make sure Ron, wasn't upset. Viola was discouraged and confronted her manager stating, "I don't feel like I have the stamina to do this for another six months." Viola's manager found a way out, by providing a new title and name for the Ron's job. She renamed the project he was working on, and cancelled it. This created an exit for Ron without having to fire him outright. The project was dropped and never completed.

Learning Byte

The system adjusted to Ron rather than Ron adjusting to the system. That isn't good business. The project did not get accomplished and lots of management time was wasted.

DO THIS: Reflect on your own style and the styles of your staff.

DON'T: Necessarily change your style, but see how it has influence on your choices and behaviors.

A challenge can also emerge when someone who has held a position of authority and command in a well-established hierarchy, like the government or private industry that is bureaucratic in style, is brought into a less formal, loosely structured organization. The transplanted employees can be seen as tyrannical unless, or until, they are able to adjust to a more laid back method of work style.

Case Example

Tom had been a ranking officer in an armed services medical corp. When he left the service he moved to a small town near his family and took a job in the local hospital. The consultant saw Tom on the first day he was hired. She found him bright and eager to be excellent and lead the "troops to greatness." The problem was, there were no troops, and the staff of this very small medical facility did not like to be treated with anything short of "friendly." They resented his approach, questioned his ethics and competency, and very shortly isolated him out of the loop of information.

Tom didn't understand. Remediation did not assist the situation. Counseling and consultation did not help. He did everything correctly and by the book and no one liked him. The CEO did not support him. In fact, the CEO thought he might be "dangerous" and dropped that hint to a few key managers to "watch out for him in case he blows." Tom's frustration grew. Eventually he was challenged directly and indeed he did "blow" by storming out of a meeting. This validated the rumor which now took on a force. Regular defusings by the consultant, some counseling sessions, and a supportive wife helped Tom work under this non-confidence atmosphere for a full year. He eventually found another professional job in a large metropolitan hospital that was run like a military base. He was valued there and so it was a good fit, but his relocation was emotionally and financially difficult. The other hospital returned to status quo.

Learning Byte

This was not a good episode for anyone. Tom didn't see the problems coming because he had come from such a successful experience. Management that had been part of the hiring process missed the style differences. They didn't think beyond eagerly factoring in the "friendly" factor because they knew Tom's family was local. What management also missed is that for the last year the hospital had been struggling to upgrade its competency evaluations for national accreditation and didn't see how Tom could have been an asset. The emotions took over the situation and the losses continued. Within 18 months this hospital lost its accreditation for an important level of emergency services. Now patients with trauma had to be transported 25 minutes further from their community to get accredited emergency services.

DO THIS: Use management skills to help people adjust to style expectations of their position or organization.

DON'T: Demand changes in style to come quickly or easily. Nurturing changes in style takes time so don't be impatient if the employee has good performance skills.

Other Changes to Expect in the Next Decade

- More women in the workforce
- More disabled in the workforce
- More minorities and racial/cultural groups represented
- Immigration laws changing the workforce
- A shortage in skilled labor
- Increase in non-English speaking workers
- Service industry will continue to replace manufacturing industry
- New jobs will require more technological training
- International competition and technological change will require different skills
- Entry level jobs will be more competitive
- Rapid turnovers
- Aging population
- More mothers with young children

- Fewer white males

(Adapted from Workforce 2000/The Hudson Institute, 1987)

- In 2002, women accounted for over 47 percent of the labor force, up from 29 percent in 1950.
- In 2002, the labor force participation rate for married mothers with children under 6 years of age was over 63 percent, up from 11 percent in 1950.
- In 2002, over 71 percent of all mothers with children under the age of 18 worked.
- In 2002, 18.4 million married families with children, almost 68 percent, had both parents working. In over 55 percent of these families, the women were working full-time, year-round.

From (www.whitehouse.gov/news/releases/2004/08/20040805-6.html)

NOW, ADD THE X FACTORS TO BUSINESS CHANGE

Now that you are beginning to think about emotional responses, and business changes, it is time to consider the "X factor." X represents the unknown, multicausal factors that contribute to emotional responses in life, including emotions in the workplace. X includes features that are known, unknown, visible, invisible and in mixed combinations. X is what intrigues scientists and lends itself to research. There is never only one X factor. But if you take change and add any X, it will create emotional response.

Factors of X can include:

1.   The Brain
Mental or cognitive approaches, learning styles, IQ ranges
2.   Past Experience
What has happened before and how has it affected or taught meaning
3.   Expectations
What is demanded from this situation? Is this new or familiar?
4.   Social Features
Does this connect to some other person or persons, present, past or future? Am I alone or do I have connections to deal with this?
5.   Personal Field State
What is going on with me right now? If this change "lands" on my field, is there already a battle going on there, or is it a calm place ready to accept change? Personal Field State includes health and mental health
6.   Location Field State
Where is this change landing in my environment? Is it a safe, dangerous, or a neutral place? What is the climate?
7.   Presentation
Is the change presented as a physical, emotional, mental, spiritual, social, sensory, or invisible threat or enhancement? Is it a good change or a bad change according to me, according to others?
8.   Time
Is this change happening now or in the future? Will it have a short or long term effect? Is this similar to changes in my past? What happened then?
9.   Control
Can I control this change? Is it out of control? Is someone controlling me? What will happen if it or I go out of control? Are others in or out of control?
10.   Human Specifics
Gender, age, culture, ethnicity, hierarchy, proximity, sensory, birth order, genetics, preferences like whether you prefer Pepsi Cola® or Coca-Cola®.
11.   Politics
Is this change associated with a political agenda of mine or someone else?
12.   Ideology
Do I believe in this change or does it go against my ideals or morals?
13.   Religion
Is this change compatible with my belief system?
14.   Physiology
Is this change going to harm me or enhance me physically?
15.   Experience

Have I done this before? Have others? Was it positive? Negative?
16.   Perception
What does this look like, mean, or symbolize to me? For others?
17.   Stress Level
Does the stress associated with this change seem familiar or unfamiliar, personal or impersonal?

HOW TO THINK ABOUT AN "X" FACTOR

Decades ago, physicians knew that putting leeches on people made them well — visible leeches created visible healings. If the patient died, it was because the leeches were not used properly. Many decades ago physicians wondered why people got sick. An invisible microbe was often the culprit. When microbes were discovered many people were healed. Scientists created antibiotics and people started to get well. Then people began dying from antibiotic usage. The scientific war between the seen and the unseen had begun.

Now, science knows that not all microbes are bad and cause disease and in fact some are useful and necessary. In the same light, not all emotions at work cause spins. Some emotions, even strong ones, can be very helpful. Some emotions, even slight, are morbid and will kill the organism of the work site. Some emotions are neutral to the work site.

In human bodies the equilibrium between good and bad microbes creates a condition called homeostasis. Homeostasis is a balance necessary for the human system to stay healthy. Homeostasis protects continuity of life. Emotional Continuity Management is a bit like trying to maintain homeostasis in the body. Homeostasis in the workplace is a goal that doesn't mean purging the system of everything challenging or stopping change. It means balancing the necessary elements to maintain equilibrium. The X factors contribute to the equilibrium or disequilibrium of the balancing elements.

To understand the simple basics of how X factors contribute to spins, you can look into the world of emotions like a scientist who has a hunch that microbe exist. Mental health experts spend their days stomping around in the Petri dishes of human emotions and many of them have only a cursory understanding of the X factors in change. So, don't be intimidated by any perceived lack of education or training you think you may have or think you may be missing. Everyone is on a learning curve. You may believe you cannot stand in the shoes of a mental health professional or psychologist, but rest assured, very few of them have ever had the competency and courage to stand in your shoes in the middle of a chaotic company spin! Be brave, and jump on in. Start reading and researching the X factors so you can do what managers do best, go where angels fear to tread, into the midst of the emotional response of your employees. Leadership is part of your job description. X factors are the parts that make up the whole.

Case Example

Sallie fell in love with Roger who drove an old beat-up green truck. Sallie had never noticed green trucks prior to her romance. Now she was aware of all trucks, especially green trucks. Her perception had changed to include all green trucks as potentially Roger's truck. She had no idea there were so many green trucks that did not belong to Roger. Because she had her first sexual experience in a green truck and since their recent violent breakup, she spent what amounted to several hours a day absent-mindedly scanning the parking lot and highway outside her office window looking for green trucks. All green vehicles emotionally distracted her and her productivity fell off the mark. The new company vehicle was a green truck.

Learning Byte

Sallie had a meeting with her manager, an older woman who was a good mentor. The manager helped Sallie refocus and encouraged her to get some more support to deal with her breakup. Sallie returned to her church and resolved her perception that all green trucks were associated with her dramatic experience with Roger.

DO THIS*: Know that people see things differently.*

DON'T: Argue about perceptions. Negotiate with people by asking about their perceptions, sharing yours, and then exploring alternative perceptions before problem solving.

Perception is an X factor that can drive emotions. Perception is based on an extremely complex set of other X factors including physiology, psychology, biology and symbolism. People perceive they have a level of control over their corner of the universe. If that changes, they perceive danger or threat. If they perceive a solution the threat diminishes. If they perceive a threat continuing, they demonstrate a number of very interesting reactions and responses. Those reactions become independent variables, or X factors. Some perceptions can be changed some cannot be changed. Perceptions are fluid so they can change and also be hidden, disguised, reformatted, ignored, rearranged into an attractive package, given different names, and have different meanings.

Case Example

Fiona had worked for HJC Incorporated since it opened. She was proud of her longevity. She clung to her perception that her longevity protected her from being fired. She knew she wasn't the fastest or brightest on the team, but was certain her contribution of time and seniority kept her a vital force. She was occasionally intimidated by new technological advances and leaned heavily on her sense of historic direction and mission for the organization. In January, the new management team advised the CEO that it would "perk up the image" which included a redesign for the logo and the letterhead. The team designed and proposed new graphics and gave excellent fiscal predictions to rationalize the change. Fiona perceived this as a personal attack because she had helped design the original logo and letterhead. She began to suspect she was being "edged out" by the new people. Her unwarranted suspicions led her to being less positive at meetings, increased her isolation, and she began to create her own self-fulfilling prophecy as people began to perceive her as "getting older and crankier." She became more rigid. The logo now became a symbol for her and the management. It took on a dimension that had nothing to do with Fiona but now was almost mythologically linked with the "old timers" and the "new guys."

Learning Byte

Management erred by not seeing this change in a historic perspective. They assumed change was something that everyone valued. This X factor resulted in the loss of loyalty from Fiona, which translated into lost time, antagonism, and tension in the company. The problem was not the change, but that no one bothered to inquire as to how that change might influence people. A simple Emotional Continuity Management adjustment in process, such as interviewing Fiona about her experience with the last re-design, or a "blurb" in an office memo or newsletter, would have given Fiona a sense of belonging that may have more easily translated into a win-win increase in loyalty.

DO THIS: Respect and honor the perceptions of others.

DON'T: Dismiss your perceptions while you are respecting and honoring those of others. Both of you might be correct.

Case Example

Joshua was offered a promotion. Everyone was surprised when he turned it down and rumors started to surface that he was leaving the company.

Learning Byte

Joshua was a good employee. He was also self aware enough to know his Personal Field State wasn't stable enough to take on the extra responsibilities. He was just recovering from a personal relationship problem and he was also working on getting his elderly parents into an assisted living situation. He didn't feel creative or organized beyond what his duties were at current levels.

DO THIS: Begin communications from a position of assuming people's perceptions are correct, for them.

DON'T: Label a perception as incorrect. Stay open in order to experience understanding the perception of someone else who can see something from a completely different angle than you.

Case Example

The company was considering a merger. The expectation was that the business would make the business more visible.

Learning Byte

Management did a survey to find out how people felt about becoming more visible and how they felt about dealing with the media. The survey discovered only four employees had any concerns because the company expectations of growth were clearly part of the mission statement. Management offered the four employees additional support and training to deal with some unresolved feelings of insecurity. Three employees felt insecurity about some technology changes. One employee felt insecure because she didn't know the expectations. When she found out she would have time to learn she relaxed.

DO THIS: *Help people grieve their perceptions if they need to change.*

DON'T: *Avoid taking the time to help people see the big picture and the details while giving them time to readjust their perceptions to the current agenda. If it isn't life threatening there is no hurry.*

EMOTIONAL RESPONSES = CHANGE + X

Now you are thinking about emotions, understand that change is normal in life and business, and see how X factors play into human emotional responses. But what is an emotional response, and what is appropriate for work? Emotional responses are the organic, natural, primal, and human energy forces of human beings, in reaction to varied stimuli of life, making life, well... life! Emotional responses are comprised of countless, amazing forces in combination with other amazing forces in complicated quantities, qualities and design. Entire scientific fields are devoted to the study of human emotional response. Researchers spend untold billions of dollars exploring complicated topics in personality, temperament, instinct, physiology, birth order, gender, developmental stage, geographic location, climate, genetic makeup or biologic difference, bias, social dimension, motivation, habit, cultural expectation, experience, belief, fantasy, and environment in a persistent pursuit of more questions than there are answers. Each answer creates more questions. Intricate scientific research data, psychological details or comprehensive depth research goes beyond the scope of this book. But managers interested in Emotional Continuity Management need a basic understanding of all these influences. Continuity means a fluid balancing and re-balancing after disturbances of all those factors. Review the list again. Doesn't it make sense that you study and find new tools and resources?

ADJUSTING TO CHANGE

Most people self-manage their physical and emotional balance by managing countless combinations of large and microscopic adjustments every moment of every day. Energy is used or misused, directed or misdirected as one system responds or reacts to a different system. Individual units and entire systems maintain a functioning balance or initiate entropy or decay. The effect of disequilibrium in any system, sets responses in motion that either stabilize or destabilize the entire mechanism. The simplest shift in balance can throw the entire balance dynamic into chaos. Sometimes such a loss of balance, in emotional terms, creates a spin. A human being can quickly respond to an emotional spin when even a simple piece of the infrastructure starts to wobble. A complicated disturbance can enact a very complicated response. The good news is that most people are healthy and manage their balancing act quite nicely. The bad news is that some people respond and react to the slightest change in environment. Some healthy people are hypersensitive. Some unhealthy people are hypersensitive.

The essentials of human response, according to top personality theorists, focus on such intangibles as the belief in free will, the specific structures of the personality (ego, traits, motives, skills, spirits, predispositions), whether someone holds a belief in a utopian principle, and any number of strengths and weaknesses. But the best way to understand how people respond in different situations is much less complicated. People are people and people are different. People have differences. Different people are different. Life stimuli are infinite. Different people experience different events, incidents, experiences, thoughts, feelings, moments, places and things differently. In terms of the workplace, different people respond to different things differently. Now, is that so hard to understand? Of course it is. But let it suffice to say that in terms of human responses at the work site, healthy employees have good days and bad days. Less than healthy employees have good days and bad days. Evil, bad, horrible, rotten people have good days and bad days. Shuffle all the influences, change + X factors, together with all the changes possible with all the people possible and all the X factors possible, and you will understand that any response is possible in any situation. So you need to be ready! Ready does not mean, "done learning." There is never going to be a universal Emotional Continuity Management plan or process that will fit everyone. If someone tells you it exists and will handle everything, then consider it dangerous.

OTHER EMOTIONAL RESPONSES MAY LOOK LIKE SPINNING

Experts in human response know, as now you know, that there is a wide range and infinite variety of possible emotional responses and reactions to infinite changes. Before you continue an exploration of human responses that turn into emotional spinning in the workplace, you also need to know there are responses that look like spinning but are not. There are responses that are clearly emotional spins. There are emotional responses that may appear like spinning but may be something quite different. Reactions originating from the following list may increase vulnerability to workplace spinning, but of themselves should not be considered emotional spinning. These emotional sub-sets may respond surprisingly well to simple positive management, affirmation, mentorship, a kind word, support system, training, an educational pamphlet, or brief EAP intervention.

The following list of spin-like reactions, impairments, or "dys-abilities" will be encountered in the workplace. It is important to treat these emotional responses with compassion and clarity to minimize the spin potential:

- People grieving the death of a significant family member, beloved friend, pet, co-worker
- People who are separating or divorcing
- Parents who are in the middle of a custody issue or other legal challenge
- Grandparents who are peripheral to a grandchild's custody issue
- Abuse survivors, male/female
- People with physical illness (self or loved ones)
- Adult Survivors of childhood sexual assault
- Previously diagnosed mental illness that has usually been well managed
- Changes in medication
- Adult children of alcoholics
- People living with active addicts/alcoholics
- People dealing with issues about their aging parents
- Addictions (active or in recovery)
- Diagnosed serious illness of a loved one
- Undiagnosed physical illness (self or loved ones)
- Ethnicity or cultural differences
- Local or national tragedy or catastrophic event

OTHER CAUSES OF EMOTIONAL RESPONSES THAT CAN TURN INTO EMOTIONAL SPINS

Blame

Personal accountability is not a curse. People really like to blame others for their problems. Blaming someone else takes the heat off. Blaming provide temporary security in the presence of a threat. It is also a classic part of sibling interaction reminiscent of "the baby did it." Workplaces often replicate the dynamics in our families of origin and unresolved family drama is played out in work sites everywhere people are thrown together. Mental Health Professionals who do interventions often hear language that sounds like a power mad older brother, or a spoiled only child, or a whiny younger baby. Blame is about keeping Mom and Dad out of your face when you are child. Blame is about keeping the boss off your back at the workplace.

There is a dysfunctional set of behaviors from people who truly extol that the world "owes them" and that "someone or something else" is responsible for their emotional dilemmas. This immaturity is the source of much annoyance in the workplace. Typically, the majority of unhealthy workers will focus their grievances on being victims of someone else. The other percentages of unhealthy workers will focus their grievances on their own failures and lack of personal competencies. The answer of course, like many things, is somewhere in the middle. Usually blame is a reaction and not a healthy process.

The following list came from a consultation done in a mid-sized health care delivery system. The employees were asked to describe the problems they wanted solved. Their list, rather than a shopping list of positives, became known as the "Gripes and Blame" list and was the source of extreme spinning and time loss:

The Gripes and Blame List

- Too many Cliques and Subgroups
- Clinical vs. Non-Clinical Discrimination
- Lack of consistency, continuity, cooperation
- Fears of revenge
- Lack of courtesy and boundaries
- Sabotage and undermining
- Night staff don't do anything right
- Day staff doesn't do anything right
- Putting up roadblocks to success
- Lack of trust and lack of integrity
- Threats and intimidations
- Negative talking about co-workers
- Blaming and backbiting
- Territorialism
- Having personal agendas
- Maliciousness and verbal aggression
- People perceiving that their position is permanent and they are not "replaceable"
- Unequal accountability/no "full buy in"
- No respect for individuals or their jobs
- Poor Communications
- Paranoia
- Unilateralism in decision making by a few without communications
- Non-compliance
- People who feel they are too important to be bothered by policy and procedures or timeliness
- Wrong focus on either external or internal customer services

Internal and External Causes

If you consider all the multiple external situations that can happen in the known and unknown universe, there are expected and unexpected people, places, things and situations that are going to create emotional response. If you consider all the internal aspects of life including, but not limited to individual age, size, gender, ethnicity, experience, location, birth order, learning style, culture, religion, and hat sizes, there are countless stimuli that may create emotional responses. Present experiences and past experience blend to make strong internal cause from external sources, or external causes for internal emotional responses.

Mental Health

Studies in 1997 suggested that approximately 28% of the adult population is affected by a mental or addictive disorder (Thomas, 2002). Mental disorders are actually quite common. Such disorders tend to be hidden and kept secret due to perceived and real social stigma. Often the appearance of mental health is easy to maintain when medications and treatments are successful. However, during extreme experiences, such as high-stress events at the workplace, exacerbations may erupt and contribute to systemic chaos and confusion. A usually calm employee may lose their capacity to function at the time when that function is in a key role or need.

Some untreated mental disorders significantly increase the chances for a workplace spin. Mental disorders are not in themselves necessarily a cause of a spin, but may increase vulnerability. Employees with well-managed mental disorders can make an excellent contribution to their companies. In a perfect workplace world, there would be no stigma attached to mental illness and an employee with a diagnosed impairment would received the same standards of accommodation as someone with a physical impairment. The ADA (American Disabilities Act) is making headway on this, but still most people with diagnosed mental disorders keep their secret as long as they are able.

Physical Health

People get physically ill. In 1997 over $100 billion was lost in productivity due to cardiovascular disease. (Thomas, 2002) When people are sick their emotional responses are affordably not the same as their healthy day emotions. Work can be a source of valued and meaningful time or a source of anguish. People who are not happy are less well. People who not well are less happy. The 'Type A' personality, who has statistically been more at risk for cardiovascular disease, is the classic example of how perceptions about work and health are linked. Management needs to pay attention to physical health as a possible cause of emotional health.

A study of 200 executives at Illinois Bell Telephone Company, half who were sick a lot, and half who were rarely sick discovered that the sick half felt changes at work were a threat to their security. The other group felt that change is inevitable and as an opportunity to grow rather than a threat to security (Pizzorno, 1996). Another study reported by Pizzorno on Navy recruits in San Diego. They discovered that it was not the quality or quantity of stress that accounted for someone becoming sick, but rather the meaning that the person attached to the events.

Stress

A recent study found that many IT managers are resisting teleworking because they fear it will increase the amount of time they are working. (Wearden, 2001) Stress is the specific importance or significance attached to something. Stress is energy placed on a system. Stress is neither positive nor is it negative. Stress is what keeps the body, mind and emotions alive. Stress in the tensing of muscles against forces of blood and tissues keeps the heart beating. Without the stress in the system, the heart would not beat. Stress can be in too small or too large of an amount. Too much stress, and the heart is overwhelmed. Too little stress and the heart stops beating. Stress in healthy doses can lead people to greatness. Stress in the wrong proportions can kill the body, disturb and distort the mind and disrupt the spirit. Stress is experienced and defined internally. It is a very individual, personal, and subjective process. It may be spoken of in external terms, but it is registered individually from within.

There are collective, current agreements on what constitute disaster, but stress is very subjective and determined by the individual experience. One person's minor annoyance can at the exact same time be another's complete, catastrophic undoing. The reason for this is that people have different perceptions, even about the same thing. A familiar children's story explains perception. The tale is of the blind men (or blind mice, depending on the version) describing their perceptions of an elephant. One describes it like a hose, having only experienced the trunk. Another describes the beast as a rope, having only confronted the tail. One describes the elephant as a great tree, hugging one of the large legs. The moral is that even similar experiences lead to very different and distinct perceptions. These perceptions are then translated into beliefs, truths, laws, moralities, and judgment as the entire issue gets quite complicated and sometimes extremely distorted. In simple terms, people are different and thus perceive life events differently, including stress.

PERCEPTIONS ABOUT STRESS

- Lay people do not have a clinical understanding of the complications of stress in either its small or extreme forms and therefore tend to minimize its effect.
- Mental health professionals may overemphasize it and overreact.
- Managers try to avoid the topic at all costs, which unfortunately may lead to "all costs."

COPING WITH STRESS

- Lay people tend to think in terms of everyday stress and have discussions around the water cooler about their accommodations or complaints.
- Mental health professionals tend to think in clinical terms like illnesses, physiological responses, fight-or-flight reactions, homeostasis-balance management, toxins, hormone and brain chemical responses, heart disease, organic responses, stimulus, cognitions, environment, genetics, and coping strategies.
- Managers distribute a pamphlet on stress reduction and cross their fingers.

RESPONDING TO INFORMATION ABOUT STRESS

- Lay people doze off after the first few moments, and decide, as the joke suggests, "what doesn't kill me makes me stronger…or funnier."
- The mental health professional would define that thinking immediately as resistance, or a coping strategy to ignore the dangers of stress.
- Managers hope to have some sort of training on this stuff because they know what is going on, but begin to fantasize about tropical islands and palm trees.

Stress causes change and stress reactions are responses to change. There is good stress and bad stress, regular stress and extreme stress. Changes at work can create both kinds. Stress can lead to an emotional response that starts internally and the may become externalized, demonstrated, and visible. That response can start a spin if the response causes stress. What an interesting and fun universe!

X FACTORS THAT WE CALL STRESS

Bills, Dandruff, Fabric Softeners That Get Caught In Your Socks, Loneliness, Phobia, Grief, Money, Guilt, Fear, Flying, Telephones, Flying Telephones, Procrastination, Low Self Esteem, Doubt, Jealousy, Envy, Money, Family Problems, Work Deadlines, Decisions, Shopping, Budgets, Lack Of Budgets, The Press, Idiots In The Office, Threats, Rumors, Success, Money, Failure, Rejections, Divorce, World Hunger, Childcare, Parenting, The Flu, Money, Separation, Work, Computers, That Woman With The Short Skirt, The Boss, The Boss's Mood swings, Your In-laws, The Kids, Giving The Kids Money, Money, The Employee Who Just Never Gives 100%, The Employee Who Always Gives 198% While Singing A Chipper Little Song And Quoting Affirmations And Always Asks If They Can Help You Do Your Work Because They Like You So Much, Pets, No One At Home Understands You, Money, Everyone Feeling Like They Can Dump On You And Doesn't Anyone Care About What A Rotten Day You've Had And By The Way Is My Weight Going Up, And What Do You Mean There Is A New Budget Cut Coming, A Child Off To College, Chronic Illness In The Family, Recent Death, Impending Death Of A Loved One, Divorce, Marriage, Pregnancy, Your Family Moving, Your Family Moving Next Door, Custody Battles, Tests For Cancer, Car Dies, Deciding To Stay Or Leave A Spouse, A Promotion With New Tasks And New Friends And New Enemies, Relocations, Political Correctness, Lack of Political Correctness, Travel, Office Politics, Performance Evaluations, Keeping Up With The Jones', Being The Jones', Starting An Affair, Ending An Affair, Divorce Of Best Friends, Having Horrible Parents, Miscarriage, Aging, Someone You Love Is Sick Or Drinking Or Using Drugs Or

Addicted To Food Or Sex Or Gambling, Taking Medications To Manage Work And Home, Downsizing, Outsourcing, Natural Disasters, Terrorism, The Terrorist Attacks of September 11, 2001, Train Bombings in Spain, the Iraq War, The Afghanistan War, The War on Terrorism, Privacy Issues, Mad Cow Disease, Global Warming, Spotted Owls.

Burnout

Not all stress is bad. Some stress motivates and some stress causes difficulty. The amount of stress a human can deal with is absolutely individual and unpredictable. Burnout is a term that has become synonymous with the accumulation of too much stress leading to a maximum overload to the system. Common terms like running on empty, tapped, fried, dry, wasted are verbal clues that an employee may be reaching a stage of burnout, or is feeling a sense of personal threat which may lead to either a solo spinout, or group decay in productivity as determined by the position of the weary worker. Other signs of pending burnout can be feelings and demonstrations associated with:

- A sense of being held hostage, trapped
- Having nothing more to give
- Helplessness
- Emotionally impotent, worthless
- Depression
- Seeing everything in terms of failure
- Loss of power
- Increased aggression, disappointment
- Increased frustration over normal tasks
- Suspicions and hostilities that are new
- Memory losses
- Forgetting details
- Agitated or irritable, restless
- Fatigue
- Physical persistent illness symptoms
- Increased desire for stimulants (alcohol, coffee, medications)
- Increase desire for depressants (sleep, medications, television)
- Social withdrawal

OVERT OR COVERT CAUSES

Business changes can be small and barely discernable. Both visible and invisible changes can cause emotional response. Close attention is sometimes necessary to see that a change is even in the works. The big, overt, obvious changes are easy to see and manage. Micro changes can be missed. What is hidden from sight, or just below the surface, eventually erupts if it is important. When it is external it can be addressed, confronted, assessed, evaluated, changed, rearranged, and measured. Those interested only in clearly visible behaviors may miss what is just below the surface. Managers need to be aware that what is below the surface has an important, and in fact critical, effect on human response. The hows, whys and wherefores are less important than the idea that what you see is never the total of what you are getting.

A weather forecaster predicts weather based on a combination of statistical relevant data, empirical research, and observable facts and signs. An expert does not discount his or her hunches. Although the well-placed hunch is not traditionally empirical, it can set the stage for increased observation acuity. Today's managers need more than basic, tried and true, standard, one-size-fits-all, traditional ways of paying attention. Today's employee will look to management for leadership based on the "now" not on "how we've always done it." Your advocacy of a new set of skills, including your expert hunches, may save yourself, your employees, and your company significant resources.

If there were no covert issues to be concerned about, there would absolutely nothing to be worried about — because as soon as you saw something, you could manage it. But that is not what happens at life or at the work site.

What if the crew of the Titanic had known that the overt tip of that now famous iceberg was only the smallest unit, a micro-sign of a deeply dangerous, potentially morbid (deadly) overt process? It was not the overt part of the iceberg that caused the catastrophic results. It was the covert, or hidden portion that did the extensive damage. The emotional losses from the Titanic accident continue to be emotionally haunting. Decades later, it is the emotional losses and not the fiscal losses that are discussed.

All human beings have secret, hidden, below-the-surface dimensions as well as outer, visible, and clear demonstrations. A healthy, covert nature lends itself to stability under duress. A distorted, dysfunctional, pathological or impaired covert nature lends itself to instability and potential risks associated with such vulnerability. Although it is not possible to see the hidden it is very possible to see the smallest units, the micro-signs, the tips of the icebergs in people, and then to make some small hunches or theories about risk. Mental Health professionals do not read minds; they watch for small iceberg tips. Not every iceberg tip is deadly. Not every sign of emotions is negative. Managers do not want to become alarmists or paranoid, and then again, which icebergs are important to keep your company afloat?

Case Example

The Titanic, the unsinkable ship, sinks.

Learning Byte

Dear Dr. Hawkins Mitchell, As I was writing my book on the Titanic it occurred to me that some of the passengers were quite famous and wealthy citizens whose personal fortunes, assets and losses associated with their deaths must have amassed great losses through multiply textured fingers of systems. The victims included captains of industry, businessmen, railroad men, bankers, merchants, publishers, Broadway producers, a presidential aide, etc. The loss of such key personnel undoubtedly threw many major companies into brief turmoil before a new 'command structure' could be laid out. And although it isn't necessary to have a "number," I can state correctly that a number of passengers aboard, when their lives were lost, affected multiple systems, agencies, corporations, etc. with an obvious "trickle" down of losses, that (with the patience of Job) could be tracked? I suppose you could then obtain microfilms of a 1912 New York newspaper or two and look at the stock pages to see how (or if) the deaths of these men influenced the stock prices of their respective companies. By the way, all of the men I listed were First Class passengers. I imagine it would be like today if Donald Trump, or Bill Gates, or Oprah Winfrey perished, all the people, places, industries who they had connections with, would feel some sort of ripple. All my best, George Behe

DO THIS: Remember that what you see may be what you get, but what you don't see may be what you get also.

DON'T: Be surprised when something hidden, or covert, pops up in the form of an emotional spin.

AUTHOR'S AFTERTHOUGHTS

Today's global marketplace is not the one that existed five years ago. Emotions are more on the surface. When Lady Diana Spencer died in a vehicular accident in France in the late 1990's, England presented the world with a new way to exhibit the public demonstration of grief. Prior to this tragedy and its subsequent collective global mourning and expressions of grief, loss, and of pain, it was typical that expressions of death were more private. Now if there is a death of a public figure, people use the Lady Diana model to express their sorrows. Mourners take flowers and teddy bears, write letters, and light candles at any site that has anything to do with the lost public figure. Driving past an extremely rural race car track in central Oregon a week after the death of racing fame, Dale Earnhardt, I saw a single inexpensive flower bouquet with an attached teddy bear duct-taped to the race track gate

I was invited to present a seminar at a State Conference of Medical Examiners and Coroners. They had become aware that their industry had changed after the Terrorist Attacks of September 11, 2001. What they reflected to me was that death had always been their private domain but that directly after the World Trade Center event, although they were waiting to be called, the fact that there were initially no corpses, found them astonished to be out of the response loop. They watched a new set of people become central in the management of the dead. They waited for bodies and none came. The deaths and the dead became public, symbolic, and overt, no longer the hidden aversion. Death was, perhaps for the first time in history, public domain. Television was showing it. What followed for the coroners and medical examiners were the arduous months and months of identification and DNA sampling of micro body parts for tedious scientific determinations. Managers in the death industry began readjusting their thinking because their employees were very upset. The Coroners wanted to explore their covert emotional bases and asked for some new tools to teach their teams and new recruits how to manage in the new environment.

What once was hidden is now overt. What used to be overt is now hidden. Emotional responses are externalized in movies and stuffed into the deep reaches of our humanity as we try to absorb all the changes.

DISCUSSION QUESTIONS

What happens if an emotional F-2 touches down in your department?

How do your employees handle stress?

How would you recognize and emotional spin in your company?

What would cause it?

How do you think the following changes affect emotions in your company?

- Increase in women in the labor force
- Paid maternity leave for men and women.
- Divorce and parenting changes
- Increase in the diagnosis of children with ADHD
- Grandparents raising kids
- Terrorism rumors and threats
- National/international tragedies which have changed perceptions (schools with metal detectors, SARS, Anthrax, Snipers)
- Addiction and domestic violence
- Multiple role management for parents, spouses
- Aging population with increasing needs for care of elderly parents

2

RISKS:
HOW DOES SPINNING
AFFECT THE BOTTOM LINE?

- *Mad cow costs Tyson Foods US$61 million January 27, 2004 (theAge.com)*

- *The cost of Depressions alone tops $70 billion in health care, work loss, as well as other expenses. By 1991, it was estimated the stress-related disorders cost approximately $150 billion annually and claimed more than 14% of insurance compensations. Stress-related absenteeism is responsible for the loss of 50 million working days each year. (Thomas 2002)*

- *Canadian Agriculture Minister Clay Serby says the total amount spent by all governments in Canada to battle the mad cow crisis is about $750 million dollars. The Canadian beef industry has been devastated since one cow tested positive for mad cow disease in May. (WelcometoMoosejaw.com, April 25, 2004)*

- *Some Data Regarding Upgrading School Security Features in Newer and Remodeled Schools Since The Columbine Shootings: (Taylor, 2004)*

- *Principal's office has large windows and overlooks the campus for better visibility. Example: Pinnacle High School in northeast Phoenix.*

- *More fences and wrought-iron gates limit access. Example: Fountain Hills Middle School.*

- *The traditional rows of separate classroom buildings are being replaced by buildings with a courtyard in the center for better visibility of the campus. Example: Tavan Elementary in east Phoenix.*

- *Classrooms have fewer windows facing the street. Windows are used primarily on the side of the classroom facing the school's interior. Example: Peralta Trail Elementary in Apache Junction.*

- *New high schools are being wired for closed-circuit televisions and security cameras. Example: New high school to be built in the Saddle Mountain Unified School District near Tonopah.*

- *Classrooms often have a door leading to the classroom next door. This provides a second exit in an emergency. Example: Cochise Elementary in Scottsdale.*

WHY YOU SHOULD READ THIS CHAPTER

How much does one hour of managerial time cost your company? Multiply your salary times the hours you spend managing emotional spins? Can your company afford this? Ask your chief financial operator if it is cost effective for you to ignore emotions. How much to you think the costs associated with increased security due to the increased issues of fear cost your company, or the companies in the examples? Each security procedure is based on an emotion: FEAR. Each security procedure costs money. Each FEAR based decision is an economic risk. How much fear can your company absorb?

BY THE END OF CHAPTER 2 YOU SHOULD BE ABLE TO

*   Translate the financial impact in the case studies to estimate risk factors if these events were to occur in your company

*   Heighten your awareness of direct and indirect costs of workplace spinning and interpret local, regional, national and international incidents into a range of costs to establish a credible base for promoting no-spin policy in your company

*   Create a document, flow chart, or other presentation material that shows your company's risks for spinning in a context of the global marketplace

*   Use the formula provided to create a cost summary of your time spent managing Emotional Continuity

OVERVIEW

CEOs and administrators, auditors and financial officers visibly shudder at the discussion of Emotional Continuity Management. They rail against it as not valuable, measurable, justifiable, or belonging to that human resources domain. Managers join in this position to keep their jobs. Some of them sneak up after a seminar and whisper desperate stories as they look about hoping their bosses won't catch them being "emotional." Some speak up at seminars the ritualized comments based on the mistaken belief that it isn't their job to know about people's feelings and emotions. They flock to programs on disaster planning and business continuity with company-specific programs and snappy lingo while quickly deferring emotional issues to another category. They roll their eyes and say, "we have an HR person for that, and I think we have a guy who will come out if we have a disaster." Sometimes more defensively they say, "Hey, I'm not my employees' clergy or spouse! If they need a counselor I send them to our EAP provider."

As they continue trying to convince themselves that managing people has absolutely nothing to do with emotional information, they follow the disclaimer with a current rant about their most difficult challenges that, of course, are all emotional in nature. The dialogue goes something like, "Oh, it's all the bickering and the little things that take up all my time. I don't know why people aren't just getting along and remaining productive. It takes all my time to keep my boss off my back, track the bottom line issues, and then I have to deal with staff that acts like they are still in high school." The few managers who straggle into a seminar about Emotional Continuity Management, and emotions in the workplace are looking for a magic bullet, a cure, a tool, or something to get some relief from the emotional content in their company. Eventually they come to understand that someone is actually listening to them and offering tools to manage. They sigh and complain that they cannot do anything about emotions at the work site and how it takes up most of their productive time managing emotional spins. Then unfortunately, many of them go out the door of the seminar, with tools in their handouts, knowing they need support, buy-on, and training that they won't get. So, they wander off to the next seminar.

Well-meaning managers share impressive stories about theatrical, emotional events and how they must grapple endlessly with tedious procedures and antiquated policies. Most are convinced that there is no way they have the capacity to know when someone is impaired, dangerous, in need of help, or an emotional risk. With few exceptions they do not feel confident about their education, expertise, or, most especially, authorization to address emotions at work. When asked about how much time and salary is spent dealing with this, they have astonishing numbers.

Take a few moments and do your own math. Consider the last few weeks, or months of your work time spent mitigating workplace emotions, then multiply it by your salary. Now, take the salary of your boss and multiply it times the hours you spend reporting on problems. Extrapolate it out for the year. Now, call a local counselor at an agency and a private practice. Ask them how much they are getting paid by the hour to do what you do every day.

THE COSTS OF SPINNING

Failing to manage or make policies and procedures for real human Emotional Continuity Management carries direct risk to an organization. Costs and overlapping streams of costs carry measurable financial consequences. From a mental health perspective it is always easy to rally around the human costs, emotional consequences, family systems difficulties and sociologic effects of mismanaged workplace feelings. The truth is that this is only half of the discussion. Emotions cost money, *big* money. The "touchy-feely" soft side of business has no leg to stand on if it does not put dollars to the test. Bottom line numbers count. And, all the soft information will be meaningless until everyone understands that emotions are financial risks. Number crunchers need to know about compassion, but the numbers matter. From a human compassion perspective numbers of dollars lost taking care of people should be irrelevant. But squishy sentiment does not keep the trucks rolling across the homeland. And if you want to have a celebration of human emotions, you need the trucker to bring the bread that is served up in the feast. No trucks means no bread! No bread means no celebration. It's all of us or none of us! The combination of fiscal risk and compassion risk blend together and become the real and measurable risks of avoiding Emotional Continuity Management.

Some Of The Bottom Line Costs Of Spinning

- Fiscal: The real costs in dollars and cents expenditures, losses, revenue streams
- Goodwill: Will people use your business or move to your competitor?
- Liability: Will your business be eaten alive by nickel and dime or catastrophic litigations?
- Global: Will your company be part of the world community or isolated to the point of no contact and ultimate extinction? Isolation is not viable.
- Other Costs: Can you think of other costs in your industry?

Fiscal

There are obvious and hidden costs associated with managing emotions at the workplace. There are costs like unaccounted health care dollars spent, counseling fees, lost vendors, clients who never pick your business because of the rude receptionist, pencils stolen and paper towels used by the obsessive-compulsive hand washer in the cubicle down the hall. A group hug isn't going to manage the fiscal risks of emotions at the work site. At the same time, putting emotions in a category that doesn't place real dollar risks on the small and large emotional spins of employees is shortsighted.

Risk Equation: Figuring the Exact Cost of Emotions in the Workplace

Your hourly salary times hours spent dealing with an emotional event, plus salary multiplied by time spent with the problem, plus the number of people affected by the spin times their salary times their hours lost, plus the salary of your boss multiplied by the time the boss who is now listening to you times the number of projected days/weeks until resolution, plus any additional ancillary costs such as FICA/taxes, services, customers lost, PR, training dollars, health care equals a number which reflects the literal cost of an emotional spin.

Case Example

A 6-hour management issue that was resolved in one day that affected 14 people for 6 hours. One customer was lost with a projected revenue stream of $4,000.00 a month=$133.00 daily (avoiding the notion that this company may have gotten the customer back, they lost only a day's revenue)

$18.00 x 6 clock hours + ($8.00 x 6 x 14) + ($38.00 x 6) + $133.00 + ancillary loss=$1,141.00 plus other expenses. That roughly works out to $190.00 an hour.

Learning Byte

Paying attention to the cost of your time managing emotions becomes a valuable resource in advocating buy-on for Emotional Continuity Management policy, training, seminars, procedures, drills, and readiness.

DO THIS: Do the Math

DON'T: Forget that every hour you spend managing emotions costs your company money.

Calculating the Costs of an Emotional Spin

Your Hourly Salary		Hours Dealing With a Spin	
	18.		6

x   =   108.

+

Number of People Effected by the Spin		Hourly Salary		Hours Dealing with a Spin	
	14		8.		6

x   x   =   672.

+

Boss's Hourly Salary		Hours Listening to You / Dealing with the Spin	
	38.		6.

x   =   228.

+

FICA / Taxes		Consultations		Revenue Lost from Customers Lost	
					133.

+   +   =   133.

+

Public Relations Costs		Training Dollars Required		Health Care Costs	

+   +   =

+

Other Costs for Your Industry		Other Costs for Your Industry		Other Costs for Your Industry	

+   +   =

=

Total Cost of an Emotional Spin
$ 1,141.00

Learning Byte

Risk Assessment Pop-Quiz: At what point does the financial loss of an emotional spin become a risk factor for your company?

DO THIS: Do the math.

DON'T: Ignore the math.

Case Example

These costs were accrued at one company over a two-month period. The company lost another twelve employees in the following eighteen months before this problem was arrested and a resolution process began. The resolution took over two years at additional costs for lost revenue, employees, trainings and consultations. (Descriptive details have been altered to protect confidentiality.)

Employee #1
Grievance: Employee-driven resentment about another staff member being assigned a new task
Outcome: Loss of this staff member to another institution

6 months severance pay	$36,000.00	
6 months insurance premium	4,200.00	
Accrued sick leave payoff	2,700.00	
Replacement during severance time	39,000.00	
Counseling	500.00	
Consultation/Trainings	15,640.00	Total: $98,040.00

Employee #2
Grievance: Customer-driven complaint about poor customer services
Outcome: Staff member became angry and denied responsibility for poor customer services. Termination and loss of an external vendor

Accrued sick leave payoff	$ 5,000.00	
Paid during suspension/investigation	4,440.00	
Paid insurance during investigation	3,100.00	
Legal investigation	6,500.00	
Counseling	200.00	Total: $19,240.00

Employee #3
Grievance: Management-driven following vote of no confidence
Outcome: Manager did not feel competent and needed significant restoring of confidence to maintain standards of practice

Paid insurance during time off work	$ 600.00	
Salary for time off	2,900.00	
3 weeks severance	3,500.00	
Counseling	350.00	
Consultations	2,000.00	Total: $ 9,350.00

Additional expenses accrued (not included in totals):
- Counseling/consultations for department for 18 months
- Advertising and recruitment expenses for new employees
- Re-training/orientations for new and existing staff
- Team building time with existing staff
- Community goodwill / public relations / vendor losses
- Replacement equipment/cost of stolen equipment
- Addiction-related costs (absenteeism, time loss, productivity)
- Additional health care (one person had several emergency room visits related to increased stress)

Goodwill

Goodwill for most companies determines longevity. Goodwill is mathematically factored by historical data, expectations of the industry, trends, and mythological predictions of future business. Predictions are fantasies. Certainly some fantasies match reality quite closely, but until a crystal ball is invented, or businesses hire psychics as consultants and their numbers are verified and repeatable, goodwill is a hope, not a sure thing. Some businesses, physicians for example, attach a "goodwill" value to the selling price of their practices. They have built up a reputation and it is a valuable asset. Clients and customers are attracted or repelled by goodwill concerns. Customer service is the subject of very expensive trainings and policy meetings for businesses that make an effort to keep people coming to their company for products or services. When people do not come, the bottom line is not maintained. And people don't come if they do not like you. This is one powerful domain of emotions at the workplace that can easily be translated into lost revenue. Large corporations spend billions on convincing the public that they are the "good guys." Loyalties shift rapidly and one day the good guys are the bad guys and revenue dries up.

The loss of goodwill can span industries and revenue streams for decades. What does the word Columbine mean to you? What did it mean 10 years ago? What about the words World Trade Center, Tylenol, TYCO, Halliburton, Enron, Exxon Valdez, or Martha Stewart? The Titanic was pitched as the safest maritime product and service in the known world. The Titanic was sold as "unsinkable." Today the word "Titanic" is synonymous with loss. Some loss, like the Titanic, spans fiscal and goodwill costs for decades.

Case Example

The Halifax Herald (May 2, 1912) received the following information from the "Insurance Press" about some of the financial losses from the Titanic sinking. (Behe, 2004) Representations of the value of a dollar in 1912 would translate into significant expenditures at today's rates

- John B. Thayer: $50,000 accident insurance
- Edgar Meyer: $47,500 life insurance
- Herbert Chaffee: $146,750 life insurance
- Benjamin Guggenheim: $25,000 life insurance
- Charles Hayes: $25,000 life insurance, $80,000 accident insurance
- William Silvey: $22,500 life insurance
- Walter Clark: $20,000 life insurance
- Isador Straus: $20,000 life insurance
- Walter Porter: $15,000 life insurance
- Albert Stewart: $15,000 life insurance
- John Cumings: $10,000 life insurance
- Walter Douglas: $10,000 life insurance
- Arthur Newell: $10,000 life insurance
- William Stead: $10,000 life insurance
- Emil Taussig: $10,000 life insurance
- Henry Harris: $5,448 life insurance
- Archibald Butt: $2,000 life insurance
- Emil Brandeis: $175,000 accident insurance
- Frank Warren: $50,000 accident insurance
- Stephen Blackwell: $33,000 accident insurance

Learning Byte

Very few companies today would use the word 'Titanic' to try to increase good will toward their company. More like performance art than business, the reputation of the show brings in the business. Goodwill is the ongoing "curb appeal" that makes the client energy flow toward and into your revenue stream. An emotional spin can redirect the flow to the extent that the goodwill moves elsewhere at an astonishing speed.

DO THIS: Consider goodwill as money on its way.

DON'T: Think people aren't paying attention to the smallest ripple of attitude.

Case Example

When the café and bakery, The Petite Pan, opened in the small town, the locals were delighted with the homemade products and the beautiful atmosphere. They flocked to the site and quickly included the owners into the community. In an uncharacteristic gesture of inclusion the traditionally isolated and emotionally closed community saw the café as good for commerce and local goodwill and the Petite Pan became the new place to meet friends and business colleagues.

Business boomed. The locals started sending their teenagers there for beginning jobs. The job turnover was surprising with the average length of employment under six weeks. It became a local joke and a point of competitive amusement, "my kid lasted five weeks," "well, my kid lasted six." No one questioned why and adults made a collective assumption that it was due to the incompetence of young workers with no skills and the money flowed into the café from all directions.

It was Tina's first job and everyone was amazed that she lasted beyond the usual two months. After four months local adults began to praise her openly and asked her what her secret was. She innocently replied, "Oh, I guess I'm just not so bothered when the owner comes at me with butcher knives and screams at me or his wife and throws things at her. I know he's sort of insane so I think it's sort of funny." Everyone was appalled and started asking their children what had happened to them. The teens shared their stories of violent tantrums between the owners that were often leveled directly at the children. The adults were humiliated that they had been so blind and had not protected their children. Business slumped dramatically. Word got around town quickly. No one sent their children there for part time jobs, no one was available to wash dishes, clear tables, or sweep floors and no one bought the baked products. The café couldn't even sell day-old bread. The business failed within weeks. The couple filed bankruptcy and left town. No one cared.

Learning Byte

Goodwill came and goodwill left. This was a lose-lose situation for everyone involved except perhaps for Tina. Her reputation as a sturdy employee became a local myth associated with the former Petite Pan café stories. Tina was hired by another company and locally celebrated as a "brave kid." She took that experience forward and was able to evolve it into a mature work ethic for herself. "I can work anywhere," she would say, "after all, I survived the Petite Café longer than anyone in town." Be that as is may, a manager or employee may get points for surviving an emotionally spinning workplace, but adults do not tolerate the same behaviors that untrained, entry level employees may accept. And, word of mouth is louder than ever with rapid speed information technology. There are no secrets that last.

DO THIS: Assume that everything is completely visible to everyone on the planet at all times and someone is keeping score.

DON'T: Ever forget that your next client is in the wings waiting to be either your client or someone else's client.

Liability

The history of litigation originally was intended to offer strength and support in holding someone to accountability. Today, it is more like a blame-and-gain game. It seems as though there is someone ready to sue someone right now because they wore the wrong hat on a Tuesday. Industries, businesses, employees and managers are at extreme risk for litigation through civil, criminal and personal liability suits. Emotions at the workplace, from extreme events such as shootings and criminal incidents to small events such as an implied sexual innuendo or racist comment, routinely end up in court. The hourly fees and retainers of legal advisors add significant costs to companies. A day in court could ruin a small business.

Managers can be blamed and scapegoated if they get caught in the middle of an emotional conflict. Personal liability in a company is an emotional and fairly political topic. The role of manager as he or she stands in the midst of in an emotional conflict is a dangerous place to be. Policies and procedures that are established to protect employees should be super-sized to protect managers. Employment Practices insurance is a growing industry and some managers are seeking personal liability insurance outside of any policy held by their company. Managers should be knowledgeable about if and how they are protected from liability.

Posturing and positioning during conflict can lead to verbal or physical threats and outright attacks. Threats of litigation are becoming more dangerous and powerful then real attacks. Legal saber-rattling from an adversary is intended to shift power so the other guy will back away first in compromise. This behavior creates emotional spin and launches future spins through implications of future terror. When managers know how they are protected from such threats they are in a better position to mediate a conflict. Managers who are afraid of being sued tend to lose their own emotional continuity if they respond from their own emotional, fear-based reactions.

When conflicts and power struggles exist it means that someone will win and someone will lose. Some battles need to be fought for justice and ethical standards; and many conflicts originate from people who only use litigation for the right reasons. There are others who use litigation or threats of litigation for the wrong reasons, to start or maintain a spin or to gain position and power. A manager needs to have total confidence that a superior or company will back them up, or support them, before they enter into a conflict or power struggle. This provides an atmosphere where the manager can feel protected and remain neutral and compassionate in the face of conflict. Rather than guarding and defending themselves or preparing their own attack, they can listen to emotionally laden content without fear. There are many models of non-violent and non-fear-based communications that can be learned to deal with conflict. And it is also a good idea to make sure having an excellent insurance policy to cover your bases.

Case Example

Marie always got A's in math. In 8th grade she brought home a D. Marie said that the teacher didn't seem to understand math and had a temper and would yell, "Hey, if you guys aren't getting this stuff it isn't my problem, you must be a bunch of retards." Marie's parent went to school and spoke to the principal and the teacher. The teacher emotionally escalated the situation and threatened to quit. The principal escalated the emotions by increasing blame toward the student and backed the teacher. The parent threatened litigation.

Learning Byte

Your clients take things seriously and so should you. Litigations are expensive and time consuming. Escalating conflicts and misunderstandings into litigation are not productive. Litigation should be used when there are significant issues, but not just to manage poor communication and power struggles. Have you had any experiences where you have seen power struggles turn into litigations? How much did they cost? What are legal fees per hour in your city?

DO THIS: Call several local attorneys and ask their fees per hour.

DON'T: Assume your company will cover your legal fees. Find out.

Global Consequences

What happens when a cow falls down on Christmas Eve? No, it isn't a children's riddle. A cow fell down in Washington State and within two months there was a global spin. In dairy communities cows are like cash. The idea that one sick cow could affect an entire ranch is less of a stretch to the imagination than thinking that a cow could launch a global economic disaster. A single cow at a ranch in Mabton, Washington led to a crisis in the international beef industry and sparked surprising risks in non-beef industries, created, public health scares, left citizens sorting out the realities from the rumors, and eventually became a college course at a university in Connecticut. The chronology of newspaper headlines from the Tri-City Herald, a local news source for the region near around Mabton, presents a fascinating picture of how one cow can create a global emotional spin in a short period.

Case Examples

(All Headlines From The Tri-City Herald, Kennewick, Washington; Associated Press; and other sources)

- Mad Cow Reported In Mabton (12/24/2003)
- Mad Cow Announcement Drains Holiday Cheer (12/25/2003)
- Sunny Dene Ranch Being Investigated (12/25/2003)
- Congress Twice Has Scuttled Plan To Restrict Sale Of Suspect Beef (12/25/2003)
- Beef Pulled From Shelves, Menus (12/25/2003)
- Mad Cow Incident Came Week After Court's Sick Animal Ruling (12/25/2003)
- Mad Cow Answers Sought (12/25/2003)
- Disease Could Ravage Industry (12/25/2003)
- Mabton In Spotlight (12/25/2003)
- Disease Could Ravage Industry (12/25/2003)
- Mabton Rallies Around Embattled Dairy Owners (12/26/2003)
- A Few Tips To Minimize Risk Of Getting Mad Cow Disease (12/26/2003)
- British Lab Confirms Mad Cow Disease (12/26/2003)
- U.S. Beef Importers Worldwide Shut Doors Amid Mad Cow Fears (12/26/2003)
- Mad Cow Disease Likely To Be Costly To Beef Industry (12/27/2003)
- Second Herd Isolated In Washington (12/27/2003)
- Tainted Holstein May Have Been Used For Various Items (12/27/2003)
- Beef Futures Fall, But Customers Still Buying Meat (12/27/2003)
- Handling Of Mad Cow Scare A Key (Bush Administration) Issue (12/27/2003)
- Holstein Traced Back To Canada (12/28/2003)
- Mad Cow Still Perplexes Scientists (12/28/2003)
- Mad Cow Disease Revives Debate (12/28/2003)
- Eyes Of Nation, World Turn To Region In 2003 (12/28/2003)
- Countries That Have Banned U.S. Beef (12/28/2003)
- Authorities Say One Herd To Be Killed, Other Still In Limbo (12/29/2003)
- News Analysis: Addressing American's Concerns About Mad Cow Disease (12/29/2003)
- Mad Cow Follows Bumper Year For Cattle Ranchers (12/29/2003)
- Many Consumers Unfazed By Mad Cow News (12/29/2003)
- Burger Chains And Steakhouses Unaffected By Mad Cow Scare (12/29/2003)
- Beef Futures Fall The Limit In Mad Cow Aftermath (12/29/2003)
- House Agriculture Committee Members Receiving Dairy Industry Money This Year (12/29/2003)
- Sheep Ailment May Hold Clues To Mad Cow Disease (12/29/2003)
- Infected Holstein Born Before Restrictions Placed On Cattle Feed (12/29/2003)
- More States May Have Received Meat From Sick Cow, But USDA Says It Is Safe (12/29/2003)
- New Methods To Test For Mad Cow Disease Would Give Results Sooner (12/29/2003)
- Japan's Mad Cow Experience Means Tough Sell For U.S. Officials (12/29/2003)
- Mad Cow Case Heightens Debate About Feed Inspections (12/29/2003)
- Dairy Industry Contributed To Key Lawmakers Who Opposed 'Downer' Ban (12/29/2003)
- Countries That Have Banned U.S. Beef (12/29/2003)
- USDA Unsure If Cattle To Be Slaughtered (12/30/2003)
- Officials Hunt 81 Additional Cows (12/30/2003)
- Agriculture Department Bans Further Use Of Sick 'Downer' Cattle For Meat, Wants Nationwide ID Stem For Cattle (12/30/2003)
- Mad Cow Isn't Result Of Trade Policy, Experts Say (12/30/2003)
- 'Downer' Decision Catches Meat Lobby Off-Guard (12/30/2003)
- Taiwan Bans U.S. Beef Imports For At Least Seven Years (12/30/2003)
- Mad Cow Scare Could Spur Move To High-Tech Livestock Tracking (12/30/2003)
- Brisk US-Canada Cattle Trade Connects Countries In Mad Cow Risks (12/30/2003)
- Countries That Have Banned U.S. Beef (12/30/2003)
- So Far, U.S. Only Contemplates Changes In Mad Cow Testing (12/30/2003)
- U.S. Delegation Arrives In South Korea To Discuss Mad Cow Case In Washington (12/30/2003)
- Meat From Holstein Sent To 8 States (12/30/2003)
- Meatpackers Say Tougher Rules Following Mad Cow Discovery Are A Good Thing (12/31/2003)

- Mad Cow Follows Bumper Year For Cattle Ranchers (12/31/2003)
- French Fries Blocked From Asian Markets (12/31/2003)
- Timing Of Mad Cow News Minimizes Impact On Ranchers (12/31/2003)
- Human Version Of Mad Cow Disease Usually Not Linked To Diet (12/31/2003)
- Farmers Won't Lose Much On Ban On Slaughtering Downers (12/31/2003)
- Mad Cow Scare Could Spur Move To High-Tech Livestock Tracking (12/31/2003)
- Federal Authorities Backtrack On Decision To Kill Calf Herd (12/31/2003)
- Officials Say Pet Owners Shouldn't Be Alarmed About Mad Cow Disease In Dogs And Cats (12/31/2003)
- GAO Report Warned Of Mad Cow Incubation (12/31/2003)
- Meat Laws Give Latino Stores A Jolt (12/31/2003)
- USDA Issues New Rules For Beef Safety (12/31/2003)
- Governor Locke Seeks Testing For All 'Downer' Cows (12/31/2003)
- Government Changes Intended To Boost Confidence In U.S. Beef Supply At Home, Abroad (12/31/2003)
- Cattle Producers Will Fight Bad Publicity About Mad Cow Disease (12/31/2003)
- Investigators Tentatively Link Mad Cow Cases To Edmonton Rendering Plant (12/31/2003)
- Cash Cows (12/31/2003)
- USDA Officials Back 30-Month Standard (1/1/2004)
- Mad Cow's Brain-Wasting Course Inspires Fear (1/1/2004)
- In Evansville, Mad Cow Doesn't Scare Lovers Of Brain Sandwiches (1/1/2004)
- Producers See More Interest In Buffalo Meat After Mad Cow Case (1/1/2004)
- Exporters Worry Beef Will Spoil During Ban (1/2/2004)
- USDA To Decide Soon On Killing Cows In Mad Cow Holstein's Herd (1/2/2004)
- From Hooves To Tendons, Asian Consumers Bought What Americans Don't Eat (1/2/2004)
- Groceries Hold Off On Selling Cow Heads For Hispanic Holiday Fare (1/2/2004)
- Iowa Lab In Forefront Of Testing For Mad Cow Disease (1/2/2004)
- Mad Cow Probe Turns To Canadian Rendering Plant (1/2/2004)
- Hide Industry Hit By Mad Cow Scare (1/3/2004)
- U.S. Beef Ban Roils Shippers (1/3/2004)
- USDA Quarantines Third Washington Herd; Some Cattle Linked To Mad Cow To Be Killed (1/3/2004)
- School Lunches Safe, Officials Tell Parents (1/4/2004)
- Mad Cow Rules Aimed Overseas (1/4/2004)
- Japan Says U.S. Safeguards Against Mad Cow Not Strict Enough (1/5/2004)
- Research Priorities Linked To Mad Cow (1/5/2004)
- Family Of Brain Diseases, Including Mad Cow, Mystify Scientists (1/5/2004)
- USDA To Kill 450 Calves In Herd Linked To Mad-Cow Holstein (1/5/2004)
- Cattle Feeding Habits Get New Scrutiny (1/5/2004)
- Utah Producers See Little Fallout From Mad Cow Scare (1/5/2004)
- As Lunch Rush Resumes, School Officials Monitoring Mad Cow Case (1/5/2004)
- Mad Cow Case Shows Risk Of Push For Protein In Feed (1/5/2004)
- Orthodox Jews Say Eating Kosher Beef Might Protect Against Mad Cow Disease (1/6/2004)
- Mad Cow Disease Puts New Spin On Farm Policy (1/6/2004)
- Have Scientists Missed Some Cases Of Mad Cow Disease In Humans? (1/6/2004)
- DNA Tests Confirm Mad Cow Holstein Came From Canada (1/6/2004)
- Cattlemen Praise Prices At Yakima Valley Auction (1/6/2004)
- USDA To Kill 450 Calves (1/6/2004)
- Market Recalls Beef Bones Linked To Mad Cow Batch (1/6/2004)
- Herd Of Calves Being Killed (1/7/2004)
- Mad-Cow Scare: Have Scientists Missed Some Cases Of Mad Cow Disease In Humans? (1/7/2004)
- Kennewick General Hospital Removes Beef From Menu (1/7/2004)
- Canada To Press Countries For Reopening Of Global Markets To Canadian Beef (1/7/2004)
- DNA Shows Cow Came From Canada (1/7/2004)
- South Florida Woman Has Mad Cow Disease (1/7/2004)
- Mad Cow Scare Revives Calls For U.S. Beef Labels In Stores (1/7/2004)

- Ranchers Wary Of Jumping Back Into Sales Ring (1/7/2004)
- Japanese Officials To Meet With U.S. On Beef Safety (1/8/2004)
- 'We Fed Legal Feed,' Say Farmers Who Raised Mad Cow In Canada (1/8/2004)
- Herd Killed Because Of Mad Cow Disease Is Buried At Landfill (1/8/2004)
- Canadian Ranchers Battered By Mad Cow Scare (1/8/2004)
- Probe Focuses On Cattle That Came From Canada With Infected Cow (1/8/2004)
- Man Learns He Ate Beef Linked To Holstein With Mad Cow Disease (1/8/2004)
- Farmers Who Raised Mad Cow Say It Was Legally Fed (1/8/2004)
- Workers Bury Calves Killed In Response To Mad Cow (1/8/2004)
- Japan To Send Team To United States To Investigate Mad Cow Case (1/8/2004)
- 129 More Cows To Be Killed (1/9/2004)
- Where's The Beef Panic? U.S. Consumers Shrug Off Mad Cow Scare (1/9/2004)
- Canada To Spend $72 Million To Expand Mad Cow Testing (1/9/2004)
- Japanese Officials Advise Against Selling U.S. Steaks Imported Before Ban (1/9/2004)
- Few Buy At Cattle Auction (1/9/2004)
- Mad Cow Investigation Focuses On Cattle That Entered Country With Infected Holstein (1/9/2004)
- 129 More Cattle To Be Killed In Mabton Herd (1/10/2004)
- Dog Sled Race Relieved By Change In Pet-Food Ban (1/10/2004)
- Mabton Rallies Around Beef And Community Members (1/11/2004)
- Officials Defend Milk From Mabton Dairy (1/11/2004)
- Nethercutt Touts Cattle Industry Changes (1/12/2004)
- Mad Cow Is A Boon To Testing Labs (1/12/2004)
- South Florida Mad Cow Victim Undergoing New Treatment (1/12/2004)
- Organic Beef Growers Determined To Cash In On Mad Cow Case (1/12/2004)
- Mad Cow Scare Revives Calls For U.S. Beef Labels In Stores (1/12/2004)
- Investigators Focus On 'Painstaking' Search (1/12/2004)
- Canadian Agriculture Minister Proposes Dialogue Aimed At Lifting Import Ban (1/13/2004)
- Japanese Delegation Reviews Mad Cow Investigation (1/13/2004)
- Evidence Suggests Unreported Cases Of Mad Cow In Humans (1/13/2004)
- Canadian Beef Industry Sends Thank You Postcards To Albertans (1/14/2004)
- Mad Cow: U.S. Investigators Conduct A Bovine Missing-Persons Case (1/14/2004)
- Small Town Accepts Decision To Become Mad Cow Killing Site (1/14/2004)
- Mad Cow Investigation Continues; Governor Plans Visit To Mabton (1/14/2004)
- Ranchers Tell Nethercutt They Want Regulations (1/14/2004)
- Mad Cow Takes Center Stage At One Of The Nation's Largest Gatherings Of Beef Ranchers (1/14/2004)
- Locke To Visit Mabton For Mad Cow Disease Meeting (1/14/2004)
- USDA Secretary Breaks Ground On New Lab To Test For Animal Diseases (1/14/2004)
- Quest Gets Permission To Ship Meat For Food Drops (1/15/2004)
- Mad Cow Takes Center Stage At One Of The Nation's Largest Gatherings Of Beef Ranchers (1/15/2004)
- Brain Sandwiches Still On The Menu In Indiana Despite Fears Of Mad Cow Disease (1/16/2004)
- North American Agriculture Officials Fail To Agree On Resuming Beef Trade (1/16/2004)
- Washington State Lawmakers Call For More Mad Cow Measures (1/16/2004)
- USDA Officials Push For National Cattle Identification System (1/16/2004)
- State Takes Steps To Better Identify Brain-Wasting Illnesses (1/16/2004)
- Tougher Mad Cow Measures Proposed (1/16/2004)
- USDA Declares 'Extraordinary Emergency' (1/16/2004)
- Cattle Groups Tell Governor They Need International Markets (1/16/2004)
- Mad Cow Discovery Shifts Focus For Washington Lawmakers (1/18/2004)
- Lack Of Modern Tracking System Hampers Mad Cow Investigation (1/18/2004)
- Consumer Groups Want More Cattle Testing, Information On Mad Cow (1/18/2004)
- Sunnyside Calf Farmer Starts Over (1/19/2004)
- Mad Cow Scare Hurts Midwest Meatpacking Belt (1/20/2004)
- Oregon-Based Interstate Meat Tries To Rebound After Mad Cow Scare (1/20/2004)
- Beef Industry To Launch Delayed Ad Campaign (1/20/2004)
- Dairy Copes With Mad Cow Fallout (1/20/2004)

- Japanese Team: U.S. And Canadian Beef Still Not 100 Percent Safe (1/20/2004)
- Hold Order Placed On Oregon Dairy In Mad-Cow Investigation (1/21/2004)
- Veneman To Brief Congress On Mad Cow Investigation (1/21/2004)
- Virginia Tech Researchers Cloning Cattle To Be 'Mad Cow-Free' (1/21/2004)
- Japan Orders Wholesalers Not To Sell U.S. Beef Products At Risk For Mad Cow (1/21/2004)
- 4 More Cows From Canadian Herd Found (1/21/2004)
- Mad Cow Scare Hurts Midwest Meatpacking Belt (1/22/2004)
- Oregon Has First Tie To Mad Cow (1/22/2004)
- Boardman Dairy Cow In Isolation (1/22/2004)
- Supermarket Uses Discount Cards To Inform Customers Of Recall (1/23/2004)
- Canadian Cows Traced To Idaho As Part Of Mad Cow Investigation (1/23/2004)
- Democrats Hit Nethercutt On Mad Cow (1/23/2004)
- United States, Japan Discuss Mad Cow Measures But Reach No Agreement On Resuming Beef Imports (1/23/2004)
- Meat Packers May Be Offered B&O Tax Break (1/23/2004)
- U.S. Delegation In Japan Says 100 Percent Testing Not Effective In Preventing Mad Cow Disease (1/23/2004)
- Herds In Three States Quarantined In Mad Cow Investigation (1/24/2004)
- Administration's Mad Cow Response Irks Both Sides (1/25/2004)
- Ranchers Still Reeling (1/25/2004)
- Beef Industry Gadfly Says Mad Cow Case Vindicates Comments To Oprah (1/25/2004)
- Search For More Mad Cow Cases About Over, Government Says (1/26/2004)
- Hastings Discusses Immigration, Mad Cow At Town Hall (1/26/2004)
- Agriculture Secretary Says U.S. Trying To Prevent Trade Problems Related To Mad Cow Disease (1/27/2004)
- USDA May Not Find All Of Herd (1/27/2004)
- Government Bans Cattle Blood In Feed, Nears End Of Probe (1/27/2004)
- 15 Cows In Connell Killed In Mad Cow Investigation (1/27/2004)
- 20 Cows From Oregon Dairy Are Euthanized (1/27/2004)
- In Wake Of Mad-Cow, Democrats Push For National Animal ID System (1/28/2004)
- Increased Testing Backed In Survey (1/29/2004)
- More Cattle Killed In Mad Cow Investigation (1/30/2004)
- Extra $47 Million Sought For Beef Safety (1/31/2004)
- Canadian Mayors To Discuss Beef Industry (2/2/2004)
- Man Who Says He Killed Mad Cow Challenges USDA (2/4/2004)
- Three More Cows Euthanized Over The Weekend (2/4/2004)
- Ag Secretary Downplays Mad Cow Risk Cited By Expert Panel (2/5/2004)
- Canadian Mayors Talk About Mad Cow Hit (2/5/2004)
- Panel: Undiscovered Cases Of Mad-Cow Likely In United States (2/5/2004)
- Panel Seeks More Mad Cow Shields (2/6/2004)
- Scientists Say Blood Donors Could Be Among People With Human Mad Cow Disease (2/7/2004)
- Fair Worries (2/10/2004)
- USDA Ends Hunt For Mad Cow Herd (2/11/2004)
- Proposed Legislation Would Make It Easier To Track Cattle (2/15/2004)
- Critics Question Findings Of Mad Cow Study (2/17/2004)
- New Form Of Mad Cow Disease Discovered By Italian Scientists (2/18/2004)
- Canada Bails Out Beef Industry (2/19/2004)
- USDA's Facts In Question (2/19/2004)
- Family Backs Mad Cow Claim (2/20/2004)
- Beef Prices Expected To Drop Because Of International Bans (2/25/2004)
- More Mad Cow Tests Loom, Says Veneman (2/26/2004)
- U.S. Beef Restraints May Soon Be Eased (2/26/2004)
- Mad Cow Criminal Probe Begins (3/4/2004)
- U.S. Extends Restrictions On Canadian Beef Imports (3/5/2004)
- Mad Cow Criminal Probe Begins (3/5/2004)
- House Seeks OK For Mad Cow Bills (3/9/2004)
- U.S. Extends Restrictions On Canadian Beef Imports (3/9/2004)

- Increased Mad Cow Testing In Works (3/10/2004)
- House Seeks OK For Mad Cow Bills (3/10/2004)
- Mad Cow Coverage By Media Discussed (3/11/2004)
- Increased Mad Cow Testing In Works (3/11/2004)
- Rapid Mad Cow Test Approved, Company Says (3/19/2004)
- Mad Cow Coverage By Media Discussed (3/19/2004)
- Mad Cow-Tainted Feed Traced To 2 Plants (3/20/2004)
- Rapid Mad Cow Test Approved, Company Says (3/20/2004)
- Canada Bails Out Beef Industry (3/23/2004)
- Mad Cow-Tainted Feed Traced To 2 Plants (3/23/2004)
- Senator Cantwell Pushes Bush To Close Mad Cow Loopholes (4/20/2004)
- Allow Mad Cow Testing (4/23/04)
- Nethercutt Aims Early at Murray (4/25/04)
- Got Cow Power? (5/9/04)
- Take Care on Downer (Cow) Ban (5/20/04)
- Mad Cow Tests to Begin Today (6/02/04)
- Mad Cow Reforms Still Lagging (6/27/04)
- Tyson Workers Protest Testing (6/30/04)
- Audit Finds Flaws in Mad Cow Testing (7/14/04)
- Veneman Defends Mad Cow Testing (7/15/04)
- Communicating Risks (8/30/04)
- Farmer's Plans to Raise More Cattle Worry Nearby Residents (9/12/04)

Case Example

According to Moneyline Telerate (February, 2004) stocks in Beef related restaurants have lowered while stocks in laboratories that test for mad cow disease have risen.

- -9.9%   Tyson Foods
- -4.7   McDonald's
- -4.2%   Wendy's
- -1.6   Smithfield Foods
- -1.5%   ConAgra Foods
- +24.8   Bio-Rad Laboratories

Case Example

Michigan based Thron Apple Valley Inc filed for Chapter 11 bankruptcy after recalling 30 million pounds of possibly contaminated meat and poultry. (McLeod, D, Business Insurance, 1999)

Learning Byte

According to Donald Bryan, Chicago-based managing director of Marsh, the brokerage unit of Marsh, Inc., the following costs should be addressed for any estimation of the economic consequences of any product recall:

- Transportation
- Storing and destroying the product
- Refunds
- Lost business
- Cleanup
- Correction of the problem, supply of replacement products, advertising, public relations, brand rehabilitation
- Customer incentive programs
- Legal costs
- Fines and reasonable costs of crisis management consultants
- Third party liabilities
- Employee-related costs, such as layoffs

DO THIS: Review the mad cow examples presented again and consider each headline individually. Then consider how many people or companies might be influenced by each headline. Then consider how many people or companies might be influenced by those secondary and tertiary influences. Think in exponential terms.

DON'T*: See any incident as an isolated event in the world market of today.*

Case Example

Dear Dr. Hawkins-Mitchell: I wanted to tell you about the four ex-employees who were working in my office two years ago are still causing me untold financial grief. One employee was an associate medical professional, fresh out of school, and this was the first private practice experience. The others were two assistants and one receptionist. The ongoing lawsuits are defamation of character and malicious slander that are costing me financially, physically and emotionally. My reputation and personal integrity in the community have had irreparable scars. My dream of moving my successful practice into a teaching institution is nearly lost. My retirement is not an option currently.

When the new doctor, Dr. Shoola agreed to the buy-in of part ownership of the practice I accepted this as a good sign and moved forward with my projects. Less than two months into the association Dr. Shoola told me there was a family emergency out of state and had to go home to live. My shock was mixed with confusion when I filtered out the medical details of the emergency, which didn't totally correspond to true medical details, and stories about a "bad-break-up" with a former lover. Dr. Shoola gave me a one-month notice of leaving. During that last month, my lawyer encouraged me to have everyone in the practice sign a confidentiality agreement. Dr. Shoola refused to sign the agreement. The entire staff had been informed that the new procedures were for everyone's protection and would now be a mandatory policy for continued employment. Dr. Shoola refused to sign and understood that it would mean immediate termination. With one week to go on the one-month notice, Dr. Shoola was terminated. This led Dr. Shoola to create four behind-doors meetings with the staff. Dr. Shoola left the state for this so-called family emergency but returned frequently for meetings with staff. Dr. Shoola took complaints and fabrications to the State Quality Control Commission and made a formal complaint of mistreatment and accused me of alcohol abuse. Coordinating efforts with former staff and personal relationships, including my former spouse with whom I was currently in divorce proceedings, apparently used this "catastrophic and emotionally traumatic" termination for a personal agenda. The effects which continue, have been, to date:

- Suspension of my medical license for 7 weeks for an investigation
- Three major malpractice lawsuits directly traced back to the encouragement from this health practitioner and former staff
- Loss of over $100,000.00 in lost production
- Anticipated losses will continue due to ongoing lawsuits including new defamation lawsuits that I will start against these former employees
- An accusation of alcohol abuse that has affected hospital status, community regard, incurred significant counseling and assessment fees. The Licensing board demanded in-patient alcohol treatment, which was assessed as not necessary from several competent Alcohol and Drug Assessment professionals who agreed this was not indicated. The Licensing board did not accept these professional assessments although the superior courts have defined them as appropriate sources for assessment. My license is still at risk due to this and ongoing litigation processes.
- Costs for Counseling and consultations
- Loss of community reputation and subsequent client losses still rising

It hasn't been a great year for my business. But if it hadn't been for the consultation we had last year, I suspect it would have been worse, because I would have taken it all personally. Now I am just approaching it as a very difficult a business issue, and not a personal emotional spin. *Best Regards, Dr. Ryder.*

Learning Byte

Emotional spinning is expensive.

DO THIS*: Take the subject seriously without being afraid of it. Do the math.*

DON'T*: Stop adding the costs when the obvious spin ends. Continue adding costs beyond the event as they continue to evolve. Some costs evolve for decades.*

Other Costs of Spinning

- Researchers at the Cornell University Institute for Health and Productivity Studies (IHPS) and the health-information firm Medstat estimate that companies' on-the-job productivity losses from *presenteeism* are possibly as high as 60 percent of the total cost of worker illness -- exceeding the costs of absenteeism and medical and disability benefits. 'Presenteeism' is the new buzzword to describe people who refuse to take time off from work, even for sick leave, because they fear losing their jobs in the current economy. (April 20, 2004 Cornell University)
- Stress-related absenteeism is responsible for the loss of 50 million working days each year. (Thomas, 2002)
- By 1991 it was estimated that stress-related disorders cost approximately $150 billion annually and claimed more than 14% of insurance compensations. (Pelletier, 1991)
- The cost of depressions alone tops $70 billion in health care, work loss as well as other expenses. (Tanouye, 2001)
- In 1997 over $100 billion was lost in productivity due to cardiovascular disease. (Thomas, 2002)
- A study by the General Accounting office found 123 plants in America that, if damaged, could expose more than one million people to toxic clouds of gas. (Kroll, 2003)
- The Impact of September 11, 2001 (Marcella, 2003)
    - 2,830 lives lost
    - 14,600 businesses directly impacted
    - Million square feet of office space lost
    - Corporate tenants displaced
    - 200,000 communication lines out of service due to network failures
- The percentage of trauma victims of September 11 that will continue to have problems and develop Posttraumatic Stress Disorder will depend on many factors, including the severity of trauma exposure. In research on disasters, prevalence rates have been: (Marcella 2003)
    - Natural disaster: 4-5%
    - Bombing: 34%
    - Plane crash into hotel: 29%
    - Mass shooting: 28%
- The following types of exposure place survivors at high risk for a range of post-disaster problems (Marcella, 2004):
    - Exposure to mass destruction or death
    - Toxic contamination
    - Sudden or violent death of a loved one
    - Loss of home or community
- The rates of Acute Stress Disorder following traumatic incidents vary, with higher rates reported for human-caused trauma. (Bryant, 2000):
    - Typhoon: 7%
    - Industrial accident: 6%
    - Mass shooting: 33%
    - Violent assault: 19%

The Costs of Protecting a Human Life

According to Kip Viscusi of the Harvard Law School, the price of an American human life is approximately $7 million. He has researched what people would pay to protect themselves from death at work, and how much they will compensate for the increased risk of death on the job. (Viscusi, 2004)

Costs of War Away from Home

Reservists and soldiers who have been deployed to the Middle East for the War in Iraq and Afghanistan come home to problems. Their employers have problems while they are away. At the time of writing of this book, over 176,000 reservists and guard members are currently deployed overseas. The numbers change as many come and go regularly while the War continues to demand military presence. Some soldiers come home to jobs that have been reassigned or outright lost to someone else.

Nathan Isaacs, a news staff writer, reported that in Ohio, a reservist committed suicide claiming it was due to the loss of a promised promotion after he got home. (Tri-City Herald, 2004) Although there are laws that make it illegal for an employer to discriminate against a reservist, terminate their jobs, or relinquish seniority, not all employers maintain the highest standards. And the need for reservists may not diminish for some time. According to Isaacs, since September 11, 2001, the number of mobilized reservists has topped 364, 477 compared to 250, 000 during Desert Storm. One employment consideration with this war is that the length of deployment is much longer than ever before. When reservists return, after a long deployment, the world has moved on, and sometimes that means their jobs are gone. The Labor Department reports as of May 2004, that reservists have filed over 3,000 work-related complaints.

Case Example

Joe is a reservist and has been deployed to a secret location. He cannot talk about it to his wife Crystal. She is in counseling because they are having marital problems. Joe has been consumed with his fears of being deployed and Crystal has gotten a job. The children are in day care for the first time. Money is tight and everyone is anxious. Crystal's counselor asks if she is concerned about Joe's safety as he goes into harms way. Her primary concern is that she is having a difficult time at work and she wants out of the marriage before something happens. Joe returns and finds everything has changed. His wife is financially emancipated, his children are older, and his civilian job has been outsourced. He tries to explain to his former boss that he didn't want to go to the Middle East and really needs his job back. The employer isn't sympathetic thinking that Joe, as a reservist, wasn't like a real soldier, and must have had a choice. The couple files for bankruptcy and divorce.

Case Example

A nurse's unit was activated and deployed to Iraq. He was a reservist and had never thought he would be in active duty. He rose to the occasion and provided excellent combat-field medicine. He saw more than he had ever expected to see in his career at home. When he returned home he had to make a very difficult transition from combat/trauma emergency medicine to treating children with fevers, old people with the flu, and skateboarders with sprained ankles.

Learning Byte

Work transitions like this are difficult. Soldiers must learn to transition quickly in order to survive. When they return from active duty they may assume that their work sites or jobs have kept up with their speed.

DO THIS: Support your employees who serve in the military.

DON'T: Drop them on their heads when they get home. Manage them well by helping them manage the changes. If their jobs are gone, help them move forward. Soldiers understand the concepts of forward and retreat and re-group. But they also operate on "no man left behind!"

Reservists, who have transitioned from the expectations of the "weekend mission" to active combat status, have changed. Many of the jobs they left at home have not changed. The fit may not work now. And, unlike a pair of jeans someone has outgrown, the receipt for exchange may have been lost. (By either the soldier or the employer.) Great employers keep the receipt and help the soldier readjust to life back in the civilian sector. Great soldiers help their bosses get ready for that with such programs as Bosslift, a program to prepare employers to help reservists.

Managers can help reservists and employers "keep the receipt" and prepare everyone for a thoughtful transition out and back. The ESGR (Employer Support of the Guard and Reserve) can help managers do this well.

The formal mission of the ESGR is to "Gain and maintain active support from all public and private employers for the men and women of the National Guard and Reserve as defined by demonstrated employer commitment to employee military service" (ESGR 2004). A practical and powerful experiential program of support for soldiers and employers is found in the Bosslift Program. Bosslift is a program the helps soldiers explain the importance of their work, so their bosses can buy-on to the value of the work they will be doing when deployed. Bosslift trips are organized to link employers and soldiers for increased support of the military mission and the need for jobs to be protected by employers. The trips are meant to remove the image of "weekend warriors" from the minds of employers. Employers are taken on simulated air combat flights, exposed to training cases, visit flight towers, tour technical schools, and have the opportunity of compare planes and equipment as well as sitting in real cockpits during takeoff and refueling.

Costs of Wars on the Home Front

- Sun Microsystems accepted $1.6 billion from Microsoft to drop an antitrust suit and agreed Friday to do business with its sworn enemy, apparently ending one of the high-tech industry's bitterest feuds. (The Associated Press, April 4, 2004)
- School in Richland was locked down by police after a 16-year-old student threatened to shoot himself. (Tri City Herald, April 4, 2004)
- Two top official at the Department of Energy resigned Friday, days after the department was sharply criticized at a congressional hearing for its handling of a program to compensate workers who became sick from their jobs at federal nuclear defense sites. (Herald Washington, D.C. bureau, April 3, 2004)
- Trains and buses in major U.S. cities may be targeted this summer by terrorists using bombs hidden in bags or luggage, federal counterterrorism officials have told law enforcement and transportation officials in a nationwide bulletin. (Associated Press, April 4, 2004)
- A band teacher was arrested on charges he had sexual contact with two female pupils. (Klamath Falls, Oregon, April 4, 2004)
- A former custodian alleging racial discrimination and retaliation has sued the Beaverton School District (Portland, Oregon, April 4, 2004)
- Secretary of State, Bill Bradbury is considering auditing the Salem-Keizer School District's contracting and purchasing practices, claiming they may have violated public contracting procedures. (Salem, Oregon, April 4, 2004)
- Tour bus filled with students hits truck, trees: 20 injured. Local television pictures showed dazed children standing on the side of the road as paramedics treated the injured. (Cocoa, Florida, April 4, 2004)
- The manager of a state unemployment office was shot to death Friday by a man upset about his jobless benefits, and another worker was wounded when he rushed to his colleague's aid. (Associated Press, April 4, 2004)
- With the jury close to reaching a verdict, a judge declared a mistrial in the grand larceny case against two former Tyco executives after a juror apparently received an intimidating letter and phone call for supposedly siding with the defense. (Associated Press, April 4, 2004)

Costs That Are Personal, Local, National, Global

Some incidents cross previously established boundaries and spin into each other. Rumors and innuendos can be at the bottom of a spin and what is seen in the final moments is only a reflection of the far-reaching consequences.

Case Example

US Airways Groups Inc. President and Chief Executive David Siegel, whose demands for cost cuts created animosity with union leaders, resigned from the nations 7 th largest airline. He led the company out of 8 months of bankruptcy. Union groups were critical of his leadership and called for his resignation. Trying to keep the company afloat with $1 billion cost cuts found labor groups balking. He will be replaced by Bruce Lakefield who has enjoyed better relations with labor groups. (Associated Press, April 2004)

Learning Byte

Who knows what really happened here except this dramatic outcome?

DO THIS: Pay attention as well as you can and know that you cannot know everything, even though you are expected to be all-knowing.

DON'T: Try to predict outcomes, but be prepared for possible complications and surprises.

AUTHOR'S AFTERTHOUGHTS

Whenever I read a newspaper now, and a headline says something like, "Executive director quits company amidst rumors of misappropriations of funds" I start doing the math in my head. The headline targets the identified culprit and suggests that some spinning process is happening, or has been happening for a long time but now has moved from the covert to the overt. I think about the employees and the managers and the spouses and the children and the counselors and the lawyers and the classroom teachers and the day-care providers and the grandparents and the spins that will be a natural consequence of this headline. I know that the headline is the tip of the iceberg. I wonder if anyone is helping the survivors? I know that no one would hire me to help because the company probably does not have a policy to debrief employees from such an emotional event. They might have a disaster plan for a tornado or a nuclear meltdown, but not an emotional spin or an employee meltdown. I feel frustrated and powerless. I know that some counselor will be making money off this tragic headline. Liquor and probably chocolate sales volume will go up. Productivity at the company involved will go down. Domestic violence, child abuse, and other nasty side effects of fear and instability will wobble the local economy. Lawyers will be making plans to take their families to Tahiti after finishing the work that has been created for them. Doctors will prescribe more antidepressants, and more pharmaceutical products are sold. Children who are stressed because mom or dad are stressed will be more likely to be targeted as ADD (Attention Deficit Disorder) when they act out their tension in the classroom. Some will be put on medications because the teachers and the parents don't know how to manage emotionally spinning children or just don't have the financial resources to be as compassionate as they would like to be. The teachers don't have the support and so they begin to spin. And perhaps no one will be there for them either. The pharmaceutical industry may benefit but pharmaceutical industry employees will be stressed, too.

I will try to get papers published and books written and seminars presented to ears that do not want to hear and think that the "soft side of business" should be left to those HR types because it has nothing to do with the bottom line. I will answer the phone in my private counseling practice and take on another client. One at a time takes a long time.

DISCUSSION QUESTIONS

- What can your company afford to spend on emotional spinning annually?

- Can you find several articles in your local paper that refer to emotions at the work site?

- If you ranked the importance of public trust, curb appeal, customer service, or reputation on a scale of 0-10 (zero meaning small and 10 meaning big), how would your company stand when compared to your top 5 competitors? What emotional issues would risk your standing? What emotional issues would enhance your standing?

SECTION II
READINESS:
Reframing, Responding, And Reactionaries

I hear stories. When I tell people I'm an Emotional Continuity Management consultant they say something like, "We had this guy we called "The Thief" because he took credit for work that wasn't his. We tried to get rid of him but he was union. Finally he moved on to another job. Now we have this manager who is driving everyone crazy. She's a player and everyone is all stirred up again." I ask, "What do you call her?"

Humans are biochemical, electrical, organic and symbolic creatures. We like flags and buttons with logos. Giving people titles and nicknames help us organize our thinking. Categories are useful to a point. Constructing policies and programs to organize our universe is useful. Vision and mission statements, company logos, and teamwork icons create templates for symbolic management. Chaos is manageable when turned into a list, document, policy, or procedure.

While many organizations and companies create volumes of procedures, policies, rules and guidelines for workplace expectations, it is not yet common to create the same organized process to organize emotional content. Emotional Continuity Management is a way to start organizing emotions by using new ideas, logos, symbols, analogies, fantasies, discussion and tools. Companies will spend countless dollars "chasing a worm" in a computer. Companies may need to spend equal dollars chasing an "emotional tornado" at work!

3

RECOGNITION:
WHAT DOES SPINNING LOOK LIKE?

One of the KNRK Disc Jockeys apologized on his Web site, posting a statement that read: "I have become so numb to the horrific things that happen in this world that I sometimes forget there are still people who feel. I in no way meant to be insensitive to anyone. My comments on this (the playing of an audiotape of the beheading of American Nick Berg by Iraqi militants on the air) were inappropriate."

Rumsfeld is trying to focus the public spotlight on the upcoming courts-martial of lower-level soldiers implicated in the Iraqi prisoner abuse, even as lawmakers ask if anyone up the chain of command is culpable. (Associated Press, May 15, 2004)

The rates of Acute Stress Disorder following traumatic incidents vary, with higher rates reported for human caused trauma.

7%   Typhoon

6%   Industrial Accident

33%   Mass shooting

19%   Violent assault

(Thomas/Bryant, 2002)

WHY YOU SHOULD READ THIS CHAPTER:

Can you predict which employees will do well during crisis and who might fall apart under duress? When everyone looks like they are doing well, why do some employees rise to the occasion while others become management nightmares? How can you tell the difference? Should you even try? Can you even discuss it? What words would you use? What is a reasonable response? What is unreasonable? What would happen to your management skills if there were a 33% increase in employees with clinically diagnosable stress disorders? Not recognizing the dynamics of human emotions at the workplace is an increasing risk factor of emergency and disaster planning. Reading this chapter will give you some new ways of seeing employees and help broaden your view about the ranges of behaviors and adjustments of your employees. You will read that different people react differently to stress, that this is normal, and to be expected.

BY THE END OF CHAPTER 3 YOU SHOULD BE ABLE TO

- Distinguish what qualities in employees suggest a higher risk for emotional spinning and draft a checklist of productive emotions and non-productive emotions specifically appropriate for your company or industry

- Increase your comfort level with terms that have been traditionally the sole domain of "mental health" managers.

- Consider yourself a Managerial Diagnostician and start using terms in your communications that include emotional dynamics or psychological language

- Increase your neutrality in conflict management

- Write a neutral but specific documentation about emotional issues

OVERVIEW

Most people do well under most, even extreme, conditions. The majority of people handle challenges, small to catastrophic, with differing levels of grace and skill. But they succeed. Then why fuss over a few "rotten apples" or emotionally dramatic people who just get upset at the drop of a hat? Aren't they just a bunch of troublemakers? Shouldn't they just mature?

The answer to these questions from an Emotional Continuity Management perspective is that managers need to manage all employees, including those who do not adjust well. Managers manage healthy people, unhealthy people, and even employees who intentionally exploit emotional variances to create chaotic environments for their own ambitions. But the single most important answer to the question of "why fuss over a few people?" is that if even one person in a system is out of balance in a way that affects anyone else, the entire system is at risk. The most difficult part of the question is the inquiry about what emotion will tip the scale and set an emotional spin reeling.

That is absolutely as unpredictable as trying to know exactly where and when a tornado will touch down. The weather or climate creates strong indications and evidence that gets us close, but the tornado seems to have a mind of its own. Human emotional nature is like that also. Just when someone creates a foolproof methodology to manage emotions, some pesky person tips the balance in an unprecedented manner and the research starts again. Science can be fun!

There are indications of higher levels of possibility in weather and emotions. If you see a clear blue sky, there is less chance for a tornado. Looming black clouds in spring in Oklahoma raise the stakes. Emotionally charged risks elevate in emotionally charged climates. Managers have to watch for looming dark clouds, and be prepared to sudden storms. Of course, there is always the clear sky day that is free from tornadoes but hosts a wildfire or earthquake. Predictions and risks are filled with variables, some constant, some not so much.

Managing workplace emotions is a bit like gambling for really big stakes. Some companies gamble that they are immune from the risks of out-of-balance emotions. They make assumptions and make hunches and have hopes. This isn't bad thinking, but it is incomplete. Hoping for the best while planning for the worst is better for business.

Case Example
Beloved teacher and coach murdered at his work site (Benton City, WA, September, 2004).
Learning Byte
Violence at the work site is real and on the rise.

DO THIS: Learn to recognize the difference between regular and irregular problems.

DON'T: Mislabel an incident just because you haven't done your homework.

Experts claim that workplace violence rarely strikes without warning, but according to a new study on the issue, the majority of the work force does not recognize those potential warning signs. A recent study commissioned by the American Association of Occupational Health Nurses Inc. (AAOHN, www.aaohn.org) indicates the need for employee education and training on workplace violence. AAOHN's study found that nearly 20 percent of the entire work force claimed they have experienced an episode of workplace violence first-hand, yet the majority still do not know what to look for when it comes to determining potential offender characteristics (Randolph, 2004).

Healthy, well-adjusted people are less likely to be caught up in a workplace spin. These same people can be caught off guard during a time of personal vulnerability, or manipulated by a career spinner. Describing the risk factors of those people who are more likely and those who are less likely to turn some incident into a spin may begin with

Spins are *less* likely to happen as a consequence of:
• The Normal Problems/Incidents of Normal People; or,
• The Abnormal Problems /Incidents of Normal People.

Spins are *more* likely to happen as a consequence of:
• The Normal Problems/Incidents of Abnormal People; or,
• The Abnormal Problems /Incidents of Abnormal People.

ANNOYANCES

Happy, healthy, well-adjusted people get annoyed. They get angry and they get sad. They experience a wide range of emotions. What makes them "well-adjusted" is that they have found methods to help them adjust. They emotionally self-correct to changes in their environment. If you are sitting in a chair and your leg feels a cramp coming on, you adjust your position to move your body away from the discomfort. This is a physical adjustment.

Emotional adjustments are the same. A brief discomfort, or even an extreme emotional pain, is managed by reorganizing an emotional position. With a minor leg cramp, most people do not need to call an ambulance or begin screaming hysterically. A heart attack is different and demands a different response. In the same light most people do not go on crying binges at their jobs, throw chairs through windows, or become snipers if they have an emotional discomfort. They adjust. If a large or catastrophic emotional crisis occurs, adjustment may take longer. But well-adjusted people have methods, ideas, and support systems to help them adjust well. Less well-adjusted people also have methods, ideas and support systems to help them adjust. They just don't do it as efficiently or effectively. Where a well-adjusted person may reach out for a supportive word from a friend or a spouse, a less well-adjusted person may reach out for a pharmaceutical product. In terms of the workplace, both approaches to adjustment may keep people working and productive. The risks increase when either the well-adjusted person or the less-than-well-adjusted person cannot put their methods in place due to stress, interference, or interruption. What impedes or interrupts adjustment increases risk. As the capacity or ability to adjust diminishes, risk increases. Minor annoyances should require minor adjustments.

Case Example

Jane always adjusted well at work, no matter the crisis. During the power outage, she could not call her support system, and her stress increased. Transportation was not available, and she was isolated from her personal comfort and support items. She had never been without her support system. She found herself taking deep breaths and silently praying herself calm.

Lydia always adjusted well at work, no matter the crisis. During the power outage, she could not call her support system and her stress increased. Transportation was not available and she was isolated from her personal comfort and support items. She had never been without her support system. She began to cry. She couldn't stop. Efforts to support her from peers led her to become increasingly agitated. She was inconsolable and began to rave about the danger of the situation and within a short period of time she was convinced that she was going to die. She was gasping for breath and calling out to God to save her before it was too late.

Learning Byte

Both women had presented the same emotional adjustment skills prior to the crisis. Jane was able to access an internal strength she had not used before. Lydia found her outer as well as inner resources unavailable in crisis. What managers need to learn from this example is that both responses are reasonable to expect. Neither response should create a crisis within the crisis. If a manager is comfortable with emotions, they can add to the calm by remaining calm in the face of the chaos. This can be very comforting, supportive, and ultimately good for recovery and business.

DO THIS: Get comfortable with emotions as part of your job. Stay calm. See chaos as an interesting feature of life and work.

DON'T: Create a crisis inside a crisis..

Well-adjusted people generally tend to have the following recognizable traits. It is reasonable to transpose these traits into opposite terms to suggest what traits less than well-adjusted people might demonstrate:

Some Traits Of Well-Adjusted Employees

- Easily let go of past grudges
- Assume the best from one another
- Seek outside feedback carefully
- Do not participate in emotional drama
- Do not initiate emotional drama
- Put clients first
- Maintain a good attitude even during challenging times
- Use the chain of command to affect change
- Use policy format to offer complaints
- Do not hide memos or information from some staff and provide it selectively to others
- Strive for cooperation
- Verbally appreciate help given
- Show respect for each other
- Model appropriate business site sense of humor
- Do not participate in humor that includes inappropriate innuendos (sexual, racial, socio-economic, political, gender bias)
- Model flexibility
- Offer examples of personal truthfulness
- Show personal accountability
- Give and receive forgiveness
- Offer clear communication
- Demand and offer equality
- Perform the highest work ethics
- Complete and follow through with assignments
- Do not engage in second-hand gossip
- Do not spread or encourage rumors
- Actively participate
- Show consideration for others
- Stand by confidentiality standards
- Act professionally in the presence of clients

- Give more than just the minimum
- Work with cooperation between hierarchies
- Show courtesy in all situations
- Listen and respond to feedback
- Able to make compromise and contribute to positive dispute resolution
- Stand behind own opinion, yet open to negotiation
- Use non-violent communication methods

Case Example

Verma had an unexpected death in her immediate family. Prior to the death she had been a very stable adult. Verma took some sick time off work. She wanted to go back to work within two weeks but knew she was not ready to resume her normal workload. With the help of her counselor and manager, she negotiated a part time schedule until she would be able to work full time. The company had an Emotional Continuity Management grief procedure that included daily post-crisis updates with management.   Her grieving followed a normal pattern of ups and downs, and within the five month post-death period, she lost only 1½ days of work due to grief adjustment. She took lunches alone for the first three months. She was excused from some nonessential meetings. Gradually, she adjusted to the difficult change in her life without significant impact on the workplace. Verma was able to appropriately continue her grief-work at home with family, with her counselor, with her manager, and returned to her pre-crisis performance level within a reasonable time frame.

Learning Byte

This was an amazing team adjustment based on a compassionate Emotional Continuity Management plan that adjusted to an uncontrollable, emotionally loaded interruption. It could have turned into a failure for everyone involved, but with the help of some carefully structured ideas, policies and plans, adjustment happened and a valuable employee was retained and supported. Verma's loyalty increased as she healed.

DO THIS: Stay in touch with your own feelings as you are managing the feelings of others

DON'T: Be afraid of feelings. Being a human being can be difficult at times. Most people are okay!

VIOLENCE

Some individuals do not do well under even the most pleasant of circumstances. Managers need to know how to spot the early signs of difficulty and trouble before they erupt into more severe incidents. News headlines of the most significant forms of violence and upheavals happening at the workplace are not uncommon. Workplace violence rarely strikes without warning. Recognizing those signs is critical to safety. Because violence at work is becoming more prevalent the Federal Bureau of Investigation (FBI) created a list of "red flag" behaviors and common warning signs, usually seen in potential offenders. These first early signs on the FBI warning list include:

- Mood Changes
- Recent Personal Hardships
- Depression
- Anxiety
- Negative behavior (e.g., untrustworthiness, lying, bad attitude)
- Verbal threats
- Past history of violence.

    (www.fhshealth.org/foh/violence.asp,

According to the FBI, workplace violence can be defined as "*any action that may threaten the safety of an employee, impact the employee's physical or psychological well-being, or cause damage to company property.*" The FBI definition is a good place to begin a discussion, and the red-flags list is a good place to start paying attention to extreme emotional spins that may turn violent. However, this list is far from exhaustive or specific enough to be much help to most managers (www.fhshealth.org/foh/violence.asp and www.fbi.gov/publications.htm).

Violence can come out of the blue with absolutely zero warning — ZERO. It can also be preceded by small noticeable changes that when connected to an event (a firing, layoff, death, divorce, reprimand, grievance, or other business change) could sometime be predictive of a potentially violent episode.

Dr. Vali's Heads-up List

- Visible change in facial expressions (grimacing, scowling, frowns, blank-stare, rapid eye movements, biting lip or inside of cheeks)
- Change in voice tone or inflection (lower, higher, quieter, louder)
- Mumbling and denying (when asked what they said, they say something like, "never mind it isn't important," "nobody ever listens to me anyway," "whatever," or some other non-response)
- Fist clenching (white knuckles, or squeezing)
- Jaw clenching (tapping or grinding teeth)
- Nervousness (leg bouncing, foot tapping, finger rapping)
- Sighing (loud dramatic sighs or deep, slow breathing that is audible)
- Uncharacteristic behaviors (loud whistling or humming, pacing, slamming, chair rocking)
- Disassociation (a sense that the person is really "somewhere else" if you a talking to them, especially in a potentially threatening situation, during a reprimand, or grievance situation)
- Personalized attacks (verbal attacks that are personalized, such as "YOU have never listened," or JOHN isn't a team player, or THE MANAGEMENT HERE is against me.")
- Sudden extreme silence (an abrupt silence that feels impenetrable followed by any of the other previously mentioned behaviors)
- Eye contact extremes (either very eyeball-to-eyeball in a threatening manner, or total loss of eye contact)
- Exit (a sudden exit from a meeting, or worksite, or threatening situation)
- Opposite Behavior (pre-violent people can also act out in an oddly charming, ingratiating manner of sugary-sweet compliance and agreement that feels disingenuous)

STRESS AND SURVIVAL

Sometimes violence erupts when someone feels as though their very survival is threatened. Severe stress can trigger the human responses for basic survival, including violence. Physically and mentally, when threatened, people have an organic default system that is much like our ancestors. Research on the topic of survival mechanisms under circumstances of stress are plentiful from experts in physiology, psychology, sociology and biology. For managers who aren't interested or don't have time to get an advanced degree in the socio-bio-psycho-physiology of the autonomic nervous system (the fight-or-flight response of the mammal *homo sapiens*) it is probably sufficient to say that trying to survive threat is natural, and that behaviors associated with the need to survive are rarely cozy and attractive. Most living creatures have a survival instinct that can be triggered by real or perceived threat.

The human survival instinct at work may be suspected with:

- Need to avoid something or someone
- A desire or need to control something or someone
- Looming fear
- Real threat
- Perceived threat
- A desire for retaliation

- A need for attention
- The urgency of ambition
- A sacrificial sense of "doing for the company"
- Working for a required reward
- Having misguided loyalties
- Seeking a path of least resistance
- Conflict avoidance
- Seeking political gain or domination
- Having an out of balance sense of accountability for self or others
- Fatigue
- Illness
- Extreme Uncertainty
- Ignorance
- Poverty
- Lack of education or training

EFFECTS OF PRIOR TRAUMA

Many people who get up and go to work each morning are survivors of previous traumatic incidents. Most people adjust to trauma without complications that impact their working performances. People are more likely to do well at work then at home if they have had a trauma. They tend to put on a "work" face and get by. Then they go home and are tormented by reactions that encroach on their well-being. More than 25,3000,000 people will persist in their reactions to trauma to the extent that they could be classified as meeting diagnostic criteria for Posttraumatic Stress Disorder (PTSD). (Thomas, 2002)

Originally studied in war veterans who demonstrated a wide range of behaviors as a result of battlefield trauma, PTSD is no longer only applied to "battle fatigue" or "shell shock." According to experts in trauma management, half of the citizens in the United States will at some time in their life be exposed to a traumatic event. Approximately 8% will demonstrate persisting emotional reactions to the trauma to the degree that they may develop a stress disorder serious enough to require professional intervention (Kessler, 1995). People who have had prior trauma are more likely to perceive a threat in some situation than others who have not experienced a trauma in a similar situation. What this means to a manager is that because the effects of trauma may not be visible, there may come some situation at work that can trigger an old trauma. An employee who is your Rock of Gibraltar can suddenly fall apart at the seams or turn violent.

Although the timing is unpredictable, the statistical possibility is predictable. If you consider that half your employees may at one time or another have a trauma event in their lives, you should be prepared to respond appropriately and effectively if that trauma reappears at the worksite. Emotional residue from an old traumatic event that is reactivated may impact your work site. A new trauma certainly will impact your work site. An emotional spin may be the result of either situation if you are not expecting it to happen. And then your lack of expectation can add more emotional content to the emotional spin.

Case Example

The business had been robbed. The consultant had been called in to do a debriefing 72 hours after the incident. The primary victim was Darcy, a young cashier who was clearly shaken by the event and had expectable reactions. Surprisingly, another employee, Martha, who was in another area during the robbery was much more unsettled and demonstrated extreme, verbally angry behavior that was not consistent with the situation. After exploration during the debriefing, Martha began discussing this robbery as if it were her personal event. This extreme anxiety upstaged Darcy who just became more quiet and cried silently. It came out during the debriefing that Martha was reliving a robbery of twenty years ago that had not been debriefed. Martha had followed the crime with thirteen years of alcohol use to cope with ongoing anxiety. Although Martha had been clean for many years, this second robbery precipitated a PTSD relapse. Her manager encouraged her to get some help and referred her to a local counselor. Some individual counseling and a few 12-Step meetings facilitated her rapid recovery from the most recent and the past crimes. Martha did not have an alcohol relapse.

Darcy entered counseling within a month because although her recovery from the robbery incident went well, her marriage began to collapse. She saw that as a result of acquiring new confidences associated with learning new skills to be a healthy survivor, the marriage changed. Her spouse escalated his alcohol consumption while Darcy began to identify how to find joy in growth and personal development. Darcy made new choices because she did not want to remain a victim. The marriage ended within a year when Darcy's husband took over the victim role and found a new lover to drink with him in his burgeoning self-pity drama. Darcy struggled with the loss of the marriage, but stayed focused on her own recovery.

Learning Byte

Employers need to pay attention to PTSD because the statistics clearly indicate that trauma is not going away, and human responses to trauma are not going away either. In a work environment, the symptoms of PTSD can be managed by using the grieving model, identifying when the symptoms are too much for your work site, and offering compassionate understanding that PTSD is a choice. People who have had trauma and are in the percentage that experience and demonstrate PTSD do not need further guilt and shame heaped on top of their trauma — they need support. Managers do not have time to be counselors, but they can make a good referral to an expert in the community who does have credentials in managing the complications of PTSD.

DO THIS: Become knowledgeable about PTSD. Take a training. Hire someone to teach you. Read a book on the topic.

DON'T: Ignore this because it is more important and more prevalent than you would like to believe! PTSD might not get you but what if it gets your teammate or partner?

Stress reactions to crime, accidents, natural or man-made traumas and disasters are normal. People who do not have any signs of stress during or after extreme incidents are not normal. They may be, in fact, at higher risk for future stress reactions. The expectation that showing emotions means weakness is an expectation that does not serve recovery.

During the earliest phases of recovery from trauma, survivors tend to exhibit mild to moderate signs and symptoms of stress. Impending or extreme danger increases the response. Most normal reactions begin by looking quite extreme, but usually these are the symptoms that do not continue over time. Extreme reactions in the early phases of recovery exist as acute or temporary reactions. The symptoms to be concerned about are the ones that may appear two to three months or more after the incident. The employee to be concerned about is the one who forces bravado or has no response to something that is obviously traumatic to everyone else. Acute stress reactions can be extreme or subtle.

Chronic problems suggest a more long-term problem. A healing curve looks like a high spike in the earliest phases, levels off for a while, and then gradually decreases. A not-healing curve looks like a high spike in the earliest phases, levels off a bit, and then either spikes up and down many times, or does not decrease. A flat-line is *not* a good sign.

Well-adjusted and not so well-adjusted people usually have similar initial reactions to traumatic events. The difference is that well-adjusted people adjust to their strong emotions, and the less than well-adjusted struggle to regain their equilibrium and may take a bit longer to get there. Showing no emotions is not adjustment, it is pathology. All people who witness trauma or catastrophe will experience some or all of the following:

- shock
- terror
- blame
- anger
- guilt
- grief or sadness
- emotional numbing
- helplessness
- unhappiness
- loss of normal concentration
- difficulty with decision making
- memory changes
- disbelief
- disorientation
- confusion
- increased nightmares
- lowered self-esteem
- difficulty taking care of self
- blaming
- intrusive thoughts/memories
- worry
- feeling unconnected

SPIN STORIES

Anyone who has worked for very long has some story about a workplace event that was emotionally challenging. These stories range from small emotional spins to large collective dramas and traumas. Some of these "spin stories" are amusing water-cooler-war-stories when they turn out well. Others have ended in tragic catastrophe for individuals, groups or companies. Emotions are going to happen to people. Emotional Continuity Management is a process that allows human beings to be emotionally human whether feelings are simple and small or escalating into a complicated, full blown, contagious group-trauma.

Managers must understand that they cannot control emotions, although they can assist in the management of them. Past emotions may blow into the present to become "here-and-now" spin feelings. Future feelings can become worrisome fantasies of gloom and doom. Feelings that originate in the past or hover in the future are impossible to control and tough to manage. The problem for managers is that an employee who suddenly exhibits the long-term effects of some old wound that has nothing to do with work may believe they need to do something to control this old stuff. That is *not* a job for managers. That is a job for someone with mental health credentials.

The whoosh of old feelings that are unexpectedly triggered by some workplace issue may surprise the individual having the spin, as much as it surprises everyone else! This old set of feelings may have been covert, or hidden in some deep emotional pocket for a very long time. Without a crystal ball or advanced degrees in psychology it is difficult to predict such an episode. Therefore, it is prudent for a manager to recognize some early signs of a change in the wind and have some tools to manage a full range of variations in emotional response. It is also important to discern which emotions are simple "solo" spins (i.e., someone is having a really bad day or a serious emotional difficulty) and those that lead to collective or contagious group emotional F-5 tornado spins. Reading the following spin stories provide an opportunity for a manager to consider what would happen to their organization if these events were occurring. Which employees in your charge would be the most vulnerable? How would such a "story" play out in your company? Would it influence the bottom-line? How would you manage it?

Case Example

A consultant company is hired to increase efficiency within a major, science-based industry. It is told that its agenda is to create a process that eliminates "dead weight." There are over 700 people in the company. One group of 40 is engaged in a project that cannot be disturbed, so they will remain exempt from the process until the project is completed. The company creates a new process, with a buzzword called Re-Focusing. Each employee must now reapply, Re-Focus, for their position. The reapplication process takes approximately 3.5 days to complete at an average expense of $100.00 per day of salary. ($100.00 x 3.5 x 700=$245,000.00) Work stops during this process. Each employee is then either rehired or let go depending on their eligibility and qualifications. 12% of the non-exempt workforce are not rehired. The other 88% are reassigned new positions. No employee is in their original job. Employees that had been with the company for decades and developed expertise in their specialty are now in new positions with no expertise. The experts, who are in the exempt group, are not available for mentorship. The experts who mentor the exempt group are not available now either. Previous mentors are now learning new jobs. Tension and anger is elevated. One employee becomes incapacitated from the stress of the situation and loses several days of work. While decisions are being made as to who goes and who stays, loyalties shift. Stakeholders become acutely aware that they are expendable. The exempt team finishes its project. They are now required to go through the Re-Focus Project. They have been out of the collective company loop and are now thrown into it somewhat after the fact. Some employees are given a large bonus with the explanation that they will be given the dollar lump sum amount "as if" they had been promoted and given a raise. However, their status in the company will not be elevated, so that their social security and retirement benefits will not reflect that change. Some employees begin to seek work elsewhere. Several employees, who are within a few years of retirement shift loyalties away from a company they have given decades of service. Their interest in projects wane. They seek support outside the company

Case Example

Dear Dr. Hawkins Mitchell, I wanted to share with you a story about my previous job. We had a very dictatorial director for just a year. He would call people into his office and ream them out. For the women he would pull out a box of tissues when they started crying. There were ample counseling costs because employees had a great need to talk about it. We didn't hire a new director for another year and throughout that time people were compelled to talk about their awful experiences with him.

The replacement director was there for about six years. He had a very bad temper and would just explode. We lost employees during his reign although he went through at least one anger management program. We lost a top-notch executive secretary, three comptrollers, and a development director. We lost board members. When another company was interviewing him he asked us, his current staff, to put in a good word for him and to "be kind." We were afraid to tell the company the truth because we desperately wanted to get rid of him; I believe that is how he keeps getting jobs! C. Mitriella

Case Example

In a higher education setting one individual responsible for writing a million dollar grant repeatedly assured people that the work was progressing when in fact the person and the process were paralyzed. Close to the deadline the individual's supervisor discovered that little had been accomplished on the grant. An organization-wide effort completed the grant at the last moment. The one-week effort to write the grant cost the institution $12,000 in lost salaries in addition to a week's disruption of five other projects. In jeopardy were services to over 800 students, over a million dollars in grant funds, and four staff positions.

Case Example

Dr. Bleuer trashed his office at the university. His students had to climb over papers, books and objects literally a foot deep. No one complained because he was a "nice guy and a good teacher" and his office hours were short. Contact with him was at a premium. His secretary, Linda, was miserable trying to keep things in order in an effort to answer business calls and manage his schedule. Early on in their association, she had assumed it was a temporary situation and that he had just been too busy. She asked him how she could help him organize. He verbally attacked Linda and warned her not to interfere with his important work with her frivolous work and an apparent need to control him. She was embarrassed and confused. When he began dumping his garbage on her work area, she was afraid to ask him not to do that. He now controlled both his and her space with his clutter. She tried to work around it to the best of her ability. Dr.

Bluer had established his intentionality from the beginning. It was not negotiable; he believed he was entitled to trash his and her space. The secretary lasted eight months.

The next secretary, Connie, found the situation exactly the same. When she appropriately asked Dr. Bluer how she could help, he repeated his offensive behavior and raged at her. Connie laughed at him and was not intimidated. Dr. Bluer laughed also and gruffly gave her permission to "figure it out and leave me alone! I don't have time." Connie spent the next five months carefully designing a system of baskets and boxes and shelves to manage the multidimensional chaos of Dr Bleuer's creative mind and chaotic style. The professor would run through the door and toss his papers at Connie. She would then toss them into one of the many baskets or containers sitting around the office. After a while she noticed that he would toss them into the appropriate box or basket. On Secretary's Day, Dr. Bluer brought Connie flowers and tossed them at her. Then he asked her if it would be okay with her if he moved all the baskets into his office since it was now too hard to come out to her office to retrieve the papers he would throw on her desk. She gladly moved those baskets into his now much more well organized office space. The flowers looked better on her tidy desk without boxes.

Case Example

Max had just quit smoking. It was his first week at work without cigarettes. He was doing well and felt good about himself. At the weekly staff meeting, it was announced that the office now had a NO SMOKING policy in effect immediately. A few people cheered, a few grumbled, and there was light-hearted banter and friendly ribbing to those who were the smokers. The policy included an EAP series on Quitting Smoking, a special smoking area away from the building, and a non-judgmental atmosphere about the change in policy.

Max took it personally and felt defensive. He felt shame and anger about his years as a smoker and now he felt angry that smokers were being judged and scorned by the administration. It made him jittery and angry. He wanted a smoke. He knew he was detoxing and wanted to quit, but now he wanted to defend his smoking friends. He remembered how glad he was that he was a non-smoker now, but felt angry for the other smokers. He wanted to rescue them. He didn't know which side he was on. It reminded him of his family of origin when his parents found out he was a smoker. They were disgusted. He remembered getting caught behind the garage by his Dad and how small he felt and afraid to show his Dad his temper. He didn't let on how he felt at work either, and so he hid his feelings. It made him feel like a small child again. He started pacing about the office grumbling and complaining. His resolve to not smoke crumbled. He went outside for a smoke with a friend. They grumbled together. Max went back in the building and fumed all day. Toward the end of the afternoon he went into the restroom and smoked. The manager came in to the restroom and reminded Max about the new policy. Max blew up and stormed out of the office in righteous indignation. This time he wasn't going to just take it like a child, he was going to do something about it!! He took his old childhood anger at his Dad out on the manager. Before he even knew what was happening, a full tilt emotional spin was launched.

Lee had just quit smoking. It was his first week at work without cigarettes. He was doing well and felt good about himself. At the weekly staff meeting, it was announced that the office now had a NO SMOKING policy in effect immediately. A few people cheered, a few grumbled, and there was light-hearted banter and friendly ribbing to those who were the smokers. The policy included an EAP series on Quitting Smoking, a special smoking area away from the building, and there was a non-judgmental atmosphere about the change in policy. Lee felt relieved.

Case Example

Jay was a social drinker. Over time his drinking behavior escalated into dysfunctional drinking. His co-worker, Keven, thought there might be cause for concern when Jay would show up on Mondays obviously slammed from the weekend. On occasion Jay would have a few drinks at lunch. His use of mints and cologne did not hide his using behaviors. Jay missed a few work days here and there, and a few times these were during critical project crunch times. He began getting disturbing phone calls from his wife on Friday afternoons, and Mondays were a waste of time after each bad weekend.

Keven had always liked Jay and they had worked together for many years. Keven had considered Jay a work buddy and didn't want to make waves or cause any trouble, but did not know how to address this distressing behavior. After all, it was not really disturbing his production too much and he could cover, but it seemed to be getting a little worse and that was unsettling. Keven decided to live and let live and figured that it was none of his business what Jay did and tried to focus on his own work.

One Friday afternoon, after Jay had taken an extra long lunch, and returned with alcohol and mints on his breath as well as slurred speech, the boss sent a fax from the main office stating that he wanted Jay and Keven to deliver some key data to the next city that was about 85 miles from their location. Road trips had strict policy and procedures including the proviso that the senior man would drive. Jay was senior and management assigned Jay a company car as the driver. Now Keven had to get in the car with an obvious drunk or make a critical decision.

Case Example

As a heterosexual, politically correct, educated, compassionate white woman, Ami was working on her personal growth and examining her attitudes about life, including being politically correct on the topics of racism and homophobia. Recently divorced and raising children alone, she felt vulnerable and worked very hard at her new job. Her worksite training had included Diversity and Racism Training. Her boss was a lesbian. Her work partner, Syleena was also a lesbian, and a woman she admired greatly. The office had several women of color in key positions and Ami was excited and felt positively obligated, challenged and inspired about exploring her inner world and developing a more sophisticated and worldly life experience. She eagerly attended trainings on diversity, conflict resolution and Gay and Lesbian issues.

During her employment at the Center, Ami occasionally worked with another lesbian, Diane. Ami didn't really like or respect Diane as a person or professional. She just didn't feel comfortable with her style at work or in person, but wanted to be a good employee and made an effort at professionalism. Diane wanted to be close friends with Ami and invited her to socialize frequently. Diane continued to engage her in conversations about non-business topics and things of a personal nature, clothes, dress, dates, and so forth. Every time Ami resisted a personal relationship, Diane protested with statements about Ami being a closed-minded white woman, homophobic, and how hurt she felt. Diane would follow Ami to lunches and even came to her home uninvited on several occasions. Ami was trying to develop a new social life and so was trying to include all her new acquaintances and workplace colleagues into her life.

Diane suggested that Ami was discriminating against her because she was a lesbian and that she should make more of an effort to 'come around" to "reality thinking." Ami was concerned that Diane might be right. After all, what did she, as a heterosexual, white, divorced woman know about real life? She decided it might be her homophobia acting up and that she was indeed a bad person by discriminating. She really didn't know what to think. She agreed to go out for lunch with Diane to "try to get beyond it." She worked harder, read more books, attended more trainings, and asked questions.

Diane became more demanding and continued to complain that Ami was discriminated against her because of her sexual orientation. This was very stressful to Ami who really did care about human beings and their oppressions. Ami tried to socialize with Diane and it just never seemed to be enough or correct. Diane insisted that she go with her to a local Gay Bar if she really wanted to know about the lifestyle. Ami felt a lot of pressure from Diane. On one occasion, after a period of soul searching and frustration she finally took the risk to confide her difficulties to Syleena. Ami explained, with some embarrassment, that she just couldn't figure out how to move forward in this endeavor of being professional and appropriate to women with a homosexual orientation. She blamed herself and said that Diane often encouraged her to "try on the shoes of being a lesbian so she could have some compassion and really understand her world." Ami told Syleena that Diane suggested to her that her husband left her for another woman because she was probably really a Lesbian. She said Diane had offered to help her get more physically comfortable with "the real truth of her feelings" by offering to have sex with her.

Syleena immediately reassured Ami. She told her, "This struggle you are having with Diane is not because she is a Lesbian, and it's not because you are a Lesbian. It is because Diane is inappropriate and may actually be a sexual predator. This behavior is completely inappropriate both personally and professionally, and it isn't about homophobia. Let's go talk to the boss together."

Where Ami may have easily tossed off male aggressive predator behavior, she was blindsided by Diane's "we're just girlfriends" intimate hugs and touching. Syleena and her boss mentored her and explained that within the Lesbian culture, just like any other culture, there are good people and less than good people.

It had never occurred to Ami that she had been attacked at her workplace by someone who used the issues of diversity and human rights to offend.

Case Example

Gary loved his workspace window. It allowed him to stay on top of his claustrophobia. He used to take medications to manage his anxieties over this, but he was doing well in his new job and discontinued the prescriptions. Management decided to upgrade the office and move desks. Everyone agreed and was excited about the new change. Gary did not want anyone to think he was weird or trying to hog the window and he became anxious. He felt stupid and weak. He couldn't express his preferences to management because he felt humiliated about his anxiety and that a small window meant that much to a grown man. His anxiety escalated and led to other self-defeating thoughts and behaviors that he had put away long ago. His production diminished. His marriage became strained. He felt like he had failed when he went to his doctor for more medications.

Case Example

Chris had an abusive childhood and managed long-term recovery with the help of a therapist and a support group. When the office changed a procedure, Chris had trouble making the adjustment and consistently forgot the new procedure. After making a number of minor errors management called Chris in to find out what was going on, and followed it with a reprimand. Chris apologized and felt horrified and ashamed, which was reminiscent of childhood abuse feelings. Chris felt helpless and lost confidence. It took a number of extra therapy sessions to address this shift, and performance evaluations suffered in the meantime. Chris lost an important promotion. A new employee cost the agency significantly more than promoting internally.

Case Example

Bill was frantic. As a Gulf War Veteran, he had been successfully dealing with his PTSD issues with weekly counseling sessions. The company decided to change health insurance providers to a managed care system that did not include mental health provisions. Bill had to decide how to handle this because he could not afford the counseling sessions out of pocket, there were no other counselors in the area that specialized in PTSD, and he knew that he needed ongoing care to manage his feelings of anger and betrayal. He started transferring his emotions toward the company that seemed to betray him. He knew this was not appropriate thinking and that his PTSD had been triggered. He didn't know what to do.

Case Example

Elijah was annoyed. The woman in the next cubicle ate all day long. If she wasn't snacking on hard candy and opening little crackling wrappers, she was eating apples, or popcorn. He couldn't see her over the cubical divider, but he could hear her shuffling about all day long as she worked, hummed little tunes, and made noises associated with either eating or preparing to eat something.

Learning Byte

Life is amazing and emotions are part of life. Spinning goes with the territory.

The old thinking that emotions were bad for the competitive edge of business now needs to be reframed to state that poorly managed emotions are bad for the competitive edge.

DO THIS: Take a few moments to remember some of your personal spin stories.

DON'T: Forget that you have survived lots of spins already and are now ready to be an expert on the management of emotional spinning.

MENTAL HEALTH CONCEPTS FOR THE MANAGER DIAGNOSTICIAN

This section of the text is not intended to be an expansive book on mental health. It is designed to give the manager an overview of human behaviors in a way that will allow him or her to make good business decisions based on a range of information — from hard data to soft, gut-level reactions or hunches backed up by rational information. This is also not intended to help you hold the hand of an employee whose pet gerbil died. Human behavior and mental health is very complicated and based on countless measurable and immeasurable variables which include genetics, experience, perception, cognition, nutrition, health, values, morals, environment, ethnicity, personalities, perceptual and learning styles, and brain function, just to mention a few. The following charts are intended to open up the previously mysterious world of human emotions in order to begin a dialogue between people who work with people. At the same time psychological information is not rocket science and SHOULD NOT BE the sole domain of one group of people.

Experts and specialists in the field of psychology and mental health spend years studying and trying to comprehend the details of their topics. They will be good resources for you. But managers who must manage in the midst of human emotional drama on a daily basis need to have competency about human emotions in order to manage people. It is astonishing to find so many managers who have no people skills and no information about emotional norms. Often this is not their fault, due to the historically exclusive nature of psychology. Some would say there is a subtle agenda to keep it mysterious and exclusive. Less than fifty years ago, an aunt or grandparent would have been considered an expert in human emotions. Today it seems a requirement to find a specialist. It is true that there are some conditions and issues that are too difficult and complicated to deal with and that makes a specialist quite useful. There are also many levels of human emotions and mental health that are easily managed and not at all mysterious.

Certainly, clinical medical or mental health diagnosis is not appropriate for managers unless they have advanced training and specialized credentials. However, when an educated and conscientious manager smells the fragrance of a freshly peeled orange, catches a brief glimpse of the color orange in the wastebasket, and finds orange peelings in the waste basket, it is absurd to think that the manager should not take the leap of faith to consider the possibility that there was an orange present in a business. And if that office has an "orange-free policy," the manager will be required to manage this. And for a manager to say something like, "Well, I'm not an orange grower so I guess I shouldn't say anything," is patently absurd. A well-seasoned manager must be able and willing to take the risk to say, "Hey, someone had an orange. I trust my perception and if I cannot, then I'll call in an orange specialist. I have list of orange experts in my policy files, so I'm safe and ready to take the risk of telling the higher-ups that there was an orange in the basket. They get to decide if it matters, but I have to manage the consequences of an orange user in my department because I also know that everyone else smelled the orange too." Contrary to some opinions, managers are human beings and with the exception of a few, are mentally healthy and would easily recognize the "smell" of someone who was exhibiting behaviors or emotions that were not reasonable for the workplace.

The combination of perceptions and direct experiences that a manager has, when documented in measurable and visible details, added to hunches and ideas, creates a more complete picture of reality when dealing with the potential range of employee emotions. Managers need permission to think outside the traditional parameters of management to include emotions as measurable risks to productive and safe employees. Managers need permission to recognize psychological features from psychological experts, from company administrators, the profession of managers, and from themselves. As you go through the following presentations of differing ways to think about emotions think about what you already know

HEALTHY, DYSFUNCTIONAL, AND PATHOLOGICAL PEOPLE

As you begin to differentiate between how to deal with the variety of emotional responses from employees, it is valuable to see them along a continuum in their level of functioning in the world. On one end of the continuum is the health employee, the poster child of mental health, company morality, function, task management, social capacity, and ethics. At the other end of the continuum would be the pathological employee, the employee who just cannot do the job, who fights and struggles with every task, is not liked by others, is abrupt or uncomfortable to be near. There is another branch of the continuum that shoots off the end of the pathological chart. That is the Emotional Terrorist who is willing and able to sacrifice others for a personal goal or agenda

Use the following analogies to begin getting more comfortable with the continuum:

The Healthy Car Analogy

If you want to take a trip, and actually get there while also enjoying the scenery, you want a car that is HEALTHY, a car that is functional. It gets you from here to there. A High Order Healthy car just needs fuel and an occasional window washing. Driving this car is a delight. A Middle Order Healthy car needs regular oil checks, tire rotations, and an occasional wiggle of the spark plugs. Perhaps the glove box gets a little stuck. It still gets you where you want to go without much effort. A Low Order Healthy car is one that requires frequent replacements of spark plugs, extra oil on a regular basis, needs to warm up before you drive it, the third gear sticks and must be wiggled just right, the outside mirrors wiggle out of place, and you never think about leaving without a spare tire. But you still get there without major concerns and you get to enjoy the scenery on the way because regular maintenance will generally keep the car functioning adequately. Some healthy vehicles look cosmetically perfect. Some look like they just came from a wrecking yard. You don't really need to worry.

The Dysfunctional Car Analogy

Dysfunctional cars might get you to your destination and they might not get you there. They need occasional or constant support to keep running. Even with constant help there is no guarantee that the dysfunctional vehicle will make it through the journey. Even with all the preparation and maintenance, it is a risk. Unfortunately, over the long haul they are vulnerable to breakdowns. High Order Dysfunctional cars usually get you there, but you have to take a few spare parts in the trunk, check the oil, watch the gauges and be on alert for random strange sounds. Middle Order Dysfunctional cars need more care and attention and the glove box doesn't even close. You are pleased if you get somewhere, and not surprised when you don't. Low Order Dysfunctional cars break down every few miles and there is no time to watch the scenery out the window. These clinkers rarely make the trip worthwhile or enjoyable due to the high level of maintenance required to micro-manage every detail. The dysfunctional car starts incurring costs. You may have to join a towing membership club, keep a cellular phone available for breakdown, or hire a mechanic to ride with you to help keep it going. Some dysfunctional vehicles look cosmetically perfect. Some look like they just came from a wrecking yard. You worry.

The Pathological Car Analogy

Pathological cars don't get you there safely, if at all. They tend to catch on fire under the hood and may explode before you even see much smoke. They may randomly swerve into oncoming traffic. The brakes may fail as you are going around an important curve and the windows don't open if it plunges into the river. The head gaskets crack under any sort of pressure. The rubber comes off the tires at 55 m.p.h. The engine might not start no matter what you give up in the process. In fact, they control the entire vacation and take up your time looking for ways around the delays. You spend time seeking other modes of transportation while hoping the vehicle suddenly turns into something functional. High Order Pathological cars sometimes have an interesting capacity for crime…they are the stolen cars that run well, but are on their own agenda. They may be confiscated before you get to your destination. And you might unknowingly become an accessory to the crime. They may appear very powerful or very calm just before they kill you with carbon monoxide. Middle Order Pathological cars are wannabes — soapbox derby cars with no motors. They have the flash but not the power. Low Order Pathological cars are usually easy to spot. They may barely be recognizable as a vehicle. Or they are the lemon cars that someone else traded in that looks good, but has been involved in a fatal accident or cleaned up after someone committed suicide in the front seat. They might look very good cosmetically, but under scrutiny do not measure up. They may look shiny in the driveway and make you look very cool, but don't put your kids in the backseat and head for the Grand Canyon because no one would survive.

THE RANGE OF HEALTHY, DYSFUNCTIONAL, AND PATHOLOGICAL EMPLOYEES

		LEVEL OF CAPACITY TO FUNCTION IN SOCIETY		
		HIGH	MEDIUM	LOW
LEVEL OF FUNCTIONING	HEALTHY	The shaker and the mover	The capable and the helpful	The well intentioned and the steady
	DYSFUNCTIONAL	The present and accounted for and troubled	The present and troubled and needy	The randomly absent, troubled and needy
	PATHOLOGICAL	The criminal and the manipulative and ill and brilliantly successful	The criminal and manipulative and ill and needy with less success	The incapable and removed from society

VARIABLES OF HEALTHY, DYSFUNCTIONAL AND PATHOLOGICAL PEOPLE

HEALTHY	DYSFUNCTIONAL	PATHOLOGICAL
Basically Happy	Basic Unhappiness	Altered States
Positive Tools	Limited Tools	Negative Tools
Skills	Limited Skills	Skills
Options	No Options Thinking	Options
Tracks Well	On and Off Track	Private Track
Reality Based	Realities Shift	Distortions
Stable	Unstable	Charismatic
Manages Loss	Fear of Loss	Controls all Loss
Flexible	Less Flexible	Rigid
Belongs	Wants to belong	Prefers Ownership
Influential	Vulnerable to influence	Exploitative

ORDERLY DISORDERS AND DISORDERLY DISORDERS

> **DISCLAIMER**: *Although these aspects may signify a potential problem, only a trained professional can evaluate whether the degree is significant enough to warrant diagnosis or treatment. Most human beings have some of each one of these aspects. It is the degree and use of these aspects which signify a potential problem. This information should not be used in any way to diagnose, treat or discriminate against any persons without the assistance of a trained, licensed or appropriately certified mental health professional such as a:*
> - *State Certified or Licensed Mental Health Counselor (Master's level or more)*
> - *State Certified or Licensed Social Worker (Master's level or more)*
> - *Licensed Psychologist*
> - *Medical Doctor or Psychiatrist*
> - *Credentialed EAP Provider (Master's level or more)*

Clinically diagnosable mental disorders come in a wide array of size, shapes and dimension and present themselves in quite a variety of equally interesting demonstrations. The Mental Health profession has, for the sake of treatment, intervention, research, and insurance reimbursements, labeled with terms like depression, anxiety, chemical dependency, schizophrenia, antisocial personality disorder, borderline personality disorder, eating disorders, sleeping disorders, thinking disorders, rage disorders and violence disorders, to name a few. Some diagnosed mental disorders have small presentations and symptoms, and others have ponderously enduring patterns of extreme and bizarre behaviors that are markedly different from what most people consider "normal" in western culture. Employees with these problems may look like everyone else, be well dressed, and show up to all meetings, but under extreme stress, medication disruptions, or other challenging circumstances, they may end up acting differently because of the way their personality seems to be structured or functioning.

How they adjust to changes at a work site can be very different. They may be very successful at adjusting under regular circumstances. Managers who know they have people on board with mental illness can usually openly discuss with them about what they might need during a crisis. Just as a manager who knows that the receptionist is diabetic and may need to call for assistance if her medications fail, managers should have the same knowledge about managing a mental illness. Chronic illness does not need to interfere in any workplace strategy. It does need to be factored into Emotional Continuity Management planning. Stress might make the person with diabetes more at risk during a crisis, but his or her daily work is not a risk factor.

Mental illness should be treated with the same deference, supported well, managed well, and taken into consideration as a risk factor. Of course, if the receptionist with diabetes keeps it a secret, or the person with a diagnosed mental illness does not disclose, the manager will be left with the risk of the unexpected response during a crisis.

A word of caution goes here. Because the world is filled with prejudice and fear, the majority of people with a chronic physical or mental disorder will NOT disclose to you. This is a business expectation and people will try to hide what many perceive as weaknesses to keep their jobs. It would be a better world if this were not true, but managing the truth of the situation means you need to have a cursory understanding of the most prevalent disorders to protect yourself from surprises. You should recognize signs and symptoms of diabetes, coronary disease, epilepsy, severe allergic reaction, contagious disease, poisoning, and have a basic knowledge of first aid and CPR. You should also recognize the signs and symptoms of a mental illness that is suddenly exacerbated.

Employees with special needs often make good employees. This has been well established in the business community. Special needs employees generally require some extra attention during a crisis. For example, employees who worked in the World Trade Center had special training to deal with evacuating people in wheelchairs in case of emergency. This training procedure saved several lives in the 2001 attacks. Disaster planners and business continuity planners take these special issues into consideration and have found that employees with special needs do well with an "emergency buddy." Some companies are advanced enough in thinking that they provide system-wide training on the emergency requirements of their special needs employees. Managers can do this if given the supportive environment required to consider all employees as valuable resources. If not, it will probably be up to you to provide services.

There are clear rules, procedures, codes, symptoms, listings and criteria that mental health providers use to establish a diagnosis of mental illness. Medical professionals are trained to tell the difference between a cold and cancer and mental health professionals are trained to tell the difference between a personality difference and a personality disorder. The diagnostician considers a full range between simple and wild possibilities and then narrows it down to the most likely. This process is called a "diagnosis of exclusion." The diagnostician further narrows down the possibilities to the most likely possibilities given the signs, symptoms, and hunches of the diagnostician. The practitioner may perform some testing prior to confirming the diagnosis or may have seen it so often that they can diagnose on the spot. Sometimes the diagnosis is so obvious that testing is not necessary.

Diagnosis is followed with the most efficient forms of treatment with ongoing assessment to determine if the condition is responding to treatment, getting worse, or improving. Mental health professionals use a tool called the *Diagnostic and Statistical Manual of Mental Disorders* (American Psychological Association, www.apa.org) to standardize the naming of the disorders. The disorders must meet a specific number of features for a specific length of time to be considered diagnosable. A few of the more prevalent diagnoses are listed below. Reviewing the following list is simply the first step for managers to think about employees as perhaps more than they may appear on the surface. Keep in mind there is a range in each of these categories and there are always exceptions. A common response when learning these labels is to diagnose everyone including yourself — don't go there! Even people without mental illness have moments in their lives where they are so temporarily disturbed that they think they are losing their minds. Mental illness is different in that it represents an enduring pattern of thinking or behaving.

PARANOIA	Suspicious that others are exploiting, harming, or deceiving him/her
SCHIZOID	Does not want and does not enjoy relationships, including with family
SCHIZOTYPAL	Odd beliefs or magical thinking behaviors that are very different than other people
ANTISOCIAL	Does not feel the need to accept the regular rules of society, does not respect laws, and repeats illegal activities
BORDERLINE	Makes significant and special efforts to avoid real or imagined abandonment
HISTRIONIC	Needs to be the center of attention all the time
NARCISSISTIC	Exaggerated sense of self importance, all life revolves around "me"
AVOIDANT	Avoids life and work activities that involve interpersonal contact, hates criticism, fears disapproval, or rejection so disapproves and rejects first
DEPENDENT	Has a very hard time making everyday decisions. Needs extreme contact for advice and reassurance
OBSESSIVE COMPULSIVE	Preoccupied with details, rules, lists, order, organization, schedules, and demands perfectionism that interferes with regular activities

Why should a manager think about mental health diagnosis? Our society continues to maintain a strong aversion to mentally ill people. Although some conditions make it impossible for people to function well, there are countless degrees of mental impairment that are well managed with medications, counseling, and support. If an employee has a diagnosed mental illness or impairment, or one that is obvious, the manager is pre-aware that there will be special issues to consider during normal and abnormal working conditions. Many businesses, for example, hire individuals with mental retardation, Downs Syndrome and developmental delays, and enjoy their contribution to the organization. A business continuity plan will usually include any special needs for these valued employees. It should be noted though that under duress, their needs may vary from the norm. This is also true for employees with other mental illnesses, diagnosed or not.

Businesses and managers have hesitated to take an active interest in the mental or emotional well being of employees due to the appropriate concern that they do not have basic or advanced training in discerning differences in wellness. Indeed, many normal behaviors of healthy people are very odd. Some mental impairments or disorders can mask themselves as other things. It is difficult for professionals to know what is going on when one symptom looks like four other things. For example, numb and tingling fingers can be caused by a pinched nerve from sitting too long in one position with your hand on a computer mouse, or be the early signs of a serious and even deadly disease. It is hard to know what is what.

A grand source of amusement to educators is that most medical students are certain they are going to die of some horrible death as they identify the symptoms for every disorder as they study. Mental health students do the same thing when they are studying symptoms of mental disorders. They know they have this or that disease, as do their friends, families, and strangers. Many of the symptoms of serious problems look a lot like regular things to start with. This is why doctors and mental health professionals use clear scientific technical tools like books, scientific studies, evaluations, tests, seminars and information sharing as well as nontechnical tools like staff meetings, discussions, ideas, and personal hunches. Technical and nontechnical data is important to an efficient diagnosis. Therefore, if you see some of these signs and symptoms in yourself, your spouse or best friend, or employee, try not to overreact. Pay attention, make a mental note, observe and ponder. Take your time. If it is not life-threatening, you will have time to make a good observation and evaluation.

If an employee appears to behave in a way which interferes with workplace functioning, then the signs or symptoms may indicate a problem or an issue which suggests an individual may be operating with a significant past, current, or emerging impairment. Your job as a manager is to be aware of this as it influences the workplace so that it does not turn into a systemic emotional spin. You do *not* need to diagnose or treat people with impairment. You *do* need to have an excellent working knowledge of impairment categories. Impaired employees deserve excellent support, referrals, information, opportunity, remediation, or release with dignity. Many organizations now provide internal treatment programs for impaired employees. Everyone has some reflection of impairment features because these are, in fact, human features.

An example of one way you can think about this is to consider that many regular people have times when they may feel a little bloated, not hungry, or are concerned with their weight. This does not interfere with work to a great degree; that is human. Someone with the clinical Mental Disorder of Anorexia is obsessively compelled to control these normal feelings in an extreme manner by not eating at all, sometimes for weeks and months to the point of near-death. They may take a sick day if they are upset over eating an almond. Missing lunch can make an average employee a bit spacey and off-track for the afternoon; anorexia can create an increasing loss of mental capacity, create secondary illnesses, and distort the decision making capacity of the individual. If someone with unmanaged anorexia is in a key position, this is an important management consideration. This employee will need management. Your other employees will, as well. Direct time loss can accrue from other employees who are concerned or angry about this person's weight loss, without understanding that their thinness is not cosmetic but unnatural.

An employee with the mental disorder of bulimia will have to control their normal feelings of eating and feeling full after a meal with forced vomiting or extreme use of laxatives. Constant vomiting or ritual laxative use can interfere with workplace tasks. The normal person may have momentary issues of fullness after food, or a desire to lose those love handles; someone with Bulimia will also have extreme responses to eating that one almond.

An employee who is clinically paranoid may think that pesky almond is tainted with anthrax. Of course in today's world that is not as paranoid as it may have been a few years ago. The difference is that the paranoid person will act on this terror in ways that are not functional. A regular employee may question the anthrax on the almonds, look for signs of white powder, and even insist that you toss the almonds out. The paranoid person will go through the same behaviors, but will take it a few more steps. They may need to have the building sealed, the counters that the almonds sat on replaced immediately, or start an emotional spin in the company that no one is safe.

It is not the *disease* that will interfere with performance — it is the unmanaged *symptoms*. Managers should know the differences between normal and abnormal reactions. A local mental health counselor or EAP professional would no doubt be more than happy to teach you what signs to watch for in your worksite.

HOW PEOPLE RESPOND TO GETTING HELP

Healthy employees are eager to find ways to make their lives easier. Regular people *like* assistance. Healthy people may fuss a bit because they perceive themselves as competent and want that acknowledgment from others. But again, healthy people adjust quickly. Dysfunctional people and those with pathology have a different response to needing or receiving help. They resist. Resistance is *interesting*.

Resistance usually indicates you have bumped up against something that creates some kind of a threat, real or perceived. People who resist opportunities to work easier and feel better are giving managers a sign that something is in the way of good and healthy responses. Resistance is a very important clue to a manager.

Here is one way to look at resistance. An ill patient comes to a doctor with symptoms and the physician diagnoses the disease and prescribes antibiotics. Most patients are interested in taking the medications if they are truly interested in health. What kind of a patient would resist the medicine? Resistance suggests sabotage, fear, or a need to control something. When patients are noncompliant about medical treatments that are simple and meant to help, and then return to the doctor complaining that "things are not better," the clinician has to take time to explore the resistance. If the patient wants a second opinion, that is not resistance — that is research. Resistance is a stronger process. Resistance is a force that is used to *control* something.

Managers bump into resistance when they offer up solutions, plans, and ideas to keep things rolling along productively and seem to hit a wall. When managers hit a wall of resistance they should take note that they have bumped into some sort of threat. Don't immediately take it personally. Stop and think, and slow the process down a little. If you resist the resistance, you will create conflict and possible spinning. Before you try to "fix" the apparent problem, first evaluate where the threat originates. The threatened person may try to suggest it is you or your idea. This is not usually the case. Someone who is not threatened can simply say, "no." Someone threatened will resist and create force to control a fear of a boundary not being respected. Managers need to respect the boundary that is created by a resistance, evaluate it, and see if what they are proposing is appropriate, necessary, and negotiable. Perhaps you can tweak your idea slightly to remove a threat. But that is a discussion that will come after you step away from the resistance.

Generally, healthy people appreciate a policy that manages emotions in the workplace because they have been interrupted by emotions and are annoyed by emotional disruption and disturbance. They welcome procedures that help everyone. Unhealthy people resist Emotional Continuity Management plans, policies or procedures because they feel the need to protect themselves from some real or perceived threat.

Responses To Emotional Continuity Management Plans

	THUMBNAIL SKETCH	RESPONSE TO ECMP
HEALTHY	Salt of the earth, fun, pleasant, groomed, inclusive, engaged with life, open, thoughtful, manage their emotions well, are open with feelings, positive and negative, are compassionate, reasonable, fairly consistent over time, have a life.	Looks forward to growth and development. May have some concerns about time involved or group commitment, but eager to see the results of more clarity and definitions of policies. No resistance.
DYSFUNCTIONAL	May be open to growth with some minor fears to larger fears, naive, young or old, has not been given the correct information, for some reason is in a weakened state, vulnerable to suggestions and influences, subject to emotional swings, able to be coerced by a stronger influences, positive or negative. Emotions are more central, may be hard worker with limited skills and options, differing levels of willingness to be taught.	Have the potential to be remediated, trained, informed and educated. May value or fear growth and development. Minor resistance.
PATHOLOGICAL	Has an agenda and a mission, willing to destroy people, places and things to protect themselves or their personal beliefs and agendas, even when masked as the "greater good." May be using individuals or the entire system for their agenda or as a legitimate cover, may target others who appear to threaten their agenda. Emotions may be central or invisible.	May resist remediation. May escalate their efforts, go underground, or leave. Emotional escalation is traceable to them and therefore easy to remedy, more difficult if they go underground or covert. Once underground they may be at risk for participating in sabotage, selling proprietary information, or other ethical violations. Early identification of these employees protects all concerned. Major resistance, either passively or aggressively, either overtly or covertly.

INTUITION AND IMPROVISATION

Millions of human beings from many different cultures, religions and traditions believe that intuition exists and has a place in life and hence in the business environment. Whether you are one of these people or not you can seek out the variety of new web sites that are blossoming on the topic of Power Hunches and the Intuitive Business. Just like any other tool, intuition can be used or discredited. That discrediting of intuition usually is accompanied by discrediting the existence of other strong human intangible experiences, like "feelings." This has not served people or business because it misses an important part of the whole. Businesses that want to operate from wholeness and not fragmentation will encourage the presence of the seen as well as the unseen, the visible and the invisible attributes that make a business work. Intuition is not the whole picture of humans, any more than rational thought is the whole picture. Good business, and excellent management make room for rational as well as intuitive thinking.

Some people have a very active intuition and others have either a slow-burner or an atrophied sense of it. Some deny its' presence, others ascribe it to the domain of the occult and hence evil. Still other try to have their intuitive nature removed through absolute use of logic and reason and others spend billions of dollars on enhancing it through mysticism and quasi-religious procedures. Perhaps all that is reasonable to discuss in terms of management practice is that there is more than meets the eye in emotional experiences, and hunches and intuition are useful parts of it.

Business scholars and research scientists are now looking at intuition with careful and serious consideration. New research is exploring how the systematic removal of the innate and instinctive human dynamic from the workplace is counterproductive. Most regular people know there is more to life than meets the eye. Business and science are slowly catching up. Since most people know (although some would hesitate to admit publicly) that there is another part of the self that isn't tangible, business has forced all attention to the product that is consumable and tangible. This is not wrong when well balanced. This is business. Billions of research dollars are spent in determining and predicting what consumers want. Wanting is not a tangible. A lot of wanting is intuitive. Another billion dollars is spent in finding out why the research didn't match up with what people actually bought. Companies are financing major studies on how to measure human intangibles in order to control markets and consumer interest. Intuition is just one of the intangibles that is being researched. Did you have a hunch about that?

Left-brain-rational-thinking-bean-counting-old-world business-types raise their collective eyebrows on the topic of intuition. The topic gets assigned into a general wastebasket category labeled that "Fuzzy, HR, Flaky, Soft, Touchy-Feely" stuff. They forget that many of the biggest business deals in history were based on "hunches." Great power hunches have led to great deals and great discoveries which have employed countless millions of workers to develop, research and implement these 'fuzzy" notions of mad business geniuses who are now rich and retired on their private island and having beverages with little umbrellas. Take some time to go on the internet and research Power Hunches and Business Intuition. You may be surprised.

Case Examples

1. The Phone Rang. Lucie knew it was her daughter before she answered it. She answered it. Her intuition made her feel warm and connected. She shared this story with her manager who also had a daughter. They enjoyed the intuitive nature of their bond with their children. The manager tended to seek out this employee for ideas about how to manage other young female employees.

2. The Phone Rang. Wendy knew it was her daughter before she answered it and had a tone of annoyance in her voice because she didn't want to be disturbed at work by her children. Wendy always ignored her intuitive connection to her children so that she could concentrate on her work and not on her feelings of guilt for leaving them with a daycare provider. Her intimate connection to her children's feelings, even when she wasn't with them, frightened her and increased her guilt. She decided it was not rational to have such feelings. She focused her energies into technology and logic and avoided all emotional connections at work. Her manager and other employees liked her work performance but didn't like to be near her.

3. Saundra had a bad feeling about Karl. She felt uncomfortable when he was around. He offered her a special position. She listened to her intuition and passed on the offer. She was going to confide in her manager but her intuition told her not to do that. Instead, she shared her concerns with her sister who lived in the same city. Later Karl was eliminated from the team for ethical violations including sexual harassment. The manager defended him until it turned out she had been involved in an affair with Karl.

4. Hillary didn't like how she felt in the presence of her manager Dylan but felt guilty because he was so nice to her. Dylan gave her special help and even offered to see her on the weekends to help her raise her job skills. She felt uneasy and odd that a manager would take such extra time but ignored her intuition in lieu of special favors. She tried to think it through and couldn't find a good reason to ignore his offers. Dylan made Hillary his assistant and became sexually aggressive with her. Hillary came to believe he was in love with her and she decided she was going to go up the corporate ladder with this manager as he grew professionally. Her inner voice of intuition continued telling her to take it slow and easy, but Dylan's affectionate solicitations were powerful, and everything he said made perfect sense. When Dylan was terminated and accused of fraudulent activities she couldn't explain why her name was on several of his project documents that included ethical and legal violations. She tried to share his rational explanations but they did not make sense now and she could not explain them. Hillary was terminated

Learning Byte

Intuition exists. You can use it as part of the picture or ignore it.

DO THIS: *Think of a time in your life where you experienced an intuitive moment*

DON'T: *Overestimate or Underestimate the value of intuition in the workplace.*

AUTHOR'S AFTERTHOUGHTS

It is absurd for me to write about this topic, because it isn't something managers want to know. The few brave souls who stand as warriors in the face of the rational machine of business and try to stalwartly advocate for intuition and human emotions risk professional "life and limb" in the effort.

I wish I had done a study on how many managers seek me after the lecture and whisper to me about their job situation. I get hugs and handshakes, knowing smiles and great evaluations. And then? Companies continue to ignore emotions. The echoes reverberate through the system, "We don't have enough money, enough time, enough training, enough staff to look at this stuff." I want to echo back, "Do the math!!!"

But then some manager tells me how they have seen all the chaos first hand. I especially remember the eyes of people in New York City in the fall of 2001. Everywhere I went the eyes bore into me with, "Did you see it? Were you here? Are you one of us?" If you want to see what the eyes of New Yorkers looked like, check out a copy of Vanity Fair, October 2001. These are the eyes of people who have had a very close-up look at something very, very scary. I see that look in managers eyes sometime as they look at me during a seminar. They see the emotions close-up and personal. And some of them are scared, and scared of being scared. Scared doesn't get promotions. Managers have "the look."

Healthy, dysfunctional and pathological people are everywhere on the planet, not just at work. Before I started doing Emotional Continuity Management consultations in companies, I knew that there was a range of people on the planet from wonderful to horrible. The first company I was hired by had an emotionally spinning person in a key position. When a beloved employee was murdered during the middle of the consultation, this employee, in a key position, convinced the majority of the staff that they didn't "need any damn counselor to talk with about feelings, because I'm here for you." She said she would do it for them and in her position of power held them hostage. Managers and line staff actually had to sneak to my private office in another city to try to deal with their emotions about the murder and their tyrannically controlling manager. I did not have an official opportunity to diagnose the manager's mental illness, but I had no doubt what it was and how it influenced the company.

DISCUSSION QUESTIONS

- What are your biases about mental illness?

- What are the biases of your company about impaired employees?

- What are some signs of behaviors that are normal in small amounts but have more risk potential if they are more frequent or extreme?

- What is your definition of healthy? Dysfunctional? Pathological?

4

REFRAMING:
WHAT DO SPINNERS LOOK LIKE?

I had to stop seeing my employees as monsters who were out to kill me. (S. Leedner, HR Health Delivery Systems Manager)

My manager looks like my ex-husband and every time he talked I would just shut down. I reframed him as a space alien who was just a fake clone of my ex-spouse and started chuckling to myself. Now I am much more open to his managing because I pretend he is from another planet that isn't hostile to earth. So when I am managing others and they give me that look of annoyance, I pretend they are from another planet also so I must treat them like guests on earth. This increases my humor and my courtesy skills. (A. Danzer, IT Manager)

But Dr. Vali, you don't understand! My manager is the most horrible witch you could imagine! I swear she rides a broom! (J. Dalaniek, Nuclear Industry Project Manager)

My manager is a wimpy, wishy-washy, person who never gets anything done. I have never met anyone so incompetent and stupid. My dog is smarter! If my manager was a dog my dog would eat him for breakfast. (I. Komneri, Medical Technology Manager)

WHY YOU SHOULD READ THIS CHAPTER

Reading this chapter may be the most odd part of this book and may appear to be the most useless and frivolous. But there is a method to this madness you are about to explore. The madness is about looking at people as if they were animals, fictional characters or mythological creatures. The method is to assist you in a mind stretch, to see beyond the regular way of looking. It is also useful to find new ways to see old things because it is much more fun.

BY THE END OF CHAPTER 4 YOU SHOULD BE ABLE TO

- Watch movies and cartoons as a means to think of new workplace characters.

- Begin to justify creative and fun activities as "research."

- Categorize emotions into predator and prey categories and identify some people who may fall into these categories.

- Determine what mix of individual styles, predator or prey, that your company requires for ultimate success

- Use your imagination at the workplace as a management tool

OVERVIEW

Human beings make mental pictures of heroes and villains. Keeping the same old pictures without an occasional adjustment can keep an outdated image as a reference point. This becomes a habit and can become a fixed or rigid belief system. Rigid thinking is not good management. Things change, people change. Thinking needs to match that living process. Most people become acculturated or comfortable with what they know. This is a comfort zone. An extreme comfort zone can become a deep rut if you keep doing the same things over and over, and seeing life through one pair of glasses. Rigid and fixed thinking do not lead toward life-long learning and flexibility that are essential attributes of the progressive manager. Emotional Continuity Management demands life-long learning and flexible thought.

Challenging your own thinking is not easy, but the outcome can be more ideas and more choices. Victims are people with limited ideas and no choices. Changing your mind and your ideas is about being progressive. Being positively progressive rather than negatively progressive is necessary to avoid bitterness. If you meet a bitter person, all you really need to know about that sad individual is they believe they have no more ideas and have lost their choices. They are locked in to whatever thinking they had when they got afraid. This is not life affirming. And it certainly is not fun-affirming.

When J. Haley, a prominent psychotherapist and expert in the techniques of family system therapy and reframing ideas was asked, "How did you ever develop the ability to get such a view of the positive side of a whole lot of things that everybody else would probably consider difficult as hell?" (Haley 1976) He presented his idea of a positive philosophical approach to helping people change by suggesting that if they could define a problem situation in a new way it usually made the problem easier to solve. He named this changing process *reframing*. Seeing things in new ways should be high on the learning curve agenda of managers. A healthy person and a healthy manager wants to learn and is not resistant or threatened by new information. An excellent manager is a perpetual student. Students are in the business of learning and managing new information. Adjustment depends on the capacity to adapt to a new idea or a new situation.

Now that you have some understanding of emotions you can use your imagination to reframe spinning into a more positive and creative perspective. Reframing is a term that means looking at a picture in a new way. For example, looking at a loud angry customer as "obnoxious" is one frame. Seeing that customer as someone who is in a grieving process through a change is another frame. Seeing that same customer as someone who is reacting to a perceived or real threat and is trying to control their natural survival and grief mechanism through aggressive posturing…is another re-frame. Seeing that person as a problem is one frame. Seeing that person as a management skills opportunity for growth is a reframe. Seeing that person as a witch on a broomstick is one frame. Seeing that same person as a cartoon witch on a broomstick changes it. Seeing that cartoon witch as an inch tall and flying a broom through space is another vision. Taking that space-flying, one-inch-tall witch and having it transform into a magical butterfly that sings opera is creative reframing. So, the witch comes to you and asks you to do a task you were avoiding. You either imagine the threat or you imagine the opera. Up to you! You can have new ideas and new choices. No one gets to mandate your imagination.

REFRAMING EMOTIONAL SPINNING

Workplace spinning is an equal-opportunity activity so can be tricky to recognize in its various formats. Trying to frame it in normal pictures could be confusing. Spinning can be intentional or accidental and takes on as many forms as there are personalities. Once a spin is started, the spinner has to adjust and readjust to the spin itself. This spinning and adjusting and readjusting leads to countless varieties, shapes, and sizes that spin into action as a spin, and a spinner, takes on a life of its own.

As a spin takes shape a spinner may become a versatile shape-shifter to continue participation. Rapidly switching forms and sizes, costumes and scripts, moods and behaviors, an intentional spinner or Emotional Terrorist might take on the characteristics of a saint one moment and the next behave like a snake. Emotional Terrorists can spin about like tornadoes one afternoon and the next morning are transformed into magical beings that are now the epicenter of tranquility. Emotional Terrorists can wear shark suits or goldfish suits. They can be as charming, charismatic, sweet and alluring as a kitten and instantly turn into a tiger. Terrorists can be your best friend or your least favorite person. The Emotional Terrorist can turn out to be your best friend or someone you would instantly expect to be a problem. In fact, frequently the identified "problem" person is not the cause of the spin but the alarm system.

Spinners are represented well by all ages, genders, colors, shapes, sizes, income brackets, educational status, religions, sexual preferences, political affiliations, ability or disability levels, marital status, training levels, and shoe size. Regular emotional spinners and Emotional Terrorists can be found in all levels of the hierarchy from long-time owners and administrators to the newest and greenest line staff. In other words, ANYONE can spin given the right set of circumstances. Reframing annoyances is just as easy as reframing extreme emotions. Small or large spins do not need to consume the worksite or your emotional well being.

Reframing

Reframing is a term used in psychology to define looking at something you have seen many times and seeing it differently. The term "reframing" when used in a discussing of emotions or emotional change originates in neuro-linquistic programming (NLP) a contemporary theory of psychology. The theory is based on assumptions and research about how the brain works and therefore how it either remains fixed or changes. In a counseling session, for example, a client may be encouraged to reframe a crisis as an opportunity for growth. A person who has been an addict may be directed in ways to reframe his or her lost years as circles in a tree that aren't lost but rather part of the entire lifespan. Reframing is creative and somewhat annoying as it takes you out of your comfort zone. When people are motivated by a crisis they tend to be more willing to reframe a situation. Even those who are short on imagination can stretch their fantasy thinking and find a new way to perceive something they have known before. In therapy, the therapist guides the reframe until the skill is self-managed. Managers need to learn how to reframe experiences so they can learn, adapt to change, and then teach others. So, read this chapter with an open mind and your imagination. Do not lock into the ideas proposed as a means toward yet another rut! Use the ideas to find your own ways of seeing, learning, and adjusting to the transformations of daily life and the business world.

Changing the Picture

How do we change what we see? We see something and trust our perceptions. But human perception is a dynamic and fluid process that changes from moment to moment. It is impossible to see all angles of any given situation while it is impossible to maintain all possible perspectives of anything. We fill in the gaps or spaces with our own ideas and belief systems, opinions and memories as well as with countless other details we create for our own comfort levels. These perceptions lock into place and if they become rigid then we become fundamentally convinced of our right-sightedness. Thus originates a conflict. The right view opposes the not-right view and the attachment to the conflicting perception creates intractable conflict. Jay Haley, author of Problem Solving Therapy (1987) wrote that "problem solving demands changes in the way a problem is perceived." Perception can be changed by reframing an idea into another picture. According to film experts, reframing means changing the view of a subject while the camera is running— either the subject moves or the camera does. In other words, the change occurs without a cut. (Glossarist, 2004) Making new movies in your mind changes how you see the world. If you don't like what you are seeing, change the film.

All organized groups develop unique mythologies. Historic events, traditions and powerful memories become icons of collective remembering. Those who do not accept the tribal myths are outsiders. Outsiders are sometimes the enemy. Stories that become a company myth can hold the organization together like emotional glue, or can fracture the company into another Us-vs-Them state. Challenging a myth can be seen as challenging the whole group. Mythologies are replete with stories of heroes and villains. Both need each other to complete the story.

Because humans are biological, chemical and symbolic, the use of metaphors, mythologies, stories and fables can be either positive or negative influences. Symbolic language is useful when learning how to manage emotions at the workplace. Metaphors are less direct and therefore can be a safer way to discuss something with strong emotional content.

Changing how you talk about emotions will be an important part of your Emotional Continuity Management style. You can use parables, fables, movies, and children's books to explore feelings. This can make a discussion less threatening. Movies, filled with metaphors and mythologies, are an excellent means to discuss emotions. It is safer to talk about an actor's reaction to a situation then to disclose your own feelings. Adding parables, fables, movie references, or symbolic metaphoric images to your management style will give you an additional tool to explore and describe emotional content.

Using metaphoric images like predators, prey and scavengers, a proactive manager may begin to see lions and vultures and bunnies at work. It takes some of the negativity off the process to "play" with the following ideas. It is one thing to think of an employee as an Emotional Terrorist or a victim of Emotional Terrorism, it is another thing to identify someone as a hungry lion on the prowl or a zebra who was not paying attention. Using these identifiers as a creative way to categorize different types of workplace critters can be a light and creative way to begin a professional dialogue or team discussion on the topic. Who works at your zoo?

Recognizing the diversity of positive and negative traits in human beings provides the building blocks necessary to resolve workplace problems. There is room for everyone on the planet, but perhaps not at your work site. Remember that in nature, not all prey are harmless and not all predators toxic. It is wise to know if your organization needs sharks to succeed, or requires goldfish to create public trust. The entire point of this nontraditional exercise in metaphors is that you need to keep your business working smoothly. What will that take? The point is not to label or diagnose individual people, but to identify what is creating chaos in the system.

As your observation skills start to change, don't be afraid to do some critical thinking and use some creative discernment. Have fun with the analogies and metaphors but use them with caution. Seeing an employee as a bunny and another as a wolf is one thing, but take caution. Any kind of problem-solving style can facilitate creative resolutions to problems or bring about a nasty lawsuit. Metaphoric reframing is no exception. Be thoughtful how you use the information. For example, it is one thing to go running to your boss screaming that your administrative assistant is a "snake in the grass." It is quite another thing to use the word "snake" like the following manager did during an Emotional Continuity Management Training workshop:

Case Example

The manager reported to her boss that she believed Shaun was a problem. She reported a variety of documented behaviors that had sent other employees into an emotional spin. When the CEO asked why she had spent time on this employee, she was able to account for numerous work hours dealing with emotional spinning in her department. As part of her report she stated a nontechnical analogy that assisted the CEO in perceiving the difficulty in her unit. She said, "It's as if Shaun is a snake in our midst and not everyone in the unit likes snakes. I want your support to pay attention and continue determining if her agenda is dangerous or just different. When I lived in the tropics a number of years ago I knew there were snakes present. I didn't need to get rid of snakes, but I did need to know which snakes were dangerous, which were annoying and which would kill me flat out. It just made sense to know the difference. I met people there who liked snakes and others who were terrified the entire time just in case they might see a snake." The CEO supported the manager's concerns.

Learning Byte

Using analogies can be fun! Not all management techniques have to be boring! Managers who have learned how to be creative are less likely to become spinners. Be thoughtful and kind and learn to laugh at the ways human beings express themselves. Reframe your difficult employees into challenges and your crisis into an opportunity. Or, pull out your managerial magic wand and poof yourself to a desert island for a well-deserved vacation. After all, you can reframe your stress also! Just don't get lost in the fantasy or begin to use it as a new and improved rut.

DO THIS: Without telling anyone, take the next few moments and create a fantasy in your imagination to reframe your workplace.

DON'T: Forget to come back to reality and get your job done.

PREDATORS, PREY AND SCAVENGERS

If you had to be on a desert island alone with another creature what kind of creature would you choose? Predators? Prey? Or Scavengers? If you were building a team, what kind of people would you choose? Predators? Prey? Or Scavengers? Quite honestly, it depends on the business you are in. Some industries need lions, others need vultures and yet others demand bunny rabbits. There should be no judgments about the business species, but it makes sense to know who you need in your zoo and what critters you are working with and why.

General Workplace Zoo Guidelines

- Predator teams work well with predators unless they start predating each other
- Prey teams work well with prey unless they become totally passive
- Scavenger teams work well with scavengers unless they divide into predator and prey
- Mixed teams work better with good management who are zoo keepers and not predators, prey, or scavengers

It is rare that lions, vultures and bunny rabbits hang out together successfully over time. Well, it might be successful for the lion and the vulture. But success is usually a win-win-win proposition. You want your competition to be outside the office, not in the office. A feeding frenzy is not a pretty sight at work! Different people and different critters can often do well in the same location, living their different lives and functions, even when not compatible. They do require clearly established boundaries and well-defined policies that significantly lower the risk for all-out warfare or a corporate feeding frenzy. In other words, they require Emotional Management.

A poor mix of categories can accidentally create a full spin process. For example, a Bunny who tries to control the natural ravages of a Lion, could be perceived as an Emotional Terrorist to a successful Lion Team. A Vulture who tried to get too much of a dead carcass before the Lions had made their exit could precipitate a spinning frenzy of power and control. On televised nature programs this is entertainment. In the workplace this is risky, disruptive, and ultimately cost prohibitive.

Costumes or Personalities

Here is another twist on this discussion. Consider for a moment what might happen if a vulture has a lion suit? Or a lion has a bunny suit? There is a difference between a talented bunny who can manage lions and vultures, or a talented lion who can balance his power to manage bunnies, and an intentional spinner or Emotional Terrorist who has multiple costumes for his own purposes of control and manipulation.

After working with someone for a while, you may be able to see past the costume to the wonderful person underneath the disguise. You may also see past the costume to see a serious dysfunction or pathological personality disorder. Mangers deal with both real people and actors in costumes and disguise for their performances.

Sometimes a very scary person is using a sweet costume or the performance mask. Sometimes a very endearing person is using a scary costume or performance. Costumes and masks can be owned or rented. Use your observation and your intuition to observe and feel who might be a shark in a rental goldfish suit, and who might be a goldfish in a rental shark suit.

Case Example

Tyler was at the Emotional Continuity Management Training and told the consultant that many years ago he had worked with a colleague that he believed was the sweetest, most caring, altruistic, hard working guy on the face of the earth. This man was perceived by Tyler as a mentor, workplace hero, true lifesaver and guru. Quite out of the blue, this "saintly" man was convicted of murdering several family members. Tyler had truly believed this man was a sweet goldfish. But it became clear that he was a shark wearing a rental goldfish suit at work. Tyler became obsessed that he had been tricked by a murderer. He could not easily accept this perceptual rift between what he saw as a goldfish and the reality of the covert shark nature. Because he no longer had faith in his own perceptions, Tyler left the job and lowered his career expectations. He returned to some earlier behaviors and began smoking marijuana. He decided if his perceptions were that far off then nothing was real. Within two years he was in poverty. It took several years and psychotherapy for Tyler to understand that he had been tricked by a professional and that he had not been stupid just because he didn't see what others eventually came to know. Tyler took his recovery seriously and was able to continue on with his career. He described himself as a goldfish sort of guy who needed a shark suit to get by in the world. He said he was now working with other goldfish. The workshop participants let Tyler know that many of them had also met sharks in goldfish suits.

Case Example

Charleen reported to law enforcement officials that the robber was about 6' 4" and around 250 pounds. The terrifying culprit threatened her life with a gun and a deep voice. When the criminal was apprehended, Charleen was appalled to find that the perpetrator was a rather small-statured, puny man who was about 5' 4" and weighed 160 pounds, had a quiet voice, and had held her up with a sock in his pocket. He had an amazing talent for looking homicidal. During a debriefing she was relieved to be told that some criminals are experts at looking like sharks while hiding their goldfish attributes.

Case Example

Evonne was a terror on wheels. She was on the top of her game, raring to go, with no obstacles to success. Luke was her meek, goldfish-like husband who didn't feel comfortable with his aggressive wife. He encouraged her to take her time as she climbed the career ladder. When recognized by a top-flight organization that saw her potential to be a successful venomous predator they offered her a blank check and the sky as her limit. The organization valued her carnivorous, shark-like nature because this was just what they were looking for to fill a key position. Evonne left the marriage and continued on to a very successful career. Luke stayed home and raised the babies after the divorce. They eventually were amicable and supportive of each other and valued the different styles they had in life. They found creative ways to spend time together with the children. Both remarried successfully and continued to do well.

REFRAMING CATEGORIES OF EMPLOYEES

> **DISCLAIMER**: *The following categories should never be used to demean, humiliate or intimidate any human beings (or critters for that matter). These metaphors and analogies should only be a source of discernment and a means to begin a new way of dealing with difficult people.*

Goldfish

Goldfish are not predators; they are prey. They show up at the fishbowl and need to be fed a few flakes every day, and generally go about their business of being nice fishes. They are neither passive, nor are they aggressive. Workplace goldfish may have opinions or feelings, ideas or agendas, but they do not interfere with the workplace environment. They are generally known as "nice people" and "good workers." They may range from very bright and extremely competent to less bright and less competent, but they know how to work within a hierarchy structure, have professional courtesy and etiquette, manage their emotions well, and make a contribution to the organization. They are able to adjust to change without causing chaos and usually have a fairly stable life away from the office. Sometimes they are invisible or quiet, sometimes a bit boring, and sometimes they are quite flamboyant, loud and opinionated. Goldfish have lovely spirits. Whether they are rowdy and opinionated or shy and unobtrusive, being in their presence is a safe place to be. They are not going to eat you. They have a deep and abiding innocence. Goldfish are lovely souls. Goldfish may be able to wear shark suits when necessary, but they usually forget to take the Acme Shark Suit Rental sticker off the front pocket.

Sharks

Sharks are predators. Sharks can sense blood miles away. Sharks have no remorse. Sharks eat goldfish for breakfast, lunch and dinner. Sharks eat sharks. They don't care. Sharks own goldfish suits which fit perfectly although they are a bit tight and rub the wrong way in the wrong places if you watch them wiggle over time. They can be syrupy-sweet, false-faced demons that bite you in the back when you think you are safe, or the dark evil worker of fear and terror. A shark may not be evil at the core but it is an opportunist and has an agenda. Even when they have no intention to feed on you because their sights are set on bigger prey, sharks just don't have cozy spirits about them. They might eat you on the road to the bigger meal. They don't care. They set off Goldfish Intuition Alarms, but usually Goldfish want to be too nice so turn down the volume of their intuition. Goldfish feel guilty just thinking that Sharks might not be safe. After all, Sharks are people too! Nice Goldfishes make excuses for Sharks right up to the point that they get eaten alive. Sharks love this Shark game.

Some companies appreciate a successful Shark taking over a Goldfish or Shark business in a bloodless coup. It is to be expected. It is not personal, it's business. Sharks are not too much of a problem in a Shark tank with other Sharks. There is a difference between a Shark who is being an efficient Shark in a pool with other Sharks and a lone Shark with a plan. An emotional predator is misanthropic.

Guppies

Guppies are young or immature fish that live in their own bubble and seem to be immune to anything around them. They are mostly harmless unless they get between a shark and its prey. If that happens they can then be diversions of disposable meat. Workplace guppies are often perceived as office mascots. They can be a young intern or summer employee who has not seasoned into the field of survivors. They are not yet well defined. They may become goldfish or they may become sharks — it is up for grabs and everyone wants to recruit them. For this reason they can be used by Emotional Terrorists for bait, meat, or rounding out a deception team. If they begin to emerge into a specific definition, they are at risk for being groomed by Sharks as allies or eaten alive to eliminate yet another pesky growing goldfish. They are perceived as generally disposable and invisible. Workplace guppies are usually well tolerated by all species, unless there is a loyalty feeding frenzy and all bets are off.

Dolphins

Dolphins flamboyantly risk their own spirit to be a mouthpiece for an organization. They are not whistleblowers, they are people who try to be agents of change. They are quick, bright, intense, sometimes cranky and cold, and usually quite opinionated. When questioned, however, you can clearly see that they have a deep investment in success of the organization and are feeling helpless and unsupported. They are willing to dive deep and leap high to keep things in working order. They may yell "Shark! Shark!" before anyone else. Where a Shark uses complaints to further its own agenda, a Dolphin is simply trying to let everyone know that there is danger nearby. Their alarms make them easy targets when they become a loud threat to a Shark. Dolphins are easy to destroy because they are highly visible. They tend to be less cuddly and cozy, more active, more verbal, and often quite more opinionated than a Goldfish. Dolphins usually survive but suffer from personal wounds. They have the mobility to leap into other ponds to survive and so they tend to leave jobs without a good recommendation for service rendered because it is easier to leave than become Shark bait. But they usually don't go quietly. They are prey, although an Emotional Terrorist will insist they have been the victims of these Dolphin "predators." Dolphins don't mind being Early Warning Witnesses to Shark presence. A Dolphin won't belabor the point for long and will move on to safer waters.

Turtles

Turtles seem to have shutters over their emotions and are difficult to read. They work hard at maintaining a professional demeanor, do not involve themselves in any workplace activity other than the business at hand, and do not engage in anything extra. They generally perceive that if they can keep out of it and just do their work all problems will disappear. These employees are dangerous, because they keep the fantasy alive that there are no dangers present in the happy little turtle bowl of life. They do not serve the process. They are the people who might tend to say, "Yeah, the Sharks were eating her, but it was none of my business." This sort of passive homicide redefines a turtle as a passive predator. In a Shark attack it is good business to take sides.

Vultures

Vultures are patient. They don't mind waiting for their food. They have a love affair with death and quietly sit on the sidelines, or circle around the playing field, waiting for a bit of dead critter. They don't care if it is a dead Goldfish or a Dead Shark; food is food. They are passively homicidal. They take no accountability for the death or destruction of prey, but willingly consume its flesh as soon as it is available. They offer no significant power of their own while are waiting. They appear neutral; they aren't. They have an opinion and a preference. They don't offer much of a threat to the predator or prey, nor do they fear the predator or prey. They know their place and will bide their time for the feast. They are not emotionally upset about the losses of the prey, nor are they particularly interested in the conquests of the predator, unless there aren't any. Then they may try to stir a few bunnies out of the bushes and wait till the killing is over. They can be at the core of some forms of spinning if they are trying to stir the bunnies out of the bushes while they are waiting. Vultures can be scavengers.

Snakes

There are poisonous snakes and non-poisonous snakes. Toxic or not, snakes have some common behaviors. For example, they slither. They have good camouflage and can slip around unnoticed in the underbrush. They are quick, self-protective, and hard to catch. Snakes can be lovely to look at. Two different snakes, one toxic and one non-toxic, can look quite similar. Both kinds are fine in a glass aquarium, but a different kind of challenge slithering around the office. They tend to move quickly and hide cleverly. Some give warnings, some do not. Some can climb trees, others can swim. Depending upon the level of toxicity, snakes are interesting zoo colleagues. Many snakes are harmless. Some snakes are poisonous. Some snake poison will make you ill. Some will kill you instantly.

Spiders

An employee who manipulates another employee using sexuality or sensuality to lure them into a web prior to biting it to death is a Spider. The web can be personal or professional but extrication becomes very difficult. The "death" can be a metaphoric killing a career or job. Spiders can go anywhere right-side-up or upside down. They like the dark. They are scary but extremely vulnerable and fragile. Real spiders, arachnids, are actually quite fragile and vulnerable. Most of them die of thirst. Workplace spiders are not so fragile and generally thirst for blood. A Spider is often defined as someone who "wouldn't hurt a fly" until their back was turned.

Chameleons

A lizard with a projectile tongue who is able to change colorations, making it easier to escape and hide. A chameleon does whatever is necessary to change masks and costumes and ideas and language to avoid anything perceived as threatening.

The list is endless, but this should give you a start of how to reframe behaviors into more creative models. Emotional Continuity Management Training discussions have run wild with grand stories of dinosaurs, rats, canaries in mines, Dobermans on the grounds, ornamental cats in the temples, the well-groomed, caged college mascots who are ceremoniously trotted out only at the big game. The weasel is often a popular favorite along with the oft-maligned skunk, pig, donkey, flea, leech and snail. What have you seen in *your* "zoo?"

Mis-Informants / Liars

Just about everyone has told a lie at some point in their life. Some lies are socially acceptable and appropriate for a situation. Please don't tell the lady in the next office that the purple dress really makes her look fat just to be an "honest" person. Just as there are pathological liars, there are pathological "truth-ers." Balance is the key. Emotional Terrorists don't like balance, they like chaos. They prefer manipulating truth and manufacturing lies for their own agendas. Emotional Terrorists use different levels and styles of lies, as do non-terrorists. However, Emotional Terrorists use a very different intentionality and purpose for their lies. And, they become very good at it. Take a moment to consider the levels and styles of lies used by sex offenders, alcoholics, bank robbers, and serial killers. They adopt comprehensive lying strategies that are beyond the imagination of healthy people. Obviously these are not your regular sort of reasonable social lies; these lies have a purpose, an agenda, an intentionality to either self-protect at all costs, maintain bulletproof status or even do harm. There are dysfunctional and pathological lies and liars.

Kinds Of Lies

- Trivial matters, false excuses to spare a feeling, flattery, harmless, inconsequential
- Lies to children about Easter bunnies, Santa Claus, the tooth fairy
- Deceptions to make a person feel better
- Inflation, exaggeration to make something sound better than it is, false praise, false encouragement, false support
- False recommendations: intentional incorrect or incomplete answers
- Fake resumes, false credentials
- Lies to protect a boss, a colleague or client
- Lies to liars
- Lies to enemies
- Not quite exacting, half truths, soft-soaps
- Lies in a crisis when innocent lives, health, safety are at risk
- Lies for no apparent reason
- Lies for the sake of lies
- Lies as games and manipulations

- Lies about lies
- Terminal lies
- Cover-up lies
- Brainwashing lies
- Corporate lies
- Accounting lies
- Political lies
- Seduction lies
- Addiction lies
- Agreed-upon group lies
- Criminal lies
- Lies about lies

Time Tyrants

Time is a precious commodity to us all. Time is Money. To most adults, time is sacred. An Emotional Time Terrorist messes with your time. They have many ways to accumulate, control, or dispose of your time. They work either actively or passively to manipulate the clock.

Look at the following list and think if you have any Time Tyrants on your team:

- Time Tyrant: So demanding about punctuality or deadlines that it is difficult to think straight under the pressure. A minute late is too much, no flexibility or patience, judgmental about other peoples' time.
- Time Thief: A procrastinator, or gets to arrive late, or asks for last-minute details at the end of the day. Uses work time for e-mail, personal calls, video games, dating set ups.
- Time Hoarders: Won't do anything extra, as if Time was their own domain, saves up leave and use it at inopportune times, will demand special time with managers and administration, asks for extra meetings.
- Time Addicts: Rigid attention or non-attention to time, unchangeable time habits no matter the situation or circumstances, work only out of a day planner, no flex time, no breathing space, Type A people, every moment used, must be "on" all the time.
- Time Misers: Makes everyone wait for them, late to meetings because of their other meetings, demands that everyone work on their clock, Scrooge-like control of other peoples' time.
- Time Victims: Always behind or ahead of time, but it is never their fault.
- Time Gamblers: Takes risks with projects, or deadlines, or lunch breaks or holiday scheduling. Doesn't take time seriously, theirs or yours, time is a game, bulletproof.
- Time Saboteurs: Will distract or employ manipulations to make themselves central in the middle of a time crunch, late to meetings, interrupt meetings, work during meetings on other projects, sidetrack other employees' time making others late.

Recognizing Tools And Weapons Of Time Tyrants

Unclear Language	Poor Communication
Distractions	Grandstanding
Red Tape	Victim Attitude
Unresolved Conflicts	Low Moral Standards
Poor Ethics	Untrained Staff
Poor Authority Chain	Unnecessary Travel
Indecision	Mistakes Without Learning
Poorly Managed Fatigue	Changing Deadline Mid-Task
Clutter	Disorder
Poor Listening	Disorganization

Gossip	Ethical Violations
Lack Of Accountability	Procrastination
Unreasonable Expectations	Won't Clean Own Messes
Blaming Others	Poor Self Care
Arriving Late	Arriving Too Early
Needing To Be Central	Avoiding Participation

MYTHOLOGICAL SPINNERS

Any study of spinning or Emotional Terrorism would be incomplete without offering a more metaphoric view of emotional assault than is contained in rational file folders. Human beings are biological, chemical and symbolic, and our human history is replete with symbols and reports of "other-world activities" which many hold sacred. While there is no intention of discussing whether or not demons or faeries exist, it is important to discuss how symbols and perception are wrapped around personal beliefs about good and evil. If a person does not accept that evil exists as the balancing force of good, this discussion will be brief. However, most adults have witnessed people whose behavior acts out the characteristics of various belief systems: saints and sinners, heroes and villains, good guys and bad guys.

People's lives are made up of countless stories. Every human being creates their own sort of mythology about their own lives. Some cultures maintain their histories through the oral tradition of story telling. Looking at the people through the eyes of myths and stories is what early humans did in their attempts to understand the world around them. It is very simple to categorize people into two groups, good or bad, hero or villain. Of course, life is much more complicated than this and holds lots of gray area between such extreme thinking. Thinking about the mythologies of the workplace, an Emotional Terrorist can be seen as a Villain. The altruistic team player might be viewed as a Hero or Heroine.

Use the following section as a creative beginning to creative thoughts or an interesting discussion. Use your imagination, play with the concepts, don't be "literal," and ask yourself if you have met any of these mythological spinners.

The Trickster

The Trickster is the employee who distracts and interrupts the serious process of the work. Perhaps they are a clown, a jester, a practical joker, or someone who likes to change the subject a lot. Tricksters might be the "funny sidekick" or someone who takes each opportunity to force a joke or pun, funny story or irrelevant detail into the conversation. A trickster attracts attention and changes the flow of the moment. One way a trickster takes territory is through humor that does not match the emotional climate of the moment.

Case Example

Jake is the Trickster who will tell the off-color story, the scatological or gross-out joke, and then make sure everyone laughs, or hears it again. He will interrupt a serious discussion with irrelevant comments, like "Oh, look, the pencil sharpener is yellow. I didn't know that. Hey, did you hear the one about the yellow woman?"

The Vampire

A vampire is an animated corpse who sucks the lifeblood from the living. They only enter when invited, but they enter quickly and do their work of destruction in record time. They are charismatic and usually attractive.

Case Example

Just a few minutes with Tim or Tia and you have no energy, no joy, no inspiration, no hope and no idea what took your lifeforce from you. Tim or Tia are always trying to be in the center of everything in a charming and charismatic way, hoping for your invitation to be the next victim. They seem to feed off others.

The Pied Piper

An employee who seductively lures the childlike energies from another employee with promises of specialness and magic. Enticing the naïve or inexperienced employee into a world that is controlled by the thinking of the Pied Piper becomes a lost-world or Dark Mountain of control. Once lost inside the mountain of control, the "child" cannot return to normal life. The Pied Piper will sometimes hold the village (company) hostage for perceived payments of entitlement.

Case Example

Arthur preys on sweet and vulnerable women who still maintain the spark of life about them, no matter their age. He is especially successful in manipulating vulnerable, middle-aged women who are in either a life or career transition. He becomes their personal guru, the wise one, the magic icon of what a Wonderful Man should be like. Charming Arthur offers a sharp contrast to an empty life or boring husband. His victim's naiveté makes them vulnerable to his spell. The victims come to believe they cannot have joy without his influence. With just a taste of this magic on her tongue, the victim is never again quite satisfied with her current life. Arthur then uses his victim to climb to his next victory.

The Succubus

A succubus is a female spirit vampire who enters uninvited, can take on the appearance of another person or personality while attempting to sexually control the victim. Victims are unaware of the danger, thinking they just had a nightmare and that the appearance of the person is the reality, rather than the demon. The victim cannot see the demon. Others may witness the demon, and try to give warning, but the victim will often defend the Succubus, even to the death of all sanity, in ignorance of its evil intention.

Case Example

Mysti-Ann is so sweet. She wants to be close to you, to be your dear and special friend. You might like her a lot, instantly, and yet you won't quite know why. She will share secrets with you and make you feel special. Mysti-Ann asks a thousand questions just to hear you talk and share your opinion. She believes in you. You believe in her. She is perky and pretty and special. You want to have a special relationship with her. You defend her. If your boyfriend, husband, co-worker, lover, buddy, or girlfriends feel threatened, it must be because they are jealous and crazy, because Mysti-Ann, the Succubus, is too innocent, sweet and needs your special care and wisdom and protection. After all, she has trusted you with her deepest self, and now you must defend her. She has picked you to be her special friend. As you see someone escalate his or her apparent jealousy and terror around Mysti-Ann, it makes her look even sweeter and more sane, innocent, and helpless. You feel as though you must protect and defend her against these odd and unwarranted attacks. You want to do things for her. You want to make sacrifices. Whatever she says must be truth. She is just a bubble of life and light. You begin to live for her sweetness and special favors. And yet, somehow you begin to feel darker and darker about everyone and everything else. You begin to isolate. People complain that Mysti-Ann stabs them in the back, but you can't see anything but her smile. You want to live in her glow and remain forever in bliss. You sabotage your career for her. Suddenly, with a smile on her face, and you in her glow, she exits abruptly to move forward with her plan. You stand reeling and have no idea that you have been exploited. You have isolated yourself from everyone.

The Incubus

The male version of the Succubus.

Case Example

Cole is so clever, so smart. He does charity work on his time off. He has adopted children from third world nations and opens doors for elderly women. People tell you he is "the best" and that he is a "catch." You want to be with him and sit at his feet. He wants to take you on his meteoric climb, or on his journey of sorrow, or on his sacred quest, or on his trek for wisdom. He invites you and you are compelled, perhaps against your better judgment, to say yes. How can you refuse his worthiness, and he has chosen YOU. He confides in you his loneliness in his quest. His marriage is not good. He just has too much to do. He hasn't had sex in a long time. But it's okay, because he must work to help pay for a homeless shelter he is sponsoring. He looks at you with those longing eyes, implying that you are the one who understands him better than anyone else in the world, "if only...." You alone are spiritually strong enough to help him reach his goals. You are his salvation for the bigger cause. You begin to fantasize ways to help serve his noble quest for light. You start sacrificing your time and energies. Even when Cole leaves you hanging for other projects, people, places, or things; he has a way of swooping back in the nick of time, just before you get the idea of the exploitation, and starts your heart going again. He inspires greatness from you. You become more energized and creative and you spend all your waking hours hoping for just a moment of his valuable time. Your time is meaningless. You dream about getting an hour with him. Or a weekend. Or a road trip. He can do no wrong. Even when he does wrong, it's okay, because he knows you will understand like no one else does because "you are special." Cole invites you on a special "mission" and you cannot or will not refuse. You sabotage everything for his briefest accolades. And when he swoops off into the sunset leaving you with the check, you pay it. And when he doesn't come back, you assume it is something wrong with you.

The Shapeshifter

A Shapeshifter wants to question and deceive. She/he may ask one question after another, but will not respond to the answers as if they mattered. The questions are only distractions to the real goal, which is to find your weakness and exploit it, or to find a way to shift his/her form around your answers. She/he is in the process of change, always. A Shapeshifter can also be someone who carries within the attributes and powers of various animals and spirits. These attributes remain hidden unless the Shapeshifter feels threatened. Then they change form (or religion, or philosophy, or opinion, or ideas, or loyalties).

Case Example

Sam is a slow-moving guy most of the time, *until* there is a particular project that needs to be done and he becomes a rabbit who darts out of the meeting.

Tim is a bit small and bird-like, *until* he takes over a meeting with a vengeance and produces well-sharpened claws to rip and shred someone else's ideas into pieces.

Mahoney is a pleasant, amiable, good hearted guy *until* he gets home alone with his wife and becomes a dark, sullen, discounting grouch.

Mike is a quiet married guy with three kids, *until* the boss is gone, then he is vicious.

Belinda is a pleasant person, conservative, subdued, *until* a male vendor comes into the office and she is suddenly a slinky cat.

Drake is the loud, obnoxious guy *until* his wife shows up.

Rip (Or Rippleena) Van Winkle

A Rip Van Winkle is someone who is in an unconscious state by self-inflicted acts of bad behaviors, or poorly considered, self-serving choices.

Case Example

William is not accountable. William is lazy and a slob. He blames everyone for all problems and makes no contribution. He is willing to be a slacker and to give every project a C- effort instead of a B or an A. William never quits, nor does he ever really join the rest of the team. This Rip Van Winkle leaves you wanting more but is unable to really do anything about it, because he just does not care that much. Rip Van Winkle, is annoying but not dreadful enough to get rid of altogether. He is more like an albatross who rarely contributes but just won't go away.

Learning Bytes

After playing with these creative ideas make your own list of identifiers in your industry or business. Be creative. Think of a category and different mythological attributes for each.
DO THIS:
- *Identify behaviors using characters from famous movie or television characters. Who is your office Scarlet O'Hara? Norma Rae? Dracula? James Bond? Superman? Wonder Woman? Lassie? Indiana Jones? Darth Vader? Neo? Oracle? Raymond? Lucy? Ethel?*
- *Identify behaviors using cartoon characters. Do you work with Nemo? Shrek? Sylvester? Tweety Bird? Woody? Mr. Potato Head? Homer Simpson? Dilbert? Stitch? Oscar the Grouch? Daffy Duck? Elmer? Powerpuff Girl? Scooby-Doo?*
- *Identify behaviors using food names. Vegetables? Ham? Chocolate Cake? Twinkies? Flambé?*
- *What mythological ideas may represent myths or metaphors inside your company? The Titanic? Remember the Alamo? Lost in Space? Return of the King? Eight Heads in a Duffle Bag? Alice in Wonderland? The Matrix?*

DON'T: Misunderstand that these ideas are meant for serious consideration and not just whimsical entertainments. Don't disregard important issues by minimizing them frivolously with silly analogies. On the other hand, take some creative ideas to reorganize your thinking.

DON'T: use any descriptor on any list to do harm. Use it to be creative, to see differently and more fully. Just because you come up with a new way of seeing someone at the workplace doesn't mean that person will appreciate your new vision or the comparison. For example, seeing someone as a vampire will help you deal with them in a different way. Telling them you see them as a vampire may create and enhance more serious spinning. The simplest disclaimer is that if you use one of these metaphors to cause harm, this automatically makes YOU a spinner.

AUTHOR'S AFTERTHOUGHTS

When I go into a company and start talking about sharks and goldfish at first I get blank stares. There is always someone who thinks I'm weird or have no real understanding of the serious nature of the business environment. But for others, I see the lights come on, faces start smiling, heads start nodding in recognition. Managers know who it is in their company that I am talking about. They have been in the trenches like me, but have not had the permission to be as creative. And that is fine. Managers will be held accountable for the language they use, and must always err on the side of caution. I get to be more outlandish as I help managers reframe their challenges. The fun part for me is when a manager who is a shark sees that I know the difference. They look around nervously in hopes that no one really heard what I said. This amuses me tremendously. The game is on. Often the sharks start distracting the proceedings at this point, and never cease to try to discredit the messenger. Their cold eyes bear down upon me during a workshop and I sense a sudden chill in the air. I recognize their evaluations later. For the first time, many of them are thinking they are not alone in their perceptions. I see the sharks getting darker and going deeper. They may even try a quick feeding frenzy as a distraction. This also amuses me because the goldfish suddenly find they have allies in one another. I encourage them to become fabulously smart goldfish if they have to swim with sharks. I show them my fantasy Shark Suit with the Acme-Shark-Rental patch. I tell them I'm a consultant so I enjoy swimming with sharks even though I am hardwired as a goldfish. I have learned to dive in and out of the shark tank or corporate pool rather quickly before the real sharks see that I have just rented a shark suit for the occasion.

My first interactions with sharks that used the succubae and incubi skills to survive were totally confounding. As a goldfish I was drawn into the warmth of the grooming and seductions and took them seriously. Then, when the hammer came down and they revealed their true intentions to do harm, I had to pull in my goldfish fins before they got caught in very sharp teeth. I have some bite marks, but got out alive. In subsequent years I tried to be an informant. That didn't work due to the covert processes and charisma factors.

Other survivors became my witnesses and helping them find ways to avoid the next danger became some of the best work I have ever done. I find it totally satisfying to help innocent people see that they are not imaging things when they feel as though they are about to be eaten alive. It is incredible to support a goldfish manager in becoming not another shark, but a fabulously intelligent, aware, awake and observant goldfish.

I have also had the dubious and intriguing opportunity to help professional sharks stay on task while not becoming distracted by a feeding frenzy in their company. I have given them permission not to feel guilty for being sharks, but how to not eat goldfish. Some businesses require sharks. Sharks are not inherently bad. Sharks serve a purpose. Sharks in your goldfish tank, however, can be a problem!

DISCUSSION QUESTIONS

- How would you manage this employee?

You meet by the coffee maker and Mel pronounces to you a rather sharp opinion about something going on in the office. You are a bit surprised, but feel a bit honored by being taken into confidence by this colorful and bright quick-thinker. Mel makes you think about your own position on the topic. You had had a strong position, but now you are seriously considering taking the stance just offered you because it does make a lot of sense after all. You go to a meeting and that particular topic is up. Opinions are varied and positional and when directly asked by your supervisor, you take a stand and speak your new position that happens to align with Mel the Chameleon. You take a risk. You look over to the Mitch who is organizing papers. You solicit Mel for backup, because Mel stated it so beautifully and eloquently earlier this morning as you both stood by the coffee maker. Mel opens his (or her) mouth and speaks the total opposite opinion with amazing clarity and powerfully argues for this opposing opinion, which is the popular stance of the supervisor, and then passes the topic back to you to "convince us that your position is even rational." You are out there alone and humiliated. Everyone praises Mel for the clarity. Later, at the water cooler, Mel praises you for your courage.

- Describe the following:
  BUNNY RABBITS
  - Describe what you might expect from a Bunny Rabbit
  SHEEP
  - Describe what you might expect from a Sheep
  OSTRICH
  - Describe what you might expect from an Ostrich
  - Make a list of other zoo animals, mythological beasts and creative images.
  - Using the following Employee Bulletin and timetable, answer the questions below:
    EMPLOYEE BULLETIN!!!

Baseball season is on!!!

All employees are expected to come at 8:00 a.m. for a brief staff meeting

All employees are invited to play

If you can't play, come and be a cheer-leader

If you can't cheer, come and bring cookies

If you have to work you are strongly encouraged to make cookies and donate them to the cheerleaders

If you are going to play, come prepared to play hard and win big!!!

We'll be playing the Acme Widgett company in two weeks — and this year we are planning to win!!!

Timetable:

7:50   Several eager players arrive in uniforms with baseball equipment ready to go

Employee A has obviously been waiting at the field for a while already

Employee B is on center stage with lots of ideas and energy

Employee C arrives in uniform but does not have a positive attitude

7:59   Majority of players are now present and ready to go

Employee D arrives in uniform with very poor attitude

Employee E and F arrive without proper equipment, in Hockey uniforms, blaming someone for not telling them the details

8:10   Staff meeting begins

8:15   Employee G and H arrive, in uniforms, with appropriate equipment

8:20   Employee I arrives in a skiing outfit

Employee J arrives, out of uniform with no information other than someone told him to show up for some sort of a staff meeting

8:22   THE PRACTICE BEGINS

8:28   Employee K shows up with everything necessary to play

8:30   Employee L never shows up. Employee M brings cookies.

8:30   Employee N is dropped off by spouse and has a black eye.

Employee O comes with a "bring-it-on" attitude and brings beer.

Questions:

•   Who is ready to play baseball and who is not?

•   Who is sabotaging the team?

•   Who do you suspect of spinning?

•   Is Employee K is beginning a spin?

•   Can you guess who had car trouble or a sick child at home? Who is lying?

•   Is Employee I is starting a spin, or if he/she is being set up for a fall by a spinning manager or secretary who gave bad information to make I the scapegoat?

•   How do you know if Employee A is the most eager to play or the one who just got there early because he/she sold company proprietary information to the other team?

•   Is 8:22 a reasonable starting time? Why? Why not?

•   What happened to Employee L?

•   How do you think the staff meeting went?

•   Is employee M's black eye something you should address? Why? Why not?

•   What needs to be managed?

5

RESPONSES: HOW CAN YOU MANAGE SPINNING?

- *Dear Dr. Vali, The grant director repeatedly assured staff that the budget was in order and produced documents to the manager that indicated this. After significant projects were put into action, it was discovered that there was no revenue to cover the project. The project had to be terminated.*

  Outcomes:

    - *The closure of a school*
    - *Cost to the state $200,000 in planning funds*
    - *Cost to the district exceeding $150,000 in unrecoverable losses*
    - *Loss of $150,000 in salaries*
    - *Two teachers and one support person lost jobs*
    - *Cost to the district and the community volunteers who developed this program includes over 3000 volunteer hours*
    - *Involved in planning and development costs worth $75,000*
    - *1200 staff hours worth $35,000 lost*
    - *Loss of credibility in the community*
    - *Loss of credibility of the Board, school district and volunteers*
    - *Ongoing lost opportunities for students with special needs*

  These people were not bad or evil people, but the outcomes of their unwillingness or inability to get help and a lack of quality management destroyed a special opportunity for this community, for some exciting and inspired teachers, and a group of wonderful young students. Sincerely, Dr. Bruce Potter, Program Director

- *The station manager quickly aired an apology, saying; "The actions of the KNRK news [94.7 FM, Portland, Oregon] morning show were insensitive, inappropriate and repulsive."*

- *Our company has laid off many employees and we are under a lot of chaos and stress at all times in our industry. Everyone is afraid all the time that their name is next on the list. There are days when I think I don't want to be a manager anymore. Then there are days when I know that when I do my best to manage some tough situation I am making it a bit better for others. That can get me out of bed in the morning. (Jane Phoenix, Weapons Project Manager)*

- *I have decided to leave nursing as a profession. I thought I was cut out for it. Then I was made a manager and all I got was grief from all my former friends. It made me physically sick. My counselor has encouraged me to find something else. I feel encouraged about this because I'm going to take time to think about it. I never really have asked myself what I wanted to do when I grew up. (Lenore Moore, former nurse manager).*

WHY YOU SHOULD READ THIS CHAPTER

Managers are in the middle of the most chaotic and emotionally charged locations on the planet earth. They stand between the emotional needs of their employees and the financial needs of their company. Oil and water are in the blender and the manager is required to lead with goodwill to all while problem-solving, making schedules, rearranging shift assignments, blessing off training dollars, and making certain that the soda machine is full of everyone's favorite soft drink. Managers need all the help they can get!

BY THE END OF CHAPTER 5 YOU SHOULD BE ABLE TO

- Make a checklist of what you need to successfully manage emotions at work making certain you include self-care and employee care.

- Choose a formal or theoretical approach to managing emotions at the workplace.

- Create a draft of compassionate interventions, policies, procedure strategies, and referrals to present to your company.

- Organize a detailed personal support system for yourself that is outside the company.

- Make contact with at least five resources that you can count on in case of emergency that will support you as you manage others.

- Pick tools that you can directly apply in your setting.

OVERVIEW

According to Anna Hahn, Crisis Program Director of the Sexual Assault Response Center, one of three females and one of four males was sexually assaulted before the age of sixteen. (see: www.RAINN.org). The number of adults raised as children in homes disrupted by alcoholism is equally disturbing. Bankruptcy filings are at an all-time high. Alcohol and drug abuse are on the increase. Within a few years, it is estimated that nearly 60% of adults will be primary caretakers of their grandchildren. Divorce statistics are escalating, with the current rate being 50% of all first marriages ending in divorce and 78% of second marriages ending in divorce (D. Mitchell, 2004). Thousands of young people are engaged in wars overseas, and the looming threat of terrorism fills much of television news air time. Advertisements for alcohol, antidepressants, erectile dysfunction and female hormone replacement products promise a life of perpetual ease and happiness. Contrary to airbrushed images of happily-ever-after, sometimes life is hard, messy, and emotional. Real people come to work each day dragging their emotional experiences with them.

Managers who (contrary to some popular notions) are human also, get caught up in the frenzy between their own emotions and those of others under their direction. Mangers work between the people who make the work happen and the people who make the rules. Working in this location, for a brave soul, is an amazing place to be. Management at its best is awesome work. But not everyone is cut out for such exhilarating and extreme daily pressure. Managers must juggle the money issues of a competitive bottom-line and the daily emotional feelings of their staff. They must see that tasks are accomplished and that people are comfortable in doing so. Once managers decide to be managers, they require good equipment to handle the job. Good management, a bit like juggling bowling balls and feathers, is a great trick if you can do it.

Real stories from real managers inspired this book. ***Creating a Spin Free Workplace©*** was originally a training program developed as a response to managers needing something between HR's good intentions, EAP's 4-6-session available referrals, out of house counseling, faddish tricks, managerial-psychobabble trends, and a magic wand. Managers needed tools, and they needed them immediately. They came to workshops and trainings and demanded practical tools that they could use the next day when they faced the dragons and demons at work. The original program was field-tested successfully with professional first responders, office secretaries, administrative professionals, physicians, hospitals, dental offices, bereavement specialists, retail managers, mental health professionals, security and terrorist experts, coroners, office managers, teachers, large corporations and small business owners. Managers wanted an active process that worked. Developing a process that combined good research, traditional mental health theories, concepts from clinical Psychotraumatology, critical incident stress management (CISM) theories and practices, international and national disaster services models, applied psychology and contemporary business theory was, at first, a daunting concept.

When managers took some of their traditional and contemporary models and added the ideas from the workshops presented in this book, they started testing and trying the tools that they redesigned for use in their companies. When they added a dash of their own common sense and creativity they felt empowered and well-grounded in science, research, theory and application. They still had to deal with exactly the same issues, but the were now acting like fearless warriors in the face of an interesting challenge, instead of hapless and hopeless victims. The managers began creating their own personalized toolkits for survival. They began to teach others how to survive. They were leaders and mentors now. Moreover, their bosses wrote letters of gratitude. Even several years after a consultation, CEO's would make a point to express "how far they had all come" since learning that emotions were not necessarily an enemy of the workplace.

The level and flexibility of any training model, including this one, must be structured to fit your specific organizational need and should appeal to all strata of individuals and employment situations. There is no standardized, universal, one-size-fits-all model. The result of establishing an Emotional Continuity Management policy should be system-wide stability that lends itself to continuity of productivity. Procedures and theories, tools and trainings should support collective or group cohesion regardless of what emotionally charged event that happens, small or catastrophic. It should support individuals who are different and companies that are different. Managers should take what they like from this collection of ideas and leave the rest. They should read, dip and skim as much information as they can from other writers and workshops. They should become consummate consumers of products designed to manage emotions. There are good people and bad people selling all sorts of products in all sorts of packages — and *you* are the only one who really knows what will work in *your* company

COMMITTING TO EXCELLENCE

The first step for a manager is to really decide if you want to manage human beings. Then, decide if you want to work toward excellence. As anyone who has worked for even a short time can attest, not every manager is management material. Management is an art and a science. To master anything takes time, energy, devotion, mentorship, practice, drills and errors. If you were going to take up a new musical instrument, you would not be playing in a symphony the first year. Even prodigy musicians need experience and training. New managers need to settle into the time it takes to learn, expect to make errors, and learn from those errors. Seasoned managers must decide if they want to become masters. Just an accumulation of years doing something does not create a master. The idea of "practice makes perfect" is not true unless the practicing is correct. A bad manager over time does not automatically turn into a good manager just because time has passed. Masters of anything are very comfortable in their roles of life-long student. True experts want to learn more. Excellence is a journey and process, not a destination.

STEPS TO EXCELLENCE

1.   DECIDE: Do you really want to be a manager?
2.   PREPARE YOURSELF: Before lifesavers jump into shark infested waters, they check their gear carefully
3.   ESTABLISH YOUR OWN SUPPORT SYSTEM: Create your own buddy-system or external cheerleaders
4.   PREPARE YOUR SYSTEM: Confirm buy-on that you will not be alone and will be well supported by your administration
5.   GO FOR IT: Jump in and give it your best. Pay attention to successes and errors.
6.   DESIGN YOUR MANAGEMENT STYLE AND PROGRAM: Look at all the options you know and create a process, style, and program that fit you and your company.
7.   RETREAT AND RECREATION: Treat yourself to a celebration, because there is a good chance no one else will know how hard you have been working!
8.   RECOMMIT: Restart the process from Step 1 for each incident you are managing.

Step 1: Deciding

If you decide, you are not a victim; you have made a choice. Once you have decided to manage, use the following tools to maintain your decision:

A.   Avoid Management Insomnia

Obviously, you are looking through this text because you are awake to the emotional problems in your company. Perhaps you have always been awake and are on top of your game, or you have been suddenly jolted into alertness because of a crisis in the workplace. Perhaps you have cleverly skipped ahead to this chapter because you already know first-hand the chaos and destruction of workplace emotional spinning. Or you are deciding whether or not to purchase the book. There are indeed many books on the market making grand promises and then leaving you once again alone in the middle of your chaos. But that's the fun of being a manager, right? Yes, it is your job to stay awake in the middle of everyone else's nightmare and remain vigilant to the details of the situation. Like it or not, you are a leader and facilitator and the potential icon for safety. You do not want to be the manager who adds another dimension of disaster inside a catastrophe. Staying awake is difficult when everyone around you appears to be sleepwalking. The only way a manager can survive for the long term is to develop a clear process of self managed care and staying awake.

B.   Review your Job Title

Your job title may give you an indication about what you are supposed to accomplish. Most managers say that figuring out what is wrong with people is not their job. If that is what you are saying, you are right — that probably is *not* your job. Your job is to pay attention, witness, evaluate, predict and document your observations and do everything you can to keep people working and productive. You then pass that information on to your bosses, experts and refer to policies, make referrals, and create mountains of documentation.

Excellent managers are in the unique position to "see" more than anyone else in the company — *if* they are awake. Some managers try to maintain a comatose state to avoid accountability, pass over the tough stuff to HR, blame, pass the buck, reorganize, manipulate and generally do whatever they can to avoid actually managing. Managing is hard work, underappreciated, and overwhelming at times. It can also be fascinating and entertaining if one stays awake and learns to absorb and endure forces of human emotions. It is not a job for wimps — it is a job for warriors. That might not be in your job description, but you know it is true.

C.   If everyone is out to get you, paranoia might be good thinking

The next obstacle to excellence is when managers suggest that all this emotional stuff is "paranoia" and that "if we spend time in fear, we won't accomplish anything." This may be true, yet the next question needs to be, "how much time do you spend dealing with employee emotions?" Do you think that time could be spent doing something more fiscally productive? If managers are very, very far from being competent, they state something like, "well nothing can happen to us, so we aren't going to spend training dollars in paranoia."

Mental Health Professionals will let you know that clinical paranoia is described in terms of an unnatural or out-of-proportion fear over time. For example, while it is healthy to fear bee stings, fires, and tornadoes, it suggests paranoia if you are compelled to spend all your time in the basement wearing mesh netting holding a hose. If, on the other hand, you have lost a house in a tornado or have a severe allergy to bees, or been in a fire, a little dose of paranoia is just good thinking and quite reasonable. Paying attention to emotions and extreme emotions is not overreacting. Spending *no* time on preparation is a dangerous overreaction. Minimization can be more dangerous than paranoia. Balance is the key: Reason and Balance. Most industries have fire extinguishers, evacuation plans, and other safety processes. This is just one more.

Managers say "I don't want to think about people in bad ways. I want to keep good thoughts about people." A good thought is a good thing. However, professional development and maturity demands that you come to understand that not everyone is a saint. There is a difference between judging a person as "bad" and making a good discernment, or a good business observation. Managers can remain professionally neutral, personally positive, and observe and document emotional behavior that is less than conducive to productivity within that particular marketplace.

It is necessary for a manager to discern whether someone's emotional behavior is positive and productive or negative and nonproductive. It is also necessary to determine when it is negative if it is due to ignorance, chronic problems, temporary circumstances, or malevolence. This leads to decisions about remediation, recovery, referral, or removal of an employee.

Step 2: Prepare Yourself

A.   Olympic Athletes Go for the Gold

Endurance for the long run takes preparation and maintenance. Imagine that you are a world-class athlete getting ready for Olympic competition. You do not just run onto the field. You do a lot of work prior to the big show. Your preparations should include physical, emotional, spiritual, and mental self-care procedures designed by you, for you. You need to warm up, suit up and show up. And if it makes you feel more confident to have a rabbit's foot in your pocket, then do so! This is *your* game and you are going to have to provide yourself with the stamina and spirit to run a marathon, not a sprint.

B.   Remain Neutral

The manager must remain neutral or will add spin to the problem. Learning to act from a neutral position is a very powerful way to manage. The mechanisms of neutrality are based on the capacity to know your own biases, feelings, opinions and positions, and then putting them aside temporarily in order to act as a mediator. A mediator does not engage in the problem or the solution. A neutral mediator acts as a facilitator of communication flow. In other words, the manager must understand the flow of the energy and not get in the way of progress by diverting it toward a personal agenda.

When a military advisor was asked what advice he would pass on to managers, he responded: "We had managers that turned out to cause more trouble than they solved and had to be let go. These managers did affect morale and productivity. My advice to managers is that I've discovered that people need an outlet for their emotions. If you have to talk to an employee who has been causing problems, approach it non-emotionally. Stay neutral, keep it professional and do not get emotional when they do. Sometimes just letting them talk with someone gets it out and gone."

C.   Determine if you have a problem or an issue

Managers must first assess if the concern on the table is a quick-fix problem or a long-term issue. The tools for one situation will be quite different from the tools necessary to approach another situation.

Management challenges come in two forms: (1) problems and, (2) issues.

(1) Problems: Acute, short-lived, addressable, fixable, solvable, tribulations and challenges

Examples: a flat tire, the sudden unexpected exit of an employee

(2) Issues: Chronic, long-term, addressable, less solvable, sometimes impossible-to-fix concerns and challenges

Examples: the poverty associated with having a bad car with bad tires and no spare, the long-term systemic disenfranchisement because messages from administration are contradictory and duplicitous in an industry that has a history of layoffs

D.   Consider the dimensions of your situation

Are you facing a dust devil or an F-5? Is it just starting or is it long-standing? Big or little? In one department, or is it systemic? Managers must take into consideration the full potential range of losses and gains of any business change, whether minor or major. They must also be on the lookout for exploitation and opportunists who will use the loss part of a change as a venue for escalating conflict and risk. An effective manager looks at potential losses and gains that may be incurred on any level of emotional, mental, physical and even spiritual realm. Change will have effect. No two people perceive a change in the same way. What is minor to one person may trigger overwhelming emotional spinning in another person.

E.   Before you ever begin, step away from the spinning

Managers must factor in considerations from the micro to the macro, and then move carefully, quietly and thoughtfully onto an observation deck, remain professionally neutral and look around to see what is going on everywhere with everyone. Everywhere! With everyone! This is the key to a good Emotional Continuity Management intervention. The manager often is overwhelmed with the specific nature of the challenge and does not step back to view the entire big picture. This is often how a major spin is enhanced as the manager engages in the problem and adds to the mix. Thank everyone for their input, make notes, document, discuss, determine…then leave the area and be alone for a while. Go out for a coffee. Take a lunch break. Sleep on it! If it is not life threatening it can usually wait until you are calm, centered, and ready to make a good management decision. Sometimes a physical break of five minutes can assist you in seeing the big picture so you do not contribute the chaos.

F.   Do your own emotional homework

Managers are in the middle of the chaos — that is your job. If you do not love that feeling, then you may not be management material. You might be a fabulous administrator or worker-bee instead. Decide if you want to be in the middle. Does it stir up your own problems and issues? Step back and evaluate the situation while also reviewing your position in the mix. How are you doing? How are you managing your own emotions? What do you think your capacity is for grief, anger, fear, and other big feelings? All feelings are natural. Managers must be better at knowing their own feelings than others must be. You do not have to control your feelings, just know them so you can manage them well.

G.   Don't fear conflict, use it

Conflict is not meant to be avoided, it is meant to be useful. When tension rises, it can lead to conflict. Conflict is normal. Conflict is not necessarily a problem or an issue. Conflict can lead to war or it can lead to creativity and invention. Gary Simmons, author of The I of the Storm, describes his method of finding peaceful solutions to conflict, and the forces that lead to a conflict storm of "competing needs, wants, and values, combined with misperception, defensiveness, and the need to be right, that create an energetic field of influence that is that storm inherent in interpersonal conflict."

Whatever analogy you use, conflict is the presence of energy that bombards or bumps into other energy. This bumping creates friction. Friction makes heat. Thus, managers feel as though they are always taking the heat from the higher-ups and putting out fires of the line workers. This is because they *are*. However, the energy, in its original state, is neutral and potentially useful. The task is to take the heat or energy and either use it for creative solutions, or return it to a neutral state so it can self-extinguish. A successful conflict resolution does not eliminate the energy but reforms or neutralizes the reactive energy.

Management turns conflict energy positive or negative. A conflict is usually about something perceived as sacred that has been threatened. This situation is someone's Holy Ground. Holy Ground is where human beings can become their best selves or their worst selves. Conflict is where you find out who you are and exactly with whom you are dealing. Conflict is a perfect means to find out what is important. Think of conflict as an excellent location for a potentially important discovery. Conflict provides a mirror so you can see where you are. Do you like how you respond to conflict? Look at your own self to see if you are missing a skill of communication. It is easy to point at the other person. Warriors and excellent managers use conflict for self-discovery.

Managers define conflict zones as their biggest challenge. However, this is where everything important is happening. The simple trick to using conflict well is to first see it as a holy spot where something good can be born. That may never happen, but it is where you begin. How you approach conflict is dependent on your opinion about conflict. If you fear it, or have had bad, violent, or terrifying experiences with conflict, do your own homework first, then move into the energy zone. A conflict does not necessarily mean a war.

When conflicting energies start spinning around, they create a sort of chaos. Chaos is the stuff of life, but you need to move slowly at this point, so you do not fall into the chaos energy. Step back, observe, check your emotional homework and then grab the skills that turn chaos into creativity. This is where a manager can shine like a beacon or go into the shadows. Managers can panic and run, join in the fight, or stand their ground neutrally and make something amazing happen.

After you have done your preparation, move forward with caution. Follow the company policy line-by-line to protect yourself and your workplace. Observe the situation at the location of conflict to see the bigger picture. Step back again if you need to take more time. Always serve the whole system. Do not try to control or block the conflict. Do not get in its way. It will have a life of its own. Take a bit more time to evaluate it within the big scope of the larger mission and see if can be used for creative value or if it is headed to create a negative effect. Use your tools and do what you can to establish the conflict as an added value. If it grows out of control, then use the bigger tools. The traditional view is that conflict means bigger weapons. Weapons do not quiet conflicts, they escalate them. Tools are useful. Weapons of mass destruction can certainly appear to end a conflict, as it burns underground until the next incident.

Step 3: Establish Your Own Support System

A. Support Yourself

Start your support system by learning how to take excellent care of yourself. This means an entire personal program and toolkit of caretaking that will support you from within.

You are a whole person! In an ideal world with ideal people, the whole person should have a repertoire and set of recipes for creating a wonderful life, at home and at work. Everyone else on the rest of the planet must strive for such balance on a daily basis. Healthy people have a plan and a process to care for their physical, emotional, mental and spiritual well-being. This book would be remiss if it avoided the whole person in favor of one of these four foundations of well-being. Take ample time to review your foundations for health as you define them. Favoring one of the four cornerstones while ignoring the others leads to operating in an unbalanced state. Doing a daily practice, discipline, or treatment of some kind in each category will keep you balanced no matter what comes your way. You need to be balanced when standing in the presence of change. *Balance* does not mean *fixed* — it can mean staying in one position for a long time, or being alert and ready to spring into action. All athletes have ways to strengthen their balance because they know how important it is to motion. Are your foundations balanced or do you put all your energies into one category at the expense of the other three?

- PHYSICAL: Exercise, diet, grooming and hygiene, movement, temperature, senses (vision, taste, touch, hearing, smelling) observing art, dancing, wearing different colors and textures, hugs or handshakes, good hand washing, breathing deeply in the morning air, music, trying different foods, a day of silence.

- SPIRITUAL: Exploring the relationship you have with whatever or whomever it is you think is in charge of the universe. Making that relationship a priority. Find a spiritual or religious practice that is yours.

- MENTAL: Challenging yourself in areas of non-expertise, in other words, if you read all the time. take a break. If you never read, pick up a book. If you read nonfiction, take a break with a cheesy novel, and if all you ever read is cheese, pick up a biography. It's okay if you take four years to read a book. It is the willingness that is important. Go to an opera, or stay at home and play a board game. Do crossword puzzles, or start a nonprofit organization and build a board of directors. Do more, or do less, but do it awake.

- EMOTIONAL: Your feelings matter mostly to you, but they do matter. You are human because you have discernment and feel differently about different things. At the end of life people generally don't regret having had a full life with emotions. If they regret, it is that they missed feeling something because they were not paying attention in the moment. Therapeutic Writing for Stress Management is an easy skill to learn to self-manage your emotions at work. It isn't about journal writing or creating narratives for posterity. Therapeutic writing can be done by doodling in the margins of your notebook during an important meeting, writing poetry on a napkin at lunch, writing your grocery list, or a number of other non-writers' tricks. (Hawkins-Mitchell, 1999)

B.   Exit Strategy

Confucius is said to have taught that "when you enter, choose your exit." A good support process is to think how you will exit if things get too much for you to manage. You do not want to linger in negativity and fear, but it is foolish to not at least make a quick check of how you might get out of a situation if it goes nasty. Most continuity plans for disaster include looking for the nearest exit, then getting on with your work.

Some decisions appear to be a good idea at the time and under certain circumstances. Then, things change and a decision may appear to have been an error. This is the nature of human experience. It should be expected. What you did not know at the time may change your opinion. This is when it may be useful to implement the Dr. Vali's "IT-SEEMED-LIKE-A-GOOD-IDEA-AT-THE-TIME" plan.

Change happens and perhaps your decision to work for this company seemed-like-a-good-idea-at-the-time. People are often more likely to end a marriage than a job! Where we might dump a distressful marriage in a flash we cling to our wretched-battering-lowlife-drunken-betraying jobs for better or worse, sickness and health, until someone's death us do part. We stay at horrible jobs stuck with awful human beings that no one in their right mind would marry! Loyalty can be a good thing. Misplaced loyalty can be insane. In our current state of economic affairs it can be easier to divorce a mate than divorce a difficult work colleague.

Date your job; don't marry it. Do not allow yourself to stay in a work situation that may be more difficult or demeaning than a bad marriage. Most people won't keep a pair of jeans if they do not fit. So, keep the receipt with any job you take on. You can change your mind. You can use the "It-Seemed-Like-A-Good-Idea-At-The-Time" exit plan, and move on. Use this job as a lesson for personal growth and then go find a job that suits you better. It may take many jobs to discover your true self. It may take many jobs inside your career of choice to find the situation where you would be inspired to make a lifetime commitment. Or it may take a change of career.

Sit in a theater and before you stuff that first handful of popcorn into your mouth, look around for the exit signs. If there is an emergency you may have saved your life. It does not mean you are leaving before the film is shown. Do the same thing in your job. Before you commit your life savings, buy a house to be close to your new job, or marry the boss' only child, look around and see if there is a healthy way out if you change your mind. It does not mean you are disloyal and it does not mean you are setting up escape. It means this is a job and not a marriage, and the world economy or your company might divorce you suddenly without notice. What would you do? Where would you go? Who are your people? How would you survive? Make a quick note of your plan, stuff it into a favorite hiding place at home, and hope you never need to read it again.

C.   Create your own Support Emotional Continuity Posse

Visualize yourself giving your speech at the Oscar Awards. You have won the award and now you stand before millions of people thanking the people who helped you get there. Being a success never means doing it alone. Pick your caregivers, cheerleaders, friends, mentors, pals, coaches, sponsors, nurturers, venting locations, buddies, sisters, brothers, and unconditional fan clubs carefully. You will need more than one place to garner support if you are going to be a master of management. Use nonhuman supports also such as journal writing, yoga, 12-Step programs, religious affiliations, exercise, good nutrition, clear water, fresh air, flowers, literature, music, and pets to nurture and care for yourself as you go out into the world of emotional management.

D.   Support your Supporters

Managers are mothers, fathers, wives, husbands and relatives to people who will support you and who will need your support from time to time. Use what you learn to pass on to your people so your circle of support strengthens. Children and spouses who are confronted with Emotional Terrorists at school and other workplaces need tools. Teach them how to use Therapeutic Writing or learn Children's Conflict Resolution techniques. (Hawkins-Mitchell, 2002) Suggest an Emotional Continuity Management training for kids to your children's teachers and encourage your spouse to create a Workplace Trauma-Toolkit© with his or her coworkers. Someone in your family may be dealing with aging parents, angry teenagers, ex-spouses, step-parenting, or other potential emotional spin risks and you can provide them with tools and training opportunities by advocating they take good care of themselves also. This will support them and you because you will have done something proactive for the people you love and you will worry a bit less about what is going on with your loved ones when you are trying to wrangle a conflict resolution with five employees that are on an emotional spin.

Step 4: Preparing the System

To convince someone that you know what you are doing can be a task in itself. To convince a boss or supervisor, CEO or your manager that you know what you are doing will mean the difference between success and non-success of your hard work. Most professionals stand on some theoretical foundation which they have come to believe in. Psychology, medicine, art and all fields of endeavor have previous masters who have organized systems of thought, called theories, that they believe define the parameters of the field at its highest order. What is your theory of management? Can you share that with your boss? Does it justify or support you management choices? Is it predicated on excellence or mediocrity?

A.   Pick a Theory

Whatever the change you want to manage, use the following composite theory as a practice exercise to start thinking about theory. Management texts are replete with management theories. Research management theories until you find the one you like and practice it until it becomes yours.

<u>Two Examples of Change Theory:</u>

Example 1: The R's Theory

1.   <u>Re-thinking</u>
      Reconsider the possibility that change is necessary
2.   <u>Re-organizing</u>
      Change needs to happen, so re-organize the system to fit the change
3.   <u>Re-modeling</u>
      Change the building or equipment to suit the change
4.   <u>Re-writing Roles</u>
      Rewrite rules and roles to adjust to the change
5.   <u>Re-warding</u>
      Enhance and entice employees to change
6.   <u>Re-lationships</u>
      Rearrange how people work together to move the system forward
7.   <u>Re-sponsibilities</u>
      Delegate help from inside and outside the organization to accommodate changes
8.   <u>Re-mediation</u>
      Retrain everyone, or specific people how to adjust to change
9.   <u>Re-organizing the industry</u>
      Become an agent of huge change that affects the entire industry to make the changes necessary

Example 2: The Easy-Does-It Theory

0 = do nothing, take no risks. Wait. EASY DOES IT!

1 = watch, observe, attend, wait, consider

2 = begin to assess, collect information, question, engage, organize, process and actively create first ideas of intervention

3 = include others, try simple ideas, support change, encourage inclusion, implement research discoveries, test systems for strength, offer encouragements

4 = increase energy, provide information, formalize processes, seek outcomes, commit to the duration of the process, develop external resources

5 = use external resources, strengthen internal resources, support infrastructure while change is being implemented

6 = demand change because the risks of no change are greater than the risks of change

B.   Consider the Diagnosis

Before a good intervention can happen, a good diagnosis must happen. Today's manager must be an Emotional Continuity Diagnostician. Managerial training may provide a basic understanding of human behavior in the guise of Keeping up Motivation, or Healthy Workplaces, or the Difficult Employee. Managers in other times in history were never intended to do the work that HR or EAPs were meant to do. Today's marketplace, with the variances of business continuity and disaster planning, demands that the manager move into a deeper understanding of human dynamics under stress.

C.   Honor your own Hunches

Managers must make some wise hunches about employees, even if it is not appropriate to "diagnose them" from a mental health clinical perspective. Just as you might have a hunch about your car needing a new intake valve, you would take it to a professional for appropriate care. Every good intervention starts with a hunch, or theory. You can go to your medical doctor with signs and symptoms and say, "I think it might be my sinuses." The doctor will check it out and confirm or deny a diagnosis before treatment. You can start with a hunch. If you call in a Mental Health Professional as a resource, most credible consultants will appreciate your hunches.

D.   Listen to Witnesses

Most people do not want to witness problems. Intentional emotional spinners do not want witnesses. Therefore, silence works well for emotional spinners until a company becomes engaged in a full force blow-out. Spinners are often quite efficient at hiding and distorting reality so that when their behaviors or intentions are eventually witnessed they scramble to rearrange the perception of the viewer. If they can discredit the witness, their position is strengthened. It is easier for the regular witness to accept a creative cover story and move back to the comfort of denial than deal with the ramifications of what they may have seen. The wonderful human brain helps with this. Like an extra eyelid on a camel that protects it from the harsh terrorism of blowing winds, our sweet, protective brains help us blink away icky emotional tornadoes.

Emotional spinners count on this. Emotional Continuity Management works to keep everyone awake, eyes open, with potential witnesses valued, not scorned. If no one has permission to spin, early signs can be addressed with compassion and humor. If no one has permission to see, the blind will no doubt lead the blind right into a tornado.

CONSIDER THE TYPES OF WITNESS

1.   Accidental: Someone unintentionally observes something out of context, inappropriate, dangerous, or incongruent because they just happen to be in the right place at the wrong time or the wrong place at the right time.

2.   Good Radar: Some people are gifted with a sense of Clear Moral Index and natural boundaries which make them able to almost smell trouble or incongruities brewing and not doubt their own perceptions and perspectives.

3.   Attuned Sensitives: Some people have well-developed, natural intuition and sensory acuity and feel safe using it. They respond to it as easily as other use a sense of sight, sound, smell and touch.

4.   Resolving Trauma Survivors: Out of necessity these people have developed or adapted accurate radar for early warning and detection of trouble. They have experienced or witnessed severe critical incidents and observed the outcomes of such events. They know that such difficulties are real and that early warnings might have served them in the past, so they are vigilant. They are great assets to a corporation when given room and support to express their witnessings. Sometimes they can come across as complainers, bitter, or arrogant with an "I-know-what-can-happen-and-everyone-who-doesn't-is-an-idiot" style. Sometimes viewed as complainers, with good support they are helpful. They terrify Emotional Terrorists, who often discredit them as "crazy."

5.   Unresolved Trauma Survivors: Quiet, fearful, high denial, blame themselves, may try to speak up, but may change their story to protect themselves or others. May give good early warnings, but will not be available to back up the claims or observations under pressure. May start strong then fade to self-protect from imagined or remembered abuse or trauma. Their information is useful to an observant manager.

6.   Co-Dependents: They have an active radar system based on their childhood survival mechanisms and also may have an overactive translator system. They can see an eyebrow twitch from across the room but they may mistranslate what it means. The asset is in their acute observational skills. The liability is in their translation of it and their fear mechanisms that suggest it is up to them to control it. They may try to fill in the gap with their own translation of what their observation means. Sometimes an eyebrow twitch is just an eyebrow twitch and sometimes it means more. An alert manager will note the witness report of the eyebrow twitch and keep alert.

7.   Intentional Spinner Witnessing: An Intentional Spinner or an Emotional Terrorist may point in a direction to distract attention or increase energy into the playing field. They may even point out their participation in the problem to make it seem as though they are self-effacing allies and actively participating in finding a solution to the problem. With this they are able to slip around for an "end run" and start a spin elsewhere. With this, they now demand that all pressure on them be removed. "It's over now, because I pointed it out" and "consequences don't matter because we are all one big happy, aren't we?" They press for instant "forgiveness" and want to just move on quickly. Any lingering at this point often leads them to create yet another event to re-distract attention.

Respecting healthy witnessing takes some practice. Although witnessing is a risk, not seeing is a greater risk. And if everyone is on board, everyone can co-witness, which lowers the individual pressure. Any witness who is not respected for their risk to witness may experience a variety of negative feelings, which can set them up to add to a spin. Whistle-blowing has given witnessing a bad name. People now fear speaking up. Instead of feeling honored and appreciated, a witness may end up:

- Feeling like a troublemaker
- Feeling like they did as a child who saw their father get silently drunk while their mother cried in the bedroom
- Feeling like they did as a molested 5 year old
- Feeling like they did when they were a battered spouse
- Feeling like a fool
- Feeling like their perceptions of reality are valueless and wrong
- Feeling stupid
- Feeling denied
- Feeling anger
- Feeling depression
- Feeling obsolete
- Feeling crazy
- Feeling useless
- Feeling frightened
- Feeling held hostage
- Feeling there is no where else to go with this and return to work feeling defeated and confused and ready to abandon loyalty to the firm

Case Example

Trudy dy saw something she does not know how to handle at work. Her co-worker, Bethany, is spreading rumors about the boss and people are spinning and getting upset. Trudy scolds herself and tells herself that she is overreacting. Bethany is an employee with a lot of seniority and Trudy is not. Everyone listens to Bethany and she has a lot of influence among the rank and file.

The waves of rumors spread like wildfire and her co-workers are getting more and more distressed. Ryan threatens to quit. Kim gets too quiet. Suzanne and Vicki Lynn spend more time whispering at the copy machine, and Jessica is taking longer lunches and does not seem to want to participate in the staff meetings. Trudy decides to risk talking to her manager and to share her observations and concerns. It is a brave moment for Trudy, who is rather shy. Trudy explains that although Bethany always gets her work done well, she is somehow able to get other people spinning emotionally. The manager wonders if Trudy might be a troublemaker.

The manager was just considering Trudy for a small promotion, but now questions it. After all, if she cannot work with Bethany on the project, it might not go well for the company. Trudy picks this up and is given the message that her intuition, observations and witnessing are not supported. When she returns to work, Bethany looks across the room at her and gives Trudy a knowing grin. Bethany knows exactly what has just happened and has won territory

Learning Byte

Now Trudy must make a difficult choice. Because her manager did not handle her witnessing well, she can: (1) work in an environment which protects an Emotional Terrorist; (2) become an annoying aggressive witness; (3) try to get other people to see it with her and become a leader of a force against the bad behavior thus escalating the problem and possibly becoming an Emotional Terrorist herself; (4) join in the spinning to be one of the gang; (5) drink heavily; (6) use the internet for her own personal life since no one cares about her; (7) go ahead and sell proprietary information to the guy who was in her face last week; (8) make plans for suicide; (9) make homicide plans; or, (10) leave. All of these options, some silly and extreme, will influence the emotional climate of the company. What would have happened if the manager had just listened to the witnessing, acknowledged the possibility that Trudy was honest, and moved with an open mind and an alert eye?

DO THIS: Explore the critical value of witnessing. with a mental health counselor or an Emotional Continuity Management consultant.

DON'T: Discredit a witness. Listen first. Evaluate later. It is not a good feeling to realize after the fact that someone "warned you" about something you didn't see.

The effective management of witnessing is quite simple. It consists of the following steps:

1.   Listen to the observations without judging, commenting, agreeing or disagreeing. Stay neutral,
2.   Make a note of the concerns for possible future reference.
3.   Say something like "Thank you, I appreciate your report and I will make a note of this information and keep my eyes open."
4.   Repeat #3 if necessary to support the witness.

If the reporter is not satisfied with this, and demands that the manager engage, it may be an Emotional Terrorist Witnessing. Most witnesses simply want to unload the report, be acknowledged, and move on. Some witnesses need more support and gratitude, but they usually do not need engagement.

A manager does not need to join, agree, investigate, act, react, deny, dance, sing or create any sort of chaos to "take a witnessing under advisement." Usually one witnessing event does not make a case unless it is criminal or life-threatening. However, a manager cannot have two witnessings if he/she blows off the first one just because it stands alone. That is, unless the manager is an Emotional Terrorist.

E.   Make a Management Toolkit

Minimum Requirements of an Emotional Continuity Management Toolkit

- Conflict resolution methods
- Communication methodologies
- Systems education
- Diversity training and cultural norms of emotions
- Icons, slogans and banners for quick recognition
- Team building strategies
- Grief work education and practice
- Control and management strategies
- Personal values tools
- Humor
- Emotional Terrorism information
- Tools for new employee orientation
- Normal and abnormal psychology basics
- How to recognize signs of traumatic stress
- Emotional self-defense
- Cultural and social hierarchy norms
- Ventilation models for debriefing and defusing
- Adjustment strategies and practices
- Stress management tools for the life span
- Physical, mental, emotional and spiritual health practices
- Resistance and creativity training
- Documentation standards for emotions
- Memos of understanding with external vendors
- Bibliographies
- Corporate models for Emotional Continuity Management
- Other resources
- Emotional tools that generalize across occupations
- A full range of emotional tools for the entire range of human emotions

- Emotional quick-fix first aid ideas with pre-arranged referrals for more serious emotional requirements
- Tools that generalize to small and large organizations without significant adjustments
- Tools that are not based in fads or trends
- Tools that are gender, cultural, socio-economic, educational, racial, and ethnically sensitive
- Tools should be designed that are cross-cultural
- Tools will work equally well for the diverse needs of executive, management and line staff. Other tools may be needed for volunteers, vendors, clients and others but should remain in step with all other tools
- Tools that are simple, understandable, and practical will be effective for use inside and outside the work setting.

Step 5: Go For It

Set your eyes on your goal, suit up, pull yourself up straight, rub your lucky rabbit's foot, take a breath and jump in to the midst of the fun. Do not be upset by initial stirs of fears and worries, this is just energy moving. As you accommodate to the energy in motion from a position of personal strength do not take chaos personally. Begin your work and manage with personal persistence striving for excellence. Start your day with a "bring it on" attitude. Reframe your vision to that of yourself as a Management Warrior seeking Excellence.

A.   Learn How to Persist

1. *Only listen to people who give you YES messages*

   Do not let the fears of other people get in the way of believing in yourself. Even if you do not believe in you, do not let others convince you that you are right. If you want to be an astronaut, give it a shot. If you do not reach the stars, okay. But in the process, you might just find that you like working with the nifty computers at Houston Control. Or you might become an armchair astronomer. If you want to be an excellent manager, use the YES's as doorways to success.

2. *Pick a goal, any goal, and do one small thing toward it every day*

   Some days are harder than others are. Once you have picked a goal, do something toward it every day. Even if today you can only muster the strength to sharpen your pencils, say aloud, "Sharpening this pencil is helping me reach my goal of _____." One 70-year-old author was asked how long it took him to write his novel. He said, "70 years." It was made into a movie after his 73rd birthday. He was in the film. If you want to be a great and beloved manager, pick a small goal to work on each day.

3. *Suit up and Show up*

   Begin to see everything as directed toward your goal. If you are watching TV, watch for programs about your goal. If you are going for a walk, consider how walking will make you stronger for your outcome. If you are eating, eat to get healthy for your goal. If you are reading a cheesy novel, use it to learn to read faster. If you are poor and alone, celebrate your freedom, because when you are successful you will be busy and up to your chin in people who want to be with you.

4. *Take time to notice the butterfly outside the window*

   As you become more involved and engaged with your visions and goals, make certain that you continue to do reality checking with nature. Spend at least five minutes each day (more if you can) looking out the window, counting snowflakes, picking flowers, sitting on the porch in the sunshine, walking barefoot, hugging trees, or weeping over sunsets. At work this can look like a quick breath of fresh air between meetings, a quiet lunch outdoors, a quick peek at the trees outside your window, or drinking a glass of water very slowly and enjoying the sweetness of the liquid going down your throat and saying to yourself, "thank you water."

5. *Don't join those who complain about the process*

In work sites, employees can quickly establish themselves into two separate groups. One group will be comprised of workers who complain about everything (and there is always ample to complain about at work) and those who do not have time or will not take time to complain. Guess which group is more successful over time? There is plenty of time to complain after tasks are completed. A good manager will allow time for an occasional group complaint-fest. This is often best handled over pizza.

6. *Make at least two new friends*

Make one friend who is just a bit less motivated and one who is just a bit more motivated than you are. Pick peers, not staff friends. Choose management peers from a different company or industry if you can. Join a management organization to meet people. Let these two different friends balance your pace. As you interact with the less motivated friend, use a little of your energy to push him/her and yourself. As you interact with the more motivated person, use a little of their energy to push yourself. Do not try to overcome the more motivated person, or rescue the less motivated person. Just notice your pace and use it to keep your energy flowing. Enjoy their success energy and persistence and to create sources and boundaries for your own forward momentum. It is also a gift to yourself to maintain old friendships with supportive people who may not be "on your train" but will act as witness to your growth and celebrate with you. There are people who love to cheer for the mountain climbers but who themselves would rather wait at base-camp. Ask climbers to join you and ask the base-camp folks to fix a cup of cocoa for you when you return with your grand stories. Both kinds of people are treasure to keep and to protect forever.

7. *Pick an appropriate time to relax with peers. Become devoted to it.*

Every Friday afternoon your staff could meet at a local café to talk, complain, laugh and regroup. The ritualized connection can be open to anyone who shows, one or all, and can be used to debrief the week so people do not have to take it home. Recreation is absolutely necessary to keep up a consistent level of persistence, create balance, provide fun stories, encourage light moments, provide places to exchange helpful tips and eliminates isolation. Isolation is very dangerous when you are striving for a goal because in isolation you can lose perspective about why you began this journey in the first place.

8. *Take care of your soulful self*

Although it is very important to care for your physical and emotional well-being while working for a goal, it is critical to care for the part of you that goes "beyond the self." Write poetry on napkins, pray, meditate, walk on the pier, compose a symphony, go back to church or synagogue, sing, smile at old people at bus stops, sew a quilt for charity, run a marathon, buy an antique, swim, watch old movies, give blood to the Red Cross, write love letters, make cookies on a rainy Sunday, wait patiently for someone, help a friend move, wash your car, paint your living room, make curtains, walk on the beach, be a birth coach, sit by a dying friend, buy a cat, take your dogs to the park, climb a tree and do whatever it takes to balance the unilateral selfish energy it takes to push toward your goal by offering service to others.

9. *Re-invent yourself as needed*

Take time to find out who you are and who you want to be in 5 years, 10 years, and 20 years. Find a mentor in someone who has succeeded in your goal; ask him or her for advice. Find someone older who will say, "Just do it now dear, because when you are my age, you will wish you had."

10. *Learn to jump hoops, even little tiny ones or ones with big flames*

Being a student, or a learner of any kind, means there are people who are "The Knowers" and they have the power for now. It's okay — because someday, you will have the power when you are the master. If you are really a master you will not forget the days you were a powerless nincompoop and you will be more mentor than tyrant. Surrendering gets either easier or more difficult as you age. Surrender can feel like freedom or death. But until you really are the One Who Knows All Things In Your Given Area of

Expertise, you can still learn. And even the Knower must learn how to be a wonderful Knower. The surrender of jumping hoops can feel bad or creative. Hoop jumping is usually a temporary event. The hoop is not the entire Truth of the Universe, it is only a hoop. Don't make it more than it is or less than it is. Masters are not necessarily any brighter or more intelligent than anyone else is, but they are more persistent than most and willing to jump through pointed flaming hoops to reach their goals and dreams. There is a story about Albert Einstein who was trying to fix a crooked paper clip. He searched for a tool to fix it and found an entire box of paperclips. He completed repairing the bent clip. Even though he did not need to, he was persistent in completing his task. When asked about this he explained that this was how he approached every problem, until it was solved.

11. *Know when to push the envelope and when to back off*

The one-minded focus necessary to reach a goal can lead some to a rather addictive process of obsessive behavior. Figure out when you are pushing it. Watch for signs like: leaving your purse in the refrigerator, forgetting to shower for much too long, talking to friends online rather than taking your dogs for a walk, yelling at your wife, screaming at your husband, thinking the world revolves around you, feeding the kids Chinese food on Thanksgiving because you forgot to buy a turkey, and screaming at friends who just "don't understand your vision." If you are hurting yourself or hurting someone else, you are off track. Maybe your goal is good and valid, but your way of getting there is inappropriate. Seek professional help if you lose yourself in your goal. It is okay to change your mind, change your vision, change your goal, and change your style. If you need to make an exit, use this phrase to explain it to friends, "It seemed like a good idea at the time, but I changed my mind." If you have a special, wonderful vision, at least go for it. Success often means you gave it a shot and re-decided.

12. *Bless yourself for Surviving*

Survival is not always a pretty sight. It takes a lot of grit and persistence to live through this life. You probably have people you have known that did not make it this far. If you are reading this, it means you are probably still alive. That's a good thing. All your faults, errors, talents, skills, efforts, mistakes, questions, answers, fears, angers, joys, resistances, problems, victories and failures have led you to Now. You are so brave. As you persist in living on Planet Earth and following your dreams and working toward achieving your personal goals, sometimes you must give yourself permission to persist and continue persisting. Sometimes no one else will encourage you. In fact, some may scorn you for pressing on. That's okay. Be noble. Be honorable. Find and create dignity in everything you do. Then, no matter how big or small your goal, when you reach it, bow deeply to yourself and say, "I AM SO BRAVE!" A wonderful benefit of this kind of thinking is that you will be able to celebrate and honor even the smallest achievements of others. What a wonderful manager you will be then! The victories of others will be neither a threat nor a joke. You will authentically celebrate success, and compassionately support errors. You will know that someone else's goal may seem small to you but it may be a Mount Everest to them. When you know what your vision for greatness is, you will be able to persist toward it while cheering loudly for other persistent people. What if there was no finish line?

B. *Know when to quit and head for shelter*

Some emotional spins are bigger than you are. Make certain that you have a best pal or resource (not a spouse or parent) outside your company that can support you and your work. The all-alone nature of management is sometimes daunting in the midst of storms. All warriors know when to quit, know where the foxhole is and all good managers know where and how they can protect themselves legally, ethically, and emotionally. If things get rough, ask yourself, "are you dating this job or are you married to it?" If you are married to the job and it becomes too much, perhaps a job-divorce will be necessary to maintain your integrity. If you are dating the job, you might just need to break up and give back the ring. No matter the situation or circumstances, it is always appropriate to work in a safe place.

C. *Have appropriate pre-arranged referrals available*

Managers are not supposed to be Mental Health Professionals. So what happens when managers recognize a major problem with one of their people? Traditionally they send them to HR or recommend an EAP session or two. Then what? The employee is still there. You may need more than these two referral resources to get through a major incident. And there is always the concern that your HR or EAP people might be the emotional problems in your company. If your resources are impaired temporarily by a traumatic event, what would you do? Some companies retain Emotional Continuity Management professionals while other businesses create partnerships and Memos of Understanding (MOU's) between agencies.

Step 6: Design Your Management Style and Program

You should know your company inside and out. Designing a management style and program needs to reflect your own personal style while fitting within the parameters of the company that pays your salary and the industry that drives the company. Try to look at the big picture and the small picture when you are researching and developing a program for your company.

A.   Your Management Design Plan Should Consider:

* Assessment of your unique and specific situation
* Making a rough-draft plan
* Checking out the plan with others
* Confirming a final, but adjustable plan
* Implementing the plan
* Assessing the plan in action
* Reorganizing the plan as necessary to adjust to changes
* Making reports and recommendations
* Writing documentations of outcomes
* Encouraging evaluation and ongoing research

B.   Obtain Buy-On

Unless you own the company, you need administrative support or buy-on to move forward. Your administrative buy-on process is perhaps the most critical of the steps in establishing an Emotional Continuity Management plan. Nothing will sabotage hard work than an upper-echelon authority dispatching your program.

KNOW THE DIFFERENCE BETWEEN CONTROL, FORCE, POWER, AND MANAGEMENT

Control   Control is an attempt to limit, restrict, stop or remove the expression of something. The desire or motivation for control is to keep something from happening or to regulate it from spreading. Emotions cannot be controlled. Nor should they be. Emotions can be managed.

Force   Force is a movement that projects a certain amount of power in one place in relationship to another place. Force creates counter-force that weakens some other area where the power has been removed to contribute to a force. Force is oppositional in that is moving against something. Hitler was a force, Germany was a power. Gandhi was a force, Non-violence is a power.

Power   Power arises from a position that carries a motive. Power is a neutral state that implies influence based on mass or volume. Power is a descriptor for determining the amount of something. David

Hawkins describes in his book <u>Power vs. Force</u>, that power arises from meaning. His research describes how power always wins over force because it appeals to what uplifts, dignifies and ennobles human beings.

Management   Management is more about organizing, handling, using or creating a process for something. If emotions are consider to simply be differing forms of energy, then management is about skillfully employing that energy into the system so that it doesn't become blocked, short circuited, explosive or diminished.

Managers need to know the differences between these concepts in order to use the ones that are most appropriate in a given situation. Historically if you consider the differences between control, management, power and force, you will readily discover the root causes of fights, conflicts, struggles, and wars. Managers need to manage. They will need to manage powers and forces without being controlling, because they will have no control over these factors. Managers do not have control. Often when managers feel this reality they begin to feel fear. Fear is a force. Faith is a power.

There are times when a manager must act as a force to oppose the winds of emotional chaos. There are other times when a manager must expose their own personal power by simply moving out of the way and letting the wind blow. This construct is something that tornado chasers understand clearly or they risk their lives. Most tornado chasers do not want to die. They simply want to understand the powers and the forces of these behemoth energies. They respect the powers and meanings of nature. They respect the forces of twisters and comprehend the comparisons between their own human energy levels and the levels associated with the storm. They do not even begin to consider controlling the tornado. They do manage themselves in the presence of these powers and forces. Emotional Continuity Management is a lot like being a tornado chaser. It is important to stand by while not being sucked into the vortex of the spin.

HOW TO MANAGE EMOTIONS

How do you manage the emotions of yourself and others? Emotional Continuity Management is a life-long learning process. People grow and develop over the lifespan and do not stop that process at adolescence. Adult learners can use the following steps to become more effective in finding comfort and pragmatic means to be in the presence of emotions in the workplace or anywhere else. The list of skills to learn are: 1) Know yourself and your feelings, 2) approach emotions with empathy, 3) flow with the motion, 4) avoid judgment, 5) express needs and wants, 6) validate, 7) express hope and gratitude, 8) pause and reflect, 9) move to problem solving, 10) and follow-up.

1.   *Know Yourself And Your Feelings*

How you feel in a situation contributes to how an emotional communication works or does not work. As a manager, you need to be on top of your own emotional game and not let others feelings take over the situation you are managing. Allowing room for feelings does not mean that feelings run the show. Feelings need to have their say in a situation but need not overwhelm it. Even big or huge feelings can come and go if they are well-managed. Remember that managed does not mean controlled. Managed does not mean denied or exploited. Your emotions matter also, but mostly to you. If you know your own feelings in a situation you can do self-care during or after the emotional situation has been resolved.

Walter Powers, a psychology professor, taught his students that if they were not aware of their own feelings during a counseling session then they were not doing it correctly. He taught that these inner feelings are excellent tools for both empathetic listening and informative response. If you feel anger, fear, embarrassment, curiosity, satisfaction or any other feeling, you can access this to discover more about the speaker and more about yourself.

2.   *Approach Emotions With Empathy*

Probably the best term to express how a manager manages the feelings of others is the word empathy. Empathy, according to Marshall Rosenberg, an expert in non-violent communication, is a "respectful understanding of what others are experiencing." If you begin a management situation with empathetic listening to your own feelings and those of another, you begin with respect to all parties. You first allow yourself to respect your own emotions to increase understanding your own experience. Then, find appropriate ways to listen and seek understanding about what others are experiencing. Empathy is respecting both sides of the exchange

3.   *Flow With The Motion*

Your feelings are on one side of a divide and the speaker is on the other side. This chasm must be crossed for communication to be successful. This separation between you and "them" creates the necessary gap to be present in any discussion of emotions. That gap is a safe place, the demilitarized zone, and the neutral ground where something will happen. It is a breathing space when feelings are big or strong. The gap should not be filled with a wall or attack language. Let the opening occur naturally. Do not rush to close the gap even in the discomfort of a time when there is no understanding. The gap is an open place where feelings can be safely exchanged. Think of a figure eight moving between two people. Imagine the flow moving easily and calmly between the two individuals.

Conflict starts when one of the individuals places a wall between that empathetic flow or begins attacking. Empathy does not imply agreement, suppression, control, or coopting to a feeling that is not on your side of the figure eight flow. A manager is open to the flow. Great managers encourage it.

4.   *Avoid Judgment*

In emotional situations, there is a natural tendency to judge the feelings at good or bad. If you do not agree with the emotion or the details of a situation, you may want to control it by making a judgment of its value. Hold your ground and let the flow continue. If it gets personal or attacking, rather than calling it bad or a failure, see that the need of the person communicating is extreme and they are expressing fear that their needs will not be met.

5.   *Express Needs And Wants*

One of the most important clarifiers in a difficult and emotional conversation is to determine the difference between needs and wants. Needs are requirements and are therefore nonnegotiable. Wants range between slight preferences to extreme desires. Needs and wants are emotionally charged feelings depending on the degree of requirement or preference. We need air. We prefer good smelling air. We need food. We prefer gourmet faire. We need clothing. We prefer comfortable clothes. We desire elegant and expensive labels. We need money. We want a raise. We need money to feed our children. We need a raise.

6.   *Validate*

Validation confirms and authorizes that a situation is within boundaries and acceptable boundaries. A validating statement sanctions it. Again, this does not mean that you agree or accept the truth of the statement or feelings expressed, but that you, as a leader authorize its presence in the discussion. By neutrally reflecting back to the speaker that they are heard they feel validated. In many cases of conflict or emotional content, this is all that is necessary to solve what may seem like an irresolvable problem. Validating that emotions are okay within certain parameters as defined by company policy, allows the feeling to be ventilated. Ventilation is movement. And movement means change. This may bring up other emotions but does not reflect intractable stagnation in a system.

7.   *Express Hope and Gratitude*

Current scientific research is confirming that positive language changes molecular structure. Words of positive expectancy and appreciation do not close the process. Managers who fear the process of emotions will usually place a wall here. Individuals who feel the need to control, rather than manage emotions, will use language that stops the flow. Someone who wants to be a tyrant or autocrat, or perhaps even an Emotional Terrorist, will take the opening and exploit it. Stopping emotional communication does not stop emotions from flowing; it merely moves the flow from one place to another. If you want that flow to move elsewhere and create unknown consequences, create a dam. If you want to be in the loop as the manager, then you need to keep the flow open by establishing a sense of future through hopeful language and gratitude. Hope words like trust, anticipate, wish for, and looking forward to, create a sense of future. Future suggests life. No hope and no future imply death. Death is the most emotional thing that humans experience.

8.   *Pause and Reflect*

Unless there is a life-threatening situation, in which case you would immediately call for backup, dial 911, or implement your emergency plan, a pause to reflect and consider is a very useful tool for managers. Pauses do not imply stoppages. Pauses are bookmarks to return to later. Pauses are brief moments to catch your breath so you are not spun up in someone's emotional tornadoes. When you take a break, define it clearly and honor that time frame. Tell your employee that you are going to take five minutes and will be back to them. Make sure it is five minutes when you return or trust will be broken and emotions will stir up again and will include an additional betrayal. You can also tell someone that you are going to sleep on it, take 24 hours to consider it, or bring it along to the next meeting in two weeks. What is important is to express it as a pause and not an end.

Reflection on an emotion is not critical thinking or evaluation. Reflection is lighter and gentler. It is a pondering, a consideration, contemplation or musing about something. This is not the time to move into cognitive, intellectual, brainstorming problem solving. This is a time to let the feelings settle down into their most clear form so that what is important stands out. Emotional energy can be chaotic, loud, spinning, and confusing. During a reflection time, you may discover that there was only one important or critical feature expressed, such as fear. Most negative emotions sift down to fear. If you can discover through gentle reflection what the fear may be, you are well on your way to begin problem-solving, because you will be addressing the real issue that created the emotion.

9.   *Move To Problem Solving*

If you have followed the steps, you are now ready to move your thinking into problem-solving strategies. This is when you can implement a style you are familiar with if it works, or do a transformation activity that will move the problem into a new light. Many managers try to problem-solve by approaching the conflict, running from it, creating a distraction, or using total avoidance. These behaviors are all about fear. Manage your own fear first before trying to manage the fears of others.

One surprisingly interesting way to problem-solve that you may never have tried is to write poetry about the concern. Poetry writing, besides being therapeutic, moves the thinking from one part of the brain to another location in the brain. You have access to many brain locations. How many do you use? Perhaps you are a manager who goes back to the same old brain location hoping to find a new trick. The standard definition of insanity is to keep doing the same thing while hoping for different results. You will still have to come back to the problem using appropriate business and industry-standard approaches based on policy and procedures. But before you move into that place that is familiar, you can explore alternative problem solving strategies that add another dimension to the information. Ann Fry, who pitches herself as the Dean of Fun at Humor University.com, provides her business clients with a pamphlet titled 139 Ways to Lighten up Your Workplace. Franz Metcalf, a Buddhist scholar teamed up with management consultant BJ Gallagher Hateley to apply the Buddha's insights to life on the job with What Would Buddha do at Work: 101 Answers to Workplace Dilemmas. Business texts will provide you with current styles and ideas like Reliability Management: An Overview, by EQE International or The Successful Manager's Handbook from Personnel Decisions.

Perhaps you want a new role model for problem solving. Study the lives of successful problem-solvers to learn how they did it. Pick someone you admire, real or a fantasy character and explore how their style could be included into yours. If you resonate with the problem-solving styles of historic figures you might enjoy Leadership the Eleanor Roosevelt Way: Timeless Strategies from the First Lady of Courage, by Robin Gerber; Power Plays: Shakespeare's Lessons in Leadership and Management, by John O. Whitney; Patton on Leadership, by Alan Axelrod; Jesus CEO: Using Ancient Wisdom for Visionary Leadership, by Laurie Beth Jones; or, Elizabeth I, CEO, by Alan Axelrod. On the other hand, maybe you want to find a new approach to old problems and need to read Winnie-The-Pooh on Management and Problem Solving, by Roger E. Allen.

Keep in mind the difference between problems and issues and remember that problems can be solved.

10. *Follow-Up*

Check back with all participants to make certain there are not lingering emotions that may spin into tornadoes.

11. *Validate*

Using the artificial technique of reflecting back to someone what you think you are hearing may at first feel awkward and "techniquey." That's because it is — until it becomes natural. Nonetheless, it is crucial to communication that you express something about what you heard and give the speaker an opportunity to clarify and simplify the message they want heard. If you hear someone correctly, according to what they want you to hear, emotions that charge the situation will begin to decrease. Being heard allows people to feel validated and valued. Being not heard leads to increased emotions and violence. It has been said that violence is simply extreme communication. If emotions are escalating, someone is not hearing.

12. *Explore options*

It is usually not helpful to problem-solve while emotions are being expressed. Problem-solving or fixing a feeling denies the value of the feeling. Exploring options is about trying to find a way to define what is precisely required or desired to address the specific feeling. When people are engaged in strong emotion, language tends to become vague and fall into words of extremes and demands as the emotional person is struggling with control. Gently helping the speaker to express specifics during this portion of the exchange is validating that you are listening and interested in their needs and wants, will help them move into a more calm and rational part of the brain where problem-solving can be seen as an option, and find real actions to solve real problems.

EMOTIONAL CONTINUITY MANAGEMENT TRANSFORMATION

Communication expertise is critical to managing the full range of emotions at the workplace. Most managers can handle annoyances and pet peeves, disappointments and minor disgruntlements. The more extreme emotions demand more skills. Violence can come loudly in bombs and guns and it can tiptoe in on quiet paws. Disaster can aggressively explode into your face or subtly disembowel your spirit through passive violence. Arun Gandhi, the granddaughter of M. K. Gandhi suggests in the forward to Marshall Rosenberg's book Nonviolent Communication: A Language of Life, that it is the positive within yourself that emerges as the alternative antidote to selfish, greedy, hateful, prejudiced, suspicious and aggressive attitudes. As long as the world sees corporate communications and demonstrations as nonpersonal and ruthless attempts to reach a bottom line, managers will have a daunting challenge to face into the winds and tornadoes of chaos with personal grounding. Some people run to the storm cellar when the slightest breeze comes. Others chase tornadoes with a resounding "bring it on" attitude.

Whatever your style and whatever winds you must face, it will serve you well and it will affirm your employees to take time to consider how you want to manage your life inside and outside the workplace and to do the hard work for personal transformation. Communication can be cooperative or life-threatening; it is up to you now to make the difference at work. *You* are the leadership. Louise Diamond writes in her book <u>The Courage for Peace</u>, "Whereas previously companies were arranged in separate, isolated, and even competitive departments, the necessities of a global market require that different parts of a single company work together seamlessly." The notion that working together can be seamless, effortless, smooth, and fluid may seem an unreachable goal for managers. Perhaps it is. But how will you know how far you can go, how much you can transform and reinvent yourself unless you "bring it on" and go for your best?

Transformative people see things differently. They see the small detail and the big picture. They find a way to combine science, art, and action in ways that inform and affirm. Einstein suggested that all that science really consisted of was everyday thought that had been refined. Refining, transforming, fine-tuning, adjusting and creating new ways to solve old problems is the hope of the global consciousness and subsequently the global marketplace. M.K. Gandhi said we must be the change we want to see in the world. Think about your favorite manager. Think about your favorite person. How would you combine the attributes of these people into a composite "you" who is the innovative management professional?

PERSONAL TRANSFORMATION AS A POSITIVE BUSINESS CHANGE

Personal transformation is a process of change. It implies that this conversion is positive and life-enhancing. Although some people can transform themselves into monsters and villains, positive transformation can lead human beings to rise to the highest potentials. Many people believe now that corporate thinking is descending into its lowest potentials, and for some organizations this is true. Others are making deep and abiding efforts to lift themselves and their colleagues up to standards that are individually enhancing and globally conscious.

Relearning something that has become a habit is hard work. Relearning at work is very hard work. Many people just want to put in their time and get home to their "real lives." Transformation means finding more than just the old, standby way to approach a problem. Many challenges are approached with the two instinctive standby options of fight or flight. Transformative thinking can dissolve obstacles rather than feeling fear or the need to increase force. Instead of pushing against an obstacle, running from it, trying to circumvent it, or standing in the front of it wanting to move forward to resolution and increasing your frustration, try something different. Try to see yourself becoming a light that dissolves through the obstacle to arrive on the other side. Transform your obstacles into pets and put hats on them. Transform your fear into humor.

It may take a few attempts to transform your old thinking into new ideas. As you stand in front of your obstacle, take a moment to look through the blockage to see what kind of manager you really want to be. Take a deep breath and be that person now. When you have done this, you have transformed an obstacle into a gateway.

Personal transformation and communication are topics that most managers understand as essential to excellence in management. Clarity in communication is vital when working with the emotions of employees. Personal transformation goes with growth and change. Workshops on communication skill building are available and plentiful. Trainings in personal transformation are abundant. If your organization does not support your communication and personal growth you will have to read books on your own, pay for workshops out of your own pocket, and advocate for training from nontraditional sources in order to develop a breadth and depth to your skill set.

Case Example

Charolette Anne was given an opportunity to have an individual meeting with the Emotional Business Continuity consultant prior to termination. She was 29 years old, a mother of three, wife, and an overwhelmed manager in a medical facility overseeing eight employees who were making an increasing number of errors. She said that her team was "acting like spoiled toddlers" and it was obvious that her skills as a mother were not serving her well in a management position. Charolette Anne reported that she had been recruited from within the ranks and had not had any training for management other than being told how bad she was doing it. The consultant asked her if she wanted to continue as a manager and she said, "Yes, I think I do. But I also love the front line work and always jump into it when I see someone making an error! And then no one likes me." With encouragement and individual consultations over a three-month period, Charolette Anne began to self-advocate for some professional management training. Although her bosses were fairly tight with training dollars the consultant suggested that the investment would be sound and so they found a low-cost, generic management skills seminar. They spent approximately $59.00 on management training.

Charolette Anne came away from her very first training session with a sense of normalization about her young age, developmental level, management skills-set, human emotions, and professional ambiguity. She learned that the ambiguous nature of management was the domain of being between the holders of powers and the line workers. She came to understand that management was like an island and she had no peers. With this insight she stopped feeling powerless, stopped trying to "make friends," and came into her own style of management. She began trying new ideas and dealing well with mistakes and false starts. A natural good humor evolved as she saw her team more like employees than naughty children. She tried creative ideas that she learned at the training and began to develop peer relationships within a manager's support group. She reinvested her energies, moved away from her annoying micro-management style, saw her team settle down, and became more confident in her position and in her personal power. This transformation spilled over to her personal life as her relationships and personal health improved. She began reading more. The company invested approximately $475 dollars on this employee, who was the 5th manager in three years that they had been considering firing for lack of skills.

Case Example

Stuart was 59 years old and didn't want to change any habits. He was tired and just wanted to retire. When the printing company went from old-style presses to computers he became increasingly depressed and anxious. His health began to waiver. He talked openly about being close to retirement so didn't believe he needed to change. Leaning heavily on his future retirement fund as his upcoming financial cushion he trudged along bitterly toward his birthday as he became sicker and sicker. His work, which depended heavily on the physical stamina of being on his feet most of the day and good eyesight, was suffering as his strength began to diminish and his vision was suddenly impaired. He lost eyesight in his left eye and had emergency surgery to remove the lens. He was then fitted for new glasses to compensate because he refused to try wearing contact lenses. Three weeks before retirement he was hospitalized with a small stroke. He recovered and returned to work in time to retire. He received a small certificate for 30 years of service. He went home. The following month the company that managed his retirement fund collapsed and went bankrupt and Stuart lost his retirement completely. With nothing to fall back on he lost hope. Within two years he passed away.

Mary Lee was 55 years old and didn't want to change any habits. She was tired and just wanted to retire on her last husband's retirement fund. When the restaurant she had worked for during the last 20 years became an espresso bar she realized she might have to change some habits. Her health began to waiver and so she consulted with some experts and decided she needed to make some personal transformations. Where once she talked openly about being close to retirement she now began thinking of starting over. She went to a local college and asked for some advice, called friends, started reading, and began rethinking her life. She leaned heavily on her ex-husband's future retirement fund as her future cushion now became an anchor and not a sail. She began working out and bought a bicycle. Her health improved. She lost weight and got stronger. Her work, which depended heavily on the physical stamina of being on her feet most of the day, got easier. She liked learning about the new coffee equipment. She had a talent for it. She decided she might try doing other new things and took on a challenge and goal that she had fantasized about for her entire life, and became a firefighter. She took training and became an Emergency Medical Responder, learned to drive the "big-rig" and to fight wilderness fires. Her body got stronger and she was having a ball. She took on another job working with young children. When she left the restaurant there was a front-page photo of her celebrating her enormous contribution to the community. Shortly after this she discovered that the fantasy retirement fund had never existed. She laughed and rearranged her finances and began remodeling her home. With nothing to fall back on, Mary Lee found hope in her spiritual journey, her own strength, her friends, her own competency and creativity, and found that her life was just taking off!

Case Example

Lily was 84 when she passed away. She was working up to the last two weeks before her death from lymphatic cancer. Her philosophy was that life was wonderful! She was a medical coder at a hospital and trained the "new kids" when they were hired. Once she complained that she was late to work because her "hip was hurting." Of course at 83 one would expect a few (or more) creaks and groans. When asked what was going on with her hip she replied, "Oh, I was swinging on a rope across a creek with my grandson and hit a shrub and bruised my hip." Her retirement party was a gala event and she wore a red dress.

Learning Byte

Transformation is either creative and moving toward life-affirming qualities, or destructive and moving toward death affirming qualities. Positive transformation is usually considered a value-added element of humans in general and employees in specific. Becoming a Transformative Manager means you encourage your people to grow and become all they can become within the framework of their given situation. And you do the same thing for yourself.

DO THIS: *Explore your own personal transformation plan. Who do you want to be when you grow up?*

DON'T: *Ever stop transforming and reinventing yourself on a regular basis.*

HOW TO BECOME A TRANSFORMATIVE MANAGER: CHANGE YOUR THINKING AND TAKE ACTION

- Find five new ways to approach any challenge
- If you can already think of five, go for ten
- Become a professional peace builder
- Read two texts on peace making
- Start your day with a life-affirming "bring it on" attitude
- Begin your day with a positive affirming statement
- Learn to be playful
- Put a small toy in your pocket (only you will know it is there)
- See your work as service
- Work can become a humanitarian process when you enjoy service
- Take the growth and become more
- Think of three difficulties you have had a how you have learned from them
- Shift your thinking
- Add a visual, auditory, kinesthetic, or tactile application to your problem-solving
- Practice new skills
- Pick a skill you are not good at yet and exercise it until you are much better
- Assist people to be more
- Encouraging people is a gift you give yourself. See potential
- Make new choices
- Take something on or let something go
- Find a personal balance
- Keep physical, emotional, spiritual and mental dynamics in equal proportions
- Use situations for creativity
- Bring art into your work, bring art into your workplace
- Open up your heart and mind
- Compassion and Intelligence are not mutually exclusive. Offer yourself.
- Accept people and situations as they are
- If this is the best it's going to get, find some peace and move on
- Hone your leadership skills
- Explore your relationship with your personal power and your presentation
- Become an icon or light in the darkness
- Add a positive dimension whenever it is appropriate
- Dream of better ways
- Read a biography of a dreamer

- Use work for spiritual growth
- Find a spiritual discipline of your choice and practice it
- Increase empowerment for yourself and others
- Encourage yourself and others to take new risks and challenges
- Plant seeds and be a kind gardener
- Be patient in the presence of change and growth. Nurture it.
- Be an inspiration
- Young people watch you to see a future. Older people watch to see hope for the future
- Let go of your opinions
- Remind yourself that it is impossible to be correct 100% of the time
- Wait
- Balance movement and non-movement times and use pauses to rest and reflect
- Believe
- Have more faith than fear
- Allow yourself to remain sensitive
- Remember the end game is usually about people
- Increase your empathy
- Make connections with people
- Soften your ego
- Big egos belong to frightened people, so become fearless
- Think highest order thoughts and ideals
- Maintain highest order ethics because you are a leader
- Think in terms of possibilities
- Air travel was a crazy idea to all but a handful of people only a few years ago
- See your work as sacred
- Revere what you do as a contribution and see the whole in the parts
- Become who it is you want to be
- Do what you have to do to continue growing as a human being

EMOTIONAL CONTINUITY MANAGEMENT ACTION POINTS

When you are confronted by an emotion, how do you manage it? If you understand that all positive emotions are based in faith in something, and all negative emotions are based in loss of faith in something — and thus fear — you can always approach negative emotions as a simple statement of fear. When you find out what the fear is, real or perceived, you can solve the dilemma without strong emotions. Fear is at the base of all negative emotion. Do not add to that fear.

Find five new ways to approach any emotion:

1. Peacefully,
2. Quietly,
3. Neutrally,
4. Gratefully,
5. Hopefully,
6. or...
7. or...
8. or...
9. or...
10. or...

- Become a professional peace-builder.
- Invite a professional mediator to help bring conflict to resolution.
- Have a conflict resolution professional or volunteer give a training on anger management.
- Start your day with a life-affirming "bring-it-on" hope.
- I can face emotions from a place of hope and affirmation.

- I am ready to face what this day brings.
- I am facing this persons emotions peacefully and neutrally.
- Learn to be playful.
- See the emotion in your presence as a cartoon critter that wants to be heard.
- Ask the person with the emotion to draw a picture of their opinion so you can be more understanding.
- Make a bulletin board for feeling art that has anonymous drawings of appropriate expressions of emotion.
- Have children of your employees do art for the office expressing feelings with crayons.
- See your work as service
- Face the emotion from a place of serving someone who has a need.
- Encourage clear expressions of their needs followed by a specific request.
- Take the growth and become more.
- Use an "I" statement to disclose a safe amount of personal information.
- Share a growth story about someone you know.
- Shift your thinking.
- Express gratitude for an emotional expression.
- Explore how an emotion offers a contribution to the work site environment.
- Practice new skills.
- Breathe slowly as the emotion is being presented.
- Stand or sit with good posture as you are listening.
- Do not let the energy of someone else's emotions enter your DNA or move into your heart. Be Teflon and not Velcro.
- Assist people to be more.
- Ask the person with the emotion how you can help them use this feeling to energize, enhance, grow, develop or create more and better ideas.
- Make new choices.
- Say no to bad timing of emotional sharing.
- Find a personal balance.
- Help employees recalibrate their emotions by supporting both expression and balance.
- Use situations for creativity.
- Use conflict to help employees explore art expressions. They can write poetry, pain, scrapbook, make music, dance or find other outlets. Some offices make cookbooks. Other offices create self-published scrapbooks and historical archives. Art can be therapeutic.
- Bring music into your workplace.
- Open up your heart and mind.
- While you are listening to the emotions of others, it is appropriate and helpful to feel your own feelings. You can use these feelings for intuitive comments.
- Accept people and situations as they are.
- Say thank you.
- Do not fight and struggle every emotion that comes your way. Some emotions pass quickly.
- Determine if this person has the capacity to grow or if they are at their maximum professional, intellectual, emotional, physical development.
- Hone your leadership skills.
- Learn to use non-violent language.
- Increase your assertiveness skills.
- Get a coach.
- Become a coach.
- Become an icon or light in the darkness.
- Use positive words.
- Smile pleasantly or gently with open eyes and raised head. Stand in good posture.
- While you listen to the feelings given you, indicate that you are interested and listening. Present an image of hope in the presence of the fear of someone else.
- Dream of better ways.
- Ask the person with the emotion about their dreams of better situations.
- Find out who originated your company and industry. What was their dream?
- Use work for spiritual growth.
- In the face of an emotion you can:
  - Be courteous

- - Be kind
  - Be loving
  - Be calm
  - Be compassionate
  - Be pleasant
  - Be good humored
  - Be open
  - Be gentle
  - Be awake
- Increase empowerment for yourself and others.
- Use positive, non-violent, affirming words and gestures.
- Plant seeds and be a kind gardener.
- Unless there is a life-threatening situation there is no hurry, so model calmness.
- Be an inspiration.
- Share a little of your story if it will help close a gap between people as a bridge to understanding.
- Let go of your opinions.
- Say, "You might be right, I'll reconsider it."
- Say, "You might be right, let me get back to you after I think about it."
- Say, "I have a very different opinion of this, yet I am interested in thinking beyond my own opinion. Perhaps there is more to this."
- Say, "I have a very different opinion of this. I doubt if I will change my opinion on this issue, but let's put all the opinions on the table and see what it looks like then. I may never swallow your opinion, but having your opinion on the table does not threaten mine, and who knows, maybe one of us can see something we haven't seen before. And if not, we can feel good about trying."
- Wait.
- Suggest a brief break or moratorium that still honors any urgent emotions needs.
- Usually emotions change over a few hours. Ask the person with the emotion to share it in less than five sentences, and then you will take a short break and come back to it. Honor the exact timing of the break and even if you can only hear five more sentences, it will be progress and things may have changed. Waiting is not postponing, delaying, avoiding or procrastinating. Be clear and exact about how long the emotional person will have to wait.
- Believe.
- Tell an emotional person that you are willing to believe them. Explain that as the manager, you will not be able to just leave it there, but that you will start all assessments with belief.
- Allow yourself to remain sensitive.
- Listening with an open heart is difficult if it is breaking or fearful but you do not need to be a machine to be a good manager.
- Tears do not discredit you. Weeping and gnashing of your teeth and throwing yourself into a puddle of person for hours will generally discredit your position of leadership.
- Great leaders do not fear a few personal tears.
- Increase your empathy.
- Be present in the moment.
- Listen slowly.
- Speak slowly.
- Ask if you are really on track with what is being shared.
- Soften your ego.
- Since you know it is okay to be wrong and human to make errors, your voice tone and attitude should reflect your willingness to learn from every situation.
- Think highest-order thoughts and ideals.
- Ask your emotional person what highest order vision they are having difficulty maintaining in this situation.
- Ask for their ideal solution.
- Tell them you will consider it as one of the possible approaches to the problem.
- Think in terms of possibilities.
- Encourage an employee sharing emotions to help you problem-solve.
- Let them know that you are the manager and are open to any and all ideas, even the most outlandish. This is called research.
- See your work as sacred.

- Do not see the emotion as the person. Human beings are either precious to you or they are expendable. If they are expendable, rethink your career.

More Tips for Managing Emotions

There is no universal standard to Emotional Continuity Management. The following list shows guidelines and not rules:

- Calm thoughts create calm actions
  You can handle this, you are a grownup and not a child.
  There will be a beginning, middle and end to this incident.
- Picture it
  Visualize a calm place where you feel safe. Do this for as long as possible before responding. Even five seconds of a calm image will help your brain respond with calming chemicals rather than anxiety chemicals. The brain is a pharmacy and you give it the prescription for anxiety or calm.
- Breathe, Breathe, Breathe
  Deep slow breaths through the nose and down to the belly. Release the breath slowly to the count of five. Begin again and repeat until settled.
- Do a Body Check-in
  Are you sweating, chewing your lip, tapping your foot, pacing, breathing shallowly, and talking rapidly?
- Pacing Exercises
  Pace yourself with a walk, writing, drawing, a trip to the restroom or water cooler, a moment outdoors, stretching, or resting quietly alone for a few moments.
- Big Picture
  Remember your big-picture mission and the fact that you decided to be a manager — so you are not a victim of this moment, it was and is a choice.
- Remember
  Feelings matter mostly to the person having them. Honor this unless you are physically unsafe. If unsafe, call 911.
- Listen
  People usually escalate their emotions when they believe they are not being heard. There is one theory that violence is simply extreme communication
- Calm voice
  In a duress situation, do not use a fake calm voice. That behavior may be perceived as condescending and create more stress. It can also imply that there is some other "secret" information that you have that the others do not have. However, try to soften the edges of your voice tone and slightly decrease the volume to model calmness.
- Gestures
  Move a bit more slowly, with less movement and gesturing. Some people read gestures at threats and may misinterpret your body as an attack.
- Know your Resources
  Know your resources!
- Don't be Stupid or Bulletproof
  Do not put yourself in an isolated, dangerous, unprotected, or risky situation or location.
- Postpone
  It is very appropriate to postpone discussions when they get too hot or overwhelming. The trick to this is to state clearly your intention to continue and define the exact time that continuation can occur if both parties are open at that time.
- No is Okay
  Saying no is okay. Saying no twice is still okay. If you are forced to say no again to make your point, the situation is escalating.

- <u>Take care</u>
  Do good self-care after an Emotional Continuity Management process.

MAKING THE EMOTIONAL CONTINUITY MANAGEMENT PLAN

You should be ready to start drafting an Emotional Continuity Management Plan for your company. Here is one form of a System-Wide model that has successfully been field tested in a variety of industries: **The Hawkins-Mitchell Spin-Free Workplace Model for System-Wide Emotional Continuity Management.**

Introduction

In order to acknowledge and balance emotions in the workplace, a systemwide approach to Emotional Continuity Management first begins with a buy-on process from the top down. Without complete buy-on from the top there will not be sufficient support to back up a manager who is confronted with the natural, subsequent challenges and resistances. If an Emotional Terrorist is in the midst of the employee pool, the manager absolutely must have support and backup from superiors.

Once the top officials, CEO's, owners and administrators buy on to the concept of managing emotions in the workplace, the process can begin by providing managers with training in the sets of tools necessary. A regular employee transitional process or a significant change can stir up emotions from small to large. Whether the changes are internal or external, natural or manmade, change is easy for some and difficult for others. This is why the exact same training program will then be introduced into the working population. Standardized trainings, follow-ups, individual recommendations, adjustments and fine-tunings comprise the introduction of any solid new procedure into a system.

When the systematic introduction of new, consistent information starts moving through the organization it always moves toward the top. The top administrator must become the containment lid for the bubbling and stirring process of system-wide change. If the administrator is committed to the theory, plan, and process the organization quickly stabilizes. If the administrator is ambiguous or oppositional, the emotional backlash will move back down toward the bottom of the system. All emotional fluctuations, grievances and anomalies are instantly reflected back into the system for integration and absorption. Or, they become more emotional substance that creates more spinning and disruption. Management is left to control all adjustments. If the manager has been trained to respond appropriately to these fluctuations the emotional content can be absorbed by a healthy system. If managers have been trained to recognize what is normal and what is a threat to containment and adjustment they can implement a variety of new tools and options to increase their effectiveness. Clear directions with consistent information stabilize the flow of emotional energy in the system as it moves toward anticipated outcomes rather than toward escalated emotional spinning.

The top-down process validates and legitimizes that everyone is on board. This significantly increases loyalty for all stakeholders. The bottom line is encouraged as outcome. At the same time, everyone sees that their emotions matter, when well managed within workplace-appropriate boundaries. If people are not on board with the process, they are quickly identified as anomalies in the system. Managers can offer them increased training, education, readjustment, reorientation, encouragement, or appropriate transition out of the system. New system standards are established with a set of expectations defined internally and internally managed. This increases stakeholder buy-on for management and line staff. Rather than escalating the 'Us vs. Them' dynamic it can become 'Us for Us.'

A well-conceived Emotional Continuity Management process provides clear definitions, reinforces company-wide expectations, and provides the entire system with easily accessible, practical, industry appropriate tools. If there is any kind of simple leak, tear, break or rupture in the system, it can be quickly repaired or managed if it is an expectation of the dynamic of change. Management will have a tool available and ready to go. If the rupture is catastrophic, management will have a cadre of resources beyond peers. It is useful to pre-train systems before there are incidents and introduce them to the resources available. During a catastrophic event, external providers can be seen as "outsiders" or "heroes." Law enforcement and fire services have discovered that when systems are in place before incidents, counseling and debriefing by external providers is seen as an internal policy decision that does not become an additional external threat in times of disaster or catastrophic challenge.

HOW SOME ORGANIZATIONS HAVE APPROACHED CREATING SYSTEM-WIDE EMOTIONAL CONTINUITY MANAGEMENT

- Hired specialized professionals for training, put them on retainers for disasters, have their people get to know them in advance so they don't appear as outsiders when the chips are down.
- Hired a field-tested Disaster Emotional Continuity Management Coach to support and train managers to deal directly with the bridge between business and emotion.
- Hosted a Consultation using resource combinations from inside and outside the company and making links with top-end, credentialed professionals in their area.
- Assigned a person or team to provide ongoing training for staff, orient new employees, write policy, create education, and establish standardized expectations while learning how to recognize the early warning signs of emotional dysfunction and to track developing emotional tornadoes on the horizon.
- Provided high-end, quality traumatology or critical incident management training for all department managers.

System-Wide Emotional Continuity Management Should Begin to Address These Questions:

Use the following questions to create a presentation document before you approach your administration to establish buy-on. A proactive position for Emotional Continuity Management begins with data that supports your position. Start your buy-on discussion with hard data, facts, statistics, fiscal risk projections and historical relevance. Follow with human-compassion-centered data that is translated into value-added benefit for your company. Show how taking care of human emotions is a fiscally advantageous, bottom-line-valuable, stakeholder-loyalty and customer-value-added business decision.

- What are the predictable fiscal consequences of an emotional spin?
- Can your Emotional Continuity Management Team manage small and large emotions?
- Is everyone ready to manage the emotions of a disaster?
- If a small spin begins, who will stop it?
- Are employees able to help themselves enough to help others?
- Do you have enough tools to manage emotional situations?
- Have you drilled and rehearsed for emotional incidents, small to large?
- Does your company have special needs employees?
- Does you company have special equipment?
- Do your employees know what to expect in case of a disaster?
- Has your entire company developed system-wide intervention strategies?
- Does anyone on your team have any specialized Emotional Continuity Management training?
- If all top managers are gone can your line staff take over the peer responsibilities?
- How will your employees know when external help is required?
- Are your people willing to call in outsiders for emotional support?
- What resources are available to all employees?
- Do you have external consultants who include teams of debriefers and trauma experts who are familiar with your business?
- Will your experts and consultants come immediately if you call them?
- Are your managers, employees, or consultants field trained in real-time disasters?

- Do your external consultants understand your people, customers, and business mission?
- What are the predictable emotional outcomes from a disaster?
- What Emotional Continuity Management tools have employees rehearsed?
- Who is familiar with the Emotional Continuity Management tools and can use them under stressful conditions?
- Does your company have unique emotional needs?
- Are there Emotional Continuity Management tools in place that increase employee understanding about what humans are likely to do under a wide range of circumstances?
- Has your entire company been trained in system-wide intervention strategies and tools?
- Who in your company has extensive and advanced psychological trauma management training?
- What Emotional Continuity Management tools would serve a simple problem, a complicated issue, or a complex emergency?
- If managers are gone, who assumes the responsibility for Emotional Continuity Management?
- How do you know when external help is required?
- Are your people willing to call in outsiders?
- Are supportive resources ready and in place if something happened today?
- Do you have external consultants and trauma experts who are familiar with your employees, your customers, your business mission, and bottom line issues?
- Will your consultants come into your disaster zone immediately?
- Are your external consultants field-trained experts?
- Have you prepared a way to manage voluntary "helpers" who will show up to disasters?
- How will you protect yourself and your company from opportunists who show up without appropriate training and credentials when you are the most vulnerable?

BUY-ON PROCEDURES SHOULD BEGIN
TO ADDRESS THESE QUESTIONS:

- How well does administration support the Emotional Continuity Management Plan?
- How completely has the Emotional Continuity Management Plan been incorporated into the Emergency Management Plan of the company?
- How well have other departments in the company been informed or notified about administrative buy-on?
- How well have other departments supported the Emotional Continuity Management Plan?
- How well supported is the need to practice and drill for emotional emergencies?
- How extensive are the opportunities to drill for emotional emergencies?
- How financially supported is the Emotional Continuity Management Plan?
- How supportive is the administration about providing opportunities for training employees in emotional management?
- How supportive is the administration about providing opportunities for training management?
- How supportive is the administration about creating cooperative partnerships with other emergency response agencies prior to a disaster or emotional event?
- How supportive is the administration about providing pamphlets, books, literature, posters, media education, and other hard-copy information on Emotional Continuity Management Planning?
- How well do personnel know what they should do in an emergency to caretake their emotions?
- How well prepared are you to manage extreme emotions in the workplace?
- How well prepared are you to manage emotions resulting from a catastrophic disaster?

STEPS FOR WRITING AN EMOTIONAL CONTINUITY MANAGEMENT PLAN

1. Research
   - Find your highest order of management style
   - Explore a variety of possible forms
   - HOW:
     - Call someone in your position in another company for an Idea Meeting
     - Read magazines and books
     - Go to workshops or classes

2. Create a Blueprint
   - Visualize your perfect style
   - Take time to sketch or write your plan
   - HOW:
     - Create a notebook or journal of ideas
     - Draw pictures and doodles of your ideal work process

3. Decide and Commit
   - Remove barriers
   - Prepare the space
   - Gather resources
   - Survive first challenges
   - Continue to commit
   - HOW:
     - Work for buy-on
     - See the big picture so there is no emergency in the planning stage
     - Continue your research and creative stages
     - Use challenges and obstacles as learning/teaching moments
     - Write and rewrite your plan as it continues to evolve into a final draft

4. Begin
   - Take actions
   - Safeguard resources
   - Survive ongoing challenges
   - Recommit
   - HOW:
     - Talk with others inside and outside your work: create networks
     - Review and strengthen your database
     - Create professional documents and forms
     - Accept and review feedback with your ideals in mind
     - Review persistence materials
     - Begin implementation stages

5. Recall
   - Review highest order ideals
   - Review original visions
   - Reconsider if appropriate
   - Recommit and Continue
   - HOW:
     - Review previous stages with ideals in mind
     - Continue to face challenges with open mind and commitment

Emotional Continuity Management Checklist

As you are creating your Emotional Continuity Training for teams and employees, you can use the following checklist to track your consistency:

- Does each module of training follow the same "scripted" procedure so that the information is uniform and repeatable?
- Is attending mandatory, because mandating attendance creates a sense of unity among participants and immediately limits options for spinning?
- Do follow-up meetings provide creative input and collaboration from all members?
- Has there been buy-on from the top? The top-down process allows the administration/management to discover what employees are on board, who are potential company emotional saboteurs, and who are simply trainable "problem children"
- Does each module include practice time and drill for new tools, language, and concept acquirement? Adjustment and absorption of new ideas takes time and familiarity.
- Do units of education or modules exceed teachable time frames? Two hours for group education is appropriate, with shorter individual consultations when required. This process should add minimum emotional impact to the organization's functioning. Do not let lengthy trainings become fodder for emotional spinning.
- Do Emotional Continuity Management trainings have written policy and clearly defined statements for:
  - Trainer qualifications
  - Company mission and team visions
  - Top organizational buy-on defined/clarified
  - Rules for mandated participation and non-negotiable consequences for non-participation
  - Expectations and timetables for skills practice and drills
  - Value added incentives for participation
- Are reproducible documents prepared for:
  - Personnel interview charts
  - Models for explaining human emotions
  - Models for explaining human responses
  - Models for conflict resolution
  - Models for grief work and trauma management
  - Self care tools ranging from simple to complex
  - Grading assessments
  - Models for managing individual differences
  - System wide back up plans
  - System wide back up plans for the back up plan

THE HAWKINS-MITCHELL FIVE-STEP SPIN-FREE WORKPLACE TRAINING MODEL FOR SYSTEM-WIDE EMOTIONAL CONTINUITY MANAGEMENT

The Five-Steps are:
1. Preparation
2. The Wake-Up Call
3. Invitation
4. Clarity and Recommitment
5. Remediation.

1.   PREPARATION

Managers begin the process by deciding exactly what they want, their expectations, how the readjustment process will lay out, who will be involved in research and development, individual committees, task forces, brainstorming sessions, and system-wide implementation. It is the blueprint of the new infrastructure. It is *not* necessary to tear down the old one while building a new framework. It *is* necessary to have a plan of action along with specialists to back up the plan. The rough draft of the Policy is created here.

Some Potential Preparation Components

- The original mission/vision statements
- All documents/policies/procedures that may be affected or changed
- Legal Counsel
- HR (Managers and above)
- Internal Auditors (Managers and above)
- Security (Managers and above)
- External mental health consultant
- External anti-terrorist specialist
- Trainers/educators
- Support staff to schedule meetings and trainings
- General timeline/deadline
- Meetings with all department heads and managers to dispel potential rumors.

It is important in this first step to have very rigid boundaries in order to protect leaks, fragmentation, generating half truth/half lies and rumors. If there is an Emotional Terrorist within this first unit, it will be evident via leaks.

2.   THE WAKE-UP CALL

After Preparation, it will be time to inform all employees, system-wide, that there is a new policy on its way to the organization; that it is positive; has nothing to do with layoffs; and, will be announced at a specific meeting (or meetings). Location and time are included in the memo or will follow within 24-48 hours.

The meeting should then be held for everyone. *Everyone must Be Mandated to Get this Initial Information.* This should not be a long, drawn-out process and in fact should only take a small period of time preferably less than an hour. Everyone should be informed in person, in group meetings, and not individual meetings, as well as in writing within a 48-hour period. There must be provisions for a make-up meeting for absent employees. Emotional Terrorists will avoid this unless it is mandated, which includes a mandated make up meeting. Terrorists will do anything to avoid this meeting.

The information given should be scripted to limit misinterpretation as well as to protect the messengers. The meeting script will announce the introduction of a new Anti-Spin Workplace Policy and present the expectation that all employees are expected to raise their consciousness about the possible effects and consequences for business and human beings in the presence of emotional spinning.

This meeting should be presented in an active, upbeat, celebratory "you-are-part-of-the-solution-or-part-of-the-problem" format strategy. This engages the collective energy and if there are Emotional Terrorists aboard they will see that there is no turning back. It is the first statement of commitment, the line drawn in the sand, the "just say no" to the dealer. This new standard must absolutely be driven by the *Zero Tolerance for Emotional Spinning or Emotional Terrorism* agenda presented by the administrative body of the organization to everyone. Emotional players will immediately try to manipulate it into something more comfortable. With a lot of built in flexibility for readjustments and realignments, trainings and support, understanding and compassion for all, the one thing that cannot be flexible is the Zero Tolerance Position.

Stage 1:

The management teams are instructed on the topic of emotions at the workplace and educated in recognition skills. They are informed of the expectations of administration and given ways to support its implementation. At these meetings there will be a period of time that managers may contribute their ideas for developing policy.

Some Potential Talking Points for Discussion

- Recognition of normal and abnormal emotions
- Statistics
- What/So What/Now what
- Denial, minimization, fears
- Wherever you work is Sacred Ground
- Predators versus Prey
- Tricks of Terrorism
- Anti-Spin Strategies
- What to expect from who and why
- Specifics of Your Industry
- Administrations buy-on support

Stage 2:

All employees are brought on board with the same scripted program given to management with a series of group meetings to accommodate all staff. All meetings must be mandatory or made up with a short turnaround, non-avoidable deadline. Period.

3.   THE INVITATION

At the end of the wake-up scripted sessions all staff, management and employees are given an invitation (either written or verbal) to become part of an Anti-Spin Action Team. After providing clear and specific information about the physical, mental, emotional, spiritual and financial danger of allowing Emotional Terrorists to run their organization, they are given an opportunity or invited to become Emotional Stakeholders. All are allowed and encouraged to describe their own view of possible emotional spinning effects in this environment (i.e., the organization's unique mission, payoffs for work ethic, personal integrity, service and care for self and others, the concerns for their own family, community, and individual success) as well as individual stories and experiences which may be useful to the group well-being.

When healthy and dysfunctional employees begin to see that it is in their best personal and collective interest to be PART OF THE SOLUTION, they generally get on board quickly and with great vigor. In fact, they are often relieved that the threat of emotional spinning or terrorism, present or future, may be identified and addressed. Many good employees have not "ratted" on their co-workers out of either fear of reprisals or a commitment to professionalism. They have been silent and miserable trying to stay out of the path of the emotional tornado. Their faith in management begins to be restored. Terrorists will immediately question the bottom line to see if it is real or going to disappear. Reinforcement of the Zero Tolerance for Emotional Spinning or Terrorism will need to be repeated.

After the invitation to join in a system-wide team-building process, it becomes immediately evident to management, usually within a few hours, who is going to support the agenda and who is going to try to sabotage it. Track all fear rumors directly back to the source and extinguish them immediately. Whining is okay, but any rumors must be stopped, assessed for spinning and intentional terrorism and completely quelled. After a very brief initial discomfort and rattling of the cages, healthy people get on with the job of recovery and cleanup, while emotional spinners and terrorists begin to reveal themselves. There will be clear, documentable, and immediate feedback.

Everyone gets the benefit of the doubt to start with — even Terrorists. All are given a small window to adjust. They must be given time to adjust, change their minds, get on board, exit, shake, shudder, and join in the new standard. Everyone adjusts at a different pace. 72 hours should be the amount of time to expect reasonable adjustment for new information. This does not mean competency, but it does mean compliance and a willingness to take the next step. Emotional Terrorists will get very, very creative to try to protract and expand the time between announcement and compliance. Those who are dragging their feet can be evaluated by their history. Management can determine through review of work history, personal observations, and appropriate grievance procedures who are the regular "slow-pokes" and who are Emotional Terrorists who are instigating resistance and sabotage. Be suspicious of everything from absenteeism to escalating stories of personal victimhood. Listen with compassion, repeat the Zero Tolerance Agenda, and move on.

Some Potential Talking Points for Discussion

- What is the critical difference between healthy venting and complaining following an appropriate grievance process to effect change, and Emotional Terrorism tactics?
- Why do some people take higher ground when others take the low road?
- What is the difference between a workplace soldier and a workplace warrior?
- What are the payoffs for becoming a workplace warrior?
- What are the ranges and levels of spinning from small to large?
- What are the differences between physical, emotional, mental and spiritual spinning?
- How are we going to help each other get on board?
- How can we support those who struggle with change?
- What are the differences between sharing our emotions and spinning?
- What are your experiences with Emotional Terrorists?
- What place do emotions fit in the workplace? Do they?
- What does it mean to be held in an emotional hostage situation in the workplace?

4. CLARITY AND RE-COMMITMENT

The bottom line must remain in place, even when challenged. Countless people stand up and decide to change their lives. They make great progress, overcome significant and daunting obstacles and are within five minutes of reaching their personal miracle when offered an "out," an easier path, a less-than-miraculous option that gets them to the land of "almost right." After grand struggles and victories, they are tired, vulnerable and ready to taste success. Cue the opportunist or Emotional Terrorist who arrives and offers them a bargain for half the price. The opportunist has radar for these moments of potential emotional cave-ins or collapse. They can almost smell the moment of critical mass and swoop in with the brightly-wrapped, sparkly rescue package. If the invitation is accepted the process can slide back to the beginning or farther.

Here's a sample of what this dynamic looks like:

Case Study

1. The mission has been announced that everyone must upgrade his or her computers from level 3.0 to level 5.0 by January 1.
2. The consultant, trainer, CEO, and management begin the work of training and helping the staff adjust.
3. Person #1 upgrades to 5.0 instantly. They have been prepared.
4. Person #2 upgrades to 5.0.
5. The system wiggles and feels a bit disrupted.
6. Person #3 upgrades to 5.0 and several others upgrade to 3.5 and 4.0. Progress is happening.
7. Several persons resist, one employee quits, others begin to whine, one starts a rumor about layoffs.
8. Person #4 upgrades to 5.0 and several others are prepared to upgrade, but want to see what administration is going to do, if the administration and management are serious.
9. Enough people are now at 4.5 or better and the old system begins to collapse in on itself.
10. There is stress and anxiety as some are catching up, others are failing and seeking help, others are waiting to see if the rumors are true so they can avoid the change, and some are getting their resumes in order. Resistance increases.
11. Person #5 upgrades to 5.0 and the system is vulnerable to total collapse. Anxiety is high.
12. December 30, the system is extremely fragile before the deadline as people upgrade, adjust, struggle, or resist. A few "slowpokes" are working hard to make the shift.
13. The expectation is that on December 31, the system will shift to the new level. Tension is elevated, some people panic, others are excited, some are concerned and fearful.
14. Two more employees bail out and jump ship, someone retires early to avoid the change, a pregnant mom exits earlier than planned. Another slowpoke upgrades unexpectedly to 5.0.

15.   CRITICAL MASS HAPPENS and all eyes look to the CEO and Management for clarity, support, recommitment, and consistency.

THEREFORE: On January 1, the CEO and management either stands by this original mission, with allowable room for minor or simple procedural and technical adjustments and reasonable catching up behaviors, or:

1.   The Project will be seen as a Test, a Hoax, a Manipulation, a trick, and a scheme.
2.   Faith collapses. Confusion Ensues. The system collapses.
3.   There is a relapse back to a level below the 3.0 standard.
4.   The program must be started all over at square one; faith has been lost, confidence has been shattered. All the work, tension, changes and challenges are now seen as vaporous in relationship to the CEO's expectation. People are confused, disappointed, lost.
5.   Those who have already done the shift to 5.0 will now readily accept positions elsewhere, usually offered them without their solicitation, where they can use their 5.0 skills that your organization has paid for in a 4.0 setting and be leaders, or in a setting that has a 6.0 expectation where they can grow.
6.   At this point you might find that the business has lost the 3.0 people and the 5.0 people and is left with the less-than-cream-of-the-crop to maintain a very challenged and confused organization. The brightest and best will leave when they lose confidence in the leadership.

5.   **REMEDIATION**

Remediation is an educational process that fine-tunes the team into the level it wants to achieve. It leaves room for missed bits of information and the natural errors associated with human beings. Any current Emotional Terrorism flurries should be Peer-Managed by the policy and Anti-Terrorism work should quickly be in the hands of managers, regular staff and on-site managers. The worker who is still working at achieving the 5.0 system but is still stuck at a 3.0 system needs more assistance. If reasonable, visible progress is being made at a reasonable pace then there should be room for support and encouragement. Healthy Employees generally transition with no difficulty if they are provided clear guidelines, training, opportunities for success and mistakes, management support, and a direct indication of personal payoffs. Dysfunctional Employees take a bit more time and attention. If they are progressing they should be supported and encourage. If they are valuable employees and have simply gotten on the wrong track, this is time well spent and usually is value-added and cost-effective.

Pathological Employees and Emotional Terrorists are generally found to be more expensive to teach than replace. Terrorists who continue resistance, sabotage progress, and do not support the policy while in fact adding fuel to tension, are now reprimanded for potential policy infractions of Emotional Terrorism. Ongoing breaking of policies or persistence in terrorist activities needs to be addressed directly and removed from a healthy system before it causes irreparable, irreversible, terminal harm.

Some Potential Talking Points for Discussion

- Ethics
- Diversity
- Trauma
- Impaired employees
- Grief work
- Survivors of prior trauma
- Addictions
- Dr. Vali's Trauma Tool Kit©
- Grievance policies and procedures
- Emotional venting models
- Business change agendas of the Company

Additional Steps

A. REVIEW RESISTANCE TO TRAINING PROGRAMS

Healthy Employees

Salt of the earth, fun, pleasant, groomed, inclusive, engaged with life, open, thoughtful, manage their emotions well, are open with feelings, positive and negative, are compassionate, reasonable, fairly consistent over time, have a life.

Response to an Anti-SPIN Policy: Look forward to growth and development. May have some concerns about time involved or group commitment, but eager to see the results of more clarity and definitions of policies. No resistance.

Dysfunctional Employees

May be open to growth with some minor fears to larger fears, naive, young or old, has not been given the correct information, for some reason is in a weakened state, vulnerable to suggestions and influences, subject to emotional swings, able to be coerced by a stronger influences, positive or negative. Emotions are more central, may be hard worker with limited skills and options, differing levels of willingness to be taught.

Response to an Anti-SPIN Policy: Have the potential to be remediated, trained, and informed and educated. May either value or fear growth and development. Minor resistance.

Pathological Employees

Has an agenda and a mission, willing to destroy people, places and things to protect themselves or their personal beliefs and agendas, even when masked as the "greater good." May be using individuals or the entire system for their agenda or as a legitimate cover, may target others who appear to threaten their agenda. Emotions may be central or invisible.

Response to an Anti-SPIN Policy: May resist remediation. May escalate their efforts, go underground, or leave. Emotional escalation is traceable to them and therefore easy to remedy, more difficult if they go underground or covert. Once underground they may be at risk for participating in sabotage, selling priority information, or other ethical violations. Early identification of these employees protects all concerned. Major resistance. Resistance can be passive or aggressive.

B. TRACK THE CONTAGION

Like a virus, Emotional Terrorism can spread between departments if the environment within the department has vulnerable units. For example, a harmless rumor that might be laughed off by two healthy employees may be taken seriously by a dysfunctional member of the team. That same rumor, used by someone with pathology, could be the last straw for the vulnerable employee. It helps to know who the players are, so that an unexpected invasion, such as a rumor or disruption, can be anticipated and stopped in its tracks. Knowing or defining the players does not mean anything must be done other than determining the risk factors involved in developing situations.

Track the Movement and Contagion of an Emotional Incident Through a System

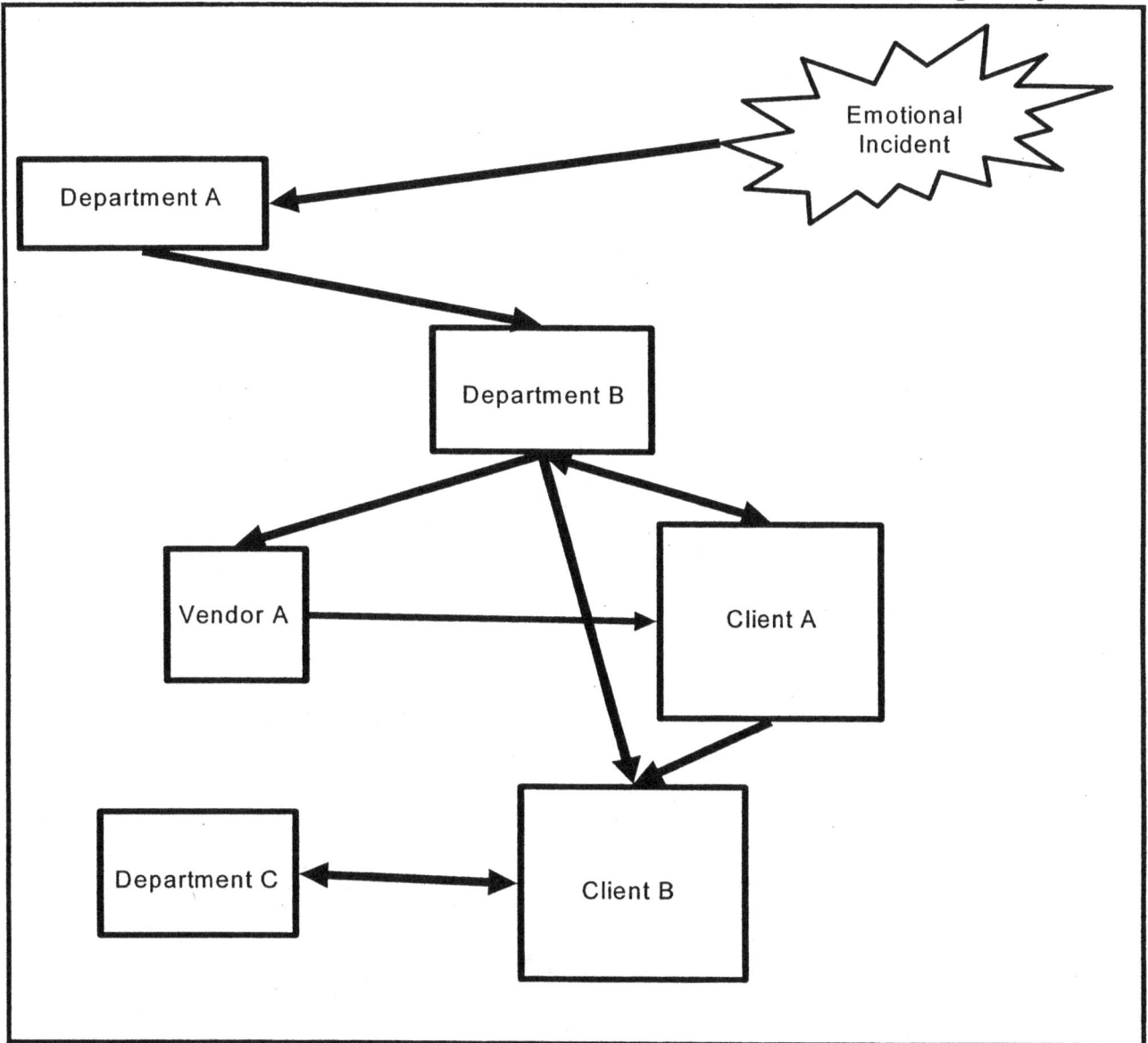

Non-Violent Non-Spinning Responses To An Emotional Spin

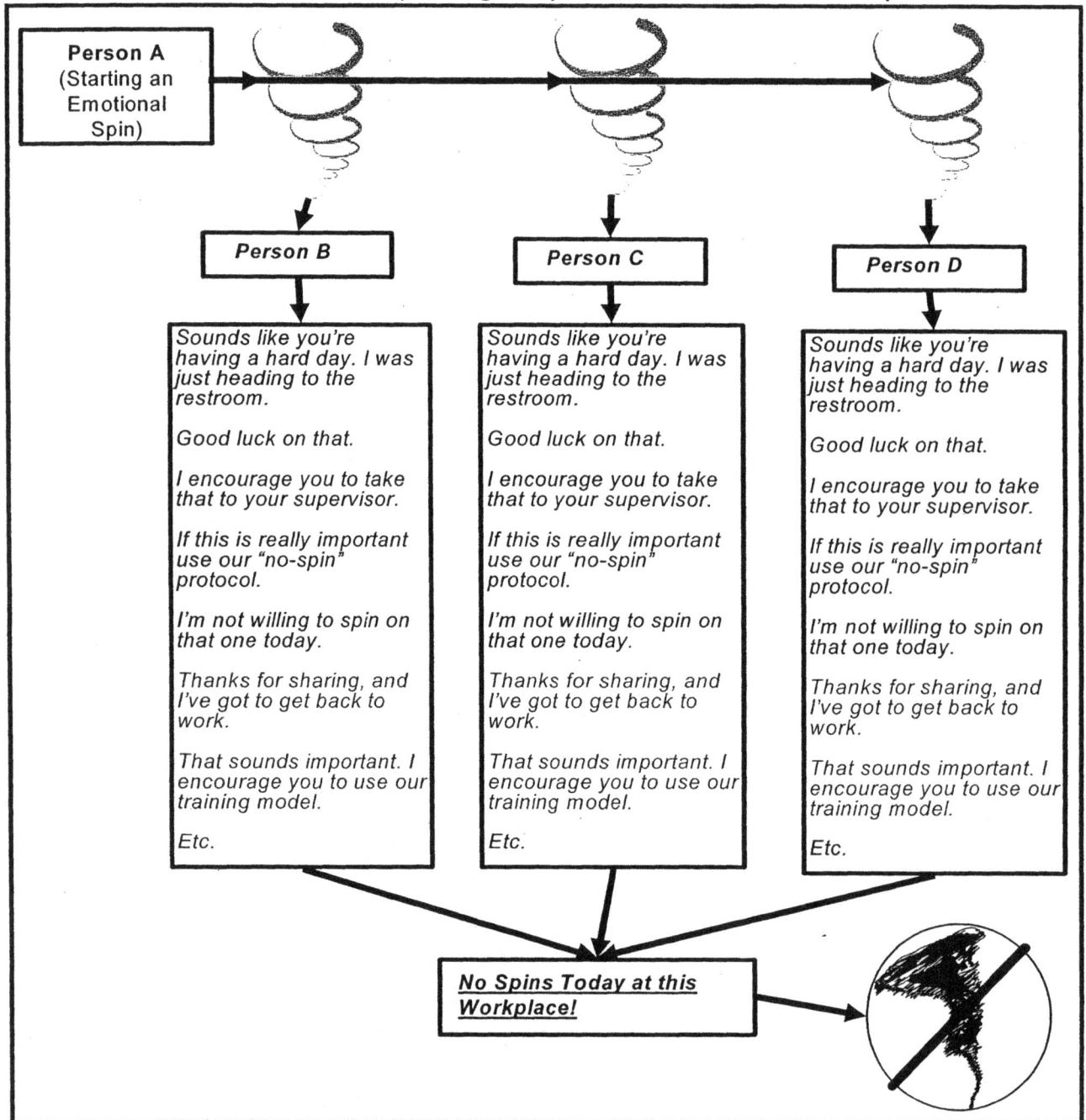

Person A (Starting an Emotional Spin)

Person B

Person C

Person D

Sounds like you're having a hard day. I was just heading to the restroom.

Good luck on that.

I encourage you to take that to your supervisor.

If this is really important use our "no-spin" protocol.

I'm not willing to spin on that one today.

Thanks for sharing, and I've got to get back to work.

That sounds important. I encourage you to use our training model.

Etc.

Sounds like you're having a hard day. I was just heading to the restroom.

Good luck on that.

I encourage you to take that to your supervisor.

If this is really important use our "no-spin" protocol.

I'm not willing to spin on that one today.

Thanks for sharing, and I've got to get back to work.

That sounds important. I encourage you to use our training model.

Etc.

Sounds like you're having a hard day. I was just heading to the restroom.

Good luck on that.

I encourage you to take that to your supervisor.

If this is really important use our "no-spin" protocol.

I'm not willing to spin on that one today.

Thanks for sharing, and I've got to get back to work.

That sounds important. I encourage you to use our training model.

Etc.

No Spins Today at this Workplace!

C.   KEEP TRAININGS CONSISTENT

- Does each module of training follow the same "scripted" procedure so that the information is uniform and repeatable?
- Is attending mandatory because mandating attendance creates a sense of unity among participants and immediately limits options for spinning?
- Do follow-up meetings provide creative input and collaboration from all members?
- Has there been buy-on from the top? The top-down process allows the administration/management to discover what employees are on board, who are potential company emotional saboteurs, and who are simply trainable "problem children."

- Does each module include practice time and drill for new tools, language, and concept acquirement? Adjustment and absorption of new ideas takes time and familiarity.
- Do units of education, or modules exceed teachable time frames? Two hours for group education is appropriate, with shorter individual consultations when required. This process should add minimum emotional impact to the organization's functioning. Do not let lengthy trainings become fodder for emotional spinning.
- Do Emotional Continuity Management trainings have written policy and clearly defined statements for:
  - Trainer qualifications
  - Company mission and team visions
  - Top organizational buy-on defined/clarified
  - Rules for mandated participation and non-negotiable consequences for non-participation
  - Expectations and timetables for skills practice and drills
  - Value added incentives for participation
- Are reproducible documents prepared for:
  - Personnel interview charts
  - Models for explaining human emotions
  - Models for explaining human responses
  - Models for conflict resolution
  - Models for grief work and trauma management
  - Self care tools ranging from simple to complex
  - Grading assessments
  - Models for managing individual differences
  - System wide back up plans
  - System wide back up plans for the back up plan

D.   REHEARSE

Follow the steps to create an Emergency Drill that includes Emotional Continuity Management as part of the scenario. Find ways to implement your emotional management skills and tools into the practice and exercise activities.

E.   RETREAT AND RECREATION

Everyone requires rest and time to play. Find ways to rest and play that work for yourself and your team. Provide a retreat, a play day, a luncheon, a surprise ice-cream party, movie tickets, hire a jazz band in the employee lounge, or whatever sounds wonderful and easy that will give respite before, during and after problems and issues and always after rehearsal drills.

F.   RECOMMIT

Take a deep breath and start again from *Step 1* and move forward because emergencies and the emotions that go with them are not going away! The daily annoyances of humans working along side humans are an expectable part of life and working environments.

STARTING AN EMOTIONAL CONTINUITY MANAGEMENT TEAM

Constructing Your Team

- Who is on your Emotional Continuity Management Team?
  Will they be trained and ready to get your company up and running during or after an incident?
- How do others respond to this team emotionally?
  Are they well thought of in the organization? Trusted? Safe?
- Who will show up?
  Have all members been trained in leadership to take over in case of loss of life?
- What does your company need to get back to 100% services?
  Can it operate at 10%? 35%?

- What qualifications are acceptable to be on the Emotional Continuity Management team? *Have they been pre-screened for PTSD from any prior catastrophic incident? Are they emotionally stable, mature, trained, and willing?*
- Have they had sufficient training? *What levels of training are sufficient for your team members and leaders?*
- Are your emergency and disaster plans specific or generalized? *What is vague and what is specific?*
- Have you tested your plan? *Has it been table talk or real-time drills and exercises?*
- Have your team member discussed and planned for emotional shock, loss, and terror? *What support does your team have to manage their feelings when they are supporting others?*
- Have all team member been trained to understand the variety of emotional reactions to expect in case of a catastrophic incident by a qualified disaster or trauma specialist or qualified Licensed Mental Health Professional?
- Who will replace you if you are not present? How would your team deal with losing you? *Does everyone know all the parts of the plan?*

Qualifications Checklist for Team Members, External Consultants, Emotional Continuity Management Trainer, Services Provider

Decide what your Best Practices and Standards are for Qualifications and then Document the following *(All licensing and certification credentials should be documented with copies of current status that can be updated on a yearly basis as needed):*

- Formal training
- Informal training/experiences
- Real time disaster experience
- Continuing education
- Licensures
- License number and date of expiration/photocopy
- Malpractice Insurance
- Specialized training
- Experience
- References
- Special skills
- Special populations skills
- Availability
- Locations
- Types of services
- Application forms/process
- Photo ID
- Criminal background check including fingerprints
- Security clearance if needed
- Vehicular background check if needed
- Signed contract for services including clear fee arrangements

Constructing Your Team Notebook

Minimum requirements should include:

- Team composition
- Chain of authority
- Exit strategies
- Member list and all contact methods
- Collect verifications of qualifications of all team members

- Verification that all team members have been screened for PTSD and prior trauma
- Plans for changes in circumstances, shifts, time off
- Complete data about will your company require to return to 100%, 75%, 50%, 25% services
- Anticipated obstacles to complete recovery
- Written plans for the Emotional Continuity Management for specific incidents, even those that appear to be unlikely:
  - tornado
  - earthquake
  - suicide
  - cyber-crime
  - shooting
  - fire
  - Emotional Terrorist
  - winter storm
  - hurricane
  - chemical spill
  - shelter in place
- Extensive lists of local, regional, national and international resourses
- A chronology of how you have tested your plans and lessons learned data
- Reproducible copies of required or preferred forms or documents
- Emergency numbers for team members and families
- Complete written policy and procedures
- Company/Administrative buy-on statement
- List of insurances and legal support
- List of all employees under the domain of the Emotional Continuity Management Team

NOTEBOOK TIPS:

- *If your team has a notebook that they can carry with them to a site, it needs pages that will be removable, pages that are covered with plastic sheet protectors, colorful enough so they can just grab-and-go out the door and not have to search for it under duress, blank lined paper for jotting notes, an attachable pen, perhaps even a backpack or carrying case that they think looks cool. The point of this is that during duress, your team needs to not have to think about anything but doing their work as calmly as possible. Looking for a bit of paper to write a phone number, or scrambling for a pen, is contraindicated for an Emotional Continuity Manager.*

- *Start collecting data for an ever-evolving team notebook with reproducible documents, forms, logos, policies, plans, procedures, checklists, guidelines, resources, requirements, and anything your team decides would assist them in emotional continuity management during an emotional incident or disaster.*

AUTHOR'S AFTERTHOUGHTS

Everyone comes to the table wanting something different. Counters want numbers; helpers want to be useful; and, managers want to manage. Setting your own goals will necessitate your understanding of your position at the table and your own personal sense of style. Extroverts and introverts will approach the process from opposite ends of the same continuum. I tell people that they cannot fail. They can learn or not learn. Successes should be studied for what went right, and failures are studied for what can go better. Spending time on blame is a waste of energy and a potential spin. Finding something to celebrate on a daily basis can keep your motivation going even in the dark nights of the manager's soul. It is the little things that keep hopes alive and spirits moving toward the goal.

Find things to be amazed about in yourself and others. After the attacks of September 11th, 2001, there was a piece circulating on the Internet about the "little things that kept people alive." Many things on the Internet should be questioned, but this one is accurate, because I was there, and I heard several of these stories first-hand from the people who experienced them. Take the time to ponder your own philosophical and theoretical basis, because these are the foundations of your daily work. Do not be afraid to ask questions. And do not let the "little things" get in your way. Read this Internet piece to start making your own perspective:

After Sept. 11, one company invited the remaining members of other companies who had been decimated by the attack on the Twin Towers to share their available office space. At a morning meeting, the head of security told stories of why these people were alive. All the stories were just about the "little things."

- *The head of a company got in late that day because his son started kindergarten.*
- *Another fellow was alive because it was his turn to bring donuts.*
- *One woman was late because her alarm clock did not go off in time.*
- *One was late because of being stuck on the New Jersey Turnpike because of an auto accident.*
- *One of them missed his bus.*
- *One spilled food on her clothes and had to take time to change.*
- *One's car would not start.*
- *One went back to answer the telephone.*
- *One had a child that dawdled and did not get ready as soon as he should have.*
- *One could not get a taxi.*
- *Then there was the man who put on a new pair of shoes that morning, took the various means to get to work but before he got there, he developed a blister on his foot. He stopped at a drugstore to buy a Band-Aid. That is why he is alive today.*

DISCUSSION QUESTIONS

- If you draft an Emotional Continuity Management Plan for your company what would be the key features necessary to get buy-on from administration and line staff

- What are your self-care tools?

- Can you write an opinion paper of your Theory of Change in business? If you can, make sure to document current event statistics and research that back up your opinions.

- What MOUs (Memos of Understanding) do you have in place now? What MOUs do you need?

- What "little things" annoyed you today? What emotions did you experience today?

6

REACTIONARIES: HOW DO YOU MANAGE EMOTIONAL TERRORISTS?

- *Arson investigators were called to a new Starbucks store after three windows were broken by some kind of incendiary device shortly before 11 p.m. Tuesday. (Associated Press, May 7, 2004)*

- *Federal regulators this week charged the National Consumer Council of deceptive claims and practices and is seeking millions of dollars in damages on behalf of NCC's customers. (Associated Press, May 7, 2004)*

- *Costco workers checked the merchandise after a woman bit into something hard in a hot dog that officers determined was a live 9 mm bullet. (Associated Press, May 7, 2004)*

WHY YOU SHOULD READ THIS CHAPTER

If you have ever worked with or for an Emotional Terrorist, you already know why you want to read this chapter, for validation. No, you were *not* crazy; that person you thought was dangerous to your mental health may indeed have been trying to make you go mad. If you have never worked with or for an Emotional Terrorist consider yourself lucky. You will want to read this chapter for self-preservation for the long-haul span of your career. If you are an Emotional Terrorist, you will want to read this chapter to find out if someone is on to you.

BY THE END OF CHAPTER 6 YOU SHOULD BE ABLE TO

- Recognize behaviors associated with Emotional Terrorism

- Create a list of emotions and behaviors that would support and encourage an Emotional Terrorist at the workplace

- Create a flow chart that tracks the streams of influence from all departments to all departments. Track how one Emotional Terrorist would influence other areas of your company

- Document the potential risks if your company had an Emotional Terrorist in a key position

- Write a rough draft policy for managing Emotional Terrorism at work. Make sure to include all strata of employees, including HR, EAP, Administration, Management, CEO, Supervisory, Line Staff, Vendors, Ancillary, Customers and so forth. Describe how any policy would change or not change depending upon the position of the Emotional Terrorist

- Watch the news or read a newspaper and find a current event that suggests Emotional Terrorism

OVERVIEW

Emotional Terrorism is an emotional and behavioral phenomenon in the workplace that has eluded business leaders for a long time. This subset of actions and emotions is at first illusive and intangible. Business writers have made attempts to deal with the visible or overt nature of these phenomena by writing about jerks at work, or angry employees or other references to people at work who are difficult. Managers have read books, gone to countless workshops, talked secretly to each other, consulted psychologists and therapists, and have found themselves unable to wrap their mind around a specific blend of human behavior that seems to go beyond the normal definitions of disruptive employees. At closer scrutiny there are three reasons this has been so difficult:

1.   Emotional Terrorists do not fall into the range of normal to dysfunctional people and need a separate category;
2.   Most managers are nice people; and,
3.   Emotional Terrorists count on nice people to struggle with the definition and use that discrepancy to gain emotional territory.

Staying good, nice, and friendly is what most human beings do. The majority of people do not like to upset other people. Emotional Terrorists have a different approach to life. They actually seek and find pleasure in the discomfort of others. As workers, managers and administrators have been concerned with productivity and not offending anyone, Emotional Terrorists have crept into workplaces and felt right at home. If Stephen Spielberg did a scary movie called *The Emotional Terrorist in the Workplace*, managers could see it on the big screen while eating popcorn. Such a public validation would create a forum for discussion. It would be out in the open. As it is now, Emotional Terrorists at the workplace continue to stir up emotional chaos and are getting away with it on a daily basis. It is time to put some light on this and make it less possible for people with an agenda of destruction to have their way.

KINDS OF TERRORISM: INTERNATIONAL AND DOMESTIC TERRORISM

> Terrorism: "the calculated use of unexpected, shocking, and unlawful violence against noncombatants (including, in addition to civilians, off-duty military and security personnel in peaceful situations) and other symbolic targets perpetrated by a clandestine member(s) of a sub-national group or a clandestine agent for the psychological purpose of publicizing a political or religious cause and/or intimidating or coercing a government, or civilian population into accepting demands on behalf of their cause." (Hudson, 1999)

For the United States, September 11th, 2001 was a horror film translated into virtual reality. When international terrorists murdered thousands of innocent workers, the word 'Terrorism' changed meaning in our national vocabulary. Terrorism now has a symbolic meaning. The word Terrorism vividly represents destruction, death, evil, fear, horror and pain.

Workplaces can be the site of international and domestic terrorism. International terrorism originates from outside the country. Domestic terrorism originates from within and is indigenous to the location. The Attacks of September 11 are an example of work sites hit by extreme international terrorism. The high school in Columbine, Colorado is an extreme example of a work site victimized by two young domestic terrorists. Information Technology professionals who specialize in disaster planning and security concerns are on the lookout for both international and domestic terrorism in the form of cybercrime.

TERRORISTS

There are religious and political, international and domestic terrorists of several varieties and levels of extremism. Psychologists, sociologists, law-enforcement professionals, legal advisors, scientists, politicians and theologians spend their days and nights trying to define, predict, explain and manage people who act in ways contrary to peace, serenity, safety, harmony and social well-being. There is no one, correct, universal answer. Any attempt at a complete answer would have to include all information that is psychological, physiological, genetic, cultural, emotional, theoretical, theological, and symbolic. The answer would have to be comprehensive. That answer does not exist. Only the question remains: why are some people hell-bent on causing problems and grief and chaos?

Terrorists are the bad guys to the victims of terrorism. Terrorists are not the bad guys to themselves and their causes. They have entitlement and are bulletproof to the extreme and they have an agenda, or mission. If you get in the way of that agenda, you may be a victim. Business texts which have attempted to couch this discussion in palpable terms have used words like 'workplace jerks,' 'bullies' or 'difficult employees.' Can you imagine calling the perpetrators of the September 11 attacks bullies, jerks, or difficult people from another country? No. They were terrorists! They had an agenda to destroy the well-being of innocent people and the consequences continue to evolve years later.

It is difficult for most rational, healthy, or moderately dysfunctional people to accept a worldview that there are people on the planet who enjoy causing pain and grief. In the abstract, people may agree there is evil, or bad people, or criminals, or icky-bad people, but most people have extreme difficulty believing that some people actually enjoy and choose such behaviors. And they have even more difficulty believing that someone would impose an agenda on them without consent. Nice people agree that there are obnoxious and aggressive people in the world, but still define them within the range of allowable differences. To discuss the presence of people who subtly, consciously, intentionally and willfully cause harm either overtly or covertly is usually too much of a challenge to normative thinking. Of course, those individuals who have had head-on run-ins with such people are well aware of their presence. The employees and citizens of New York, Pennsylvania and the Pentagon are now well aware that terrorists exist. Amazingly, there are still people outside that circle of direct experience who are not comfortable thinking that there are people running about the planet with hidden agendas and covert plans to cause horror. These naïve innocents are to be blessed and then quickly educated!

EMOTIONAL TERRORISM

> *Emotional Terrorism: "Domestic terrorism that uses human feelings for ammunition." (Hawkins-Mitchell, 2001).*

Emotional Terrorism is everywhere. It can be found in homes, churches, synagogues, shopping centers, Parent-Teachers Association meetings, city council meetings, and anywhere that people live, work and play. Emotional Terrorism at work is a significant risk. International and domestic terrorism are now factored into business risk management. Emotional Terrorism must also be seen as risk.

The fact that international or domestic terrorism has emotional roots, (someone is very, *very* upset about something) should immediately translate into the awareness that Emotional Terrorism is a constituent of these other forms of terrorism. Perhaps one way to discuss Emotional Terrorism at the workplace is to describe it as Big Terrorism's little cousin. Nevertheless, the agenda of either BIG or LITTLE terrorism is the same: *control through the use of terror*. All terrorists have a common agenda. That agenda is to create fear, chaos, havoc, terror and destruction in any way possible in order to have some sense of control, make a statement, divert attention, or call attention to something.

Mean, evil, bad, horrible, icky, intentionally dangerous, unconscionable, criminal, vile, scary, seductive, dangerous people exist. And they work with you. One very simple and horrifyingly daunting statistic may convince you. It is a statistic that is hidden from public view because of its nature and implications. In the United States, there is at least one registered sex offender for every square mile of earth. This statistic represents ONLY the ones who are registered. What makes you think they do not work with you? Or go to church with you? Or shop at the local market with you? Or sit with you at a PTA meeting? They do. And some of them are reading this book. If this does not get your attention, nothing will. Knowing a statistic like this just is not enough. Protection of the vulnerable from the inherent risks of such dreadful behavior demands much, much more attention. Knowing that this statistic is a reality makes it difficult to continue making good management decisions that are based on a belief that "people are good" and kind. Instincts must be challenged. Nice and trusting instincts do not work when dealing with a sex offender. Their thinking process is completely different from regular people who would never consider harming a child for their own gain. Regular instincts do not work with Emotional Terrorists either. Their thinking process is completely different from regular people who would never consider harming a co-worker for their own gain. Terrorists do not operate by the same rules as regular people.

Emotional Terrorism at Work

Businesses and managers need new language to deal with the ranges of terrorist challenges at work. A disgruntled worker who arrives with a gun is obviously a workplace terrorist. The employee who systematically disembowels someone's reputation through gossip and innuendo is no less destructive. One workplace terrorist will make the nightly news. One will not. Both have far reaching consequences.

Emotional Terrorists are people who have an agenda to destroy the well-being of others using emotionally loaded information, behaviors, innuendoes, direct assaults, inferences, rumors, and language to establish either disruption or decay within a system with no regard to the emotional well-being of others and to the benefit of a personal, albeit private or collective mission of control. Instead of hand grenades and weapons of mass destruction, they use emotions, vulnerabilities, implications, innuendoes, gestures, rumors, subtlety, victimhood, deflection, games and power plays to take territory and cause harm. These are not regular, healthy, well-adjusted or nice people. If you consider the statistics of active sexual predators, criminals, addicts, or untreated mental illness it must make sense to you that statistically you will meet these charming folks at work! Emotional Terrorists do not live in isolation, nor do they wear black hats to identify themselves. Emotional Terrorists have taken some of the least pleasant human attributes, dysfunctions and pathologies and turned them into an art form.

Case Example

The security guard at the shopping center was laughing to himself. The custodian noticed that every time the guard walked around a certain corner, he was chuckling. Finally the custodian asked, "Hey Leo, what's funny?" Leo looked long and hard at the custodian, and answered, "Nothing man, I'm laughing so I don't go crazy. I was just told that it was now my job to keep tabs on the mall's Santa because he apparently just fondled some kid. A parent complained, but the evidence wasn't specific enough to bust him for one report! So I am trying to manage this by imagining a bunch of us guards taking the Santa down and cuffing him for being a pervert! I have a little girl at home and the idea of her sitting on his lap makes me want to kill him!" The custodian nodded and added, "Yeah, I got in trouble here at work because I used a curse word last week, and this guy can have little girls on his lap for his pleasure all day long."

Learning Byte

An Emotional Terrorist counts on your innocence, ignorance and naivete to groom you for their own agenda. The only place you can see Emotional Terrorism is in its effect. And the effect of Emotional Terrorism in the workplace is emotional spinning. This real example of an Emotional Terrorist at the work site is disturbing. Situations like this — and worse — do happen. How would you manage the guard's emotions if you were his manager? What if you were the custodian's manager? What if you were the Santa's manager?

DO THIS: Know beyond a shadow of a doubt that Emotional Terrorists are counting on your denial to keep their secret.

DON'T: Let Emotional Terrorists hold you or anyone else emotionally hostage. Shine a light on them so they can scurry back into the shadows and play nice with everyone else, or go somewhere else.

Emotional Terrorists maintain control over people by holding them hostage inside their own illusions of power and control. Terrorists do not feel obliged to live within the framework of regular society. Think about how someone might hold a company hostage emotionally.

Case Example

Dear Dr. Hawkins Mitchell, I had an employee in a very responsible position in back-office management with my medical assistants and production. This employee was constantly setting little traps or setting off small incendiary emotional bombs that would go off regularly and disrupt production, set one assistant against another, or position herself to be a hero to repair the damage. These deliberate acts caused so much chaos and trouble that it was difficult to access just who the culprit was. After your Emotional Terrorism Consultation, I learned how to detect this kind of behavior and created a concise exit procedure for anyone with this kind of destructive personality. This had gone on for approximately six months before the consultation and afterwards I was able to see how this very large problem created conflict in my small office of seven. We had conflict because every day this employee created conflict. During her interview, she had lied about her ex-employer in such a creative way that I did not even bother checking her references. I was totally taken in by the "nice" woman. When I did call her previous employer after I fired her, that employer shared that she had treated him and his other employees in the same manner.

The last incident that I observed was one in which she was working diligently to destroy group morale during coffee breaks by berating my best producer. It finally came to my attention when this very valuable employee nearly quit. Finally, I had observed enough and documented enough of the other disruptive behaviors to know the difference between what she said and what she actually did behind the scenes. With the termination of this disruptive employee, an Emotional Terrorist, the office has returned to a very peaceful environment. Thank you for the consultation, it continues to work!

Sincerely, Dr. Smith

Learning Byte

This "nice" doctor took the risk to see his employee as more than just a problem. She was more than a troublemaker. She was an individual who *enjoyed* disruption. There are people who get disease and there are people who are carriers of disease. Interestingly enough, carriers do not get the symptoms and do not appear sick. In fact, compared with the reactions to these individuals, they may look good! This Emotional Terrorist went from job to job carrying disruption and chaos. After talking with the doctor, he had continued to track her movements in the community, and discovered that she had a long history of being at jobs for only a few months and leaving a trail of very expensive chaos. The lesson this doctor learned was that being "nice" to children and pets is one thing. Being nice as a CEO was an error. He had to sacrifice some of his valued niceness to become slightly more aware that some employees are not nice and therefore do not respond to nice interventions.

DO THIS: While maintaining your kind heart, find a way to temporarily put your "niceness" aside in order to stay safe. Learn the difference between being nice and being compassionately smart.

DON'T: Put yourself at risk.

As a malignant tumor that does not respond to chemotherapy may require removal, the only rational option for an Emotional Terrorist who does not respond to appropriate 'nice' interventions that would get the attention of nice people may be amputation: removal through termination. Transferring the employee simply moves the malignancy elsewhere as a stopgap. Eventually the disease will appear elsewhere in the system. The Roman Catholic Church has recently become aware of how a simple logistical relocation of a priest who has sexually exploited children does not end the problem. Moving an offender to a different diocese work site is a stopgap response that is ineffective when someone is an offender. Their behavior goes with them. The same is true with even a less severe representation of Emotional Terrorist. There comes a time when it does not serve the company to keep a malignant person employed. Managers must be the ones to track the effects of one employee on others.

Attributes and Behaviors of the Emotional Terrorist

There are at least seven principle attributes of Emotional Terrorists. The difficulty is that as soon as a perpetrator reads these, they are quite capable of rearranging the criteria for their own purposes. Emotional Terrorists are experts at using information to deny accountability, manipulate a vulnerable person or situation, educate others in their ways, groom new victims or recruits, litigate to gain position, or defend their own threatened innocence. That is the bad news. The good news is that the following attributes are impossible to disguise over time. A persistently neutral, businesslike, pleasant, courteous, and boundaried approach to an Emotional Terrorist just drives them nuts. If they cannot control a situation, they can adapt, migrate or change.

1.   ENTITLEMENT

Most healthy and dysfunctional people work at growing and evolving appropriate self-esteem to a point where they can realize that they are good and indeed deserve good things in life. Emotional Terrorists take that normative behavior and escalate the healthy idea of *deserving* to another level. They not only deserve, they are *entitled* well and beyond anyone else. Where the idea of "I want and deserve good things" can lead to appropriate self care and compassion to others, entitlement leans toward justification and rigid self-aggrandized thinking which affords permission to "take from" someone else in order to get the deserved or entitled goal, object, or outcome.

Entitlement is subsidized by a sense of personal victimhood, real or perceived. Entitlement rationalizes the accumulation of property, territory, or rights from someone else as perfectly correct within the context of its own motives for control. Entitlement thinking creates a cause-and-effect thinking structure that does not include external data. For example, an Emotional Terrorist will not consider the needs or wants of someone else because their agenda, cause, or motives are a bit, or a lot, more justified. Victimhood is increased and entitlement leads to increased accumulation needs. This sort of victimhood may begin with a real event or loss, but it is perpetuated and increased beyond the realm of true victims. Some individuals or groups actually work out contrived victimhood for litigated dollars. It is not unheard of that someone with a whiplash injury may not truly be injured. In certain parts of Asia in the 1970s, it was not unheard of for locals to throw themselves in front of automobiles of Americans and then claim entitlement to life-long financial support. Opportunists are not victims.

True victims are people without choices. Someone who is hit by a car is a victim. If you were molested as a young child or adolescent, you were a victim. This kind of victimhood is nonnegotiable because children do not have the power to choose. People and survivors who are true victims generally make every human effort possible to move away from victimhood status, away from self-entitlement and the identification of vulnerability.

Example Of Differences In Motives For Wanting A Day Off

- **Wanting**: I want a day off, because I have worked hard.
- **Deserving**: I deserve a day off, because I have worked hard.
- **Entitlement**: I work harder than anyone else does, so I am entitled to time off. I have special rights. I'll get my manager to let me have next Tuesday off. I don't care that Susan is at her mother's funeral that day. Who takes care of me? After all, didn't I bring donuts last month? What did I get for that?

- **Emotional Terrorism Entitlement**: I don't deserve this treatment, why should I do all the work when I can get Mary to do it for me and I'm out of here? I'm entitled to extra time off and since I have Mary under my control, I think while I'm at it I will make it look like she isn't working as hard as I am. So, she can work for me and take the rap for me later. And if the manager doesn't give me the day off I'll start telling people he's having an affair.

2.   BULLETPROOF

Being bulletproof is an interesting term that finds its psychological origins in topics of addiction. Addicts are said to be "bulletproof" when their disease has taken the normal course of decay to the point where they have a belief that they can do anything without consequence. Addicts who are reaching advanced stages of their disease might think they can drive under the influence and not get caught because they are too smart, or are safe from reproach due to their "cleverness" and ability to "handle their liquor" or know when to stop. Such behaviors are typical of those used by people who are operating with a sense of entitlement. The distorted thinking suggests to them a level of immunity not held by "normal" people. Somehow, they become outside the laws of social norms and even nature.

Being bulletproof in it most nonproductive form typically shows itself in the later stages of addiction, criminal activity, and Emotional Terrorism. A somewhat milder form of being bulletproof is seen in first responders who think they can survive what "normies" or civilians cannot even handle on TV. They run into burning buildings, take down violent thugs, clean up blood and guts off highways, and leap buildings in a single bound. In this career, it is necessary and useful to have a level of this thinking to act and survive out in the field of their "work site." This overlay of capacity is called "image armor." Cops and Firefighters carry a lot of it. They are allowed!

Bulletproof is something different. Bulletproof is when people, including those with image-armor, push that thinking too far, to a point beyond which they take risks that are not reasonable to take. Bulletproof people believe they are beyond the domain of what "regular" people must accept. Law enforcement and fire service professionals with image armor survive in severely risky situations. But if they see themselves a bulletproof they may put themselves and others on their team at risk.

At the workplace, bulletproof employees are somehow mysteriously special, unique and above all, unquestionably correct. They truly believe they are untouchable. For example, a bulletproof employee might blatantly steal and brag about it. They are so convinced of their unique status that they try to eliminate anything that does not fit into their picture. Anything that threatens that picture or threatens their sense of being bulletproof, is suspect and dangerous, and must usually be eliminated. Bulletproof employees are beyond the scope of social behaviors, morals, taboos, expectations, guidelines, laws, and the other rights and comforts of others humans. They do not really think that the rest of the universe is much of their concern. Bulletproof people consider themselves untouchable and are completely surprised when consequences arrive.

The term Greeks used for bulletproof thinking was *hubris*. Hubris is an inappropriately escalated level of pride that precedes a mighty fall to humiliation. When employees start thinking they are bulletproof, immune, safe, or untouchable, trouble is not far behind. Most regular human beings know they are mortal and fallible and are concerned and thoughtful when taking dangerous risks. Someone who is bulletproof has a different approach to risk.

The early signs of Emotional Terrorism can start with a small level of hubris. The lowest level of hubris belongs to people who are just simply obnoxiously arrogant. These people are not Emotional Terrorists unless they impose non-consensual agendas on others based on their sense of entitlement and arrogance. Emotional Terrorists evolve the level of their hubris to risk taking. Over a period of time they will take increasingly bigger risks. They may start with verbalizing more entitlement, rising to a sense of not caring how their behaviors effect others, until they see themselves as more and more omniscient and omnipotent, and begin to carry an odd sort of rigid new rules about themselves which allow them to do things that are over-the-top. At first the behaviors may possibly look brave and useful. Then, as the behaviors become more rigid, the individual is less approachable, less malleable, and less willing to be "managed" by anyone else.

Examples Of Workplace Bulletproof Behaviors:

- An active alcoholic or addict who drives a company car while under the influence
- A cyber-hacker who keeps at it, thinking he/she won't be caught
- Having an affair with a co-worker, practicing unprotected sex and hoping not to get HIV or that it will affect working conditions
- Coming to work intoxicated
- Using a work computer for pornography
- Using company resources for personal gain and assuming no one will know
- Assuming terrorism only happens to the other guy

3.   ANTAGONISTIC

Antagonistic behaviors are the natural consequences of conflict between forces or tensions — a pulling apart of substances where that pulling diminishes one side. Antagonism is hostile. Emotional Terrorists create an atmosphere of tension and conflict that is almost palpable, even when hidden behind polite behaviors. In fact, an overlay of polite on top of a depth of antagonism is standard fare for the Emotional Terrorist. Home ground is overt courtesy with an undertone of something miserable and angry.

Passive-aggressive behaviors are antagonistic. Antagonism is a bit like a game to an Emotional Terrorist. It is the playing field where people are vulnerable. Set up an antagonistic dynamic and watch the fun! An antagonist especially enjoys finding people who are vulnerable and pushing them a little bit until they are just slightly emotionally off balance. They then shrug their shoulders and say, "Gee I didn't know you were so sensitive." Or they tease someone and say, "Oh, I'm just kidding, that was a joke. Don't you have a sense of humor?" Or they like to stir up anger in a group, tease someone, belittle, or just act in an edgy sort of way that keeps the general tension up. This makes it much less boring for the antagonist. They have an amazing capacity to keep conflict going even in the midst of peacemakers. They use direct or indirect methods, whichever work best.

Antagonism is often directed at management. This is different then normal whining and moaning about management. An Emotional Terrorist will use antagonism to stir up the emotions of others. Claiming that someone else has to be the "problem" of all the tension in the office will effectively deflect accountability away from himself or herself and onto someone else. It is a good trick. When people are suspicious and nervous, the terrorist has taken some ground. "Antagonists are individuals who, on the basis of non-substantive evidence, go out of their way to make insatiable demands, usually attacking the person or performance of others. These attacks are selfish in nature, tearing down rather than building up, and are frequently directed against those in a leadership capacity" (Haugk, 1988).

4.   ENTRENCHED   .

Emotional Terrorists do not quit. They do not back down. They dig their heels in for the long haul and take a position that is fixed and unshakable. Flexibility and negotiation are not the domains of Emotional Terrorists. They are deeply rooted in their positions rather than shared interests. Whereas individuals may be narcissistic, selfish, self-centered, or egotistical, the Emotional Terrorist goes beyond these personal interest behaviors. They take such self-indulgences and raise them to a level of "cause." In international terrorism, individuals have been known to participate in suicide or homicide in the name of a particular cause. Emotional Terrorists at the work site symbolically mimic this in their willingness to sacrifice others for their rigid belief system, and see themselves as martyrs in the process.

Entrenchment is easily recognizable in a discussion. You may be offering ideas and concepts for negotiation, and someone who is entrenched in their position will not budge. In fact, they will not bend. In mediations, the entrenched person will rarely even see that there is a workable solution for all. This is not a concept that fits within the realms of entrenchment. Entrenchment is more all-or-nothing, win-lose, with-us-or-against-us thinking. Most healthy people will eventually apologize, open up, bend, flex, leave, cry, stop, laugh, move on, or adjust in some way. In other words, they will make movement. Emotional Terrorists will move only to regroup their agenda and hit it from another angle. An Emotional Terrorist does not let anything deter from their goal of control of something, someone, or somewhere.

Case Example

Dear Dr. Vali, Barb's attitude had always been curt, but it had escalated over the last few years. We had worked on the same big public project several times, and the last time I was her manager. She offended the client and staff and so it was decided that it would be the last year she was put on the project. She was gently informed through what I call a "soft message." In as positive a frame as possible, I let her know that it was apparent she no longer enjoyed this assignment and would be relieved of it. I let her know that we wanted her to be comfortable and that the plan was to find her another assignment to do something that she liked better. She left the meeting and it felt positive. Apparently, her first stop after our meeting was to tell a vulnerable staff member, Lois, that she had been "fired." Lois was crushed and believed that managers had betrayed Barb. For the next several months, Lois was consumed by her emotions and spent several hours a day ruminating. As her manager, I did not know the connection and was confused by Lois' sudden emotional demise.

Barb's attitude did not improve and in fact started to deteriorate. She e-mailed lengthy complaints to the rest of the staff that outlined her unfair treatment. This was a surprise to everyone since no one had been in on the situation. Everyone became upset. Now everyone was stirred up. My manager informed me that I had to inform Barb that she had to "mend relationships." Barb's response was an interesting decision to not speak with anyone. This lasted for over nine months. If a work-related task involved speaking, she was excruciatingly sparse with words, and there were no exchanges of what I would call normal talk. If she walked down the hall and someone said "hello," she would not respond. My manager and I spent countless hours trying to ameliorate this tension.

The process for firing people in our company is too daunting to use easily. HR tried using mediation but lost neutrality and became a covert agent for Barb who was able to deflect her anger in blame. Our HR person became an ally for her and started to add to the tension by taking sides. Trying to avoid the discomfort and conflict, the entire team avoided Barb in the hallways or meetings. Managers were now spending two to three hours a day trying to deal with the "emotional debris caused by this emotional tornado" that blew through every day. In all honesty, I had some personal "intuition" a year earlier but did not want to sound like an alarmist so now I felt awful for not speaking up earlier.

One of my acquaintances is a counselor, and at another meeting I found myself spilling out my distress. I told him the whole story about Barb's snit and explained that this communications company had over 4,000 employees with no policy for impaired employees unless they were "bleeding from the eyes, or directly caught drunk or using drugs." The counselor suggested that behavior at work that included nine months of no speaking was more than a "snit." He said it was entrenched behavior and Barb was holding the company hostage. The counselor recommended that a don't-make-waves policy was not doing anyone a service and suggested that perhaps this employee was in need of care. The suggestion that Barb needed help was never considered. The possibility that she might harm herself or someone else had never been considered. The counselor asked if there was an EAP policy in place. I told him there was, but it had to be called in by the HR person who "didn't want to bother anyone." When asked how much of Barb's dramatic avoidance behaviors had affected the team, I said, "At first we were consumed by it, and now we barely care." My manager just thought she was obnoxious and my feelings about her were more emotional. I was beginning to hate this woman! My counselor friend suggested that Barb was entrenched in something, which is beyond the normal scope of an acute (short term) temper tantrum, emotional outburst, hurt feeling, snit, or disappointment. Quite honestly, I had never considered that perhaps Barb was impaired rather than just an "obnoxious person."

I have decided to take your advice and look at this from a different angle. I never thought about Emotional Terrorist before and now, with that and what my counselor friend said, I am seeing a different picture. I am planning on meeting with my manager and discussing it with her. Sincerely, Maureen

5.   <u>MULTI-TALENTED</u>

Managers need new ideas, new tools, and new ways of seeing people because Emotional Terrorists are always thinking up new ways to create chaos. International and domestic terrorists like to catch people who are asleep on the job or not paying attention. Emotional Terrorists are no different. They will create, re-create, and turn themselves inside out to achieve their agenda. Emotional Terrorists have to be multi-talented, with many diverse skills to accomplish their mission. This is why as a manager you need to be more talented then the Emotional Terrorist. Look at the following list of tools and techniques available to an Emotional Terrorist and consider what you might have to have in your toolkit or emotional arsenal to manage these workplace challenges. The annoying thing about preparing for terrorism of any kind is the necessity of having to see things through *their* eyes. Knowing that ethical people cannot see through unethical eyes any more than a sane person can see through they eyes of someone who is mentally ill, managers must still begin the tedious process of thinking beyond their own niceness to find creative solutions and risk preventions.

Tools And Techniques Of An Emotional Terrorist

- Lying to a supervisor or co-worker
- Tampering with files or documents
- Harassment
- Use or misuse of company resources
- Knowledge of schemes or practices that take advantage of the company
- Requests for confidential information
- Sharing and withholding information
- Access or control over proprietary information
- Rumors and gossip
- Contributing or withholding support to individuals or key team members
- Time card reports falsified or inaccurate
- Inaccuracies
- Inappropriate acceptance of gifts, gratuities, entertainment
- Manipulation of data
- Security tampering
- Overt theft
- Manipulated expense reports
- Failure to follow through
- Incomplete tasks
- Abandonment of tasks
- Selling or marketing business practices
- Conflicts of interest
- Substance abuse
- Insider information abuse
- Unethical recruitment practices
- Downplaying public safety
- Unnecessary trainings and time-consuming meetings followed by consequences for tasks not finished
- Maintaining only minimum legal or code compliances
- Inappropriate responses to reports of danger, whistle-blowing, or common knowledge
- Poorly managed customer relations
- Corporate spying, losses of security, disclosure of security information
- Accepting or making inappropriate political contributions per industry standards
- Price fixing, gauging, hoarding
- Ignoring laws about immigration
- Not abiding by drug laws
- Avoiding tax laws
- Corruption of public officials or private individuals
- Dangerous sexual practices

- Using company technology to further addictions, crime, or sabotage
- Antitrust violations
- Creating pressure which leads to the misconduct of others

6. ABLE TO ATTRACT INNOCENT SUPPORTERS

Emotional Terrorists count on innocent nice people to further their causes. They use their many skills, tools and techniques to accomplish this. Emotional Terrorists are sometimes seen as heroic to the naïve. They become the gallant spokespersons for the truth, often seen as brave activists, guides or gurus. They project themselves as victims, and innocent people are often gullible to this line and are hooked into the martyred cause for justice. Anarchists, fascists, and dictators have used this ploy throughout history to get other people to do their dirty work so they can remain the pure hero or heroine. Some people have personalities that lead them to be followers who cannot or will not think for themselves. Others are afraid, passive, lack imagination, short sighted, or bored. Some people follow leaders without question. Other people join Emotional Terrorists to create a spin and have no idea that they have been exploited. Emotional Terrorists have a talent for recruitment by making their followers feel special, entitled and eventually bulletproof. Of course, it is the Emotional Terrorist that maintains control over the one flack jacket, parachute or life ring, but does not hesitate to volunteer someone else to step into the line of fire, jump first or swim through the sharks first. Thinking how people respond to group energy explains how Emotional Terrorist can be contagious and symbolically, as well as occasionally literally, fatal to the follower. The Emotional Terrorist does not mind sacrificing the employment or reputation of someone else to maintain his or her own job. If a manager is a leader an Emotional Terrorist may not hesitate to do whatever they think is necessary to erode that position of authority.

7. CHARISMATIC OR TRAGIC

Two powerful methods that Emotional Terrorists use to attract supporters are the demonstration of charm and sadness. Charisma calls on the weak by suggesting a special luckiness if the charismatic person accepts their presence. Luck will somehow rub off and special good feelings are assumed a next small step away. Disenfranchised employees will seek strength from anywhere if they feel the ship is sinking. Managers need to find ways to be attracting and appealing leaders to counterbalance the exploitive charismatic appeal of Emotional Terrorists.

Tragic or sad performance from Emotional Terrorists appeal to helpers, lost nurturers, co-dependents, and the need-to-feel-needed people. The charms of an Emotional Terrorist who drops a head, sighs, tries to talk and doesn't finish a sentence, sits a bit apart from the group, rubs a forehead, leaves early, asks questions that have no clear answers, raises their hand to ask a question — then when called on says, "never mind, it wasn't important," and generally appears sad, are compelling. These and other behaviors draw energy toward the Emotional Terrorist. Remember, an Emotional Terrorist does not really want to share, partner or collaborate. They may appear to be inclusively charismatic or inclusively needing constant help, but the purposes behind these activities are self-focused and exploitive. Charisma and tragic behaviors are extremely deniable by the Emotional Terrorist. Charisma denial is characterized by "I was just helping" and tragic denial is characterized by "I just was trying to get some help." The word "just" is the tipoff. A sentence that begins with "just" is usually associated with either entitlement or denouncement of accountability.

8. HOSTAGE TAKERS

Emotional Terrorists take people and workplaces hostage. When people are held emotionally captive at the work site because they have to be there from nine to five, the risk potential for Emotional Terrorism elevates. The work site is a perfectly constructed container for chaos because no one can leave. An Emotional Terrorist will use this captive audience to pull off an emotional incident, then sit, and watch the consequences unfold like a soap opera they are writing themselves. Think of this as an "emotional drive-by shooting" where the victims cannot even call for help or run away. And tomorrow it may happen again because that Emotional Terrorist is going to be at the work site again. Hapless employees in this drama may not even know they roles they have been assigned until they are given a script from the Emotional Terrorist. The cast assignments of good guys and bad guys, heroes, heroines and villains when written by the Emotional Terrorist instead of the manager make the director of the show in question. Who is writing the script in your department? Who is running the show? Can anyone get out of the work site hostage environment long enough to get a new perspective? Are doors open?

Warning Signs of Emotional Terrorism Activities

- Intangible feelings, hunches, intuitions, sense, or opinion that something is "going on" with no specific data to confirm or deny
- Grooming: a systematic, unnatural approach to relationship control that appears upon close scrutiny to be contrived and gainful
- Contact escalations: interactions get more frequent
- Early spinnings: small emotional events increase
- Covert works: reports of trouble without evidence
- Rejection of approach: suggestion of problems met with resistance, denial
- Early signs of entrenchment: rigidity
- Overt signs: visible tensions and emotional reactions with no real data
- Accusations: blame statements or inferences
- Side Attacks: indirect blame, accusations, complaints
- Overt visible behaviors: demonstrations and activities, documentable data
- Gathering of forces: small or large groups spending time processing issues
- Direct attacks: specific demonstrations, behaviors and complaints
- Ultimatums: provocations, challenges
- Threats: intimidation, pressure, bullying, coercion
- Repetition: Continuing or repeating any or all earlier signs, even with increased risk, in order to demonstrate a willingness to continue for absolute control

The Gotchas

The Gotchas are verbal clues that an emotional process is going on in your midst. Managers are trained to see the obvious signs of annoyance, discomfort, dissatisfaction, and outright trauma or catastrophic emotional incident. The Emotional Terrorist is also trained or aware of these, and finds it more useful to work "under the radar" with more subtle language. The language of Emotional Terrorism is easily deniable with an innocent laugh, distraction or direct lie. Remember, Emotional Terrorists do not hold to the same accountability as the regular employee, so a lie is not an issue if it will further their cause. Lies come in all sorts of language and form. The Gotchas are lies with strings attached. The strings are a leftover feeling of guilt, shame, discomfort, and confusion often attached to a need to defend or attack. Even the so-called positive grooming statement has an edge of something sticky that just does not hold true.

Gotchas

a. After all, you are my new best friend
b. Ha! Ha! I caught you in an error
c. You are the most special person in the world
d. Everywhere I go people don't get it
e. I won't stop until I get what I want
f. What will it take to get you on board?
g. I'm watching you no matter what until you fail
h. I'm an expert and you are not
i. Righteous indignation
j. I'm a victim of all this
k. You aren't going to share this with anyone, are you?
l. I was just joking, what's wrong with your sense of humor?
m. Can't you take a joke?
n. Maybe you're too sensitive
o. I have the ear of the boss and can tell him what you want

p.	I thought we were close friends, but obviously not
q.	Promise you won't tell anyone this
r.	If you tell anyone this I'll get fired (you'll get fired)

GUIDELINES TO MANAGING EMOTIONAL TERRORISM

If you have become aware, or been made aware that someone under your management is an Emotional Terrorist it may become eventually necessary for you to interact with the individual. These are guidelines, not rules or laws of the Universe. In other words, you will have to find your own way through this process using your style, within the context of the situation, and the dimensions of your company and industry. The interview process below offers some good suggestions as to how to avoid obvious pitfalls and traps of working with someone who does not follow the same guidelines as you do. Being clear about what you are doing, where you are going, and how you are going about it, will give you the upper hand; the sense of presence necessary to manage someone who is cunning, baffling, tricky, subtle, upset, chaotic, manipulative, angry, frightened, controlling, or in some rare cases just plain "evil."

Remember that the goal is usually to keep this person employed and employable. Remember that the snake in the bucket can be a good snake or a bad snake if the lid is efficient. You may be the first person to ever contain and lid an Emotional Terrorist. They usually don't like that. However, the good news is that some Emotional Terrorists internally long for boundary settings from someone, and settle right down into very compliant participants. This is the best-case scenario and one you should have forefront in your mind as the process unfolds. *Plan for the worst, but expect the best* is a good beginning. Using a bit of humor, you might think of yourself as an animal trainer who likes the critter, but doesn't want it to chew up your slippers. You may not need to train, punish or eliminate the beast. The simple act of you taking your hierarchical authority and letting the Emotional Terrorist know that you are the alpha leader of the pack may settle things down immediately. Sometimes the challenge for control or power can be easily dissolved with a silent presence that originates from a feeling that is fearless. How many times have you heard the expressions, "never let them see you sweat," or "they can smell your fear?" This is true with Emotional Terrorists as well. You absolutely need to understand your own bottom line, your own strengths, your weaknesses, use your own support systems, and have a deep abiding faith in that system. Emotionally it is impossible to be in fear and in faith at the same time. Therefore, you must be on top of your own faith-game to walk into a situation fearlessly. Ask yourself the following questions before you begin:

In What Do You Have Faith?

- Your company policy
- Your industry standards
- Your training
- Your credentials
- Your authority
- Your information
- The hierarchy, chain of command
- Your interview skills
- Your team
- Your exit strategy
- Your listening and evaluating skills
- Your own intelligence
- Your own ability to discern truth
- Your intuition
- The information given you by a witness
- Data
- Observations
- Hunches
- Experience
- Your bosses

- Your mission
- Your imagination
- Your people
- Your God or Higher Power
- Your resume is current
- That people are generally good
- That even Emotional Terrorists can adjust
- That no matter what you do you are home after work and safe
- That if you do not know what to do, you have good resources to aid you

Once you have faith in something, you will not as easily slip into fear. Of course, if you survived the Titanic, you might not have absolute faith in boats and find yourself slightly hesitant to get in another boat. In the same way, if you have come up against an Emotional Terrorist in your past, you might wonder if the effort to deal with all of this management process is worth the work. Although this is a valid thought, it is also a doorway to fear. This is why it is essential throughout the process of managing to decide and re-decide if you truly want to be a manager. If you do not have faith in your decision to manage, you will not operate from a position of strength. Emotional Terrorists smell your fear and will dive deep into that fear with a variety of unique or custom-designed Gotchas.

Case Example

Wendy, the manager, was ready to deal with the Emotional Terrorist in her department. Lou, who had created turmoil for weeks, was sitting in a chair in her office. Before the meeting, Wendy had called her mentor for support, taken some deep breaths, had a moment to walk outdoors and relax, and she was now on top of her game. Before she was able to start the procedure of redirecting Lou's energies, he said, "I suppose you're going to discipline me for complaining." A year before her training, Wendy thought, she would have fallen for that Gotcha and responded, thus losing her position. Today she had faith in her capacity to not be unbalanced, and made a neutral sound, "Oh" and moved on with her agenda.

Learning Byte

Wendy knew that if she responded with a defense or attack that she was lost. If she tried to control his Gotcha she was lost. If she ignored it totally, he would still have gained ground, because it would have been seen as a success. Responding with a neutral "oh" gave her the power in the moment. She began her interview from a strong position so she could control the flow of the conversation. Thus, totally discounting any value in Lou's emotions or words, Wendy ran the show.

DO THIS: Remain calm in the presence of an Emotional Terrorist. Remember that you are the good guy. Do your best!

DON'T: Worry if you feel shaky or get tricked. Remember, these men and women are well practiced at this. Don't forget that it isn't about you. You are just the Victim du Jour.

Managing an Emotional Terrorist

Management and *Terrorism* have a number of common denominators. The words include concepts and actions. Both words imply that there are rules and policies to follow, work within specific procedural activity formats, a level of predictability, and consequences that affect others. What is different about the two is that most managers, unless they are terrorists themselves, work inside the lines. The respect authority, work within the chain of command, operate through guidelines and principles, and adhere to generally accepted norms. Terrorists count on this and employ their imaginations to work within and around all these normative boundaries.

A story from a manager of a small company brings this difference to light as she was trying to out-think an Emotional Terrorist in her workplace. She had been working with other managers for months trying to teach them the necessity of creative management of difficult employees, and during a spin-free workplace consultation came up with a way to teach the value of "out-thinking" the problem makers and managing Emotional Terrorists.

Case Example

Delores was a senior manager in a private school. One early spring morning a staff member came running into her office reporting that there was a big snake in the schoolyard. Delores quickly assessed, to her discomfort, that as a manager it might indeed be her responsibility to remove the snake to protect the children and staff. So, she proceeded to go out into the field with an ax. Just as she was about to destroy the snake, she felt dozens of little eyes and big eyes on the back of her head. She turned around to see little noses pressed against windows and staff faces with worried expressions. They were all wondering what she was going to do with that snake! Delaying her initial organic disgust of snakes, she stopped her homicidal intent, returned to the school, got a bucket, and proceeded to go through the emotional and physically difficult challenge of catching the snake alive. She wanted to do it without causing the children or staff to be unduly upset and without doing harm to her self. To her surprise, she no longer wanted to actually harm the snake. She just needed this threat gone. She succeeded, with some help from another brave staff member. This strategy later became a written policy, the 'Snakes in the Schoolyard' Policy.

Snakes In The Schoolyard Policy:

1. At least two (2) employees with gloves approach the snake. Snakes squirm toward the easiest direction to escape, the path of least resistance. With two people, the snake has no escape route. The snake catchers must not fear snakes. But gloves are required for better performance.
2. Whichever employee grabs the snake must immediately toss it into a bucket with a lid. One of the employees must then immediately secure the lid. The real trick to Snake Removal is the lid. Without the lid, the snake escapes and you must do it again. Spending your time catching the same snake over and over is not efficient and is not good business practice.
3. Once you contain the snake you must take it into the school, let the children see that it is not hurt. Because children have imaginations and like to see even crawly things cared for correctly.
4. Later, transport the snake elsewhere, off the premises, a long way away from where you work, and dispose of it.
5. If the snake is Toxic, call in a professional.

Learning Byte

The Outcome? Generally, everyone is happy. Managers, staff, the children, and if done well, even the snake. The manager did disclose privately, "Of course, you know, Dr. Vali, that if this type of snake came to my house, I'd just chop its head off, but workplace snakes are different." With that comment, the manager had the concept of how to manage a workplace terrorist. She removed the word snake from the policy and developed a procedure for her team that they understood. The company had recently been challenged by a workplace Emotional Terrorist in human form, and after the snake incident, the manager was able to show her staff how to protect the company, clients, themselves and even the Emotional Terrorist from being harmful.

DO THIS: Learn what snakes are toxic and what snakes are harmless.

DON'T: Assume that all snakes must be removed. Some snakes can do very well with micro-management if they have solid and well-defined boundaries (lids).

Some Tips To Deal With Emotional Terrorists

- Do the best you can
- Trust your intuition, don't worry if no one else is noticing
- Do not seek feedback from staff
- Watch, wait, listen
- Easy does it, time will reveal demonstrations
- Don't take covert behaviors personally
- Be confident and also seek support
- Document tension levels and situations even if there is no external data
- If you think something is going on, you might be right, so stay alert
- Rest when you are able and practice good self care for surviving the long haul
- Re-decide if you want to be a manager and re-group your energies and resources
- Continue with other projects and stay awake

Running a Meeting with an Emotional Terrorist

Although a certain amount of interaction with Emotional Terrorists has a hidden or covert nature, there are also times that you will have to be in direct contact with a known Emotional Terrorist in your office. If you have determined that an employee is an Emotional Terrorist, you can proceed to manage them by paying attention to a few careful steps to avoid falling into their control.

- Set up a meeting with nonnegotiable times in your power place
- Stay neutral
- Be clear and firm; do not let the Emotional Terrorist call the shots
- Have a witness, or note-taker present
- Demand clear boundaries. If the employee is more than five minutes late for any reason courteously cancel that meeting and reschedule a new one at your convenience.
- If the employee has an emotional reaction to your boundary, stay firm and courteous, and make a notation of their reaction if it is verbal or nonverbal
- Be courteous and business-like throughout the meeting
- Make certain the environment is businesslike, and seating is hierarchical
- No food or snacks, this is not "friendly" — this is business
- Begin with the issues at hand
- Do not allow discussion until you are done with meeting agenda
- Listen and take notes, but do not engage in a discussion
- Remain neutral. Make notes on your emotions and deal with them at a later time and well removed from the Emotional Terrorist
- Avoid questions. Approach all questions as if they were hand grenades with the pins already removed
- Do not defend, attack, or make personal comments
- Do not share your personal opinions
- Do not praise or support
- Keep it neutral and business only
- If the tension rises or the meeting becomes emotional, or the Emotional Terrorist gains any ground, take a five-minute break, and start over or cancel the meeting and reschedule on your terms.
- Close the meeting with a "thank you" by standing up and formally eliminating any opportunity to continue with emotionally loaded comments. If there are lingering statements, comments, attacks, defenses, or trailing comments, repeat the thank you as a punctuation mark at the end of a sentence. Repeat as often as needed to close the meeting courteously. If absolutely necessary, repeat the words "thank you" in a neutral tone as you are opening the office door and indicating that it is over, and time to leave.

Become an Expert in Using Communication Models

Communication models are not one-size-fits-all. Finding a style that fits your personality is important to competency and confidence. Whether you study Rosenberg's model of "Non-Violent Communication," or your Grandmother-s "Be-Nice-to-Everyone" model, is up to you. There are styles that are more functional at the workplace, especially when dealing with difficult people, bullies, jerks and Emotional Terrorists. One such model, described in the tool section of this book, is called the *Drama Triangle*. Stephen Karpman created a model of communication within a psychological model called transactional analysis that efficiently removes the power plays from any interaction. If you see an interaction a bit like a game model, the three roles in the Drama Triangle would be *victim*, *persecutor* and *rescuer*. Taking on any of these roles is a dangerous position. As the roles shift quickly from one to another, anyone playing this game will be caught in a veritable unending spiral of emotional conflict. Moving away from any of these three roles will lead to neutrality and a position of clarity that will move any discussion away from emotional content to business content.

AUTHOR'S AFTERTHOUGHTS

Managing the creative attributes of Emotional Terrorists takes calm, quiet, non-emotional persistence. In the face of tornados at work, you are the calm place, the shelter, the cellar or the quiet serenity model for your staff. If you spin, all will be lost. If you get into anger, fear or blame, all will be lost. If you become a victim, a rescuer or a persecutor, all will be lost. If you are tranquil and persistent over time, that will become the tone of your leadership and the higher ground that your team will go to when under duress. If everyone on your team is on the same page, the Emotional Terrorist will not have a place to spin or create chaos, so they eventually lose control, lose interest, and either become compliant or move on to their next target. I have found that once managers get the hang of this they truly enjoy the refined, professional power of being in a neutral position. The pressure is off and they are able to access their own opinion, ideas, intuitions and creative ideas. I have seen them sit up a little taller, have softer expression on their faces, laugh more frequently, and relax in the knowledge that what they have been doing is actually very, very hard. They give themselves some permission to feel a bit proud of their work. Good managers are a brave lot!. A suggestion I give managers who are trying for the first time to experience neutrality, is to think of themselves as Switzerland. I remind them that Switzerland, as a nation, maintains a politic of neutrality. This is not a weak position in the world. In fact, Switzerland is where the Geneva Convention was held, where Swiss bank accounts are considered the safest, where there are Swiss Army Knives and the best chocolate. The Swiss have a very powerful and well-trained army. They know they have the capacity to defend and attack, but choose not to do so. In that choice, they have remained world leaders and safe haven as neutral ground. They do not participate in the Karpman Drama Triangle sorts of politics of the rest of the world. After I explain Swiss neutrality as a model of strength, I remind them of the chocolate part. It is obvious to me that after any enduring challenge of remaining neutral in the midst of conflict, chocolate is indicated. This is not carte blanche for a binge feeding frenzy, but rather honoring the tradition of many warriors to finish a battle with a "wee bit of chocolate."

DISCUSSION QUESTIONS

- Without identifying anyone specific, can you describe an Emotional Terrorist you have worked with in your career history?

- What was their overt behavior like?

- What about their covert behaviors?

- What were the long-term consequences of this employee's actions or non-actions?

- Watch the local newspaper for one week and count how many accounts suggest the presence of an Emotional Terrorist in a workplace.

- Why would it be to your company's benefit to keep an Emotional Terrorist on the payroll?

- Why would it be a risk?

SECTION III
READINESS:
TOOLS FOR EMOTIONAL
CONTINUITY MANAGEMENT

I hear stories. When I tell people I'm an Emotional Continuity Management consultant they say something like, "I've heard about emotional stuff at conferences... but how do you really do anything about people's feelings at work? What tools are there? How can you quantify emotions? How can you make policies about human feelings? Oh yeah, we've had people who created so much conflict and chaos that it was unbelievable. But can anything actually be done about it?"

Indeed no one can mandate emotions nor can they predict and control the human mind, but work needn't be a madhouse. There are countless user-friendly tools available to better manage your own emotions and the emotions of others. Psychologists, mental health counselors, human resource professionals, management trainers, social workers, coaches, and people who attend 12-Step Meetings have better tools than most companies. Why? Emotional Continuity Management is not rocket science, nor the exclusive domain of some secret psychology club! Although historically businesses haven't had the time or inclination to put Emotional Continuity Management tools in place, times have changed.

Companies that would spend millions on software tools, customer surveys, and ergonomic furniture need to spend dollars on Emotional Continuity Management tools, too. And the best emotional management tools are simple to use. The following chapters introduce a few tools that have been well tested in real work sites with real people under real conditions. Just as everyone in a company needs to know how to use the fire extinguisher, everyone on your team needs to know how to use emotional readiness tools for whatever may happen. Continuity planning is about readiness. Emotional Continuity is about emotional readiness.

7

READINESS:
TOOLS FOR MANAGING IN
THE MIDST OF EMOTIONAL CHAOS

WHY YOU SHOULD READ THIS CHAPTER

Mastery takes practice and rehearsal. Review the list of attributes of well-adjusted people to increase your recognition skills for evaluation. In other words, if you are starting to play the violin and people are still wincing at the squawks and screeches, you may be making progress, but you still need to work on it. You should be able to tell if your tools are working by how you feel and how people are responding.

BY THE END OF CHAPTER 7 YOU SHOULD BE ABLE TO

- Have a working knowledge of several Emotional Continuity Management tools

- Recognize the Drama Triangle before you start implementing any Emotional Continuity Management tool

- Determine if you or your organization have a Duty to Warn (mandated reporters) in the case of dangerous or risk taking behaviors

- Know the stages of grieving and how they may appear in the workplace

- Know when you need help

WHAT THE EXPERTS SAY ABOUT
EMOTIONAL CONTINUITY MANAGEMENT TOOLS

"Tools? Take a break, give yourself permission to say no, rest, eat healthy and exercise. My own personal favorite: laugh. Over the years in the EMS business I have seen many people suffer from "emotional bankruptcy" My own experience of this was with the 4th dead baby call in a couple of weeks. We were extricating a car passenger and the baby she had been holding fell out from underneath the dash. She had been feeding the baby at the time of the accident. We had another call and I was unable to get out of the ambulance. I was paralyzed. I took myself off the call list and didn't ride for 6 months." — Patti Courson, Director of Emergency Management Services, Kennewick, Washington.

HOW TO MANAGE FEELINGS OF LOSS

- Big feelings are okay. Making good choices about how to act out those feelings is important. Adults have choices.
- Move through the stages of grief. (Denial, Bargaining, Anger, Depression, Acceptance) Remember that avoidance of any stage only postpones the inevitable. It is okay to stay in one stage as long as necessary, just don't move your furniture into any particular stage. It is also okay to move back and forth between stages for a while until you are emotionally equipped to complete a stage. This takes some time.
- Avoidance accumulates emotional slush which can become fixed and rigid over time,
- Healing means being willing to go through all the stages several times and then doing it again. It is like going through a tunnel and coming out the other side, or going around a baseball diamond until you get back to home plate. Each time this is successfully accomplished there is potentially more compassion, wisdom and meaning to the loss. By going through the process again it becomes more familiar and less threatening.
- The degree of energy in grief is related to the inherent value of the loss. Grief levels can only be determined by the person experiencing it. This is determined by their perceptions alone. Other perceptions can influence this, but it is very personal.
- Work is an appropriate place to express feelings of loss within some appropriate guidelines and boundaries. It is not necessary or healthy to pretend loss does not exist. Neither is it healthy to express grief constantly or make it central in the workplace. It is helpful to find an honest, open, and measured balance in the workplace. If that balance is lost, there should be no shame, although it may be appropriate to take time to rebalance feelings.
- An old measure of correct grieving suggested by Native American tradition is that the only way to release sorrow is to tell your story 1,000 times. Silence does not serve the grieving process. Find safe listeners. Create safe places to share grief stories.
- Establish a quiet and safe time separate from business to discuss feelings.
- Don't start a feelings discussion with complaints.
- Think out your feelings and write them out.
- Take your time.
- Remember that emotions do not make people weaker.
- Use your energy wisely. Pace yourself.
- Feel your emotions without the aid of anesthesia from drugs, alcohol, food, sex, overwork, gambling or other numbing devices

HOW TO MANAGE TENSION

There are many ways to cope with tension. Some ways are healthy, some are dysfunctional, while other ways can be dangerous. Avoiding tension through the use of anesthesia is an overwhelmingly simple, accessible and eventually pointless process. Numbing oneself with the anesthetics of illegal or prescription drugs, alcohol, gambling, sex, shopping, eating, exercise, work or other activities delays the process of experiencing genuine and authentic feelings and ultimately complicates resolution. In the long run the continued use of anesthesia makes tension much worse as the system begins to consider the anesthesia as normal and requires more to maintain the status quo. There is no such thing as "the first one is free" because the long-term costs prohibit the value of the first dose. Dependency leads to addiction and addiction is *not* a tension antidote.

The most remarkable antidote for managing tension is to not resist it. What you resist, persists. In its earliest phases anxiety is simple tension. If you can just go ahead and feel the tension and do some minor adjustments it often just goes away. Tension that increases or turns to anxiety may be something other than tension.

There is a phrase that is useful in psychology that lets the therapist know if it a simple event or a more complicated incident: "If it is Hysterical It may be Historical." What that means is that if the feelings go beyond a normal range of experience into bigger and bigger emotions it is likely that it has tapped into some old belief system, bad experience, trauma or memory stored in the brain. Regular daily grind tension should dissolve rapidly with a few deep breaths, a coffee break, a walk around the block, a phone call to a support person, a minor complaining, or a yoga sun-salutation. In other words, normal tension is normal. Try first to get creative with your own tension and turn it into an ally. Find out first about yourself and your style of taking care of tension. Let the energy of tension rise and fall like a wave in the ocean. If it continues rising and rising like a tsunami tidal wave, it may not be tension. This is also true for your employees. You can help them "ride the waves" or pay attention to see if they are falling off their surfboards and drowning. Translate the idea of tension into a metaphor of surf waves of energy. Then you may be able to try one of the following techniques to "play" with the energy of tension at work:

- During a high-tension project invite everyone to wear Hawaiian shirts to work
- Laugh at tension and sweep it out of your mind
- Give tension a first name or character image
- Take your tension out for ice cream or sugar free yogurt
- Have an Annual Tension At Work Day in your office with awards
- Come dressed as your favorite fantasy Drama Triangle character
- Have a Biggest and Smallest Tension of the Week Bulletin Board (that spider, the power outage, the day 49 people called in with the flu, current events, broken vending machine)
- Play with your tension. Buy it a toy. Buy it a blanket. Make it a paper hat!
- Hire Tension Experts to give Anti-Tension trainings
- Create a Tension Support Group
- Delegate someone on your "anti-tension team" to come up with a Tension Motto, Logo, or Mascot (put small bungee cords on name tags on "Fight-the-Tension day," make a poster depicting a room filled with long-tailed cats and rocking chairs)
- Create a never-ending collection or list of things that demand tension, such as:

rubber bands	tympani drums
dramatic theater	waiting for the envelope to be opened at Oscars
April 15th	a cat hunting a bird
muscle groups	trampolines
elections	Stephen Spielberg, Steven King, Alfred Hitchcock

HOW TO SET BOUNDARIES

A boundary is a real or perceived edge, limit or border between yourself and someone else. The boundary can be physical such as a fence, wall, or cubicle. It can be emotional, such as not sharing a personal story, or mental, as in protecting your intellectual properties. A boundary can be spiritual in the sense that you can allow someone to share a religious opinion, or not. We place boundaries to protect and enhance our lives. Boundaries can frame good art or keep an invasion from your sacred ground. When you give someone a boundary it is quite reasonable for them to ask if you meant it. If you repeat your boundary one more time, clearly, calmly, and sincerely, a healthy person will accept that as your truth and not press forward, risking a potential crossing of your boundary. If the person asks again, and they are told no, they should move on and accept *no as meaning no.* When a boundary is not accepted after three clear messages, it is possible you are dealing with a dysfunctional or a pathological employee. This is an excellent early warning sign for spin potential.

When boundary-crossing behavior continues it is important to give another quiet and clear message to establish the firm reality of the boundary. Establishing a boundary more *clearly* does not mean *louder*. Clearer means being very specific and simple. There should be no need for detail or explanation. No means no. If the demands or behaviors escalate you may need help in getting your message across. This can be a good time to have a policy in place. For example, if an employee makes a personal advance and asks another employee on a date, and there is no policy against it, this is not necessarily a boundary crossing. It may be an exploration. It is not necessarily inappropriate to ask. However, if the answer is a clear "no," the exploration ends. The reply message requires neither violence nor volume. If it becomes more challenging or difficult to maintain or hold the boundary in place, this is significant information. The ease or difficulty in establishing clear boundaries demonstrates an indication of the agenda of the person crossing the boundary. The key to a verbal boundary is this: *Yes means Yes, No means No,* and *Maybe means Maybe.* The answer must not have a hidden giggle, nod of the head, or shake of the head that is incongruent with your words. If you don't know, say, I Don't Know, please get back to me later.

Case Example

Paul asked Erin out for a dinner date. Erin said "No, thank you." Paul was disappointed and quietly asked, "Are you sure?" Shelly replied, "This isn't a good time for me to go out." He said, "May I ask again another time?" Erin said, "Sure, in a few months, check back." Paul waited for five months before approaching Erin again. They went out to dinner and enjoyed themselves.

Case Example

Jerry asked Shelly out for a dinner date. Shelly said, "No, thank you." Jerry was disappointed and said, "Oh, come on Shelly, I know that Jim asked you out, but he's sort of dull. If you go out with me we'll have a ball!" Shelly replied, "Yes, Jim did ask me out, and I also told him that this isn't a good time for me to go out." Jerry replied, "What's the matter? Aren't I your type?" Shelly replied, "This isn't a good time in my life to go out with someone, but thanks anyway." Jerry escalated with, "Well, I'm not just anyone, come on Shelly, let's go out and have dinner, it'll be my treat if it's about the money!" Shelly said, "no, thank you." Jerry was angry now at being rejected. He walked away. The next afternoon Jerry approached Shelly with, "hey, are you free tonight? I have tickets to a movie." Shelly replied with, "No, thank you." Jerry came back in a few days with another invitation. Shelly replied, "No, thank you." Jerry asked Shelly, "Are you sleeping with Jim?" Shelly responded, "That isn't an appropriate question." She left the room. Jerry started a rumor that Shelly was having an affair with Jim and now was being cold and unfriendly to all the other people in the office. The rumor came back to Shelly after she inquired why people were not speaking to her. Shelly filed a harassment grievance and Jerry was terminated. The company spent thousands of dollars dealing with Jerry's boundary issue.

HOW TO NORMALIZE ACUTE STRESS REACTIONS

Most people can keep their emotions in line at the workplace. They don't fall apart and have tantrums and crying binges all day. If they do it is clear that something is seriously wrong and they have too much stress or tension in their life. But even normal, healthy, well-adjusted adults have bad days, and suffer from acute episodes of stress and tension. Ideally, people should not fear this nor should businesses fear these events. Normalizing stress as part of the human experience takes a lot of pressure off of everyone. In fact, it is usually a bonding process between "survivors of stress" to share tension and stress stories which often increases team loyalties, somewhat like fox-hole buddies. "We did it! Good for us!" Normal tensions should come and go like waves and a good management team can support their people by handing out the surfboard wax, or hollering a rousing "SURF'S UP, GANG" cheer. Normal, regular, run-of-the-mill emotional spins are not a problem, and, in fact, can add color to a dreary workplace. But if spinning does not rapidly resolve, or becomes a repetitive cycle something else is happening.

Case Example

Jason was in a foul mood. He was late to the staff meeting and did not contribute. Toward the end of the meeting the manager asked Jason what was going on. Jason growled that he was having trouble with the new computer upgrade. The manager stopped the team and announced to all, "Hey, I hear Jason is the only one in the office who wants to throw the computers out the window? Are we going to let him be the only one having that much fun?" The team stopped and cheered and was loud and unruly for two or three minutes. During the uproar, while everyone was complaining and laughing and grumbling publicly, the manager quietly asked Lou, a senior staff member, to pop in and give the tea, a bit more encouragement and support. Lou offered one-on-one training at the end of the week to Jason or anyone who wanted some extra time. Jason refused with, "nah, I'm actually getting it. It's just I didn't sleep last night because my son was up with the flu the entire night." The manager shared that his wife was down with it also. The work continued with good production levels throughout the day, with the team making humorous references to vicious things they wanted to do with their computers.

HOW TO MANAGE GRIEF: YOURS AND OTHERS

Elizabeth Kübler-Ross described five stages that people go through with losses through death: Denial, Bargaining, Anger, Depression, and Acceptance. Other losses necessitate we go through the same stages in either an abbreviated form or equally as pronounced. The level of loss is self-defined and based on the individual's perception of the value of the loss. No one can ascribe value or lack of value to another human being. Values are self-validating and supported by personal experience.

Mental health professionals will attest that although there is no absolute standard way anyone goes through the stages of loss, moving through all the stages would define grief work as accomplished and minimize the risk of being stuck in a stage for a protracted period. Moving through grief is like moving through a tunnel. Feelings inside the tunnel can be viable, fluid, erratic, weighty, vague, explosive, quiet, energized, controlling, vacant, passive and aggressive. There is no one right expression of these feelings. It takes moving through the tunnel to get to the proverbial "light at the end of the tunnel."

What is often missed is that all change creates a loss. Change can offer gain as well but always with a price of loss. If you choose one path, you will have to lose the other path either temporarily or permanently. You may gain the value of the chosen path and lose the value of the lost path. There may be no judgment of right or wrong in this, but the choice necessitates a loss of some sort. With every loss there is some level of grief work. The entire process of going through the tunnel to adjustment may last five minutes if it is a small loss. It does not take a death to have a loss. It does not take a death to go through the stages of loss.

Example

I lost my pen! It is a favorite pen. I am a writer. I will need my pen to continue writing my poetry.

1.   Denial

This is the "as-if" stage. There is no awareness that the pen is missing, so I continue my life "as-if" it will be there when I require it. I go about my business. I plan to write this afternoon with my favorite pen and I have no concept that my pen is gone. I naturally act "as if" my pen still exists where I left it in my mind.

But the pen is gone and this thought does not change the facts.

2.   Bargaining

I go to my studio to write. Wanting my pen now, the energy of that desire begins to stir within me. I move from a rather blank thinking place to a more active thinking of "I want my pen NOW." Energy moves toward my goal and I begin to work my thoughts in order to create the end I desire. I am trying to anticipate and control the outcome. I want to shorten the gap between me and my pen. My bargaining thoughts continue: "When I get my pen I will keep it close to me or on a string around my neck so I won't have to look for it like I am right now." "When I find my pen I will write all the time, go to church, be nicer, etc." I may even engage others in my attempt to control by asking someone, 'Will you help me take care of my pen?"

But the pen is gone and this thought does not change the facts.

3.   Anger

Now the energy increases as bargaining, the earlier control mechanism, did not control the situation or produce the pen. This energy must go somewhere. The first place it goes is outward, toward anger. The loss cannot belong to me, therefore it must belong to someone else. The energy now begins to sputter, spurt or explode outward away from the self into forms of blame, shame, anger, rage, accusations, defiances, attacks and rebellions. I may shout angry accusations like, "Who took my pen?" "You were supposed to help me. You are a jerk." "You hated my writing."

But the pen is gone and this thought does not change the facts.

4.   Depression

The energy production, still unsuccessful in producing the pen, now makes a U-turn and blame, shame, anger, rage, accusations, defiances, attacks and rebellions are now directed away from others and toward self. In depression I may believe "I'll never write again", "I was never any good anyway", "I picked the wrong person to help me protect my pen."

But the pen is gone and this thought does not change the facts.

5. Acceptance

Acceptance does not mean joy and celebration. Acceptance is the arrival at a clear awareness of the situation. The loss is real. The loss has meaning. Gains are seen, losses are absorbed, and gradually there is a return to a more stable energy. I come to believe "My pen is gone. I liked that pen a lot. I will live through this loss, but I will remember it each time I write or see a pen like the one I lost."

But the pen is gone and this thought does not change the facts.

HOWEVER, LIFE HAS MOVED ON. AND SO SHALL I.

Once such a minor grief is completed through the cycle, it will recycle again and again, usually in smaller doses and briefer cycles. A reminder of the loss may trigger the residue from a past stage. But eventually the recycling resolves more quickly. If the loss is severe the stages may hold the same energy and strength but usually are more fluid, less fixed, and less likely to become locked. A loss that is perceived as small, although it must follow the same stages, has less depth and usually resolves more quickly. The cycles may come quickly at first but with less force over time.

The frivolous example of losing a pen is useful to explore grief work because most people can discuss loss if it is about something as inane and commonplace as a pen. Most adults have experienced losses in their lives. That does not mean they are efficient at grief work. A person can be in one stage of grief about one loss, while in another stage about another loss, or change. You can be in anger about your pen and acceptance about your receding hairline or expanding waistline. You can be in bargaining about your receding hairline or expanding waistline and pitch an anger fit because your favorite pen is missing. Humans go through countless changes and losses and gains on a daily basis. Two people experiencing the same loss will perceive its value differently and may be in very different stages at the same time.

HOW TO MANAGE INFLEXIBLE EMPLOYEES

Growth can be annoying. It is uncomfortable. People don't like to be uncomfortable. But without that struggle they can become fixed and rigid. Many conflicts are born from people who have either temporarily or permanently lost their flexibility. Inflexible people become positional and become used to, or comfortable in the position they pick. They may forget that they began a project with a group Shared Interest. They become fixed in their thinking and now they have a new goal, a new agenda: themselves. Inflexible people take a deeper positional stance and their opinion, rather than being a place for discussion, creativity or group brainstorming, becomes a Personal Holy Grail. They fear losing ground or territory and feel compelled to fight and to defend their place. They begin to see their only choices as Fight or Flight. Standing Ground is tough work.

An effective manager must discover why an inflexible person has become positional in a conflict situation. If the inflexibility is situational, the manager may assist them in restoring or remembering the original goal, thus reclaiming flexibility. The manager must assist them in refocusing on the original Shared Interest.

Flexible people are less likely to develop into Emotional Terrorists. Inflexibility is often triggered by a perception of fear or loss of control. Helping get inflexible people back on a safe track into shared interests can restore their faith and hope, limit potential isolation, and be a first step in successfully resolving rising tensions, conflicts and disputes. It moves people away from fear and back into faith. Good faith resolutions are the product of moving away from rigid positions toward shared interests and goals.

Case Example

Kathleen had been with the company for 23 years. She was not growing any more and was getting stuck in her positions. She had a difficult time adjusting to the high-speed tensions of her staff which consisted of eight younger women. Half of the young women were from one ethnic group and the other half represented a different ethnic group. Kathleen had refused diversity training, thinking she didn't have a problem with "those other people, except that they sure didn't work as hard as the other girls." Not only was she insensitive to differences, she forgot why she was there in the first place and had begun to mismanage her additional role of protecting the perception of her organization in the community. She stated that she "had been doing this for 23 years and didn't need any more training, it was these young girls who need the training." She clearly showed favoritism to her ethnic group and was also not particularly sensitive to the agendas of young, working women. The entire department she managed was turning against her and she had no idea that she was at risk of being replaced. Her supervisor asked her if she was willing to learn some new skills. She balked at the idea of additional training because she was fixed in her belief that "they" were the problem, not her. Getting her to bend and flex took a lot of management time. Fortunately, she was given the time and opportunity to reclaim the Shared Interest Mission of her organization. She was a valuable employee with an excellent background. The challenge was that her good performance record had isolated her and she had lost touch with the growth of the industry. Because her supervisor was able to see the bigger picture, the entire issue slowly began to dissolve into a neutral event as the positions were honored and the shared interests were rekindled for all employees.

HOW TO REMAIN NEUTRAL AND GROUNDED

Neutral: *impartial, not taking sides, disinterested, non-aligned*

Grounded: *steady, firm, sturdy, balanced, whole*

Remaining neutral and well grounded in the face of spinning is the only effective position. Employees should just step away from the spin, and defer management to managers. Managers should carefully gather information, evaluate and synthesize data, reevaluate, and gather more data while keeping an eye on the big picture of the organizational mission. An effective manager becomes a bit like Switzerland. Switzerland maintains its neutrality partly due to the fact that it is a very powerful country with an extremely well trained and expertly prepared military power to back it up if necessary. Unless it becomes necessary to defend themselves or attack someone else they will just remain neutral and operate from the observation deck. If Switzerland did not have a powerful army as a contingency, it would be more difficult to remain neutral. If management does not have the backing of effective policy and solid, supportive CEO or Administration, it is very difficult to remain neutral in a battle against regular conflicts, much less the more derisive and distorted conflicts associated with workplace emotions and Emotional Terrorism.

Standing ground and remaining neutral in the face of conflict is a learned skill and can become an art form. Like all skills it takes a willingness to learn. Unfortunately, many adults think they have learned it all. It is uncomfortable to be new at something. Remember, most people don't like being uncomfortable. Conflict is uncomfortable, and managing conflict can be quite uncomfortable. Managing conflict in the midst of personal discomfort takes energy and life force, plus it takes being a neutral grown up.

Remember that growth can happen in the presence of conflict. The seed must be in conflict with its hull to germinate. This is life. Without life, growth stops and decay begins. Decay is evidence of the end of life force. When growth stops death is not far behind. Effective managers need to keep up their own personal life force to manage the rigors of managing other peoples' life force. Then they take all that energy and turn it into grounded neutrality. This is daunting work. Not everyone is cut out for it. Managers have to balance great self-care while being in the presence of a range of things that most people only read about or see on television.

This is particularly difficult when managers have been promoted from within ranks. Perhaps someone is a brilliant nurse or administrative assistant. This does not mean they have had ANY management training. This must be attended to for good management. Spend training dollars to let managers learn how to manage. This is a brilliant investment!

To stay neutral, try to see the bigger picture of the system in working order. Use self-care models and transformation ideas to find your own central core.

Managing Conflict or Threatening Emotions

- Communicate limits ("I won't allow you to scream at me").
- Share your personal feelings ("I feel upset when you raise your voice").
- Exit. Leave quietly without explanation and refuse to join conflict.
- Identify how the conflict may be something you will need to address, but that you are not the conflict. The person escalating owns the conflict.
- Breathe, relax, breathe, stay calm and quietly grounded. Think of the conflict as a set of burning boats trying to port in your harbor, but you do not let them tie up on your dock. You will watch these burning boats sail away into the sunset.
- Keep your office doors open when in a conflict situation.
- Remember that conflict is a temporary condition. Conflict can be turned creative.
- Soften your voice while continuing to speak your truth.
- Do not use escalating language, gestures, body language, or make threats.
- If someone crosses your boundaries emotionally, it may be necessary to enlist assistance.
- If you ask someone to stop a behavior and the behavior continues you may need to ask twice. If they do not respond after two requests it is appropriate to exit the situation. You may inform them that you will continue this discussion at a later date, but that the emotional content is too loaded at this time.
- Document your experience after the fact, not during the event.
- If someone crosses your boundaries physically call 911, security, or scream for help.
- If you are male, screaming for help in a dangerous situation is appropriate. Many men are needlessly attacked because they assume they can "talk themselves out" of an escalating situation and think it isn't masculine to seek help. There is nothing un-masculine about needing help if someone is threatening your well-being and you are isolated.

A Conflict Resolution Management Checklist

- Don't mix business with pleasure or displeasure
- Treat the other party like a business associate
- Use recordkeeping
- Use third parties to communicate when it is indicated or agreed upon
- Be on time and honor agreements made
- Focus on the problem not the blame
- People in business give one another the benefit of the doubt
- Prepare for meetings
- Let go, move on, don't fight, do business
- Keep feelings in check
- Do not make assumptions
- Keep your dignity
- Use common courtesy
- Do not tattle
- Use a "we can do this" attitude
- Use negotiating skills
- Do not seek or expect emotional support
- Make and keep appointments
- Use appropriate timing
- Keep personal information out of the business
- Monitor your own body language and voice tone
- Spend 25% of the time defining your position and 75% of the time exploring your shared interests
- Review the meeting to check for understanding
- Differences do not automatically mean failures
- Disagreements can lead to clarity

Relationships contain two elements: *Business* and *Emotions*. Remain a business professional while you also take care of your emotions. Emotions matter. But they matter mostly to YOU. Business communication is different than emotional communication. Pay attention to your words, tone, body language, and agenda to maintain a business relationship at work. Business isn't cozy and intimate — that's okay. Make sure you get your cozy intimacy needs met in appropriate venues so you do not depend on your business contacts to meet those needs and preferences.

Conflict Resolution 101 in Five Minutes

The Core Training for Conflict or Dispute Resolution can be taught in approximately five minutes. Becoming an expert takes longer.

PART ONE: POSITIONS

- In a conflict, people take positions
- Those positions reflect their opinions and values
- Positions are forces of energy which do not appear to be similar in any way
- Positions are stuck and fixed, rigid, nonnegotiable, win-lose
  1. A position reflects Wants, Preferences, Needs and the smaller picture.
  2. Needs are non-negotiable. Wants are flexible and negotiable.
  3. Preferences range between a minor and a major preference and can be flexible.
  4. Locked, Rigid, or Fixed Positions are unproductive to forward movement.
  5. Flexibility does not mean giving up a position, it means bending, or finding "flex points." Flex points are micro-units of positions which can be wiggled to find movement.
  6. Flexing a position only serves if parties have a Shared Interest. As soon as positions have been defined, turn energies to shared interests.

PART TWO: SHARED INTERESTS

- To move toward resolution people must move away from positions to shared interests.
- Positions are important and sacred and need not be sacrificed to find a shared interest.
- Shared interests are win-win discussions, although flexibility, compromise, and negotiation may mean everyone doesn't "win" everything they want
  7. Shared Interests are what originally brought the parties together and now reflect the basis of any continued relationship and the bigger picture
  8. Spend only 25% of the time defining position
  9. Spend 75% defining, remembering, and working at clarifying Shared Interests and exploring micro-units of possible flex-points
  10. If both parties have a Shared Interest in keeping a conflict going, it will go on. If both parties have a Shared Interest in resolving the conflict there is hope that it will be resolved.
  11. One kind of resolution is in the discovery that there will not be a resolution
  12. A party can maintain a position and work for Shared Interest
  13. If the mission is about controlling someone or something, resolution is difficult to achieve.
  14. Resolution does not always mean agreement. Resolution can be an "agreement to peacefully never agree but get on with the Shared Interest Anyway." This is a way to honor differences and yet move forward.
  15. If part of the collective mission is about honoring the self and others, resolution is not as difficult to achieve even with fixed positions. The focus returns to the Shared Interest and parties move on and continue to look for creative solutions to their different visions.
  16. Creative Solutions come from generating as many options as possible.

HOW TO USE ALL YOUR RESOURCES

Brains are wonderful. So much is present within the small space between the ears. But there is so much more. There are millions of resources that express countless ideas and opinions, some wonderful and some not so much! But if the ONLY resource you use is your own brain, you are either sadly mistaken about its use as a complete reference source, you have delusions of grandeur, you are bulletproof, or you live on an island in the middle of an ocean.

Move through everyone you know with an open mind and listen to ideas that come from the top and bottom of the chain of power. It is not unusual for the least powerful person in an organization to have the clearest idea of what is going on in the system. To miss any link is like missing a chapter in a book: you never know which sentence in which paragraph in which chapter may be critical to the plot.

Managers should pay attention to which employees want to learn and which employees resist new information. An employee who is not open to new information is a risk. They are either sadly mistaken about their own use as a complete reference source, they have delusions of grandeur, are bulletproof, or live on an island in the middle of the ocean. Real experts are open to learning more. Be suspicious of an expert who sees themselves as the be-all and end-all resource of even their own field of expertise.

Expand Your Data Base

- ask questions
- demand off site training hours
- read books, magazines, pamphlets
- look at bibliographies for other book ideas
- eavesdrop on conversations when your are out for coffee
- surf the internet, see movies
- travel out of town
- take a class
- listen to the radio
- attend free lectures
- look at community bulletin boards
- go to counseling
- hire a consultant
- get a life coach
- grab free pamphlets at conferences, ask questions of speakers at workshops
- talk to your counterpart at the competition
- go out for coffee with someone you meet at a seminar, ask more questions
- go to used book sales, the library,
- talk with people more important than you
- talk with people less important than you
- seek wisdom from children, talk with a reference librarian
- read a doctoral dissertation or a masters thesis
- seek wisdom from traditions and people from other cultures
- ask your parents or grandparents for opinions before they are gone
- always keep your eyes and ears open for a new thought; be curious

THE EMOTIONAL CONTINUITY MANAGEMENT QUICK-FIX

When emotions start spinning, your employees need your support. And they may need that support immediately to stop a spin. Emotional zingers, guilt trips, shamings, verbal innuendoes, and outright attacks can hit even the most stable employee sideways when least expecting it. Emotions that are subtle or profoundly upsetting can come on suddenly and out of the blue — and in most universes, these forces hit the most available and vulnerable target of the moment. If it isn't you then you might have a chance to do a quick-fix to stop the spin.

Emotions matter to the person having those feelings. If the emotions are coming from an Emotional Terrorist it is important to recognize that, if you are a target, you are simply their current squeaky toy, blue-plate special, target of the moment, soup of the day or "victim du jour." It probably is not about you. You may have contributed to the environment of emotions, or triggered some feelings for someone else, but feelings come from within and are always a response to how someone puts meaning into an experience. Someone who has had previous trauma or abuse may have a tendency to turn an emotional content into a personal event. The emotions of someone else do not originate inside of you.

It is important to make an effort to not allow your emotional response to be part of a spin process, small or large. Your emotions matter also, but mostly to you. Take your feelings to an appropriate source of support, a friend outside the office, partner, spouse, family member, EAP provider, counselor, clergy, journal or yoga class. Take care of your feelings without engaging in the agenda of someone else. Avoid the drama triangle.

A.   GO NEUTRAL

Healthy emotional variances come and go. Emotional Terrorists do not want to spin out of control themselves, they want you to do that for them so they can control the emotional situation. This allows them to justify their reality, make you the "bad guy" and walk away clean. It is a very powerful control mechanism. The trick with this is to just go emotionally flat. Do not engage. Do not agree or disagree. Respond to their device with a neutral, "*oh,*" or "*I will take that into consideration,*" or "*why do you ask?*" or "*I will get back to you on that later,*" or "*I was just heading to the restroom, I'll get back to you.*"

B.   STEP AWAY

Literally move back a step, and then redirect your progress or energy to an entirely different place. If you are stuck in a corner, cubicle or office space, take one step back and stand firmly grounded on two feet with arms at your sides in a relaxed manner, visualize yourself moving backwards and away from the emotional debris, or make a position change in your chair that suggests you are changing the situation. Taking a break reorients the energy flow. It can be useful to say, "Can you just hold that thought until I return from the restroom?" Excuse yourself and come back to the room and position yourself in a neutral way.

C.   SILENCE

There are times when silence is the perfect response to aggressive behavior. Breathe quietly and wait quietly and see if the person you are dealing with either escalates or de-escalates the situation.

D.   NO EYE CONTACT

Although making no direct eye contact or too much eye contact is a favorite mechanism that Emotional Terrorists use to control or invalidate you, you can use it also. Use your eyes to hold a position as you step back and exit from an uncomfortable situation.

E.   BOUNDARY GESTURES

Raise one hand, palm forward, in a "stop" gesture, with a very clear neutral phrase, such as, "*not here, not now,*" or "*I need to be elsewhere, could we take this up later if it is important?*" or "*thanks for your input on that, and I will have to move on with what I was doing,*" or "*oh, I understand what you are saying, so let's stop here for now,*" or "*this sounds important to you, and I'm just on my way to the copy machine, perhaps we/you/I should discuss it with the supervisor,*" or "*this does not sound like business to me, it sounds like emotions and so we will need to establish a different venue for this discussion.*"

F.   CLOSED PHRASES

Closed phrases are more socially acceptable ways to say, NO. They end the conversation without being extremely abrupt while leaving no room for discussion. They can sound like, "*this is certainly a good topic to discuss with the boss,*" or "*since our Anti-Terrorism training, I have decided to not even start to go there with anyone,*" or "*now that I understand how rumors get contagious, I am sure being careful with what I discuss with people. But I hope you bring that up at the next staff meeting when everyone is present.*"

G.   NO SPINNING ALLOWED

If you recognize an unavoidable spin coming your way take a moment to get grounded. Take a few deep breaths, and brace yourself for the blow. Know this is temporary. Know that you can survive more readily if you don't go spinning off with the emotions of someone else. See yourself as well grounded and safe. Let the emotional tornado blow itself out and then use the proper hierarchy process to report any danger if necessary. Make every effort not to add to the spin when reporting the spin. Make good choices and try not to be manipulated by the grand or subtle spinnings of others. Let dust devils go by. Report tornadoes. Pay attention to dust devils that gather speed and force.

H.   TAKE CARE OF YOUR FEELINGS

If someone attacks you emotionally, you may have a wound that needs care. Your feelings count, but usually not to the person who attacked you. Honor your feelings and give them reasonable attention and care. Take it to a trusted friend off the site. Write in your journal. Share at a 12-Step Meeting. Call your spouse or sister. Do not dump on others any more than you would lift the edge off of every bandage to show someone the goo of your skinned knee. It's yours. You are responsible to take care of it. You are grown up. If you need help, get it. If the attack is big then feel no humiliation in seeking more significant help. Even little boo-boos deserve a nice bandage. Big wounds require bigger bandages, and sometimes more gauze. Unless you are completely taken out you need to take care of your own feelings. When you are recovered and secure report the attack forward through the appropriate grievance procedure rather than random venting to co-workers that may injure them or start other spins. Take care of yourself because you are valuable.

I.   TEMPORARY

Know that storms are temporary. Some of them are nasty even if they do have a natural, very brief, lifecycle. Remember, problems can be fixed and issues can be resolved. If there is no life-threatening situation time is not an enemy and can be used for healing and resolution.

J.   STAND ON THE OBSERVATION DECK

Do whatever it takes to stay neutral in your observations. For example, you can pretend to be standing on the observation deck of a spacecraft. You are surrounded and protected by a force field. You see an alien approaching you. It speaks through a translator device and has a human form. You know it is not really human because you have been in this part of the galaxy before. You listen. The alien spews emotional content your direction. Because you know it is alien-speak you can offer a courteous remark from your safe perspective and then get back to the command post to carry on with your own mission. Later you may think to yourself, "*wow, that was an emotionally agitated alien walking around here, I wonder who let it loose? Oh, well, I guess they'll let anyone work on this ship.*"

K.   PRETEND

As you stand on your observation deck you can get through a lot of minor emotional spins by playing and pretending. No one else needs to know you have created a fantasy to survive your work site chaos. Keep it to yourself and smile pleasantly in the face of chaos. After all, you are royalty who is being held captive and must weave sticks into gold before 5:00 p.m. The evil gremlin King who is trying to distract you from your work has been sent from the Evil Witch's castle to try to keep you from your release. You cannot let on that you know, so you politely turn him away with a regal phrase and return to your weaving. Or no one knows that you are The Secret Weapon Goalie on the Olympic Hockey team and your coach has planted you in this office to learn skills in deflecting the emotional hockey pucks. You know your task is to avoid being hit in the head by the puck, but also to drop it back into play. You don't own the puck but you must keep standing as it is being hurled at you at 599 m.p.h. The crowd roars!

L.   ACT OUT A LITTLE (a little)

Be a little silly and slightly whimsical in a way that no one else will notice. It is useful and healing to shake off the "nasties" with a dose of humor that causes no harm. Keep a small toy in your pocket. Collect jokes in your day planner. Wear your socks inside out. If you get a paper cut put a cartoon character bandage on it and send yourself a get-well card. As Oscar Wilde was once attributed as saying, "Life is much too important to be taken so seriously!" The only way this works is to keep it to yourself. Someone may be doing very important work and your whimsy could cause harm. This is small whimsy you do to entertain yourself.

M.   OVERACT

Sometimes it stops someone in their tracks to react to an overreaction with another overreaction. Be careful and make very good choices, but it can be very powerful to provide a fun-house mirror reflection back to someone. For example, someone comes to you with a rumor. Listen politely. If you suspect that they are trying to make a spin, offer them the reminder that spinning isn't appropriate and if it is a real problem, they should use the chain of command. This is supportive to someone who is in distress. If, on the other hand, this is an Emotional Terrorist who demonstrates that they are not really interested in problem-solving, and if you think you can get away with it, throw your hands in the air, or fall down on the floor and pretend to weep uncontrollably while raving about the potential ramifications of this rumor to yourself, your unborn grandchildren, national security, global warming, the ecosystem of lint, the spiritual well being of the Maharaja LeBlommbia's Quest for Interplanetary Peace and the migratory status of Canadian Geese in the Northwest. Then stand back up, quietly dust yourself off, and say, "You are right, this is so important that I think we either need to tell our manager, write a formal grievance, or would you just like me to spread this around the office with your name on it?" Again, although this is a theoretically sound process that has been used in therapeutic settings for decades, you must be very careful with whom you use it in the office.

N.   SEEK BEAUTY

Go to the window and look for beauty. Go outdoors for thirty seconds and take a breath of air. Even a cement walkway is beautiful if you take a moment to consider its texture, solidity, how it came to be there, the humans who put it there, the water that was used to mix it and how it came from the sea and the clouds, the sun and wind that dried it that leave each day and return at dawn, the feet that walk across it that were once the feet of small children with sweet innocent smiles, and the ants which scurry across what must seem to them a rugged terrain in a never ending cycle of life. Emotional Terrorists hate beauty and grace. Appreciation for beauty does not support the agenda of destruction. Beauty is life-affirming and not life-alienating. The power of beauty dismantles negativity. Take a beauty break to regroup your emotions on a regular basis and always after a brush with anything that is Anti-Beauty.

O.   DEVELOP A PERSONAL PRACTICE

Develop a personal recovery practice and do something wonderful for your body, mind, emotions and spirit on a daily basis. This will keep your emotional immunity in top working condition. Develop your own sacred recipe for self care, joy, beauty, persistence, whimsy, connection and peacemaking.

P.   DISCOVER YOUR INNER-SELF

Listen to an Emotional Terrorist closely from your observation deck to discover your own vulnerabilities. Learn more about your own fears by seeing the reflections off the mirrors of others. Each experience we have either takes us forward or moves us backward. Life is about moving forward. You started this life in perfection and innocence and this is your true nature. Find out how this applies to you now and how it applies to you at work. No matter how many times you have been dropped on your head by people and situations you are an adult and can not make the choice to use life for life affirming or for life alienating.

HOW TO MAKE A TOOLKIT FOR MANAGING EMOTIONS

The best tools to facilitate strong employee revenue are those that will be efficient for the entire range of human emotions — from daily annoyances to catastrophic trauma. Although different tools should be used for the variety of issues and problems at work, managers should consider tools that match incidents throughout the entire recovery process. Be good consumers. There are many trendy and faddish hot items available in the Emotional Continuity Management marketplace. As you are developing your Emotional Continuity Management plan, it may be helpful to think of your plan as a recipe box or well-stocked toolkit. Emotional Continuity Management plans should contain essentially the same foundational ingredients. Review the list below as you develop your shopping list. Then consider the tools in the rest of the chapter as a place to start trying different methods. As you get more advanced and creative, you will want to explore other tools and create your own.

Minimum Ingredients of an Emotional Continuity Management Toolkit

- Conflict resolution methods
- Communication methodologies
- Systems education
- Diversity training and cultural norms of emotions
- Icons, slogans and banners for quick recognition
- Team building strategies
- Grief work education and practice
- Control and management strategies
- Personal values tools
- Humor
- Emotional Terrorist information
- Tools for new employee orientation
- Normal and abnormal psychology basics
- How to recognize signs of traumatic stress
- Emotional self defense
- Cultural and social hierarchy norms
- Ventilation models for debriefing and defusing
- Adjustment strategies and practices
- Stress management tools for the life span
- Physical, mental, emotional and spiritual health practices
- Resistance and creativity training
- Documentation standards for emotions
- Memos of understanding with external vendors
- Bibliographies
- Other resources
- Corporate models for Emotional Continuity Management

Your Toolkit Should Also:

- Provide emotional tools that generalize across occupations
- Provide a full range of emotional tools for the entire range of human emotions
- Provide emotional first aid and have arrangements in place for more serious emotional requirements
- Generalize to small and large organizations without significant adjustments
- Avoid trends and fad solutions
- Be gender and ethnically sensitive
- Be cross-cultural
- Work equally well for the diverse needs of executive, management and line staff.
- Offer simple, understandable, and practical tools for use both inside and outside the work setting

HOW TO CREATE AN EVALUATION FORM FOR EMOTIONS

You can create a ratings chart that helps identify emotional content as positive or negative. It will not necessarily be scientifically valid but it may be useful to begin a conversation with your team, or it may help you do some self-evaluations. Put whatever you are concerned with on a chart and circle the number that best reflect your feeling state at just this particular time. Knowing there are no right or wrong answers, you can take the moment to explore your answers to determine learning or training priorities.

Example

Rate your level of positive or negative emotions about the following from -5 (negative feelings) to +5 (positive feelings):

Your customers	-5	-4	-3	-2	-1	0	+1	+2	+3	+4	+5
Current trends in your industry	-5	-4	-3	-2	-1	0	+1	+2	+3	+4	+5
Your product or service	-5	-4	-3	-2	-1	0	+1	+2	+3	+4	+5
Career opportunities	-5	-4	-3	-2	-1	0	+1	+2	+3	+4	+5
Your competition	-5	-4	-3	-2	-1	0	+1	+2	+3	+4	+5
Competitive threats	-5	-4	-3	-2	-1	0	+1	+2	+3	+4	+5
Future of the company	-5	-4	-3	-2	-1	0	+1	+2	+3	+4	+5
Future of the Industry	-5	-4	-3	-2	-1	0	+1	+2	+3	+4	+5
Management	-5	-4	-3	-2	-1	0	+1	+2	+3	+4	+5
Opportunities for career growth	-5	-4	-3	-2	-1	0	+1	+2	+3	+4	+5
Opportunities for personal growth	-5	-4	-3	-2	-1	0	+1	+2	+3	+4	+5
Support	-5	-4	-3	-2	-1	0	+1	+2	+3	+4	+5
Security	-5	-4	-3	-2	-1	0	+1	+2	+3	+4	+5
Emergency preparedness	-5	-4	-3	-2	-1	0	+1	+2	+3	+4	+5

Some Traits of Well-Adjusted Employees

- Easily let go of past grudges
- Assume the best from one another
- Seek outside feedback carefully
- Do not participate in emotional drama
- Do not initiate emotional drama
- Put clients first
- Maintain a good attitude even during challenging times
- Use the chain of command to effect change
- Use policy format to offer complaints
- Do not hide memos or information from some staff and provide it selectively to others
- Strive for cooperation
- Verbally appreciate help given
- Show respect for each other
- Model appropriate business site sense of humor
- Do not participate in humor that includes inappropriate innuendos (sexual, racial, socio-economic, political, gender bias)
- Model flexibility
- Offer examples of personal truthfulness
- Show personal accountability
- Give and receive forgiveness
- Offer clear communication
- Demand and offer equality
- Perform the highest work ethics
- Complete and follow through with assignments
- Do not engage in second-hand gossip
- Do not spread or encourage rumors
- Actively participate
- Show consideration for others
- Stand by confidentiality standards
- Act professionally in the presence of clients
- Give more than just the minimum
- Work with cooperation between hierarchies
- Show courtesy in all situations
- Listen and respond to feedback
- Able to make compromise and contribute to positive dispute resolution
- Stand behind own opinion, yet open to negotiation

The Range of Healthy, Dysfunctional, and Pathological Employees

<table>
<tr><th rowspan="2"></th><th rowspan="2"></th><th colspan="3">LEVEL OF CAPACITY TO FUNCTION IN SOCIETY</th></tr>
<tr><th>HIGH</th><th>MEDIUM</th><th>LOW</th></tr>
<tr><td rowspan="3">LEVEL OF FUNCTIONING</td><td>HEALTHY</td><td>The shaker and the mover</td><td>The capable and the helpful</td><td>The well intentioned and the steady</td></tr>
<tr><td>DYSFUNCTIONAL</td><td>The present and accounted for and troubled</td><td>The present and troubled and needy</td><td>The randomly absent, troubled and needy</td></tr>
<tr><td>PATHOLOGICAL</td><td>The criminal and the manipulative and ill and brilliantly successful</td><td>The criminal and manipulative and ill and needy with less success</td><td>The incapable and removed from society</td></tr>
</table>

HOW TO MANAGE EMOTIONS

There is no universal standard to Emotional Continuity Management. The following list are guidelines and not rules. Start here, but create your own personal list!

- <u>Calm thoughts create calm actions</u>
    You can handle this, you are a grown up and not a child. There will be a beginning, middle and end to this. incident.
- <u>Picture it</u>
- *Visualize a calm place where you feel safe. Do this for as long as possible before responding. Even five seconds of a calm image will help your brain respond with calming chemicals rather than anxiety chemicals. The brain is a pharmacy and you give it the prescription for anxiety or calm*
- <u>Breathe, Breathe, Breathe</u>
    Deep slow breaths through the nose and down to the belly. Release the breath slowly to the count of five. Begin again and repeat until settled.
- <u>Do a Body Check-in</u>
    Are you sweating, chewing your lip, tapping your foot, pacing, breathing shallowly, and talking rapidly?
- <u>Pacing Exercises</u>
    Pace yourself with a walk, writing, drawing, a trip to the restroom or water cooler, a moment outdoors, stretching, or resting quietly alone for a few moments.

- Big Picture
  Remember your big-picture mission and the fact that you decided to be a manager, so you are not a victim of this moment, it was and is a choice.
- Remember
  Feelings matter mostly to the person having them. Honor this unless you are physically unsafe. If unsafe, call 911.
- Listen
  People usually escalate their emotions when they believe they are not being heard. There is one theory that violence is simply extreme communication
- Calm voice
  In a duress situation, do not use a fake calm voice. That behavior may be perceived as condescending and create more stress. It can also imply that there is some other "secret" information that you have that the others do not have. However, try to soften the edges of your voice tone and slightly decrease the volume to model calmness.
- Gestures
  Move a bit more slowly, with less movement and gesturing. Some people read gestures as threats and may misinterpret your body as an attack.
- Know your Resources
  Know your resources!
- Don't be Stupid or Bulletproof
  Do not put yourself in an isolated, dangerous, unprotected, or risky situation or location.
- Postpone
  It is very appropriate to postpone discussions when they get too hot or overwhelming. The trick to this is to state clearly your intention to continue and define the exact time that continuation can occur if both parties are open that time.
- "No" is Okay
  Saying no is okay. Saying no twice is still okay. If you are forced to say no again to make your point, the situation is escalating.
- Take care
  Do good self-care after an Emotional Continuity Management process.

WHAT IS YOUR DUTY TO WARN?

Some professionals are required by law to report violence or threats of violence. They are called *mandated reporters* and must, by law, call professional agencies to report even a suspicion of threat risks. You may voluntarily become a mandated reporter by deciding you will take the risk to have someone upset with you if you are overly concerned in error.

The state of our world today suggests that you are best served by overreacting rather than underreacting to your intuition. You will not have to make the final judgment that someone is at risk. You can call in the experts. Mental health professionals, law enforcement, child protective services or other appropriate agencies need to be called in if you ever are concerned about violence. The rule of thumb for managers is that it is better to err on the side of being overly concerned than it is to read a name of one of your employees on the front page the next morning after you did nothing. Memorize the phone number for your local Crisis Hotline. You can always call them for advice and let them make the decision if you are overly concerned. That is what they are trained for and will be available for you 24 hours a day, 7 days a week.

Listening for Suicide Risk

- A direct statement of the intention to commit suicide
- A specific plan
- History of attempts
- Vague statements about suicide or their own funeral
- History of depression
- Hopelessness or recent losses
- Alcohol or drug use
- Ill health
- Impulsivity
- Stressful events
- Adolescent or elderly
- Access to or availability of weapons

Risk of Homicidal Behavior

- Direct threats
- Access to or availability of weapons
- Substance Abuse
- History of past acts of violence
- History of explosive, persecutory, paranoid, suspicious, angry, hostile behaviors
- Verbalized a plan to do an action
- Verbalized an identified victim
- Apparent unwillingness to collaborate during a conflict

_____ LOCAL CRISIS HOTLINE

_____ LOCAL MENTAL HEALTH

_____ EMERGENCY NUMBERS

Remember that the number for 911 in most communities is "911." It is easy to remember for a reason

THE DRAMA TRIANGLE

The drama triangle is a model for communication first described by Stephen Karpman from the psychological theory of Transactional Analysis. (Karpman, 1968). The model can be used to look at human interaction like a game with three players: The Victim, The Rescuer, and The Persecutor. As the game is played, no one wins. The roles are exchanged and repeated in a vicious cycle of exchange that moves each player into the other role to maintain the game. As the game continues, The Victim attacks The Persecutor for "crimes" and thus now becomes The Persecutor through the use of blaming. The Persecutor now is The Victim. The Rescuer may step in to offer assistance to The Victim, which threatens The Persecutor, who is now The Victim by way of The Rescuer. The Victim may join The Rescuer and both may now attack The Persecutor, who becomes The Victim by the attack and uses it to justify another attack or hook another Rescuer…and the game continues until someone steps out of the cycle and becomes a non-player.

The non-player, although seen as a player by the others, can remain in the setting but will take on a neutral, nonparticipating role. This may be seen as a rescue, an attack, or a martyr (victim) stance, but if it is maintained over time, players will either end the game or move on to solicit new players.

There are real victims in life. If you are hit by a car, attacked by a terrorist, molested, assaulted, and so forth, you are a victim. The victim in the Karpman Drama Triangle puts adhesive on the back of their wrist and attaches it to their forehead in an ongoing "poor me" position.

There are real persecutors. Terrorists, offenders, and criminals are not playing. They are dead serious.

There are real rescuers. Law enforcement, nurses, fire fighters, EMT's, teachers, counselors, social workers and other "good guys" are not playing the triangle game, but must watch that they aren't rescuing people who do not want to be rescued.

Individuals who play the Drama Triangle do it for the game itself. If you stop playing, eventually they will move on because you are not playing. They may up the ante, or raise the stakes significantly to entice you to continue being a player, but if you move away from the triangle, you will eventually feel better and be more useful.

An old classic drama triangle is seen in the melodramatic scene of the sweet and innocent heroine tied to the railroad tracks by the evil villain as the handsome hero rides in just in the nick of time. This is endemic to our collective sense of theater. Hollywood knows that the archetypical evil-doer must kidnap the helpless victim so that the hero as agent 007, Superman, martial arts master or mistress, or even cartoon figure sweeps in to save the weak and the known world for the betterment of humanity. The drama triangle is everywhere, but that does not necessarily mean we have to play it out at the work site with theatrical dimensions. Even if your company is part of the industry that promotes or supports the drama of victims, rescuers or persecutors it doesn't mean your workplace has to replicate the soap opera within the work environment. Watch a soap opera or CNN to see how the triangle plays out. Now watch your work site for how you may be unconsciously playing.

The Drama Triangle

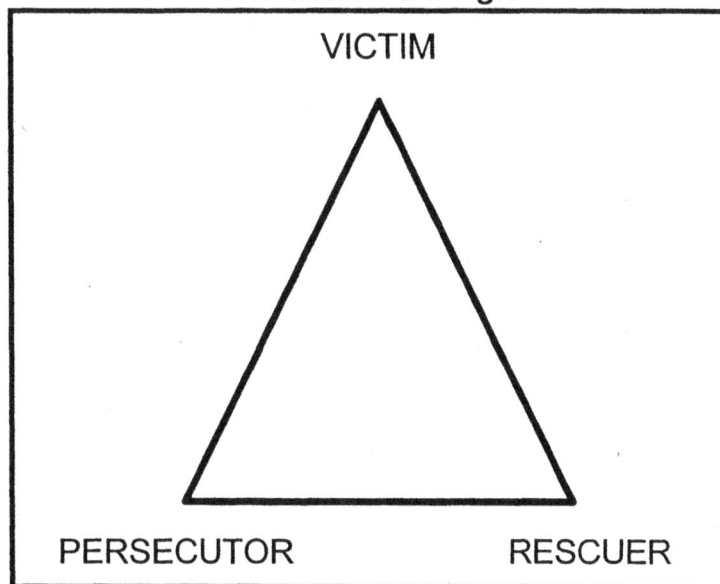

VICTIM

PERSECUTOR   RESCUER

How to Manage the Emotions of Others Through Defusing and Debriefing

The following guidelines are a compilation of strategies based on a number of well-tested interventions. The information has been adapted from voluntary organizations, professional associations, counseling techniques, traumatic events interventions, debriefing and defusing models, and applied psychology. Managers can be trained in any such specialties to gain more knowledge in how to support and encourage individual or group emotional recovery. Although a brief overview of defusing and debriefing are included in this text, most managers should not attempt to facilitate these processes without specific training and practice. There are many agencies and consultants who will teach these techniques for basic and advanced competencies.

PART ONE: Brief Intervention and support — individual or group

(20 minutes maximum; this intervention is meant to defuse, calm, validate and support in order to manage an immediate emotional context. It is not intended to be used for recovery, restoration, mitigation, counsel, or to remove emotions. It is a first-level management response that acknowledges and slightly ventilates the top level of emotions)

Step One
> Put the situation or event into the Big Picture context

Step Two
> Ask what happened, and listen

Step Three
1. Support the individual in your own natural style
2. Remember that emotions are natural
3. Remind them it will take time to recover
4. Give good self-care advice
5. Let the individual know more help is available
6. Encourage going about normal routines as much as possible
7. Give reassurances and support for future support
8. Help to develop a plan of action for the immediate time
9. Keep all responses private

PART TWO: Next Step of Intervention and Support — individual or group

(As long as it takes, usually 2-3 hours in length and approximately 72 hours after an incident. This process is intended to go more into depth about events and feelings. It is NOT ever intended to critique performance or task accomplishment, be mental health counseling, or evaluative. This is meant to debrief, support, allow, educate, relieve and ventilate deeper level emotions)

1. Introduce yourself and ask others to just share their names if unknown
2. Make no critiques, let people know that will happen, but at a different time
3. Maintain and establish privacy, confidentiality, or who will be informed
4. Assure that everyone is safe, and that everyone in the room should be here
5. It is useful to do this process with peers as the presence of supervisory personnel can intimidate people from sharing their emotions, and supervisors will generally not share their feelings in the presence of subordinates
6. Ask everyone to explain their role in the situation
7. Offer an opportunity to share any thoughts and memories
8. After step seven is done, offer an opportunity to share emotions
9. Ask if there is any emotions that are lingering about and causing ongoing stress
10. Ask if there is anything that someone is having a difficult time with or a specific idea, image, feeling or thought that is persisting
11. Offer education that it is natural to have all these feelings
12. Don't hurry any part of the discussion, let it evolve naturally
13. Encourage participants to continue normal activities as much as possible, and reassure that it will take time to recover but that most people recover
14. Give assurances that seeking help is appropriate and acceptable. Provide a list of resources available
15. Decide if anyone needs help making a plan of action for short or long term recovery
16. Remind participants again that recovery takes time and they may do this process again if needed

THE ENTER AND EXIT TOOL:
A COMPASSIONATE "BACK TO WORK" MODEL

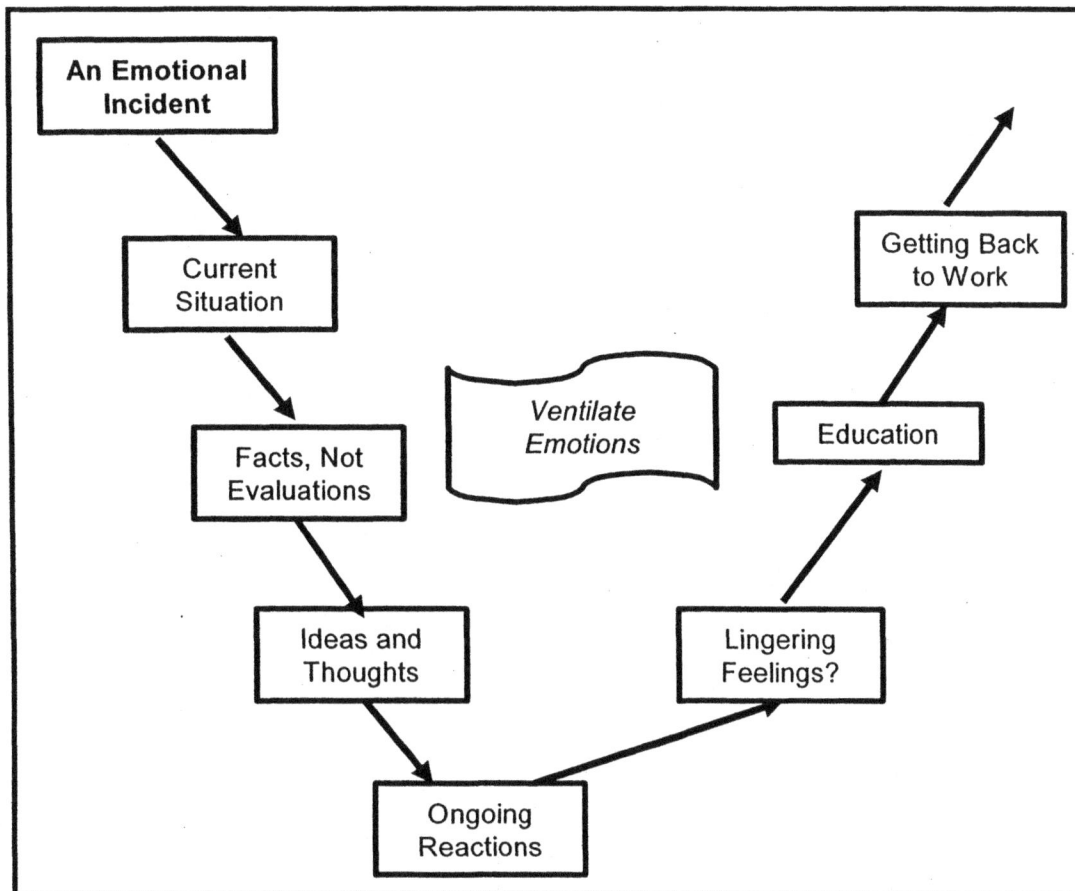

An Emotional Incident → Current Situation → Facts, Not Evaluations → Ideas and Thoughts → Ongoing Reactions → Lingering Feelings? → Education → Getting Back to Work

Ventilate Emotions

AUTHOR'S AFTERTHOUGHTS

I often meet resistance to the topic of managing emotions at work. I'm not surprised anymore when someone verbally attacks me, or my ideas. There are people who just do not want to deal with the soft-sided emotional contents of business, are themselves dysfunctional, afraid, threatened by their own humanity, or just plain mean/ I understand. But when I run into someone who seems to be on a mission to make me look bad I find it interesting. I use my tools and move into a non-spinning zone of neutrality to avoid taking it personally or getting worked up into someone else's emotional frenzy. Then I teach the drama triangle. Difficult people are now surrounded with individuals who know that it is relatively easy not to participate in collective chaos. This is a good moment for me when I see an entire group of people relieved to stop spinning. It's a great moment for them also because from this point forward they have a portable tool to avoid the chaotic agenda of someone else. They are now equipped to identify anyone who wants to contribute to the team and anyone who would rather stir up emotional sabotage.

DISCUSSION QUESTIONS

- What emotional management tools do you have now?

- What tools do you need to survive the long haul of your working career?

- What tools can you teach?

- Under what circumstances would you call 911 immediately?

- Under what circumstances would you report a crime to you boss? To law enforcement officials?

- Can you list 37 things you are grieving right now? Can you identify the stages?

8

READINESS:
TOOLS FOR MANAGING IN THE
MIDST OF BUSINESS CHANGE

WHY YOU SHOULD READ THIS CHAPTER

Reading this chapter will begin to give you an idea of the complexity of Business Change. It often comes as a shock to a manager when an employee has an outburst or termination incident over something that appears insignificant. It is equally surprising when someone can absorb a massive catastrophic event with apparently no effect.

BY THE END OF CHAPTER 8 YOU SHOULD BE ABLE TO

- Create a list of any minor or major changes your company has made during the last week

- Define and discuss business changes in terms of a grieving process

- Write a business plan for emotional readiness for the full range of emotional potentials, annoyances to catastrophes

WHAT THE EXPERTS SAY ABOUT EMOTIONAL
CONTINUITY MANAGEMENT TOOLS

"Changes in organizations influence the members of the organization. Changes in organizations call issues of safety into question requiring that people find new processes to assure their emotional security. The tools of change need to incorporate tools that address these shifts in emotional security.

"In the classic military and factory models of the workplace the emotional well-being of workers was not a significant issue. Employees did their work and went home. Any outburst of emotion was dealt with as a disciplinary problem. In modern organizations companies need the creativity and full potential of every person. They cannot afford to waste any resources. Emotionally unhealthy workplaces waste creativity, collaboration and intelligence. Staff that carry significant unresolved emotion may waste valuable creativity, collaboration and intelligence. — B. Edward Bohart, Ed.D., Community College Director of Educational Talent Search and Upward Bound, Astoria, Oregon..

EXAMPLES OF BUSINESS CHANGE

Changes, small and large
Remodeling/Painting
Outsourcing/Downsizing
Awards/Loss of Awards
Personal Tragedies
Organizational Change
Furniture Arrangements
Redefinitions of Tasks
Illness of a Co-worker
Suicide/Murder of Co-worker
Marriages/Divorces/Affairs
Natural Disasters
Hirings and Firings
Local/National/International News Events
A New Water Cooler
Technology glitch

Moving the Pens
Changing Letterhead/Logos
Re-Sizing/Layoffs
Losses
Catastrophic Trauma
Project Groupings
Access to People/Information
New Administration
Death of Co-worker
Rumors of Changes
Computer Upgrades
Economic Changes
Policy Shifts
A New Custodian
Resizing
Scandal

HOW TO EVALUATE EMPLOYEE READINESS FOR CHANGE

Does your employee:

Believe the change is necessary?	Yes	No
Fear the change?	Yes	No
Think management doesn't care?	Yes	No
Fear consequences of the change?	Yes	No
Believe the change will happen?	Yes	No
Perceive they are being exploited?	Yes	No
Disagree with the timing?	Yes	No
Agree with the change?	Yes	No
Support the change?	Yes	No
Respect change leadership?	Yes	No
Make contribution to change making choices?	Yes	No
Receive encouragement to change?	Yes	No
Get support for normal resistance?	Yes	No
Understand grief and loss with change?	Yes	No
Believe emotions are appropriate at work?	Yes	No
Express extreme anger or fear?	Yes	No

Lack confidence or skills to change?	Yes	No
See management as Us or Them?	Yes	No
Understand all the details of the change?	Yes	No
Feel lost in rumors and vague information?	Yes	No
Know the details of timing?	Yes	No
Have clear understanding of expectations?	Yes	No
Have opportunity to separate tasks from feelings?	Yes	No
See an end point in sight?	Yes	No
Feel they are in the loop?	Yes	No
Care?	Yes	No
Enjoy chaos?	Yes	No
Demand change?	Yes	No
Understand policy and procedure?	Yes	No
Have their own support network?	Yes	No
Feel welcomed into decision making meetings?	Yes	No
Trust management?	Yes	No
Feel prepared?	Yes	No
Feel open to complain without consequence?	Yes	No
Expect a celebration at the end of the change?	Yes	No

AUTHOR'S AFTERTHOUGHTS

Resistance is not a bad thing. It is a natural fear reaction. Fear of the unknown and fear of the real or perceived known stirs up a need to control outcome. Managers cannot "control" these resistances but do need to learn how to manage them. Making people feel safe is an art and a science with specific tools. Managers must first manage their own fear.

DISCUSSION QUESTIONS

- What is the smallest change you have experienced that created an emotional response? What were you afraid of?

- What is the largest change you have experienced that created an emotional response? What were you afraid of?

- What is the smallest and largest change in your company that created an emotional response? Identify the fear base.

- Can you make a timeline of predictable changes that may occur in your company in the following year? What about in your industry?

- Do some personal soul searching and evaluate your own resistance to change. Do you know your change style?

9

READINESS:
TOOLS FOR MANAGING
IN THE MIDST OF SPINNING

WHY YOU SHOULD READ THIS CHAPTER

This chapter offers you a set of tools that will help you reconsider the consequences of emotions that get out of control at work. If you begin to visualize emotions as a tornado you can start to quantify its damage potential. This will give you a means to discuss the need for Emotional Continuity Management for training or buy-on considerations. The chapter includes a tool to help you calculate the exact cost of an emotional incident.

BY THE END OF CHAPTER 9 YOU SHOULD BE ABLE TO

*   Quantify emotions by using the scale provided
*   Recognize observable attributes of en emotional incident
*   Calculate the exact costs of emotional management

WHAT THE EXPERTS SAY ABOUT EMOTIONAL CONTINUITY MANAGEMENT TOOLS

"As a teacher trainer, I have led violence prevention workshops. Sometimes, teachers are victims of violence because their inability to manage their own emotions mingles explosively with an adolescent's inability to manage his or hers. This is not just a book for the private sector. Emotional Continuity Management tools can save lives in tumultuous inner-city schools!" — Hal W. Lanse, Ph.D., Teacher Trainer, New York City, New York.

DR. VALI'S EMOTIONAL TORNADO SCALE ©

Range	Damage	Potential Behaviors and Examples
VV-0	None	Normal general whining, non-specific complaints about life's annoyances and daily challenges. No demand for alignments. Share and vent.
		I hate Mondays when everything is a mess.
VV-1	Noteworthy	Specific complaints focused on specific people and issues. Some expectation for alignment.
		Joe never cleans his desk. Don't you think he" a loser?
VV-2	Significant	Specific complaints focused on specific people and issues. Elevated emotional charge, more expectation for alignment and support. Early generalized references to outcome.
		Joe's a loser, he is such a slob. Don't you just hate his desk? We should do something about him!
VV-3	Critical	Specific complaints focused on specific people and issues. Increased emotional charge, elevated demands for alignment. More references to outcome and generalized plans for actions.
		I can't stand Joe. It's driving me crazy. Why don't we tell management and get him out of here. Let's ask Sue to join us.
VV-4	Extreme	Specific complaints focused on specific people and issues. Increased charge, elevated demands for alignment and allegiance. Specific demands for outcomes, and specific plans and direct actions.
		It's got to be Joe or me. Even Louise hates his attitude. We're going to the union and getting him out of here. I heard he had an affair.
VV-5	Catastrophic	Specific complaints focused on specific people and issues. Increased emotional charge, elevated demands for alignment, allegiances and loyalties, with threats of abandonment. Demands for outcomes at all cost. Actions being taken. Threats.
		Sue won't help us get Joe out of here. She must be having sex with him too. We can get rid of her easy, just go to HR and tell them she's not doing her work. I'll hide some of her project data and then she'll either join us or get out of here.

Observations on the Attributes of an Emotional Tornado

Use this practice sheet to write about emotional observations:

Describe your observations:	
Volume….	
Speed….	
Force….	
Area (crossing boundaries) ….	
Location ….	
Point of Origin….	
Size….	
Range….	
Levels….	
Frequency….	
Duration….	
Describe your hunches:	

Some Early Recognizable Signs of a Spin

Incongruent Giggling	Avoidance
Malicious Compliance	Non-Compliance
Blame Statements	Eye Contact
Body Language	No Eye Contact
Littering	Procrastination
Gossiping	Self Projection
Unsolicited Opinions	Avoidance Of Tasks
Not Returning Phone Calls	Humiliation
Excessive Perfumes	Inappropriate Humor
Unsolicited Religious Evangelism	Trashing Shared Space
Invalidation	Anger
Seductions	Minimizing
Leaving Tasks 1/4 Undone	Innuendo
Whisperings	Raised Eyebrows
Nagging	Dismissing
Ignoring	Interrupting
Discrediting	Partial Truth
Partial Lie	Arrogance
Intimidation	Distance
Disgust	Corrections
Jealousy	Inattention
Boredom	Incongruence
Denial	Unwillingness
Criticism	Questions
Intimacy	Manipulations

Poor Grooming
Negation
Poor Hygiene
Outbursts
Excessive Perfume
Illegal Activities
Incongruent Perkiness
Non-Completion Of Agreements
Negative Facial Expressions
Rebelling Against Dress Code
Loud Stereos In Quiet Spaces
Teasing
Jokes
Illicit Love Affairs
Starting Rumors
Guilt Language
Cursing

Compliments
Poor Boundaries
Untreated Health Issues
Drug/Alcohol Abuse
Offensive T-Shirts/Clothes
Sexual Innuendo
Demanding Praise
Gestures
Mind Games
Power Plays
Manipulative Silences
Harassment
Eating Loudly During Meetings
Spreading Rumors
False Charm
Shame Language
Exclusions/Racism

THE "WHAT'S UP?" CHECKLIST

You observe a behavior that makes you wonder if "something is up" with the employee. It is not time to confront them, because you are just going to watch for now. Use the What's Up Questions Checklist to begin evaluating observable, emotional behaviors or begin thinking about feelings in the work site. Do not ask 'Why' questions at this point of your exploration. Ask the following action questions first:

What, Where, When, Who, How, Which, How many, How often?

- Is this behavior due to a new circumstance?
- Is this behavior temporary or has it been ongoing?
- How long has this behavior been observed? By whom?
- Exactly when did this behavior begin?
- Is this behavior consistent or intermittent?
- How many people have seen this behavior?
- How many people have seen this behavior and not mentioned it?
- If this behavior escalates what might happen?
- If this behavior de-escalates what might happen?
- Does this behavior cause harm to anyone or anything?
- Is there a specific place, person or thing that is associated with this behavior?
- Is this behavior consistent with your sense of the employee's personal style?
- Has this behavior happened before?
- Is this behavior in any way associated with an anniversary of some previous incident?
- Has this behavior been influenced by outside forces or inside forces?
- Is this behavior due to interactions with people or equipment?
- Which performances or tasks does this behavior impact?
- Who has this behavior influenced?
- Is this behavior in any way life threatening?
- If you confront this behavior what might you anticipate as a response?
- Is there any way this behavior could be helpful to a creative solution?

HOW TO TALK ABOUT FINANCIAL ISSUES WITHOUT MAKING A SPIN

Managers must sometimes discuss fiscal and bottom-line topics with employees. Employees can use discussions about money, economics, fiscal and bottom-line ideas to spin. Most people have deep and abiding opinions, hopes and fears about their money. People have an emotional relationship with money. Money talk can stir up the most stable person into emotions about their survival and security. Discussions about money should be dignified, supportive, encouraging, positive, and thoughtful.

- Become familiar with all the fiscal details before you share
- Never share anything that is a partial, rumor-producing, tidbit of information
- Create several different ways to share budget or financial information to match the multiple learning styles of your team
- Concentrate on positive outcomes
- Do not mix business with emotions
- Find leadership in your team from people who appear comfortable with financial context
- Ensure that everyone knows the goals and how their work fits into the small and big picture
- Justify cost-consciousness by showing how it creates personal value added benefits
- Develop ways for financial department leaders to meet with non-financial department leaders to discuss how their teams can value one another
- Take a course or offer courses on marketing, customer services, finances, or budgeting
- Create buy-on by asking team members what they would do if they owned the company
- Involve your people whenever possible
- Have your CFO create a tutorial or workshop for employees who are far removed from the financial end of the company
- Have your employees create a tutorial or workshop for financial officers who may be far removed from client or direct services
- Understand how financial information impacts each department

CALCULATING THE COST OF SPINNING

Use this chart to calculate costs of time spent managing emotions with your staff.

Calculating the Costs of an Emotional Spin

Your Hourly Salary		Hours Dealing With a Spin		
	x		=	

+

Number of People Effected by the Spin		Hourly Salary		Hours Dealing with a Spin		
	x		x		=	

+

Boss's Hourly Salary		Hours Listening to You / Dealing with the Spin		
	x		=	

+

FICA / Taxes		Consultations		Revenue Lost from Customers Lost		
	+		+		=	

+

Public Relations Costs		Training Dollars Required		Health Care Costs		
	+		+		=	

+

Other Costs for Your Industry		Other Costs for Your Industry		Other Costs for Your Industry		
	+		+		=	

=

Total Cost of an Emotional Spin

$

AUTHOR'S AFTERTHOUGHTS

The first time I started using the Tornado as a metaphor for emotional storms was right after I experienced my first tornado event in Bloomington, Indiana. I had already experienced significant earthquakes, a couple of typhoons and other disasters, but this was my first tornado. I was with 300 bright and happy people headed out for a night of music and art. The sirens went off and the fun ended. No one was hurt. No one died. In fact, after the emergency, there were no visible signs that anything had happened. But I had observed 300 different emotional reactions to the same event. When it was over and everyone went home I was aware that I had witnessed something important and had my eyes opened for similar circumstances.

The next time I observed a similar phenomenon with the same emotional "feeling" was in a work site where a new administrator had been hired. Within only a few hours of his entry a bright and shiny workplace was turned into a chaotic emotional nightmare. There was no visible damage. No one died. People went home at night. But unlike the tornado event, everyone had to come back to the storm the next morning! Within a few weeks the emotional and fiscal toll was extreme.

DISCUSSION QUESTIONS

- What are the early warning signs of an emotional spin?

- How much can your company afford to spend on emotions that are counterproductive?

- What are your personal emotions about money?

- How would you like to be treated during a financial discussion?

10

READINESS: TOOLS
FOR MANAGING IN THE MIDST
OF EMOTIONAL TERRORISM

WHY YOU SHOULD READ THIS CHAPTER

Because Emotional Terrorism is domestic terrorism that uses human feelings for ammunition, nice people don't want to think about it. Assuming that you are a nice person, the reason you need to read this chapter is to address and absorb the reality that there are employees who have an agenda to destroy the well-being of others, using emotions as weapons. They are prepared for you and you need to be prepared for them. They are getting better at what they do and you need to be better at recognizing them while protecting yourself and others. They hope you don't get this information. They will discredit this topic. They will distract you and encourage you to be nicer. You need to read this chapter because Emotional Terrorism is real and it isn't going to go away anytime soon.

BY THE END OF CHAPTER 10 YOU SHOULD BE ABLE TO

• Use the warning signs checklist and recognize the attributes of Emotional Terrorism

• Address your own emotions about the topic

• Discuss the topic of Emotional Terrorism within the framework of your position and become an advocate of creating policy to protect your company and yourself

• Recognize stories in your local media that indicate Emotional Terrorism was an aspect of the issue reported.

WHAT THE EXPERTS SAY ABOUT EMOTIONAL CONTINUITY MANAGEMENT TOOLS

"Emotional Terrorists will manifest an atmosphere that will create constant turnover so that managers are always replacing, re-educating, or training new employees, which is fiscally expensive. Tools for victims, since you just can't always easily get rid of Emotional Terrorists if they have good performance skills, help weary employees continue to work in the face of this kind of adversity." — Cheryl Coppinger, Administrative Specialist, CH2M Hill; Hanford Group, Inc.; Board of Directors, National Managers Association, Chapter 395, Richland, Washington.

Emotional Terrorism Early Warning Signs Checklist

- Harassment
- Lying to a supervisor or co-worker
- Tampering with files or documents
- Use or misuse of company resources
- Knowledge of schemes or practices that take advantage of the company
- Requests for confidential information
- Sharing and withholding information
- Rumors and gossip
- Withholding support to the office team
- Time cards or reports falsified or inaccurate
- Inappropriate acceptance of gifts, gratuities, entertainment
- Security tampering
- Overt theft
- Manipulated expense reports
- Failure to follow through
- Selling or marketing business practices
- Conflicts of interest
- Substance abuse
- Insider information abuse
- Unethical recruitment practices
- Downplaying public safety
- Minimum legal compliances
- Inappropriate responses to whistle-blowing
- Poorly managed customer relations
- Accepting or making inappropriate political contributions
- Price fixing, gauging
- Ignoring laws about immigration
- Not abiding by drug laws
- Avoiding tax laws
- Corruption of public officials
- Dangerous sexual practices
- Antitrust violations
- Creating pressure which leads to the misconduct of others

WARNING SIGNS OF EMOTIONAL TERRORISM ACTIVITIES

- Intangible feelings, hunches, intuitions, sense, or opinion that something is "going on" with no specific data to confirm or deny
- Grooming: a systematic, unnatural approach to relationship control that appears upon close scrutiny to be contrived and gainful
- Contact escalations: interactions get more frequent
- Early spinnings: small emotional events increase
- Covert works: reports of trouble without evidence
- Rejection of approach: suggestion of problems met with resistance, denial
- Early signs of entrenchment: rigidity
- Overt signs: visible tensions and emotional reactions with no real data
- Accusations: blame statements or inferences
- Side Attacks: indirect blame, accusations, complaints
- Overt visible behaviors: demonstrations and activities, documentable data
- Gathering of forces: small or large groups spending time processing issues
- Direct attacks: specific demonstrations, behaviors and complaints
- Ultimatums: provocations, challenges
- Threats: intimidation, pressure, bullying, coercion

- Repetition: Continuing or repeating any or all earlier signs, even with increased risk, in order to demonstrate a willingness to continue for absolute control
- Lying to a supervisor or co-worker
- Tampering with files or documents
- Harassment
- Use or misuse of company resources
- Knowledge of schemes or practices that take advantage of the company
- Requests for confidential information
- Sharing and withholding information
- Access or control over proprietary information
- Rumors and gossip
- Contributing or withholding support to individuals or key team members
- Time card reports falsified or inaccurate
- Inaccuracies
- Inappropriate acceptance of gifts, gratuities, entertainment
- Manipulation of data
- Security tampering
- Overt theft
- Manipulated expense reports
- Failure to follow through
- Incomplete tasks
- Abandonment of tasks
- Selling or marketing business practices
- Conflicts of interest
- Substance abuse
- Insider information abuse
- Unethical recruitment practices
- Downplaying public safety
- Unnecessary trainings and time consuming meetings followed by consequences for tasks not finished
- Maintaining only minimum legal or code compliances
- Inappropriate responses to reports of danger, whistle-blowing, or common knowledge
- Poorly managed customer relations
- Corporate spying, losses of security, disclosure of security information
- Accepting or making inappropriate political contributions per industry standards
- Price fixing, gauging, hoarding
- Ignoring laws about immigration
- Not abiding by drug laws
- Avoiding tax laws
- Corruption of public officials or private individuals
- Dangerous sexual practices
- Using company technology to further addictions, crime, or sabotage
- Antitrust violations
- Creating pressure which leads to the misconduct of others

How to Translate the Snakes-in-the-Schoolyard Policy
To Manage Difficult Employees and Emotional Terrorists

1.   At least two (2) employees with gloves approach the snake. Snakes squirm toward the easiest escape direction, the path of least resistance, and with two people, the snake has no escape route. The snake catchers must not fear snakes. But gloves are required for better performance.

   a.   *A manager, with the support of their manager, approaches the employee in question. The manager creates an environment that has appropriate boundaries, an office, a meeting room, a safe place that is clearly a workplace environment. The manager informs the employee that she/he is operating in association with her/his manager and may even include another person to take notes of the meeting. The manager has prepared himself/herself in advance to manage personal emotions, and plans a post-meeting self-care activity. If the manager has fear it is essential to have someone else present. Preparation is essential.*

   b.   *At least two (2) employees approach the Emotional Terrorist. Emotional Terrorists head toward the easiest escape direction, the path of least resistance, and with two people, the ET has no escape route. Managers must not fear Emotional Terrorists but support is required for better performance.*

2.   Whichever employee grabs the snake must immediately toss it into a bucket with a lid. One of the employees must then immediately secure the lid. The real trick to Snake Removal is the lid. Without the lid the snake escapes and you must do it again. Spending your time catching the same snake over and over is not efficient and is not good business practice.

   a.   *The meetings should not dally around conversations or other personal and potentially emotional data. The manager must grab the content of the meeting first and describe the issue in clear statements that are non-emotional in language. The employee will respond immediately to language of attack or blame. Accountability is the key and the manager needs to clearly state the situation first, before there is an opportunity for the employee to squirm out of the situation by counter attack using justification, entitlement, charisma, or tragic language. Inform the employee about policy. Describe administrative position that affirms that policy. Settle into the process of repeating the information quietly and calmly if the employee attacks or defends. The employee will test the lid to see if it is held in place.*

   b.   *Whichever employee connects with the Emotional Terrorist must immediately define the boundaries. Managers must then immediately secure the lid of boundaries with clarity. The real trick to Emotional Terrorist removal is the lid. Without the lid the Emotional Terrorist escapes and you must do it again. Spending your time catching the same Emotional Terrorist over and over is not efficient and is not good business practice.*

3.   Once you contain the snake you must take it into the school, let the children see that it is not hurt, because children have imaginations and like to see even crawly things cared for correctly.

   a.   *One technique that is very powerful after such a meeting is to walk quietly back to the employee's workstation with them. Carry your posture straight, place a pleasant expression on your face, and escort the employee back to their cubicle while quietly discussing non-emotional content, such as a new contract in the future, a company picnic, the state of the technology advances in the company. Stay neutral. If that is not possible, stay quietly pleasant. Always leave your door open after such a meeting to let other employees feel as though you are not hiding, fearful, or did something that you feel ashamed about. It is a powerful option to walk quietly about the work site and do some small task that shows other employees that you are calm, to model calmness for them. If the difficult employee acts out at this time the other employees will be able to observe that behavior and remain more neutral themselves. After you leave the area people will try to discover what happened. They will have to make their own assessment of the situation, but you will continue to model your openness to inclusion. If the difficult employee continues to act out it will eventually become apparent that you are not the source.*

   b.   *Once you contain the Emotional Terrorist you must allow it to stay in the company so that the other employees can see that it is not hurt. Distressed employees have imaginations and like to see even Emotional Terrorist cared for correctly.*

4.   Later, transport the snake elsewhere, off the premises, a long way away from where you work, and dispose of it.

   a.   *If the problem has not been solved you may need to call the employee back into your office and reiterate the policy and remind them that this is a time for them to show their commitment to the policy by encouraging them not to stir up the emotions of other employees, because that is a considerable distraction to the workplace. You may assign them some EAP intervention, set them up for a personal training, or give them a small amount of time away from the job site to reconsider their behavior choices. This can be an extra hour for lunch, a ten minute break, a day off with or without pay, a probation period, or temporary suspension. If the choice is suspension you will have to communicate clearly to the rest of the staff how to support the employee. One of the biggest mistakes a manager can make at this point is to get defensive or secretive.*

   b.   *Later manage the relocation of the Emotional Terrorist elsewhere, off the premises, a long way away from where you work, and establish closure.*

5.   If the snake is Toxic, call in a professional.

      a.   *If the employee is not able to manage the emotional boundaries of your company there are a number of low-level interventions available prior to termination. EAP providers, trainings, remediations, second chances, workshops, college classes, consultations, and external counseling can be offered or provided. If none of this helps, then termination may be more cost-effective and emotionally effective for the individual and the whole organization.*

      b.   *If the Emotional Terrorist creates a toxic environment, call in an Emotional Continuity Management consultant.*

AUTHOR'S AFTERTHOUGHTS

Whenever I begin talking about Emotional Terrorism, nice people get twitchy. People who do not want to move out of their comfort zone suggest I'm overly dramatic. Those who have never confronted Emotional Terrorism question my motives. Others who have witnessed, been hurt, or challenged by an Emotional Terrorist thank me. They whisper their story about someone who has caused untold grief to themselves or others.

Whenever I begin talking about Emotional Terrorism, Emotional Terrorists get twitchy. They want to know what I know. They usually heckle me and try to discredit me for a while. I find it amusing. The only thing they truly fear is recognition and exposure.

I have seen too many harsh consequences of Emotional Terrorism not to be a siren. It was never the role I wanted in life, but I don't mind. I have met enough Emotional Terrorists in my work to want to help the good guys. And I have met enough good guys who are ready to set up early warning systems at their work sites rather than being taken by surprise ever again.

DISCUSSION QUESTIONS

- Why do you think people do not want to address the issue of Emotional Terrorism?

- What experiences have you had with Emotional Terrorism?

- How would you warn people?

11

READINESS:
TOOLS FOR MANAGEMENT
SELF-CARE

WHY YOU SHOULD READ THIS CHAPTER

Your work and career is a marathon, and not a sprint. For this reasons alone you need to pace yourself and take excellent care of you. If you don't take care of yourself, who will?

BY THE END OF CHAPTER 11 YOU SHOULD BE ABLE TO

- Decide if you want to be a manager and learn how to re-decide on a daily basis
- Define your own best practices using the self-care checklists
- Scrutinize your ethics
- Establish a personal practice of emotional, mental, spiritual and physical self-care.

WHAT THE EXPERTS SAY ABOUT
EMOTIONAL CONTINUITY MANAGEMENT TOOLS

"It is of utmost importance to have the right amount of emotional tools at the workplace. It is the place we spend much of our lives, and the need to be secure and balanced at work sets the stage for the remainder of our time away from the workplace. Most important in my line of work is empathy, understanding, compassion, thick skin, the ability to disassociate yourself from the task that must be performed and keeping a good sense of humor." — Dan Blasdel, Franklin County Coroner, Pasco, Washington.

Self-care Questionnaire: Do I Want to Be a Manager?

- Why do I do this work?
- Who do I serve?
- What do I believe about the service I provide?
- How do I "take on" work and how do I "let go" of work?
- How do I feel about my failures? The failures of others?

- What do I fear the most?
- Do I have needs to control anything?
- Do I perceive people as essentially good and whole or essentially bad and flawed?
- What is the biggest secret about myself?
- What are my values of beliefs concerning:
    - work
    - recreation
    - marriage
    - divorce
    - children
    - men
    - women
    - alternative sexual orientations
    - abused people
    - people who abuse
    - disabled people
    - age
    - fighting
    - justice
    - power
    - weakness
    - poverty
    - wealth
    - thin people
    - overweight people
    - religions not my own
    - cultures not my own
- Do I give the "right" answers but feel different inside?
- Where did my biases, values, beliefs, ethics originate?

HOW TO MANAGE YOUR OWN SELF CARE

You are a whole person! In an ideal world with ideal people, the whole person should have a repertoire and set of recipes for creating a wonderful life, at home and at work. Everyone else on the rest of the planet must strive for such balance on a daily basis. Healthy people have a plan and a process to care for their physical, emotional, mental and spiritual well-being. This book would be remiss if it avoided the whole person in favor of one of these four foundations of well-being. Take ample time to review your foundations for health as you define them. Favoring one of the four cornerstones while ignoring the others leads to operating in an unbalanced state. Doing a daily practice, discipline, or treatment of some kind in each category will keep you balanced no matter what comes your way. You need to be balanced when standing in the presence of change. Balance does not mean fixed — it can mean staying in one position for a long time, or being alert and ready to spring into action. All athletes have ways to strengthen their balance because they know how important it is to motion. Are your foundations balanced or do you put all your energies into one category at the expense of the other three?

Create your own self-care practice. First, fill in the chart provided with what you do now in each category. Then, with a colored pen or pencil, collage, or other creative form, add what you would like to change or add to your self-care regimen in the next weeks, months and years. Use the examples provided to being thinking about your self care.

- **PHYSICAL**: Exercise, diet, grooming and hygiene, movement, temperature, senses (vision, taste, touch, hearing, smelling) observing art, dancing, wearing different colors and textures, hugs or handshakes, good hand washing, breathing deeply in the morning air, music, trying different foods, a day of silence.

- **SPIRITUAL**: Exploring the relationship you have with whatever or whoever it is you think is in charge of the universe. Making that relationship a priority. Find a spiritual or religious practice that is yours.

- **MENTAL**: Challenging yourself in areas of non-expertise, in other words, if you read all the time. take a break. If you never read, pick up a book. If you read nonfiction, take a break with a cheesy novel, and if all you ever read is cheese, pick up a biography. It is okay if you take four years to read a book. It is the willingness that is important. Go to an opera, or stay at home and play a board game. Do crossword puzzles, or start a non-profit organization and build a board of directors. Do more, or do less, but do it awake.

- **EMOTIONAL**: Your feelings matter mostly to you, but they do matter. You are human because you have discernment and feel differently about different things. At the end of life people generally do not regret having had a full life with emotions. If they regret, it is that they missed feeling something because they were not paying attention in the moment.

Personal Toolkit

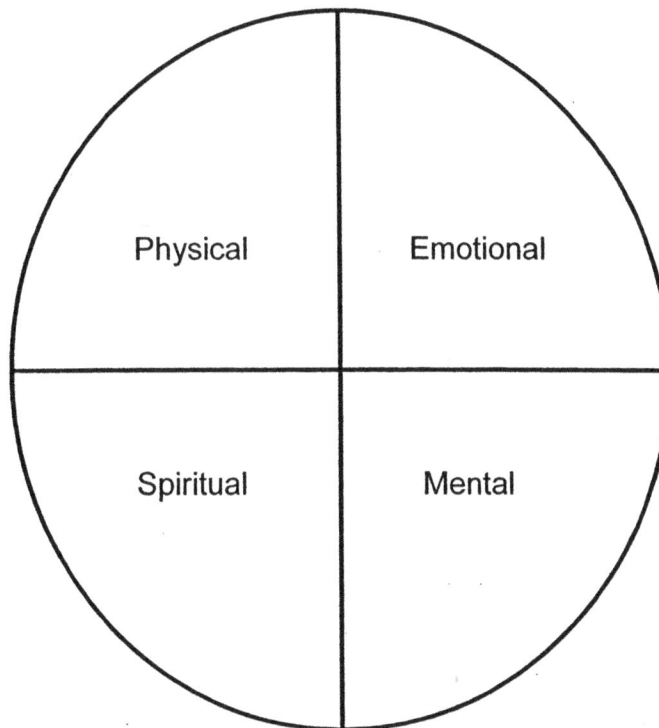

Physical	Emotional
Spiritual	Mental

How to Enhance Your Emotional Value as a Manager

- Avoid critical behaviors
- Remember to express your highest ideals
- Humor is appropriate when it is appropriate
- Remember the big picture of the mission
- All critical incidents are temporary so take the extra moments to make certain you are responding at your highest level
- Feelings and emotions are good, yours and theirs
- Respect is not just a song by Aretha Franklin
- Become approachable
- Do not interrupt to interject you opinion
- Relax
- Sarcasm is never useful
- Posture sets a tone
- Pleasantness is possible even during conflict
- Detach from the people to see the issue or problem
- Assume people are telling the truth first

- Become comfortable with your strengths
- Become comfortable with your weaknesses
- Give people an opportunity to maintain their dignity, even when they are wrong
- Solicit other opinions
- Seek to understand others
- Be an advocate for reconciliation
- Take breaks
- 'Please' and 'thank you' are classics
- Know the difference between formal and informal meetings
- Only take notes when necessary
- Express your feelings and opinions clearly and simply when possible
- Optimism is stronger than pessimism
- Appropriate praise does not make you lose power
- Courtesy and kindness can work at the jobsite
- Listen with attention
- Speak with a pleasant tone
- Pay attention to what your face is doing: grimace, rolling eyes, smiling
- Do not fear losing all personal power with an apology, it builds bridges
- Do not use an apology to take power, or the bridge will collapse
- Remember people are generally good
- Remember bad people do exist
- Try different ways to interact with different people
- Ask appropriate questions
- Confront issues and not people
- Do not avoid discussing personal issues that may impact your employees: death of a loved one, pet, divorce, birthday, wedding, graduation

How to Manage a Self-Evaluation

After filling out this questionnaire, determine the areas you want to change or keep the same. What would help you be your best?

Am I consistent?	Yes	No
Do my words match my actions?	Yes	No
Do my gestures match my words?	Yes	No
Am I condescending or sarcastic?	Yes	No
Do people trust me?	Yes	No
Do I trust myself?	Yes	No
Do I anticipate others' concerns?	Yes	No
Am I curious?	Yes	No
Am I flexible?	Yes	No
Am I on task?	Yes	No
Am I on task emotionally?	Yes	No
Do I think results are more important than people?	Yes	No
Am I comfortable with my own emotions?	Yes	No
Am I comfortable with the emotions of others?	Yes	No
Am I open to learn from everyone?	Yes	No
Do I maintain my commitments and follow through?	Yes	No
Do I make excuses and blame others?	Yes	No
Do I value and work well with differences?	Yes	No
Am I having any fun?	Yes	No
Do I avoid conflict?	Yes	No
Do I foster conflict?	Yes	No
Do I enjoy leadership?	Yes	No
Are my communications purposeful?	Yes	No
Are my interactions calm?	Yes	No
Are my interactions chaotic?	Yes	No

Do I manage problem solving without taking it personally?	Yes	No
Do I have good support?	Yes	No
Do I have good resources?	Yes	No
Do I share credit with others?	Yes	No
Do I approach or withdraw from problem solving?	Yes	No
Do I have neutrality skills?	Yes	No
Do I motivate others?	Yes	No
Do I serve as an example of top ideals and ethical standards?	Yes	No
Do I reward?	Yes	No
Do I punish?	Yes	No
Do I back up my people?	Yes	No
Do I encourage others to grow?	Yes	No
Do I create obstacles?	Yes	No
Am I an obstacle?	Yes	No
Do I ask others to do what I will not do myself?	Yes	No
Do I laugh?	Yes	No
Do I relax?	Yes	No
Do I rise to the occasion?	Yes	No
Am I where I want to be?	Yes	No
Am I growing and learning on a daily basis?	Yes	No
Do I make realistic promises?	Yes	No
Do I protect confidentiality or sensitive data?	Yes	No
Am I honest?	Yes	No
Can I admit error?	Yes	No
Can I admit error graciously?	Yes	No
DO I FOLLOW A CODE OF ETHICS?	YES	NO

HOW TO EXPAND YOUR EMOTIONAL VOCABULARY

The next time someone asks "How are you?" use a more accurate word from the emotions list. Say something other than an automatically ritualized "Fine."

Festive	Contented	Relaxed	Calm	Satisfied
Serene	Peaceful	Joyous	Ecstatic	Enthusiastic
Inspired	Pleased	Grateful	Cheerful	Lighthearted
Buoyant	Surprised	Optimistic	Spirited	Vivacious
Brisk	Sparkling	Merry	Generous	Hilarious
Exhilarated	Playful	Elated	Jubilant	Thrilled
Restful	Keen	Intent	Zealous	Ardent
Avid	Anxious	Desirous	Proud	Sorrowful
Unhappy	Depressed	Melancholy	Gloomy	Somber
Dismal	Heavy-hearted	Quiet	Mournful	Dreadful
Dreary	Flat	Blah	Dull	Moody
Sulky	Out of sorts	Low	Discontented	Discouraged
Disappointed	Concerned	Sympathetic	Compassionate	Choked up
Embarrassed	Shameful	Ashamed	Useless	Worthless
Ill at ease	Injured	Isolated	Offended	Distressed
Pained	Suffering	Worried	Crushed	Despairing
Tortured	Lonely	Pathetic	Cold	Warm
Upset	Hot	Resentful	Irritated	Enraged
Furious	Annoyed	Provoked	Offended	Sullen
Indignant	Irate	Wrathful	Cross	Cranky
Sulky	Bitter	Frustrated	Grumpy	Breathless
Fuming	Stubborn	Belligerent	Captivated	Confused
Awkward	Bewildered	Encouraged	Mindless	Courageous
Confident	Secure	Independent	Lonely	Reassured

Bold	Brave	Daring	Silly	Heroic
Hardy	Determined	Loyal	Petrified	Impulsive
Concerned	Fascinated	Engrossed	Scared	Curious
Inquisitive	Creative	Sincere	Appalled	Skeptical
Distrustful	Suspicious	Dubious	Fortunate	Uncertain
Evasive	Wavering	Hesitant	Whimsical	Perplexed
Indecisive	Hopeless	Powerless	Out of step	Helpless
Defeated	Pessimistic	Uptight	Threatened	Immobilized
Paralyzed	Tense	Hollow	Dismayed	Shallow
Empty	Strong	Weak	Awed	Weary
Repulsed	Tired	Alive	Hesitant	Feisty
Close	Loving	Sexy	Suspicious	Tender
Passionate	Aggressive	Assertive	Doubtful	Passive
Humble	Mixed-up	Envious	Worried	Jealous
Preoccupied	Cruel	Distant	Pressured	Bored
Cooperative	Fearful	Frightened	Dependent	Timid
Shaky	Apprehensive	Terrified	Nervous	Panic
Tragic	Hysterical	Alarmed	Crunched	Cautious
Shocked	Horrified	Insecure	Burdened	Impatient

Checklist for Maintaining Safe and Best Practices

- Stay in touch by attending industry conferences
- Stay in touch by attending management conferences
- Take continuing education units
- Expand your credentials by new certifications, diplomat status, degrees, initials
- Review best practices in your industry and raise your own standards
- Become the leading expert in your practice so you can be an expert witness to establish best practices standards in your industry
- Get Employment Practices Insurance from your industry
- Know your company's insurances and liabilities to evaluate your safety
- Determine your risks of liability by considering your industry, clients served, standards and practices policies of competency, and how "loose you play" with ethics
- Caretake your supervisory relationships by knowing that these chains are not necessarily a blanket of trust. Determine the clear level of liability held by any of your actions, or the actions of your employees, or upper management. Outline the liability parameters of all parties who can be held liable, or who can hold you liable.
- Know the difference between formal supervision and peer consultation in terms of your liability.
- Have a written policy about privacy, confidentiality, and protection procedures to protect yourself and your staff.
- Keep at least a brief documentation of all meetings.
- Understand that in today's world there is no such thing as privacy. Be thoughtful about what you put on paper, say over a telephone, copy, reproduce, or put into your computer.

The Faith Checklist

In what do you have faith and to what degree?

•	Your company policy			*Yes*	*No*
•	Your industry standards		*Yes*	*No*	
•	Your training			*Yes*	*No*
•	Your credentials		*Yes*	*No*	
•	Your authority			*Yes*	*No*
•	Your information			*Yes*	*No*
•	The hierarchy, chain of command		*Yes*	*No*	
•	Your interview skills			*Yes*	*No*
•	Your team			*Yes*	*No*
•	Your exit strategy			*Yes*	*No*
•	Your listening and evaluating skills			*Yes*	*No*
•	Your own intelligence			*Yes*	*No*
•	Your own ability to discern truth			*Yes*	*No*
•	Your intuition			*Yes*	*No*
•	The information given you by a witness			*Yes*	*No*
•	Data			*Yes*	*No*
•	Observations			*Yes*	*No*
•	Hunches			*Yes*	*No*
•	Experience			*Yes*	*No*
•	Your bosses			*Yes*	*No*
•	Your mission			*Yes*	*No*
•	Your imagination			*Yes*	*No*
•	Your people			*Yes*	*No*
•	Your God or Higher Power			*Yes*	*No*
•	Your resume is current			*Yes*	*No*
•	That people are generally good			*Yes*	*No*
•	That even Emotional Terrorists can adjust			*Yes*	*No*
•	That no matter what you do you are home after work and safe			*Yes*	*No*
•	That if you don't know what to do you have good resources			*Yes*	*No*

The "How Am I Doing?" Ethics Questionnaire

Do I:

•	Obey the law?	*Yes*	*No*
•	Talk my questions and concerns out with others?	*Yes*	*No*
•	Choose who I share my concerns and questions with carefully?	*Yes*	*No*
•	Prepare for any potentially challenging consequences of honesty?	*Yes*	*No*
•	Trust my perceptions?	*Yes*	*No*
•	Use my intuition?	*Yes*	*No*
•	Use my head?	*Yes*	*No*
•	Check and double check?	*Yes*	*No*
•	Participate in activities that I would not want to see on the front page of the newspaper or on the local or national news?	*Yes*	*No*
•	Will what I do stand the light of day?	*Yes*	*No*
•	Do I have a code of ethics?	*Yes*	*No*
•	Do I even know what the word "ethics" means for me?	*Yes*	*No*
•	Do I work in an ethical environment?	*Yes*	*No*
•	Would I accept being the recipient of this action?	*Yes*	*No*

AUTHOR'S AFTERTHOUGHTS

Most people know their own body temperature while having no idea about the state of their emotional, mental or spiritual well-being during normal much less during abnormal situations. As a mental health provider, disaster educator, and trauma counselor I consider it an ethical issue to know what's going on with me before I dare ask a client what is going on with them! My personal performance standards demand that I know my own self so I can take care of me before I have the audacity to help anyone else. Otherwise I might be unconsciously hoping my clients will take care of me rather than me serving them.

I won't work with anyone if I'm not at least at 86% of my best self. I don't expect to be at 100% every day. I allow for fluctuations. But at a certain level I need to take care of me first. Self-care is not antithetical to being a professional, a helper, a manager, an employee or a useful human being. If you don't take care of you, who will?

DISCUSSION QUESTIONS

• What is your normal emotional temperature? How do you take care of your feelings if they are hurting?

• What were the rules in your family about taking care of yourself? Were you taught to believe that self-care is selfish?

• Have you ever talked to a lifeguard or first responder and asked them what they do to make certain they are in their best state to serve others? What are they taught about risking their lives to save others?

12

READINESS: TOOLS FOR DEVELOPING AN EMOTIONAL MANAGEMENT CONTINUITY PLAN

WHY YOU SHOULD READ THIS CHAPTER

Business infrastructure is comprised of mission, policies, procedures, strategies, rules, regulations, and countless documentations. This blueprint of a business is the cohesion or glue that keeps it together. A system is only a system if it works systematically. The same is true about Emotional Continuity Management as a method for addressing the emotional infrastructure of an organization.

BY THE END OF CHAPTER 12 YOU SHOULD BE ABLE TO

- Compose a set of statements addressing company vision, mission and philosophy that include emotions as integral infrastructure to success

- Produce a document that you can use to evaluate emotions

- Draft an Emotional Continuity Management Policy using the guidelines given, adjusting it to the standards of your industry

- Use soft and hard technical assessment checklists to establish a compassionate back-to-work emotional standard.

WHAT THE EXPERTS SAY ABOUT EMOTIONAL CONTINUITY MANAGEMENT TOOLS

"Most major corporations proactively protect their data to assure business continuance during a disaster through the development of disaster recovery plans and business continuity plans. The devastating effect of 9/11 awakened many companies to the value of their personnel. After all, what good is protecting your data and systems when no one is available or emotionally prepared to go back to work?

Since 9/11 there has been an increase in the development of Crisis Management plans as part of the continuity program addressing the people issues. A comprehensive continuity management program must also include an emotional continuity management policy. This is crucial to the survival to a company. Employees being the most valuable asset, companies must have a program in place to deal with the emotional effects a crisis or disaster. Emotional stress has great implication to the mind and body making some employees incapacitated to work. Ignoring this can be one the greatest mistakes a company can make for its survival." — Raymond A. Jean, Managing Consultant, Business Resilience and Continuity Consulting for a Fortune 500 company, West Hartford, Connecticut.

WRITE OR REWRITE THE MISSION STATEMENT

The old joke about how hard it is to remember the mission of emptying the swamp when up to your chin (or whatever) in alligators still applies when discussing a company or personal mission statement. Most human beings can quickly get distressed when they forget their goals. Distressed people are at risk for emotional spinning. When employees begin asking, "Why am I doing this?" they may also begin to ask questions like, "What else could I be doing?" They begin to question authority. Loyalties start to shift. Perceptions of success and failure begin to distort. In other words, when employees cannot see where they are going and why, they start to look around for direction. Managers can be leaders or absent when this happens. A good leader gives mission direction frequently.

Because people and life and work are living forces it is necessary to review and revise a team mission on a regular basis. People change, business changes, communities change and the mission should reflect the most current language, concepts, ideas and visionary goals. If the mission is old and wonderful it can remain the same as it is given a fresh paint job of words and language. If the mission is truly based on solid ground it should survive the changes of time. Knowing that there are subtle changes in language every few years and that even the meanings of words themselves change will keep the mission alive and contemporary. Monitoring a mission statement asks if everyone is still on board. It seeks to know if everyone in the same book. It is hard to get employees on the same page if they aren't even in the same book!

Your personal or company mission statement can be as simple or as complicated as necessary to define and elaborate the reasons you are doing what you do. It's up to you after all, it is *your* organization. It is useful to write your own mission statement. Why are YOU doing what you are doing?

A Mission Statement can be simple:

<u>The Acme Widget Company Mission Statement</u>:

We Travel to Other Places and Do Nifty Stuff!!!

A mission statement can also be poetic and complicated:

<u>The Kirsha Foundation© Mission Statement</u>

Provides children and adolescents, birth to twenty six, free access to the Arts, Education, and Creative Envisioning activities in order to encourage, enhance, and expand the belief, participation, protection, and understanding that young people have a vital role in the Universe.

The Kirsha Foundation institutes and funds programs, projects, and activities that enlighten, launch, protect, vitalize, educate, exchange, and celebrate contributions which transform Fear into Hope, Loss into Meaning, Aloneness into Collaboration, Conflict into Peace, and Ideas into Masterpieces.

What Are the Mission Statements of These Companies?

IBM   APPLE   WALMART   DISNEY

HOW TO WRITE A VISION STATEMENT

You see where you want to be but how are you going to get there? You are on a journey to your goal but the image of the trip is vague. You need an image or a vision of the goal and the trip. A team vision is the collection of action points which keep the journey on track and in sight. A vision statement suggests the scenery or landmarks on the road toward the mission. Whatever your organization's mission, the vision is the how, what, and wherefore of the process to keep on track. An easy way to increase risk for emotional spinning is to turn a team into a band of wandering emotional nomads. Employees on a mission with no map are at a greater risk for an Emotional Terrorist ambush. Emotional Terrorists are keen to employ lost and vulnerable employees into their own mission process and have creative ways to sell their vision agenda. Managers need to lead the way with simple to understand maps and visions of the journey.

A way to create one kind of vision map is to try the following exercise with your team:

1. Each team member writes ten simple and clear positive words that describe the essence of your mission. (i.e. Compassion, Service, Winning, Satisfaction, Health, Money, Delicious Food, Clean Engines, Best of Show, Fast, Excellence, Famous, Safety, etc.)
2. Throw all the words in a hat.
3. Rank order the top ten words.
4. Break into groups and randomly assign each group one word
5. Take that word and develop a positive phrase and action statement for each word
6. Take all those collective efforts and put them together to make The Grand Vision Statement. Then the team can vote for the directive vision statement based on the Grand Vision Statement.

Example: If one of the top ten words was VISION, a group could take that word and make a symbolic vision statement using the letters of the word:

V   Visualize the Future
     (We are Moving from the Past through the Present into the Future)
          1. Proposed action
          2. Proposed action
          3. Proposed action
I   Intentions
     (Our intentions are to work for a Higher Purpose choosing Light over Darkness and being our best selves)
          1. Proposed action
          2. Proposed action
          3. Proposed action
S   Stop all Sabotage
     (Our journey is a long one, so we will discourage all behavior which sabotages our successful arrival at destination)
          1. Proposed action
          2. Proposed action
          3. Proposed action
I   I and Thou
     (We take care of ourselves and each other)
          1. Proposed action
          2. Proposed action
          3. Proposed action
O   Owning the Process
     (We are stakeholders in this mission and own the process we develop)
          1. Proposed action
          2. Proposed action
          3. Proposed action

N   Naming the Mission
         (We name our Mission "Service" and make a commitment to find new ways to provide it for our
         clients)
                    1. Proposed action
                    2. Proposed action
                    3. Proposed action

HOW TO CREATE A BUSINESS PHILOSOPHY

A business philosophy is the belief structure upon which the business develops. It is the conceptual skeleton, infrastructure, or foundation. Philosophies explain or examine the concepts, truths, doctrines and systems of thoughts of something. All businesses are based on the covert or overt philosophies of their originators. Philosophies are the driving force or energy underneath the mission and action of the work.

Do you know or can you guess the philosophies of the following business organizations? Ask or research these companies to see what they stand for philosophically. What are their mission statements and visions? Each organizational philosophy represents its origins, its people and its products.

Mrs. Fields Cookies	Budweiser
Sisters of Charity	Ben and Jerry's Ice Cream
The Mafia	Disney
Goodwill Industries	Halliburton
Girl and Boy Scouts	Wal-Mart
American Medical Association	Starbucks

Case Example

Philosophy: *All Work is Sacred*

A group of hospital employees were asked why they should be motivated to "do the right thing." They answered with comments about morality, professionalism, and personal values. When it was suggested that one philosophy behind doing the right thing was that All Work Was Sacred and therefore they worked on Sacred Ground they stared with blank expressions and had no response. The consultant suggested that they worked on sacred ground because people were born in this hospital and people died in the hospital also. Clients they served were coming into the world, trying to stay in the world, or leaving this world. The consultant suggested this meant sacred ground to her. They had not thought of that, but liked it. Then several employees offered their own personal philosophies and remembered their medical training and the philosophical foundations they had learned years earlier. The consultant helped them organize a philosophical statement that reflected their beliefs about their work.

But how could a fast food restaurant, a dental practice, a childcare center or a corporate headquarters be Sacred Ground? What about an automobile factory, nuclear waste facility or brokerage firm? Most offices do not host birthing rooms or morgue tables. Of course, babies have been born in offices and employees have died of heart attacks at work. Employees have died falling down elevator shafts and conceived new life on a top of a desk in the last cubicle. This does not necessarily make a location "sacred," but finding what is sacred to you or your employees about work is an excellent way to keep people feeling good about their work. People generally attend well to whatever they accept as sacred, be it a religion or a sports event. Find out what is sacred to a person, honor it even if you don't hold it sacred yourself, and you will go a long way to being a peacemaker at work. Wars are usually over people fighting about protecting what they define as sacred. Work is no different.

Case Example

A couple was having marital difficulties and did not understand each others' careers. She was a massage therapist. He was a bridge builder. When it was suggested that they both worked under the philosophy of maintaining important infrastructure so people could live their lives in comfort, they looked each other in the eyes and began to cry. It had never occurred to them that they were in the same book, but on different pages.

Case Example

Two weeks after 9/11 the client said, "My kid works at the World Trade Center, but I think he is still alive. And he's with his best friend. They always meet in that pizza place in the lower part of the towers to talk all their big important stuff. This was their sacred domain. So I think they must have found each other and are down there drinking the sodas for free waiting to be rescued."

Three weeks after 9/11 the client said, "I guess I don't think they are coming out now. But I tell you what, that pizza place now is part of where heaven starts. And pizza is sacred food."

Maybe you can't consider your work as sacred, and your worksite as Sacred Ground. If such theological vapor is too much for your sharply pointed rational mind, try playing with the following philosophical discussion. See if it works. Play with it. Wrap it around your mind to see if it fits. If not, it doesn't matter. Philosophies are Sacred Ground and very personal. There is nothing more sacred than discussing sacred ground with someone who holds the opinion that there is nothing sacred.

A Rational Approach to "See All Work as Sacred Ground" Exercise

1. If you believe in any sort of a "God," then wherever you are God is, which makes every location Sacred Ground.

2. If you don't believe in any sort of God, or any sort of higher power, being or essence which is larger than you, then Sacred, in the traditional, more theological sense of the word, might not work for you. Ask yourself what you hold Sacred, meaning valued above all things. If the answer is "nothing" then your vision of "nothingness" is what you hold sacred. Most people do hold something dear, precious and unreservedly unique. This is their Personal Sacred. Although the concept of sacredness is usually associated with religious or spiritual ideas, many people hold their own rational thought as sacred. If you are one of those people take the exercise the next logical step:

3. Wherever you go, there you are, and so is your mind, your consciousness, your beingness, and whatever vessel contains your rational thinking apparatus. Wherever you are must be Sacred to you, even if it is Sacred to you alone. If you perceive yourself all alone in an otherwise hostile universe, then you should take great care to protect yourself and those around you and your location from harm. Because that which effects your location in an adverse way may compromise the container of Your Rational Mind which you consider your sacred. If you hold the absence of Sacredness sacred, then maintaining that belief is sacred to you, or you would give it up easily.

4. It's just good business to have a good philosophy, and "Work is Sacred" is just as good as other philosophies. Terrorists recognize and respect their Sacred Ground. This is where they love to operate. Or, they love to invade yours. Sacred ground is where people are the most vulnerable and fear risking the most. People don't like to gamble on Sacred Ground so they are easy prey to someone who is willing to risk it all. And Terrorists don't hesitate to risk your sacred ground at the drop of a hat. The great terrorists of the 20th Century have all recognized Sacred Ground; that is why they have fought to control it. They enjoy sending other peoples children, our most sacred possessions, into the battlefields for their agendas. They have enjoyed putting our children at risk, or our holy sites in harm's way. Of course they are horrified when a random missile fragment hits their Sacred Ground. Immediately they cry "foul' from their sacred entitlement.

5. Conflicts and wars can be started by the challenges associated with defining what is sacred and what is not. On some level, all wars are Holy Wars. One side wants to protect its' Sacred. The other side wants to protect or accumulate Sacred. No one wants to "surrender." Siblings fight over a sacred toy, husbands and wives fight over who controls the stuff or the sex or the money or the kids. Movies like *Changing Lanes, War of the Roses, Lord of the Rings, Braveheart*, and countless others are cinematic examples of battles for sacred ground. If every one and every place were defined as sacred, there would be no wars. Ever. We would spend our days honoring the Sacred

of others while celebrating our own Sacred. Wars take a lot of energy, resources, time, and money. War is life alienating. Unless your mission is War, and your work is based on the philosophy that Death is valuable, then it probably does not serve your agenda to ignore the Sacred in all things. But then again, is War *your* Sacred? When Peace is Profitable, Peace will prevail. In the meantime it is useful to wade around in philosophical questions and discussions to help you define where you are really coming from either personally, professionally or from an organizational perspective.

6.   Conflict at work over sacred ideas, equipment, attitudes, salaries, secrets, opinions, rumors, agendas, or anything else is costly.

HOW TO DEVELOP A WORKING MANAGEMENT THEORY

A theory is an assumption. A theory is an idea based in possibilities but not necessarily in fact. A good theory should create more questions then answers. An excellent theory will simply be a container for questions to be researched. A familiar theory like The Theory of Relativity proposed by Albert Einstein created a huge container for daunting questions. Business theories are not generally as grand as this. But perhaps your business theory is not well-conceived or is vague, and you need to define it more clearly. How do you go about that? You start where you are.

You start with the question. If you have a question about why tornados seem to hate trailer courts, you may use it to begin your research. A theory does not answer the question but acts as the framework around the question or questions. A theory is the collection of questions, thoughts, or general principles that attempt to explain something. Science is based on various theories or sets of theories that are constantly tested to determine facts as true or untrue. Theories are the source of grand debates as they are agreed upon as valid or argued about until determined as factual or inaccurate. Gravity, for example, is another theory that has been well tested. Most people agree upon its relevancy. However, because no one can completely comprehend its true nature, the questions of gravity are still determined as a theory because they cannot completely be validated as indisputable fact.

One interesting aspect of theories is not only that they lead to more questions, but they also highlight the exceptions. These exceptions can lead to more questions and research with also can lead to more theories. Space flight was principally driven by countless theories that NASA continues to test, succeed, fail and re-test again. In the wake of all these theories countless discoveries, strategies, anomalies, disappointments, terrors, victories, and more questions have emerged.

Business Management Theories are readily available and should also be tested for relevancy and workability. A simple example of a Business Management Theory is that, "the work gets done when people show up." This is a lovely theory that may or may not be true. To test it, everyone should stay home next Monday and see what happens. Or come to work and spend the day reading magazines. Another Business Management Theory might postulate that work gets done more quickly with the presence of music, or the colors in the office determine attitudes, or safe people are happy people, or if there is a disaster everyone will be more than willing to show up and do their jobs. Interesting theories, but are they facts?

What theories are operating at *your* company?

Examples of Management Theories

1.   Maintain consistency with products and services
2.   Work from a philosophy of win-win
3.   Avoid dependence on outside markets
4.   Reward success
5.   Implement training at all levels
6.   Improve daily
7.   Remove barriers
8.   Do not fear fear, use it to grow

9. Make peace when possible
10. Expect quality and motivation

Examples of Emotional Continuity Management Theories

1. Support emotions as a normal part of human experience
2. Develop excellent resources for management of emotions, small and large
3. Encourage employees to discuss feelings as part of their productivity
4. Discourage emotional spinning at the worksite while allowing room for expression of personal feelings
5. Create an appropriate support system for emotionally impaired employees
6. Eliminate tension when they interfere with productivity at a cost effective level as predetermined by management or administration
7. Mitigate conflict with open communications
8. Work for reconciliations
9. Institute training and advanced training in conflict resolution for all strata of employees
10. Become a beacon of success with both strong business leadership and strong emotional leadership

HOW TO WRITE A RULE BOOK

Guess which employees do not like rules, laws and regulations? You guessed it! Emotional Terrorists operate by their own sets of rules. But they don't adhere to or appreciate the use of rules that create order, peace, awareness, accountability, compassion, and reason. Each business has to design, implement and police its own rules according to specific industry standards, products, services, missions, visions, policies and goals. Rules can be inhibitive and punitive, or they can add to a cohesive sense of order and direction. Most civilized peoples agree that a ruleless society breeds chaos. And if you recall, chaos is what Emotional Terrorists use to exploit situations for their own agenda.

There are already rules for safety and procedural process and rules for social order in your organization. There are rules that everyone is comfortable with and rules that make people nervous. Some rules trigger emotions in people who have been abused or held in oppressive environments. These employees may struggle with authority but will eventually adjust well if they are supported. This is different than Emotional Terrorists who are merely trying to take authority away from someone to have it themselves.

A pleasing rule that your company might use is one from the health care industry, that when translated from the Latin states "First Do No Harm." This exquisite concept from medical traditions could be a practical and compassionate rule for all human beings. Doing no harm is often translated into some version of a Golden Rule "Do unto others" guideline. Of course doing no harm also means doing no harm to the self. A trained lifeguard does not jump into the churning surf on a rescue mission until well grounded in personal safety. It serves no one to risk your own well-being impulsively if your well-being can easily be safeguarded with a simple piece of equipment like a rule, an idea, tool, or policy. It is important to develop safe boundaries, guidelines and backup systems, but establish operating rules prior to the onset of any process. When you are ready then you can make your own rulebook.

What are the current rules of your organization or industry? Does everyone play by the same rules? Who wrote your rulebook? Does your competition use that rule book also? Sports, games and work are easier when the rules are understood and when all the other teams are playing by the same rules. Most managers try to create a team spirit where everyone is in the same book. If you want your company to operate like a baseball team you need to ask yourself if you have a baseball team or just a bunch of people who happen to show up at the same time in the same place — but with different agendas. Emotional Terrorists have their rules and rulebooks, so it makes sense that you should also. Read the following list and think about the rules in your company. Read the list again as you might if you were an Emotional Terrorist. Rules are rules, and games are games.

A Sample Rulebook

Rule #1:   You are either IN or OUT

Like the saying goes, nobody is just a "little bit pregnant." You either are or you are not. In the same way nobody on staff, in any capacity, is a little bit part of the staff, you either are or you are not. It is called commitment, loyalty, or focus.

In many areas of life there are gray areas. If you are on a team there is no gray, you are in or you are out. Being on a team means getting off the proverbial fence and deciding allegiance. In or Out defines the essence of the Us-or-Them competitive nature of the universe. Good Guys and Bad Guys, Our Home Team vs. The Other School, Shirts and Skins, Guys against the Gals, Winners and Losers. When you are on a team, whether it be a team bound for glory or a team bound for selfish purpose, there is a natural occurring boundary of belongingness once goal-centered activities begin. As energy is directed and devoted to purpose, those who are with that driving force become more clearly defined as being "Us or Them," insiders or outsiders, a player or an observer, active or passive. Even passive observers define their allegiances by who they are cheering for, the t-shirts they buy, and the banners they wave. This is called membership, allegiance, alignment, engagement, joining forces, signing up, good faith, and loyalty. "Are you with us or against us?"

Rule #2:   No Tornadoes Allowed

You can't be on the team if you are a Tornado personality. Tornadoes risk the goal being met, so team members need to manage their emotions within a certain agreed-upon level.

Tornadoes are forces that do not adhere to a policy of "for the good of the all" and have their own agendas, usually destructive. All teams, whether positive or negative, ultimately eliminate any disruptive Tornado personality from their ranks due to its unpredictable and uncontrollable nature. Tornado personalities are eliminated because they are risky to the goals and produce non-productive forces.

Rule #3:   You are Self Accountable

If you are not in good shape, are injured, sick or distracted, you are less focused on our mission and might become a risk to our success. We want you strong and committed. We are willing to help but you also need to be willing to do self-care. You are valuable. Take care of yourself.

"To thine own self be true" is a good place to start being accountable. Many psychologists believe that all behavior, good, bad or ugly, is chosen for the sole purpose of self care, enhancement, protection or survival. Philosophers love to discuss the roots of altruism. Be that as it may, people who do not take care of themselves first, become fragmented and less able to make clear and accurate perceptions over time. Survival is our natural, instinctive order. This is a human default position. We can rise above that to join with civilization in groups and teams, but not if we are not safe and whole at our core.

Rule #4   You are Accountable to Others

Pulling your weight, being there for others in a crunch, backing each other up, loyalty, support, honor and celebration makes the sum of our parts bigger than each unit alone. We are valuable. Help us take care of us.

Team accountability can also be called Loyalty or Affiliation. If you are wearing a team's colors, you represent the team. In today's global marketplace there are such diverse affiliations that adherence to loyalty levels and obligations depend upon the team mission and goals. But in most industries it is clear, within that framework, which loyalties are counterproductive.

Rule #5   Team Members Contribute and Anticipate

You do your part and when you are not center court you still remain in active anticipation in case the ball is tossed your way.

Picture an NBA Basketball team member dribbling a ball down the court. He bends his knees slightly, slows his pace, scoops up the ball to pass it to someone and no one is available. The other members are doing their nails, talking on cell phones, making arrangements for dinner, primping, on the internet, talking to the guy on the bench, or just gazing into space. Team members anticipate the next play with the goal in mind. They are alert, alive, awake and enthusiastic. They are present and accounted for. Team members know that the ball might be tossed their way, and sometimes the pesky ball just comes flying. They are in a heightened state of expectancy and tuned in.

Rule #6   Drills and Rehearsals are Not Negotiable

No one gets to the Olympics, the Superbowl, or Carnegie Hall without constant, consistent, daily, repetitive practice, drills, practice, drills and more drills.

Practice makes perfect is an invalid statement. If you are practicing it incorrectly,

it will never be perfect. Perfect practice makes perfect. But practice. Now, do it again.

Not unlike a mathematician who finds the worth in trying to solve the unsolvable Pi, our team members are committed to the process as well as the outcome.

Rule #7   Suit Up and Show Up for the Games

You can't play if you aren't here, physically, emotionally, spiritually, or mentally. Wherever you go... there you are. So be here when you are here.

If there is a game on Thursday, team members suit up in the right uniform, grab the right equipment and get to the playing field a few minutes early. It doesn't matter what team you are on, you are either there or you are not there. If you do not show up and play you eventually get cut from the list. People can work at less than 100%, but what percentage of "presence" can your organization tolerate? The neurosurgery industry should demanded 100%.

Rule #8   Study the Rulebook and Watch for Changes

All life is about change. Stay current.

Healthy people pay attention and learn to adjust when necessary to grow with the team. Living things are constantly in a process of change and you may need to adapt to unexpected and unpredictable things on a regular basis. You may have been hired because you are a star, but a star only remains a star if they stay one step ahead. You may have been hired because you are a steady contributor, keep it up, and you may end up the star if the star slows down and tries to ride the wave of yesterday and gets bullet proof. Stay awake.

Rule #9   Just Say No

Healthy adult behavior is about making good choices. To not be a victim or a perpetrator means making choices which are ethical and appropriate and having the faith that those choices will serve to lead you and perhaps your organization to higher ground. Higher ground is a good place to be when the floods come.

Emotional Terrorists are like drug dealers who deal a nasty substance called FEAR. They spread a line of fear like cocaine and invite you to snort it up. In fact, they may actually put your nose in it hoping you will get hooked instantly. Nice people don't even see it coming. Emotional Terrorists can deal you a fear snort in a variety of interesting and subtle forms. The targeted person may feel a sense of specialness and power and then fear they are going to lose that status. The targeted person may fear for their reputation, status, job or general security and the dealer will "reassure" them to groom dependence. Dealers groom their victims. Once the drug is in your system, you are a hostage to how it plays out in the system. Once a FEAR THOUGHT is in the system, it has to work its way out, just like any other drug. Sometimes it just slips through and is ventilated, and other times it may hit an important organ and all bets are off. Sometimes it kills instantly. If someone deals you a chemical drug at work you'd probably say NO. But if someone offers you the drug of Fear, in the form of a rumor or threat or scary idea that may affect your job security, you might just snort it up into your spirit and become afraid. Do the same thing as if they were offering you heroin publicly. Just back away from the dealer and say "no." Fear is probably the most powerful drug that can be put into the human system or organizational system. It comes in a variety of pretty and ugly packages. The forms are as varied as the dealers.

HOW TO ESTABLISH CRITERIA

Criteria are standards. One excellent criteria might be called "Best Practices." Business criteria are based on industry standards and defined in specifics according to the company needs and preferences. Criteria can be arranged in such categories as performance, economics, or ethics. An industry, business, or individual can develop a list of behavior criteria that become the baseline for best practices. A criteria can establish the standards of practices for hiring, promoting, evaluating, auditing, filing grievances, or terminations.

The following list is a set of criteria developed by a health care delivery team when they were invited to set standards of best practices and establish their criteria for their unique team's view of excellence. The team wanted to communicate to each other what they hoped to see from one another and from themselves. Each member wrote their own criteria, and then a list was complied eliminating duplications. Their team had been disrupted by Emotional Terrorism and they wanted to avoid future upheavals. After developing a list of industry standards and expectations for their job performances, they began to discuss ways of managing past, present, and future emotionally disruptive outbreaks by using this list to create their own No-Emotional-Terrorists-In-Our-Department policy. The team graded each other on these standards on an ongoing basis to maintain a peer driven criteria for excellence.

Case Example
Fiona Feenie Memorial Hospital's Widget Packing Department
Criteria for Team Excellence
As a team, we will strive to:
- Let Go Of Past Grudges
- Assume The Best From One Another
- Seek Outside Feedback Carefully
- Not Participate In Emotional Drama
- Not Initiate Emotional Drama
- Remember We Are Not Victims Because Adults Have Choices
- Put Clients First
- Maintain A Good Attitude
- Use The Chain Of Command To Effect Change
- Use Policy Format To Offer Complaints
- Show All Memos To All Staff Always
- Strive For Cooperation
- Verbally Appreciate Help Given
- Show Respect For Each Other
- Model Appropriate Business Site Sense Of Humor
- Not Participate In Humor Which Includes Sexual Innuendos
- Model Flexibility
- Be Examples Of Personal Truthfulness
- Show Personal Accountability
- Give And Receive Forgiveness
- Offer Clear Communication
- Demand And Offer Equality
- Perform The Highest Work Ethics
- Complete Follow Through
- Not Engage In Second Hand Gossip
- Not Spread Or Encourage Rumors
- Actively Participate
- Show Consideration For Others And Courtesy In All Situations
- Stand By Confidentiality Standards
- Be Professional In Front Of Clients
- Give More Than Just The Minimum
- Work With Cooperation Between Hierarchies

HOW TO CREATE A BACKUP STRATEGY

One of the most annoying things about a disaster is that they are not predictable. Just when you make a plan, there is an exception. For this reason you need an excellent, well rehearsed, system-wide strategy... *and* a backup strategy. The most successful and simple backup strategy is to train everyone to be part of the project. This is useful if your life or emotions depends on anyone else. You want everyone to know what you know, or more!

As you have already learned, disasters create extremes in emotions. If a strategy that is intended to keep people calm fails... the emotions escalate. This can create even more chaos that will add more emotion to the situation. If your emergency responder team or your Emotional Continuity Management team is out of town when the disaster hits, who can use the fire extinguisher? Does everyone have a walkie-talkie or know where the keys are? If a fire extinguisher fails, what's next? Do you have a box of baking soda nearby? Are the numbers 911 written in big print on all the telephones? Because it remains difficult to predict the future, any good plan and safe strategy requires an equally good back up strategy.

A backup strategy can be simple or complicated. If the first strategy works there is no need for a second line of defense. However, if the first strategy does not work a second strategy must include preparing for consequences of that failure. For example, if a fire extinguisher fails, and the fire continues to burn during the failure of that original strategy, the fire will continue to consume fuel while you are implementing the second line of strategy. How would that influence your choices? Would emotions be more calm then or more stirred up? There is a story about a group of people in one of the World Trade Center towers who were making their exit and a stairway was blocked. Some of them went back upstairs. Some of them found another way out. A touching story in An Oral History of September 11, 2001 (Fink,2002) about the team of accountants who carried the disabled gentleman down a hundred of flights of stairs is a poignant example of why the system needs to be on board with strategy building. Strategies and backup strategies save lives and assist in business and Emotional Continuity Management.

Case Example

Miss Kim worked well with people and disabled children and was well respected in her work. She was an artist, musician and writer who also had a great capacity for being comfortable with very difficult and challenged students. She was also very comfortable with challenging creatures like bees, wasps and spiders. In her classroom she was often the one enlisted to come remove the scary insects. She truly enjoyed rescuing crawly things and felt good about setting them free back into their natural environment. Her motto was "you don't have to hurt something just because it scares you." Her mentorship in the office gave some employees the courage to carry a few spiders outside without squashing them under a shoe. They found themselves feeling good about this and began challenging each other to "save a spider." The back up strategy was to call Miss Kim!

How to Make Hard Technical Data & Soft Technical Data Assessments

Part One: the Hard Technicals

The following is a guideline for anyone trying to develop a hard paper evaluation, auditing criteria, or assessment policy. You can use the following to create policy, set standards of excellence, define best practices, create documentation, or begin appropriate dialogue about your company's requirements for excellence.

- Ongoing Evaluation of Training Standards and practices of HR staff/CEU's/Credentials
- Training Standards and practices of EAP, Third party providers, medical providers/mental health providers
- Hiring Practices: psychological screenings
- Firing Practices: risk assessment
- Security Professional Standards: CEU's, Credentials
- Security screening for all Security for Drugs, Psychology, Criminal Background, PTSD

- How are people taught to catch or react to discovery of fraud
- Criteria standards for Disaster Preparation/Management
- Correlations between sick days and project agendas
- Absenteeism patterns
- Grievance patterns
- Health dollars spent
- Mental Health dollars spent
- Employee satisfaction
- Employee perceptions
- Vendor satisfaction
- Vendor perceptions
- Community satisfaction
- Community perceptions
- Competency standards of all interagency support interventions
- Level and credibility of intervention specialists and options with industry standards
- Industry standards for impairment interventions
- Participation patterns for interventions/treatments/consultations
- Emerging patterns of behavior at 30/60/90 and 365 days after hire
- Post hiring/Post firing/Post retirement or transition follow-up procedures

Part Two: the Soft Technicals

The following is a guideline for anyone trying to develop a hard paper evaluation of soft-sided information. It can be turned into and auditing criteria, or assessment policy. This information can be turned into checklists, discussion points, impressions to share, didactic data points, or action points. You can use the following to create policy, set standards of excellence, define best practices, create documentation, or begin appropriate dialogue about your company's requirements for excellence.

- How does it feel to be in the presence of this person?
- Demonstrations: body language, voice tone, gestures
- General Hygiene
- Strength Or Weakness Of The General Infrastructure
- Strength Or Weakness Of Relationship Links
- Power Balances Or Imbalances
- Real Or Perceived Power
- Commitment To The Organization
- Commitment To Self/ Others
- Loyalty Links
- Rigidity/Flexibility
- Sense Of The Big Picture: Mission
- Sense Of The Small Picture: Units
- On Same Page As CEO/Management/Agendas
- Self Perception
- Discrepancies Between Self And Other Perception
- Level Of Satisfaction
- Communication Skills/Styles
- Willingness To Learn
- Willingness To Contribute
- Willingness To Mentor
- Willingness To Change
- Willingness To Self Disclose
- Willingness To Self Evaluate
- Comfort With Own Humanity
- Perception Of The Organizational Change: Past/Present/Future
- Perception Of The Organizations Change's Effect On Self/ Others
- Language Of Enhancing Or Demeaning Self Or Others
- Whining, Victimhood, Aggression, Anger, Blame, Shame, Fear, Hostility, Rumors, Threats, Apathy
- Once again, how did it feel to be in the presence of this person?

HOW TO CREATE A GRADING POLICY

A team grading activity may assist teams to identify, clarify, and create goals. Use a traditional academic grading system to develop a GPA (grade point average) using both business (performance tasks) and emotions (feelings). Create an anonymous report card which has been developed using the criteria, missions, visions, and rules already determined by your business practice. Make certain everyone has the exact same kind of writing tool, forms, and room to work to protect anonymity. After collecting the forms and grouping the data, destroy the grade cards to protect all employees.

Business and Emotions in the workplace are like oil and water. They reside in the same container, but do not mix well. Both are necessary when people are employed to make money. You cannot toss one out and leave the other hanging, and finding the balance between the two is quite a challenge. Since ignoring one for the other is unreasonable, it is helpful to separate the two in determining office Terrorism. Remember, these are Guidelines, not laws.

Making Anonymous Opinion Grade Report Cards

Part 1: Business Only

1. List the name of every employee
2. Based solely ONLY on PERFORMANCE CONTRIBUTION, everyone give everyone a letter grade (i.e. A+, A, A-, B+, B, B-, C+ C, C-, D+, D, D-, F)
3. Add all the grades and divide by the number of employees
   i. to establish your PERFORMANCE G.P.A.
   ii. (A=4, B=3, C=2, D=1, F=0)
4. If your organization is between an A+ and a C-, then the first order of business is to relax and recognize that WHATEVER IS GOING ON, YOUR BUSINESS IS MAKING It on an PERFORMANCE LEVEL at least adequately. There may be room for improvement, but you can begin by acknowledging the success it has at the moment. Even C businesses survive. D businesses need help. F businesses usually fail without extreme changes.
5. Decide on the PERFORMANCE G.P.A. that is reasonable for your organization, your bottom line. Remember that A's are great, but B's are quite good, and C's are average and while often not preferred may be acceptable.
6. Determine what, if anything, you need or want to do to develop PERFORMANCE improvement management to elevate or maintain the current G.P.A.
7. REPEAT IN 3-6 MONTHS

Part 2: Emotions

1. List the name of every employee
2. Based solely ONLY on EMOTIONAL CONTRIBUTION, everyone give everyone a letter grade (i.e. A+, A, A-, B+, B, B-, C+ C, C-, D+, D, D-, F)
3. Add all the grades and divide by the number of employees to establish your EMOTIONAL G.P.A. (A=4, B=3, C=2, D=1, F=0)
4. If your organization is between an A+ and a C-, then the first order of business is to relax and recognize that WHATEVER IS GOING ON, YOUR BUSINESS IS MAKING It on an EMOTIONAL LEVEL at least adequately. There may be room for improvement, but you can begin by acknowledging the success it has at the moment. Even C businesses survive. D businesses need help. F businesses usually fail without extreme changes.
5. Decide on the EMOTIONAL G.P.A. that is reasonable for your organization, your bottom line. Remember that A's are great, but B's are quite good, and C's are average and while often not preferred may be acceptable.
6. Determine what, if anything, you need or want to do to develop EMOTIONAL improvement management to elevate or maintain the current G.P.A.
7. REPEAT IN 3-6 MONTHS

<u>Report Card Learning Bytes</u>

- IF YOU HAVE people who are in the C- to F category in either performance or emotions you should   ask why they are on your team? How are they serving this company? Are they a risk? Can their GPA be changed?
- If low grades are reflected on just on one or two vote cards, is it reasonable to think these negative reflections came from a personal enemy or a witness?
- If there is a large discrepancy between the performance grade and the emotions grade there exists a problem or issue that requires management attention.
- If someone is an A+ in one area and a D in another there exists a problem or issue that requires management attention.
- If someone is consistent in both areas you have information about where training investment dollars and leadership energy should go.
- If someone is an A+ person do they need/deserve more/less training than the C+ person?
- Would training maintain the grades, lower, or elevate them?
- If the grades do not change after a 3-6 month period, what is your next plan?

<u>Use the following traditional academic scoring standards to create an anonymous grading project</u>

A+	4.2	B-	2.7	D	1.0
A	4.0	C+	2.2	D-	.7
A-	3.7	C	2.0	F+	.2
B+	3.2	C-	1.7	F	.0
B	3.0	D+	1.2		

DOCUMENTATION CAN BE YOUR BEST FRIEND

- If you are asked five years from now to defend yourself, will you have documentation to protect yourself and your part of the story?
- What level of documentation will be necessary to underwrite your risk?
- Did you notify all parties with whom you shared information?

Simple Documentation Can Include Formal or Informal Notes

- When and where did this meeting happen?
- Why was the employee in your office?
- What happened?
- What was the emotional environment?
- Describe the dilemma or concern.
- What was said?
- What plans or recommendations were made?
- What are potential risks to these plans or recommendations?
- Did you discuss any potential risks?
- How did you intend to follow through with recommendations?
- Did you follow through?
- Did the employee follow through?
- When?
- Who else was involved in this action?
- What phone calls or meetings occurred in association with this action?
- Were there any other emotional responses that should be noted?

HOW TO DOCUMENT EMOTIONAL TERRORISM

If an Emotional Terrorist is under a contract or the support of a union template, dealing with an Emotional Terrorist could be a prolonged process. The goal may not be to remove them from the team. It may work better to micro-manage an Emotional Terrorist until they are either on board, compliant, or exit voluntarily. Removal is not always the best strategy because there is always another Emotional Terrorist with an excellent resume just waiting in the wings to fill the next empty slot.

When there is clear, unambiguous policy spelling out expectations, management is certainly within their rights to reprimand and remediate. If such a policy is in place, even in its earliest formats and rough drafts, and an employee does not respond or honor it, you will immediately have some excellent information. This information becomes worthwhile criteria for documentations, reprimands, trainings, remediations, or removals. Include your legal staff and HR management to organize the paper documentation chain to support and maintain the policy. A written policy is mandatory when dealing with an Emotional Terrorist or they will turn the problem back on you.

A document may include the following attributes:

- *We (the organization, the members of the task force, the department, individuals) set the policy on this date*
- *This is the policy (full written document/history/mission/statistics/justification)*
- *The policy was explained to all employees on this date (trainings)*
- *Opportunity for training and advanced information was provided in this format*
- *Ongoing and secondary training options were available and recommended to all employees*
- *This worker did not respond/or responded in specific manners not within expected levels (document specifics and how it links to policy)*
- *This worker was individually encouraged to review expectations and given ample opportunity to gather increased information, training, mentorship, or other third party assistance in achieving adequate standards (options offered, dates, training opportunities, private meetings, consultations, EAPs, etc.)*
- *Policy on Adequacy Standards Repeated (clarify expectations between the A+ and the C- expectations of compliance to policy)*
- *This worker was encouraged to attend specific trainings or learn specific procedures to assist in their getting on board with these opportunities. All impediments to their participation were removed in the following way (time off, transportation, per diem, etc.)*
- *This worker was again encouraged to attend special trainings or procedures to assist in their getting on board with these opportunities. All impediments to their participation were removed in the following way (time off, transportation, per diem, etc).*
- *The worker did not respond (specific non-compliance reports)*
- *The worker was given another good faith fair warning, clarification and opportunity to address expectations (List next trainings, individual meetings, consultations, educational opportunities offered)*
- *Compliance successful (date, examples, support evidence)*
- *Compliance failed (date, examples, support evidence)*
- Recommend extended training or dismissal (The organization must determine the cost variances and value added benefits of ongoing extended training for behavior adaptation over the costs of rehiring or re-training another employee.)

Documentation Example

1. _____(company name)_____ established a_____(policy name)__ on __(date)
2. A copy of the policy is attached
3. Trainings on this policy were given to all employees on _____(dates)_____
4. Ongoing training was offered to all employees and announced through the following communications and in the following formats: _____(formats)_____, _____ (advertising)_____
5. _____(name)_____ did not respond to the company expectations for this policy within expected levels (document specifics and how it links to policy, including a section on "intangibles, impressions, and intuitions")
6. _____(name)_____ was individually encouraged to review expectations and given ample opportunity to gather increased information, training, mentorship, or other third party assistance in achieving adequate standards (options offered, dates, training opportunities, private meetings, consultations, EAPs, etc.)
7. Policy on Adequacy Standards and Expectations were reviewed and repeated on the following dates in the format specified: _____(dates)_____
8. _____(name)_____ was encouraged to attend special trainings and offered mentored or tutorial procedures to assist compliance by _____
9. Any reported impediments to their participation was removed in the following way (time off, transportation, per diem, etc.)
10. _____(name)_____ was again encouraged to attend special trainings or procedures to assist in compliance and impediments to their participation was removed in the following way (time off, transportation, per diem, etc.)
11. _____(name)_____ responded with/ did not respond (specific non-compliance reports)
12. _____(name)_____ was given another good faith fair warning, clarification and opportunity to address expectations (List next trainings, individual meetings, consultations, educational opportunities offered)
13. Compliance successful (date, examples, support evidence)
14. Compliance failed (date, examples, support evidence)
15. Costs associated with non-compliance to policy to date (The organization must determine the cost variances and value added benefits of ongoing extended training for behavior adaptation over the costs of rehiring or re-training another employee.)
16. Recommendations
17. Notifications
18. Signatures, Witnesses, Additional Information
19. Follow-up

HOW TO WRITE A NEW EMOTIONAL CONTINUITY MANAGEMENT POLICY

Many organizations have infrastructure based on management policies and procedures. The procedures get things done and the policies are the frameworks or principles to guide the flow. When things break down policies are reviewed and rewritten. Policies are more than guidelines and less than laws and can be used to direct system energy, block the flow, or create disruptions.

Policy Writing Guidelines: (Not Laws)

1. A policy is a course or management of methods and actions which guide and determine present and future decisions or practices
2. There are many of ways to formulate policy depending upon industry standards and expectations
3. Some policy is better than no policy. Policy can be a safety net or an impediment to movement
4. Good policy is part science and part art combining data, facts and aesthetics necessary to keep the flow moving forward
5. Policy is a framework so should be open and fluid

6.   Incorporates ethics
7.   Spells out the rules clearly, avoiding misinterpretation
8.   Is written in clear and simple language

Policy can be general and/or specific:

General	Specific
A No-spinning-at-the-workplace policy	No gossip policy
Dress code policy	No slogan T-shirts policy
Anti-harassment policy	No sexual jokes policy
No drugs policy	No smoking policy
Non-discrimination policy	No mandatory age retirement policy
Special needs policy	Policy to hire ⅓ disabled for staff

A well-written policy has roots and flexibility. The roots must come from the administrative level of support. This is absolutely necessary for any policy to withstand any winds which may come. Without this support, the policy will necessarily fail as it blows away in the dust if challenged.

Flexibility adds the bend and movement to a policy so that it does not become fixed and rigid over time. The sources of flexibility should be gleaned from the specific daily demands at your work site or in your industry and include any cultural, ethnic, economic, or emotional dynamics that are part of the place the policy is intended to serve. It should offer protection and openness. There needs to be enough flexibility to serve production as well as the people who perform the production. A policy should serve the bottom line concerns of the company, the community, the global marketplace, and in the best of all worlds…the Planet Earth! Policies should be living forms and not rigid statutes set in mental concrete.

HOW TO WRITE AN ANTI-EMOTIONAL TERRORISM POLICY

An Anti-Terrorism policy should be strong enough to withstand an F-5 Emotional Tornado. That means any policy you craft needs amazing roots and an incredible amount of flexibility. When any policy is in place it becomes exquisitely clear who the players are. This is even more clear when creating a policy to manage an Emotional Terrorist at the work site. Emotional Terrorists will offer grand and creative resistance. A strong policy clarifies the boundaries and that can set up a reactionary environment until the policy is standardized, tested and supported by the administration. Those employees who do not like boundaries, like Emotional Terrorists, will feel compelled to act, react, respond, go overt, go covert, or create spinning in others. While other employees whine and complain and inevitably either exit or adjust to the situation, Emotional Terrorists will escalate their agenda to not be bound by the rules of others. The creation of a policy often illuminates a hidden terrorist instantly if their resistance becomes visible. Knowing and expecting this is useful if you are grounded in good theories and procedures prior to implementation and announcements of new policy.

The following is an introduction to how you might start thinking how you are going to develop components for your *No Emotional Terrorism at the Work Site* Policy:

A "No-Spinning-Allowed" Policy

a.   Develop and define the limitations your organization is able or willing to manage if confronted by emotional disruptions from small to catastrophic
b.   Demand Zero Tolerance for going beyond the level defined as tolerable by your organization
c.   Build into the policy enough room to handle the strong human emotions of extenuating circumstances, natural disasters, man made disasters, and unexpected events
d.   Build into the policy a pre- and post-Disaster Emotional support and Management program such as Critical Incident Stress Management, Defusings, Debriefings, Training, Counseling, EAP, or Ongoing Intervention Strategies

e.   Create a close relationship between Legal, Human Resources, Security, Internal Auditing and Administration to develop procedures to track, evaluate, and measure Emotional intangibles and to protect all employees from Emotional Terrorists. This should be part of any Disaster Plan

f.   Provide ongoing training for all strata of employees in the areas of understanding normal as well as abnormal human emotions and their relationship to the business world, and what happens to real people.

g.   Supply ongoing training in Human Emotions Management to all staff (All means ALL. Anyone left out becomes a risk.)

Emotional Continuity Management Trainings Checklist

As you are creating your Emotional Continuity Training for teams and employees, you can use the following checklist to track your consistency:

- Does each module of training follow the same "scripted" procedure so that the information is uniform and repeatable?
- Is attending mandatory, because mandating attendance creates a sense of unity among participants and immediately limits options for spinning?
- Do follow-up meetings provide creative input and collaboration from all members?
- Has there been buy-on from the top? The top-down process allows the administration/management to discover what employees are on board, who are potential company emotional saboteurs, and who are simply trainable "problem children."
- Does each module include practice time and drill for new tools, language, and concept acquisition? Adjustment and absorption of new ideas takes time and familiarity.
- Do units of education, or modules exceed teachable time frames? Two hours for group education is appropriate, with shorter individual consultations when required. This process should add minimum emotional impact to the organization's functioning. Do not let lengthy trainings become fodder for emotional spinning.
- Do Emotional Continuity Management trainings have written policy and clearly defined statements for:
- Trainer qualifications
- Company mission and team visions
- Top organizational buy-on defined/clarified
- Rules for mandated participation and non-negotiable consequences for nonparticipation
- Expectations and timetables for skills practice and drills
- Value added incentives for participation
- Are reproducible documents prepared for:
    - Personnel interview charts
    - Models for explaining human emotions
    - Models for explaining human responses
    - Models for conflict resolution
    - Models for grief work and trauma management
    - Self-care tools ranging from simple to complex
    - Grading assessments
    - Models for managing individual differences
    - Systemwide back up plans
    - Systemwide back up plans for the back up plan

Administrative Buy-on Evaluation

(Rate the following between 1=Low and 10=High)

How well does administration support the Emotional Continuity Management Plan?
1   2   3   4   5   6   7   8   9   10

How completely has the Emotional Continuity Management Plan been incorporated into the Emergency Management Plan of the company?
1   2   3   4   5   6   7   8   9   10

How well have other departments in the company been notified about administrative buy-on?
1   2   3   4   5   6   7   8   9   10

How well have other departments supported the Emotional Continuity Management Plan?
1   2   3   4   5   6   7   8   9   10

How well supported is the need to practice and drill for emotional emergencies?
1   2   3   4   5   6   7   8   9   10

How extensive are the opportunities to drill for emotional emergencies?
1   2   3   4   5   6   7   8   9   10

How financially supported is the Emotional Continuity Management Plan?
1   2   3   4   5   6   7   8   9   10

How supportive is the administration about providing opportunities for training employees in emotional management?
1   2   3   4   5   6   7   8   9   10

How supportive is the administration about providing opportunities for training management emotional management?
1   2   3   4   5   6   7   8   9   10

How supportive is the administration about creating cooperative partnerships with other emergency response agencies prior to a disaster or emotional event?
1   2   3   4   5   6   7   8   9   10

How supportive is the administration about providing pamphlets, books, literature, posters, media education, and other hard-copy information on Emotional Continuity Management Planning?
1   2   3   4   5   6   7   8   9   10

How well do personnel know what they should do in an emergency to caretake their emotions?
1   2   3   4   5   6   7   8   9   10

How well prepared are you to manage extreme emotions in the workplace?
1   2   3   4   5   6   7   8   9   10

How well prepared are you to manage emotions resulting from a catastrophic disaster?
1   2   3   4   5   6   7   8   9   10

Qualifications Checklist for External Consultant or Emotional Continuity Management Trainer or Services Provider

Document the following:

- Formal training
- Informal training/experiences
- Real time disaster experience
- Continuing education
- Licensures
- License number and date of expiration/photocopy
- Malpractice Insurance
- Specialized training
- Experience
- References
- Special skills
- Special populations skills
- Availability
- Locations
- Types of services
- Application forms/process
- Photo ID
- Criminal background check including fingerprints
- Security clearance if needed
- Vehicular background check if needed
- Signed contract for services including clear fee arrangements

Steps for Writing a Quality Emotional Continuity Management Plan

Research
Find your highest order of management style
Explore a variety of possible forms
>HOW:
>Call someone in your position in another company for an Idea Meeting
>Read magazines and books
>Go to workshops or classes

Create a Blueprint
Visualize your perfect style
Take time to sketch or write your plan
>HOW:
>Create a notebook or journal of ideas
>Draw pictures and doodles of your ideal work process

Decide and Commit
Remove barriers
Prepare the space
Gather resources
Survive first challenges
Continue to commit
>HOW:
>Work for buy-on
>See the big picture so there is no emergency in the planning stage
>Continue your research and creative stages
>Use challenges and obstacles as learning/teaching moments
>Write and rewrite your plan as it continues to evolve into a final draft

Begin

Take actions
Safeguard resources
Survive ongoing challenges
Recommit
> HOW:
> Talk with others inside and outside your work: create networks
> Review and strengthen your data base
> Create professional documents and forms
> Accept and review feedback with your ideals in mind
> Review persistence materials
> Begin implementation stages

Recall

Review highest order ideals
Review original visions
Reconsider if appropriate
Recommit and Continue
> HOW:
> Review previous stages with ideals in mind
> Continue to face challenges with open mind and commitment

Beginning an Emotional Continuity Management Team

Part One: **Constructing Your Team**
- Who is on your Emotional Continuity Management Team?
  - *Will they be trained and ready to get your company up and running during or after an incident?*
- How do others respond to this team emotionally?
  - *Are they well thought of in the organization? Trusted? Safe?*
- Who will show up?
  - *Have all members been trained in leadership to take over in case of loss of life?*
- What does your company need to get back to 100% services?
  - *Can it operate at 10%? 35%?*
- What qualifications are acceptable to be on the Emotional Continuity Management team?
  - *Have they been pre-screened for PTSD from any prior catastrophic incident?*
  - *Are they emotionally stable, mature, trained, and willing?*
- Have they had sufficient training?
  - *What levels of training are sufficient for your team members and leaders?*
- Are your emergency and disaster plans specific or generalized?
  - *What is vague and what is specific?*
- Have you tested your plan?
  - *Has it been table talk or real-time drills and exercises?*
- Have your team member discussed and planned for emotional shock, loss, and terror?
  - *What support does your team have to manage their feelings when they are supporting others?*
- Have all team member been trained to understand the variety of emotional reactions to expect in case of a catastrophic incident by a qualified disaster or trauma specialist or qualified Licensed Mental Health Professional?
- Who will replace you if you are not present? How would your team deal with losing you?
  - *Does everyone know all the parts of the plan?*

Part Two: **Constructing Your Team Notebook**

Minimum requirements should include:
- Team Composition
- Chain of authority
- Exit strategies

- Member list and all contact methods
- Collect verifications of qualifications of all team members
- Verification that all team members have been screened for PTSD and prior trauma
- Plans for changes in circumstances, shifts, time off
- Complete data about will your company require to return to 100%, 75%, 50%, 25% service levels
- Anticipated obstacles to complete recovery
- Written plans for the Emotional Continuity Management for specific incidents, even those that appear to be unlikely:
  - tornado
  - earthquake
  - suicide
  - cyber crime
  - shooting
  - fire
  - Emotional Terrorist
  - Winter storm
  - hurricane
  - chemical spill
  - shelter in place
- Extensive lists of local, regional, national and international recourses
- A chronology of how you have tested your plans and lessons learned data
- Reproducible copies of required or preferred forms or documents
- Emergency numbers for team members and families
- Complete written policy and procedures
- Company/Administrative buy-on statement
- List of insurances and legal support
- List of all employees under the domain of the Emotional Continuity Management Team

HOW TO SEE PAST THE STAGES OF GRIEVING TO THE ONGOING STAGES OF RECOVERY

There is no *recovered* in *recovery*. There is change. But recovery is not an endgame. Recovery is a process. There really is no such thing as 'recovered' in human experience. If you take the phases of any incident from beginning to end, you should see that there is evolution but even an ending will evolve into a new beginning which means more change and more losses to adjust. There is an effect that can be called *resolution*, but even that is an evolving process as it changes form over time. Knowing this, it is still useful to assist, support, and encourage resolutions that help employees return to productivity at work. Understanding that life has cycles and rhythms may help you manage people who just will not stay in the same emotional framework as Kubler-Ross's five stages describe. Here is one roadmap for recovering process:

DENIAL	PRE-INCIDENT	The "as-if" stage that does not have control over future expectations
BARGAINING	INCIDENT	Whatever is happening in the "now" is causing some effect, consequence.
		During incident there are countless possible responses and reactions
ANGER	DURATION	Losses of control continues
DEPRESSION	DECAY	Losses continue and awareness of consequences emerge
ACCEPTANCE	END	A calm, an end of incident chaos
ANGER	DURATION	Losses continue to emerge

DEPRESSION	DURATION	Losses continue to emerge
REPLAYS	TRANSITION	Memories, replays, recriminations, reframes, reviews, remorse
ENERGY	RECOVERING	Choice making, positive or negative decisions are established for healing or continued duration
ADJUSTMENTS	RECOVERING	Memories stored, reviewed, categorized, ritualized, reframed
ADJUSTMENTS	RECOVERING	Adjustments continue over time
ADJUSTMENTS	RESOLUTIONS	Adjustments continue over time and are contained in active memory and perception sites of the brain which now directly affect future perceptions, beliefs, attitude behaviors, opinions and decisionmaking

Personnel Interview Form

When you do an Emotional Continuity Management Process, you may want to interview employees for witnessing, or planning. Use this form, or create your own, to track the interview data:

Reference Information: (why this interview is requested, by whom, in reference to what concern)

Date _____   Time _____ Location _____

Interviewer Name _____ Title _____ Department _____

Interviewee Name _____ Department _____ Title _____

Comments made:

o

o

Impressions and Observations:

o

o

Summary of Recurrent Themes

o

o

Possible Contribution Factors or Causal Supports

o

o

Other Information

o

o

Recommendations:

      Short Term

o

o

      Long Term

o

o

      Follow-Up Recommendations

o

o

Signatures _____

Copies sent to _____

Sample Scheduling Form for Mandatory Meetings

(NAME OF YOUR DEPARTMENT)
Individual Meetings: Circle one: OPTIONAL   MANDATORY
Wednesday, August 6th
12:00-12:30   _____
12:30-1:00   _____
1:00-1:30   _____
2:00-2:30   _____
2:45-3:15   _____
Thursday, August 7th
9:00-9:30   _____
9:30-10:00   _____
10:00-10:30   _____
10:30-11:00   _____
11:30-12:00   _____
Wednesday, August 23rd   (*Only if prearranged with manager and consultant*)
12:00-12:30   _____
12:30-1:00   _____
1:00-1:30   _____

AUTHOR'S AFTERTHOUGHTS

The first time I presented this information to a group of internal auditors, although in agreement with the concepts, they assured me that unless the concepts were quantifiable, businesses would not be receptive to including standards for emotions within their best practices evaluations. I listened. And although not everyone is as tuned into measurement as an auditor, the point was well taken. The challenge became not only to convince companies that Emotional Continuity Management is critical to success, but to provide a means to identify, assess, and evaluate human emotions in a way that is productive and compassionate. A few people suggested producing a profiling tool. As a mental health professional it has always been my opinion that such instruments deny unique differences. And as soon as a standard is established a new anomaly appears. This is a good thing. Life is ever shifting and adjustment means paying attention to those movements. Rigidity is life threatening. So, how do you document emotions?

The solution was quite simple: collect data and report your findings. Use both hard data (observations) and soft data (intuitions, feelings and impressions) to create a full picture.

It has been my observation that people tend to feel whatever they feel. What people do with those feelings should be the only piece that is up for question. For example, wanting to scream at work may be a very appropriate feeling. Screaming at work may not be acceptable. On the other hand, if you are a professional sports person and your job includes attending sports events, screaming may be perfectly acceptable behavior. Even in this situation there are limitations such as not screaming in the face of the referee or directly into the television camera.

Companies that begin the difficult process of establishing hard and soft guidelines for emotions in the workplace are going to do better than their competition. The reports of less confusion, chaos and upheaval on a daily basis are my feedback. Companies go for longer periods of time without having to stop productivity to manage an emotional incident. If this sounds valuable to you, then perhaps your company can handle the ambiguity of the dynamics between hard and soft data of emotions.

DISCUSSION QUESTIONS

- How many "feeling" words are included in your company mission or vision statements?

- What is your personal set of rules about emotions? What did your family teach you about emotions?

- Can you compare your company with another company in your industry in terms of philosophy? How are they the same? How are they different? Does your company or industry have an emotional philosophy?

- How would Emotional Continuity Management be a valuable strategy for success in your company?

13

READINESS: TOOLS FOR MANAGING INCIDENTS AND FOR DRILLING

WHY YOU SHOULD READ THIS CHAPTER

The expression "Practice Makes Perfect" is *not* correct! If you are practicing something incorrectly, doing it over and over and over will not correct it. The phrase should be, "Practice Something Perfectly to Maintain Perfection." The only way to attain anything close to perfection is to practice until you discover your errors, get feedback and make corrections. Emergency, Disaster and Readiness drills need to address the physical and the emotional needs of your people. Reading this chapter will get you started in seeing how to include emotions in your regular emergency drill practices.

BY THE END OF CHAPTER 13 YOU SHOULD BE ABLE TO

- Include emotions as a component in previously established disaster or emergency drill policies and practices

- Initiate an Emotional Management Continuity drill for your company

- Produce an emergency assistance resource list for managing big emotions

- Define strategies for managing emotions before, during and after a disaster

WHAT THE EXPERTS SAY ABOUT EMOTIONAL CONTINUITY MANAGEMENT TOOLS

"Conflict is inevitable, in fact it is desirable if we are to grow and change in meaningful ways. But the conflict that helps us progress is not the destructive conflict of anger and violence. This type of conflict only creates fear as well as more anger and violence, the antithesis of growth. Managers as well as world leaders need tools that encourage people to use disagreement positively to help construct the reality of the greater vision and prevent destruction on local and global levels. Hopefully, skill and practice in using such tools can be the next pandemic."
— Sharon G. Frizzell, Instructional Designer and Communicative Skills Instructor, Command Technologies, Inc. (An MTC company), Silver Springs, Maryland.

An Emotional Continuity Management Event Hot Sheet

Fill out this hot sheet if there is an incident:

- What is the nature of the event?
- What is the scope of the emotional impact?
- How much geography/territory is involved? (i.e., a fire in the break room, a devastated community or a devastated one block radius, a 48 car pile up in front of the main entrance to the worksite, death of one colleague, death of many colleagues)
- Who is in charge, authority/command structure? (Who do I report to?)
- Has there been property damage?
- Who has authority for restoring the property damaged?
- Have people been displaced, injured, or killed?
- How many victims are involved?
- What are their ages if known?
- Are any children involved?
- Will the children's needs be treated separately from adult needs? Elderly? Special Need/disabled?
- Are there any fatalities?
- What are the general nature of any injuries? (mild, moderate, severe, catastrophic)
- Will I have access to medical information?
- How many support staff will be involved?
- Support systems and teams in place now? On the way?
- How long will I be expected to respond?
- Will I be safe? How will that be accomplished?
- Is there a dress code? Or is there any special circumstances where clothing or footwear should be a factor? (i.e. weather, walking through rubble, ethnic or cultural needs, attire for funerals)
- Is the entire staff trained in full range of disaster protocols from shelter in place to full evacuation?
- Has the entire staff been trained in what emotions to anticipate during this kind of incident?
- Are there cultural, religious, political, or ethnic variables that I should know or understand?
- What languages will be spoken? Will there be translators?
- Am I covered by company liability insurance or my own? Or both?
- What duties am I expected to perform or am responsible for providing?(i.e. debriefings,defusings, counseling, crisis response, medication assessment, diagnosis, mediation, communications, transportation, referrals, hand-holding)
- What paperwork will be required to manage this incident? Do I have all the required forms?
- What are the Mental Health or Disaster Professional qualifications necessary to deal with this?
- Who else will be helping me on this?
- Will I be fed, housed, provided for, given chocolate?
- Will there be an expectation of continuous service, or will there be opportunity for self care, support for me if I need it, breaks, days off, etc.
- What are my other resources?
- If I find that the situation is beyond my scope, expertise or personal tolerance, or if I become ill or injured or incapacitated, what is the protocol for a professional exit strategy and will that be supported
- Who will take over my assignments?
- What are the qualifications of the disaster team?
- What are the qualifications of the Emotional Continuity Management Team?
- How do I protect myself and my team first?
- What is the emotional environment needed for rapid recovery?
- What is the physical environment (locations on-off site, recovery equipment, communications, paper/pencils, water bottles, cell-phones, toilet paper) needed for rapid recovery?
- Do we have event specific planning strategies?
- Memos of understanding, agreements, contracts with Local, National and Global Resources?
- Have we tested this plan?

Drill and Rehearsal Form

<u>Checklist:</u>
- Establish full buy-on administratively
- Pick your team
- Assign roles
- Determine leadership or authority chains
- Define the emotional needs of your company
- Decide on what kind of drill you will have
- Establish timetable
- What is the purpose of the drill?
- What are five specific objectives you will seek?
- What documentation will be required?
- Create and write the emergency and emotional scenarios
- Make participant assignments
- Consider how you would manage a real emergency or unexpected event if one occurred during the exercise
- Make a detailed list of all activities, small and large
- List emotions that you wish to exercise and the interventions you would use
- Decide on how you will evaluate the exercise after it has been completed
- Conduct the drill
- Collect documentation
- Analyze data
- Celebrate the closure of the drill formally
- Debrief participants and planners without critique
- Planners evaluate the success or failure of goal achievements
- Lessons learned
- Add or subtract necessary components for the next drill
- Decide on what training will be necessary and who will get it
- Schedule the next drill
- Send written thank yous to all participants. No memos, real letters.

Additional steps:
- "*This is a Drill*" instructions given
- Identification Tags
- Evaluations should focus on positive points
- Have fun
- Add a surprise
- Associated agencies participation
- Drill a full range of emotions from small to large, annoyances to catastrophic
- Participants told to maintain their acting roles until excused from the drill.
- Notifications
- Exit information
- Practice mock debriefings
- Debriefing schedule
- Formal thank yous
- What questions will you need answered to make good decisions?
- What resources will you need in each case?
- What resources will you activate immediately?
- What resources will you put on stand-by?
- How will you approach administration, employees, vendors and ancillary participants?
- What plan will you write?
- What policies for emotions will you want in place?
- What people with what qualifications will serve you best?
- What level of emotional impact will this possibly have?
- What risks will there be for solo or group emotional spinning?
- What tools will you use to manage the emotions of employees?

- How will you take care of your self as you participated?
- What would be the estimated costs of this for your company?
- Outline the performance tasks that must be accomplished
- Outline the emotional components for yourself, the staff, and the community that you must accommodate as the process evolves.
- What emotions are likely to be demonstrated?
- What might be a surprise emotion?
- How will you manage the emotions of your employees and clients?
- What fears or concerns can you anticipate because they were exposed to a potential health threat? Exposed to injury? Exposed to death?
- How will you plan for managing: (see the Emotions List in above)

Fear	Anger
Rage	Terror
Sadness	Concern
Ambivalence	Hysteria
Boredom	Numbness
Confusion	Shock
Horror	Disgust
Disappointment	Grief
Denial	Horror
Grief	Disgust
Disappointment	Withdrawn
Irritated	Rancorous
Pessimistic	Impatient
Passive	Aggressive
Nervous	Embarrassed
Edgy	Sensitivity
Serious	Frivolous

How to Set up a Drill

1. Establish full buy-on administratively
2. Determine leadership
3. Prepare with paper drills and table-talks prior to simulation drills
4. Define the goals of the drill
5. Develop appropriate and safe logistical settings
6. Develop appropriate scenarios
7. Create scenario assignments
8. Consider management of a real emergency or unexpected event during the simulation
9. Review plans and gather feedback
10. Conduct the drill
11. Collect results
12. Celebrate the closure of the drill formally
13. Debrief participants and planners without critique
14. Planners then can evaluate the success or failure of goal achievements
15. Add or subtract necessary components and schedule next drill cycle
16. Send thank yous to all participants
17. What questions will you need answered to make good decisions?
18. What resources will you need in each case?
19. What resources will you activate immediately?
20. What resources will you put on stand-by?
21. How will you approach administration, employees, vendors and ancillary participants?
22. What plan will you write?
23. What policies for emotions will you want in place?
24. What people with what qualifications will serve you best?
25. What level of emotional impact will this possibly have?

26. What risks will there be for solo or group emotional spinning?
27. What tools will you use to manage the emotions of employees?
28. How will you take care of your self as you participated?
29. What would be the estimated costs of this for your company?
30. What would be the estimated costs for your company if it was unprepared for a real emergency?

Tips for Success of Drills

Clear Notifications:
> *Always state "THIS IS A DRILL" when making phone calls or contact calls during the drill. Remember when Orson Wells read the story War of the Worlds on radio and some people really thought the Earth was being invaded by aliens? People are fun! And, people are nervous. Our world is scarier than it was a few years ago. It is better to be cautious than to create more emotional impact. It is critical to inform and notify all players and anyone who might be concerned that this is not a drill.*

Identification Tags:
> *For the same reasons as above, and for ease in managing the Participants, all members should have visible and highly identifiable temporary identification that is collected after the drill.*

Time them well:
> A drill during a layoff phase is dangerous. A drill during an earthquake is pointless and dangerous.

Evaluations should focus on positive points:
> *Negative critiques destroy buy-on. Attempt to phrase weaknesses and losses in positive "can-do-better-next-time" language.*

Have fun:
> *Simulations can be fun and exciting when people are motivated to do their best for the sake of everyone else.*

Add a surprise:
> *The unexpected is where drills show holes in preparation. Don't add anything extreme, but include a small twist to make it interesting.*

Ask other experts to play with you:
> *Go to your local fire department, hospital or chapter of the American Red Cross and ask someone to help you plan your drill.*

Drill a full range of emotions:
> *Include all feelings from small to large, annoyances to catastrophic.*

Maintain the illusion:
> *Encourage participants to maintain their acting roles until excused from the drill.*

Explain exit strategies and ending calls:
> *Inform your participants how they can exit the drill if it becomes distressful. Also inform everyone when or how the drill will conclude.*

Debrief even when it is a drill:
> *Make certain any individual who exits a drill have a mandatory debriefing to deter people who simply want to exit the process so they can go home early, and protect participants who may really have difficulty. This also gets people into the good habit of debriefing.*

Pleases and Thank-yous:
> *Courtesy goes a long way to create closure and future buy-on. Write a formal thank you letter to all participants.*

How to Make an Emergency Assistance Resource List

DISASTER CONSULTANT
    Local Contact Person:
    National phone number:
    Local number:
    Website:
    Other:

EMOTIONAL HEALTH PROVIDER
    Local Contact Person:
    National phone number:
    Local number:
    Website:
    Other:

MENTAL HEALTH PROVIDER
    Local Contact Person:
    National phone number:
    Local number:
    Website:
    Other:

MEDICAL SERVICES PROVIDER
Local Contact Person:
    National phone number:
    Local number:
    Website:
    Other:

WEATHER SERVICES
    Local Contact Person:
    National phone number:
    Local number:
    Website:
    Other:

HOMELAND SECURITY (HS)
    Local Contact Person:
    National phone number:
    Local number:
    Website:
    Other:

DEPARTMENT OF JUSTICE (DOJ)
    Local Contact Person:
    National phone number:
    Local number:
    Website:
    Other:

FEDERAL EMERGENCY MANAGEMENT
AGENCY (FEMA)
    Local Contact Person:
    National phone number:
    Local number:
    Website:
    Other:

DEPARTMENT OF ENERGY (DOE)
    Local Contact Person:
    National phone number:
    Local number:
    Website:
    Other:

ENVIRONMENTAL PROTECTION AGENCY (EPA)
    Local Contact Person:
    National phone number:
    Local number:
    Website:
    Other:

DEAPARTMENT OF HEALTH AND HUMAN SERVICES (DHHS)
    Local Contact Person:
    National phone number:
    Local number:
    Website:
    Other:

U.S. DEPARTMENT OF TRANSPORTATION
    Local Contact Person:
    National phone number:
    Local number:
    Website:
    Other:

DEPARTMENT OF DEFENSE (DOD)
    Local Contact Person:
    National phone number:
    Local number:
    Website:
    Other:

NATIONAL TRANSPORATION SAFETY BOARD (NTSB)
    Local Contact Person:
    National phone number:
    Local number:
    Website:
    Other:

AMERICAN RED CROSS
    Local Contact Person:
    National phone number:
    Local number:
    Website:
    Other:

LOCAL LAW ENFORCEMENT
    Local Contact Person:
    National phone number:
    Local number:
    Website:
    Other:

FIRE DEPARTMENT
    Local Contact Person:
    National phone number:
    Local number:
    Website:
    Other:

EMERGENCY MEDICAL SERVICES
    Local Contact Person:
    National phone number:
    Local number:
    Website:

Other:
PUBLIC WORKS
    Local Contact Person:
    National phone number:
    Local number:
    Website:
    Other:
EMOTIONAL AND MENTAL HEALTH SERVICES
    Local Contact Person:
    National phone number:
    Local number:
    Website:
    Other:
24 HOUR CRISIS HOT LINE
    Local Contact Person:
    National phone number:
    Local number:
    Website:
    Other:
VOLUNTEER SERVICES ASSISTANCE ORGANIZATIONS
Salvation Army
    Local Contact Person:
    National phone number:

Local number:
Website:
Other:
Critical Incident Stress Management Teams
    Local Contact Person:
    National phone number:
    Local number:
    Website:
    Other:
Spiritual Support Network
    Local Contact Person:
    National phone number:
    Local number:
    Website:
    Other:
D'Mort (Death support)
Search and Rescue
Dive Rescue
Ski Patrol
K-Nine Search and Rescue
HAM Radio Network
WHAT ELSE WILL YOUR COMPANY NEED?

Managing Before, During and after a Disaster

BEFORE

Acknowledge

Acknowledge that there is a probability that at some time there will be a disaster that has an effect and consequences for your company

Brainstorm

Make a list of all possible disasters that could ever, even in wildest imaginings, touch your company directly or indirectly

Buy-on

Establish hierarchical buy-on for your company. If you company refuses to acknowledge the probability that there will be a disaster that has an effect and consequences for your company, dust off your resume and look elsewhere. Denial is not good business.

Plan

Create a list of partnerships, interventions, resources, policies, procedures, ideas, concepts, supplies, and contingencies for even the wildest imagined disaster

Narrow

Narrow down your full list to the top ten possibilities

Training

Get training for anyone who might be involved in any disaster, from the line staff to the authority players in key positions. Training can consist of a small pamphlet to significant formal education opportunities

Partners

Pre-plan partnerships with local, state, and federal responder agencies and private disaster industry professionals. Write memos of understandings, pay for retainer fees, and publish a list for everyone on your staff. You never know if you will be there to make the calls.

Normalize

Make disasters a normal discussion in meetings, and planning sessions as you would any other part of company business. Disasters are a "normal" part of life and need addressing in a coherent and open manner in the same spirit you would discuss the furniture in the office.

Learn

Although everyone is doing fine, this is an excellent time to seek more management training.

DURING

Self Care

It is always appropriate to take care of yourself first

Survive

Do what is appropriate to survive a disaster

Expect

Expect emotions of all forms, from immobilized screaming to hysterically funny giggling fits.

Remember

Recall the stages of grieving: Denial, Bargaining, Anger, Depression, Acceptance. Add to this blaming, resistance, minimizing, aggrandizing and emotional response and reaction surprises that you haven't anticipated.

Remind

Remind yourself and others that all disasters have a beginning, a middle and an end. Beginnings are easy, and ends are a relief. Middles are crazy makers and seem to last forever…but they do not!

Learn

Although this is a difficult time for everyone, it can be an excellent time to seek more management training.

Review

Review the BEFORE guidelines and repeat what is necessary to stay on track.

AFTER

Manage

Remember that the disaster cannot be controlled, but you can manage through it. Face the changes and work through the transitions between the activity of the disaster and the end of the disaster when changes have been completed.

Expect

Don't be surprised. Encourage yourself and others to not ne surprised. There is no "going back" before the disaster, there is only moving forward "after" the disaster. Help people move forward.

Involve

Involve people in managing themselves and others. In disasters there is a tendency for people to either help others or become looters. Involve people in helping, even if it is a fabricated task like "we need someone to empty the wastebaskets." Busy people become more focused and feel more security. The rubric is that in an abnormal situation, it is helpful to do something that seems normal. Washing dishes, sweeping, dusting, organizing a phone tree, serving water, and other such banal and mundane tasks may keep people from sliding into an emotional abyss of helplessness. An employee who has "power and control" over the wastebaskets may feel less overwhelmed by the power of the disaster and may return to competent functioning more quickly.

Listen

Listen. Don't argue, discredit, disagree, or deny people their own perception of reality. People will adjust and recover in their own way at their own speed.

Okay

Human emotions are okay. Don't avoid or discourage emotions from your employees. If you feel uncomfortable with emotions find someone who isn't and gently direct people that direction. Do not block the healthy process of emotional recovery or it may come back on you.

Pay Attention

After a disaster the rhythm of work has fits and starts as it readjusts to its new flow. Try to move with it without resistance. See or feel it as a choreography with new dance steps. Two steps forward, one step back. One step forward, two steps to the side and two steps forward. Take your time. You will "feel" your new footing soon. Don't be afraid to ask questions or check your footwork from time to time. You don't want to step on toes, but you also don't want to miss a beat. Everything will be uncertain which will then be followed by what seems like rigid certainty… which will then again decay into chaos as it moves back into a more resolved new form. Take your time. Take your time. The disaster is over now, you have time to figure it all out.

Insist

Insist on being in the loop for information sharing. If you are out of the loop your anxiety will increase and so will your employees' anxiety. It is better to say, "I don't know, but I'll find out as soon as I can," than to say, "I have no clue" and leave people in the dark with no sense of leadership.

Communicate
Share information, listen, wait, exchange ideas, avoid rumors, seek facts, present facts, offer patience, peace, procedures and protocol.

Support
Support your people. Know they can handle information better than innuendo. People can handle ambiguity if they are in the loop. Waiting is very hard for most people under duress, so make a formal "what should we do while we are waiting" process. Put things in writing when you can. A quick-fix bulletin board for memos or messages is very supportive for groups of people. Expect people to be distracted. It might help to have a television in the office for a few days. Let people watch it while they are working. Put it in the center of the work site and not the employee lounge. Don't make employees pretend nothing happened. That will make you look crazy. Expect random outbreaks of group talking when incidents change. Check up on people to find out if they are in the loop or feel like they are.

Open up
Acknowledge stress, yours and theirs. It's okay to say you are stressed even when you are in a management position. It gives you more credibility and makes you more accessible. This doesn't mean a crying jag with your staff necessarily, although tears do not destroy leadership potential. Don't hesitate to ask for help. Quick check-ins with employees, without getting deeply involved in their emotions is very helpful. It is called defusing and takes the edge off the emotions as a brief respite and release. Find a place where you can defuse also. It should not be with another employee that you are managing.

Debriefings
Create opportunities to debrief your employees. You can train your people to do it, find volunteers, hire professionals or consultants who have been specially trained in mental health disaster practices.

Avoid
Do everything you can to stay away from group blame-frenzy behavior.

Continue
Continue to communicate and move forward, check in with people to see if they are moving forward, or if they are beginning to lose ground and need a different kind of intervention.

Persist
Persist in assisting people who may need ongoing management support. During normal situations people need leadership. Before, during and well after a disaster people need to keep their focus through the well balanced position of leaders. Workers who may have lost capacity to work due to loss of technology or services that existed before the incident will need specific leadership to stay connected to the job.

Learn
Although this is a difficult time for everyone, it can be an excellent time to gain more training.

Review
Review the BEFORE and DURING guidelines and repeat what might be useful or necessary to stay on track. There may be another disaster in your future.

Lessons Learned
In the absolutely most intensely positive manner you can muster after all of this, review every step, BEFORE, DURING AND AFTER, with an eye of successes and areas that need improvement.

Celebrate
Celebrate your survival!

Memorialize
Plan ahead for the one year anniversary or remembrance moment of the event. Create an annual commemoration for your office. Delegate the task if necessary to someone who would benefit emotionally from the process of creating tribute.

Phases of Disaster Planning to Consider

PLANNING PHASE *(prior to a disaster incident)*
- Define qualifications necessary for Emotional Continuity Management team membership and leadership
- Select and interview applicants
- Provide training and continuing education
- Provide regular training and practice drills
- Plan task assignments, authority lines, and delegations of responsibility
- Create a disaster buddy system

- Chain of command structure should be provided to all employees
- Contractual relationships with external disaster services providers

IMPLEMENTATION PHASE (during a disaster incident)
- Provide a central location for communications for your team and outside teams
- Do a disaster buddy check-in
- Initiate pre-planned task assignments, authority lines, and delegations of responsibility
- Coordinate responses
- Coordinate lines of supply, equipment, and information
- Assess needs with an ongoing process of open communications
- Provide a clerical manager for support
- Provide other support services such as communications, logistics, supply
- Orient team to the specific event
- Define event status and review plan
- Profile the participants of the event
- Collect resources, make network connections, implement memos of understanding,
- Create a blueprint of actions for immediate response and build in plan for long term
- Make task assignments
- Continue training as needed with regular updates and support
- Review short term response
- Begin discussions of intermediate and long-term responses
- Continue status updates, consultations, liaisons, MOU's, and provider partnerships
- Provide expert consultations and trainings
- Support staff and manage self-care
- Defuse as needed
- Document activities

RECOVERY PHASE (after an incident)
- Debrief participants and team members
- Continue self-care
- Maintain liaisons and links with other network connections
- Ongoing training should continue
- Discussions on lessons learned
- Wrap up details
- Paper work completion, filings, recordings
- Support process over the long term no matter how long it takes
- Send thank you letters
- Support and encourage buddy sets and support and reorganize around any buddy losses
- Provide memorials and commemoration programs
- Acknowledge and give appropriate recognitions
- Return to phase one and begin new phase of recruitment for planning for next disaster

Increasing Competency of Your Own Emotional Continuity Management

With every incident ask:
- What can I learn from this?
- Why would I need to continue to hang on to hurt feelings?
- What fear does this expose for me? Why am I vulnerable?
- What sacred issues of mine are at risk or being threatened?
- Can I think of ways to let this go?
- Did I take this issue personally?
- Was it really about me?
- Can I use my spiritual practice and move on?
- Could I let this incident simply pass?
- Would I let incident simply pass?
- When will I allow this incident to simply pass?
- Can I give myself permission for the feelings I had?
- Is this temporary or permanent?

- Did I make a positive or negative contribution?

AUTHOR'S AFTERTHOUGHTS

Preparation is just good thinking. The interruption of business to practice physical evacuations or emotional debriefing appears to be an annoyance until you actually need these skills in reality. Drills with first responders, the American Red Cross, and with Critical Incident Stress Management teams have taken my valuable time. I have whined about volunteering my time to "practice." Then an incident happens and I can't say enough about the value of drills. I practiced. Now it makes sense. Now it is rational and not a waste of my time. I get it.

Whenever I return from a disaster I am humbled by how grateful I am that someone went ahead of me and tipped me about what it would look like. The faces and names, the debris and the details may be slightly different but the general texture is the same. And what is always the same is that people are having emotions. I have drilled and rehearsed my Emotional Continuity Management practices and am not surprised when a human emotion is presented to me. I know what to do. And if it is beyond me I know who to call. I am not bullet-proof so I anticipate that I might have some emotions. Sometimes I do. Sometimes I do not. But no matter what, my mission is to be helpful and not add to the disaster. I have my feelings. They matter mostly to me. Ignoring my emotions is neither healthy nor useful. Extensive research on Post Traumatic Stress Disorder backs me up on this.

My colleagues who specialize in IT (Information Technology) Disaster Planning and Business Continuity Management have taught me well. My physical well-being is my hardware. My emotions are my software, and I participate willingly in drills to protect them both.

DISCUSSION QUESTIONS

- What drills are practiced on a regular basis at your company? Does your organization drill for all contingencies, even the most unpredictable?

- How would you suggest a company include drilling for emotional reactions during a drill?

- Do you think drills should be voluntary or mandatory? Why?

14

READINESS:
TOOLS FOR MANAGING DIVERSITY
IN A GLOBAL MARKETPLACE

WHY YOU SHOULD READ THIS CHAPTER

Under duress, people begin to express their deeper selves, hidden selves, and emotional selves. These differences can be honored and managed well or can contribute to more chaos including warfare at the office. Human beings feel comfortable when thinking is organized into familiar categories and feel uncomfortable when those categories fail to hold together. When people are uncomfortable they begin to have emotions and struggle to recreate the categories to recreate a sense of safety and cohesion. This is normal. Safety feels better than danger and differences feel dangerous. Knowing about differences makes people feel safer. Safer people are more productive.

BY THE END OF CHAPTER 14 YOU SHOULD BE ABLE TO

• Conduct a group discussion on the topic of global diversity and how it influences your business

• Do an inventory of your own strengths and weaknesses in managing differences

• Implement a diversity training that includes emotional diversity

WHAT THE EXPERTS SAY ABOUT EMOTIONAL CONTINUITY MANAGEMENT TOOLS

"Among the lessons learned in the aftermath of the Hotel New World disaster (March, 1986), in which psychological and psychiatric intervention was provided for such an event for the first time in Singapore was the recognition of the need for a psychological support plan for such an incident." — F.Y. Long, Clinical Psychologist.

HOW TO BEGIN THINKING ABOUT DIVERSITY AND GLOBAL EMOTIONS

To work in a global marketplace you must first know your own position before you can support emotions of your employees as they interface with international issues, people, products, goods and services. Emotions about global markets, international competition, outsourcing, goods and products, and hiring from outside home nation can turn into large spins quickly if not well managed. Many employees are at ease with other people from other ethnic, racial or global origins. Some employees are ill at ease. Some others are hostile and angry for a variety of reasons. As a manager you first start with your own position and determine your relationship with the global economy. These are simply questions and consideration to begin thinking about how you feel and how others may feel about global marketplace issues. The debate over outsourcing is one place this comes into play. The world is getting smaller and angrier lately, so it is essential to think these questions through:

- Consider your connections to global industries and marketplaces, people and products
- Do you encourage discussions about cross cultural similarities and differences in your industry. Does your company open dialogues?
- How do differences serve your industry?
- Explore diversity from a larger perspective than your own opinion.
- Take workshops, attend symposia or lectures on world affairs
- Read as much as you can about other nations
- Read the newspaper from your country and other international press
- Do you think accepting other points of view and opinions means you agree?
- Could you learn another language, or at least some basic courtesy phrases
- Would you participate in a community activity that celebrates ethnic or cultural values
- Track world events with an atlas, globe, or wall map of the Earth
- Invite someone from another global perspective to have a job-share day with peers
- Consider if your company includes or excludes any part of the global community
- Evaluate if your company serves or harms any other part of the global market
- Start a book club, discussion group, or think-tank that considers international issues

Checklist

- What actual revenues and profits come from international markets?
- Does growth depend on global markets?
- Do hiring practices expect to include global citizens?
- Are vendors, suppliers, clients or producers come from outside your nation?
- Do you have international competition?
- Is your company owned by national or international interests?
- Are any of your services outsourced internationally?
- How do your employees feel about global issues?
- What percentage of your employees are not citizens of your country?
- Are there free trade agreements or international contracts associated with your company or your industry?
- What are current emotional trends about your international partners, are they friendly or antagonistic?
- Does any of your technology require international connections, training or service?
- Does your company require security? Are security requirements or procedures any different for international participants in your industry or company?
- Has your entire staff been trained in international diversity issues?

HOW TO DO A QUICK-CHECK OF DIVERSITY KNOWLEDGE

When working in international markets if you are trying to make a sale, organize a project or save a contract, you may need to do some research first. Some nations have strong emotional responses to even small errors in etiquette and severe reactions to behaviors that shatter sacred laws or cultural taboos. Answer and discuss the following diversity questions:

- Does every culture nod their heads to acknowledge yes?
- Are gifts from your company automatically seen as valuable internationally?
- Is it always appropriate to use a first name in an introduction?
- Do all individuals shake hands in formal greetings?
- Do you know if red is a safe color or does it mean something?
- Will being late for a meeting have different consequences in different cultures?
- Are there foods that are cross-cultural?
- Is it appropriate to eat during a business meeting in all cultures?
- Are there activities that are offensive to some cultures and celebrated by others?
- Do all cultures have the same financial philosophy?
- Do all cultures share your work ethic?
- Which cultures would avoid working with female employees?
- Does your company recognize the emotional impact of religious practice?
- Does music, art, dance or theater hold the same meaning in all cultures?
- When are shoes required in a meeting? Hats and head coverings?
- Is it always appropriate to wear jewelry or religious symbols?
- What international markets would be damaged by loss of face?
- Do you know the consequences of inappropriate behavior with each of your global partners or competitors?
- Do all nations carry the same credentialing processes? Academic standards?
- Do you know international laws? Should you?

Personal Diversity Inventory

- Where were you born?
- When were you born?
- Did this influence who you are today?
- Where are your parents from? Grandparents? Spouse/Partner?
- How many siblings in your family and what birth order are you? (oldest, youngest, middle, third of seven)
- What adults had a major influence in your life and why?
- What were your traditions and holiday celebrations?
- What makes you unique or comes from your unique upbringing?
- What has been your most positive memorable encounter with someone from another culture/race?
- What has been your most negative memorable encounter with someone from another culture/race?
- Describe a time you have experienced prejudice, discrimination, or a feeling like you didn't "belong."
- What are your hobbies, activities, or personal interests?
- What is there about you that no one could tell by looking at you?
- Have you ever traveled or lived outside your own nation?
- How does that experience influence your thinking?
- If you have never traveled outside your own nation, how do you think that would influence your thinking?
- Do you think diversity is a significant issue in the workplace?
- How do you think diversity issues directly or indirectly influence you in the workplace?

The Hawkins-Mitchell "Potato Theory" for Brief Diversity Trainings

Step One
- Give everyone a blank 3 x 5 card
- Have the word POTATO on a piece of paper or 3x5 card
- Show the word POTATO to the participants
- Instruct them to look at the word silently

Step Two
- Instruct participants to write down the first thought, single word or image that they had when they saw the word
- Collect the cards

Step Three
- Congratulate participants for completing all the basics necessary for an introductory training on diversity.
- Display the cards. Did everyone have the same image?

Step Four
- Now for the advanced course. Contemplate the following question:
    After seeing the simple, uncomplicated, 6 letter word, POTATO, and considering what image entered into your perceptual field first. what is your "Core Truth" about POTATO?
- Some people imagine a baker with sour cream and chives
- Some people visualize fries with ketchup
- Some people see chips with clam dip
- Some see mashed with gravy
- Some see dirty brown lumps out of the garden or farm
- Some see tater tots
- Some see zebras
- Other see scalloped
- Still others see rice
- Some will see Idaho
- Others think yams or sweet potato pie
- Someone might not even know what a potato is
- Others are concerned with the correct spelling of the word
- Someone is analyzing potato futures on wall street
- Some see death, because of an allergy to potatoes
- Another sees poverty because that's what they lived on as children
- Some see the potatoes flying across the room when their marriage broke up and there was that violent night when their spouse was drunk and he/she threw the dinner against the wall and there were mashed potatoes all over the wall when the police came
- Some see lunch
- Others see dinner
- Others see breakfast home fries
- Others see chicken food because chickens eat anything
- And others refuse to participate in this exercise

Step Five
- Now, try to convince the person sitting next to you that YOUR Reality Picture is the absolute, sacred, 100% right-on true CORRECT MENTAL PICTURE OF the universal truth for the word POTATO.
- Now convince them that their truth is in error.

Step Six
- Be grateful that there is NO MANDATING THE HUMAN MIND or the entire world might be filled up with millions and millions and millions of You. And that could mean no French fries. Unless that's what you thought about and then there would be nothing else. Nothing. And only an Emotional Terrorist demands that the world reflect their reality alone.

Short of brainwashing, there is very little control over the mental translation of even a simple word like POTATO. How much more complex are other ideas, words, concepts, and dynamic considerations in our vast human experience? We all want people to hear and understand us. This is human nature. But there is a significant difference in hoping for understanding and trying to control or manipulate other people away from their own thinking. Everyone's personal thoughts are sacred.

Therefore, if you care to work successfully with any other human being, you must understand that they hold sacred truths. If you wish to know what is sacred to them, to honor them, first know what is sacred to you. Everyone has the right to their own sacred truths unless they cause harm to others. If your sacred truth kills mine, then we have a war. You don't have to agree with others to honor their sense of what is sacred to them. It's okay that you find it quite odd, weird, bad or wrong that a coworker thought about zebras when you were thinking of mashed potatoes. But so what? This is not tricky. It is simple. We honor diversity because the universe is diverse. And why would someone make it tricky unless they had another agenda?

Note that Emotional Terrorism is *not* a diversity issue. Diversity is about honor, and Emotional Terrorists do not honor the sacred of others. Some Emotional Terrorists will use diversity as a disguise to hide behind. They will claim "entitlement" because they are different or misunderstood. They will become activists in order to further their agenda of controlling yet another group. After some rather simple scrutiny you may find that Emotional Terrorists are not seeking honor for all but exclusivity and control of their agenda. With further scrutiny it will become clear that they in fact want to persuade you to eliminate someone or something that does not match their preferences. Managers must not let the importance of diversity become exploited by an Emotional Terrorist.

AUTHOR'S AFTERTHOUGHTS

Sad is sad. Happy is happy. Fear is fear. And anger is anger. Psychology may appear complicated, but human feelings are rather simple. Most people want to feel happy, safe, and comfortable and they are willing to do a lot to feel that.

Because of my rather interesting life, philosophically and theologically I have come to my own conclusions about the nature of human life on planet earth. My personal experiences working at Ground Zero did challenge and change some personal and professional ideas I had previously assumed were "true." What didn't change was a belief that it is the similarities in human existence that bind us and not our differences. Differences are important and add color and texture to our lives but during crisis, physical or emotional, differences should become secondary to survival.

DISCUSSION QUESTIONS

- What are your personal rules about diversity? Do they differ from the agenda of your industry?

- What people, places, and things are so different from you that you would avoid them if you could?

- How is diversity a relevant issue in terms of your company's bottom-line?

- In what ways is diversity a component of Emotional Continuity Management?

SECTION IV
READINESS:
Rubble, Rehearsal And Resources

I hear stories. When I tell people I'm an Emotional Continuity Management consultant they say something like, "Our business survived the tornadoes but a year later we were still shaken up." Or, "If we only would have had a plan and a drill that we could have rehearsed a few times, we might not have been taken by surprise when there was a mass layoff."

When we were children we had fire drills at school. Some of us had earthquake drills, tsunami, volcano, tornado, and even duck-and-cover-nuclear-attack drills. The bell would ring and out we'd go to our assigned waiting spot. Children do that today. Bomb threats and violence at school has created an increased need for emergency drills.

Most businesses have a little laminated card by the exit with arrows and circles and squares defining the evacuation route in case of a fire. But how do you drill for a Greedy CEO who is sabotaging the company? How do you find your evacuation route away from the lady in the cubicle next to yours who is obviously out of control?

As long as we live on Planet Earth some sort of disaster is right around the corner. It is a fact of life. The news media make disasters look like a surprise! Disaster is normal fare for living. One should expect disaster every day. This doesn't mean you should live in your basement. It does mean that it is intelligent to know where your basement is on the outside chance that you may need to fun to it quickly. To think disasters are out of the norm is denial at best and insanity at worst.

Thinking, planning, preparing and drilling for disasters is not paranoia. Thinking, planning, preparing and drilling for disasters is intelligent. People who feel prepared are happier. They can relax and forget about disaster because they know what to do if one pops up. They can get on with life. Employees who feel prepared are happier. They can relax and forget about disaster because they know what to do if one pops up. They can get on with work.

It is a fact that people who have within their minds the concepts of what might happen during a disaster are statistically less likely to suffer the long-term effects of the disaster. People who avoid the topic are at greater risk for long-term emotional consequences as a result of a disaster.

When hit with a 6.9 earthquake one early morning, there was no time to think about what to do. And I was in no mood to sort out my choices at that moment. I did what I had been practicing and drilling. I followed up with emotional self-care. I had been drilling that also. When in my first (hopefully last) tornado, I was deeply grateful for the people who had drilled for tornadoes because I didn't have a clue what to do... I was in denial and laughed, thinking it was a joke. They were moving quietly and quickly to the basement as I stood like a deer in headlights.

I have rehearsed being neutral during a conflict. If an angry and raging employee verbally attacks me, I don't have time to think about what to do. Their feelings are immediate and I need to have an Emotional Continuity Management skill ready to go.

I have rehearsed really listening to people. If a grieving and weary employee verbally risks sharing with me their tender story, I don't have time to think about what to do. Their need is immediate and I need to have an Emotional Continuity Management skill ready to go.

I have rehearsed and drilled debriefing employees. If something needs ventilation I am ready. I use the tools I teach. They serve me and they serve others well. And I want you to have them all, the ones I offer and anything else you can get to make your life easier!

15

REDUCTIONS, RUINS, AND RUBBLE: WHEN ARE THE SPINS FROM DISASTERS THE ULTIMATE SPIN?

- *Hundreds of tiny earthquakes reported at Mt. St. Helens (KCBD,com, Lubbock Texas; ABCNews.com. 9/28/04.*

- *Swarms of quakes in Mount St. Helens crater (Seattlepi.com, 9/28/04)*

- *"The senior flight attendants hadn't had a substantial raise since the 1970's, and it was very important to get a good contract for them and others. We did come to a tentative agreement in June of 2001. It was overwhelmingly ratified on September 12, 2001. On September 10, I flew down to Dallas for a meeting with American Airlines to discuss the implementation schedule for the contract…. we were on the phone when the second plane struck…. All I know is that for two whole years I was obsessed with the contract and suddenly it seemed so unimportant. It was twenty-four hours before the ballot count, and nothing seemed to matter anymore." Laura Glading, Union Representative, Association of Professional Flight Attendants (Fink, 2002)*

- *"The mayor of Union Point, Georgia apparently committed suicide Thursday morning, hours before a grand jury was to hear fraud charges against him that could have sent him to prison for life." (Associated Press, May 14, 2004)*

WHY YOU SHOULD READ THIS CHAPTER

- On September 26, 2004 the northwest of the United States began to read current and disturbing news about Mt. St. Helens rumbling, 20 years after she had blown.

- Elevation of Mount St. Helens before it erupted [20 years ago]: 9,677 feet; after: 8,363 feet; volume of resulting landslide, the largest in history: 3.3 billion cubic yards.

- Velocity of the volcanic blast: 200 to 335 mph; blast-zone area: 230 square miles; timber blown down: 4 billion board feet, enough to build 300,000 two-bedroom houses. Volume of ash carried eastward by wind: more than 540 million tons; area over which it fell: 22,000 square miles; time needed for ash to circle the Earth: 15 days.

- Number of historically active volcanoes (those once active that could become active again) in the United States: 53; where they are found: Alaska (43), Hawaii (5), Washington (2), California (2), Oregon (1).

- Number of historically active volcanoes in the world: 539; share found on the Pacific Ocean plat''s turbulent rim, dubbed the "Ring of Fire:" 66 percent; countries with more volcanoes than the United States: Indonesia (76) and Japan (63).

- Deadliest eruption ever: Tambora (Indonesia, in 1815); deaths: 92,000, including 82,000 from starvation in the aftermath. *(Mt. St. Helens website)*

Disasters are catastrophes and calamities. They are tragedies that render a victim or victims either temporarily or permanently unable to manage regular activities. Disasters leave people in their wake feeling unsettled and powerless. A disaster can come and go in a few seconds in a tornado, or chronically sap life away from its victims in a decade-long drought. A disaster can be felt through the loss of a family breadwinner or a beloved child. A work disaster can be the result of a natural disaster. It can also result from the consequences of a job loss, ruined reputation, business bankruptcy, community alienation, public scandal, death of co-worker, violent incident, criminal incident, or terrorism attack. Disasters can be a destructive force of nature or the consequences of individual tyrannical agendas directed from one human being to another human being or specific group. Disasters can be random or predicted by professional forecasters. The one thing that is predictable is that disasters happen daily, and rarely when you are expecting them.

BY THE END OF CHAPTER 15 YOU SHOULD BE ABLE TO

- Understand the different types of disasters and the management steps to take before, during and after a disaster strikes

- Create a presentation showing the direct and indirect costs of disaster to a business in your industry or in your region. If you have historical references for your industry or region make certain you include fiscal data.

- Design and implement a training program, paper, presentation, or pamphlet for employees that explains what to expect emotionally during and after a disaster

- Establish liaisons, partnerships, and memos of understanding for services between your company and experienced disaster management specialists

OVERVIEW

A disaster is a complicated event affecting numerous connections, intersections, links, and systems of people, places, things and ideas. Disasters produce changes in human emotions that are both predictable and unpredictable. The regular ways of relating do not work during or immediately following a disaster. Normal cues are missing, images are distorted, and normal emotions and thoughts are temporarily incongruent. Mental health professionals who have been specially trained in disaster management know the unique needs of people in these distorted experiences.

Managers need to have at least a basic understanding of disaster exercises, tools, practices, procedures, and resources because they may be the only people available that the staff trusts. If your staff does not trust you before a disaster, a disaster will not increase their sense of safety. If the manager is clueless and unprepared for a disaster, or has no concept about the effects of disaster on human emotions, chaos can increase and escalate the emotional consequences.

After a catastrophic event, it is often the quiet, centered, and calm voice during the event that a victim remembers. A calm voice of compassion that is resonating with reason and security is the loudest guiding force when madness is swirling noisily about, chaos is ripping apart the fabric of the known, and cacophony is jumbling up signals and signs that have before this moment made sense. Imagine for a moment the stairwells in the World Trace Center building during the earliest morning evacuations. People unsure of the situation quietly and quickly followed well-practiced procedures guided by managers reminding them of the drills they have done before. Now imagine a firefighter calling a child out from under his hiding place in a burning home. As the firefighter manages strong inner emotional content, the child hears a voice of authority, calm, and direction. Managing during a disaster is not about controlling the disaster; it is about managing the emotions of the moment. Disasters have a beginning, middle, and an end. Each stage is managed a bit differently. In addition, there is a pre-disaster phase where the real planning is formulated and rehearsed.

CHANGES OCCURRING WITH DISASTER

During a disaster, changes in divisions of work, power, authority and perceptions are appropriate expectations.

Power

Power creates change in people during regular interactions and dramatically during disasters. In terms of control, influence, capacities or strengths during a disaster it is the disaster that holds the power. Normally powerful people can be brought to their knees and usually powerless people can rise to superhuman abilities. The hierarchy power structures of any organization may be made impotent by the superceding power of a disaster.

Case Example

The family came in for counseling — two parents and five children. Four of the children had genetically determined terminal illnesses. The parents were distraught and disoriented, and apparently had been for a long time. After a few minutes into the session, the counselor realized she was talking, but no one was listening or hearing. She scanned the family. The one child who had not been diagnosed with the illness was seven years old and paying very close attention to the counselor. The therapist realized that the seven year old had all the power in the family. She leaned over and quietly asked the child, "Am I mistaken, or are you the power in this group?" The child, with open wide eyes astonishingly responded, "Well, somebody has to be in charge!"

Work

Work stops during a disaster unless you work in the disaster industry. Expecting anyone to continue normal activities is at the least unreasonable and at the worst unethical, inhuman, and perhaps even insane. Expect and support a reasonable period of time between the end of the incident and the return of any level of normalcy. The specific details of the disaster should define those expectations.

Case Example

The team showed up to work after the bombing. They were terrified and distraught, but did not want to appear as if they were abandoning the company. They also wanted to help or keep doing something normal. The manager engaged the Emotional Continuity Management plan and instructed the team that work would be a slow-down force until further notice. Team members knew their emergency assignments and some people knew they could go home and still be "on the team" for the duration. The team set up a television in the center of what was left of the office space, someone got food, another employee set up chairs around the TV, and emergency buddies checked in with each other. Not much work was done for the first three days, but everyone felt emotionally connected.

Authority

Professionals who work in the disaster industry recognize the need for clearly understood lines of command during a disaster. Incident command is set up to provide incident management or authority procedures in charge of the on-scene process of a disaster. They initiate response, assess the situations, and manage resources. This command operation becomes the icon, flag or base of operations that keeps workers on track in the chaos. In your company, you may need to either be the incident manager during a disaster or delegate one. You also need to create a procedure in the event that you are not available. One of the most difficult discussions after any disaster can be dealing with a manager who was injured, absent, on vacation, or not present for any reason during a disaster where they had authority.

Case Example

The city official had not been re-elected when the disaster hit. He suited up, showed up, and became the emotional focus point for the survivors. He passed the torch to the next duly elected official as soon as the incident began to wind down.

Perceptions

There is an understanding among mental health disaster workers that any victim, emergency responder or mental health disaster worker (including themselves) that they meet during or after a disaster will be in an "altered state of consciousness." The degree of that alteration of thinking is the variable. It is never a question of "if" there is an altered state — only "how altered is it" will be the relevant issue. This means that brains that are processing information in a distorted manner because of the influence of the incident do not operate like brains not under duress.

Victims and responders are "under the influence" of the disaster and need to be managed like anyone under the influence of a powerful drug. The brain release significant amounts of brain chemicals directly into the brain-blood barrier, the body releases fight-or-flight hormones, blood moves away from the extremities (hands and feet and brain) toward the center of the body (belly) and digestion stops. People under this influence can do some very odd, silly, heroic, bizarre, unexpected and dangerous things. The word "shock" is a term that most people understand, but it is inadequate to define the long terms effects of disaster influence. Post-Traumatic Stress Disorder (PTSD) is a good example of the long-term effects. A mother running into a fire to save her child and coming out cradling a sofa pillow in her arms and singing to it as if it is her child because she truly "sees" it as her child is not an unusual, albeit tragic, example of an altered state of consciousness designed by disaster.

Case Example

October 10, 2001. The mother was sitting with the trauma counselor. Her son was in the World Trade Center when it collapsed. Weeks had passed. She was calmly explaining to the counselor that she knew her son was still alive and sitting in the basement of the building with one of his work buddies. She explained a well-constructed belief that the friends had found each other during the collapse, had run down to the pizza place in the basement of the buildings, and were under a table eating pizza and drinking bottled water. This distressed but confident mother was surrounded by her family that had already come to believe that both the son and the friend were lost. Compassionately patient with this mother, they did not challenge her altered state and quietly waited with her. She repeated her story to anyone who would listen. She in fact, sought out new audiences as often as she could find anyone to listen. Her story became her lifeline ritual.

Learning Byte

The counselor knew not to challenge the story and had instructed the family not to disturb her belief system, informing them gently that it would resolve into reality in its own time. The counselor did not agree with the mother, nor did she disagree. She remained powerfully neutral and listened. This allowed the mother to modify her story a little bit each time she told it. By the end of the week, the mother was open to the beginning images of her son's death. She was starting to accept the possibility that her son was gone and her brain began to accept the capacity to integrate the enormity of this horrifying information. Her first movement toward this was when the mother reached out and took the hand of the therapist, looked the counselor in the eye and said, "It's been a long time down there, I don't think the pizza would still be any good, do you?" The counselor held her hand and said gently, "I don't know, if it was New York Pizza, it might be good no matter what? What do you think?" The mother began to cry.

DO THIS: Honor the enduring power and ongoing dynamic of disasters.

DON'T: Hurry the process.

Declaring a Disaster

When a public disaster happens, although the victims may quickly decide it is a disaster for them, there are strict local, state, and federal guidelines they must be met for an official declaration. These declarations are the templates that control funding, provide emergency relief services, offer public assistance, initiate debris clearance, repair and demolitions, deliver replacements, create emergency housing, grant loans or grants, provide counseling, launch search and rescue teams, arrange for transportation, introduce mass care and feeding, begin mutual aid, start any necessary changes to laws or regulations, provide any tax relief, management or provision of restoration costs, and give immediate and long term financial support or relief. See www.disastercenter.com and www.fema.gov if you would like to read some of the language of Executive Orders and laws concerning official declarations of disaster. The thumbnail sketch of authority is:

- Local disasters are declared by the governing body of a city when conditions are beyond the control of the services, personnel and equipment of the local government.
- State of Emergency is the declaration made at the state level by the governor when conditions of extreme peril to the safety of persons and property exists.
- Major disaster is declared at the federal level by the president when resources of local, state and private relief organizations will not suffice.

Resources

Before, during and after a disaster there are many agencies and trained professionals available to help a manager prepare their employees for crisis. Agencies can be local, county, state, or federal and include paid and volunteer staff. The agencies that are federally mandated to respond to disasters each have a specific turf or area of specialized response. Each of the following agencies, except the Red Cross, are federally funded. The American Red Cross receives no money from the government, although it has been congressionally mandated to respond to disaster. The Red Cross depends entirely on the donations of citizens and yet must respond to disaster.

Assistance Organizations

(This list is not exhaustive, and due to the current nature of the global environment may not be correct for the next 45 minutes. It is important to stay current with what assistance organizations are tasked with, what their turf is, what level of authority they have, who is the spokesperson nationally and locally, and how each organization may influence your company's recovery in the case of a disaster of any level or duration)
- Homeland Security (HS)
- Department of Justice (DOJ)
- Federal Emergency Management Agency (FEMA)
- Department of Energy (DOE)
- Environmental Protection Agency (EPA)
- Deapartment of Health and Human Services (DHHS)
- U.S. Department of Transportation
- Department of Defense (DOD)
- National Transporation Safety Board (NTSB)
- American Red Cross (Arc)
- Local Law Enforcement
- Fire Department
- Emergency Medical Services
- Public Works
- Volunteer Services and Organizations: Southern Baptist Church, Salvation Army, Critical Incident Stress Management (CISM) Teams, D'Mort (Death support), Search and Rescue, Dive Rescue, Ski Patrol, K-Nine Search and Rescue, HAM Radio, and more.

TYPES OF DISASTERS

Natural Disasters

Natural disasters come in many shapes and sizes and originate from a variety of sources that are essentially indigenous to the elements of life on planet Earth: fire, air, water, and earth with include such amazing disastrous effects as:

- Floods
- Hurricanes
- Tsunamis
- Tornadoes
- Earthquakes
- Thunderstorms
- Wildfires
- Volcanoes
- Winter Storms
- Drought
- Heat Waves

Some experts include biological and chemical disasters in this category due to the natural order of biology and chemistry of the earth. In that discussion, someone always says, "well then Man Made Disasters are natural also." Nevertheless, the purpose of this book is not about such distinctions, because no matter the cause or strata of a disaster, human beings will have an emotional response.

Case Example

What had just been a small brush fire was now a potential catastrophe. Heidi, a seasoned manager, was calm and did well with multi-tasking until she heard that the fire was headed toward her home. She had to decide whether to stay at work or go home to evacuate her house. She suddenly became immobilized and was unable to make simple decisions for herself or others.

Learning Byte

Do you have your roles defined? Do you have your own emergency plan for your family and pets? How would you manage your own personal concerns in the face of a natural disaster at your work site? How would you handle your work site responsibilities if your home or family were involved in a disaster?

DO THIS: Make your own emergency management plan for you and your family before you make one for your company.

DON'T: Wait.

Man-Made

Some catastrophic incidents, although real in consequence, are induced through the direct or indirect influence of people. There is an argument that suggests that since people are part of nature, there is no such thing as an unnatural disaster. Be that as it may in theory, many "man-made" disasters would be avoidable if people had not been involved. Terrorism is *absolutely* a man-made disaster.

Case Examples

- *March 28, 1979, Reactor 2 at the Three Mile Island nuclear power plant suffered a partial meltdown. Over 2,000 personal injury claims filed*
- *October 1983, Vehicle bombing of the U.S. marine and French Army barracks in Lebanon, kills 295*
- *December 1988. The bombing of Pan Am Flight 103 over Lockerbie, Scotland, kills 270*

- *February 1993. The vehicle bombing of the World Trade Center*
- *April 1995 bombing of the Alfred P. Murrah Federal Building, Oklahoma City, kills 168*
- *October 2000 bombing of the USS Cole, kills 17*
- *September 11, 2001, Terrorism in three sites kills thousands*
- *October-December 2001, Bioterrorism incidents with anthrax kills several*

Case Example

Toby worked in the hospitality industry and had significant professional accomplishments, was well regarded and saw an excellent future in the company. Toby lost several personal friends during the World Trade Center disaster on 9/11/01. He attended several memorials and funerals and struggled to support friends who were now widows and widowers. He grieved privately to not further disturb these friends. When Toby asked for time off to attend funerals the management gave him permission to go but reproached him for not "getting over it." After the third memorial, Toby was fired and was unable to find a new job for over a year. While dealing with the emotional losses, he also lost income. Unable to pay rent he lost a home. He applied for financial assistance from several sources that were publicly fundraising to support victims of 9/11 as well as state, federal and local agencies. Toby did not qualify because he was not related to any of the deceased. He had to relocate for work and thus lost even limited emotional support systems. He eventually found part-time commission work but was laid off within a couple of months due to downsizing and remains underemployed, with no benefits and no savings.

Case Example

Melinda, a health care delivery manager had a full career including responding to many traumatic events. This professional was well seasoned. The terrorist bombing was catastrophic, but Melinda was not directly influenced and offered up managerial services to assist in the emergency recovery work. During the initial recovery work, she had no personal difficulty, although appropriately touched by the scope of the event. The event turned "personal" when this employee caught sight of the small crumpled body of a deceased child. Melinda had purchased some novelty apparel for a grandchild earlier in the week. The deceased child was wearing the same novelty apparel. Melinda personally identified with the scene, lost capacity to function in the event, and left the worksite unannounced.

Case Example

Dear Dr. Hawkins Mitchell, I would be glad to tell you my thoughts about how I have seen managers in difficult and potentially disastrous situations. As you know, I'm in the military. We currently have about 2000 people in my unit including military and civilian workers. We haven't had a natural disaster, but we have been threatened by one several times. Most of the employees deal with the possible problem well, but some do react to even the mere threat of an event. These people panic easily and would not deal with a big problem very well. I call them the "sky-is-falling" people. Managing them is difficult. As a military installation we deal with some weather-related issues but we also deal with the man-made stuff, you know, possible terrorism. We are sort of on alert for that everyday. A lot of money and time have been invested in getting prepared for a possible event. Some employees feel that security is just a bother because "nothing ever really happens here." They're more worried about work slowdowns than the big picture that includes contingency planning and exercises.

Sometimes it is the people themselves that create temporary disaster. We have several threats of violence cases each year. In our unit if an employee is even slightly angry, they are sent home until a doctor says it is safe for them to return. Talk about work slowdown! Managing disasters is hard work on top of my regular workload! Respectfully, Sgt. Major Jones

Case Example

From the New York Times, February 20, 2004

An article by Sarah Kershaw reports a lack of safety exists at the Hanford nuclear cleanup site in Richland, Washington. For five decades, the nuclear industry has been the center of industry in the Tri-Cities area, Kennewick, Pasco and Richland. 11,000 workers face the cleanup tasks. The original 70-year cleanup deadline is now cut to 35 years. The fact that a cleanup project of this magnitude is dangerous is not a stretch of the imagination. Dr. Tim Takaro, a clinical assistant professor at the University of Washington who deals with Hanford workers on a regular basis, was quoted as saying it was dangerous. Not only is the community dealing with the danger, now it faces investigations and scrutiny of even more daunting proportions. Legal battles over health, past, present and future, are running rampant in a community of workers who are responsible for over 177 underground tanks that hold 53 million gallons of toxic radioactive wastes which, according to Kershaw contaminated 270 billion gallons of groundwater near the banks of the Columbia River. Apparently, Dr. Takaro is finding workers with illnesses and reports 45 incidents of 67 workers needing medical attention within approximately an 18-month period, suggesting the presence of toxic leaks. A Government Accountability Project, a nonprofit group pressing legal actions, reports: "Hanford is in the process of creating a new generation of sick and injured workers."

CORPORATE-MADE DISASTER

Layoffs

According to the Bureau of Labor Statistics, the definition of a Mass Layoff is a situation involving least 50 persons at the same establishment, each of whom has filed an initial claim for unemployment benefits during a consecutive five-week period. The Bureau of Labor Statistics reported 18,963 Mass Layoff Events in 2003.

Alan Downs wrote in the cover flap of his book *Corporate Executions* (1995) that "Layoffs are utterly destructive of everything they are mistakenly thought to fix. The twisted carnage of human dignity and squandered corporate assets left in the layoff wake must be brought into the light of public inquiry and debate." In 2004, the discussion must include the highly charged, politically rabid debates over the Outsourcing of America and Corporate Greed Scandals. These high drama events are matched daily by small disasters like the loss of a retirement fund, pension plan, health care plan, or early retirement program.

Outsourcing

Outsourcing is a concept that has evolved over the last few decades into something more complicated than just sending jobs elsewhere. Companies have always looked for cheaper labor and have found a willing marketplace in third world countries. But researchers (Forrester Research, 2004) have reported that over 79% of 700 people surveyed think it will eventually hurt the U.S. economy; more than 40% of 7,300 top executives thought the same; and, approximately 3.32 million jobs will be outsourced by 2015. Service professionals are feeling a backlash of losing jobs to workers overseas and then not finding a replacement job at home. These same researchers believe as many as 200,000 service jobs may be lost each year for the next decade. Some corporate thinkers see this as opportunity. Others see it as a disaster. Whatever the outcome of the debate, emotions are running high.

John Cook writes in the March 10, 2004 *Seattle Post-Intelligencer* that the word outsourcing " has evoked far-reaching emotions in the past year, prompting presidential candidates and labor groups to decry its practice and economists and chief executives to defend it as a natural progression of the economy." Albert Marcella, author of *Outsourcing, Downsizing, and Reengineering* (1995,2004) identifies eight categories of potential victims of outsourcing and downsizing:

- Senior executive management
- Line management and human resources staff
- Downsized or Outsourced Employees - the "Victims"
- Remaining Employees - the "Survivors"
- Spouse, significant other, life partner of the "Victims"
- Children of the "Victims"
- Local Communities
- Society at Large

Beyond the fiscal risks and political opinions surrounding the topic of outsourcing and downsizing, the soft risks of human feelings and emotions are plentiful. Human emotional capital risks rapidly translate to fiscal risks. Emotional Continuity Management planning means that the long-term emotional needs of human beings are factored into risk categories and approached with interventions that maintain the energy flow of the system.

Some Potential Emotional Risks of Outsourcing

• Loss of concentration	• Isolation
• Decreased resilience	• Passive-Aggression
• Elevated anxiety	• Discouragement
• Distraction	• Betrayal
• Altered moods	• Fear
• Passivity	• Despair
• Disorientation	• Disassociation
• Disempowerment	• Distrust
• Invalidation	• Failure
• Dejection	• Depression
• Aggression	

Case Example

Ed had been earning $72,300 a year. He was laid off because his job was outsourced overseas. He lost his retirement nest egg in the recent stock market crunches. He is collecting unemployment and trying to sell some of his collectibles online and in antique markets. He said, "I lost my job and it isn't coming back."

Learning Byte

Although there are fiscal benefits to using outsourcing to compete in trade markets there is a strong emotional backlash that is becoming a hot political topic as the export of local jobs, trained people, and skilled workers is seen as risk by some and opportunity by others. This probably depends upon where your job security stands. Fears about outsourcing may become more critical to risk than actual outsourcing.

DO THIS: Find out all you can about the pros and cons of outsourcing.

DON'T: Panic. Grieving tools will help you adjust to any changes that you may need to make.

Greed and Scandal

Is it true that taking a paper clip home from work is a crime? Where is the line between grabbing a paperclip to avoid stopping at the store on the way home, taking a box of paper clips because you are not being watched, taking a case of paperclips because you are entitled, and selling paperclips out the back door to the Paper Clip Black Market?

If greed is a desire to have more of something than is actually needed, managing the emotions of a corporate gluttony or self-indulgence means using some sort of a moral compass to define boundaries for desire based on entitlement. Desire is an emotion that is human and therefore manageable. Desire to the point of greed is dysfunctional and can be pathology.

A Review Of Corporate Scandal

(Compilation adapted from www.CitizenWorks.org)

1.   Adelphia Communications; John Rigas (quit) — Under investigations by the SEC and two federal grand juries for multibillion dollar, off-balance-sheet loans to its founders, the Rigas family. Former CEO Rigas, his son and former CFO Timothy Rigas were arrested for securities fraud. SEC, 2 federal grand juries and an internal investigation. Stock drop since 1/14/2000: -99.75%.

2.   AES; Dennis W. Bake — Use of secured equity-linked loans (SELL) that grossly inflated revenues and bolstered stock prices. These loans are not carried on the company expense sheets, since they are paid back by issuing stocks--further diluting value and ownership of company. Posted $445 million loss so far this year (2002).

3.   AOL Time Warner; Robert Pittman — Accused of erroneously inflating advertisement revenue to keep stock prices inflated assuring greater stock price through mega-merger with Time Warner. Stock down 59% in 2002.

4.   Arthur Andersen LLP; Joseph Berardino (quit) — Company found guilty of obstruction of justice; David B Duncan, former partner, accused of ordering the destruction of Enron-related papers, plead guilty to obstruction of justice. Obstructed justice in the Enron investigation. Other scandals include: WorldCom (3.9 billion in hidden expenses); Boston Market Trustee Corp (Agreed to pay $10.3 million to in suit claiming a façade of corporate solvency);. Baptist Foundation of Arizona ($217 million settlement); Department 66 ($11 million settlement); Sunbeam ($110 million settlement); 6. Colonial Reality ($90M settlement); Waste Management ($75 million settlement) DOJ investigation.

5.   Bristol Myers; Fred Schiff (resigned); Peter Dolan — Accused of purposefully inflating sales by offering incentives to wholesalers--including warnings that it planned to raise prices--in order to meet last year's revenue expectations. SEC investigation. Posted lowest stock price since 1996

6.   Cendant; Henry Silverman — paid $2.83 billion to shareholders after internal audits revealed CUC Intl. (which merged with HFS to form Cendant) inflated income by $500M through fraud and accounting errors.

7.   Citigroup; Sanford I. Weill — Congressional investigators testified that CitiGroup helped Enron Corp and others set up "sham" transactions to alter their finances. These transactions included loans that allowed Enron to hide nearly $4 billion of debt. Stock down 48%.

8.   CMS Energy; William T. McCormick Jr., CEO (resigned); Rodger Kershner, general counsel and senior vice-president (resigned) — Disclosed it overstated revenue by nearly $4.4 billion in 2000 and 2001 by using artificial "round trip" energy trades. Number of lost jobs: 50; stock drop since 1/14/2000: -56.78%

9.   Computer Associates; Charles Wang — Agreed to a $638,000 penalty in April to settle charges with the Justice Department that it violated pre-merger rules after announcing it would acquire Platinum Technology Inc. SEC investigation. Stock drop since 1/14/2000: -73.58%

10.   Cornell Companies Inc.; Steven W. Logan (removed) — Pending Class action suit claims Cornell and its officials of making misleading statements on behalf of shareholders. Arthur Andersen questions "unusual $3.7 million retainer" to Lehman Bros Holdings Inc. Stock down over 50%

11.   Duke Energy; R. Priory — Investigations into "round trip" energy trades with other energy producers to inflate volumes and revenues. These falsified trades added $1B to revenues over three years.   SEC, the Commodity Futures Trading Commission and CA state regulators and attorney general class action lawsuits. $8,831,475 in total compensations.

12.   Dynegy; Chuck Watson (ousted) — Tried to merge with Enron; target of several federal probes into alleged sham trades aimed at artificially pumping up revenue and volume. Dynegy's longtime chief executive, Chuck Watson, resigned in May, and it has announced a major restructuring. SEC, the Commodity Futures Trading Commission and California state regulators and attorney general. Stock drop since 1/14/2000: -64.97%.

13. El Paso; William Wise — Identified 125 "round trip" trades used to bolster revenues and market share. SEC, CFTC, Houston US Attorney's office lawsuits.

14. Enron; Ken Lay (left company) — Once the nation's largest energy trader, collapsed into the largest-ever U.S. bankruptcy on Dec. 2 amid an investigation surrounding off-the-book partnerships that were allegedly used to hide debt and inflate profits. SEC and DOJ investigations; team of attorneys representing investors and employees in civil lawsuits. Stock drop since 1/14/2000: -99.80% layoffs: 6,100.

15. General Electric Corporation — Jack Welch (retired); Jeffrey Immelt: (1) GE Capital is a primary financial backer to WorldCom, providing a financial crutch to the corporation that would go on to file the largest bankruptcy claim in the history of the US; (2) Largest corporation to lack an independent board; (3) 77% of GE's 401k's was invested in company stock as of 2001; (4) GE paid its independent auditor three times as much for non-audit fees in 2000, Congressional inquiry into the lending practices of JP Morgan and Citigroup, both of which were partners with GE in lending to WorldCom. The stock down 38% on the year.

16. Global Crossing; Leo Hindery, Gary Winnick — faces probes by the SEC and the FBI regarding its accounting practice and for allegedly engaging in network capacity swaps with other telecommunications firms to inflate revenue; CEO acknowledges that Global Crossing's actions "may in some fashion [have] misled the market." SEC, DOJ; pending; over 60 investor fraud lawsuits in total. Stock drop since 1/14/2000: -99.87%.

17. HPL Technologies, Inc.; David Lepejian (former CEO, founder) — Facing charges that corrupt accounting practices inflated stock prices following IPO, allowing executives to sell 85,500 shares at inflated prices. Also facing charges of violating Security Exchange Act of 1934. Company expects to restate profits for 2001 and 2002. Class action lawsuit pending. Company stock halted on NASDAQ since 7/26/2002 following 72% drop.

18. ImClone Systems Inc.; Samuel Waksal (arrested) — Charged with insider trading, under investigation by a congressional committee to determine if it correctly informed investors that the U.S. Food and Drug Administration had declined to accept for review its experimental cancer drug; Samuel Waksal, former chief executive of ImClone, was arrested June 12 on insider trading charges. DOJ, Congressional litigation. Pending. Company stock drop since 1/14/2000: -52.34%

19. JP Morgan Chase & Co.; William B. Harrison — Congressional investigators testified that JP Morgan Chase helped Enron Corp and others set up "sham" transactions to alter their finances. These transactions included loans that allowed Enron to hide nearly $4B of debt. Senate committee on government affairs.

20. Kmart; Charles Conaway — SEC investigating accounting and other practices. The company investigated whether it improperly accounted for vendor allowances and has since changed its practices. SEC, and internal investigations. Company stock drop since 1/14/2000: -91.02%.

21. KPMG; Michael J. Donahue — SEC alleges accounting missteps by KPMG that allowed Xerox to post knowingly erroneous profits/earnings SEC investigations.

22. Lucent Technologies; Henry Schact — Adjusted 2000 revenues by $679 million, spurring SEC investigation. Also investigating whether vendor financing played an improper role in sales. Company stock drop since 1/14/2000: -93.39%

23. Merrill Lynch & Co.; David H. Komansky — Agreed to $100 million settlement with New York State Attorney General regarding charges it tailored stock research to win investment banking business. Suspended two employees including Martha Stewart's broker after an internal probe relating to sale of ImClone shares.

24. MicroStrategy; Michael J. Saylor — Settled without admitting wrongdoing an SEC suit accusing it of backdating sales contracts to meet quarterly financial estimates and other improper revenue recognition practices. Company stock drop since 1/14/2000: -99.07%

25. Network Associates; George Samenuk — Investigations regarding whether it hid expenses and overstated revenue from 1998 to 2000. Company stock drop since 1/14/2000: -28.25%

26. Pricewaterhouse Coopers; Sam DiPiazza — Accounting scandals include: (1) Phar-Mor: overestimation of profits; (2) Gazprom: suits over false and misleading statements; (3) Pinnacle Holdings: accounting violations; (4) Avon Products: accounting violations; (5) PwC Securities: independence standards. SEC investigations: settled three investigations involving Pinnacle Holdings, Avon and PwC Securities with SEC with $5 million fine.

27. Qwest Communications; Joseph P. Nacchio (quit) — Under investigations to determine if it inflated revenue for 2000 and 2001 through capacity swaps and equipment sales SEC investigations.

Department of Justice, FBI, Denver US Attorney's office Company stock drop since 1/14/2000: -88.35%

28. Reliant Energy; R. Steve Letbetter — Admitted it inflated revenue by counting artificial "round trip" energy trades. Under SEC investigation for accounting matters and energy trades relating to restatement of profits. Number of lost jobs: 50.

29. Rite Aid; Robert G. Miller — Indicted for fraud after it inflated profits by $1.6 billion from 1997-1999. Scandal missed by auditor KPMG which resigns as auditor for company.

30. Sunbeam; Al Dunlap (ousted) — SEC files accounting fraud suit against 4 executives. Executive Albert J. Dunlap settles for $15 million. Auditor Arthur Anderson settles shareholder suit for $110 million.

31. Tyco International. Ltd.; L. Dennis Kozlowski (quit and indicted on 11 felony counts) — Under investigation into whether executives used corporate cash to buy art and a home. Tyco's former chairman, Dennis Kozlowski, resigned June 3, a day before being indicted for evading about $1 million in sales taxes from art purchases. Accused of improperly creating "cookie jar" reserves that were supposed to cover merger costs but instead were drawn on to boost profits; and improperly "spring loaded" earnings from acquisitions by accelerating their pre-merger outlays. SEC, Manhattan District Attorney's office and company's internal investigation. Pricewaterhouse Coopers: collected $37.9 million in consulting fees in 2001 Company stock drop since 1/14/2000: -55.15% layoffs: 11,000.

32. Vivendi Universal; John-Marie Messier (forced to quit) — May incur $1.1 billion charge as the result of off-balance-sheet accounting. Attempted to add $1.5 billion in net profit in deal relating to sale of British Sky Broadcasting Group PLC (MSNBC 7/02/2002). Moody's relegated Vivendi's credit rating to "junk bond status" (New York Times 7/02/2002)

33. Waste Management; Maurice Myers — Overstated income from 1992-1996 by more than $1 billion; Anderson pays $7 million fine to SEC for issuing false and misleading reports as well as part of $229 million shareholder settlement.

34. WorldCom Inc.; Bernard Ebbers (quit; under fire for borrowing $408M from WorldCom to cover margin calls), John Sidgmore — Hid $3.85 billion in expenses, allowing it to post net income of $1.38 billion in 2001, instead of a loss. Charged with fraud by SEC. New York State pension fund files $300 million suit. New York State Comptroller filed a motion in Federal District Court saying New York State pension fund lost more than $300 million because of fall in stock price; House Financial Services Committee subpoena four executives to testify, and all take the fifth. Number of lost jobs: 17,000; stock drop since 1/14/2000: -96.90%

35. Xerox; / Rick Thoman — Xerox said June 28 it would restate five years of results to reclassify more than $6 billion in revenues. In April, the company settled charges that it used "accounting tricks" to defraud investors. Allaire also sold $16 million in stock before earnings were recalculated and shares fell nearly 80% (New York Times 4/7/2002). Number of lost jobs:1,500; stock drop since 1/14/2000: -67.53%.

Other Disaster Data: Costs and Frequency

There are many other kinds of disasters. There are technological disasters, biological disasters, communicable disease disasters, chemical disasters, financial disasters, weapons-of-mass-destruction disasters, sociological disasters, and some would say there are symbolic and political disasters. What all kinds of disasters have in common is that they are expensive and they are frequent.

All disasters are costly financially. A single-family home fire can cost millions to a family living in a low-income housing project dwelling. A chemical spill can deplete city emergency responder funds. A technology disaster can level a company. A corporate scam can leave thousands of people without their nest egg. An emotional disaster is usually attached to every disaster. The emotional costs, not those defined by mental health and counseling fees, can leave an individual, family, or company unable to recoup losses. A disaster crosses all boundaries of mental, physical, emotional and spiritual safety causing serious loss, destruction, hardship, unhappiness, and sometimes death. The following collection of data is only a sampling of statistics from recent incidents. There are a number of web sites that offer daily updates and yearly archival information. For example, The Disaster Center web site,

www.disastercenter.com, offers extensive data on disasters and disaster management. It is worth your time to open the site just to review the collection regarding:
- The 100 most expensive natural disasters of the 20th century
- The 100 most deadly natural disasters of the 20th century
- The 100 most expensive technological disasters of the 20th century
- The 100 most deadly technological disasters of the 20th century.

The following compilations are small samplings of disaster costs and frequencies.

(The following statistics were released by the National Oceanic and Atmospheric Administration (NOAA) in April 2004; http://www.ncdc.noaa.gov/oa/reports/billionz.html)

COSTS

--- 2003 ----
- Southern California Wildfires, Late October to early November, 2003. Dry weather, high winds, and resulting wildfires in Southern California. More than 743,000 acres of brush and timber burned, over 3700 homes destroyed; at least $2.5 billion damage/costs; 22 deaths.
- Hurricane Isabel, September, 2003. Category 2 hurricane makes landfall in eastern North Carolina, causing considerable storm surge damage along the coasts of NC, VA, and MD, with wind damage and some flooding due to 4-12 inch rains in NC, VA, MD, DE, WV, NJ, NY, and PA; estimate of over $4 billion in damages/costs; at least 47 deaths.
- Severe Storms and Tornadoes, Early May, 2003. Numerous tornadoes over the Midwest, MS valley, OH/TN valleys and portions of the southeast, with a modern record one-week total of approximately 400 tornadoes reported; over $ 3.1 billion in damages/costs; 41 deaths.
- Storms and Hail, Early April, 2003. Severe storms and large hail over the southern plains and lower MS valley, with Texas hardest hit, and much of the monetary losses due to hail; over $1.6 billion in damages/costs: no deaths reported.

---- 2002 ----
- Widespread Drought, Spring through early Fall, 2002. Moderate to Extreme drought over large portions of 30 states, including the western states, the Great Plains, and much of the eastern U.S.; estimate of over $10.0 billion in damages/costs; no deaths.
- Western Fire Season, Spring through Fall, 2002. Major fires over 11 western states from the Rockies to the west coast, due to drought and periodic high winds, with over 7.1 million acres burned; over $2.0 billion in damages/costs; 21 deaths.

---- 2001 ----
- Tropical Storm Allison, June, 2001. The persistent remnants of Tropical Storm Allison produces rainfall amounts of 30-40 inches in portions of coastal Texas and Louisiana, causing severe flooding especially in the Houston area, then moves slowly northeastward; fatalities and significant damage reported in TX, LA, MS, FL, VA, and PA; estimate of approximately $5.1 billion in damage/costs; at least 43 deaths.
- Midwest and Ohio Valley Hail and Tornadoes, April, 2001. Storms, tornadoes, and hail in the states of TX, OK, KS, NE, IA, MO, IL, IN, WI, MI, OH, KY, WV, and PA, over a 6-day period; over $1.9 billion in damage/costs, with the most significant losses due to hail; at least 3 deaths.

---- 2000 ----
- Drought/Heat Wave, Spring-Summer, 2000. Severe drought and persistent heat over south-central and southeastern states causing significant losses to agriculture and related industries; estimate of $4.2 billion in damage/costs; estimated 140 deaths nationwide.
- Western Fire Season, Spring-Summer, 2000. Severe fire season in western states due to drought and frequent winds, with nearly 7 million acres burned; estimate of $2.1 billion in damage/costs (includes fire suppression); no deaths reported.

FREQUENCY

DISASTERS 2004 JANUARY 1– SEPTEMBER 20

Source: http://www.fema.gov/news/disasters.fema?year=2004

Major Disaster Declarations

•	09/20	West Virginia	Landslide, Severe Storm, Flooding
•	09/19	Pennsylvania	Tropical Depression
•	09/19	Ohio	Severe Storm, Flooding
•	09/19	Pennsylvania	Flooding, Severe Storm, Tropical Depression
•	09/18	Georgia	Hurricane
•	09/18	North Carolina	Hurricane
•	09/17	Puerto Rico	Landslide, Tropical Storm
•	09/16	Florida	Hurricane
•	09/15	Mississippi	Hurricane
•	09/15	Alabama	Hurricane
•	09/15	Louisiana	Hurricane
•	09/15	South Carolina	Tropical Storm
•	09/10	North Carolina	Tropical Storm
•	09/04	Florida	Hurricane
•	09/03	Virginia	Severe Storm, Tornado, Tropical Storm, Flooding
•	09/01	South Carolina	Hurricane
•	09/01	Indiana	Severe Storm, Tornado, Flooding
•	08/26	N. Mariana Islands	High Surf, High Winds, Typhoon, Flooding
•	08/26	Nevada	Fire
•	08/13	Florida	Tropical Storm, Hurricane
•	08/06	Pennsylvania	Severe Storm, Flooding
•	08/06	Kentucky	Severe Storm, Flooding
•	08/06	West Virginia	Landslide, Severe Storm, Flooding
•	08/03	Kansas	Severe Storm, Tornado, Flooding
•	08/03	New York	Severe Storm, Flooding
•	07/29	Guam	High Winds, Tropical Storm, Flooding
•	07/29	N. Mariana Islands	Flooding, High Surf, High Winds
•	07/20	South Dakota	Flooding, Severe Storm
•	07/16	New Jersey	Severe Storm, Flooding
•	06/30	California	Flooding
•	06/30	Arkansas	Flooding, Severe Storm
•	06/30	Michigan	Severe Storm, Tornado, Flooding
•	06/18	Wisconsin	Flooding, Severe Storm
•	06/15	Virginia	Flooding, Severe Storm, Tornado
•	06/11	Missouri	Flooding, Severe Storm, Tornado
•	06/10	Kentucky	Landslide, Severe Storm, Tornado, Flooding
•	06/07	West Virginia	Landslide, Severe Storm, Flooding
•	06/08	Louisiana	Severe Storm, Flooding
•	06/03	Indiana	Flooding, Severe Storm, Tornado
•	06/03	Ohio	Severe Storm, Flooding
•	05/25	Iowa	Severe Storm, Tornado, Flooding
•	05/25	Nebraska	Severe Storm, Tornado, Flooding
•	05/07	Arkansas	Landslide, Severe Storm, Flooding
•	05/05	North Dakota	Ground Saturation, Severe Storm, Flooding
•	04/29	New Mexico	Severe Storm, Flooding
•	04/23	Illinois	Tornado, Severe Storm
•	04/21	Massachusetts	Flooding
•	04/10	Federated States of Micronesia	Typhoon
•	02/19	Oregon	Winter Storm, Severe Storm
•	02/13	South Carolina	Ice Storm

•	02/05	Maine	Severe Storm, Flooding
•	01/26	Ohio	Landslide, Severe Storm, Flood
•	01/13	American Samoa	Heavy Rain, Surf, Cyclone
•	01/13	California	Earthquake

Emergency Declarations

•	04/02	North Dakota	Snow Storm
•	03/03	New York	Snow Storm
•	01/26	Maine	Snow Storm
•	01/15	New Hampshire	Snow Storm
•	01/15	Connecticut	Snow Storm
•	01/15	Massachusetts	Snow Storm
•	01/15	Maine	Snow Storm

Fire Management Assistance Declarations

•	09/14	Hawaii	Kawaihae Road Fire
•	09/13	California	Old Highway Fire
•	09/04	California	Geysers Fire
•	09/03	California	Pattison Fire
•	09/02	California	Bear Fire
•	09/01	Alaska	Taylor Complex Fire
•	08/26	Nevada	Andrew Fire
•	08/20	Oregon	Bland Mountain #2 Fire
•	08/14	California	French Fire
•	08/14	California	Lake Fire
•	08/12	Washington	Mud Lake Fire
•	08/11	Washington	Fischer Fire
•	08/11	California	Bear Fire
•	08/11	California	Oregon Fire
•	08/10	Alaska	Bolgen Creek Fire
•	08/08	California	Stevens Fire
•	08/07	California	Calaveras Fire Complex
•	08/04	Oregon	Redwood Highway Fire
•	07/30	Washington	Elk Heights Fire
•	07/30	Washington	Deep Harbor Fire
•	07/26	Nevada	Robbers Fire
•	07/21	California	Crown Fire
•	07/18	California	Melton Fire
•	07/18	California	Foothill Fire
•	07/14	Nevada	Waterfall Fire
•	07/14	California	Pine Fire
•	07/14	California	Mataguay Fire
•	07/14	California	Hollow Fire
•	07/14	California	Lakeview Fire
•	07/06	Washington	Beebe Fire
•	07/03	Colorado	McGruder Fire
•	07/01	Alaska	Boundary Fire
•	06/30	Nevada	Verdi Fire Complex
•	06/28	Arizona	Willow Fire
•	06/18	New Mexico	Bernardo Fire
•	06/16	Utah	Brookside Fire
•	06/09	Arizona	Three Forks Fire
•	06/05	California	Gaviota Fire
•	05/25	New Mexico	Peppin Fire
•	05/04	California	Eagle Fire
•	05/04	California	Cerritos Fire
•	04/01	Colorado	Picnic Rock

DISASTERS 2003
Major Disaster Declarations

- 12/19 Federated States of
  Micronesia   Typhoon
- 12/09 US Virgin Islands   Flooding
- 12/09 Virginia   Flooding, Severe Storm
- 11/21 Puerto Rico   Landslide, Severe Storm, Flooding
- 11/21 West Virginia   Landslide, Severe Storm, Flooding
- 11/07 Washington   Severe Storm, Flooding
- 10/27 California   Wildfire
- 09/26 Pennsylvania   Severe Storm, Tropical Storm, Flooding
- 09/23 West Virginia   Hurricane
- 09/23 Delaware   Tropical Storm
- 09/20 Delaware   Hurricane
- 09/20 District of Columbia   Hurricane
- 09/19 Maryland   Severe Storm, Hurricane
- 09/18 Virginia   Hurricane
- 09/18 North Carolina   Hurricane
- 09/12 New Hampshire   Severe Storm, Flooding
- 09/12 Vermont   Severe Storm, Flooding
- 09/05 Indiana   Severe Storm, Tornado, Flooding
- 08/29 New York   Severe Storm, Tornado, Flooding
- 08/23 Pennsylvania   Flooding, Severe Storm, Tornado
- 08/01 Ohio   Flooding, High Winds, Tornado
- 08/01 North Dakota   High Winds, Severe Storm
- 07/29 Tennessee   Heavy Rain, High Winds, Severe Storm
- 07/29 Florida   Severe Storm, Flooding
- 07/21 Nebraska   Tornado, Severe Storm
- 07/17 Texas   Hurricane
- 07/15 Ohio   Flooding, Severe Storm
- 07/14 Arizona   Wildfire
- 07/11 Indiana   Severe Storm, Tornado, Flooding
- 07/02 Kentucky   Flooding, Landslide, Tornado
- 06/21 West Virginia   Landslide, Severe Storm, Flooding
- 06/06 American Samoa   Flooding, Landslide
- 06/06 Arkansas   Severe Storm, Thunderstorms, Tornado
- 06/03 Kentucky   Landslide, Severe Storm, Tornado
- 05/23 Mississippi   Severe Storm, Tornado
- 05/15 Illinois   Severe Storm, Tornado, Thunderstorms
- 05/14 Maine   Winter Storm
- 05/12 New York   Winter Storm
- 05/12 Alabama   Severe Storm, Thunderstorms, Tornado,
- 05/10 Oklahoma   Tornado, Thunderstorms
- 05/08 Tennessee   Flooding, Severe Storm, Tornado
- 05/06 Missouri   Thunderstorms, Tornado, Flooding
- 05/06 Kansas   Thunderstorms, Flooding, Tornado
- 04/26 Alaska   Winter Storm
- 04/25 Florida   Tornado
- 04/24 Mississippi   Tornado, Flooding, Thunderstorms
- 03/27 Virginia   Winter Storm, Flooding, Landslide
- 03/27 North Carolina   Ice Storm
- 03/20 Tennessee   Winter Storm, Flooding
- 03/14 West Virginia   Winter Storm
- 03/14 Kentucky   Winter Storm
- 03/14 Ohio   Winter Storm
- 02/04 Oklahoma   Ice Storm
- 01/08 South Carolina   Ice Storm

- 01/06 Arkansas · Ice Storm
- 01/06 Federated States of
  Micronesia · Typhoon

Emergency Declarations

- 09/23 Michigan · Power Outage
- 09/23 New Jersey · Power Outage
- 09/23 Ohio · Power Outage
- 08/23 New York · Power Outage
- 04/09 Colorado · Winter Storm
- 03/27 New York · Winter Storm
- 03/20 Delaware · Winter Storm
- 03/27 Rhode Island · Snow Storm
- 03/20 New Jersey · Winter Storm
- 03/14 Pennsylvania · Winter Storm
- 03/14 Maryland · Winter Storm
- 03/14 District of Columbia · Winter Storm
- 03/11 New Hampshire · Winter Storm
- 03/11 Connecticut · Winter Storm
- 03/11 Massachusetts · Winter Storm
- 03/11 Maine · Winter Storm
- 02/26 New York · Winter Storm
- 02/01 Louisiana · Loss of the Space Shuttle Columbia
- 02/01 Texas · Loss of the Space Shuttle Columbia

Fire Management Assistance Declarations

- 11/20 South Dakota · Mill Road Fire
- 11/12 Colorado · Buckhorn Creek Fire
- 10/29 Colorado · Overland Fire
- 10/29 Colorado · Cherokee Ranch Fire
- 10/28 California · Whitmore Fire
- 10/26 California · Simi Fire
- 10/26 California · Cedar Fire
- 10/26 California · Paradise Fire
- 10/26 California · Mountain Fire
- 10/25 California · Verdale Fire
- 10/25 California · Old Fire
- 10/23 California · Grand Prix Fire
- 10/21 California · Pass Fire
- 09/06 Oregon · Cove Road Fire
- 09/06 Washington · Needle Fire
- 09/06 California · Bridge Fire
- 09/02 Oregon · Herman Creek Fire
- 08/21 Montana · Flathead Fire Zone
- 08/20 Colorado · Lincoln Complex Fire
- 08/20 Oregon · Booth Fire
- 08/19 California · Locust Fire
- 08/13 Montana · Cherry Creek Fire
- 08/13 Montana · Missoula/Mineral Fire Zone
- 08/11 Montana · Hobble Fire
- 07/25 California · Canyon Fire
- 07/25 Colorado · Cloudy Pass Fire
- 07/25 Montana · Robert Fire
- 07/25 Montana · Wedge Canyon Fire
- 07/23 Montana · Missouri Breaks Complex Fire
- 07/22 Oklahoma · Big Rock Fire
- 07/16 Washington · Okanogan City Fire
- 07/15 Nevada · Robb Fire
- 07/15 Utah · Causey Fire

•	07/14	Arizona	Kinishba Fire
•	07/12	Washington	Middle Fork Fire
•	07/11	Nevada	Red Rock Fire
•	07/03	California	Railroad Fire
•	06/29	California	Tejon Fire
•	06/28	California	Sawmill Fire
•	06/25	New Mexico	Atrisco Fire (Formerly Bosque Fire)
•	06/21	Arizona	Ash Fire
•	06/18	Arizona	Aspen Fire
•	06/17	Nevada	Highway-50 Fire (Formerly Spooner Fire)
•	05/18	Hawaii	Waikoloa Village Fire
•	05/10	New Mexico	Walker Fire
•	01/07	California	Pacific Fire

Learning Byte

It is never a question of "if" there will be an incident, only "when."

Case Example

The new manager was directed by her boss to write an emergency contingency plan that would take care of the staff. She was given a budget to hire a consultant. The consultant asked if she had written into the plan directions for sheltering in place. The manager didn't think it was necessary and didn't want to make waves.

Learning Byte

The physical location of the company was within five miles of a nuclear plant, within thirty miles of a chemical weapons storage facility, on an earthquake fault and in an area that has severe weather and a recent history of wildfires. The manager could not imagine a situation that would necessitate her staff being in the building overnight... much less for three or four days. The consultant asked the manager what kind of "emotional waves" would there be if the need arose and no one had been trained or prepared for the possibility. What do you think? Every company should have a shelter in place plan to manage such real incidents as a winter storm, chemical accident in the area, terrorist event, or any other surprise and unexpected reasons for a company shelter-in-place lockdown.

EMOTIONAL CONTINUITY MANAGEMENT BEFORE, DURING AND AFTER A DISASTER

Now that you know there is a disaster brewing somewhere all the time, everywhere, you will know that every day you are either pre-disaster, current-disaster, or after-disaster. That will make your job easier. Many companies gamble that they will have a long, long time before (if) they have a disaster. It is a much more rational policy to assume that you will have a disaster tomorrow and anything you do today will help you survive it. Emotional Continuity Management is not about being paranoid, but it is about being emotional alert that disasters happen. The statistical majority of people that wear seatbelts is higher than those who need them during an accident. Risk-takers gamble. Unfortunately, that gamble influences others if you do not manage the seat belts of your charges, your children. Managers need to make certain their employees have on their disaster seatbelts as they move forward. Good parents protect themselves and their children. Good managers protect themselves and their colleagues before something happens.

BEFORE

Acknowledge — Acknowledge that there is a probability that at some time there will be a disaster that has an effect and consequences for your company.

Brainstorm — Make a list of all possible disasters that could ever, even in wildest imaginings, touch your company directly or indirectly.

Buy-on — Establish hierarch buy-on for your company. If you company refuses to acknowledge the probability that there will be a disaster that has an effect and consequences for your company, dust off your resume and look elsewhere. Denial is not good business.

Plan — Create a list of partnerships, interventions, resources, policies, procedures, ideas, concepts, supplies, and contingencies for even the wildest imagined disaster.

Narrow — Narrow down your full list to the top ten possibilities.

Training — Get training for anyone who might be involved in any disaster, from the line staff to the authority players in key positions. Training can consist of a small pamphlet to significant formal education opportunities.

Partners — Pre-plan partnerships with local, state, and federal responder agencies and private disaster industry professionals. Write memos of understandings, pay for retainer fees, and publish a list for everyone on your staff. You never know if you will be there to make the calls.

Normalize — Make disasters a normal discussion in meetings, and planning sessions as you would any other part of company business. Disasters are a "normal" part of life and need addressing in a coherent and open manner in the same spirit you would discuss the furniture in the office.

Learn — Although everyone is doing fine, this is an excellent time to seek more management training.

DURING

Self Care — It is always appropriate to take care of yourself first.

Survive — Do what is appropriate to survive a disaster.

Expect — Expect emotions of all forms, from immobilized screaming to hysterically funny giggling fits.

Remember — Recall the stages of grieving: Denial, Bargaining, Anger, Depression, Acceptance. Add to this blaming, resistance, minimizing, aggrandizing and emotional response and reaction surprises that you have not anticipated.

Remind — Remind yourself and others that all disasters have a beginning, a middle and an end. Beginnings are easy, and ends are a relief. Middles are crazy makers and seem to last forever... but they do not!

Learn — Although this is a difficult time for everyone, it can be an excellent time to seek more management training.

Review — Review the BEFORE guidelines and repeat what is necessary to stay on track.

AFTER

Manage — Remember that the disaster cannot be controlled, but you can manage through it. Face the changes and work through the transitions between the activity of the disaster and the end of the disaster when changes have been completed.

Expect — Don't be surprised. Encourage yourself and others to not be surprised. There is no "going back" before the disaster, there is only moving forward "after" the disaster. Help people move forward.

Involve — Involve people in managing themselves and others. In disasters there is a tendency for people to either help others or become looters. Involve people in helping, even if it is a fabricated task like "we need someone to empty the wastebaskets." Busy people become more focused and feel more security. The rubric is that in an abnormal situation, it is helpful to do something that seems normal. Washing dishes, sweeping, dusting, organizing a phone tree, serving water, and other such banal and mundane tasks may keep people from sliding into an emotional abyss of helplessness. An employee who has "power and control" over the wastebaskets may feel less overwhelmed by the power of the disaster and may return to competent functioning more quickly.

Listen — Listen. Don't argue, discredit, disagree, or deny people their own perception of reality. People will adjust and recover in their own way at their own speed.

Okay — Human emotions are okay. Don't avoid or discourage emotions from your employees. If you feel uncomfortable with emotions find someone who isn't and gently direct people that direction. Do not block the healthy process of emotional recovery or it may come back on you.

Pay Attention — After a disaster, the rhythm of work has fits and starts as it re-adjusts to its new flow. Try to move with it without resistance. See or feel it as a choreography with new dance steps. Two steps forward, one step back. One step forward, two steps to the side and two steps forward. Take your time. You will "feel" your new footing soon. Don't be afraid to ask questions or check your footwork from time to time. You don't want to step on toes, but you also don't want to miss a beat. Everything will be uncertain, which will then be followed by what seems like rigid certainty... which will then again decay into chaos as it moves back into a more resolved, new form. Take your time. Take your time. The disaster is over now, you have time to figure it all out.

Insist — Insist on being in the loop for information sharing. If you are out of the loop your anxiety will increase and so will your employees' anxiety. It is better to say, "I don't know, but I will find out as soon as I can," then to say, "I have no idea!" and leave people in the dark with no sense of leadership.

Communicate — Share information, listen, wait, exchange ideas, avoid rumors, seek facts, present facts, offer patience, peace, procedures and protocol.

Support — Support your people, knowing they can handle information better than innuendo. People can handle ambiguity if they are in the loop. Waiting is very hard for most people under duress, so make a formal "what-should-we-do-while-we-are-waiting" process. Put things in writing when you can. A quick-fix bulletin board for memos or messages is very supportive for groups of people. Expect people to be distracted. It might help to have a television in the office for a few days. Let people watch it while they are working. Put it in the center of the worksite and not the employees' lounge. Don't make employees pretend nothing happened. That will make you look crazy. Expect random outbreaks of group talking when incidents change. Check up on people to find out if they are in the loop or feel like they are.

Open up — Acknowledge stress, both yours and theirs. It is okay to say you are stressed even when you are in a management position. It gives you more credibility and makes you more accessible. This does not necessarily mean a crying jag with your staff, although tears do not destroy leadership potential. Don't hesitate to ask for help. Quick check-ins with employees, without getting deeply involved in their emotions, is very helpful. It is called defusing and takes the edge off the emotions as a brief respite and release. Find a place where you can defuse also. It should not be with another employee that you are managing.

Debriefings — Create opportunities to debrief your employees. You can train your people to do it, find volunteers, hire professionals or consultants who have been specially trained in mental health disaster practices.

Avoid — Do everything you can to stay away from group blame-frenzy behavior.

Continue — Continue to communicate and move forward, check in with people to see if they are moving forward, or if they are beginning to lose ground and need a different kind of intervention.

Persist — Persist in assisting people who may need ongoing management support. During normal situations people need leadership. Before, during and well after a disaster people need to keep their focus through the well-balanced position of leaders. Workers who may have lost capacity to work due to loss of technology or services that existed before the incident will need specific leadership to stay connected to the job.

Learn — Although this is a difficult time for everyone, it can be an excellent time to gain more training.

Review — Review the BEFORE and DURING guidelines and repeat what might be useful or necessary to stay on track. There may be another disaster in your future.

Lessons Learned — In the absolutely, most intensely positive manner you can muster after all of this, review every step, BEFORE, DURING AND AFTER, with an eye of successes and areas that need improvement.

Celebrate — Celebrate your survival!

Memorialize — Plan ahead for the one year anniversary or remembrance moment of the event. Create an annual commemoration for your office. Delegate the task if necessary to someone who would benefit emotionally from the process of creating tribute.

MANAGING DISASTER ANNIVERSARIES

Most adults remember vividly where we were when John F. Kennedy was shot. Children may have seen adults weep for the first time, or felt sickened by the television coverage or were confused as they sorted out how this would affect everyone and everything. A person did not need to be in Texas to feel the ripples of that day. Decades later, people still discuss where they were when JFK was shot.

For many adults and children, the tragedies of September 11, 2001 were their first connection to a historical event. People everywhere saw the television footage over and over. They saw the reactions of others. Emotions ran high and to the extreme. People wondered and waited to see what horror would be next. Psychological and Emotional Terrorism — one planned goal of the terrorists — spread as everyone wondered where the next target would be.

People closest to the terrorist actions suffered the most directly. A recent study found eleven percent of New York City children now suffer Post-Traumatic Stress Disorder, and fifteen percent suffer agoraphobia, a fear of public places, because of the attack. Even if you were not in New York City, Washington, D.C. or Pennsylvania on September 11, 2001, you were exposed to a trauma. Children and adults everywhere continue to have difficulties dealing with their emotional experiences. Anxiety symptoms and sleep difficulties are on the rise since September 11 (Mitchell, 2002).

When someone approaches the one-year anniversary of a disaster, noted trauma experts know that this is a difficult day for many adults and children. Tremendous media coverage can be expected in some cases. In other cases, the individual suffers in solitude over an extreme personal incident. Memory images replay again and again, and thoughts and feelings resurface. Some children regress behaviorally and academically around the anniversary of a trauma. Some adults do, also. Fears, worries, or nightmares may come back. Some adults and children will do well; others may have surprisingly strong reactions. David Mitchell, who created a series of writing journals for disaster anniversary management, writes, "As a Disaster Manager and counselor I have seen how ignoring or mishandling anniversaries can create more emotions than the original event. The National Institute of Mental Health and the University of Illinois Extension Disaster Resources agree when they say that children and adolescents, if given support, will recover almost completely from the fear and anxiety caused by a traumatic experience within a few weeks. However, some children and adolescents will need more help perhaps over a longer period of time in order to heal. Grief may take months to resolve, and may be reawakened by reminders such as media reports or the anniversary of the death. And some of the effects of long-term disruptions may not surface immediately; problems may not surface until weeks, months, or even a year following the disaster" (Mitchell, 2002).

Managers need to be actively involved in open acknowledgment of anniversary events and emotions. They can lead the team or create a team that will provide support, validation, space, and memorial events for everyone. If someone has had a personal loss or trauma on your team, ask how he or she wants to spend that day. If the team has had an incident, help them organize an appropriate tribute. It can be formal and elaborate, or it can be one minute of silence. That is up to you and your company needs. However, ignoring the moment can create an emotional backlash of anger and pain that combines with old memories and feelings of the original event that can become distorted into a full blown emotional spin. Certainly, the compassionate thing is to take the time to honor the moment. The fiscally responsible thing is to invest some down time for people's emotions that will allow employees to emotionally regroup and return to productivity.

AUTHOR'S AFTERTHOUGHTS

I was born in the middle of a 7.1 earthquake and so have always felt that I had some proprietary ownership of disaster in general. I managed in a variety of professional and personal roles during earthquakes, floods, range fires, tornadoes, typhoons, winter storms, and volcanic eruptions. I lived 35 miles away from Mt. St. Helens when she blew her top the first time. I live near a river that is wild and floods on a fairly regular basis. I live in the shadow of a nuclear site and a chemical weapons depot that are only a few miles from my front door. I experienced direct assault as an act of terrorism when I was in Asia in the 1971. A military guard set vicious guard dogs on me as we walked on a public beach. The soldiers were amused as the dogs bit through my boots. Later that same year I saw the aftermath of a plane that had been used as a weapon to fly into the home of a national leader. That one didn't ever make the news.

When my daughter died unexpectedly, followed within a couple of weeks by the sudden death of my mother, I was sure that I had more knowledge than many about surviving duress and disaster. I went back to work but how I managed those days was not the same as before. When I went to work as a trauma counselor directly following the attacks of September 11, 2001, I experienced more than anticipated. The dynamics and complications associated with disaster and terrorism were beyond even my amazing imagination. But I had my first trauma flashback as I recalled the horrifying day I was notified of my daughter's death, which was also on a September 11th.

I was a well-trained professional with depth experiences in trauma management, disaster, Critical Incident Stress Management, Red Cross Disaster Mental Health Services, Psychotraumatology, advanced degrees and lots of direct experience...and I got to feel more and learn more! My learning curve for disasters includes knowing without a shadow of a doubt the following truths:

- *Disasters are sacred, because they hold places for miracles*
- *Disasters are scary, because they are bigger than me*
- *You can never learn enough to know everything to be perfectly prepared*
- *You cannot really prepare for the unimaginable*
- *You cannot control disasters, but you can manage the aftermath*
- *Most Disasters are natural*
- *Unnatural disasters create the exact same emotions as natural disasters*
- *Disasters are only truly disastrous if you have no meaning in your life*
- *Disasters are completely unpredictable*
- *People are completely unpredictable*
- *Life is amazing and fun and divine and odd and scary and miraculous and messy and painful and silly and wonderful and short, and disasters are part of life*
- *I have a lot more to learn about disasters, and management, so stay tuned.*

DISCUSSION QUESTIONS

- What types of natural disasters are typical of your region of the earth?

- What types of man-made or other kinds of disaster could happen in your region of the earth?

- Have any of your employees experienced a disaster in the past? If so, what kinds, where and how did it affect them?

- What disaster management agencies are up and running in your location? Your city? State? Region? How can you make partnership agreements with them in advance of a disaster, natural or man made?

- How much has your company spent on IT disaster preparation? How much has your company spent on Human Emotions disaster preparation?

ACTIVITY

Answer the following questions for your company:

- What resources you have in your immediate vicinity? What can you have here in one hour, one day, three days, one week?

- During disaster, various agencies have clear guidelines. What might your company need in case of any sort of disaster from the various resources, including: federal, state, county, city, Red Cross, Voluntary agencies, hospitals, health care delivery professionals, suicide prevention, ambulance companies, vendors, funeral directors, coroners, poison control, veterinarians, humane associations, search and rescue, fire, ski patrol?

- What else might you need for your company? What is specific to your region's weather, the shape of your building, the composition of your employees, or geographic situation? Think it through now. Do you need to have supplies to shelter in place?

16

REHEARSAL:
WHY PLAN, EXERCISE, AND DRILL
FOR THE UNEXPECTED?

"Everyone thought we were crazy for drilling and preparing for terrorism." — Jerry Hauer, former Director of the NYC office of Emergency Management, testifying before the 9-11 Commission, May 19, 2004)

"There are many reasons why a manager should continually drill, test, conduct exercises and train for the unexpected. However, there are countless more reasons managers cite for NOT engaging in these activities. Unless management has a lock on predicting the future, the reality is hard to ignore. It is not if a disaster will happen but only when. The drilling, testing, and training for the unexpected prepares both individuals and organizations for the inevitable." — Albert Marcella, Ph.D., Business Automation Consultants

WHY YOU SHOULD READ THIS CHAPTER

Emergency responders practice and rehearse their tools, equipment, skills and emotions on a regular basis because they know that the next incident is just around the corner. It is their job description, passion and profession to be prepared. A few short years ago corporate thinking assumed, like the just about everyone else, that such preparation was the sole domain of emergency first responders and medical personnel. Unfortunately that bubble is burst and now we know better. Reading this chapter will get you ready to get ready for any Emotional Continuity Management crisis.

BY THE END OF CHAPTER 16 YOU SHOULD BE ABLE TO

- Design and implement a drill, exercise, or round-table discussion using the practice examples so you can be the most well prepared company in your industry.

- Based upon specific issues from within your own industry, create a set of potential risk scenarios, small and catastrophic, and plan three different approaches to minimize the risk to your company from emotional incidents.

- Choose the tools, interventions, resources, and responses your company would use in each example. Include the full range of human emotions from irritations and annoyances to catastrophic reactions of trauma and violence. Become a good consumer.

- Write an industry-specific document that uses technical and nontechnical intervention strategies that could be used as a management assessment documentation, including a variety of intervention strategies. Develop a presentation of drill costs vs. disaster costs.

- Telephone your local law enforcement or fire department and have them teach you about drills and how they manage emotions before, during and after an incident.

OVERVIEW

Emergency contingency experts contend that drilling and exercising for unexpected catastrophes is critical to speedy recovery. As any number of disaster managers can attest, there are times when infrastructure and technology survive or can be replaced, but if your employees are consumed by their emotions all the trendy technology in the world will not calm those emotions. Machinery cannot lead the recovery of the emotions of human beings. Only other human beings can do that.

Practicing emotional emergency drills is different from drilling for emergency technology or structure disruptions. It is difficult for most people to pretend to have feelings the first few times and can feel somewhat ridiculous. Students who have practiced the techniques of role modeling, drama students, and extroverts may enjoy filling the roles of emotion actors during your first practice drill. Red Cross volunteers would probably be more than happy to show you how to "play disaster." Although everyone will know this is artificially staged, employees and Emotional Continuity Management team members can begin to think through their responses and develop a repertoire. One of the intriguing parts about creating a drill which includes the emotional component is that once the veneer is gone and everyone is given collective permission to "play" you may be surprised at how real it feels, how introverts become extroverts, and how engaged your participants become in the process. You should have a mental health professional available in case someone becomes unexpectedly authentically distressed.

Case Example

The Emotional Continuity Management Trainer had prepared the company volunteers on what to expect in case of a real chemical weapons emergency. The drill was going along smoothly until there were two unexpected events. First, one of the volunteer victim actors had a real psychological panic attack and began screaming uncontrollably. Most of the volunteers assumed it was part of the act of participating in a lifelike emergency drill. When she did not stop in a few minutes the team realized that the drill had turned into a real event and followed their guidelines to assist the authentically distressed participant.

The second unexpected surprise was when a planned surprise turned into an emotional disturbance. Like other disaster drills the planners wanted to throw in a few surprises to see how people would respond. Unbeknownst to the participants in the exercise, the trainers had asked the coroner to send a team of deputies to practice death notification. When the deputies and the coroner arrived, and began asking for assistance from the participants to notify a family member about a "death," the company team slipped from practicing emotions to real emotions. Facing the coroner brought up a ripple of terror in the exercise that was unexpected. Because the scene of the drill had been so well staged, several participants began to question if this was a drill or a real event. One mental health professional became so visibly upset that she was relieved of her duty. Another volunteer stepped forward to address the issues, now uncertain if it was real or drill. The team continued to follow procedures although distressed and managed well by using previously practiced methods. The volunteer took a quiet leadership role and directed others to assist one another with their emotional concerns.

Learning Byte

Both these unexpected emotional events became the entire focus of the exercise. Although the drill involved over twelve responder agencies with various exercise agendas, it was the unexpected emotional events in each setting that became the focus. Post-drill debriefing exercises turned into real debriefings of emotions. Reality had imposed on the fantasy. Drills and exercises provided a back-up system to rehearse managing the emotions that incidents such as these may create.

DO THIS: Factor in the concept of Emotional Continuity Management (which include Post-Traumatic Stress Disorder training, Stress Management, Debriefing, and Defusing as well as normal and abnormal and mental health considerations) into your drills.

DON'T: Have drills in close proximity to a real event in your community; include people who have had recent trauma; or, involve children in the drills. Don't have a mock drill without a post-drill mock-debriefing by trained individuals.

DRILLS

Emergency responders drill their technical tasks and their emotional tasks. They learn teamwork techniques to support and enhance performance and emotional stability. The buddy system or check-in process keeps people on track emotionally during distressing incidents. Post-incident training usually requires a debriefing process of some sort that allows participants to ventilate their emotions. First responders have discovered that individuals who caretake their emotional equipment as well as their technical equipment are less likely candidates for PTSD and generally have a more durable career. The concept is that toxic emotions enter into the human system during an incident and must find a way to exit. That exit can be healthy or dysfunctional, but the emotions will come out. If they do not exit they will remain in the system and cause toxic and potentially terminal damage on the system. Debriefing does not "fix" feelings. It only allows them appropriate ventilation so they don't build up to a dangerous and toxic overload that can either explode, or go deep underground to cause hidden damage.

A well conceived drill verifies the Emotional Continuity Management plan, increases goodwill for a job well done, demonstrates weaknesses and strengths, identifies additions or subtractions to the plan, increases buy-on for stakeholders and protects companies from the liability risk of not being employee-centered. The old adage of "practice makes perfect" is only applicable if the practice that is done is correct. Practicing something incorrectly over and over does not make it perfect, unless your goal is to make it perfectly wrong. In fact, an abbreviated definition of insanity is doing the same wrong thing over and over, expecting different and better results

All emergency management organizations practice and evaluate their tools and techniques to fine-tune their systems. Critiques and table-talks are arranged to hash over the successes and failures of plans and procedures. These generally cognitive, businesslike and non-emotional exchanges are arranged to find the weak links, missed ideas, or new data necessary to update emergency responses. New information provides new ideas.

Some organizations have the forethought to include the emotional components into their planning exercises. Some local chapters of the American Red Cross, for example, participate in expansive community emergency exercises that include a number of different agencies and responder components. They often include in the prepared scenario a number of actors who will demonstrate what a real victim may present at the scene. These actors and actresses are often community volunteers who enjoy the opportunity to be covered with products called "mélange" that simulate blood and gore. Some volunteers allow themselves to be put in body bags and others volunteer to act as grieving relatives. Firefighters, law enforcement professionals, health care teams, security guards, city officials, and coroners act out their roles in these scripted dramas while disaster mental health responders artificially comfort the fake survivors. These drills and exercises have been shown to be priceless opportunities to think through what might really happen in a similar situation.

Case Example

The Emotional Continuity Management Planner had been previously ignored by the other members of the emergency contingency team who focused primarily on IT recovery. She stated at one planning meeting, "What have you planned to do if people jump off the bridges. This community has five bridges and people do unexpected things during disasters." The team looked at her and scoffed that no one in their right mind would do that. They began to move the discussion forward until she continued, "During a disaster there are people who are temporarily not in their right minds. It happened in New York during the attacks. People jumped off bridges into the bay to either escape or swim toward their children who were in schools across the bridges."

Learning Byte

The team reconsidered and began discussions of how the community would respond to people's emotional reactions during a disaster.

DO THIS: Invite Mental Health professionals who have been trained in disaster responses and have had field experiences to planning meetings.

DON'T: Let someone who has the title but not the credentials or experience dismiss the needs of Emotional Continuity Management during this phase of your planning

In recent years businesses have not had to consider themselves "emergency responders." This is no longer valid. With the instability of today's world you may find yourself in a situation where you must respond immediately and with clarity to save your own life or the lives of your co-workers. The extreme situation that managers of corporate offices in the World Trade Center towers experienced early in the morning of September 11, 2001 has served as a "wake-up-call" to many businesses to come up with Emotional Continuity Management plans to handle the emotional impact of a large-scale event. If you think your little company might be immune to such drama because you are in Padiddle, South Nowhere and all you do is make little widgets and have five employees, think again. Consider natural disasters, disgruntled employees, a random psychopath with a weapon, rumor, layoff, national economic events that shut down your communications system, a community transportation tragedy, or a disrupted shipping process or the completely unthinkable event that makes the national headlines because no one in their "right mind" would have guessed that such a horror could have happened at little-ol' Padiddle, South Nowhere in the lobby of the What's-Up Widget Company! But CNN is on its way! The weirdest and most random things can happen, because life is unpredictable.

Case Examples

- Headline: Roof Collapses at Shopping Mall.
- Headline: Drive-By Shooting Kills Local Fast-Food Restaurant Customers
- Headline: Widget Inc. to Lay Off 43,000 Employees By June 30
- Headline: Cure Found For Common Cold, Destroys Health Care Industry, Millions Out Of Work
- Headline: Pacific Northwest Storm Shuts Down Columbia Gorge, Trucks Held Up For Sixth Day
- Headline: Local Business Owner Dies in Auto Accident
- Headline: Read Your Own Paper Tonight and Think Of How Many People Were Emotionally Challenged At Work Today

Case Example

"When the January, 1998 Ice Storm took Upstate New York by surprise, Niagara Mohawk Power Corporation was able to deploy trained critical incident management staff to the County Emergency Operations Centers in the most highly affected rural counties. The employees had trained and exercised with police, fire, EMS, and government emergency responders in the Public Safety Critical Incident Management course at Onondaga Community College where a simulation board had been the focus of training involving all disciplines in the same class. The training paid dividends again that year when the Labor Day windstorm knocked out power to 250,000 customers. The Onondaga County Executive called upon the power company to loan their Emergency Planning Manager to the County to direct their EOC.

Bottom-line losses to the power company were $25,000,000 and $125,000,000 respectively from the two storms. Still later in September that year, the company was able to deploy trained crews to Puerto Rico to aid in the response and recovery to Hurricane Georges." *Thomas Phelan, PH.D.*

Learning Byte

This technical discussion of drills can be seen in statistics of cost-effectiveness. How to translate the emotional statistic would be extrapolated by a manager who knew how his or her people were doing through this. What people felt scared or discouraged after the first storm? Who felt successful and jubilant after the second storm? And who went to Puerto Rico? Most businesses do not factor into their plans the personal comments or salient emotional features in a situation that is charged. The mythology around not complaining, or a big-girls-and-boys-don't-cry mentality, has been dissolved through the tears spent at disaster sites. It is a myth that people cannot do work and have feelings at the same time. Firefighters and law enforcement, military and medical employees have discovered that emotions are present in every human situation. When reading or listening to Tom Phelan, the pride he has of his team's success is visible. Pride is also an emotion. How would you manage pride of success in your company? Is pride an emotion that can slow down productivity? How? Is it an emotion you can use to increase production? How? What would that look like in your company?

DRILLS AND REHEARSALS FOR EMOTIONS

There are scores of emergency planning texts available that can help your company formulate a drill. For example, you can take an IT contingency book and retranslate the technological risks into emotional risks. What are your company's emotional mainframe, software, hardware, database, applications, platforms or communications systems? In other words, who are your strong leaders, your soft followers, your knowers, your doers, your standard-bearers and your communicators? Or, you could call an emergency management provider in your community and ask them to help you create a drill. This book also offers some guidelines. What is important to know is that a drill doesn't need to be fancy but it does need to be formalized.

Best practices say that a drill should be mandatory, well-planned and regularly scheduled. Until participants have had some practice in drilling, a surprise exercise would cause too much emotional stress, and that is the opposite goal you would want to have. Emergency preparedness drills which include emotions are intended to prepare participants for a traumatic event and to give participants confidence that they can survive. If the real deal happens, it has been rehearsed and will have a less shattering effect than something that is considered unthinkable. Unthinkable incidents happen and people are emotionally overwhelmed by the difficulties of incorporating totally new ideas during extreme duress.

- **Paper-Drills**: A paper drill is just that, a drill on paper. It is a combination of scenarios and written guidelines provided to leadership to pre-think their concerns. The data is collected and shared with all departments.

- **Table-Talks**: A table talk or tabletop drill is one that is held around a table. In other words it is all talk and no physical action. It is an opportunity for participants to share and talk through their concerns, ideas and expectations to become familiar with each other, emergency policies, procedures and exercise compliances.

- **Dress Rehearsal or Walk-Through**: A physical practice of the elements of the drill. One step away from the table-talk and two steps away from paper. More real, but very controlled.

- **Job Function:** This drill tests specific jobs, people, or departments.

- **Evacuation Drill:** Participants act out an evacuation with simulated hazards, like stairways with participants acting like dead bodies, mélange, smoke, debris, and loss of communications. Surprises are built into the drill and the plan will need to adapt to the situation.

- **Full Simulation**: A full simulation is a real-time action replication or mock-up of what a disaster might look like and feel like. Although it is artificial it is the closest proximity to real-time incidents. The most labor intensive type of drill, simulations may prepare employees more for a real disaster than any other form of drilling. An emergency situation is simulated as closely as possible. This exercise should include all company participants, emergency personnel, local emergency agencies, others.

How to Set up a Drill for Emotional Continuity Management

- Establish full buy-on administratively
- Determine leadership
- Prepare with paper drills and table-talks prior to simulation drills
- Define the goals of the drill
- Develop appropriate and safe logistical settings
- Develop appropriate scenarios
- Create scenario assignments
- Consider management of a real emergency or unexpected event during the simulation
- Review plans and gather feedback
- Conduct the drill
- Collect results
- Celebrate the closure of the drill formally
- Debrief participants and planners without critique
- Planners then can evaluate the success or failure of goal achievements
- Add or subtract necessary components and schedule next drill cycle
- Send thank-yous to all participants
- What questions will you need answered to make good decisions?
- What resources will you need in each case?
- What resources will you activate immediately?
- What resources will you put on stand-by?
- How will you approach administration, employees, vendors and ancillary participants?
- What plan will you write?
- What policies for emotions will you want in place?
- What people with what qualifications will serve you best?
- What level of emotional impact will this possibly have?
- What risks will there be for solo or group emotional spinning?
- What tools will you use to manage the emotions of employees?
- How will you take care of your self as you participated?
- What would be the estimated costs of this for your company
- What would be the estimated costs for your company if it was unprepared for a real emergency?

Tips for Success of Drills

- **Clear Notifications** — Always state "THIS IS A DRILL" when making phone calls or contact calls during the drill. Remember when Orson Wells read the story *War of the Worlds* on radio and some people really thought the planet was being invaded by aliens. People are fun! And people are nervous. Our world is scarier than it was a few years ago. It is better to be cautious than to create more emotional impact. It is critical to inform and notify all players and anyone who might be concerned that this is not a drill.
- **Identification Tags** — For the same reasons as above, and for ease in managing the Participants, all members should have visible and highly identifiable, temporary identification that is collected after the drill.
- **Time them well** — A drill during a layoff phase is dangerous. A drill during an earthquake is pointless and dangerous. A discussion after an earthquake might be useful for planning the next drill.
- **Evaluations should focus on positive points** — Negative critiques destroy buy-on. Attempt to phrase weaknesses and losses in positive "can-do-better-next-time" language.
- **Have fun** — Simulations can be fun and exciting when people are motivated to do their best for the sake of everyone else.
- **Add a surprise** — The unexpected is where drills show holes in preparation. Don't add anything extreme, but do include a small twist to make it interesting.

- **Ask other experts to play with you** — Go to your local fire department, hospital or chapter of the American Red Cross and ask someone to help you plan your drill.
- **Drill a full range of emotions** — Include all feelings from small to large, annoyances to catastrophic.
- **Maintain the illusion** — Encourage participants to maintain their acting roles until excused from the drill.
- **Explain exit strategies and ending calls** — Inform your participants how they can exit the drill if it becomes distressful. Also inform everyone when or how the drill will conclude.
- **Debrief even when it is a drill** — Make certain any individual who exits a drill have a mandatory debriefing to deter people who simply want to exit the process so they can go home early, and protect participants who may really have difficulty. This also gets people into the good habit of debriefing.
- **Pleases and Thank-yous** — Courtesy goes a long way to create closure and future buy-on. Write a formal thank you letter to all participants.

Case Example

Viola, the full-time private administrative assistant to a school administrator, answered the phone as usual. A voice on the other end was screaming about "the explosion." Viola realized it was a parent trying to find out if his child was safe. Viola quickly learned that many people were dead in the same neighborhood where her children were in school. Because she had exercised for emergencies, she was able to stay on the phone to support other parents who were calling the office in a panic although she was near panic herself. The other parents were calling because they were trapped away from the school by emergency road closures. Viola answered so many calls and had such terror for her own children that she could barely breathe. She remembered her training and knew she could get through and get help later. Her new boss, who had not received Emotional Continuity Management training yet, came into the office and demanded why she had not done her regular tasks. Although her first reaction was an emotion bordering on hysteria, she took a deep breath and calmly explained the situation to her boss.

Learning Byte

What could Viola have done differently? What could her manager have done differently? What emotions were at play here by all the individuals in this situation?

Case Example

The office manager Denise opened the doors early in the morning to find a huge lizard in the center of the office. It was a large harmless lizard, but a reptile nonetheless. She screamed and when the next person came in to work right behind her they took action to remove it. Yes, they called 911. Emergency responders came, called animal control, and removed the creature. A week later there was another lizard. One afternoon a client came through the door screaming that there was a lizard hanging down from the gutters outside near the entrance to the store. Everyone was now in a panic. Animal control, emergency responders and company leadership were called in and the lizard problem was addressed.

There were no more lizards. Three years later Denise was still nervous about lizards under her desk and co-workers, vendors, and customers frequently teased her.

Learning Byte

Although no one could have predicted the lizard problem in this company, they did not take the time to consider the potential of such unexpected events and plan ahead. The interesting thing about this company is that its work was associated with responding to the emergencies of others and spent significant money in trainings to deal with the emotional needs of their clients. One of the weakest spots in care models is the lack of attention many emergency responders have to their own care needs. Business leaders need to plan for the unexpected. Even drilling for something that will never happen puts employees at ease when in an unknown situation because they have created a space in their thinking for "emergency emotions."

Creating a Space for Emergency Emotions

Drilling and exercising for emotions events allows the brain to make a space for the experience. Post-Traumatic Stress Disorder is an extreme consequence of seeing or experiencing something extreme that is unexpected and potentially life threatening or in the presence of a real death. The mind says, "Some perception in my inner worldview has been shattered forever." The difference between trauma and difficulty lies in the perceptual distortion presented by the incident. For example, a firefighter will generally not become traumatized by fire. On the other hand, someone who has never seen a large fire can become traumatized when they see flames roll across a floor like an ocean wave. That same firefighter, who is seasoned to fire, may develop PTSD the first time he sees an eyeball rolling across the floor. That is not something the mind is prepared to see the first time. Some firefighters would say, "oh, gee, there goes another darn eyeball. That's the third one this week." Another firefighter might find this was their emotional last straw.

To manage severe emotions well includes creating a place in the brain for the possibility of new and challenging information. It is as though you see an Unidentified Flying Object land in your patio. Even if you are a believer, your brain will now have to accommodate the image in real-time. If you believe in UFOs, your worldview includes UFOs. If you do not believe in UFOs, your world may be temporarily or permanently shattered. If your company has UFO drills, even if you don't believe in them, and a UFO lands in your lunchroom at work, your brain will have already begun the initial process of accommodating to the concept of how your team will help each other respond in unexpected events, and will be less likely to shatter into emotional pieces. Of course, it is not really necessary to drill specifically for unexpected UFO invasions in the lunchroom, or for the possibility or horrors like rolling eyeballs. What is helpful is to create an emotional climate where your employees can begin to develop a repertoire of thoughts, ideas, words, and images to manage emotions that may surface during an incident. So many people with PTSD report that no one would talk to them about their feelings, especially at work.

AUTHOR'S AFTERTHOUGHTS

When I took piano lessons I was constantly annoyed by the requirement of playing scales over and over and over. When I gave my first large concert performance my fingers went in the right places even though my heart was pounding with stage fright.

When I went to New York City in September of 2001 I knew what my job was, even though my mind and heart were shattered by recent events. I had participated in many disaster drills, and in fact had been involved in a large multi-agency aviation disaster exercise when I was called on to go to NYC. When I arrived at my post my practice apparently paid off because I left the scene knowing that my humble contribution of services helped. Rehearsing, practicing and drilling in advance, preparing my own support team to be ready to take care of me when I returned, calling people at home daily, laughing when laughter was available, crying when crying was appropriate, carrying my self-care tools with me, remembering the policies and procedures of the work and the situation, and managing emotions from small to huge all helped me to do my job, and continues to make an ongoing contribution to my recovery. The unexpected is somehow less daunting when you rehearse for the unexpected. Sometimes it seems silly and pointless. Other times it is precious.

I am reminded of a story I read about British soldiers in POW camps during World War II. Apparently, they had a higher rate of survival than others because they continued to rehearse and drill even when incarcerated. They would arise at the proper time, make a formation, do calisthenics, and mime regular activities like eating, shaving, and drinking tea in elegant imaginary teacups in an effort to maintain a sense of order within the chaos. These soldiers were prepared and ready for whatever came up. When rescue came up, they were in better shape then their counterparts who had not drilled on a daily basis.

I am a strong advocate of improvisational music, therapy and life in general. My personal affirmations include gratitude for spontaneity and astonishment at the mysteries of life. I am also keenly aware that there is order in the universe and that disasters, catastrophes, terrorist events, traumas and even minor inconveniences disturb our order, and thus cause us to be in an altered state in our efforts to regain order. I tell my clients that it is not the fear or difficult emotions that are the problems in life, it is the desire to hire a moving truck and relocate your emotional furniture into the drama and stay there. I encourage people to feel their feelings fully and then move forward with their feelings as an active, energetic part of their full texture. Feelings are okay. And, we still have to get things done. There used to be a toy produced called Weebles® (Hasbro, 1969). They were small people shapes that had a rounded base so that when a child pushed the toy it would wiggle but not tip over. The advertisement for the toy went something like, "Weebles, they wobble but they don't fall down!" I call real survivors "Weebles" when they can maintain some integrity with their own human emotional experience and get the job done.

The week of September 11, 2001, I was scheduled to participate in a multi-agency aviation disaster simulation emergency drill. Hundreds of people were involved. The leadership thought it might be appropriate to cancel the drill under the circumstances. Everyone involved stated something to the effect that, more than ever, we needed to drill. The emotional contexts of the participants were profound during the drill. Although we had all drilled many times before there was a new meaning to the practice. It was the first time that my teams really saw the need for post-drill debriefing, using my drill buddy systems plan, personal emotional support for one another, and really using the Emotional Continuity Management tools they had learned from me in countless, tedious trainings. It was the first time team members thanked me for pounding into their heads that, during a real event, they would have unexpected emotions. It was the first time a significant and powerful leader who had been a major obstacle to the addition of Emotional Continuity Management during disaster drills made a special effort to thank me for pre-training his employees. They knew what to do and called in the proper resources from within their own company.

DISCUSSION QUESTIONS

The following case examples are real, true-life, experiences. Details have been altered to protect privacy. The exercise activities are designed to give you an overview of the problems and issues of real-life experiences. Use the scenarios below to practice with the activities:

Activity 1 — Give your planning team 3x5 cards. Give them 15 minutes to make as many wild and unlikely risk scenarios as they can imagine. Toss the cards into a box and draw them randomly. Discuss each potential emergency scene or risk for two minutes. Focus only on what emotions might be demonstrated or experienced by your employees in each situation.

Activity 2 — Choose several different scenarios and estimate the average costs of these emotional events if they happened in your company.

Activity 3 — List what emotions might happen in each scenario. List positive and negative emotions. Find five or more ways to manage the emotions in yourself or a coworker.

Activity 4 — Create a paper or table-talk drill for your company based on one of the scenarios.

Activity 5 — Implement a drill based on the scenario of your choice or one you create.

Activity 6 — Find five more ways you can say, define, describe, or give examples of the following words. Where do these words belong in discussing the scenarios? What emotional demonstrations do they suggest?

emotions	managing emotions
emotional reactions	support
emotional climate	help
appropriate	resistance
inappropriate	conflict
emotional triggers	change

REHEARSE AND DRILL SCENARIOS

Scenario A — Your community is located within 50 miles of a Mad Cow outbreak. You manage a food industry company that has contracts with health care services and other local contracts. You manage 34 full and part-time staff that work in two shifts. Your boss had informed you that your team must remove all beef from the venue.

Scenario B — You just found out that you are pregnant and you have not told anyone yet. A co-worker discloses that she is leaving early today to have an abortion and wants you to finish her assignment without telling anyone.

Scenario C — There is a running joke in the office about mentally handicapped people. Your brother has schizophrenia. Someone tells you a new joke.

Scenario D — You have been struggling with weight loss for two years, a daily struggle. Co-workers make fun of "fat" people. There is a potluck lunch today and your boss asks if you are coming.

Scenario E — Your new boss takes you and a colleague out to lunch, and insists on driving after a few martinis. Last year a dear friend was killed by a drunk driver.

Scenario F — You have diabetes. Do you tell your colleagues how to help you if you become ill?

Scenario G — You cheated on your time cards. A coworker finds out.

Scenario H — Your spouse is an alcoholic. There is trouble at home. The boss wants you to work overtime. This means your alcoholic spouse will be driving the children home from school.

Scenario I — You are a member of Alcoholics Anonymous and you have been sober for two years. You are being scorned for being a party-pooper by associates who party on the weekend. They think you don't like them. They invite you out again.

Scenario J — You are gay. You have not told anyone. Someone asks you what you think about gay marriages and if you know any gay people.

Scenario K — You are taking anti-depressants to tolerate your difficult working situation. At a meeting you are asked what improvements might help the organization.

Scenario L — Your religion doesn't allow you to work on Saturday. Saturday is the championship game for the Company Bowling League. Bowling is at the center of all social events and social discussions throughout the year. Bowlers are more likely to get the promotions and often are given opportunities to travel to out of town conferences.

Scenario M — You are having an affair with a co-worker. Your lover tells you about another co-worker who is committing fraud.

Scenario N — You accidentally intercept a love letter on company letterhead to a co-worker on your team.

Scenario O — Your boss asks you to do something that frightens you.

Scenario P — Your co-worker asks you to help cover up an error she made.

Scenario Q — Your co-worker tells you an unsavory secret about your boss.

Scenario R — The National Weather Service has upgraded the hurricane to a category 4 and recommended evacuation. You are hosting a group of visiting industry professionals from a foreign nation. Their translator just walked out of the meeting.

Scenario S — An employee that left the company a year ago, before you were hired, comes into your office with a weapon claiming he was mistreated by the last manager.

Scenario T — Your company is forced to Shelter in Place for two days because of a toxic chemical spill. (A truck overturns, a railroad car goes off the track, a local chemical plant has a fire, etc.)

Scenario U — Your boss has a sudden heart attack and dies in the employee lounge during Bring-Your-Children-To-Work Day.

Scenario V — A toilet overflows during the weekend causing major foul flooding in your office.

Scenario W — There is one confirmed case of Smallpox reported in the United States. (Contact your local health department, the CDC - Center for Disease Control, or WHO - World Health Organization) to find out the profound ramifications of this terrifyingly real possibility.

Scenario X — You suspect one of your employees is a sex offender.

Scenario Y — Your company has an Emotional Terrorist in a key position. This employee begins to focus attention on your management skills.

Scenarios Z —
- You have a snake in your office
- A rumor of outsourcing has erupted
- Mass layoffs are threatened
- Someone in the company has committed cyber crime
- Money is missing from the cash drawer

- The office manager is not following through on tasks and is calling in sick frequently
- The boss changes his/her mind every time something is almost finished
- You work in tornado alley in the Midwest and new employees are hired who have never been near a tornado
- Your office is on an earthquake fault
- 15% of your employees are related to active duty military units deployed to the Middle East. The news this week is not good.
- Four of your employees are pregnant and the office is scheduled for repainting
- Two of your employees have been married to the same man
- Two of your employees have been married to the same woman
- Someone in your company has a child die
- An employee starts showing signs of mental illness
- Someone in your company is devastated by the loss of a beloved pet
- One of your employees insists on rearranging key equipment and the rest of the staff is upset
- 23% of your workforce are military reservists called to active duty
- A key employee disappears
- Your competitor raises the stakes and you lose a valuable client
- An employee has a chronic cough
- Office communications have been disrupted
- Your company files for bankruptcy
- There have been news stories about toxic leaks. There is an odd smell at your office. Someone starts vomiting.
- Someone forgot to "save" an important 83-page document and it was lost
- Your office shares a common wall with another company that has had a fire
- You hate your HR manager
- Your HR manager hates you
- A scandal implicates your company
- A severe winter storm collapses trees onto important job performance equipment
- An employee who is a combat veteran is upset with the War in Iraq
- The office is infested by termites
- Transportation to your office has been disrupted

17

RESOURCES: DO YOU HAVE GOOD INFORMATION?

"I just didn't know what to do or where to turn. Employees were quitting left and right and everyone else was upset. Someone came up to me and asked me if I had a book about how to manage their anger because anyone who went to the EAPs were quickly "released" for some reason or another. I had nothing to offer except tell them to go to some bookstore or the library. I felt helpless. I had never considered the possibility that our boss was an Emotional Terrorist until the workshop. Now I have resources like crazy! I'm a survivor of corporate insanity!"

Jeanne, Middle Management and Workshop Participant

WHY YOU SHOULD READ THIS CHAPTER

It may appear easier to just use what you already know. Obstacles to ongoing learning are numerous and compelling. Time is the biggest challenge to most hard working people. Never, though, has anyone felt worse after an emotional incident than the person who avoided learning the one thing that may have helped. Most managers are already overwhelmed and do not have time to read the fine print, explore creative options, ponder new concepts, or luxuriate over intuitive data about unpredictable incidents. And most managers are where the buck stops if something goes horribly, horribly wrong.

BY THE END OF CHAPTER 17 YOU SHOULD BE ABLE TO

- Develop your own bibliography of favorite resources

- Start a company library with books on emotional management topics

- Provide an appropriate resource guide for employees

- Have ample data for proactive Emotional Continuity Management

- Assign or delegate employees to create an Emotions At The Workplace task-force, that does not necessarily include HR or EAP specialists

- Delegate a team to create an employee pamphlet or brochure with includes local, regional, state and national reference for emotional care and support

- Construct an information and referral network with extensive resource materials including professional resources in your community, websites, tools, educational strategies, trainers (local and national), interventionist specialists, trauma counselors, CISM (Critical Incident Stress

Management), books, annual conferences on disaster and emotions, and emergency response resources (local, state, federal)

OVERVIEW

Life-long learning is not a job for the weak! But, then again, neither is management. The often misplaced mythology of strength equals power should be replaced by the daily humility of understanding what is left to know in the world far outweighs whatever we think we know today. A powerful person does not fear being a student.

Finding good resources is like finding a good mechanic or dentist. You can close your eyes and point to a name in the phone book, or you could ask around. You can find people you trust and ask them to suggest books, movies, videos, audiotapes, seminars, workshops, speakers, classes and organizations that will lead your life long learning process in the direction you so desire.

LIFE-LONG LEARNING

As I mentioned earlier in this text, not all people are destined or adequately wired to be managers. The best managers factor in a portion of their work time for education. Perhaps it will be to read one paragraph a day from a favorite or new book. Some managers find it easier to lump education into week-long seminars. The value of seminars is great as long as the education keeps moving forward on a daily basis. In other words, it is reasonable to go to a dentist in an emergency, but daily brushing and flossing will minimize those urgencies. It is reasonable to call your mechanic when the car breaks down, but daily maintenance care minimizes those urgencies.

As you review the resources in this chapter you should begin to get the idea of what you want to know as well as what you need to know. You will also experience your own resistance to change.

Use what you have. Get more stuff. Work with internal auditors, outside agencies, libraries, consultants, counselors, teachers, law enforcement and firefighter professionals, universities, community colleges, adult education programs, consultants, critical incident stress management volunteers, EAP providers, HR providers, books, videos, trainers, and whatever you can find to research, develop and evolve a program for Emotional Continuity Management which will protect yourself, your workers, and your industry.

Help others to learn. Advocate for trainings. Allocate funds and provide training dollars. If you have a small to nonexistent budget, find local volunteers or create a library at work. Go to used book sales and buy books. Give your team time to learn. Provide them with resources. Do what ever it takes to grow your resources and availability to them. Make slogans, write mottos, use bulletin boards and sandwich boards if they work at getting people on board with the challenges of balancing business and emotions and avoiding emotional chaos or emotional ignorance in the workplace.

REFERENCES

American Red Cross, Weapons of Mass Destruction Overview, ARC 3079-2, October, 2002

Behe, George, Titanic: Safety, Speed and Sacrifice, Transportation Trails, 1997

Cook, John, Seattle Post-Intelligencer, March10, 2004

Coppinger, Cheryl, Richland, Washington

Down, Alan, Corporate Executions, AMACOM,1995

Ekman, Paul, Emotions Revealed, Times Books, 2003

Fink, Mitchell and Mathias, Lois, Never Forget, an Oral History of September 11, 2001, HarperCollins, 2002

Friedman, Howard, Allyn and Bacon, Personality: Classical Theories in Modern Research, 2003 (2nd edition)

Frizzell, Sharon G., Silver Springs, Maryland

Fry, Ann, Laughing Matters, Better Way Press, 2004

Hahn, Anna, Sexual Assault Response Center, 2004

Haugk, Kenneth, Antagonists in the Church, Ausberg, 1988

Hawkins, David, Power vs. Force, Hay House, 2002

Hawkins-Mitchell, Vali, Conflict Resolution: Use of Writing with Children, for Montessori Project, Inner Directions, 2002

Hawkins-Mitchell, Vali, Creating a Spin-Free Workplace, Inner Directions, 2002

Hawkins-Mitchell, Vali, Creative Writing Series for Trauma of Children (Journals and Teacher/Parent Guidelines), Inner Directions, 2003

Hawkins-Mitchell, Vali, Dr. Vali's Survival Guide: Tips for the Journey, Emerald of Siam, 1999

Hawkins-Mitchell, Vali, Dr. Vali's Trauma Toolkit: Surviving Crisis and Trauma Management for Professionals, Inner Directions, 1999

Hawkins-Mitchell, Vali, Emotional Micro-Terrorism at the Workplace, Inner Directions, 2001

Hawkins-Mitchell, Vali, Employee Relations Bulletin, Simon & Schuster, 1995-2000

Health and Safety Executive, No. HSG218, Sudbury, June 2001

Health at Work, 1991

Hudson, Rex, Who Becomes a Terrorist and Why, Lyons Press, 1999

Isaacs, Nathan, Tri-City Herald, 2003 and 2004

Jean, Raymond A., West Hartford, Connecticut

Karpman, Steven, Fairytales and Script Drama Analysis, Transitional Analysis Bulletin. 7:39-43, 1968

Kessler, R., Archives of General Psychiatry, 1995

Kroll, J, Homeland Insecurities, Economist, August 2003

Kubler-Ross, Elizabeth, On Death and Dying, Scribner, (reprint), 1997

Kubler-Ross, Elizabeth, Death: The Final Stage of Growth, Engelwood Cliffs, 1975

Lanse, Hal W., Ph.D., New York, New York

Lewis, Gerald, Critical Incident Stress and Trauma in the Workplace, 2003

Long, F.Y., Psychological Support in Civil Emergencies: the National Emergency Behavior Management System of Singapore, International Review of Psychiatry, vol. 13, 2001)

Marcella, Albert, Business Continuity, Disaster Recovery and Incident Management Planning: A Resource for Ensuring Ongoing Enterprise Operations, Institute of Internal Auditors, 2004

Marcella, Albert, Outsourcing, Downsizing, and Reengineering: Internal Control Implications, Institute of Internal Auditors, 1995

Mask, Tori, Weebles: Weebles Wobble But They Don't Fall Down, 2003

McLeod, Douglas, Business Insurance, April 1999

Mitchell, David and Hawkins-Mitchell, Vali, Parenting After Divorce: Mandated Seminar Guide for Divorcing Parents, Inner Directions, 1997

Mitchell, David W, Anniversary Trauma Journal, 2002

Myers, Diane, Disaster Response and Recovery, A Handbook for Mental Health Professionals, 2003

Pelletier, K.R. Healthy People – Healthy Business: Perspectives in Behavioral Medicine,

Phelan, Thomas D., President, Strategic Teaching Associates

Pizzorno, Joseph, Total Wellness, Prima, 1996

Randolph, Susan, AAOHN, Occupational Hazards, January 2004

Schaef, Anne Wilson, The Addictive Organization, Harper, 1988

Simmons, Gary, The I of the Storm, Unity House, 2001

Solomaon, Michael, Marketing: Real People, Real Choices, Prentice Hall, 2003

Tanouye, E, Mental Illness: A Rising Workplace Cost, Wall Street Journal, August 2001

Taylor, Bill, Arizona Republic Research, May 2004

The Economist, January 2004

The Glossarist, Film Dictionary, 2004

Thomas, Jay C, Handbook of Mental Health in the Workplace, 2002

Wearden, Graeme, ZDNet UK, 2001

Westerheide, Joe, Director, A Chance to Change

Workforce 2000, The Hudson Institute, 1987

WEB SITES

www.cornell.edu	Cornell University, Web Research, May 2004
www.citizenworks.org	Citizens Works, May 2004
www.bls.gov	U.S. Department of Labor Bureau of Labor Statistics, May 2004
www.esgr.org	Employer Support of the Guard and Reserve, May 2004
www.eeoc.gov	Equal Employment Opportunity Commission, May 2004
www.disastercenter.com	The Disaster Center, May 2004
alertnet@reuters.com	Reuters Global News May 2004
www.humoru.com	Ann Fry's Humor University May, 2004
www.fema.gov	Federal Emergency Management
www.fema.gov/kids	FEMA for Kids: The Disaster Area
www.qm2.org	Management Briefing
www.eapcism.com	Critical Incident Stress Management. for the Workplace, April 2004
www.RAINN.org	Rape, Abuse, and Incest National Network
http://www.openix.com/~johnfh3/	Mt. St. Helens Website
www.ABCNEWS.com	ABC News
www.Seattlepi.com	Seattle Post Intelligencer (newspaper)
www.KCBD.com	Radio KCBD, Lubbock, Texas

ASSESSMENT TOOLS

Traumatic Events Questionnaire (TEQ) Lauterbach and Vrana, 1996. (Fires/explosions, industrial and farm accidents, witnessing death or violent crime, other life-threatening situations)

Traumatic History Questionnaire (THQ), Green, 1993. (Serious accident at work, toxin exposure, Handling bodies, Present at a crime, other injury)

Traumatic Stress Schedule (TSS) Norris, 1990 (Crime involving force or threat, motor vehicle accident and injury, other terrifying or shocking experience)

Impact of Event Scale, Horowitz, Wilner, and Alvarez, 1979. (Links personal reactions to trauma)

Assessing Psychological Trauma and PTSD, Wilson, Keene, 1997. (Provides specific steps that Mental Health providers can use to create assessment that is tailored to occupations specifics)

TOPICAL BIBLIOGRAPHY

BUSINESS TOPICS

Allen, Roger E., Winnie-The-Pooh on Management and Problem Solving, Routledge, 1998

Axelrod, Alan, Elizabeth I CEO: Strategic Lessons from the Leader Who Built an Empire, Prentice Hall Press, 2002

Axelrod, Alan, Patton On Leadership, Prentice Hall Press, 2001

Carter, Jay, Nasty People: How to Stop Being Hurt by Them Without Becoming One of Them, Contemporary Books, 1989

Collins, James C., Good to Great: Why Some Companies Make the Leap...and Others Don't, Harper Business, 2001

Covey, Stephen, Seven Habits of Highly Successful People, Free Press, 1990

EQE International, Reliability Management: An Overview, ABS Consulting, 2000

Gerber, Robin, Leadership the Eleanor Roosevelt Way: Timeless Strategies from the First Lady of Courage, Portfolio, 2003

Johnson, Spencer, Who Moved My Cheese, Putnum, 1998

Jones, Laurie Beth, Jesus CEO: Using Ancient Wisdom for Visionary Leadership, Hyperion, 1996

Metcalf, Franz, What Would Buddha Do at Work?, Seastone, 2001

Personnel Decisions, The Successful Manager's Handbook, Personal Decisions, 1992

Richmond, Lewis, Work as a Spiritual Practice: A Practical Buddhist Approach to Inner Growth and Satisfaction on the Job, Broadway, 2000

Roberts, Wess, Leadership Secrets of Attila The Hun, Warner, 1990

Rosner, Bob, Working Wounded, Warner, 1995

Whitney, John O, Power Plays: Shakespeare's Lessons in Leadership and Management, Simon and Schuster, 1992

Witten, Donna, Enlightened Management: Bringing Buddhist Principles to Work, Inner Traditions, 2000

BUSINESS CHANGE

Caplan, Gayle, Survivors: How to Keep Your Best People on Board After Downsizing, Davies-Black, 1997

Goldberg, Beverly, Empty Cubicles: Employee Retention When Downsizing — Avoid The Anxiety Created By Layoff, Brown Herron, 2002

Marks, Mitchell Lee, Charging Back Up the Hill: Workplace Recovery After Mergers, Acquisitions and Downsizings, Jossey-Bass, 2003

Wooward, Harry, Aftershock: Helping People Through Corporate Change, John Wiley, 1987

DIVERSITY

Aron, Elaine, <u>The Highly Sensitive Person</u>, Broadway Books, 2000

Briles, Judith, <u>Gender Traps</u>, McGraw-Hill, 1996

Gardenswartz, Lee, <u>Diverse Teams at Work</u>, McGraw-Hill, 1995

Neubauer, <u>Nature's Thumbprint</u>, Columbia University Press, 1996

Ornstein, Robert, <u>Evolution of Consciousness</u>, Simon and Schuster, 1992

Ornstein, Robert, <u>The Roots of the Self</u>, Octagon Press, 1995

ETHICS

Anderson, Nancy, <u>Work with Passion</u>, New World Library, 1995

Belasco, James, <u>Teaching the Elephant to Dance</u>, Plummer, 1991

Blanchard, Kenneth, <u>The Power of Ethical Management</u>, William Morrow, 1988

Bolman, Lee, <u>Leading with Soul</u>, Jossey-Bass, 2001

Carter, Stephen, <u>Integrity</u>, Perennial, 1997

Chappell, Tom, <u>The Soul of A Business</u>, Bantam, 1994

Daniels, Neil, <u>The Morality Maze</u>, Prometheus Books, 1991

Daniels, Aubrey, <u>Bringing Out the Best in People</u>, McGraw-Hill, 1999

DeMars, Nan, <u>You Want Me To Do What?</u>, Fireside, 1998

Downs, Alan, <u>Corporate Executions</u>, Amacom, 1995

Ekman, Paul, <u>Telling Lies</u>, R.S. Means Company, 1992

Fournies, Ferdinand, <u>Why Employees Don't Do What They're Supposed to Do</u>, McGraw-Hill, 1999

Frank, Robert, <u>Passions Within Reason</u>, Norton, 1989

Halberstam, Joshua, <u>Everyday Ethics</u>, Penguin, 1994

Kidder, Rushworth, <u>How Good People Make Tough Choices</u>, Fireside, 1994

Krause, Donald, <u>The Art of War for Executives</u>, Perigee, 1995

Pritchett, Price, <u>The Ethics of Excellence</u>, Pritchett & Hull, 1993

Roberts, Wes, <u>Leadership Secrets of Attila the Hun</u>, Warner, 1990

Terkel, Susan, <u>Ethics Encyclopedia</u>, Facts on Fire, 1999

ANGER AND VIOLENCE

Lerner, Harriet Goldhor, <u>The Dance of Anger: A Woman's Guide to Changing the Patterns of Intimate Relationships</u>, Quill, 1997

Rubin, TI, <u>The Angry Book</u>, Touchstone, 1998

Sonkin, Daniel Jay, <u>Learning to Live Without Violence: A Handbook for Men</u>, Volcano Press, 1997

Weisinger, Hendrie, <u>Dr. Weisinger's Anger Work-Out Book</u>, Perennial, 1985

SEXUAL HARASSMENT

Eberhardt, Louise, <u>Confronting Sexual Harassment</u>, Whole Person Associates, 1995

Morris, Celia, <u>Bearing Witness</u>, New Page Books, 2001

Preston, Cheryl G., <u>When No Means No</u>, Carol Publishing, 1993

Rutter, Peter, <u>Sex, Power and Boundaries</u>, Bantam, 1996

WRITING FOR SELF CARE

Baldwin, Christina, <u>Life's Companion, Journal Writing as a Spiritual Quest</u>, Bantam Books, 2001

Capacchione, Lucia, <u>The Power of Your Other Hand</u>, New Page Books, 2001

Fox, John, <u>Poetic Medicine</u>, Putnam Publishing Group, 1997

Goldberg, Natalie, <u>Writing Down the Bones</u>, Shambhala, 1986

Kaye, Peggy, <u>Games for Writing</u>, Farrar, 1995

Lamott, Anne, <u>Bird by Bird</u>, Ancor Books / Double Play, 1995

Nachmanovitch, Stephen, <u>Free Play</u>, Jeremy P. Tarcher, 1991

Pennebaker, James, <u>Opening Up: The Healing Power of Confiding in Others</u>, Avon, 1990

Shaughnessy, Susan, <u>Walking On Alligators</u>, Harper, 1993

Voytilla, Stuart, <u>Myth and the Movies</u>, Michael Wiese, 1999

TRANSFORMATION AND PEACEBUILDING

Chodron, Pema, <u>When Things Fall Apart</u>, Shambhala, 1997

Coelho, Paulo, <u>Warrior of the Light</u>, Perennial, 2003

The Dalai Lama, <u>The Art of Happiness</u>, Riverhead, 1998

Davis, Laura, <u>I Thought We'd Never Speak Again</u>, Quill, 2002

Dwoskin, Hale, <u>The Sedona Method</u>, Sedona Press, 2003

Diamond, Louise, <u>The Courage for Peace</u>, Conari, 2000

Foundation for Inner Peace, <u>A Course in Miracles</u>, Foundation of Inner Peace, 1985

Frankl, Viktor, <u>Man's Search for Meaning</u>, Pocket, 1997

Goldsmith, Joel, <u>The Infinite Way</u>, DeVorss, 1997

Goldsmith, Joel, <u>The Art of Meditation</u>, Harper, 1956

Hay, Louise, <u>Meditations to Heal Your Life</u>, Hay House, 1994

Keeney, Bradford, <u>Improvisational Therapy</u>, Guilford, 1990

Kipfer, Barbara, 14,000 Things To Be Happy About, Workman, 1990

Kushner, Harold, How Good Do We Have to Be?, Little Brown and Company, 1996

Kushner, Harold, When Bad Things Happen to Good People, Avon, 1981

Muhs, William, 99 Sayings on Peace, New City Press, 2003

Nahmad, Claire, The Book of Peace, Journey, 2003

Reeve, Susyn, Choose Peace and Happiness, Red Wheel, 2003

Rivers, Frank, The Way of the Owl, Succeeding with Integrity in a Conflicted World, Harper, 1997

Simmons, Gary, The I of the Storm, Embracing Conflict, Creating Peace, Unity House, 2001

TuTu, Desmond, God Has a Dream: A Vision of Hope for Our Time, Doubleday, 2004

Winkler, Gershon, Magic of the Ordinary, Recovering the Shamanic in Judaism, North Atlantic, 2003

ADDICTION AND RECOVERY

Beattie, Melody, Co-Dependent No More: How to Stop Controlling Others and Start Caring for Yourself, Pinnacle Books, 1992

Carnes, Patrick, A Gentle Path Through the Twelve Steps, Hazelden, 1993

Covington, Stephanie, A Woman's Way Through the Twelve Steps, Hazelden, 1994

Evans, Patricia. The Verbally Abusive Relationship, Adams Media Corporation, 1996

Halpern, Howard. How to Break Your Addiction to a Person, MJF Books, 1997

Martha Cleveland, Chronic Illness and the 12 Steps, Hazelden Publishing and Educational Services, 1999

Mellody, Pia, Facing Love Addiction: Giving Yourself the Power to Change the Way You Love, Harper, 1992

RELATIONSHIPS

Bennett, Madeline. Sudden Endings: Why Husbands, Wives and Lovers Walk, Out on Long, Loving Relationships, Pinnacle Books, 1992

Cloud, Henry, Boundaries, Zondervan, 2002

Hendrix, Harville, Keeping the Love You Find: A Guide for Singles, Atria, 1993

Johnson, Robert A, He , Harper and Row, 1989

Johnson, Robert A, She, Harper and Row, 1989

Johnson, Robert A, We, Harper and Row, 1989

McCann, Eileen, The Two-Step: The Dance Toward Intimacy, Grove, 1985

SEXUAL ISSUES

Bass, Elen, Beginning to Heal: A First Book for Survivors of Child Sexual Abuse, Perennial, 1993

Buxton, Amity Pierce, The Other Side of the Closet: The Coming Out Crises For Straight Spouses, IBS Press, 1991

Byerly, Carolyn, The Mother's Book: How To Survive The Molestation of Your Child, Kendall / Hunt, 1992

Carnes, Patrick, The Betrayal Bond, Health Communications, 1997

Davis, Laura, Allies in Healing: When the Person You Love Was Sexually Abused as a Child, Harper, 1988

Davis, Laura, Courage to Heal, Harper, 1988

Ells, Alfred, Restoring Innocence, Healing the Memories and Hurts That Hinder Sexual Intimacy, Thomas Nelson, 1991

Engel, Beverly, Partners in Recovery, Ballantine Books, 1993

Frank, Don, When Victims Marry, Thomas Nelson Inc. 1990

Gil, Eliana, Outgrowing the Pain, Dell Publishing Co., 1988

Gil, Eliana, Sexualized Children, Self Esteem,1992

Gil, Eliana, The Treatment of Adult Survivors, Selfesteem, 1988

Graber, Ken, Ghosts in the Bedroom, Health Communications, 1991

Grubman-Black, Stephen, Broken Boys/Mending Men, The Black Burn Press, 2002

Hansen, Paul, Survivors and Partners, Heron Hill Publishing Co., 1991

Helfer, Ray, Child Abuse and Neglect: The Family and the Community, Addison-Wesley Publishing Co., 1976

Hindman, Jan, Just Before Dawn, Alexandria Association, 1989

Hunter, Mic, Abused Boys: The Neglected Victims of Sexual Abuse, Ballantine Books, 1991

Karr-Morse, Robin, Ghosts from the Nursery, Atlantic Monthly Press, 1999

Lew, Mike, Victims No Longer: Men Recovering from Incest and Other Sexual Child Abuse, Perennial, 1990

Mease, Bill, How Can I Help Him?, Hazelden, 1992

Paul Monette, Becoming a Man, Harper San Francisco, 1993

Sanders, Timothy, Male Survivors: 12 Step Recovery Program for Survivors of Childhood Sexual Abuse, Ten Speed Press, 1991

U, Bob, Adults Anonymous: Molested As Children, Hazelden, 1991

Wood, Wendy, Triumph Over Darkness, Beyond Words Publishing, 1993

PARENTING

Ahrons, Constance, The Good Divorce: Keeping Your Family Together When Your Marriage Falls Apart, Quill, 1998

Bloomfield, Harold, Making Peace in Your Stepfamily, Hyperion Books, 1994

Burns, Cherie, Stepmotherhood: How to Survive Without Feeling Frustrated, Left Out, Or Wicked, Three Rivers Press, 2001

Connie Dawson, Growing Up Again: Parenting Ourselves Parenting our Children, Hazelden Publishing and Educational Services, 1998

Fisher, Bruce, Rebuilding: When Your Relationship Ends, Impact Publishing, 1999

Folberg, Jay (Editor), Joint Custody and Shared Parenting (2nd edition), Guilford Publishing, 1991

Kingman, Daphne Rose, Coming Apart: Why Relationships End and How to Live the Ending of Yours, Conari Press, 2000

Magid, Ken and Schreibman, Walt, Divorce Is... A Kid's Coloring Book, Pelican Publishing Co. 1980

Ricci, Isolina, Mom's House, Dad's House: Making Shared Custody Work, Collier, 1980

Roosevelt, Ruth, Living in Step, McGraw-Hill, 1977

Smoke, Jim, Growing Through Divorce, Harriet's House, 1971

Teyber, Edward, Helping Your Children With Divorce, Jossey-Bass, 2001

Wallerstein, Judith , Second Chances: Men, Women, and Children a Decade After Divorce, Ticknor and Fields, 1990

Wallerstein, Judith, Surviving the Breakup: How Children and Parents Cope with Divorce, Basic Books, 1980

Ware, Ciji, Sharing Parenthood After Divorce: An Enlightened Custody Guide for Mothers, Fathers, and Kids, Viking 1982

Warshak, Richard, Divorce Poison, Regan, 2001

Wolf, Anthony, Why Did You Have to Get a Divorce and When Can I Get a Hamster?, Noonday, 1995

PROSPERITY

Chopra, Deepak, Creating Affluence, New World Library, 1993

Hill, Napoleon, The Think and Grow Rich Action Pack, Plume, 1972

Laut, Phil, Money is My Friend, Trinity, 1978

Parker Editorial Staff, The Parker Prosperity Program, Parker, 1967

Ponder, Catherine, The Millionaires of Genesis, DeVorss & Company, 1976

Roman, Sanaya, Creating Money, Keys to Abundance, HJ Kramer, 1988

PET LOSS

Anderson, Moira, Coping with Sorrow on the Loss of Your Pet, Alpine, 1996

MYTHOLOGY

Campbell, Joseph, The Power of Myth, Anchor, 1991

Hort, Barbara, UnHoly Hunger, Shambhala, 1996

Johnson, Robert A, Owning your Own Shadow, Harper, 1991

Jung, Carl, Man and His Symbols, Dell, 1997

Scheirse-Leonard, Linda, On the Way to the Wedding, Shambhalla, 1994

Stoker, Bram, Dracula, Candlewick Press, 2004

Voytilla, Stuart, Myth and the Movies, Michael Wiese, 1999

Zweig, Connie (Edited by), Meeting the Shadow, Tarcher, 1991

DISASTER AND TRAUMA

Cohen, Barry, Managing Traumatic Stress Through Art, Sidran Press, 1995

Herman, Judith, Trauma and Recovery, Basic, 1997

Mitchell, Jeffrey, Critical Incident Stress Debriefing, Chevron, 1995

Wilson, John, Assessing Psychological Trauma and PTSD, Guilford Press, 1996

ADULT ADD AND ADHD

Gordon, Michael, The Down & Dirty Guide to Adult ADD, GSI, 1996

Halverstadt, Jonathan Scott, ADD and Adult Relationships, Contemporary Medical Education, 1998

Hartmann, Thom, Complete Guide to ADHA:Help for Your Family at Home, School and Work, A Hunter in a Farmer's World Book, Underwood, 2000

Kelly, Kate, You Mean I'm Not Lazy, Stupid or Crazy?! A Self-Help Book for Adults with Attention Deficit Disorder, Tyrell & Jerem Press, 1993

Kilcarr, Patrick, Voices from Fatherhood : Fathers, Sons and ADHD, Brunner/Mazel Publisher, 1997

Latham, Peter, Tales From the Workplace, JKL Communication, 1996

Murphy, Kevin, Out of the Fog: Treatment Options and Coping Strategies for Adult Attention Deficit Disorder, Hyperion, 1995

Nadeau, Kathleen, Adventures in Fast Forward: Life, Love, and Work for the ADD Adult, Taylor and Francis, 1996

Sudderth, David, Adult ADD: The Complete Handbook: Everything You Need to Know About How to Cope and Live Well With ADD/ADHD, Prima Lifestyles, 1997

Weiss, Lynn, ADD on the Job: Making Your ADD Work for You, Coopersquare, 1996

CHILDREN'S BOOKS: Ethics and Problem Solving

Bierhorst, John, <u>The Woman Who Fell From the Sky</u>, Harper Collins, 1993

Cameron, Polly, <u>I Can't Said the Ant</u>, Scholastic, 1961

Cooper, Helen, <u>The Bear Under the Stairs</u>, Bantam, 1994

Feldman, Christina, <u>Stories of the Spirit, Stories of the Heart</u>, Harper, 1991

Granowski, Alvin, <u>Goldilocks and the Three Bears/Bears Should Share: Another Point of View</u>, Steck-Vaughnm, 1995

Hawkins-Mitchell, Vali, <u>A Wiggly Girl Sits Still</u>, Inner Directions, 2002.

Hawkins-Mitchell, Vali, <u>Bad Bracelet Club</u>, Inner Directions, 2003.

Hawkins-Mitchell, Vali, <u>Christofer Faces the Day</u>, Inner Directions, 2003.

Holliday, Virginia, <u>Bantu Tales</u>, Viking Press, 1970

Kent, Jack, <u>There's No Such Thing as a Dragon</u>, Golden, 2001

Lobel, Arnold, <u>Ming Lo Moves the Mountain</u>, Harper Trophey, 1993

Maddern, Eric, <u>The Fire Children</u>, Penguin, 1993

McCarthy, Tara, <u>Multicultural Fables and Fairy Tales</u>, Scholastic, 1999

Porter, Eleanor, <u>Pollyanna</u>, Wordsworth, 1994

Seieska, John, <u>The True Story of the 3 Little Pigs</u>, Puffin, 1996

Trivizas, Eugene, <u>The Three Little Wolves and the Big Bad Pig</u>, Alladin, 1997

Young, Ed, <u>Seven Blind Mice</u>, Penguin, 2002

TRADITIONAL FABLES

<u>Henny Penny (or Chicken Little)</u>

<u>The Elves and The Shoemaker</u>

<u>The Emperor's New Clothes</u>

<u>The Little Train</u>

<u>The Pied Piper</u>

AUTHOR'S AFTERTHOUGHTS

One of my most valued mentors told me that if I was not learning from every client then I was doing something wrong. This has been good advice and became a personal motto as I was learning. Then, when I became the Fabulous and Amazing Dr. Vali, that advice was an icon and it was already a practice habit. It has served me well. Just when I think Ive "seen it all and heard it all" I find myself in learning mode from someone in my private practice or consulting work who has a new story. I listen.

I tell my students and clients about one of my favorite learners. He is a gentleman who could barely read. He came to my office to learn how to be a better father after his divorce. He loved his children but didn't feel competent. He knew he wasn't going to get a college degree, had no time for seminars, and of course was almost illiterate. He was so eager to be a great dad that we worked out a way for him to have life long learning. I helped him find a book he thought he might like to read if he had time and was a better reader. He bought his own copy of the book. First I showed him that it was definitely okay to make notes, underline, or write on the pages of the book. After all, it was his book. Then I showed him how to tear out one page at a time. After all, it was his book. He then took that page and folded it carefully and put it in his pocket. Then when he was taking a lunch break at his work, relaxing, or in some other place that was quiet he would pull out that page and plug away at reading it. Sometimes he'd only get through a sentence. But then he would ponder that sentence for a long time. I encouraged him not to worry about how long it took, but to take the information inside his good spirit and to have some faith in himself and his kids. This gentleman kept at it, and his children adore him. They see him as a man who is willing to learn, to make effort, and invest in something important. He gets an A+ from this Ph.D. and is an inspiration to me to get up each morning at dawn and read about something I need to learn even if it is just a sentence or two. I hope this chapter encourages you to expand your knowledge base.

NEXT-TO-THE-LAST THOUGHTS

When I train companies on Emotional Continuity Management I encourage workshop participants to consider forces in nature that create conflict. I talk about tornadoes and the spins. I also talk about where the spin is not. Over the years I have become fascinated with the topic of Nothingness as an energy source and a resource for de-escalating spins. Using Nothingness as a form of nonviolent, non-resistance to conflict has made me a better counselor, and conflict resolution mediator, friend, enemy, wife and mother. I am even nicer to my big silly border collie that must jump on me every chance he gets. I am learning that many times doing Nothing is quite useful.

For a long time I contemplated the Power of Nothing as it came to my attention (from many sources) that all conditions in the universe possess more space than matter, more empty than full, more open than closed, and more peacefulness than conflict. Years ago a teacher suggested I try to meditate on what was not present. My poor little brain worked on that one for quite a long while. I was looking for the something of Nothing. I eventually found I could quiet my busy mind quickly by thinking about the space between my spinning molecules and atoms rather than thinking about the pain in my left elbow. I thought about the space where the pain was not. I did that when I birthed my babies when I was taught to rest between contractions, because I could catch my breath when "nothing" was happening.

I learned more about this when I lived 422 feet away from the Pacific Ocean. The time between tides is called slack-tide. It is a moment between the tide coming in and the tide going out when is appears as though Nothing is happening. Fishermen taught me that this is the most important time to pay attention to the sea, because this was where everything was going to happen next. My senses, perceptions, and training suggested I focus on what "was" rather than what "was not." I live in a society of consumers that always wants more. Most industries and many companies support the concept that more is better.

Don't misunderstand — I like stuff! A lot. And shopping makes me a happy girl! And at the same time I am becoming quite more comfortable in the presence of Nothing. It is a quiet place. Sweet. Nothing is a location inside me and outside me that provides balance. It is a place and a non-place where the 'me' that is me does not react out of fear, misperception, judgment or anger. I simply am. Nothing seems to be the location to find everything! Many of my favorite teachers and authors have said this and have tried to lead me to this place over many years. I was looking too hard! Nothing does not lend itself well to words so there are, of course, countless books trying to describe Nothing in scientific, psychological, cognitive, physiological, biological, sociological, and spiritual language. I buy lots of books.

Becoming defensive during a conflict means I perceive a threat. It may be real, it may be Nothing. What if there wasn't a threat? What would I resist? Would I be more present in a challenging situation? Would I be more useful, more kind, more intrigued, more compassionate? Would I support life affirming creative productivity? Would I become like some sort of martial arts whiz and breathe an Ohm through my body and rise above conflict to offer my noble wisdom in some fortune-cookie language? I hope not. That would so NOT be me! Yet, on the other hand, I have learned that peacefulness is a powerful position to take in a conflicting situation. Nothing leaves me open to options. Victims have no options, so I become quite less frightened.

To manage emotions that are starting to spin, I need to first know what is going on with me. I need to feel my feelings, take care of what is missing for me, determine my position and then ask what my shared interest is with the other human in the situation. If I am not dealing with someone pathological or an Emotional Terrorist, then I may assume that our shared interest is peace and calm, justice and love and all those other non-tangible emotions that we humans equate with "happy." If I take my position from the center of my Nothingness I tend to become peaceful, quiet, sweet, and balanced. I am ready to listen without feeling threatened. Then I won't be pushing the situation into more energy of conflict by adding my force to the spin. I can make better choices.

An emotional spin, like the spinning winds in nature, only happens when forces collide. Many different forces exist in the universe without having to collide! If there is Nothing to bump into, the wind just moves wherever it needs to go. My task to provide a space for Emotional Continuity is to pay attention, listen, open up, breathe, stay balanced and calm, and not put up an energy field that collides into another energy field that contributes to the spinning. This is where problem solving can begin. It is science. It is art. It is esoteric. It is good business. It is happy.

I'm getting better at this process without becoming condescending, caving to other powerful forces, creating more conflict, or needing to make a hasty escape. I watched one of my dearest teachers die this year. She died the way she lived, with grace. For several years she did everything she could to attend to her situation without conflict. She approached her illness with attention but without resistance and stood in the Nothingness as she problem-solved her choices. Eventually she apparently found it more useful to move toward the open spaces sweetly than resist the forces that were colliding inside and outside of her. I have seen many children make this same choice as they smiled sweetly through their deaths, surrounded by loving families who either were fighting and grasping to keep them present inside the world of something, or breathing their last sweet breaths with them as they released them to the next something.

I learned over the course of my life how to fight. It seemed that I needed to for a very long time. Being born during an earthquake I think made me a bit scrappy to start with, and being raised by wolves helped. Trauma and drama in my life added to the mix. But toady I know that real change doesn't have to come through fighting, resisting and conflict. I have had the gift of seeing how people in catastrophic disasters, birthing rooms, deathing rooms, hospital rooms, conference and boardrooms, living rooms and courtrooms have made choices to center themselves and take a position of Nothingness in order to have Everythingness. These people stay 100% present in the moment and authentically manage their own Emotional Continuity while having energy to spare to offer compassion to someone else! Finding your own path to this is the stuff of warriors. Go for it!

Vali Hawkins Mitchell

APPENDIX I
THE HAWKINS-MITCHELL
SPIN-FREE WORKPLACE MODEL
FOR SYSTEM-WIDE EMOTIONAL
CONTINUITY MANAGEMENT

INTRODUCTION

In order to acknowledge and balance emotions in the workplace, a systemwide approach to Emotional Continuity Management begins with a buy-on process from the top down. Without complete buy-on from the top there will not be sufficient support to back up a manager who is confronted with the natural, subsequent challenges and resistance. If an Emotional Terrorist is in the midst of the employee pool, the manager absolutely must have support and backup from superiors.

Once the top officials, CEOs, owners and administrators buy on to the concept of managing emotions in the workplace, the process can begin by providing managers with training in the sets of tools necessary. An ordinary employee transitional process or a significant change can stir up emotions from small to large. Whether the changes are internal or external, natural or man-made, change is easy for some and difficult for others. This is why the exact same training program will then be introduced into the working population. Standardized trainings, follow-ups, individual recommendations, adjustments and fine tunings comprise the introduction of any solid new procedure into a system.

When the systematic introduction of new, consistent information starts moving through the organization it always moves toward the top. The top administrator must become the containment lid for the bubbling and stirring process of systemwide change. If the administrator is committed to the theory, plan, and process the organization quickly stabilizes. If the administrator is ambiguous or oppositional, the emotional backlash will move back down toward the bottom of the system.

All emotional fluctuations, grievances and anomalies are instantly reflected back into the system for integration and absorption. Or, they become more emotional substance that creates more spinning and disruption. Management is left to control all adjustments. If the manager has been trained to respond appropriately to these fluctuations the emotional content can be absorbed by a healthy system. If managers have been trained to recognize what is normal and what is a threat to containment and adjustment, they can implement a variety of new tools and options to increase their effectiveness. Clear directions with consistent information stabilize the flow of emotional energy in the system as it moves toward anticipated outcomes rather than toward escalated emotional spinning.

The top-down process validates and legitimizes that everyone is on board. This significantly increases loyalty for all stakeholders. The bottom line is encouraged as outcome. At the same time, everyone sees that their emotions matter, when well managed within workplace-appropriate boundaries. If people are not on board with the process, they are quickly identified as anomalies in the system. Managers can offer them increased training, education, readjustment, reorientation, encouragement, or appropriate transition out of the system. New system standards are established with a set of expectations defined internally and internally managed. This increases stakeholder buy-on for management as well as line staff. Rather than escalating the "Us vs. Them" dynamic, it can become "Us for Us."

A well-conceived Emotional Continuity Management process provides clear definitions, reinforces company-wide expectations, and provides the entire system with easily accessible, practical, industry-appropriate tools. If there is any kind of simple leak, tear, break or rupture in the system, it can be quickly repaired or managed if it is an expectation of the dynamic of change. Management will have a tool available and ready to go. If the rupture is catastrophic, management will have a cadre of resources beyond peers. It is useful to pre-train systems before there are incidents and introduce them to the resources available. During a catastrophic event external providers can be seen as "outsiders" or "heroes." Law enforcement and fire service organizations have discovered that when systems are in place before incidents, counseling and debriefing by external providers is seen as an internal policy decision that does not become an additional external threat in times of disaster or catastrophic challenge.

HOW SOME ORGANIZATIONS HAVE APPROACHED CREATING SYSTEM-WIDE EMOTIONAL CONTINUITY MANAGEMENT

- Hired specialized professionals for training, put them on retainers for disasters, have their people get to know them in advance so they don't appear as outsiders when the chips are down.
- Hired a field-tested Disaster Emotional Continuity Management Coach to support and train managers to deal rectly with the bridge between business and emotion.
- Hosted a Consultation using resource combinations from inside and outside the company and making links with top-end credentialed professionals in their area.
- Assigned a person or team to provide ongoing training for staff, orient new employees, write policy, create education, and establish standardize expectations while learning how to recognize the early warning signs of emotional dysfunction and track developing emotional tornadoes on the horizon.
- Provided high-end, quality traumatology or critical incident management training for all department managers

System-Wide Emotional Continuity Management Should Begin to Address These Questions:

Use the following questions to create a presentation document before you approach your administration to establish buy-on. A proactive position for Emotional Continuity Management begins with data that supports your position. Start your buy-on discussion with hard data, facts, statistics, fiscal risk projections and historical relevance. Follow with human-compassion-centered data that is translated into value-added benefit for your company. Show how taking care of human emotions is a fiscally advantageous, bottom-line valuable, stakeholder loyalty and customer value-added business decision.

- What are the predictable fiscal consequences of an emotional spin?
- Can your Emotional Continuity Management Team manage small and large emotions?
- Is everyone ready to manage the emotions of a disaster?
- If a small spin begins, who will stop it?
- Are employees able to help themselves enough to help others?
- Do you have enough tools to manage emotional situations?
- Have you drilled and rehearsed for emotional incidents, small to large?
- Does your company have special needs employees?
- Does you company have special equipment?
- Do your employees know what to expect in case of a disaster?
- Has your entire company developed system-wide intervention strategies?
- Does anyone on your team have any specialized Emotional Continuity Management training?
- If all top managers are gone can your line staff take over the peer responsibilities?
- How will your employees know when external help is required?
- Are your people willing to call in outsiders for emotional support?
- What resources are available to all employees?
- Do you have external consultants who include teams of debriefers and trauma experts who are familiar with your business?
- Will your experts and consultants come immediately if you call them?

- Are your managers, employees, or consultants field trained in real-time disasters?
- Do your external consultants understand your people, customers, and business mission?
- What are the predictable emotional outcomes from a disaster?
- What Emotional Continuity Management tools have employees rehearsed?
- Who is familiar with the Emotional Continuity Management tools and can use them under stressful conditions?
- Does your company have unique emotional needs?
- Are there Emotional Continuity Management tools in place that increase employee understanding about what humans are likely to do under a wide range of circumstances?
- Has your entire company been trained in system-wide intervention strategies and tools?
- Who in your company has extensive and advanced psychological trauma management training?
- What Emotional Continuity Management tools would serve a simple problem, a complicated issue, or a complex emergency?
- If managers are gone, who assumes the responsibility for Emotional Continuity Management?
- How do you know when external help is required?
- Are your people willing to call in outsiders?
- Are supportive resources ready and in place if something happened today?
- Do you have external consultants and trauma experts who are familiar with your employees, your customers, your business mission, and bottom line issues?
- Will your consultants come into your disaster zone immediately?
- Are your external consultants field-trained experts?
- Have you prepared a way to manage voluntary "helpers" who will show up to disasters?
- How will you protect yourself and your company from opportunists who show up without appropriate training and credentials when you are the most vulnerable?

Buy-On Procedures Should Begin to Address These Questions:

- How well does administration support the Emotional Continuity Management Plan?
- How completely has the Emotional Continuity Management Plan been incorporated into the Emergency Management Plan of the company?
- How well have other departments in the company been informed or notified about administrative buy-on?
- How well have other departments supported the Emotional Continuity Management Plan?
- How well supported is the need to practice and drill for emotional emergencies?
- How extensive are the opportunities to drill for emotional emergencies?
- How financially supported is the Emotional Continuity Management Plan?
- How supportive is the administration about providing opportunities for training employees in emotional management?
- How supportive is the administration about providing opportunities for training management
- How supportive is the administration about creating cooperative partnerships with other emergency response agencies prior to a disaster or emotional event?
- How supportive is the administration about providing pamphlets, books, literature, posters, media education, and other hard-copy information on Emotional Continuity Management Planning?
- How well do personnel know what they should do in an emergency to caretake their emotions?
- How well prepared are you to manage extreme emotions in the workplace?
- How well prepared are you to manage emotions resulting from a catastrophic disaster?

STEPS FOR WRITING AN EMOTIONAL CONTINUITY MANAGEMENT PLAN

1. **Research**
    Find your highest order of management style
    Explore a variety of possible forms
    HOW:
    >   Call someone in your position in another company for an Idea Meeting
    >   Read magazines and books
    >   Go to workshops or classes

2.   **Create a Blueprint**
      Visualize your perfect style
      Take time to sketch or write your plan
      HOW:
            Create a notebook or journal of ideas
            Draw pictures and doodles of your ideal work process

3.   **Decide and Commit**
      Remove barriers
      Prepare the space
      Gather resources
      Survive first challenges
      Continue to commit
            HOW:
            Work for buy-on
            See the big picture so there is no emergency in the planning stage
            Continue your research and creative stages
            Use challenges and obstacles as learning/teaching moments
            Write and rewrite your plan as it continues to evolve into a final draft

4.   **Begin**
      Take actions
      Safeguard resources
      Survive ongoing challenges
      Recommit
      HOW:
            Talk with others inside and outside your work: create networks
            Review and strengthen your data base
            Create professional documents and forms
            Accept and review feedback with your ideals in mind
            Review persistence materials
            Begin implementation stages

5.   **Recall**
      Review highest order ideals
      Review original visions
      Reconsider if appropriate
      Recommit and Continue
      HOW:
            Review previous stages with ideals in mind
            Continue to face challenges with open mind and commitment

Emotional Continuity Management Checklist

As you are creating your Emotional Continuity Training for teams and employees, you can use the following
checklist to track your consistency:

•   Does each module of training follow the same "scripted" procedure so that the information is uniform and
      repeatable?
•   Is attending mandatory because mandating attendance creates a sense of unity among participants and
      immediately limits options for spinning?
•   Do follow up meetings provide creative input and collaboration from all members?
•   Has there been buy-on from the top? The top-down process allows the administration/management to
      discover what employees are on board, who are potential company emotional saboteurs, and who are
      simply trainable "problem children."
•   Does each module include practice time and drill for new tools, language, and concept acquirement?
      Adjustment and absorption of new ideas takes time and familiarity.
•   Do units of education, or modules exceed teachable time frames? Two hours for group education is
      appropriate, with shorter individual consultations when required. This process should add minimum

emotional impact to the organization's functioning. Do not let lengthy trainings become fodder for emotional spinning.
- Do Emotional Continuity Management trainings have written policy and clearly defined statements for:
    - Trainer qualifications
    - Company mission and team visions
    - Top organizational buy-on defined/clarified
    - Rules for mandated participation and non-negotiable consequences for nonparticipation
    - Expectations and timetables for skills practice and drills
    - Value added incentives for participation
    - Are reproducible documents prepared for:
        - Personnel interview charts
        - Models for explaining human emotions
        - Models for explaining human responses
        - Models for conflict resolution
        - Models for grief work and trauma management
        - Self care tools ranging from simple to complex
        - Grading assessments
        - Models for managing individual differences
        - System wide back up plans
        - System wide back up plans for the back up plan

THE HAWKINS-MITCHELL FIVE STEP SPIN-FREE WORKPLACE TRAINING MODEL FOR SYSTEM-WIDE EMOTIONAL CONTINUITY MANAGEMENT

The Five-Steps:
1. Preparation
2. The Wake-Up Call
3. Invitation
4. Clarity and Recommitment
5. Remediation.

1. PREPARATION

Managers begin the process by deciding exactly what they want, their expectations, how the readjustment process will lay out, who will be involved in research and development, individual committees, task forces, brainstorming sessions, and systemwide implementation. It is the blueprint of the new infrastructure. It is not necessary to tear down the old one while building a new framework; it is necessary to have a plan of action and specialists to back up the plan. The rough draft of the Policy is created here.

Some Potential Preparation Components

- The original mission/vision statements
- All documents/policies/procedures that may be effected or changed
- Legal Counsel
- HR (Managers and above)
- Internal Auditors (Managers and above)
- Security (Managers and above)
- External mental health consultant
- External anti-terrorist specialist
- Trainers/educators
- Support staff to schedule meetings and trainings
- General timeline/deadline

Meetings with all department heads and managers to dispel potential rumors. It is important in this first step to have very rigid boundaries in order to protect leaks, fragmentation, generating half truth/half lies and rumors. If there is an Emotional Terrorist within this first unit, it will be evident via leaks.

2.   THE WAKE-UP CALL

After Preparation, it will be time to inform all employees, system wide, that there is a new policy on its way to the organization, that it is positive, has nothing to do with layoffs, and will be announced at a specific meeting (or meetings). Location and time are included in the memo or will follow within 24-48 hours.

The meeting should then be held for everyone. EVERYONE MUST BE MANDATED TO GET THIS INITIAL INFORMATION. This should not be a long, drawn-out process and in fact should only take a small period of time, less than an hour. Everyone should be informed in person, in group meetings, not individual meetings, and in writing within a 48 hour period. There must be provisions for a make up meeting for absent employees. Emotional Terrorists will avoid this unless it is mandated, which includes a mandated make up meeting. Terrorists will do *anything* to avoid this meeting.

The information given should be scripted to limit misinterpretation and to protect the messengers. The meeting script will announce the introduction of a new Anti-Spin Workplace Policy and present the expectation that all employees are expected to raise their consciousness about the possible effects and consequences for business and human beings in the presence of emotional spinning.

This meeting should be presented in an active, upbeat, celebratory "you-are-part-of-the-solution-or-part-of-the-problem" format. This engages the collective energy and if there are Emotional Terrorists aboard they will see that there is no turning back. It is the first statement of commitment, the line drawn in the sand, the "just say no" to the dealer. This new standard must absolutely be driven by the Zero Tolerance for Emotional Spinning or Emotional Terrorism agenda presented by the administrative body of the organization to everyone. Emotional players will immediately try to manipulate it into something more comfortable. With a lot of built-in flexibility for readjustments and realignments, trainings and support, understanding and compassion for all, the one thing that cannot be flexible is the Zero Tolerance Position.

Stage 1:

The management teams are instructed on the topic of emotions at the workplace and educated in recognition skills. They are informed of the expectations of administration and given ways to support its implementation. At these meetings there will be a period of time that managers may contribute their ideas for developing policy.

Some Potential Talking Points for Discussion

- Recognition of normal and abnormal emotions
- Statistics
- What/So What/Now what
- Denial, minimization, fears
- Wherever you work is Sacred Ground
- Predators versus Prey
- Tricks of Terrorism
- Anti-Spin Strategies
- What to expect from who and why
- Specifics of Your Industry
- Administrations buy-on support

Stage 2:

All employees are brought on board with the same scripted program given to management, with a series of group meetings to accommodate all staff. All meetings must be mandatory or made up with a short turnaround, non-avoidable deadline. Period.

3.   THE INVITATION

At the end of the wake-up scripted sessions all staff, management and employees are given an invitation (either written or verbal) to become part of an Anti-Spin Action Team. After providing clear and specific information about the physical, mental, emotional, spiritual and financial danger of allowing Emotional Terrorists to run their organization, they are given an opportunity or invited to become Emotional Stakeholders. All are allowed and encouraged to describe their own view of possible emotional spinning effects in this environment (i.e., the organization's unique mission, payoffs for work ethic, personal integrity, service and care for self and others, the concerns for their own family, community, and individual success) as well as individual stories and experiences which may be useful to the group well being.

When healthy and dysfunctional employees begin to see that it is their best personal and collective interest to be PART OF THE SOLUTION, they generally get on board quickly and with great vigor. In fact, they are often relieved that the threat of emotional spinning or terrorism, present or future, may be identified and addressed. Many good employees have not "ratted" on their co-workers out of either fear of reprisals or a commitment to professionalism. They have been silent and miserable trying to stay out of the path of the emotional tornado. Their faith in management begins to be restored. Terrorists will immediately question the bottom line to see if it is real or going to disappear. Reinforcement of the Zero Tolerance for Emotional Spinning or Terrorism will need to be repeated.

After the invitation to join in a System Wide Team-Building process, it becomes immediately evident to management, usually within a few hours, who is going to support the agenda and who is going to try to sabotage it. Track all fear rumors directly back to the source and extinguish them immediately. Whining is okay, but any rumors must be stopped, assessed for spinning and intentional terrorism, and completely quelled. After a very brief initial discomfort and rattling of the cages, healthy people get on with the job of recovery and cleanup, while emotional spinners and terrorists begin to reveal themselves. There will be clear, documentable, and immediate feedback.

Everyone gets the benefit of the doubt to start with. Even Terrorists. All are given a small window to adjust. They must be given time to adjust, change their minds, get on board, exit, shake, shudder ,and join in the new standard. Everyone adjusts at a different pace. 72 hours should be the amount of time to expect reasonable adjustment for new information. This does not mean competency, but it does mean compliance and a willingness to take the next step. Emotional Terrorists will get very, very creative to try to protract and expand the time between announcement and compliance. Those who are dragging their feet can be evaluated by their history. Management can determine through review of work history, personal observations, and appropriate grievance procedures who are the regular slow-pokes and who are Emotional Terrorists who are instigating resistance and sabotage. Be suspicious of everything from absenteeism to escalating stories of personal victimhood. Listen with compassion, repeat the Zero Tolerance Agenda, and move on.

Some Potential Talking Points for Discussion

- What is the critical difference between healthy venting and complaining following an appropriate grievance process to affect change, and Emotional Terrorism tactics?
- Why do some people take higher ground when others take the low road?
- What is the difference between a workplace soldier and a workplace warrior?
- What are the payoffs for becoming a workplace warrior?
- What are the ranges and levels of spinning from small to large?
- What are the differences between physical, emotional, mental and spiritual spinning?
- How are we going to help each other get on board?
- How can we support those who struggle with change?
- What are the differences between sharing our emotions and spinning?
- What are your experiences with Emotional Terrorists?
- What place do emotions fit in the workplace? Do they?
- What does it mean to be held in an emotional hostage situation in the workplace?

4.   CLARITY AND RE-COMMITMENT

The bottom line must remain in place, even when challenged. Countless people stand up and decide to change their lives. They make great progress, overcome significant and daunting obstacles and are within five minutes of reaching their personal miracle when offered an "out," an easier path, a less-than-miraculous option that gets them to the land of "almost right." After grand struggles and victories, they are tired, vulnerable and ready to taste success. Cue the opportunist or Emotional Terrorist who arrives and offers them a bargain for half the price. The opportunist has radar for these moments of potential emotional cave-in or collapse. They can almost smell the moment of critical mass and swoop in with the brightly wrapped, sparkly rescue package. If the invitation is accepted the process can slide back to the beginning or farther.

Here's a sample of what this dynamic looks like:

1.   The mission has been announced that everyone must upgrade his or her computers from 3.0 to a 5.0 level by January 1.
2.   The consultant, trainer, CEO, and management begin the work of training and helping the staff adjust.
3.   Person #1 upgrades to 5.0 instantly. They have been prepared.
4.   Person #2 upgrades to 5.0.
5.   The system wiggles and feels a bit disrupted.
6.   Person #3 upgrades to 5.0 and several others upgrade to 3.5 and 4.0. Progress is happening.
7.   Several persons resist, one employee quits, others begin to whine, one starts a rumor about layoffs.
8.   Person #4 upgrades to 5.0 and several others are prepared to upgrade, but want to see what administration is going to do, if the administration and management are serious.
9.   Enough people are now at 4.5 or better and the old system begins to collapse in on itself.
10.   There is stress and anxiety as some are catching up, others are failing and seeking help, others are waiting to see if the rumors are true so they can avoid the change, and some are getting their resumes in order. Resistance increases.
11.   Person #5 upgrades to 5.0 and the system is vulnerable to total collapse. Anxiety is high.
12.   December 30, the system is extremely fragile before the deadline as people upgrade, adjust, struggle, or resist. A few "slowpokes" are working hard to make the shift.
13.   The expectation is that on December 31, the system will shift to the new level. Tension is elevated, some people panic, others are excited, some are concerned and fearful.
14.   Two more employees bail out and jump ship, someone retires early to avoid the change, a pregnant mom exits earlier than planned. Another slowpoke upgrades unexpectedly to 5.0.
15.   CRITICAL MASS HAPPENS and all eyes look to the CEO and Management for clarity, support, recommitment, and consistency.

THEREFORE: On January 1, the CEO and management either stands by this original mission, with allowable room for minor or simple procedural and technical adjustments and reasonable catching up behaviors, or:

1.   The Project will be seen as a Test, a Hoax, a Manipulation, a trick, and a scheme.
2.   Faith collapses. Confusion Ensues. The system collapses.
3.   There is a relapse back to a level below the 3.0 standard.
4.   The program must be started all over at square one; faith has been lost, confidence has been shattered. All the work, tension, changes and challenges are now seen as vaporous in relationship to the CEO's expectation. People are confused, disappointed, lost.
5.   Those who have already done the shift to 5.0 will now readily accept positions elsewhere, usually offered them without their solicitation, where they can use their 5.0 skills that your organization has paid for in a 4.0 setting and be leaders, or in a setting that has a 6.0 expectation where they can grow.
6.   At this point you might find that the business has lost the 3.0 people and the 5.0 people and is left with the less than cream of the crop to maintain a very challenged and confused organization. The brightest and best will leave when they lose confidence in the leadership.

5.   REMEDIATION

Remediation is an educational process that fine-tunes the team into the level it wants to achieve. It leaves room for missed bits of information and the natural errors associated with human beings. Any current Emotional Terrorism flurries should be peer-managed by the policy and Anti-Terrorism work should quickly be in the hands of managers and regular staff and on-site managers. The worker who is still working at achieving the 5.0 system but is still stuck at a 3.0 system needs more assistance. If reasonable, visible progress is being made at an appropriate pace then there should be room for support and encouragement. Healthy employees generally transition with no difficulty if they are provided clear guidelines, training, opportunities for success and mistakes, management support, and a direct indication of personal payoffs. Dysfunctional employees take a bit more time and attention. If they are progressing they should be supported and encourage. If they are valuable employees and have simply gotten on the wrong track, this is time worth the effort and usually value-added and cost-effective.

Pathological Employees and Emotional Terrorists are generally found to be more expensive to teach than replace. Terrorists who continue resistance, sabotage progress, and do not support the policy while in fact adding fuel to tension, are now reprimanded for potential policy infractions of Emotional Terrorism. Ongoing breaking of policies or persistence in terrorist activities needs to be addressed directly and removed from a healthy system before it causes irreparable, irreversible, terminal harm.

Some Potential Talking Points for Discussion

- Ethics
- Diversity
- Trauma
- Impaired employees
- Grief work
- Survivors of prior trauma
- Addictions
- Dr. Vali's Trauma Toolkit© (Hawkins-Mitchell, 1999)
- Grievance policies and procedures
- Emotional venting models
- Business change agendas of the Company

ADDITIONAL STEP

A.   REVIEW RESISTANCE TO TRAINING PROGRAMS

HEALTHY EMPLOYEES

Salt of the earth, fun, pleasant, groomed, inclusive, engaged with life, open, thoughtful, manage their emotions well, are open with feelings, positive and negative, are compassionate, reasonable, fairly consistent over time, have a life.

Response to an Anti-SPIN Policy: *Look forward to growth and development. May have some concerns about time involved or group commitment, but eager to see the results of more clarity and definitions of policies. No resistance.*

DYSFUNCTIONAL EMPLOYEES

May be open to growth with some minor fears to larger fears, naive, young or old, has not been given the correct information, for some reason is in a weakened state, vulnerable to suggestions and influences, subject to emotional swings, able to be coerced by a stronger influences, positive or negative. Emotions are more central, may be hard worker with limited skills and options, differing levels of willingness to be taught.

Response to an Anti-SPIN Policy : *Have the potential to be remediated, trained, and informed and educated. May either value or fear growth and development. Minor resistance.*

PATHOLOGICAL EMPLOYEES

Has an agenda and a mission, willing to destroy people, places and things to protect themselves or their personal beliefs and agendas, even when masked as the "greater good." May be using individuals or the entire system for their agenda or as a legitimate cover, may target others who appear to threaten their agenda. Emotions may be central or invisible.

Response to an Anti-SPIN Policy: *May resist remediation. May escalate their efforts, go underground, or leave. Emotional escalation is traceable to them and therefore easy to remedy, more difficult if they go underground or covert. Once underground they may be at risk for participating in sabotage, selling priority information, or other ethical violations. Early identification of these employees protects all concerned. Major resistance. Resistance can be passive or aggressive.*

B.   TRACK THE CONTAGION

Like a virus, Emotional Terrorism can spread between departments if the environment within the department has vulnerable units. For example, a harmless rumor that might be laughed off by two healthy employees may be taken seriously by a dysfunctional member of the team. That same rumor, used by someone with pathology, could be the last straw for the vulnerable employee. It helps to know who the players are, so that an unexpected invasion, such as a rumor or disruption, can be anticipated and stopped in its tracks. Knowing or defining the players doesn't mean anything must be done other than determining the risk factors involved in developing situations.

Track the Movement and Contagion of an Emotional Incident Through a System

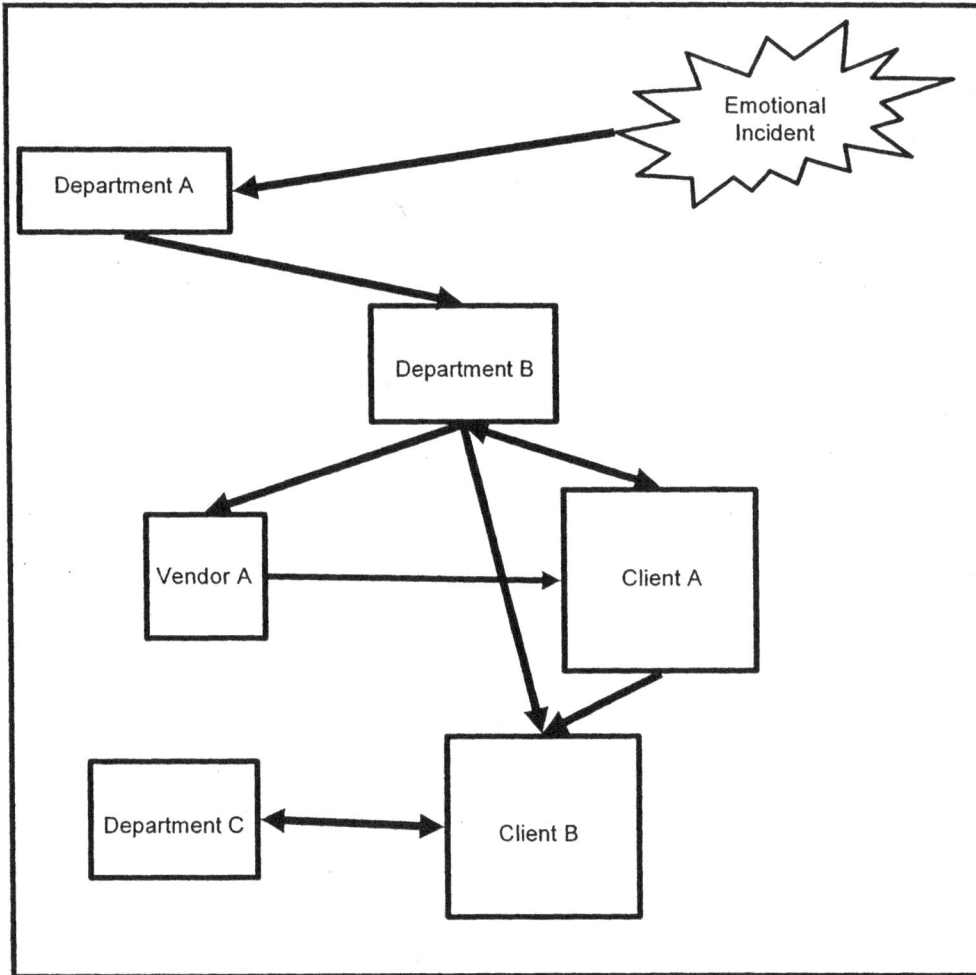

- Emotional Incident
- Department A
- Department B
- Vendor A
- Client A
- Department C
- Client B

Non-Violent Non-Spinning Responses To An Emotional Spin

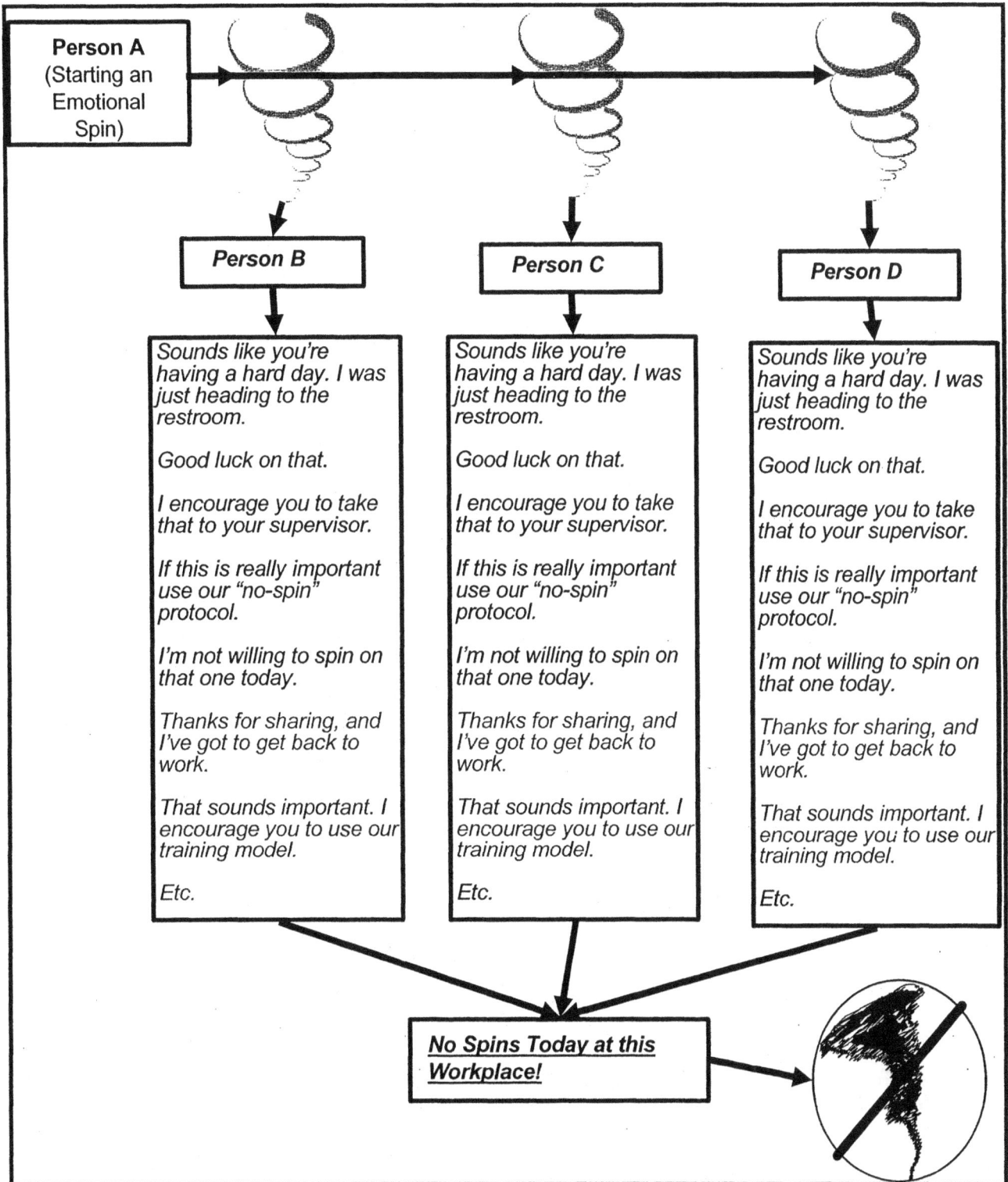

Person A
(Starting an
Emotional
Spin)

Person B

Person C

Person D

*Sounds like you're
having a hard day. I was
just heading to the
restroom.*

Good luck on that.

*I encourage you to take
that to your supervisor.*

*If this is really important
use our "no-spin"
protocol.*

*I'm not willing to spin on
that one today.*

*Thanks for sharing, and
I've got to get back to
work.*

*That sounds important. I
encourage you to use our
training model.*

Etc.

*Sounds like you're
having a hard day. I was
just heading to the
restroom.*

Good luck on that.

*I encourage you to take
that to your supervisor.*

*If this is really important
use our "no-spin"
protocol.*

*I'm not willing to spin on
that one today.*

*Thanks for sharing, and
I've got to get back to
work.*

*That sounds important. I
encourage you to use our
training model.*

Etc.

*Sounds like you're
having a hard day. I was
just heading to the
restroom.*

Good luck on that.

*I encourage you to take
that to your supervisor.*

*If this is really important
use our "no-spin"
protocol.*

*I'm not willing to spin on
that one today.*

*Thanks for sharing, and
I've got to get back to
work.*

*That sounds important. I
encourage you to use our
training model.*

Etc.

**No Spins Today at this
Workplace!**

C.   KEEP TRAININGS CONSISTENT:

- Does each module of training follow the same "scripted" procedure so that the information is uniform and repeatable?
- Is attending mandatory because mandating attendance creates a sense of unity among participants and immediately limits options for spinning?
- Do follow up meetings provide creative input and collaboration from all members?
- Has there been buy-on from the top? The top-down process allows the administration/management to discover what employees are on board, who are potential company emotional saboteurs, and who are simply trainable "problem children."
- Does each module include practice time and drill for new tools, language, and concept acquirement? Adjustment and absorption of new ideas takes time and familiarity.
- Do units of education, or modules exceed teachable time frames? Two hours for group education is appropriate, with shorter individual consultations when required. This process should add minimum emotional impact to the organization's functioning. Do not let lengthy trainings become fodder for emotional spinning.
- Do Emotional Continuity Management trainings have written policy and clearly defined statements for:
    - Trainer qualifications
    - Company mission and team visions
    - Top organizational buy-on defined/clarified
    - Rules for mandated participation and non-negotiable consequences for non-participation
    - Expectations and timetables for skills practice and drills
    - Value added incentives for participation
    - Are reproducible documents prepared for:
        - Personnel interview charts
        - Models for explaining human emotions
        - Models for explaining human responses
        - Models for conflict resolution
        - Models for grief work and trauma management
        - Self care tools ranging from simple to complex
        - Grading assessments
        - Models for managing individual differences
        - System wide back up plans
        - System wide back up plans for the back up plan

D.   REHEARSE

Follow the steps to create an Emergency Drill that includes Emotional Continuity Management as part of the scenario. Find ways to implement your emotional management skills and tools into the practice and exercise activities.

E.   RETREAT AND RECREATION

Everyone requires rest and time to play. Find ways to rest and play that work for yourself and your team. Provide a retreat, a play day, a luncheon, a surprise ice-cream party, movie tickets, a jazz band in the employee lounge, or whatever sounds wonderful and easy that will give respite before, during and after problems and issues and always after rehearsal drills.

F.   RECOMMIT

Take a deep breath and start again from Step 1 and move forward because emergencies and the emotions that go with them are not going away! The daily annoyances of humans working along side humans are an expectable part of life and working environments.

STARTING AN EMOTIONAL CONTINUITY MANAGEMENT TEAM

CONSTRUCTING YOUR TEAM

Who is on your Emotional Continuity Management Team?

Will they be trained and ready to get your company up and running during or after an incident?

How do others respond to this team emotionally?

Are they well thought of in the organization? Trusted? Safe?

Who will show up?

Have all members been trained in leadership to take over in case of loss of life?

What does your company need to get back to 100% services?

Can it operate at 10%? 35%?

What qualifications are acceptable to be on the Emotional Continuity Management team?

Have they been pre-screened for PTSD from any prior catastrophic incident?

Are they emotionally stable, mature, trained, and willing?

Have they had sufficient training?

What levels of training are sufficient for your team members and leaders?

Are your emergency and disaster plans specific or generalized?

What is vague and what is specific?

Have you tested your plan?

Has it been table talk or real-time drills and exercises?

Have your team member discussed and planned for emotional shock, loss, and terror?

What support does your team have to manage their feelings when they are supporting others?

Have all team member been trained to understand the variety of emotional reactions to expect in case of a catastrophic incident by a qualified disaster or trauma specialist or qualified Licensed Mental Health Professional?

Who will replace you if you are not present? How would your team deal with losing you?

Does everyone know all the parts of the plan?

QUALIFICATIONS CHECKLIST FOR TEAM MEMBERS, EXTERNAL CONSULTANTS, EMOTIONAL CONTINUITY MANAGEMENT TRAINERS, SERVICES PROVIDERS

Decide what your Best Practices and Standards are for Qualifications and then Document the following:

(All licensing and certification credentials should be documented with copies of current status that can be updated on a yearly basis as needed)

- Formal training
- Informal training/experiences
- Real time disaster experience
- Continuing education
- Licensures
- License number and date of expiration/photocopy
- Malpractice Insurance
- Specialized training
- Experience
- References
- Special skills
- Special populations skills
- Availability
- Locations
- Types of services
- Application forms/process
- Photo ID
- Criminal background check including fingerprints
- Security clearance if needed

- Vehicular background check if needed
- Signed contract for services including clear fee arrangements

CONSTRUCTING YOUR TEAM NOTEBOOK

Minimum requirements should include:

- Team Composition
- Chain of authority
- Exit strategies
- Member list and all contact methods
- Collect verifications of qualifications of all team members
- Verification that all team members have been screened for PTSD and prior trauma
- Plans for changes in circumstances, shifts, time off
- Complete data about will your company require to return to 100%, 75%, 50%, 25%
- Services
- Anticipated obstacles to complete recovery
- Written plans for the Emotional Continuity Management for specific incidents, even those that appear to be unlikely:
    - tornado
    - earthquake
    - suicide
    - cyber crime
    - shooting
    - fire
    - Emotional Terrorist
    - winter storm
    - hurricane
    - chemical spill
    - shelter in place
- Extensive lists of local, regional, national and international recourses
- A chronology of how you have tested your plans and lessons learned data
- Reproducible copies of required or preferred forms or documents
- Emergency numbers for team members and families
- Complete written policy and procedures
- Company/Administrative buy-on statement
- List of insurances and legal support
- List of all employees under the domain of the Emotional Continuity Management Team

NOTEBOOK TIP: If your team has a notebook that they can carry with them to a site, it needs pages that will be removable, pages that are covered with plastic sheet protectors, colorful enough so they can just grab-and-go out the door and not have to search for it under duress, blank lined paper for jotting notes, an attachable pen, perhaps even a backpack or carrying case that they think looks cool. The point of this is that during duress, your team needs to not have to think about anything but doing their work as calmly as possible. Looking for a bit of paper to write a phone number, or scrambling for a pen, is contraindicated for an Emotional Continuity Manager.

Start collecting data for an ever-evolving team notebook with reproducible documents, forms, logos, policies, plans, procedures, checklists, guidelines, resources, requirements, and anything your team decides would assist them in emotional continuity management during an emotional incident or disaster

Use the following pages to start your TEAM NOTEBOOK:

Disaster Emotional Continuity Management Checklist

PLANNING PHASE (prior to a disaster incident)

- Define qualifications necessary for Emotional Continuity Management team membership and leadership
- Select and interview applicants
- Provide training and continuing education
- Provide regular training and practice drills
- Plan task assignments, authority lines, and delegations of responsibility
- Create a disaster buddy system
- Chain of command structure should be provided to all employees
- Contractual relationships with external disaster services providers

IMPLEMENTATION PHASE (during a disaster incident)

- Provide a central location for communications for your team and outside teams
- Do a disaster buddy check-in
- Initiate pre-planned task assignments, authority lines, and delegations of responsibility
- Coordinate responses
- Coordinate lines of supply, equipment, and information
- Assess needs with an ongoing process of open communications
- Provide a clerical manager for support
- Provide other support services such as communications, logistics, supply
- Orient team to the specific event
- Define event status and review plan
- Profile the participants of the event
- Collect resources, make network connections, implement memos of understanding,
- Create a blueprint of actions for immediate response and build in plan for long term
- Make task assignments
- Continue training as needed with regular updates and support
- Review short term response
- Begin discussions of intermediate and long-term responses
- Continue status updates, consultations, liaisons, MOU's, and provider partnerships
- Provide expert consultations and trainings
- Support staff and manage self-care
- Defuse as needed
- Document activities

RECOVERY PHASE (after an incident)

- Debrief participants and team members
- Continue self-care
- Maintain liaisons and links with other network connections
- Ongoing training should continue
- Discussions on lessons learned
- Wrap up details
- Paper work completion, filings, recordings
- Support process over the long term no matter how long it takes
- Send thank you letters
- Support and encourage buddy sets and support and reorganize around any buddy losses
- Provide memorials and commemoration programs
- Acknowledge and give appropriate recognitions
- Return to phase one and begin new phase of recruitment for planning for next disaster

BEFORE

Acknowledge — Acknowledge that there is a probability that at some time there will be a disaster that has an effect and consequences for your company

Brainstorm — Make a list of all possible disasters that could ever, even in wildest imaginings, touch your company directly or indirectly

Buy-on — Establish hierarchical buy-on for your company. If you company refuses to acknowledge the probability that there will be a disaster that has an effect and consequences for your company, dust off your resume and look elsewhere. Denial is not good business.

Plan — Create a list of partnerships, interventions, resources, policies, procedures, ideas, concepts, supplies, and contingencies for even the wildest imagined disaster

Narrow —   Narrow down your full list to the top ten possibilities

Training — Get training for anyone who might be involved in any disaster, from the line staff to the authority players in key positions. Training can consist of a small pamphlet to significant formal education opportunities

Partners — Pre-plan partnerships with local, state, and federal responder agencies and private disaster industry professionals. Write memos of understandings, pay for retainer fees, and publish a list for everyone on your staff. You never know if you will be there to make the calls.

Normalize — Make disasters a normal discussion in meetings, and planning sessions as you would any other part of company business. Disasters are a "normal" part of life and need addressing in a coherent and open manner in the same spirit you would discuss the furniture in the office.

Learn — Although everyone is doing fine, this is an excellent time to seek more management training.

DURING

Self Care — It is always appropriate to take care of yourself first

Survive — Do what is appropriate to survive a disaster

Expect — Expect emotions of all forms, from immobilized screaming to hysterically funny giggling fits.

Remember — Recall the stages of grieving: Denial, Bargaining, Anger, Depression, Acceptance. Add to this blaming, resistance, minimizing, aggrandizing and emotional response and reaction surprises that you haven't anticipated.

Remind — Remind yourself and others that all disasters have a beginning, a middle and an end. Beginnings are easy, and ends are a relief. Middles are crazy makers and seem to last forever…but they do not!

Learn — Although this is a difficult time for everyone, it can be an excellent time to seek more management training.

Review — Review the BEFORE guidelines and repeat what is necessary to stay on track.

AFTER

Manage — Remember that the disaster cannot be controlled, but you can manage through it. Face the changes and work through the transitions between the activity of the disaster and the end of the disaster when changes have been completed.

Expect — Don't be surprised. Encourage yourself and others to not ne surprised. There is no "going back" before the disaster, there is only moving forward after the disaster. Help people move forward.

Involve — Involve people in managing themselves and others. In disasters there is a tendency for people to either help others or become looters. Involve people in helping, even if it is a fabricated task like "we need someone to empty the wastebaskets." Busy people become more focused and feel more security. The rubric is that in an abnormal situation, it is helpful to do something that seems normal. Washing dishes, sweeping, dusting, organizing a phone tree, serving water, and other such banal and mundane tasks may keep people from sliding into an emotional abyss of helplessness. An employee who has "power and control" over the wastebaskets may feel less overwhelmed by the power of the disaster and may return to competent functioning more quickly.

<u>Listen</u> — Listen. Don't argue, discredit, disagree, or deny people their own perception of reality. People will adjust and recover in their own way at their own speed.

<u>Okay</u> — Human emotions are okay. Don't avoid or discourage emotions from your employees. If you feel uncomfortable with emotions find someone who isn't and gently direct people that direction. Do not block the healthy process of emotional recovery or it may come back on you.

<u>Pay Attention</u> — After a disaster the rhythm of work has fits and starts as it re-adjusts to its new flow. Try to move with it without resistance. See or feel it as a choreography with new dance steps. Two steps forward, one step back. One step forward, two steps to the side and two steps forward. Take your time. You will "feel" your new footing soon. Don't be afraid to ask questions or check your footwork from time to time. You don't want to step on toes, but you also don't want to miss a beat. Everything will be uncertain which will then be followed by what seems like rigid certainty…which will then again decay into chaos as it moves back into a more resolved new form. Take your time. Take your time. The disaster is over now, you have time to figure it all out.

<u>Insist</u> — Insist on being in the loop for information sharing. If you are out of the loop your anxiety will increase and so will your employees' anxiety. It is better to say, "I don't' know, but I'll find out as soon as I can," than to say, "I have no clue" and leave people in the dark with no sense of leadership.

<u>Communicate</u> — Share information, listen, wait, exchange ideas, avoid rumors, seek facts, present facts, offer patience, peace, procedures and protocol.

<u>Support</u> — Support your people. Know they can handle information better than innuendo. People can handle ambiguity if they are in the loop. Waiting is very hard for most people under duress, so make a formal "what should we do while we are waiting" process. Put things in writing when you can. A quick-fix bulletin board for memos or messages is very supportive for groups of people. Expect people to be distracted. It might help to have a television in the office for a few days. Let people watch it while they are working. Put it in the center of the worksite and not the employee lounge. Don't make employees pretend nothing happened. That will make you look crazy. Expect random outbreaks of group talking when incidents change. Check up on people to find out if they are in the loop or feel like they are.

<u>Open up</u> — Acknowledge stress, yours and theirs. It's okay to say you are stressed even when you are in a management position. It gives you more credibility and makes you more accessible. This doesn't mean a crying jag with your staff necessarily, although tears do not destroy leadership potential. Don't hesitate to ask for help. Quick check-ins with employees, without getting deeply involved in their emotions is very helpful. It is called defusing and takes the edge off the emotions as a brief respite and release. Find a place where you can defuse also. It should not be with another employee that you are managing.

<u>Debriefings</u> — Create opportunities to debrief your employees. You can train your people to do it, find volunteers, hire professionals or consultants who have been specially trained in mental health disaster practices.

<u>Avoid</u> — Do everything you can to stay away from group blame-frenzy behavior.

<u>Continue</u> — Continue to communicate and move forward, check in with people to see if they are moving forward, or if they are beginning to lose ground and need a different kind of intervention.

<u>Persist</u> — Persist in assisting people who may need ongoing management support. During normal situations people need leadership. Before, during and well after a disaster people need to keep their focus through the well balanced position of leaders. Workers who may have lost capacity to work due to loss of technology or services that existed before the incident will need specific leadership to stay connected to the job.

<u>Learn</u> — Although this is a difficult time for everyone, it can be an excellent time to gain more training.

<u>Review</u> — Review the BEFORE and DURING guidelines and repeat what might be useful or necessary to stay on track. There may be another disaster in your future.

<u>Lessons Learned</u> — In the absolutely most intensely positive manner you can muster after all of this, review every step, BEFORE, DURING AND AFTER, with an eye of successes and areas that need improvement.

<u>Celebrate</u> — Celebrate your survival!

<u>Memorialize</u> — Plan ahead for the one year anniversary or remembrance moment of the event. Create an annual commemoration for your office. Delegate the task if necessary to someone who would benefit emotionally from the process of creating tribute.

Administrative Buy-On Evaluation

(Rate the following between 1=Low and 10=High)

How well does administration support the Emotional Continuity Management Plan?

1   2   3   4   5   6   7   8   9   10

How completely has the Emotional Continuity Management Plan been incorporated into the Emergency Management Plan of the company?

1   2   3   4   5   6   7   8   9   10

How well have other departments in the company been informed or notified about administrative buy-on?

1   2   3   4   5   6   7   8   9   10

How well have other departments supported the Emotional Continuity Management Plan?

1   2   3   4   5   6   7   8   9   10

How well supported is the need to practice and drill for emotional emergencies?

1   2   3   4   5   6   7   8   9   10

How extensive are the opportunities to drill for emotional emergencies?

1   2   3   4   5   6   7   8   9   10

How financially supported is the Emotional Continuity Management Plan?

1   2   3   4   5   6   7   8   9   10

How supportive is the administration about providing opportunities for training employees in emotional management?

1   2   3   4   5   6   7   8   9   10

How supportive is the administration about providing opportunities for training management emotional management?

1   2   3   4   5   6   7   8   9   10

How supportive is the administration about creating cooperative partnerships with other emergency response agencies prior to a disaster or emotional event?

1   2   3   4   5   6   7   8   9   10

How supportive is the administration about providing pamphlets, books, literature, posters, media education, and other hard-copy information on Emotional Continuity Management Planning?

1   2   3   4   5   6   7   8   9   10

How well do personnel know what they should do in an emergency to caretake their emotions?

1   2   3   4   5   6   7   8   9   10

How well prepared are you to manage extreme emotions in the workplace?

1   2   3   4   5   6   7   8   9   10

How well prepared are you to manage emotions resulting from a catastrophic disaster?

1   2   3   4   5   6   7   8   9   10

Emotional Continuity Management Event Hot Sheet

Fill out this hot sheet if there is an incident: (can be used for Drills)

- What is the nature of the event?
- What is the scope of the emotional impact?
- How much geography/territory is involved? (i.e. a fire in the break-room, a devastated community or a devastated one block radius, a 48 car pile up in front of the main entrance to the worksite, death of one colleague, death of many colleagues)
- Who is in charge, authority/command structure? (Who do I report to?)
- Has there been property damage?
- Who has authority for restoring the property damaged?
- How many victims are involved?
- What are their ages if known?
- Are any children involved?
- Will the children's needs be treated separately from adult needs? Elderly? Special Need/disabled?
- What are the general nature of any injuries? (mild, moderate, severe, catastrophic)
- How many support staff will be involved?
- Support systems and teams in place now? On the way?
- How long will I be expected to respond?
- Will I be safe? How will that be accomplished?
- Is there a dress code? Or is there any special circumstances where clothing or footwear should be a factor? (i.e., is the entire staff trained in full range of disaster protocols from shelter in place to full evacuation?
- Has the entire staff been trained in what emotions to anticipate during this kind of incident?
- Are there cultural, religious, political, or ethnic variables that I should know or understand?
- What languages will be spoken? Will there be translators?
- Am I covered by company liability insurance or my own? Or both?
- What duties am I expected to perform or am responsible for providing? (i.e., debriefings, defusings, counseling, crisis response, medication assessment, diagnosis, mediation, communications, transportation, referrals, hand-holding)
- What paperwork will be required to manage this incident? Do I have all the required forms?
- What are the Mental Health or Disaster Professional qualifications necessary to deal with this?
- Who else will be helping me on this?
- Will I be fed, housed, provided for, given chocolate?
- Will there be an expectation of continuous service, or will there be opportunity for self care, support for me if I need it, breaks, days off, etc.
- What are my other resources?
- If I find that the situation is beyond my scope, expertise or personal tolerance, or if I become ill or injured or incapacitated, what is the protocol for a professional exit strategy and will that be supported
- Who will take over my assignments?
- What are the qualifications of the disaster team?
- What are the qualifications of the Emotional Continuity Management Team?
- How do I protect myself and my team first?
- What is the emotional environment needed for rapid recovery?
- What is the physical environment (locations on-off site, recovery equipment, communications, paper/pencils, water bottles, cell phones, toilet paper) needed for rapid recovery?
- Do we have event-specific planning strategies?
- Memos of understanding, agreements, contracts with Local, National and Global Resources?
- Have we tested this plan?

How to Set up a Drill

1.   Establish full buy-on administratively
2.   Determine leadership
3.   Prepare with paper drills and table-talks prior to simulation drills
4.   Define the goals of the drill
5.   Develop appropriate and safe logistical settings
6.   Develop appropriate scenarios
7.   Create scenario assignments
8.   Consider management of a real emergency or unexpected event during the simulation
9.   Review plans and gather feedback
10.   Conduct the drill
11.   Collect results
12.   Celebrate the closure of the drill formally
13.   Debrief participants and planners without critique
14.   Planners then can evaluate the success or failure of goal achievements
15.   Add or subtract necessary components and schedule next drill cycle
16.   Send thank-yous to all participants
17.   What questions will you need answered to make good decisions?
18.   What resources will you need in each case?
19.   What resources will you activate immediately?
20.   What resources will you put on stand-by?
21.   How will you approach administration, employees, vendors and ancillary participants?
22.   What plan will you write?
23.   What policies for emotions will you want in place?
24.   What people with what qualifications will serve you best?
25.   What level of emotional impact will this possibly have?
26.   What risks will there be for solo or group emotional spinning?
27.   What tools will you use to manage the emotions of employees?
28.   How will you take care of your self as you participated?
29.   What would be the estimated costs of this for your company
30.   What would be the estimated costs for your company if it was unprepared for a real emergency?

Tips for Success of Drills

Clear Notifications — Always state "THIS IS A DRILL" when making phone calls or contact calls during the drill. Remember when Orson Wells read the story War of the Worlds on radio and some people really thought the Earth was being invaded by aliens. People are fun! And people are nervous. Our world is scarier than it was a few years ago. It is better to be cautious than to create more emotional impact. It is critical to inform and notify all players and anyone who might be concerned that this is not a drill.

Identification Tags — For the same reasons as above, and for ease in managing the Participants, all members should have visible and highly identifiable, temporary identification that is collected after the drill.

Time them well — A drill during a layoff phase is dangerous. A drill during an earthquake is pointless and dangerous.

Evaluations should focus on positive points — Negative critiques destroy buy-on. Attempt to phrase weaknesses and losses in positive "can-do-better-next-time" language.

Have fun — Simulations can be fun and exciting when people are motivated to do their best for the sake of everyone else.

Add a surprise — The unexpected is where drills show holes in preparation. Don't add anything extreme, but include a small twist to make it interesting.

Ask other experts to play with you — Go to your local fire department, hospital or chapter of the American Red Cross and ask someone to help you plan your drill.

Drill a full range of emotions — Include all feelings from small to large, annoyances to catastrophic.

Maintain the illusion — Encourage participants to maintain their acting roles until excused from the drill.

Explain exit strategies and ending calls — Inform your participants how they can exit the drill if it becomes distressful. Also inform everyone when or how the drill will conclude.

Debrief even when it is a drill — Make certain any individual who exits a drill have a mandatory debriefing to deter people who simply want to exit the process so they can go home early, and protect participants who may really have difficulty. This also gets people into the good habit of debriefing.

Pleases and Thank-yous — Courtesy goes a long way to create closure and future buy-on. Write a formal thank you letter to all participants.

Drill and Rehearsal Checklist

- Establish full buy-on administratively
- Pick your team
- Assign roles
- Determine leadership or authority chains
- Define the emotional needs of your company
- Decide on what kind of drill you will have
- Establish timetable
- What is the purpose of the drill?
- What are five specific objectives you will seek?
- What documentation will be required?
- Create and write the emergency and emotional scenarios
- Make participant assignments
- Consider how you would manage a real emergency or unexpected event if one occurred during the exercise
- Make a detailed list of all activities, small and large
- List emotions that you wish to exercise and the interventions you would use
- Decide on how you will evaluate the exercise after it has been completed
- Conduct the drill
- Collect documentation
- Analyze data
- Celebrate the closure of the drill formally
- Debrief participants and planners without critique
- Planners evaluate the success or failure of goal achievements
- Lessons learned
- Add or subtract necessary components for the next drill
- Decide on what training will be necessary and who will get it
- Schedule the next drill
- Send written thank yous to all participants. No memos, real letters.

Additional steps:
- "This is a Drill" instructions given
- Identification Tags
- Evaluations should focus on positive points
- Have fun
- Add a surprise
- Associated agencies participation
- Drill a full range of emotions from small to large, annoyances to catastrophic.
- Participants told to maintain their acting roles until excused from the drill.
- Notifications
- Exit information
- Practice mock debriefings
- Debriefing schedule
- Formal thank yous
- What questions will you need answered to make good decisions?
- What resources will you need in each case?
- What resources will you activate immediately?
- What resources will you put on stand-by?
- How will you approach administration, employees, vendors and ancillary participants?
- What plan will you write?

- What policies for emotions will you want in place?
- What people with what qualifications will serve you best?
- What level of emotional impact will this possibly have?
- What risks will there be for solo or group emotional spinning?
- What tools will you use to manage the emotions of employees?
- How will you take care of your self as you participated?
- What would be the estimated costs of this for your company?
- Outline the performance tasks that must be accomplished
- Outline the emotional components for yourself, the staff, and the community that you must accommodate as the process evolves.
- What emotions are likely to be demonstrated?
- What might be a surprise emotion?
- How will you manage the emotions of your employees and clients?
- What fears or concerns can you anticipate because they were exposed to a potential health threat? Exposed to injury? Exposed to death?
- How will you plan for managing: (*see the Emotions List above*)

Fear	Anger
Rage	Terror
Sadness	Concern
Ambivalence	Hysteria
Boredom	Numbness
Confusion	Shock
Horror	Disgust
Disappointment	Grief
Denial	Horror
Grief	Disgust
Disappointment	Withdrawn
Irritated	Rancorous
Pessimistic	Impatient
Passive	Aggressive
Nervous	Embarrassed
Edgy	Sensitivity
Serious	Frivolous

Emergency Assistance Resource List

DISASTER CONSULTANT
    Local Contact Person:
    National phone number:
    Local number:
    Website:
    Other:
EMOTIONAL HEALTH PROVIDER
    Local Contact Person:
    National phone number:
    Local number:
    Website:
    Other:
MENTAL HEALTH PROVIDER
    Local Contact Person:
    National phone number:
    Local number:
    Website:
    Other:
MEDICAL SERVICES PROVIDER
Local Contact Person:
    National phone number:

    Local number:
    Website:
    Other:
WEATHER SERVICES
    Local Contact Person:
    National phone number:
    Local number:
    Website:
    Other:
HOMELAND SECURITY (HS)
    Local Contact Person:
    National phone number:
    Local number:
    Website:
    Other:
DEPARTMENT OF JUSTICE (DOJ)
    Local Contact Person:
    National phone number:
    Local number:
    Website:
    Other:

FEDERAL EMERGENCY MANAGEMENT AGENCY (FEMA)
    Local Contact Person:
    National phone number:
    Local number:
    Website:
    Other:

DEPARTMENT OF ENERGY (DOE)
    Local Contact Person:
    National phone number:
    Local number:
    Website:
    Other:

ENVIRONMENTAL PROTECTION AGENCY (EPA)
    Local Contact Person:
    National phone number:
    Local number:
    Website:
    Other:

DEAPARTMENT OF HEALTH AND HUMAN SERVICES (DHHS)
    Local Contact Person:
    National phone number:
    Local number:
    Website:
    Other:

U.S. DEPARTMENT OF TRANSPORTATION
    Local Contact Person:
    National phone number:
    Local number:
    Website:
    Other:

DEPARTMENT OF DEFENSE (DOD)
    Local Contact Person:
    National phone number:
    Local number:
    Website:
    Other:

NATIONAL TRANSPORATION SAFETY BOARD (NTSB)
    Local Contact Person:
    National phone number:
    Local number:
    Website:
    Other:

AMERICAN RED CROSS
    Local Contact Person:
    National phone number:
    Local number:
    Website:
    Other:

LOCAL LAW ENFORCEMENT
    Local Contact Person:
    National phone number:
    Local number:
    Website:
    Other:

FIRE DEPARTMENT
    Local Contact Person:
    National phone number:
    Local number:
    Website:
    Other:

EMERGENCY MEDICAL SERVICES
    Local Contact Person:
    National phone number:
    Local number:
    Website:
    Other:

PUBLIC WORKS
    Local Contact Person:
    National phone number:
    Local number:
    Website:
    Other:

EMOTIONAL AND MENTAL HEALTH SERVICES
    Local Contact Person:
    National phone number:
    Local number:
    Website:
    Other:

24 HOUR CRISIS HOT LINE
    Local Contact Person:
    National phone number:
    Local number:
    Website:
    Other:

VOLUNTEER SERVICES ASSISTANCE ORGANIZATIONS
Salvation Army
    Local Contact Person:
    National phone number:
    Local number:
    Website:
    Other:

Critical Incident Stress Management Teams
    Local Contact Person:
    National phone number:
    Local number:
    Website:
    Other:

Spiritual Support Network
    Local Contact Person:
    National phone number:
    Local number:
    Website:
    Other:

D'Mort (Death support)
Search and Rescue
Dive Rescue
Ski Patrol
K-Nine Search and Rescue
HAM Radio Network
WHAT ELSE WILL YOUR COMPANY NEED?

Sample Scheduling Form for Mandatory Meetings

(NAME OF YOUR DEPARTMENT)

Individual Meetings: *Circle one*: OPTIONAL   MANDATORY

<u>Wednesday, August 6th</u>

12:00-12:30   _____

12:30-1:00   _____

1:00-1:30   _____

2:00-2:30   _____

2:45-3:15   _____

<u>Thursday, August 7th</u>

9:00-9:30   _____

9:30-10:00   _____

10:00-10:30   _____

10:30-11:00   _____

11:30-12:00   _____

<u>Wednesday, August 23rd</u>   (*Only if prearranged with manager and consultant*)

12:00-12:30   _____

12:30-1:00   _____

1:00-1:30   _____

APPENDIX II
SUMMARY:
WHAT YOU NEED TO KNOW TO MANAGE EMOTIONAL TERRORS IN THE WORKPLACE AND TO PROTECT YOUR BUSINESS' BOTTOM LINE

1. **LEARN TO MANAGE IN THE MIDST OF EMOTIONS**
   - Be comfortable managing the emotions of others and yourself before, during and following an emergency or emotionally charged incident
   - Be able to describe the emotional scope of any incident
   - Know how emotions are appropriate to the workplace
   - Know why emotions are an essential part of management domain
   - Know what management skills or tools are necessary to manage emotions
   - Differentiate between emotions that are healthy, dysfunctional, and pathological
   - Be able to discuss the full range of emotional responses from small to large
   - Take a proactive stand to initiate discussion about emotions at the workplace
   - Be able to explain how emotions are to be expected and accepted while at the same time viewed as a financial risk potential at the workplace
   - Be able and willing to move any discussion about emotions at the workplace beyond the dismissible "touchy-feely" elements of emotions toward clear evidence of financial and other risks
   - Recognize emotions and risks associated with violence, mental illness, stress, Post Traumatic Stress

2. **UNDERSTAND HOW CHANGE INFLUENCES EMOTIONS**
   - Be able to discuss the differences between minor changes and major changes in terms of their potential emotional consequences
   - Know how changes in society, tradition, fads, trends or industry influence emotional content at your work site
   - Know which employees are most likely to resist change and when to expect it

3. **KNOW HOW DISASTERS INFLUENCE EMOTIONS**
   - Know what specific disasters may be typical of your location
   - Know the different kinds of disasters and what emergency preparation is necessary for expected and unexpected incidents
   - Have an emotional continuity plan for before, during and after a disaster

4. **BE ABLE TO REFRAME EMOTIONS**
   - Use imagination, intuition, metaphor and humor as creative ways to reframe emotions

5. **UNDERSTAND AND RECOGNIZE SPINNING**
   - Be able to define and characterize issues associated with the challenges of managing human emotions at the work site and explain the concept of workplace spinning to your employer or employees as you develop a buy-on procedure
   - Have a full understanding about what emotions are appropriate in your work site during normal operations and abnormal operations
   - Have a full understanding about what emotions are inappropriate in your work site during normal or abnormal operations
   - Know when emotions are spinning and when they are not spinning

- Avoid contributing emotional energy to a spin in progress
- Be able to recognize early warning signs of an impending emotional spin
- Be able to discuss the causes of emotional spinning using professional language in a variety of professional settings
- Be able to incorporate intuition, soft non-technical data, and hard-copy technical data in your analysis of emotional spinning
- Be able to document a position justifying the value of a spin-free workplace

6. **UNDERSTAND THE FINANCIAL RISKS OF SPINNING**
   - Be able to calculate the costs of managing emotional spinning
   - Be able to calculate the costs of not managing emotional spinning
   - Research what your company can afford to spend on emotional spinning
   - Interpret local, regional, national and international incidents into a range of costs to establish a credible base for promoting no-spin policy in your company
   - Document and create presentation materials representing financial and other risks of emotional spinning

7. **KNOW HOW TO USE TORNADOES TO DESCRIBE EMOTIONAL SPINNING**
   - Know the attributes of an emotional tornado
   - Use tornado attributes to evaluate emotions
   - Understand the risks of inappropriate emotions at the workplace
   - Make use of the tornado analogy to discuss current events

8. **UNDERSTAND AND RECOGNIZE EMOTIONAL TERRORISM**
   - Be able to define and give examples of international, domestic, and emotional terrorism
   - Know the attributes, behaviors, systemic influence, fiscal risks, early warning signs, techniques, language, and tools used by emotional terrorists

9. **KNOW THE GUIDELINES TO MANAGING EMOTIONAL TERRORISM**
   - Be able to describe in detail your personal weaknesses and strengths
   - Become competent in the use of the drama triangle

10. **CREATE A WELL STOCKED EMOTIONAL MANAGEMENT TOOLKIT**
    - Develop a comprehensive list of compassionate interventions, policies, procedures, strategies, and referrals in place to manage emotions
    - Consistently employ continuing education, well developed support systems, and ongoing skills development for professional growth
    - Know the steps to prepare your company systemically for excellent emotional management
    - Be well prepared for emotional management by establishing competency in the use of tools in the following areas:
      - Conflict resolution methods
      - Communication methodologies
      - Systems education
      - Diversity training and cultural norms of emotions
      - The use of icons, slogans and banners for quick recognition
      - Team building strategies
      - Grief work education and practice
      - Personal values tools
      - Appropriate use of humor
      - Emotional terrorism information
      - Normal and abnormal psychology basics
      - How to recognize signs of traumatic stress
      - Emotional self-defense
      - Ventilation models for debriefing and defusing
      - Adjustment strategies and practices
      - Stress management tools for the life span
      - Physical, mental, emotional and spiritual health practices
      - Resistance management skills
      - Documentation standards for emotions
      - Memos of understanding with support services
      - Extensive resources

- Make sure your toolkit includes tools which:
  - Generalize across occupational strata
  - Generalize across a full range of human emotions
  - Generalize to small and large companies
  - Include emotional quick-fix techniques
  - Are not based in fads or trends
  - Are gender, cultural, socio-economic, educational, racial, and ethnically sensitive
  - Can apply to volunteers, vendors, clients
  - Are simple, understandable, and practical

11. **CREATE A PERSONAL "GO FOR IT" ATTITUDE**
    - Establish a life long learning plan
    - Develop your unique set of persistence tools
    - Have a clearly defined exit strategy
    - Chose and defend your personal and professional management design
    - Frequently determine if you really want to be a manager
    - Decide if you need more training and advocate for it for yourself.
    - Continue to seek additional training in emotional management

12. **OBTAIN ADMINISTRATIVE BUY-ON**
    - Create and implement a detailed buy-on plan for administration and line-staff

13. **IMPLEMENT A SPIN-FREE TRAINING MODEL**
    - Develop an emotional continuity plan or spin-free model for managing emotional spinning in your company
    - Review and finalize administrative buy-on for this process
    - Implement this policy in your company

14. **DEVELOP AN EXTENSIVE BUSINESS CONTINUITY RESOURCE INVENTORY**
    - Establish liaisons, partnerships, referral sources, and memos of understanding for services between your company and local and national disaster and emotional support specialists
    - Create and maintain a library of books, web sites, and audio visual materials to help for yourself and your employees deal with the full range of emotions, small to catastrophic

15. **UNDERSTAND THE VALUE OF REHEARSALS AND PRACTICE DRILLS FOR YOUR EMOTIONAL CONTINUITY PLAN**
    - Know how to create and execute an Emotional Management Continuity Drill
    - Execute an Emotional Continuity Management Drill for your company

ABOUT THE PUBLISHER

ROTHSTEIN ASSOCIATES INC.

Brookfield, Connecticut USA

info@rothstein.com

www.rothstein.com

203.740.7400

888.ROTHSTEin (888.768.4783)

THE ROTHSTEIN CATALOG ON DISASTER RECOVERY

www.DisasterRecoveryBooks.com

THE ROTHSTEIN CATALOG ON SERVICE LEVEL MANAGEMENT

www.ServiceLevelBooks.com

THE ROTHSTEIN CATALOGS ON SERVICE LEVEL MANAGEMENT and DISASTER RECOVERY have served as these industries' principal resource for 1,000+ books, software tools, videos and research reports, since 1989.

They are divisions of Rothstein Associates Inc., an international management consultancy focused on crisis management, risk mitigation, disaster recovery, business continuity and service level management, since 1985.

A complimentary CD-ROM containing our catalogs will be sent upon request to: info@rothstein.com.

OTHER BOOKS AND RESOURCES FROM ROTHSTEIN ASSOCIATES INC.

www.rothstein.com

SERVICE LEVEL AGREEMENTS: A FRAMEWORK ON CD-ROM FOR IT AND TECHNOLOGY
10th Edition, by Andrew Hiles

Now every IT services professional can have effective SLAs! SERVICE LEVEL AGREEMENTS: A FRAMEWORK ON CD-ROM FOR IT AND TECHNOLOGY brings together all of the critical elements needed to build a Service Level Agreement, with extensive templates, examples and tools. It reflects the combined expertise and SLA development experience from over 50 man-years of consulting effort.

THE COMPLETE GUIDE TO I.T. SERVICE LEVEL AGREEMENTS: MATCHING SERVICE QUALITY TO BUSINESS NEEDS
3rd Edition, by Andrew Hiles

Covering all aspects of Information Technology Service Level Agreements (SLAs), this essential manual is a step-by-step guide to designing, negotiating and implementing SLAs into your organization. It reviews the disadvantages and advantages, gives clear guidance on what types are appropriate, how to set up SLAs and to control them. An invaluable aid to IT managers, data center managers, computer services, systems and operations managers.

CREATING A CUSTOMER-FOCUSED HELP DESK: HOW TO WIN AND KEEP YOUR CUSTOMERS
by Andrew Hiles & Dr. Yvonne Gunn

This volume and the companion product, Help Desk Framework CD-ROM came about as a result of the authors' own practical experience in Help Desk operation and management and of hundreds of workshops the authors have conducted world-wide over the last fifteen years. It is intended to be a practical reference guide, but the suggestions, checklists and templates all need to be interpreted and amended in the light of the culture, technology, service maturity and constraints of each individual organization.

SERVICE LEVEL AGREEMENTS: A FRAMEWORK ON CD-ROM FOR SERVICE BUSINESSES
by Andrew Hiles

Brings together the critical elements needed to build a Service Level Agreement for service or supply businesses (non-technology focused), with extensive templates, examples and tools.

SERVICE LEVEL AGREEMENTS: WINNING A COMPETITIVE EDGE FOR SUPPORT & SUPPLY SERVICES
by Andrew Hiles

This book holds the key to creating enduring, satisfying and profitable relationships between customer and supplier. It shows how both internal and external services and supply can be aligned to meet business vision, mission, goals, critical success factors and key performance indicators. The techniques described will help you balance service cost against quality, leading to competitive advantage and business success. They can be applied to any industry, to any supply or support service. They have been used by leading companies internationally - and they work!

BUSINESS THREAT AND RISK ASSESSMENT CHECKLIST WITH CD-ROM   by Edmond D. Jones
This manual contains checklists that an individual or group may use to evaluate the threats and risks which may impact an organization's campus, facility or even specific departments within the organization. Each of the checklists shown in this manual and a cover page that may be used to assemble your own checklists are contained on the CD that accompanies this manual.

MORE BOOKS AND RESOURCES FROM ROTHSTEIN ASSOCIATES INC.

BCM FRAMEWORK™ CD-ROM   by Andrew Hiles

BCM Framework consists of a number of easily tailored modules that are selected from our database of client work from a combined total of over one hundred years of consultancy experience - modules that are hand picked as the most relevant to your own situation, culture, organization, equipment platform and infrastructure. It contains documents, examples, checklists and templates covering each of the Disaster Recovery Institute International's and Business Continuity Institute's ten disciplines, model project plans, questionnaires and Business Recovery Action Plans for with Organization Schematics and role descriptions, with some vital - and often forgotten - actions included. These are in MS Word®, MS Excel® and MS Project® formats designed to be easily tailored to your organization's needs.

ENTERPRISE RISK ASSESSMENT AND BUSINESS IMPACT ANALYSIS: BEST PRACTICES
by Andrew Hiles

This book demystifies risk assessment. In a practical and pragmatic way, it covers many techniques and methods of risk and impact assessment with detailed, practical examples and checklists. It explains, in plain language, risk assessment methodologies used by a wide variety of industries and provides a comprehensive toolkit for risk assessment and business impact analysis.

AUDITING BUSINESS CONTINUITY: GLOBAL BEST PRACTICES   by Rolf von Roessing

"The work not only provides a general outline of how to conduct different types of audits but also reinforces their application by providing practical examples and advice to illustrate the step-by-step methodology, including contracts, reports and techniques. The practical application of the methodology enables the professional auditor and BCM practitioner to identify and illustrate the use of good BCM practice whilst demonstrating added value and business resilience." - Dr. David J. Smith, MBA LL.B(Hons), Chairman of the Business Continuity Institute, Education Committee

BUSINESS CONTINUITY AND HIPAA: BUSINESS CONTINUITY MANAGEMENT IN THE HEALTH CARE ENVIRONMENT   by James C. Barnes
Edited by Deborah Barnes, Philip Jan Rothstein, FBCI

This book examines business continuity planning as adapted to encompass the requirements of The Health Care Portability and Accountability Act of 1996, or HIPAA. We examine the typical business continuity planning model and highlight how the special requirements of HIPAA have shifted the emphasis. The layout of this book was designed to afford assistance, hints, and templates to the person charged with the task of implementing business continuity planning into a healthcare organization.

BUSINESS CONTINUITY PLANNING: A STEP-BY-STEP GUIDE WITH PLANNING FORMS ON CD-ROM *(Third Edition)*   by Kenneth L. Fulmer, CDRP

This popular book for those new to business continuity gives a step-by-step outline filled with precise instructions, risk and business impact analysis guidelines and forms for creating your basic business continuity blueprint. It serves as a workbook for those organizing a plan and as a guidebook for those responsible for implementation. Clear and complete, Business Continuity Planning will prove an invaluable resource and guide for managers, owners and planning coordinators. Endorsed by The Business Continuity Institute (BCI) and The Disaster Recovery Institute International (DRII).

DISASTER RECOVERY TESTING: EXERCISING YOUR CONTINGENCY PLAN
Philip Jan Rothstein, Editor

From this book, the contingency planner can understand more than just how to test: why to test, when to test (and not test) and the necessary participants and resources. Further, this book addresses some often-ignored, real-world considerations: the justification, politics and budgeting affecting recovery testing. By having multiple authors share their respective areas of expertise, it is hoped that this book will provide the reader with a comprehensive resource addressing the significant aspects of recovery testing.

BUSINESS CONTINUITY PROGRAM SELF-ASSESSMENT CHECKLIST WITH CD-ROM
by Edmond D. Jones

This book and companion CD-ROM contains a comprehensive set of questions assess the status of an organization's business continuity program. The questions may be used by a new or experienced business continuity planner to assess the overall program to determine those areas needing work. The same checklists can be used by internal or external audit or by others having a responsibility for evaluating an organization's business continuity program.

Inner Directions LLP

COUNSELING AND EDUCATION SERVICES
2815 VAN GIESEN ST., RICHLAND, WA 99354
(509) 942-0443

VALI HAWKINS MITCHELL, PH.D., LMHC
DAVID W. MITCHELL, M.A., LMHC

Vali is available for seminars, trainings, consultations, private coaching, public speaking events, critical incident stress debriefings, EAP (Employee Assistance Programs), and other programs custom designed to fit your organization.

vali@owt.com
www.drvali.com
www.emotionalcontinuitymanagement.com
www.kirshafoundation.org
www.triartgallery.com

INNER DIRECTIONS, LLP PROVIDES THESE AND OTHER SERVICES:

- Emotional Continuity Management Training and Consultation
- Confidential Counseling and Coaching for Professionals
- Critical Incident Stress Management Debriefings and Consultations
- Employee Assistance Counseling (EAP)
- Conflict Resolution and Dispute Mediation
- Writing Services and Writing Education for Creative Business Writing
- Keynote Speakers and Over 30 different workshop and training topics including:
    - Emotional Continuity Management
    - Pre-Disaster Planning
    - Persistence Training and Personal Coaching
    - Mediation Training
    - Conflict And Dispute Resolution
    - Violence In The Workplace: From Annoyance To Catastrophic
    - Addictions In The Workplace
    - Managing Cyber-Addictions At Work
    - Grace Under Pressure
    - Living Well With Chronic Medical Illness
    - The Use Of Programmed Writing For Anxiety Reduction
    - Long Term Trauma Management
    - Mental Health Survival First Aid Tool Kit
    - Workplace Grief, Anger, Ethics, Diversity, and Time Management Programs
    - Parenting / Step Parenting / Parenting After Divorce Programs
    - Creative Writing For Business Managers
    - How To Help Your Staff And Stay Okay
    - Stress Management
    - Teambuilding And Power Management
    - Having A Meaningful Work And Creating A Soulful Workplace

ABOUT THE AUTHOR

Vali Hawkins Mitchell, Ph.D., LMHC is a Licensed Mental Health Counselor and holds a Doctorate in Health Education. She consults nationally in the field of Emotional Continuity Management and has pioneered the development of this field (www.emotionalcontinuitymanagement.com). Two decades of disaster work — in the shadow of Mount St. Helens, the Hanford Nuclear Site and the Umatilla Chemical Weapons Depot — have provided her unique perspectives on the emotional nature of disaster planning.

Her assignments at numerous incidents include serving at the site of the World Trade Center attacks. She has served as co-clinical director of the Southeast Washington Critical Incident Stress Management team and is a member of the Disaster Services Human Resources System with the American Red Cross. Providing advanced trainings in trauma and disaster management, dispute resolution, critical-care health topics, and Emotional Terror in the workplace has kept her busy serving a wide range of industries and employees with a unique "been there, done that" style. The highest praise she has received has been from first responders who have recognized her contributions and style as authentic by pronouncing her "one of us."

Author of *Dr. Vali's Survival Guide: Tips for the Journey* and a series of children's books on Trauma Management and Dispute Resolution, Dr. Vali is also a Family Trauma Counselor providing services to hospitals, medical facilities, physicians, nurses, and families dealing with medical trauma. Co-owner of Inner Directions, LLP, she maintains a busy private counseling practice. (www.DrVali.com)

Also active in the arts, she is the founder and Executive Director of the Kirsha Foundation (www.Kirshafoundation.org), a non-profit organization that provides free access to the arts for youth age birth to 26, and is co-owner of the Tri-Art Sculpture Gallery (www.triartgallery.com) with her business partner and husband David Mitchell. Currently living in Richland, Washington surrounded by a cherry orchard on the bank of the Yakima River, when she isn't kayaking or trying to save a tree in her yard that has become eagle habitat, she teaches workshops and consults with businesses using the methods outlined in this book.

Vali Hawkins Mitchell, Ph.D., LMHC
Inner Directions, LLP
2815 Van Giesen
Richland, WA 99354
509-942-0443
vali@owt.com

EMOTIONAL TERRORS IN THE WORKPLACE:
PROTECTING YOUR BUSINESS' BOTTOM LINE
Emotional Continuity Management in the Workplace
By Vali Hawkins Mitchell, Ph.D., LMHC

Philip Jan Rothstein, FBCI, Editor

ISBN 1-931332-27-4

REGISTRATION AND *FREE* CD-ROM

If you purchased this book *other* *than* directly from Rothstein Associates, please fill out and return this form to register for future updates, and for your complimentary CD-ROM containing **THE ROTHSTEIN CATALOG ON DISASTER RECOVERY**. (*If you purchased this book directly from Rothstein Associates – The Rothstein Catalog On Disaster Recovery – you are automatically registered; be sure to let us know if your address changes*).

To qualify for future updates and receive your complimentary CD, please fill out this form completely and return it by fax to 203.740.7401, email to info@rothstein.com, or mail to the address below.

PRODUCT: **EMOTIONAL TERRORS IN THE WORKPLACE**

ISBN 1-931332-27-4

First Name _____   Last Name _____

Company/Organization _____

Department/Mail Station _____   Title _____

Street Address _____

City _____   State/Province _____

Zip/Postal Code _____   Country _____

Email address _____   Phone _____

Where Purchased _____   Purchase Date _____

Check here if you would you like to receive a complimentary subscription to our email newsletter, **BUSINESS SURVIVAL™: BUSINESS CONTINUITY FOR KEY DECISION-MAKERS** (*be sure to include your email address above!*) ☐

Check here if you would like to receive a complimentary CD-ROM containing the latest version of **THE ROTHSTEIN CATALOGS ON DISASTER RECOVERY and SERVICE LEVEL MANAGEMENT**, the industry's principal resource for hundreds of books, software tools, videos and research reports since 1989. ☐

THE ROTHSTEIN CATALOG ON DISASTER RECOVERY
ROTHSTEIN ASSOCIATES INC.

4 Arapaho Rd.
Brookfield, Connecticut 06804-3104 USA
203.740.7444   Fax 203.740.7401
info@rothstein.com

www.rothstein.com

THE ROTHSTEIN CATALOG ON DISASTER RECOVERY

www.ingramcontent.com/pod-product-compliance
Lightning Source LLC
Chambersburg PA
CBHW080410270326
41929CB00018B/2976